Christology in the Indian Anthropological Context

European University Studies

Europäische Hochschulschriften
Publications Universitaires Européennes

Series XXIII

Theology

Reihe XXIII   Série XXIII

Theologie
Théologie

Vol./Bd. 287

PETER LANG

Frankfurt am Main · Bern · New York

Mathew Vekathanam

Christology in the Indian Anthropological Context

Man-History-Christ:
Christ, the Mystery of Man
and of the Human History
An Evaluative Encounter
with K. Rahner and W. Pannenberg

PETER LANG
Frankfurt am Main · Bern · New York

CIP-Kurztitelaufnahme der Deutschen Bibliothek

Vekathanam, Mathew:

Christology in the Indian anthropological
context : man - history - Christ: Christ, the
mystery of man and of the human history ; an
evaluative encounter with K. Rahner and W.
Pannenberg / Mathew Vekathanam. — Frankfurt am
Main ; Bern ; New York : Lang, 1986.
(European University Studies: Series 23,
Theology ; Vol. 287)
ISBN 3-8204-9776-5
NE: European University Studies / 23

ISSN 0721-3409
ISBN 3-8204-9776-5

© Verlag Peter Lang GmbH, Frankfurt am Main 1986

printed in Germany

DEDICATED
TO THE BLESSED VIRGIN MARY

PREFACE

This dissertation was undertaken as a partial fulfilment of the requirements of Doctorate at the University of Würzburg; we have handled our topic, however, with personal conviction and pleasure. We found this task also academically quite interesting. The inspiration for this work should actually be traced back to the time of our theological studies in Bangalore, India, and our work for the degree of Licentiate in Theology at the Gregorian University in Rome. But, it has to be acknowledged that our theme took this concrete shape as a result of our many discussions with Prof. Alexandre Ganoczy, who has been kind enough to moderate this work putting so much of his time at our disposal, inspite of his additional responsibilities in the last two years as the Dean of the theological faculty. Our sincere thanks for his encouragement, creative criticism and valuable suggestions. We also remember with gratitude the role of Prof. Norbert Klaes especially in historically differentiating and methodically modifying some of the basic concepts in the first part of our work. We would also like to express our sincere thanks to Prof. Walter Simonis for his service as the 'Korreferent' of this inaugural dissertation.

Without the help of many, in one or another way, this work would not at all have been realizable. We thank Herr Konrad Schäfer for his timely and generous assistance in getting the manuscript typed and Frau Gertrud Bauer for taking care of its technical side. Our thanks are due in a special way to the brethren of the Carmelite Monastery of Würzburg, where we spent most of our time in Germany, to P.Dr. Ulrich Dobhan OCD, provincial of the Bavarian Province, for his generous help towards the publication of this work and the 'Verlag Peter Lang, Frankfurt-Main' for accepting this dissertation into the theological series of 'the European University Papers'.

Our sincere thanks are above all due to our own Carmelite Province of Malabar, India, and its Provincial Rev. Fr. Ephrem Parathazham OCD, for generously putting at our disposal sufficient time and other facilities for the completion of this work. We are conscious of our obligation to many more; even if all are not individually mentioned, we acknowledged with gratitude our indebtedness to all of them....

Würzburg
18.05.1986   Mathew Vekathanam OCD

TABLE OF CONTENTS

Abbreviations   xxi

Some Models of Sanskrit Pronunciation   xxiii

General Introduction   1

PART ONE

THE VEDANTIC CONTEXT OF THE INDIAN CHRISTOLOGY

FROM AN ANTHROPOLOGICAL VIEW-POINT:

THE DIVINE HORIZON IN MAN

Introduction   8

Chapter I
The Reality of God and the Concept of Brahman

A. The Indian Henotheism: Gods and God   19

B. Brahman, the Absolute (Nirguna)   23
    1. The Etymology of 'Brahman'   24
    2. 'Neti, Neti' Laksanas: The Way of Negation   26
    3. Brahman as 'Sat-Cit-Ananda'   28
        a. Brahman as 'Satyasya Satyam':
           Real of the Real, Truth of the True   30
        b. 'Prajnanam Brahma':
           Brahman as Consciousness   33
    4. The Concept of 'Maya' and the Problem of the World   34

C. 'Saguna Brahman' and the Concept of 'Isvara'   39
    1. God as Isvara: The Lord of all Being   40
    2. The World as the 'Deha' (Body) of God   42
    3. Isvara and His Triadal Manifestations as 'Trimurti'   46
        a. Brahma   47
        b. Visnu   48
        c. Siva   49

Conclusion to Chapter One   51

Chapter II
Man and the Reality of 'Atman'

A. The Vedantic Concept of Man   55
    1. The Dicovery of 'Atman'   57
    2. The Relation between Atman and Brahman   63
        a. Atman-Brahman Identity   63
        b. Atman as Part of Brahman   65

B. Man in Bondage   68
    1. 'Karma' and the Question of Sin   68
    2. 'Samsara'   74
    3. The Important Anthropological Implications of the
        Doctrine of 'Karma-Samsara'   78
        a. The Caste System   78
        b. The Position of Man in the Animal Kingdom:
            Panpsychism   82
        c. Fatalism and Human Freedom   84

C. The Vedantic Understanding of the Human History   86

Conclusion to Chapter Two   93

Chapter III
The Vedantic Search for Salvation

A. Salvation as Liberation from Karma-Samsara   95

   1. The Quest for the Beyond   95

     a. The Concept of 'Moksa': Heaven and Hell
       in the Vedas   96

     b. 'Moksa' as Liberation from 'Karma-Samsara' in
       the Upanisads   99

   2. 'Anubhava' and 'Saksatkara'   100

   3. The Role of Self-Discipline (YOGA) and Spiritual
     Guide (GURU) on the Way of 'Saksatkara'   108

     a. Yoga: Self-Discipline   109

     b. Guru: The Spiritual Guide   112

B. The Paths towards 'Saksatkara'   117

   1. Karma-Marga: The Path of Deeds   118

   2. Jnana-Marga: The Path of Knowledge   122

   3. Bhakti-Marga: The Path of Loving Devotion   127

C. The Quest for a God-Man   134

   1. The Concept of 'Avatara'   134

   2. 'Krsnavatar'   138

   3. Avatara in further Reflection   145

Conclusion to Chapter Three   153

Conclusion to Part I   154

PART TWO

THE DIVINE IN HUMAN HISTORY

AS VISUALIZED BY THE INDIAN CHRISTOLOGICAL APPROACHES

Introduction   158

Chapter IV
The Universal, Advaitic Christ

A. **Jesus Christ within the Context of the Vedantic**
    Question of 'the Religion' in Religions   161
    1. The Fundamental Universality of All Religions and
        the Primacy of the Vedanta   162
        a. The Equality of all Religions   162
        b. The Theory of 'Ishtam': Personal Religious Preference   167
        c. The 'Sanatana Dharma' as 'the Religion' in Religions   169
    2. Christ as Part of Sanatana Dharma   173
        a. The Universal Christ-Principle   174
        b. The Oriental Jesus   176
        c. The Advaitic Yogi   179
    3. The Advaitic Christ within the Category of Avatara   183
        a. Jesus Christ, the Example of Man's Potential Divinity   183
        b. Christ, One among Many Divine Manifestations   187

B. **The Vedantic Isvara and the Christ Principle**   196
    1. The Christ Unknown   196
        a. The Universal Divine Mystery   197
        b. The Mystery and Its Name   201
        c. The Christ-Principle in the Trinitarian Context   205
    2. Isvara, the Christ   208
    3. Jesus of Nazareth and the 'Christ':
        The Name and the Supername   212

C. The Universal Christ and the Problem of Historicity   216

   1. The Irrelevance of Jesus' Historicity   216

   2. The Meta-Historical Christ   220

      a. Christ's Historical Singularity and His Uniqueness   221

      b. Historical Identification and Personal Identity   223

Conclusion to Chapter Four   226

Chapter V
Jesus Christ from the Point of View of His Historical Uniqueness

A. Jesus Christ, the Ultimate within the Bounds of
    Human History   230

   1. The Sonship of Jesus Christ   230

      a. Montotheism and Incarnation   231

      b. The Problem of Christ's Divinity   232

      c. Jesus Christ, the Son of God   234

   2. Jesus Christ and the Divine Humanity   235

      a. The 'Pantheism' of the Will   237

      b. God the Father and Christ the Son   240

      c. The Divine Transparency of Christ's Sonship   242

   3. Christ within the Context of Evolution   245

      a. The Pre-existence of the 'Logos'   246

      b. Evolution of the Divine Humanity   248

      c. Jesus Christ, the New Creation   249

B. The Mystery of the Divine Incarnation:
    Jesus - God and Man   252

   1. The Divinity of Jesus Christ   252

      a. 'Saccidananda' and the 'Cit-Logos'   252

      b. Jesus Christ, the Self-Manifestation of the Triune God 256

      c. The Divine Consciousness of Jesus   260

2. Jesus, the true Man   263
   a. The Humanity of Jesus in the Context of 'Maya'   263
   b. Jesus' 'Manushya Svabhava'   267
   c. The 'Sat Purusha': True Man   269
3. Jesus Christ, the God-Man   272
   a. 'Nara-Hari' - God-Man   272
   b. The Five 'Kosha' (Sheaths) and the 'Ciracit'
      (Eternal Logos)   274
   c. 'Tadatyma' in the 'Brahmanya Purusha'   276

C. The Historical Incarnation in the Context of the
   Mythical Avatars   **278**
   1. Incarnation and 'Avatar'   278
      a. The Significant Parallels   278
      b. Jesus Christ, the Avatar par Excellence?   281
   2. Jesus Christ, the Mystery of Human History   286
      a. History and Myth   286
      b. History and Reality   289
   3. Jesus Christ, the Historical Fulfilment   292
      a. The Fulfilment of the Vedantic Aspirations   293
      b. The Fulfilment of the Avataric Quest   295

Conclusion to Chapter Five   299

Chapter VI
The Universal Relevance of Christ's Uniqueness in History

A. Christ, the 'Mahaguru': The Great Teacher of Mankind   **303**
   1. The Sermon on the Mount   304
   2. Jesus Christ, the Ethical Teacher   305
   3. 'Ahimsa' in Practice   309
   4. The Vedantic Sadguru   311

B. **The Saving Role of Jesus Christ in Human History**   **315**

  1. The Question of Sin and the Vedantic Problematic   315

    a. The Vedantic Reaction   316

    b. The 'Original Sin' and the 'Actual Sin'   317

    c. The 'Maya' of the Will   321

  2. The Saving Fact of Christ   322

  3. The Redemptive Act of Christ   322

    a. The Mystery of the Cross   328

      i. The Scandal of the Cross   328

      ii. The Supreme Example of the Cross   331

      iii. Suffering for the Sake of Love   333

      iv. The Redemptive Sacrifice   335

    b. The Relevance of Christ's Resurrection for the Human History   340

      i. Resurrection and the Advaitic Illumination   341

      ii. The Eschatological Matter-Spirit Integration   342

      iii. Love as Life Conquering Death   344

    c. Towards an Indian Pneumatology   348

      i. The Non-Personal Spirit   349

      ii. Jesus Christ and His Redemptive Universality   349

      iii. The Indwelling Spirit (Antaryamin)   351

  4. The Universality of Christ's Salvation in the Indian Context   354

    a. The Salvific Value of Hinduism   354

    b. The 'Anonymous Christians' and the 'Anonymous Christianity'   358

C. **'Khristanubhava': The Liberating Experience of Christ**   **363**

  1. The Nature of Christ-Experience   364

    a. Christ-Experience and God-Experience   364

    b. 'Khrista-Sayujya'   367

    c. The Trinitarian and Communitarian Dimensions of Christ-Experience   368

2. The Pluriformal Dimensions of 'Khristanubhava':
   Jesus Christ, Our 'Brahma Marga' - The Way   371
   a. Karma-Marga: The Way of Action   372
   b. Jnana-Marga: The Way of Knowledge   374
   c. Bhakti-Marga: The Way of Loving Devotion   377
3. The Christian 'Prema-Marga' (Love as the Way) and
   the Call to Social Concern   382
   a. The Indian Problematic   382
   b. The Social Dimensions of Indian Christology   384

Conclusion to Chapter Six   387

Conclusion to Part II   389

PART THREE

AN EVALUATION FROM THE THEOLOGICAL PERSPECTIVES
ESPECIALLY OF KARL RAHNER AND WOLFHART PANNENBERG

Introduction   394

Chapter VII
Christ, the Universal Mystery of Man

A. Man's Transcendental Horizon: The Mystery of 'Atman'
    before the Mystery of 'Brahman'   397
    1. The Transcendental Aspect of Human Experience   397
        a. The Human Existence as a Radical Question   398
        b. The Human Transcendence in 'Jnana':
            The Gnoseological Aspect   399
        c. Transcendence in Freedom and Love   403
    2. The Whiter (Woraufhin) of Human Transcendence   404
        a. The Incomprehensible Mystery   405
        b. The Mystery of Fullness (Purnam)   407
        c. 'Prajnanam Brahma': Consciousness and Person   410
    3. Man as the Event of God's Self-Giving   413
        a. Man, the Rational Animal - 'Zoon logikon'?   413
        b. Man as Orientation to the Mystery of Fullness   415
        c. The Anthropological Turn in Theology   418

B. Transcendence in Process   419
    1. History as the Event of Transcendence   420
        a. Spirit in the World   420
        b. The Historical Mediation of Transcendence   423
        c. The Question of the Vedantic Panpsychism   424

xviii

2. Revelation as History 426

   a. Unity of Truth and the History of Truth 426

   b. The Historico-Eschatological Character of Revelation 429

   c. God-Knowing and God-Talk 432

3. The Tragedy of History 435

   a. The Limitedness of Human Transcendence:

      The Question of Man's Divinity 436

   b. The Hard Realities of Sin and Suffering 437

   c. 'Karma-Samsara' and the 'Original Sin' 439

C. The Mystery of Christ as the Mystery of Man 442

1. 'Transzendentale Christologie' 442

2. 'Suchende Christologie' 446

   a. Anthropological Reduction? 447

   b. Search in History 448

   c. 'Fides ex auditu' 449

3. Christological 'Historiophobia'? 451

Conclusion to Chapter Seven 456

Chapter VIII

Jesus of Nazareth, the Unique Mystery of Human History

A. The 'Jesus is God' - Problematic 459

1. Jesus of Nazareth as the Image of Man and as the

   Image of God 459

   a. Jesus, the Image of Man 459

   b. Jesus, the Image of God 462

   c. Jesus, the Mystery of the God-Man 463

2. The Christological Formula of Chalcedon and the

   Indian Problematic 465

3. Can God 'become'? 473

   a. 'Pre-Existence' or 'Mission'? 473

   b. Incarnation and the Virgin Birth: 'Hieros gamos'? 477

   c. The Divine Consciousness of Jesus:'Visio immediata'? 480

B. **The Historical Destiny of Jesus**   **485**

   1. 'Dharma' and 'Basileia':

      The Message of the Kingdom   486

   2. Jesus' Crucifixion: A Suffering God?   489

   3. Vicarious Substitution?   494

C. **Eschatological Saviour**   **499**

   1. Jesus' Resurrection: Eschatology versus History?   500

   2. The 'Basileia' in 'Prolepsis'   505

   3. The Resurrection and the Re-Incarnation   511

      a. Death and Immortality   512

      b. 'Re-Incarnation' and 'Purgatory'?   513

      c. 'Eschaton' Now   516

Conclusion to Chapter Eight   518

Chapter IX
Jesus Christ, the Mystery of Man and of the Human History

A. **The Universality of the Unique**   **521**

   1. Jesus' Uniqueness in Question   521

   2. The All-Inclusive Uniqueness   524

      a. Jesus' Anthropological Uniqueness   525

      b. Jesus' Historical Uniqueness   526

      c. Jesus' Revelational Uniqueness   528

   2. The Advaitic Synthesis of Polarities   530

B. **Salvation - A Christian Monopoly?**   **533**

   1. The Universality of Salvation   533

   2. 'Anonymous Christian' - the Indian Problematic   538

   3. 'Extra Christum nulla salus' - and the Salvific

      Value of Hinduism   542

C. 'Khristanubhava' and 'Brahmasaksatkara':
   Christ (-ology) in Experience   546
   1. Self-Experience and god-Experience   547
   2. The Trinitarian Dimension of Christ-Experience   552
   3. The Mysticism of Altruistic Love   559

Conclusion to Chapter Nine   565

Conclusion to Part III   567

General Concluding Perspectives   569

Footnotes   575

A Select Bibliography   759

ABBREVIATIONS

For the abbreviations of Collections, Periodicals etc. we follow, with some minor obvious alterations:

Karl Rahner et al., (Hrg.), Sacramentum Mundi. Theologisches Lexikon für die Praxis, Band 1, Freiburg/Basel/Wein, 1967, SS. XIII-XXXI.

The biblical abbreviations are taken from: Raymond E. Brown et al. (Edd.), The Jerome Biblical Commentary, New Jersey, 1968, p.xxv.

The documents of Vatican II are indicated by the initial letters of the first two words of the original latin texts.

Some well-known abbreviations are not specially mentioned here.

Abbreviations of Some Important Hindu Scriptures

Ait.Up.	:	Aitareya Upanisad
Br. Up.	:	Brhad-aranyaka Upanisad
Chand. Up.	:	Chandogya Upanisad
Isa Up.	:	Isa Upanisad
Ke. Up.	:	Kena Upanisad
Kat. Up.	:	Katha Upanisad
Kau. Up.	:	Kausitaki Upanisad
Mandu. Up.	:	Mandukya Upanisad
Mund. Up.	:	Mundaka Upanisad
Pr. Up.	:	Prasna Upanisad
Sat. Br.	:	Satapatha Brahmana
Svet. Up.	:	Svetasvatara Upanisad
Tait. Up.	:	Taittiriya Upanisad

Other Abbreviations

Bd., Bdd., (Vol., Vols.)	:	Volume(s).
bes., (esp.)	:	especially
CM	:	Clergy Monthly
Ed., Edd., (Hrg.)	:	Editor(s)
Hrg., (Ed., Edd.)	:	Editor(s)
IES	:	Indian Ecclesiastical Studies
IJT	:	Indian Journal of Theology
ITS	:	Indian Theological Studies
JDh	:	Journal of Dharma
p., pp., (S., SS.)	:	Page(s)
Repr.,	:	Reprint
S.B.E.	:	Sacred Books of the East
		ed. by F. Max Müller
S., SS., (p., pp.)	:	pages
Tr.	:	Translation, Translator
Vol., Vols., (Bd., Bdd.)	:	Volume(s)

SOME MODELS OF SANSKRIT PRONUNCIATION

(For details on romanized Sanskrit charachters and pronunciation Cfr.: Monier-Williams, A Sanskrit-English Dictionary, Oxford, 1964 (1890).

Advitīyam	Kāma	Prāṇa	Śiva
Amśa	Kauṣītaki	Praśna	Smṛti
Ānanda	Khristānubhava	Prēma	Śruti
Ananta	Kośa	Pūrṇa	Sthūla
Antaryāmin	Kṛṣṇa	Puruṣa	Sūkṣma
Apauruṣeya	Kṣatriya	Puruṣārtha	Sūkta
Āśrama	Kuṇḍalinī	Rakṣa	Sūrya
Astēya	Lakṣaṇa	Rāma	Sūtra
Ātman	Līlā	Rāmānuja	Svabhāva
Avatāra	Liṅga	Rāmāyaṇa	Svetāśvatara
Bhagavadgītā	Mahābhārata	Ṛgvēda	Taittirīya
Bhāṣya	Mahāvākyāṇi	Ṛsi	Tīrtha
Bṛhad-āraṇyaka	Maitrī	Saccidānanda	Trimūrti
Brahmacārin	Mandūkya	Ṣad-Darśana	Uddhānam
Brāhmaṇa	Mārga	Śakti	Upaniṣad
Chāndokya	Māyā	Sākṣatkāra	Vāc
Darśana	Mōkṣa	Samānatva	Vāhana
Daśāvatāra	Muṇḍaka	Sāmavēda	Varṇa
Dēha	Nāmarūpa	Saṁkhya	Varuṇa
Dikṣa	Nārāyaṇa	Saṁsāra	Vāyu
Dvēṣa	Nāstika	Saṁskṛta	Vedānta
Ēkam	Natarāja	Sanātana	Vibhūti
Gāyatrī	Nirākāra	Śankara	Viśiṣta
Guṇa	Nirupādhika	Sannyāsin	Viṣṇu
Hiraṇya	Nirvāṇa	Śarīra	Vivāha
Īśvara	Nirviśeṣa	Śāstra	Vyāsa
Itihāsa	Parā	Savitṛ	Vyūha
Jāti	Prajāpati	Śikṣa	Yajamāna
Jnāna	Prakṛti	Śiṣya	Yūpa .

GENERAL INTRODUCTION

This work is undertaken as a small contribution towards a better understanding of the Christ-Mystery as the mystery of man and his history in the Indian context. The mystery of Christ is so rich, deep and extensive that it cannot be limited to a particular philosophical system or theological representation. Each culture has the fundamental Christian right to accept Christ in its own way, if it acknowledges him as its fulfilment and as the ultimate answer to its radical religious search. The acceptance of the mystery of Christ does not imply an equal acceptance of centuries of 'cultural dust' accumulated on it in a different cultural situation. Each people should have, in the universality of Christian fellowship, tradition and magisterial unity, the possibility to encounter Christ in its own socio-cultural and philosophical context. An 'imported' Christ is a 'foreign matter' that will easily be rejected from any self-respecting cultural 'organism'. An understanding of Christ should grow in each people out of their own cultural back ground.

The 'inculturation' of the Christ-Mystery as the mystery of man and his history could proceed in a dialectic process. In India, for example, the Indian cultural heritage has to be the starting point, the thesis, which is to be transformed and fulfilled by the anti-thesis, the Christ-Mystery, as it is encountered in the purity of the sources of Revelation resulting consequently in a reasonable and salutary synthesis called Indian Christology. If in the first centuries the Greco-Roman cultural and philosophical milieu could serve to make Christ understandable, it has to be accepted that the Indian philosophical categories are no less suitable as a frame of expression for the Christ-Mystery. It is highly problematic when, instead of Christ, the whole 'Christ-vision' of a particular philosophy or culture is imposed on a different one as the only valid way of Christo-logizing, in which case the process of a healthy theological dialectics is throttled or even unjustly manipulated!

It is also an undeniable fact that there are formidable problems which are to be faced in accepting any philosophy or culture to interpret Christ in a given context. In presenting Christ one also will have to be faithful to the core of the Christ-Mystery, to his person, message and work. The rampant contradictions and irreconcilable positions that can emerge in such a contextualization can by no means be overlooked. Just as the Church had to 'christianize' many of the hellenistic presuppositions in the first centuries, so also a process of 'christianization' - not hellenization or westernization- in traditional patterns of Indian thinking is indispensable in any process towards an Indian Christology. That implies both a demythologization and a re-mythologization of Indian philosophy and western Christan theology to come to a systematized reflection about Christ which is at the same time genuinely Indian and Christian. 'Myth' has here, of course, a positive meaning as a 'category' of understanding and expression which differs from people to people.

The emancipation of the Indian way of thinking and talking about Christ from western patterns does not mean in any way a break from the rich Christological traditions of that part of the Church. The 'europeanized' Christianity and Christian thinking should not be considered as a rival or hindrance to the Indian mode of thinking about Christ and living him, but rather it is a valuable complementation, an enriching help and even a valuable guide to the process of Christologization in India. The long Christological tradition of the west is a patrimony of the universal Church which is at the disposal of every part of it. The Indian vision of Christ is also not a counter-vision, separating it from the Christian unity of faith and fellowship, but a complementary vision indispensable also for the beauty and theological richness of the Church that rejects nothing that is 'true and holy' in the lives of other peoples which it considers as a 'ray of that Truth which enlightens all men' (Vatican II, Nostra aetate, no. 2).

In this perspective, our work is divided into three parts:
(1) In the first part we aim at a simple, logical and clear presentation of the Indian anthropological context, especially of the Vedanta, in which the Christ-Mystery has to take root. Regarding this part we would like to make it clear at the very outset that it is not meant as an extensive elaboration of the Vedanta in all its minute details. We have no intention of investigating all the marginal and intricate questions connected with it especially because, in our judgement, that is not of immediate relevance for the extremely limited scope of our topic and for a sufficient and credible context-setting, which alone is our goal. Sufficient differentiations will be made without, however, exaggerating them beyond the requirements of our dissertation taken in its

entirety! Besides, there is also no scarcity of literature in this field for an advanced Indologist, as our bibliography would clearly show, and we do not think of substituting them. Nevertheless, we consider our first part to be of importance for us, because the subsequent parts would not be sufficiently intelligible without the categorial clarifications we make in this part. So, we limit ourselves to the essentials which are indicative and not exhaustive!

(2) In the second part we make an analytical systematic and critical survey of how the Indian thinkers, both Hindu and Christian, have so far confronted the Mystery of Christ. Here our Christological concern gets special emphasis.

(3) In the third part we deal with the main problems facing the development of an authentic Indian Christology and how the views of two of the representative theologians of the West, Karl Rahner and Wolfhart Pannenberg, could react in the direction of a mutual complementation and perhaps even of mutual correction! Karl Rahner and W. Pannenberg are sought out in this evalutative part of our work not just because they are two knowledgeable representatives of the German catholic and protestant theologies - we do not ignore that there are many schools in both confessions! - but mostly because they are evidently concerned with the two major problems which the Christ-Mystery has to face in the Indian and Vedantic context, namely: the uniqueness of Jesus of Nazareth, the Christ, both anthropologically as the absolute bringer of salvation and historically as the culmination of the process of world-history towards a necessary fulfilment. They seem to us to be good dialogue-partners for an emerging Indian Christology. In the third part we also make an attempt to sort out our own personal anthropo-christological conclusions to which this research could lead us.

It is to be mentioned here that, as our bibliography would amply testify, many authors have written on Indian theological topics and a good number of research works have been done in various universities on themes which are relevant for Indian theology. They are mostly in the fields of missiology and inter-religious dialogue. Works of comparative study are also not rare. Worthy of mention here are doctoral dissertations of authors like K. Klostermaier, J. Mattam, A. Mookenthottam and H. Barlage and contributions by others like R. Antoine, P. Antes, R.H.S. Boyd, H. Bürkle, J.B. Chethimattam, R. De Smet, J. Neuner, K. Dockhorn, M. Dhavamony, S.J. Samartha, P.D. Devanandan, Dom Le Saux,

4

M.M. Thomas, R. Panikkar and D.S. Amalorpavadass, to mention only a few. But we have not yet seen a systematic work that amply examines the Indian anthropology and history from a Christological point of view as we try to do in the following pages. Another point of novelty in this work is our encounter with the anthropo-historical and Christological views especially of Karl Rahner and Wolfhart Pannenberg which bridges the different currents of thought encouraging mutual correction and complementation. Though this work is principally dogmatic in character, its missiological, pastoral and dialogico-ecumenical implications are also not unimportant.

The title of our work contains an important term, 'Mystery', which needs some clarification. In our use, 'Mystery' is by and large a boundary concept (Grenzbegriff) and we take it as is explained by Rahner especially in his article 'Über den Begriff des Geheimnisses in der katholischen Theologie' in Schriften zur Theologie, Bd. IV, SS.51-99. Further elaboration of this concept of Rahner could be found in K.P. Fischer's 'Der Mensch als Geheimnis - Die Anthropologie Karl Rahners' and in 'A Rahner Reader' by Gerald McCool (London 1975, especially pp.108-132). We will be referring to this point in the third part of our work especially in chapter VII. An adequate conceptualization of 'mystery, however, is impossible because it signifies what is beyond all conceptualities. From the human point of view it is the sum total of human transcendence, which is evident to us but at the same time hidden from us, which is awe inspiring and distant while being at the same time within us and fascinating! It will be in this sense that we will be mostly using the term 'Mystery' and not just in its meaning in common parlance as the hidden, secret and abscure truth or religious doctrine. In considering Christ as the Mystery of man and of the human history we are not dealing just with one of the doctrines of Christianity but with the mystery of all worlds and times. Our thesis is that Jesus, the Christ, is the ultimate manifestation of the transcendent reality of man and his history which, of course, does not exhaust or eleminate the depth and incomprehensibility of transcendence!

It is inevitable that we meet with many Sanskrit words in the course of our work. In transliterating them, we follow with minor adaptations the system proposed by the 'Congress of Orientalists' at Athens in 1912. Due to typographical reasons, however, the symbols of pronouncations are not repeated with each word. The list of pronouncation at the beginning of our work gives ample guidance. The English translation of most of the Sanskrit texts are taken from the books shown in our bibliography no.3. The Bible quotations, as a rule, are from the English edition of 'The Jerusalem Bible' and the biblical abbreviations from 'The Jerome Biblical Commentary' edited by R.E. Brown et al. The footnotes are given, of course, in numerical sequence, but at times there are omissions of numbers due to practical reasons. Similarly, some footnote-numbers are repeated, in which case they are distinguished by additional alphabets. The works we have used are acknowledged in the footnotes; our 'Select Bibliography', however, mention those works which have considerable significance for our topic.

PART ONE

THE VEDANTIC CONTEXT OF INDIAN CHRISTOLOGY

FROM AN ANTHROPOLOGICAL VIEW-POINT:

THE DIVINE HORIZON IN MAN

INTRODUCTION

To make clear what we mean by 'the Vedantic Context', it is necessary to refer shortly to the general Hindu milieu in which Vedanta is situated. Hinduism has behind it a long history of about 5000 years. Our concern here, however, is not to describe all the aspects of 'this immense mythological banyan-tree with its roots spread out over the whole extent of the Indian subcontinent[1], but only to shed some light on the 'Vedanta' and those aspetcs of Hindu life leading to it and immediately deriving from it. Vedanta is the sum and substance of Hinduism and especially the cornerstone of modern Hinduism.[2]

Hinduism is generally described as an immense socio-religious phenomenon defying all definition; it is more a way of life, a culture, than a religion in the strict sense[3] with a founder, dogma or defining hierarchy. Hinduism is a 'parliament of religions'[4] or a 'league of religions' than a single religion with a definite creed.[5] It is similar to a forest or a jungle where 'beautiful trees grow side by side of poisonous ones'[6]. It is the result of the blending of the advanced culture of the indigenous Dravidians and other aborginal elements dating back to about 3000 B.C[7] with the socio-religious practices and beliefs of the conquering Aryans who entered India about 2000 B.C.[8] C.B. Papali, a noted Indologist, describes Hinduism as 'the religion of the Indo-Aryans which, through millenia of evolution from within and absorption of elements from without, has grown into a complex mass of religious, philosophic and social systems, loaded with the traditions and myths of all peoples that at various times entered into its fold[9].

The term 'Hinduism' refers to the 'ism' or the world-vision of the people who settled down on the banks of the river Sindhu called 'Indu' or 'Hindu' by the Persians. The 'Hindus' moved later to the whole of the subcontinent. Later on in the course of centuries the word 'Hindus' gained a particular religious connotation and gradually distinguished itself from the 'Indians', the word that stands for the whole population of the Indian peninsula regardless of religious differences.[10] From the socio-cultural point of view it is quite correct to say with some reservations that all Indians are Hindus. Besides, since the vast majority of Indians, more than 82 per cent, belong to the Hindu religion, we have excluded from our work, for the sake of thematic concentration, other non-Hindu religious groups in India as a cultural background for the development of an Indian Christology. Special mention must be made in this regard about Islam, the religion of more than 10 per cent Indians! The Islamic traits in Indian life, according to our opinion, are neither genuinely Indian in origin nor have they got integrated into the Indian cultural life-stream. Other minor non-Hindu religious groups, according to the nature of our topic, are too insignificant to claim our attention in the present work.

As a religion 'Hinduism is a conglomeration of miriads of beliefs, but each individual Hindu is involved with only a fraction of them. He clings to them in a vital fashion, whereas his interest in all other beliefs or tenets is merely intellectual so that he has no difficulty in admitting their general validity - at least for others - even if they contradict one another'[11]. In its long evolution Hinduism has grown like a snow-ball absorbing on its way everything, even irreconcilables, resulting in a complex and indefinable socio-religious phenomenon distinguishing it sharply from other religions.[12] Certain beliefs and practices are yet considered essential to Hinduism: (1) Divine Revelation of the Vedas, (2) Faith in Karma-Samsara, (3) Mukti or Moksa conceived as the ultimate liberation of man, (4) Observance of Varna-Asrama-Dharma, ie. the duties of caste and stages of life.[13] We will be dealing with all of these points in the course of our work in so far as they are relevant to our theme. Now it is necessary for us to have a look at the religious scriptures of Hinduism, some of which are of extreme importance for our work.

The corpus of the sacred literature in Hinduism is divided into three categories: (1) Sruti: What is heard, (2) Smrti: What is remembered and (3) Sectarian Works which are also considered by some as forming a part of Smrti.[14]

The period of Sruti is called the Vedic Period (2OCO BC-6OO BC). The Vedas are the most sacred compositions of India, 'the oldest literary record in the Indo-European languages' [15]. 'Veda' from the root 'vid', [16] to know, to see intellectually, literally means 'sacred knowledge' or the sacred wisdom contained in the revealed texts, which constitutes the primary authority in religious matters. [17] The Rgveda, Samaveda, Yayurveda and Atharvaveda form the earliest part (ca. 1OOO BC) of Vedic literature. [18] They are together called Vedic Samhitas (collections) and they are collections of hymns, incantations and sacrificial formulae. [19] They are songs to the gods and not messages from gods to men. Originally 'Veda' meant only Rgveda, [20] the other three being later additions. To the Samhita of Vedas the sacrificial texts called 'Brahmanas' (8OO BC - 6OO BC) were later added. [21] In reaction to the sacrificial systems, the sages (Rsis) retired to the forests giving rise to the 'Aranykas', forest treatises (ca. 6OO BC) [22], which culminated in the Upanisads, as a fulfilment of the Vedic aspirations. Of these, the Rgveda and the Upanisads deserve our special consideration especially in the context of our theme.

The oldest Indo-Europian monument is the Rgveda [23] composed in Sanskrit or Samskrta [24] and handed down from generation to generation through oral transmission. [25] The mass of Rgveda might have taken a long time to produce and Max Müller is of the opinion that now we may not have even a hundredth part of those poems of the Vedic period. [26] The Rgveda is 'without the shadow of a doubt, the oldest book of the Aryan family of nations', says Ragozin. [27] The oldest monument of the literature of Indians is at the same time the oldest monument of the Indo-European literature which we possess. [28] It is earlier than the literature of Greece and Israel and reveals a very high level of civilization. [29] The Rgveda comprises 1O17 hymns in 1O books and presents 'the first adventures of the human mind made by those who sought to discover the meaning of existence and man's place in life' [30].

The Upanisads develope the Vedic ideas. It is the end, the perfection or culmination of the Vedas. Chronologically also the Upanisads come at the end of the Vedic period. They represent the central aim, meaning, the conclusion and the goal of the teaching of Vedas. Because of their subtlity Upanisads were taught to the pupils only at the end of the 'Vedic course' [31]. Because of these reasons the Upanisads are rightly called 'Vedasya antah' or 'Vedanta', Veda's end. The authority of the Vedas may be to a great extent due to the inclusion of Upanisads in the Vedic corpus.[32]

The literal meaning of 'Upanisad' is 'sitting down near' (upa=near, ni=down, sad=to sit). It stands for the mystery, secret (rahasyam) communicated only to a few tested pupils who sat near the teacher with devotion to truth in the quietitude of the forest hermitages.[33] Some translate 'Upanisad' as a substantive from the root 'sat', to loosen, to reach or to destroy with 'upa' and 'ni' as prefixes and 'kvip' as termination, to mean the 'Brahma-knowledge' by which ignorance is loosened or destroyed.[34]

There is no universal agreement on the number of Upanisads. They are counted from 10 to as many as 200. In S. Radhakrishnan's opinion the principal Upanisads are 16 in number.[35] The earliest prose Upanisads: Aitareya, Kausitaki, Chandogya, Kena, Taittiriya and Brhadaranyaka together with Isa and Katha belong to the 8th and 7th century B.C. They are pre-Buddhistic;they are the Vedanta in the original form and are the earliest philosophical compositions of the world.[36] The other Upanisads were most probably written before 300 B.C. The names of renouned Rsis like Yajnavalkya, Svetaketu, Sandilya, are associated with the Upanisads, but the authors of the Upanisads remain unknown. They must be products of different schools as the different currents of aupanisadic thoughts show. The Upanisads may be described in the words of S. Radhakrishnan as 'the highest and purest expression of the speculative thought of India. They embody the meditations on great matters of a succession of seers who lived between 1000 and 300 B.C. In them....we have the earliest attempt at a constructive theory of cosmos, and certainly one of the most interesting and remarkable'[37].

The Samhitas, Brahmanas, Aranyakas and Upanisads together constitute the revealed literature, what is heard (sruti), of Hinduism. They are considered to be eternal (nitya), immemorial and timeless (sanatana) because their truths which were always in the mind of God are said to be breathed out by God or visioned by the seers who spoke out of the fullness of their illumined experience. The Rsis (sages) were men of direct vision with absolute certainty about what they 'saw'. These truths are not discovered or thought out by the seers but revealed to them by the Divine. The revealed Word of God is impersonal, authorless (apauruseya) ie. independent of any individual author.[38] The human role in its composition was minimal; the sages were like 'mirrors' reflecting passively the eternal truth they encountered. Those who transmitted it had no part to play in its composition or expression unlike the biblical inspiration in which God is the principal author and the human authors are given an active instrumental role.[38] The revelation takes place in a bipolar interaction, namely, man's contemplation (tapah-prabhava) and the grace of God (deva-prasada).[39] So it has a subjective and objective character.[40] As it is the revelation of God it is infallible. It is, however, not an account of God's dealings with man in history, but a gradual revelation of the meta-historical truth about the being of God and man.[41] They are to be accepted without questioning. Those who denied the eternal, impersonal and infallible character of the Vedas are called 'Nastikas',unbelievers.[42] Because of the scrupulous attention given to keep up the originality of the Vedas, they have survived 25 centuries in remarkably good shape.[43]

The Vedas have dominated Indian philosophy, religion and life for almost 3000 years. Every subsequent philosophical development had to show itself to be in accord with the Vedas. The Vedas and among them especially the Upanisads had great influence also beyond the geographical boundaries of India both in the east and in the west. The mysticism of Persian Suphism, the logos-doctrine of neo-platonism, the Alexandrian Christian mysticism, the philosophy of the great German thinkers of the 19th century like Schopenhauer etc. may be traced to the Upanisads.[44] Schopenhauer observes that 'from every sentence of [the Upanisad] deep, original and sublime thoughts arise, and the whole is pervaded by a high and holy and earnest spirit. In the whole world.... there is no study.... so beneficial and so elevating as that of the Upanisads. They are products of the high wisdom. They are destined sooner or later to become the faith of the people'[45].

'Smrti', what is remembered, is the next group of religious literature. They are all Hindu religious writings of human origin in agreement with the doctrines of the Sruti. The period of Smrti begins at about 600 B.C; the period of reaction against the established Hindu system marks between 600 B.C and

300 A.D. followed by the pauranic period, 300-1200 A.D. The period of reaction marks the origin of heterodox groups like Buddhism and Jainism. Smrti shows the Hindu attempt to reassert itself against such sects even to the point of reabsorbing them into the Hindu fold. The three main divisions of Hinduism based on Vedic gods, ie. Vaisnavaism (the cult of the solar god Visnu), Saivism (the cult of Siva) and Saktism (the cult of the power of Siva in a personified feminine form), became popular in this period. In its widest sense Smrti includes: (1) the six Vedangas (limbs of the Veda, namely, Siksa: phonetics, Chandas: metre, Nirukta: etymology, Vyakarana: grammar, Jyotisa: astronomy, and Kalpa: ceremonial), (2) Aphoristic compositions or Sutras, (3) Dharmasastra ie. law books, (4) Itihasas, epics like Ramayana, the first national epic of India, and Mahabharata together with the Bhagavadgita, (5) 18 Puranas and 18 minor puranas: collections of tales regarding gods, creation, heroes etc., (6) Nitisastra: collection of moral precepts and edifying fables.[46]

Among the Smrti works, the Ramayana and Mahabharata have achieved great importance and have come to be regarded as 'the Vedas of the common folk'. Ramayana is the story of the crown prince of Ayodhya and Mahabharata depicts the great battle between two branches of the same royal family, the Pandavas and the Kauravas. The Mahabharata is an immense work, the longest poem in the world,[47] more than seven times the length of Iliad and Odyssey combined.[48] This epic poetry of India developed alongside the later Upanisads before the Christian era. In the sixth book of this great epic we have 'one of the finest gems of world literature, the famous Bhagavad-Gita (the Lord's Song), a short poetical composition of exquisite beauty, philosophico-mystical in character and a perennial source of inspiration to the Hindu intelligentsia'.[49]

The Bhagavadgita is most probably a work all by itself composed independently of Mahabharata and later added to it. The author of Gita is unknown. Some call him Vyasa,[50] and the date assigned to it is 5th cen. B.C. There is no general agreement. The text of Gita may have received many alterations in subsequent times.[51] There is a german tendency initiated by Garbe and continued notably by Rudolf Otto to dig out an Ur-Gita from under what they considered to be a mass of strictly irrelevant metaphysics.[52] R. Otto is of the opinion that the original Gita was composed of the chapters 1, 2, 10, 11 and 18 of the present Gita and that might have been a part of Mahabharata.[53]

The Bhagavadgita is called an Upanisad in a derived sense since it receives its main inspiration from that remarkable group of scriptures.[54] In this sense it may also be justly considered as forming a part of Vedanta. Krsna, the hero of Gita says: "Through all the Vedas it is I who should be known, for the maker of Vedanta am I, and I know the Vedas"[55]. The Gita is also called the 'layman's Upanisad'[56]. It tries to reconcile the apparently unreconcilable philosophical tendencies of Hinduism[57] in a syncretic whole[58] with a desire to be 'all things to all men'[59]. Gita is a resume of the essentials of the whole Vedic teaching as contained in the Upanisads[60] and so may be called the 'essence of all the Upanisads[61] and is venerated almost as a Sruti literature inspite of its strictly Smrti character. It could be read even by the Sudras and women who normally had no access to the strict Sruti.[62] It is even known as the 'New Testament' of Hinduism.[63] As it is the most popular[64] of all Hindu Scriptures it was also taken seriously and commented by later philosophers especially the Vedantins. It is also a fact that the Gita represents not any particular sect of Hinduism but Hinduism as a whole, not merely Hinduism but religion as such, in its universality without limit of time or space.[65]

The growth of heterodox sects like Buddhism and Jainism constituted a threat to the Vedic religion and the philosophers found it necessary to give rational foundation for the Vedic positions. This effort of rationalization and systematization resulted in the various systems of Indian philosophy called the Sad Darsanas, the six schools. They were based on Brahmasutras, systematization of aupanisadic thoughts in treatises called Sutras (clues) written in the form of aphorisms. 'Darsana' literally means vision. The main six philosophical Darsanas are:[66] Nyaya, essentially a system of logical analysis that adopted the atomic cosmology of Vaisesika. Smakhya which is an a-theistic philosophy of purusa-prakrti (active and passive principle) dualism which supports the Yoga-darsana that proposes techniques of integration of human faculties to achieve the sound balance of purusa and prakrti. Purva or Karma Mimamsa (early investigation) concerned with the proper interpretation of Vedas and

the conditions effective for vedic sacrifices and finally Uttara or Jnana Mimamsa (later investigation) which is concerned with the knowlegde of Brahman
and Atman, the reality of God and the reality of man. This last one, most
commonly known as 'Vedanta Darsana', was based on the Brahmasutra of
Badarayana called 'Vedanta Sutra' (ca. 200 A.D.). For many centuries the
Vedanta Sutra stood supreme and normative in the Vedantic school. This
particular philosophical trend is called 'Vedanta' due to the fact that it was
an attempt to re-interpret 'the basic truths of Vedas in the light of the aupanisadic revelation'[67] . The tripple canon (Prasthanatraya) or the basic text
of the Vedantic school are: (1) The Upanisads, (2) The Bhagavadgita and (3) The
Vedanta Sutra.[68]

The Vedantic philosophers wrote commentaries (Bhasya) on the Prastanatraya
and in the Vedanta itself different directions developed. The most famous
among them is the Advaita (non-dualism) first exposed by Gaudapada (ca.
500 A.D.) reaching the highest level of prestige through Sankaracharya (788-
820 A.D.) born at Kalady in today's Kerala.[69] Sankara's most important work
is his Bhasya on Vedanta Sutra.[70] Another important Vedanta school is that
of Ramanuja, said to have been born about 1017 A.D at Sri Parambattur
near Madras,[71] and his philosophy is known by the name 'Visistadvaita', qualified non-dualism, which has still great impact on the Vedantic thinking. Sankara
and Ramanuja are the most important and the most representative of the
Vedantic philosophers. Other Vedantic schools of lesser influence are the
'Dvaitadvaita' (dual-non-dual doctrine) of Nimbarka, born ca. 1162, the 'Dvaita'
(dualism) of Madhva (1197-1276) and the 'Suddhadvaita' (pure non-dualism)
of Vallabha, born ca. 1479.[72]

Hinduism went through a period of Moslem influence (1200-1757) [77] and that
helped the resurgence of monotheism, disregard for caste distinctions and
image worship and it was also the golden age of vernacular religious literary
works in India. In the period of western colonialism that followed, HInduism
absorbed many of the 'westernized' Christian ideas and that helped to a period
of renaissance in Hinduism (from 1757) under various reformers and reform
movements especially of the 19th century. Together with it followed a resurgence of Vedanta and Neo-Vedantins together with a general desire 'to adapt
the traditional beliefs and practices to the demands of the times (e.g., Gandhi,
Radhakrishnan, etc.)' [78].

In our work our attempt is to place the Indian understanding of Jesus Christ in the anthropological background of the Vedanta. In the Light of the above given introduction, the notion of Vedanta should be defined for our purpose to include the Upanisads which necessarily demands reference to the Rgveda, the Bhagavadgita which is considered as the essence of Upanisads and the Vedanta Darsana especially as it is represented by Sankara and Ramanuja. Thinkers of the other Vedantic schools like Nimbarka, Madhva and Vallabha seem to be of insignificant influence in todays Indian thinking. Nimbarks's 'Dvaitadvaita' is very similar to the philosophical position of Ramanuja. Vallabha's 'Suddhadvaita' is by and large a blend of the so-called pantheistic monism of Sankara and the theistic trends of Ramanuja. The 'Dvaita' of Madhva owes a lot to the dualistic Samkhya philosophy with a lot of Vedantic adaptations. His 'Dvaita' is also rightly called 'Savisesadvaita'. The basic tenets of the above mentioned philosophers are in one or another way implied in the systems of Sankara and Ramanuja. So we think it not necessary to bring them explicitly into our discussion. Such an approach is also followed by the modern interpreters of the Vedanta, the Neo-Vedantins, like Vivekananda, S. Radhakrishna and others, who also will be given considerable attention with the required differentiations as will be evident in the course of our work! It must also be clear from the very outset that we do not treat all the aspects of Vedanta itself in all its extensiveness, but only what is of immediate relevance for our topic. The fact that we make such a limitation of the topic does not mean that all other sources are ignored; they will also be considered in so far as they stand in immediate relevance to the Vedanta, of course with the necessary brevity. It is, however, an undeniable fact that Vedanta did not remain just as one of the Darsanas but permeated all of Hinduism and can be called even the cornerstone of modern Hinduism.

We have explained what we mean in our work by the word 'Vedanta'. We would like to make clear in this context that we do not reduce the vastly diverse Hindu thought patterns in India into the system of the Vedanta. We hold, however, that the Vedanta is the most representative of all Indian systems and we limit our investigation to this without questioning the validity of another possible approach. We also do not put all the different currents of thought into a single 'pot' indiscriminately. In the progress of our work we will be making adequate effort to differentiate historically the various schools and thought patterns in the Vedanta itself which can rightly be considered as the foundation of Hinduism and its crown! A similar approach to the Vedanta is also seen in Christian authors like P. Johanns, Abhishiktananda, P. Chenchiah, R. Panikkar, M. Dhavamony and many others as is evident from our bibliography.

Another point we would like to stress is that the main concern of this first part is anthropological through and through. Even the notion of God is seen from an anthropological stand-point. As S. Radhakrishnan observes, 'the main concern of Indian thought is with the status of man, his ultimate goal. Nature and God are treated as aids to help man to attain security of being, peace of mind. The main interest of Indian thought is practical. Philosophy is a guide of life'[74].

It is because of the basic anthropological character of the Indian enquiry that it expresses very often the Divine Mystery 'through an unspent fruitfulness of myths'[75]. It is, however, important that we distinguish between the truths of Hinduism, especially of the Vedanta, and the myths in which they were very often clothed. Perhaps even more than in the philosophical speculations of the Vedantic sages do we find expressed in these ancient and manifold myths the deep religiosity and the transcendent, divine horizon of the Indian soul.[76] Because of the anthropological and existential importance of myths, occasional reference to them has been found indispensable in our attempt to 'draw' the Vedantic context.

In the above pages we have tried to contextualize Vedanta in the general historical milieu of Hinduism. As the intention of our work is to outline a 'Khristavidhya', an Indian Christology, in the background of the anthropology of the Vedanta, we will be giving attention to three topics in this first part: God, Man, God-Man. In short, we are concentrating our attention on the Divine horizon in man as seen by the Vedanta!

It is also important to keep in mind that the context in which Christology has to develop in India is not that of a fossilized philosophical structure, a Vedanta of the past! While investigating the possibility of accepting the Vedantic categories into anthropo-Christological thinking, we do by no means intent to ignore the present Indian socio-economical context. A Christological dialogue in India, in order to be dynamic and fruitful, has to take place not merely in the realm of ideas, but in the midst of the realities of every day Indian existence. Christology has to grow out of the totality of the Indian experience that is inevitably bound up with the socio-economical factors of development today. We intend to give special attention to this particular point in Chapter VI, even though our attention is concentrated on the philosophical categories in the first three chapters.

A reasonable objection could be raised regarding our method of approach to the Vedanta. Is our approach to the Vedanta after all objective? It is not prejudicial and an assault against the Vedanta to subordinate and accommodate it to our personal goal and system by deducing anthropological and historical conclusions motivated by our Christological concern and not warrented by the Vedanta itself? Is it not a selective approach to take what suits us and to ignore the rest? It is true our concern is primarily Christological. It is also true that inspite of all our attempts at historical differentiations and conceptual distinctions we cannot do justice to the whole complex system of the Vedanta. It is also not our purpose! Our approach to the Vedanta is motivated by the particular nature of our question (Fragestellung) and topic. In this context an exhaustive presentation of all the intrinsic aspects of the Vedanta is neither possible nor required! That does not mean that we are prejudicial and not objective. We take only what is relevant for us, but we respect the context of the texts in all its objectivity and reserve for us the right to make conclusions which may not be directly intended by the texts. This is a legitimate approach in any scientific investigation and is demanded for a concentrated approach to the topic. Many Hindu scholars like S. Radhakrishnan, Aurobindo, Satprakasandanda and Akhilananda, to mention only a few, have also done the same in their approach to the Christian faith and world vision. They speak, for example, of the 'Hindu view of Christ' (Akhilananda) and of 'Jesus Christ in the light of the Vedanta' (Satprakasananda). A good many Christian theologians also have followed a similar method: 'To Christ through the Vedanta' (P. Johanns), 'Indische Weisheit - Christliche Mystik: Von der Vedanta zur Dreifaltigkeit' (Dom Le Saux alias Swami Abhishiktananda), 'The Vedanta Philosophy and the Message of Christ' (P. Chenchiah), 'The Crown of Hinduism' (J.N. Farquhar), 'The Vedanta Philosophy and the Message of Christ' (Carl Keller) etc. Further, it could be also said that Karl Rahner's approach to Heidegger or W. Pannenberg's use of Hegel are also definitively adaptive without being selective, prejudicial and consequently non-objective. So we would like to emphasize clearly that, inspite of our special concern, our approach to the Vedanta is objective and not prejudicial and so our method is quite legitimate.

CHAPTER I

THE REALITY OF GOD AND THE CONCEPT OF BRAHMAN

Man's understanding of God is implicitly and unthematically man's understanding of himself. Every search for God is basicly a search for the meaning of one's own existence. The anthropological conception of a particular people can never be understood without taking into consideration their theological preconceptions, especially their concept of God.

Our first concern in the analysis of an Indian anthropology is the analysis of the Indian man's understanding of God. Every question in the search for the ultimate meaning of existence implicitly contains an answer, corresponding to the question itself and ultimately to the one who puts the question. This particular approach is justified especially because our study is principally an attempt to investigate the manifestation of the divine horizon, aspect or element in man.

A. The Indian Henotheism: Gods and God

The archeological escavations in Mohenjo-Daro and Harappa, the Indus valley cities inhabited by the sophisticated pre-Vedic Indian agriculturalists, point to the possibility that the Dravidians and other non-Aryans practised the worship of many gods who were represented by concrete and material symbols.[1] The two main Indus valley cults were phallic worship and sacrifice to the mother goddess.[2] Besides the phallic 'lingam' archeologists could also unearth fragments of the statues of the 'cosmic dancer' and the three-faced yogi.[3] These evidences of image- worship indicate the tantalizing possibility of a long mythological and polytheistic tradition which might have reached its zenith about 2500 BC. In the Indus valley, however, there was a notable absence of temples although at Mohenjo-Daro a public building housing a bathingpool with chambers, probably prefiguring the holy bathing-places of later India, is conspicuous.[4]

The Aryan invaders who overthrew the ancient Indua valley civilization about 1700 BC had their own gods[5] ; but in their forms of worship (Vedic yajna) there was no room for the image of any god.[6] The Vedic gods were mainly personifications of the powers of nature. Their chief god was Indra, god of the storm, whose weapon was the thunderbolt. The natural forces - sun, wind, sky, thunder, fire, rain etc. - were the revelations of personal living gods possessing mind and will; idol representations were for them unnecessary and they could not evidently be contained in man-made tempels.[7] Fire was the most common representation of gods in Vedic times.[8] Though the Vedic gods are largely personifications of the powers of nature the Vedic religion cannot be explained as nature-worship; natural phenomena were transposed to a mythical plane. The Vedic hymns have much of occultism and mysteriousness; the gods mean much more than what their etymology signify. Each god is an assemblage of divine powers, of diverse origins and with several levels of significance.[9]

In the late Rigvedig period the gods began to be represented anthropomorphically in the form of idols.[10] In the Aganiic period the Deity venerated was represented by some visible emblem, a tool like a sword or a club, a tree, a stone, a picture or a statue which after being consecrated by a priest was looked upon as a visible presence of the personal God.[11]

The presence of the Divine in the midst of men, the irruption of the Divine into the profane is what is emphasized by the Hindu idol worship. The Divine and the profane are the two aspects of the same reality; the two fields are not entirely separated nor even superimposed on each other, but rather identical. The Divine cannot however be adequately comprehended or circumscribed by the spatio-temporal.[12] The Hindu has a deep sense of this Divine or Sacred which is diffused throughout nature penetrating every thing and every person. The Divinity can be foculized in a particular person or object through a process of ritual or mental purification, making manifest (avirbhuta) what was latent (avyakta).[13] But even when the deity is conceived in an anthropomorphic manner, it is generally supposed to be pure spirit. The relation between god and the idol is extrinsic; matter cannot be 'transubstantiated' into the deity.[14] In a consecrated idol there is only a special presence (visesadhisthana) of God who is immanent in all beings (sarvadhisthana).[15] After the consecration the divinity is supposed to assume the idol as his body which results in his real presence (samnidhya) and self-manifestation (avirbhava). The assuming of the idol form is considered as a great condescension on the part of God.[16]

It is evident that idolatry ministers to some of the most powerful and most valuable of man's religious instincts. That is the reason why it has played such a great part in the religious history of human race. Even great nations like Babylon, Greece and Rome that rose to great power and influence in the ancient world bowed down to idols. It is no wonder that the Indians are no exceptions to this general phase in the development of religons.[17] The making of images is a response to the eager human desire to know God's nature and character. The idols meet this need. God comes down from the sphere of thought and imagination to the level where he can be touched and seen, concretely adored and prayed to; man sees how the revered Being is like; man can gaze on his great features, read his character and carry away a picture of the Divine in his heart.[18] It is a sign of man's effort to reach beyond and above the sense-reality. This consciousness of the sacredness of things and persons may represent an admirable search and yearning after God, even if due to human weakness this movement towards God becomes vitiated by idolatry.[19] The above reference to the idolatry and image worship in India has great relevance for our work as we shall see later especially in reference to the mystery of the Divine Incarnation and the presentation of Jesus Christ as the "Image of God".

The gods in Vedic times are often reckoned as thirty-three in number and are divided into three groups of eleven for each of the three worlds: earth, air and heaven.[20] In the ages that followed there was an endless proliferation of myths and puranas and the number of gods and goddesses increased to no less than 330 millions, 'as many indeed as hairs on the skin of a cow'.[21] P. Fallon writes: "All the tribal gods and goddesses of the many races which have made up India's population, many heroes and sages, mythical personages or historical characters have.... been absorbed by Hinduism; all are worshipped, all are invested with the transcendent nature of [God].[22] They are legion; its not possible to enumerate them. Even demon-worship had its place in some obscure sectors of popular Hinduism. C.B. Papali remarks: "Certainly the devil is not worshipped as an object of love and adoration, but as an object of fear, as one to be kept out of mischief by occasional gifts. To the same category belongs the worship of serpents and other noxious creatures".[23]

So far we have spoken of Vedic polytheism. The Vedic polytheism was of a special kind. It made a peculiar turn not elsewhere observed but noticed only in India. There are evidences in the Vedas that the crude polytheism gradually developed to what Max Müller calls 'Henotheism'.[24] Pre-eminence began to be attributed to one god without asserting that he is the only God; it was an attempt at a unity to mitigate the the multiplicity of gods. M. Dhavamony writes:

> "It (henotheism) is a belief in single gods, each in turn standing out as the highest. It is defined as 'the belief in individual gods alternately regarded as the highest', the god addressed being for the moment treated as the supreme deity. This god alone is present to the mind of the worshipper; with him for the time being is associated everything that can be said of a divine being: he is the highest, the only god, before whom all others disappear." [25]

The same author states further that 'henotheism' is to be distinguished from a Greco-Roman model of modified monotheism in which one god (Zeus or Jupiter) emerges as the one god, ruler of the rest of the gods. 'None of the Vedic gods becomes the supreme God, undisputed king of gods and men. The different gods coalesce into one another with the result that they lose their identity'.[26] The Vedas address Indra, the god of lightning and thunder, Agni, the fire-god presiding over sacrifices, Varuna, the king of the universe who fashions and upholds heaven and earth, Surya, the sun-god, or Prajapati, the creator and protector of the world as the supreme deity in successive hymns.[27] The predominant idea of henotheism is that various gods are only different forms of a single divinity. The Rgveda says: "What is but One, the wise call by diverse names."[28] And again: "Him with fair wings, though only One in nature, wise singers shape, with songs, in many figures."[29]

Even the unsophisticated Indian villagers somehow realize that the numerous deities are but aspects and manifestations of the One Absolute. Each one chooses his 'ista devata', the deity which appeals to him the most, if he cannot concentrate on the formless and nameless Spirit; at the same time some respect and attention will also be paid to other aspects of the Absolute represented in other forms.[30] We will be discussing this question further in Chapter IV in reference to the manifestation of the Divinity in Jesus Christ.

The story of polytheism, or as in the case of India 'henotheism', is the story of man's search for God. Even in its most primitive form it is an expression or manifestation of the divine horizon in man, his transcendental constitution. It is an acknowledgement of the Mystery beyond the reach of one's own efforts even if it finds its expression as agnosticism as a Bengali author puts:

"The Hindu is fundamentally an agnostic, ie., has never believed in the possibility of human intelligence ever to unravel the mysterious eternal truths of the universe..... he has ever felt to be at complete liberty to imagine and invent whatsoever God or Gods he chooses to adore. He has not feared to conceive the Divinity as He, She, It or They..... he has endowed his own creation or invention with any attributes he likes for the time being..... His polytheism or henotheism is based essentially on his agnosticism."[31]

Our discussion so far on henotheism, polytheism and idols in Hinduism has great importance for our work especially because of its relevance to the question of the three persons in one God that is essential for the Christian understanding of the Divine Incarnation, the self-manifestation of God, as we shall see in Part II and later in Part III.

B. Brahman, the Absolute (Nirguna)

We will be using the Indian term for God, 'Brahman', time and agian in our work especially in reference to the divine horizon in man. Hence it is necessary to clarify the concept of 'Brahman' at the very outset. The Vedic Indians were sufficiently logical to realize that if the endless variety of the world suggests numerous deities, the unity of the world suggests a unitary conception of the deity. The religion of the Vedas consisted in the worship of the great and powerful gods whom men sought to propitiate with gifts and sacrifices. In the period of the Brahmanas it was believed that the sacrifices had a power of its own which gave men mastery even over gods. But cults and sacrifices lost their hold on the reflective minds of the Upanisadic sages whose religious craving and philosophical introspection brought them to the Ultimate Origin and Cause of every thing.[32] They understood that the real that lies behind the tide of temporal change is one, though we speak of it in many ways. Instead of denouncing the worship of the various deities as a disastrous error, they led the worshippers of the many deities to the worship of the one and only God by a process of reinterpretation and reconciliation.[33] By association and interconnection each god was thought to share in the perfections and functions of his fellow-gods, each god gradually merged into the other and finally each god merged into the All.[34] To this major principle the sages gave the name 'Brahman'.[35]

1. The Etymology of 'Brahman'

'Brahman' is a neuter noun and is derived from 'brh', to grow or to burst forth, a notion connected with development, gushing forth, bubbling over, ceaseless growth (brhattvam). Growth and development especially in their marvellous order (rta) is a incomprehensible fact, a mystery which is fascinating and at the same time terrifying, to which Rudolf Otto gives the name 'Sacred'.[36] So the word 'Brahman' can be roughly equated with 'the Sacred'. It can stand for sacred utterance,[37] · sacred Word (Vac), sacred formula, sacred chant sacred action etc. It could have also meant prayer, hymn, magic formula,[38] sacred knowledge or Veda, then the power inherent in them,[39] lastly, the Supreme Power.[40] Since the 'Sacred' as manifested in ritual was felt to be the bond that linked temporal man with what is eternal, 'Brahman' came to represent 'the Eternal' as it is in itself beyond space and time and as it manifests itself in the phenomenal world.[41] So 'Brahman' meant originally the all-pervading and selfexistent Power.

Sankara derives the word 'Brahman' from the root 'brhati', to exceed (atisayana) and means by it eternity, purity etc. For Madhava 'Brahman' is the one in whom the qualities dwell in fullness: "brhanto hy asmin gunah".[42]

'Brahma' is the masculine form of 'Brahman'. Neither the neuter form 'Brahman' in the above mentioned sense of an eternal principle or supreme power, nor the masculine from 'Brahma' appear in the Rgveda.[43] In the Rgveda 'Brahman' means only sacred knowledge or utterance,[44] hymn, incantation or Word (Vac).[45] Some scholars, however, interpret some of the Rgveda passages as allusions to 'Brahma'.[46] But Brahma is represented as the creater in the late Vedic and subsequent works.[47]

The 'Brahman' without the change of form has also a masculine application. In this case it means the one who is imbued with the power to make the sacred utterance. He can be a god or a man.[48] Later on it began to refer exclusively to a man, the priest, and that occurs in the Rgveda with a change in accent as 'Brahman' or 'Brahmin'[49] As a particular caste later on took on the priestly duties this caste began to be called 'Brahmana'. Brahmana means also the name of the sacrificial texts of the Vedic Corpus. In these texts 'Brahman' denotes the ritual and is generally understood also as the omnipotent Supreme Power, the Primal Principle and the Guiding Spirit of the universe, all comprehensive Creative Principle and the Cause of all existence: "Verily, in the beginning, this (universe) was the Brahman. It created the gods, it made them ascend these worlds; Agni this (terrestrial) world, Vayu the air, and Surya the sky...."[50] This refers to Brahman as the cosmic unifying principle.

The influence of old Vedic cosmologies and the resulting figurative and anthropomorphic thinking might have prevented the early Indian visionaries from grasping fully the stupendous notion of Brahman as the all pervading all inclusive Power as later developed by the aupanisadic sages.[51] The Upanisads testify eloquently the earliest Indian attempts of Brahma-jijnasa or enquiry into the nature of the Supreme Reality. The Vedanta commentators like Sankara and Ramanuja further developed this doctrine. S. Radhakrishanan formulates the principal concern of the Upanisads as follows:

> "To the pioneers of the Upanisads, the problem to be solved presented itself in the form, what is the world rooted in? What is that by reaching which we grasp the many objects perceived in the world around us? They assume, as many philosophers do, that the world of multiplicity is, in fact, reducible to one single, primary reality which reveals itself to our senses in different forms. This reality is hidden from senses but is discernible to the reason. The Upanisads raise the question: what is that reality which remains identical and persists through change?"[52]

Brahman is the answer to this question. As this question took manifold forms and expressed diverse concerns, the concept of Brahman also began to undergo a gradual process of development in various philosophical directions. There are two classical Vedantic ways of approaching the concept of Brahman: (1) the way of negation and, (2) the way of affirmation.

The Brahman that is thus arrived at is called "Nirguna Brahman".[52a] ie. Brahman without accidental attributes. "Guna" means a quality or endowment which a substance has and which is really distinct from that substance.[52b] As Brahman is Absolute as we shall soon see, there cannot be in it a distinction of 'having' and 'being'. In this sense the supreme Brahman is also called 'nirakara' (without form or bodily shape) and 'nirupadhika' (free from all determinations or characters).[52c]

2. 'Neti Neti' Laksanas: The Way of Negation

About Brahman Brhadaranyaka Upanisad asks this question: "By what can we know the universal knower?"[53] The Upanisads themselves give the answer: It is that from which our speach turns back along with the mind, being unable to comprehend its fullness:

> "There no eye can penetrate,
> No voice, no mind can penetrate:
> We do not know, we do not understand
> How one should teach it."[54]

It is that which the tounge of man cannot truly express nor human intelligence conceive:

> "I do not think, 'I know it well',
> I do not know, 'I do not know';
> He of us who knows It, knows It,
> He does not know, 'I know it not'.
> Who thinks not on It, by him it is thought:
> Who thinks upon it, does not know,-
> ununderstood by those who unterstand,
> By those who understand not understood."[55]

Therefore, we describe the Absolute in negative terms. Brahman is beyond our human categories and defies all description: "All speech together with mind turns away unable to reach it."[56] In this case we have to deny to Brahman all misleading human categories. This is the function of the negative or "Neti Neti" laksanas. They point to Brahman by excluding from it all misleading and unsuitable predicates because Brahman is beyond the sphere of predication. It would be better to say no more of it than 'Not this, Not this'. Once we define it we limit the unlimitable and circumscribe the uncircumscribable. Therefore the Upanisads indulge in negative accounts, that the Real is not this, not this. It is:

> "Not gross, not subtle, not short, not long, not growing, not shadowy, not dark, not attached flavourless, smell-less, eye-less, ear-less, speechless, breath-less, mouth-less, not internal, not external, consuming nothing, consumed by nothing:"[57]

For the Isa Upanisad the Supreme One (tad ekam) is without qualities and attributes, neither existent nor non-existent: "without sinews, without scar, untouched by evil",[58] and the Brhadaranyaka Upanisad says of Brahman: "This Self - (What we can say of it but) 'No, no!' It is impalpable, for it cannot be grasped; indestructible, for it cannot be destroyed; free from attachment, for it is not attached (to anything), not bound,..."[59] The Kena Upanisad strikes however a more positive chord in its negative approach to Brahman. Even though Brahman is beyond all thought and undertandign and speech. It is the condition of the possibility ("Bedingung der Möglichkeit") - to use a Rahnerian expression as we shall see in the third evaluative part - for all understanding and speech: Brahman is:

> "That which cannot be spoken by speech, but by which the speech is made possible; that which cannot be thougnt by the mind, but by which, they say, the mind thinks; that which cannot be seen by the eye, but by which the eye is made to see; that which cannot be heard by the ear, but by which the ear is made to hear; that which does not breath, but by which the breath is made possible, know that alone to be the Brahman, not this which they worship outside."[60]

It is to indicate the inapplicability of empirical determinations that the Upanisads attribute to Brahman contradictory predicates: "It does not move and yet it moves. It is far away and yet it is near."[61] These attributes, while affirming the transcendent character of the Supreme (Para Brahman) does not deny his immanence (Apara); He is both inside and outside the world.[62]

This view of of the Upanisads in making the negative approach to Brahman is also supported by the Bhagavadgita. It also speaks of the Supreme as the "unmanifest, unthinkable and unchanging"[63], neither existent nor nonexistent: "Within all beings, yet without them; unmoved, It yet moves indeed; so subtle is It you cannot comprehend It; far off It stands, and yet how near It is."[64]

Shortly said, the 'Neti Neti' approach to Brahman emphasizes that It is the Absolute beyond all multiplicity, change, division or relation. Nothing can be predicated of Brahman because all qualifications or attributions would go counter to the very absoluteness and unicity of the Supreme Reality. To know It correctly one must resort to negation, the "Neti, Neti" (not this, not that) method proposed by the Upanisads. Brahman in this aspect is the Godhead itself than God apprehended as the Creator, Ruler or Saviour.[65]

He is not even person in the ordinary sense of the term; He is actually It and therefore impersonal. Any description or definition makes It into something. It is nothing among things to which human categories can be applied. As S. Radhakrishanan affirms: "It is non-dual, advaita. It denies duality. This does not mean, however, that the Absolute is non-being. It means only that the Absolute is all-inclusive and nothing exists outside it."[66] It goes without saying that the above mentioned "Neti, Neti" approch corresponds to the "Via negationis" of the gnoseological analogy proposed by the scholastic philosophy. We will he referring to this point later.

3. Brahman as 'Sat-Cit-Ananda'

No finite concept or word can really express the infinite Being, Brahman. To say that the nature of Brahman cannot be defined does not mean that It has no essential nature of Its own. Negative characteristics should not mislead us into thinking that Brahman is a nonentity. The negative indications or Laksanas[67] mean only that Brahman should not be defined by empirical and accidental features, for they do not belong to Its essence.[68] We need some positive indications to designate the Absolute Reality. The Brahma-laksanas can have validity only if they are based on Its 'svarupa' or essential nature. The negative or "Neti, Neti" laksanas point to Brahman by excluding from It all unsuitable predicates. This negative step should lead us ultimately to a positive approach to Brahman. The necessity of combining the negative with the positive approach is very emphatic in the statement of Kathopanisad:

"Not by speech, not by mind,
not by sight can he be apprehended.
How can he be comprehended
Otherwise than by one's saying, "He is"?
Unseen, unspeakable, ungraspable, unthinkable,
Unnamable, without distinctive marks, tranquil (santa)
Benign (siva), without a second (a-dvaita)." [68a]

The positive indications or Svarupa-laksanas give us some enlightenment about the proper nature of Brahman and the Sruti contains as just seen some 'Svarupa-laksanas' which are direct indications of the proper form (svarupa) of Brahman.[69] These indications should not be taken just in the ordinary meaning of their terms. The positive terms also should be subjected to a process of interpretation which take us beyond the ordinary meaning to the most elevated, supra-mundane meaning (paramartha).[70] R. De Smet writes: "In this process we move along a threefold ascending path through causality (hetubhava), negation (apavada) and elevation (paramartha-laksana), according to the suggestions of the context."[71]

According to the Taittiriya Upanisad, the only way in which Brahman can be positively described is: "Brahman is Reality, Knowledge, Infinite" - "Satyam jnanam anantam brahma".[72] As the Real of the real,[73] Brahman simply IS (asti) and hence Sat or Being is the most suitable designation for It. If Brahman is the Ultimate Being, It is the sole Knower and includes all knowledge and thus the very essence of Its being is understanding (Vijnana):[74] It is wholly a mass of wisdom (prajnana)[75]; It is Consciousness itself (Cit).[76] There can be no limitation for such a Being; it is therefore Infinite (ananta).[77]

If the Absolute (Brahman) is pure existence (Sat), pure thought (Cit) and infinity (Anantam), It must be free from change, deacay and suffering; It must be pure Bliss (Ananda). There are some who are of the opinion that Ananda is the nearest approximation to the Absolute Reality;[78] and that is why while Taittiriya Upanisad describes the Brahman as "Real, Intelligence, Infinite" (Satyam jnanam anantam Brahma)[79], Brhadaranayaka Upanisad designates It as "pure Knowledge and Bliss" (Vijnanam Anandam Brahma).[80] The Tait. Upanisad also affirms that those who know the Brahman as Reality, Knowledge and Infinity shares in the Bliss of Brahman: "He who knows Brahman as Reality, Knowledge and Infinity, hidden in the depth of the heart and in the highest ether or farthest space, he enjoys all blessings, at one with the omniscient Brahman."[81]

The Taittiriya Upanisad describes the episode of a pupil who seeks after the nature of Brahman.[82] Brahman is seen as that from which these beings are born, that in which when born they live, and that into which they enter at their death. The pupil seeks what reality conforms to this account. It cannot be matter (anna) because matter cannot account for the forms of life. Life (prana) again cannot be the ultimate principle, for conscious phenomena are not commensurate with living forms. As consciousness (manas) itself has different grades - the consciousness of an animal and a man are not the same - that also cannot be the ultimate principle. Could intellectual consciousness (Vijnana) then be Brahman? Even that is incomplete because it is subject to discords and dualities. There must be a further principle, a deeper one, which has led to the development of matter, life, mind and intellectual consciousness. The pupil ultimately apprehends the self-evident Reality and the Supreme Unity that lies behind all the lower forms. This Ultimate principle is the Bliss of fulfilled existence (Ananda). There the search ends and he comes to the conclusion that Reality is Satyam (truth), Jnanam (Consciousness), Anantam (Infinity) which taken together is Spiritual Bliss (Anandam).[83] Once more it is to be observed as Sankara remarks, the Taittiriya Upanisad statement "satyam jnanam anantam Brahma" is not a definition of Brahman, but a designative statement; these words refer to Brahman in their primary meaning.[33a]

As S. Radhakrishan rightly observes, Sat (Being), Cit (Consciousness, and Ananda (Bliss) are different phrases for the same being:

> "Self-being, self-consciousness and self-delight are one. It is absolute being in which there is no nothingness. It is absolute consciousness in which there is no non-consciousness. It is absolute bliss in which there is no suffering or negation of bliss. All suffering is due to a second, an obstacle...."[84]

We will be considering the concept of Ananda later in chapter III of this part of our investigation especially when we will be analysing the reality of 'Anubhava' or experience. We would like to mention here also that the concept of 'Saccidananda' will be playing a significant role later in our discussion of the divinity of Christ in Chapter V and in reference to the trinitarian dimension of the Christ-experience especially in Chapters VI and IX corresponding to the notion of God-realization, which we will be developing in Chapter III. For the present we pay some detailed attention to the most important characteristics of Brahman, namely, 'Sat' and 'Cit'. As Ananta (Infinite) is a necessary consequence implied in Sat and Cit, a further analysis of it is not required for our work.

a. Brahman as Satyasya Satyam: Real of the Real, Truth of the True.

Brhadaranyaka Upanisad declares that Brahman is Satyasya Satyam - the Reality of the real, the source of all existing things.[85] We may speak of reality in three levels: (1) Pratibhasika satta or phenomenal reality which is like dreams having existence only in the mind, (2) Vyavaharika satta or empirical reality, the realities of our common and day to day experience and (3) Paramarthika satta or transcendent reality which is Brahman.[86] Brahman cannot be said to 'have' existence as in the case of the other above two, the world of finite beings, which are real only for practical purposes.[87] Brahman IS existence; in It there is no dualism between 'having' and 'being'; and consequently It is not subject to change. Brahman is beyond the opposition of 'having' and 'being'. In Its Truth It reconciles the definite 'being' and the indefinite 'becoming'; therefore the designation of Brahman as 'satyasya satyam'[88] is justified: Sat (=being) + tyat (=indefinite) = Satyam (=true).[89]

Since Brahman is the Real every thing depends on Brahman for their existence. Brahman is the source of all beings to which all existence aspire. Brahman is the principle that unifies, makes into ONE, the diversity of realities.[90] As 'satyasya satyam' Brahman is the ONE without a second (ekam eva advitiyam). We read in the Chandogya Upanisad:

> "In the beginning, my dear, this was Being only, - one, without a second. - Some say that, in the beginning, this was non-being, only one, without a second. From that non-being sprang Being. But how could it be so, my dear? - said he; How could Being be born of non-being? In fact, this was Being only, in the beginning, one, without a second."[91]

This statement regarding the primacy of the Oneness of Being over multiplicity is a key statement in the Indian philosophical tradition. This 'Sat' is unique, source and origin of all beings; as the ultimate basis of all reality it remains hidden from ordinary experience.[92]

The One perceived as the ground of all being in Indian thought is a positive category. As J.B. Chettimattam observes:

> "...it is not the negative "one" of Plotinus, which simply isolates the Absolute from everything else, as transcendent and ineffable, excluding being and even intelligence. Nor is it the amorphous one of the pleroma of the Gnostics, which is simply a non- distinguished crowd of entities. This is also not the "one" of Plato, which is merely an ideal and model for all to imitate, but outside of them all. [As a positive category] all things are in the One without adding anything to its superabundant fulness. Yet, it is in the heart of each being as its innermost reality. This "One" does not leave out any metaphysical residue. All are in Him in His supreme unity, and He is in all without being multiplied."[93]

The expressions like 'ekamevadvitiyam' (one only without a second) is seen already in the early Upanisads to denote an impersonal, eternal, self-existent unifying principle.[94] This Brahman is invisible, ingraspable, eternal, without qualities; it is the imperishable source of all things;[95] all this really is Brahman (sarvam khalvidam Brahma); in it every thing is born, everything exists and everything is absorbed (tajjalana).[96]

This being so, the title 'Param Brahma[97] (the Supreme Great) is most applicable to Brahman. Ramanuja observes that Brahman "primarily denotes that which has greatness of essential nature"[98] and only secondarily and in a derivative sense those things which are relatively great. The Upanisadic designation of Brahman as Purnam (plenitude) expresses the same idea of Brahman's greatness expressed by the Taittiriya Upanisad. The opening prayer of Isa Upanisad is an indication of the greatness of Brahman and Its presence in all things: "...that is Fullness, this is fullness; fullness is derived from the Fullness. Even after the fullness is drawn from the Fullness, Fullness remains as such."[99] Sankara gives great emphasis to the the aspect of the greatness of Brahman characterising Him as 'bhuman', fullness, as comprehensive of the essential characteristics of God.[100]

The Param Brahma is also 'param Tattvam'[101] (the immutable ground) beyond all change. Change is the dynamism of a finite reality to stability and immutability. Such a dynamism is not present in the Reality that is Fullness itself. The mystic monosyllable OM (AUM)[102] represents Brahman in His fullness and the ground of all being; the past, present and future are all included in this one sound and every thing is implied in it.[104] 'Om' co-ordinates all speech and represents the totality of the world; it is the Absolute Sound.[104] The Omkara (utterance of Om) has consequently a salvifying and liberating effect,[105] because it represents the Fullness of Brahman Himself.

In conclusion to our discussion of 'Brahman' as 'Satyasya Satyam' it could be mentioned that this explanation is surprisingly similar to the Christian understanding of God as 'ipsum esse subsistens'. God is the Real of the real and the Truth of the true! We will be evaluating the concept of 'Purnam' (God as the Mystery of Fullness) later in Chapter VII with the help of Karl Rahner and Wolfhart Pannenberg.

b. 'Prajnanam Brahmā: Brahman as Consciousness

In the Upanisads, consciousness is the basic note of real existence.[106] If Brahman is 'Satyam', the only one who truly is, who alone is immutable,[107] It has to be fully in Itself and shining by Itself, which characteristic is designated by the term Prajnanam, Cit or Jnanam.[108] The noblest and most comprehensive thing that comes within the realm of our own experience is consciousness. But our consciousness suffers from a subject-object dichotomy, knowing subject and known object. When we speak of the ultimate Reality as Consciousness this subject object distinction cannot come into question because a reality circumscribed by an object cannot be the Ultimate reality. An object is a determining factor and any determination contradicts the very meaning of the Ultimate Reality.[109] When we say that the Ultimate Reality is Consciousness, Prajnanam Brahma,[110] we arrive at a conclusion from the desire to know and the tendency to unify all our experience in an ultimate ground.

This ultimate ground or pure intelligence (Prajnana) is the meeting point of subject and object. The various factors which distinguish our acts of knowledge do not and cannot belong to the essence of pure consciousness. In pure Consciousness there is no question of 'becoming' conscious through sensory experience,[112] there do not exist various 'grades' of consciousness as in the case our waking state, dreaming state and dreamless sleep. These various grades do not pertain to the essence of knowledge and consciousness. 'Only the common factor in these varying states constitutes the ideal condition.[113] This common factor is pure Intelligence (Cinmatra) or a sense of 'I'[114] which is the ground of all forms and modes of expressions of reality. This is the Absolute Reality, pure self-awareness (bodharupa), the Brahman which forms the basis of everything as the Aitareya Upanisad states: "All this is guided by intelligence, is based on intelligence. This world is guided by intelligence. The basis is intelligence. Brahman is intelligence."[115] As Sankara observes, this Intelligence is so pure that It does not admit even the subject-object, knower-knowledge-knowable distinctions.[116] Brahman is the Supreme Intelligence which includes the knowledge of all other things (sa brahmavidyam sarvavidpratistam);[117] by knowing Brahman everything else is known.[118] The one who knows Brahman also gets out of the gnosiological subject-object dichotomy and himself becomes Brahman (Brahmaved brahmaiva bhavati)[119]

As Brahman is pure Consciousness, the Upanisads apply to Him the analogy of light which stresses His character of selfluminosity. Brahman is Intelligence itself, while all other things are made intelligible. Brahman shines by Himself but all other things shine only in his reflection. The light of Brahman illumines everything ; but He himself is not illumined by any:

"The sun shines not there, nor the moon and stars,
These lightnings shine not, much less this (earthly) fire:
After Him, as He shines, does everything shine,
This whole world is illumined with His light."[120]

This Brahman as the ultimate source of all consciousness is named 'Param Jyotih' (Supreme Light).[121]

Our analysis of 'Brahman' as consciousness is of great relevance for our topic especially because of the importance of a consciousness Christology in the Indian context as we shall see later in Chapter IV and also due to the intimate relation between consciousness and person as we shall discuss in our evaluation in Chapter VII. We will also have to distinguish there between God's being consciousness itself and man's having it, which constitutes the difference between God and man!

4. The Concept of 'Maya' and the Problem of the World

The 'way of negation' and the 'way of affirmation', the two steps which we have discussed in reference to the process of knowing Brahman leads to the question of 'Maya', which is supposed to explain Brahman's relation to the world and the possibility of understanding Brahman starting from the things of this world. The scholastic notion of analogy, both ontological and epistomological, does a similar function by 'via affirmationis', 'via negationis' and 'via elevationis'. Inspite of the apparent similarity between 'analogy' and 'Maya', there are certain specific characteristics for the notion of 'Maya' as we shall see below, which are important in determining the relation between God and the world, the God-man relationship and consequently the very nature of man himself and the final goal to which he is destined!

Brahman is beyond the reach of thought and voice. He is absolute and qualityless (Nirguna) and inconceivable (Acintya). He is the One without a second (Ekam-advitiyam). Every thing outside him is only unreal (an-rta). In this context how can we explain the undeniable fact of this world including human beings? This world cannot be Brahman because this is fundamentally limited. At the same time there cannot BE anything other than Brahman. This world confronts us as a big paradox. The search for a solution of this problem has been one of the major concerns of Hindu thinking. Even the Samhita raises this preoccupation in its famous creation hymn:

> "In the beginning there was neither being nor non-being,
> there was no atmosphere, nor the sky beyond it.
> What was there then? wherein was it concealed?
> was it perhaps in the depth of the waters?
> Death there was not, nor immortality,
> nor was there token of night or day;
> but that One Being was breathing without breath,
> apart from it there was nothing whatsoever.
> Who knows for certain, who shall here declare it?
> whence was it born, whence came this creation?
> The gods themselves were born after this world's production;
> then who can know from whence it has arisen?"[122]

The Upanisads provide various elements of the answer to this most difficult question as C.B. Papali writes:

> "....those ancients were faced with three alternatives: to admit a real world coeternal with God compromising thereby his absolute sovereignty; or regard the world as a real emanation or evolution of God sacrificing His immutability; or finally maintain the absolute perfection and immutability of God and deny the reality of the world. All these explanations are attempted in the Upanisads, but the overall tendency of their speculation is in favour of the last alternative, absolute monism: God alone is real, all the rest unreal....Faced by the necessity of choosong between the perfection of God and the reality of the world, those ancients.... sacrificed the world to save God."[123]

Brahman is the One Reality to which nothing can be added and from which nothing can be substracted. Therefore the reality of nature, man and even gods must be understood in terms of absolute dependence on Brahman. 'Nothing can be or work or think and nothing can be properly grasped and known apart from Brahman'.[125] Whatever exists owes its being to Brahman.[126] There are various metaphors to show how this universe takes its origin from Brahman while the Brahman remains ever-complete and undiminished. Brahman is the cause of the phenomenal world as the spider is the cause of its web, and fire the cause of sparks: "As a spider goes out (of itself) by (means of its) treads, as tiny sparks leap out of the fire, so from this self [Brahman] issue all life-breaths (prana), all worlds, all gods, all contigent beings."[127]

The origin of the world from Brahman should not be unterstood as a creation from nothing. 'God does not create the world but becomes it. Creation is expression. It is not the making of something out of nothing. It is not making so much as becoming. It is the self-projection of the supreme. Everything exists in the secret abode of the supreme'[128]. The world has to be traced to the power of the Supreme. We will be referring in Chapter VII to the similarity of Hegel's philosophy to the above mentioned position.

"Maya" is the most common word used to express the reality of the world and its relation to the Nirguna Brahman. 'Maya' is most commonly translated as 'illusion', but its real meaning is much deeper. We read in the Svetasvatara Upanisad that this world is the result of Maya, cosmic illusion:

"This whole world the illusion-maker projects out of this (Brahman)
And in it by illusion the other is confined.
Now, one should know that nature is illusion,
And that the mighty Lord is the illusion-maker."[129]

Here Brahman is described as the 'Mayin'. To translate 'Mayin' as 'illusion-maker' is correct, but in this context it is not sufficient and even misleading. 'Mayin' can be best translated as 'the wonder-working powerful being'[130]. Maya does not imply that the world is simply and only an illusion or is absolutely non-existent. Maya is the word used to denote the world's absolute dependence on Brahman. 'While the world is dependent on Brahman, the latter is not dependent on the world. This one-sided dependence and the logical inconceivability of the relation between the Ultimate Reality and the world are brought out by the word, "maya". The world is not essential being like Brahman; nor is it mere non-being. It cannot be defined as either being or non-being'[131]. The world has its roots in Brahman, though it does not constitute the nature of Brahman. 'The world is neither one with Brahman nor wholly other than Brahman'[132].

Etymologically speaking "Maya" is derived from the root, ma, to form, to build; it stands for the capacity to produce forms. 'There is no suggestion that the forms, the events and the objects produced by maya or the form-building power of Brahman, the mayin, are only illusory'[133]. Maya states that Brahman without losing his integrity is the basis of the world, the root cause of the universe. The world does not carry its own meaning; but it is not annulled or cancelled by the Beyond. If the world is unreal by itself it is real as based on Brahman.[134] It is not utter non-existence. The emphasis is on the dependence of the world on Brahman. 'The relative rests in the absolute. There can be no echo without a noice. The world is not self-explanatory; it is not the cause of itself. It is an effect'[135]. It is not a reality by itself, but a given reality.

Since the reality of the world is not ultimate and it is only an empirical reality, there is a serious possibility that it becomes a source of illusion for us. The world can be very deceptive, because Brahman is not immediately visible to the human faculties of perception. Even then the world is not a deception, but only an occasion of deception, for us. The world and its changes conceals and obscures Brahman (tirodhana) from our view; we cannot easily pierce behind the universe and its activities.[136] The Bhagavadgita itself speak of the world as delusive in character, because the manifested world hides the real from the vision of the mortals.[137] In this case the world becomes a source of delusion.[138] Why is it so? There is no answer to this question; it is only to be accepted as a given realty.[139]

The illusory nature of the world, explained and elaborated by the Upanisads and the Bhagavadgita, were later interpreted by philosophers in exaggerated terms. There is, ofcourse, a non-dualistic trend in some of the Upanisads as we have seen above; this trend found its systematization and chief defence in a later period in Sri Sankara, 'who made Advaita or Non-Dualism, the chief metaphysical school in India. According to him, the world of our experience has only a relative value, namely of a stepping-stone towards the realization of the Real'[140]. The position of Sankara is best stated by Ramanuja as follows:[141]

"Brahman alone, who is pure intelligence and hostile to all characterising attributes, is real; all other things than Him ... are merely assumed
to exist in Him, and are unreal."[142]

"Unreality is that, which, being grounded upon what is perceived, is
liable to be stultified by means of the knowledge of things as they actually are."[143]

A rope mistaken for a snake is a classical example of Sankara to explain
the illusory nature of the world. The rope is real; the interpretation given
to it as snake is the result of illusion caused by our ignorance (Avidhya).
We will be dealing with 'Avidhya' more elaborately in chapter II of this part.
Sankara's system of philosophy has been most commonly misunderstood as
monism. Sankara's thought represents Advaita; Advaita means non-dualism
which need not necessarily be monism. It is true that such expressions as:
Satyam Brahma, jagad mithya (Brahman alone is real, the world is false),
Sarvam khalv-idam Brahma (Verily this whole world is Brahman) could be
understood or interpreted in monistic or acosmic terms. In the philosophy
of Sankara, 'a' only negates the world as a reality added to or beside the
Absolte. It is not false, but only non-real (anrta).[144] But as R. De Smet observes, 'Sankara's language kept to such heights that the lower genius of many
a so-called disciple and, more commonly, of the neo-Vedantins of today could
not keep pace with him, and they have turned this transcendentalism into
an unpalatable brand of pantheism'[145].

We will be further elaborating the implications of the concept of 'Maya'
for Christian anthropology and Christology later in Chapter V especially in
reference to Brahmabandhab Upadhyaya's explanation of the Christian faith
in creation and the true humanity of Jesus Christ. Our above discussion of
'Maya' is also relevant for our consideration of the transcendence and immanence of God and the God-man relationship as understood by Karl Rahner
and Wolfhart Pannenberg later in our evaluative part especially in Chapter VII.
A proper understanding of the relation between God and man and the nature
of this world in relation to God is also, as we shall see in Chapter IX, important
for a genuine Christian spirituality.

C. 'Saguna Brahman' and the Concept of 'Isvara'

Nirguna Brahman is God considered in His absolute transcendence. The immanent aspect of God is given emphasis by the expression 'Saguna Brahman'.
God in His absolute simplicity, perfection and unicity is 'Nirguna'; in His
undeniable relation to the world He is understood as 'Saguna'. 'Nirguna' and
'Saguna' are two terms which are often not properly understood. "Guna" means
an accidental quality which a substance 'has'. Since we cannot make a distinction in God between 'having' and 'being' in the strict sense God is Nirguna
and cannot be Saguna, metaphysically speaking. But man cannot live by metaphysics alone. Metaphysical facts regarding God must also be made understandable to the ordinary man. So the intention in considering God as Saguna is
pedagogical ano therefore the concept of Saguna Brahman should not be considered as contradictory to Nirguna Brahman; both are actually complementary.
While the understanding of God as Nirguna Brahman reached through the
'Neti-laksanas' and through the 'Svarupa-laksanas' designating Him as "Saccidananda" are correct and more accurate, the saguna understanding of God
is anthropomorphic and accommodated to ordinary speech. The transcendence
of God does not cancel His immanence.[146]

It is also to be mentioned that to render 'saguna' as personal and 'nirguna'
as impersonal is very attractive and common, but quite incorrect! The Sanskrit
language has actually no equivalent for 'person'[146a] as it is fixed in the traditional Christian theology as 'subsistens distinctum natura intellectuali' - distinct and complete subsistent characterised by intelligence and free will,
which is applicable to the finite man and the infinite God. Regarding the
application of the concept of person to Brahman R. de Smet observes that
'it is evident that nirguna Brahman verifies this [classical] definition [of person]
and corresponds perfectly to the notion of God as defined in the great Councils
of the Christian Church [ie. Nicea and Chalcedon] - abstracting ofcourse,
from his definition as Holy Trinity. On the contrary, the notion of 'saguna'
Brahman is anthropomorphic and cannot have any but a merely pedagogical
value'[147]. Our discussion regarding the distinction of 'Nirguna Brahman' and
'Saguna Brahman' are of great relevance for us especially in our consideration
of the immanent trinity and the economic trinity as we shall see later in
Chapters IV and VII.

1. God as Isvara: The Lord of all Being

In the history of Hinduism various terms have been used to express the idea of God emphasizing His relation to the world. The most important of them are: Deva, Bhagavan and Isvara. 'Div' is the root of Deva, which means 'shining, fair, good' and therefore God. [147a] Bhagavan or Bhagavad, which is another term for Supreme God, is he who is 'bhaga' which means dispenseer of good fortune, giver of gifts. Prosperity, dignity, distinction, excellence, majesty, loverliness, beauty etc. are the ideas connected with Bhagavan. He is the Glorious One, the Adorable, the Holy One, the Blessed Lord. [147b]

The title Isvara is a very important and common designation for God. Its root is 'Is', to own, to possess, to be powerful, to command, to rule, to reign. In the Vedic literature 'Isvara' [148] means the power of a ruler, lord or master or even the divine power. The Isa Upanisad and Katha Upanisad use the term Isvara with a theistic accent. [149] There we see a tendency to conceive the Supreme Being in personal terms and distinct from the universe. Here the term 'personal' is to be understood not as a static one, just in the ontic sense as in the case of Nirguna Brahma, but as a dynamic one. Isvara as personal God is understood as being capable of loving relationship. 'Isvara' has a monotheistic overtone. This term stands for a personal dynamic God who in His transcendence is never in absolute distance like the Nirguna Brahman from this world of human beings. He is the Divine Transcendence immanent in the world. The idea of God as origin, sustainer, and indweller of the universe and of the human self and at the same time distinct from them all is denoted by 'Isvara'. Although each Hindu sect calls its own deity 'Isvara', by and large Isvara stands as a non-sectarian term very comprehensive in significance and can be used as a synonym to God. [150]

Isvara is to be considered as the Saguna aspect of Nirguna Brahman, who is supra-personal, completely transcendent and is absolute silence. Brahman is to be apprehended in two ways. 'Both the Absolute and Personal God are real; only the former is the logical prius of the latter' [151]. Hence there are two forms of Brahman, the unmanifest and the manifest, the formless and the formed, the timeless and the temporal, the higher and the lower. Accordingly there are also two forms of 'Brahma-Vidhya' (knowledge of God), the higher and the lower. Isvara is Brahman Himself considered in His power of manifestation.[152] The two are like two sides of one reality. So the distinction between Nirguna Brahman and Isvara, Brahman in itself and Brahman in the universe, the transcendent beyond manifestation and the transcendent in manifestation, the indeterminate and determinate (nirguno guni) is by no means exclusive.[153] The difference is only one of stand-point and not of essence, between God as He is and God as He appears to us.[154] The Supreme in its absolute self-existence is Brahman (nirguna), the Absolute as the Lord containing and controlling all is Isvara.[155] Dr. Radhakrishnan is of the same opinion. Nirguna and saguna Brahman are not two kinds of Brahman, but the same Brahman described in different ways. He further analyses the Absolute Reality in four poises or statuses: (1) the Absolute Brahman, (2) the Creative Spirit or Isvara, (3) the World-Spirit (Hiranya-garbha), and (4) the World (Viraj)[156] The most important point that he wants to stress is that Isvara is the development or manifestation of the Absolute or Nirguna Brahman. This attempt to distinguish between transcendent Brahman (Para Brahman or Nirguna Braman) and the empirical Brahman (Apara Brahman or Isvara) has strong support in the Upanisad: "There are, assuredly, two forms of Brahman: the formed (murta) and the formless (amurta)...the stationary and the moving, the actual (sat) and the yon (tya)."[157] The Bhagavadgita also accepts the the Supreme as having two forms, higher (para) and the lower (apara).[158] But the whole stress of Bhagavadgita is on the Personal God or Isvara which for the Gita is Krsna, who is even identified with the 'highest Brahman'[159] and even considered as the base supporting Brahman and in this sense surprisingly above Brahman.[160] For Gita the Absolute Brahman and the Supreme Personal God are all Krsna, the human manifestation of God (Avatar). We will be dealing with the question of Avatar more elaborately in chapter III of this part and the question of Jesus Christ as the definitive manifestation of God in the subsequent chapters.

Bhagavadgita may be considered as the crowning of Indian theism.[161] Eventhough it considers sometimes Brahman as the Absolute and Imperishable,[162] and at other times identifies Brahman with Krsna, the personal God the overall trend is to subordinate Brahman to the Personal God: "For I am the base supporting Brahman, immortal changeless, and (supporting) too the eternal

law of righteousness and absolute bliss".[163]   Brahman for Gita is the womb
into which personal God implants His seed.[164]   In Gita 'Brahman' has various
meanings; it can stand even for material nature or liberated self or even
sacrifice,[165] but the Supreme God, the most sublime Person and the highest
Brahman is Krsna, the anthropomorphic, incarnate God: "Highest Brahman,
highest home, highest vessel of purity are you. All seers agree that you are
the eternal and divine Person, primeval God, unborn and all-pervading Lord."[166]
It cannot, however, be denied that some passages of Gita can be pantheistically understood.[167]   But the most prominent message of Gita is that God
is not an impersonal Absolute but the lover of man's soul.[168] He is presented
in Saguna terms with anthropomorphic figures: father, comrade, beloved,[169]
who is capable of loving relationship with man, in human terms.[170] For Gita,
Isvara (the Saguna Brahman) is more important than the Brahman beyond
attributes. Das Gupta writes:

> "...according to Gita the personal God as Isvara is the supreme principle,
> and Brahman, in the sense of a qualityless, undifferentiated, ultimate
> principle as taught in the Upanisads, is a principle which, though great
> in itself and representing the ultimate essence of God, is nevertheless
> upheld by the personal God or Isvara."[171]

Inspite of the anthropomorphic overtones of Gita in presenting the Isvara,
it may be said that the idea of God's love for man is present in the Gita
for the first time in the religious literature of India, although not in that
radicality as seen in the New Testament. In chapter IV we will he referring
critically to the attempt of some Indian theologians to identify the notions
of "Christ" and "Isvara"!

2. The World as the 'Deha' (Body) of God

Ramanuja is the most known philosopher who supplied serious justifications
for a theism that is of great value to popular Hinduism. For Ramanuja also
the Reality is one and undivided (aprthak) Brahman, but it is not as Sankara
held absolutely simple but internally complex (visista). The Reality is only
one, but Ramanuja speaks of three reals: (1) the Lord (Isvara) who is the
Cause of everythings, (2) the world of conscious (cit) beings, (3) the unconscious material universe (acit).[172]

For Ramanuja the Supreme God is Isvara or Visnu who is identical with the Brahman of the Upanisads. The souls and the world form a unity and are the body (deha) of Isvara; they are real, but they depend on Him and are nothing apart from Him. God is composed of a body (deha) and soul (dehin). The body may be defined: "that substance which a conscious entity can use and support entirely for its own purposes, and which in its essence is exclusively subordinate (sesa) to that entity".[173] According to this definition of Ramanuja, the soul (dehin) transcends the body, but the body is one with it as its natural instrument, accessory, effect, mode, field of action (ksetra) and dominion.[176] The relationship between God and this world, his body, a part (amsa), is characterised as 'bhedabheda' ie. difference-non-difference. As a philosophical system Ramanuja's method is called 'visistadvaita' or qualified non-dualism in contrast to the advaita or non-dualism of Sankara.

In Ramanuja there is also a distinction between 'deha' and 'sarira' eventhough both can be translated as body. 'Deha' emphasises the material aspect of the body. Its root is 'dih' which means the composite of elements or matter. Sariram (sru+iram) is body considered in its relation to the soul: it is supported by the soul, completely controlled by it, entirely subordinated to the soul and ordered to serve the purpose of the soul. When Ramanja explains the world as the body of Isvara, he takes body or deha in this particular sense of 'sarira'.[178]

For Ramanuja, Brahman is the highest reality, but not without attributes. The world and God are one just as body and soul are one; the world is genuine and real; it is no deception or illusion. God and the world are at the same time unchangeably different. Before the world came to existence it was already in God in a potential form. The world is not made from something alien, a second principle but is produced by the Supreme out of His own nature; He is the instrumental and material cause of the world. In creation, the world that was already present in God in potential form developed into 'name' and 'form' (namarupa). This world is not only God's body but also His remainder (isvarasyasesa) and that shows the absolute dependence of the world on God.[179]

The distinction that Ramanuja makes is not, as Sankara does, between true and false, real and illusion, but between the permanent and the perishable.

The Lord who is indestructible (sattva) is the ground of all perishable beings (asattva).[180] The entities do not detract from the absolute simplicity and infinite perfection of Brahman, because they are not entities independent of Brahman, but they are His modes and body; they are the Visesana (attribute) of God.

A Viśesana or attribute, for Ramanuja, is the quality of the substance. Though a Viśesana has its origin in the substance, it does not change the nature of the substance. What is essential for an attribute or Viśesana is that it does not form a part of the essence of the substance or subject, nor add anything to its essential perfection, but has its own particular nature distinct from that of the subject and is at the same time entirely dependent upon it. [181] The souls and the world are in this sense Viśesana or attributes of Brahman. The analogy that is used to explain this is that of flame and light; light is dependent on flame, but it is not flame.[182] The Absolute of Ramanuja is not Nirguna Brahman, but Visista-Brahman (differentiated Absolute).

Unlike Sankara, Ramanuja puts great emphasis on the personality of God, not just in a static sense as is valid also in the case of Nirguna Brahman but in a dynamic and to some extent anthropomorphic sense. The fourth Sutra (aphorism) of Badarayana presents Brahman as "that being the highest object of human pursuit" (Tat tu samanvayat). For Ramanuja this is an affirmation that God is not just a relationless Reality with absolutely no concern for this world, but It is a He, a person capable of entering into personal relations; He is not something, but some One. He is not just the adhara (ground) of all being[183], nor is he merely the 'satyasya satyam' (impersonal truth), but He is in fact the Purusottama (Supreme Person).[184] As the Supreme person, He is One who is deeply involved in the life of every man as the guide and inner ruler (Antaryamin) or as the leader of men (Narayana).

Sankara has given us an excellent theory of God, at the cost of the reality of the material world; but Ramanuja 'fulfils our desire for a philosophy of man and nature which Sankara had failed to satisfy'[185]. It is not the 'idea', however excellent, of an Absolute Being that constitutes active religion, but the intense personal relationship between God and man. But Ramanuja's system has also very serious defects. Due to an absence of the notion of efficient causality, which is the cause of all things and gives beginning to all things, the world of finite beings is explained as eternal and subtle modes of Brahman. Eventhough he is opposed to all kinds of pantheism, the accusation of pantheism or panentheism levelled against his 'Visista-Advaita' is difficult to avoid because the finite beings are said to be eternally existent in Brahman as modes or attributes, which are actually contrary to the absolute simplicity of God which Sankara is eager to defend. In so far as both Sankara and Ramanuja do not recognize the pure efficient causality of God in creating finite things from nothing, the only two possible ways of conceiving the world of beings are as 'Maya' (Sankara) or as 'Visesana' (Ramanuja). Both may find justification in the Upanisads. It may also be said that the absolutistic and theistic views of the Upanisads are not exclusive of each other and that Sankara and Ramanuja emphasise different aspects in the teachings of the Upanisads.[186]

Both the position of Sankara and Ramanuja do not explain satisfactorily the transcendence of God and his immanence so convincingly as is done by the Judeo-Christian notion of creation. We have to affirm both the autonomy of this world - the freedom of man included - and its dependence on God. We will be evaluating this point further in Chapter VII.

3. Iśvara in His Triadal Manifestation as 'Trimurti'

There are some apparent and interesting parallels between the Christian Trinity and the Hindu Trimurti. But the differences are Substantial as we shall see below and later especially in Chapters IV and VII.

Iśvara is the highest manifestation of the One Supreme God. He is the personal God and to Him are attributed the three functions in relation to the world, namely that of creation, protection and destruction. Isvara becomes Brahma, Visnu and Siva when His three functions are taken separately.[187] God with His creative ideas is Brahma. God who pours out His love and is perpetually at work saving the world is Visnu. This creation is brought to its perfection and end by God in His aspect as Siva.[188] Trimurti literally means 'having three forms'. The Supreme Being considered in His three-fold cosmic functions is Trimurti;[189] it also presents God as the beginning, middle and the end of every thing.[190] These three manifestations of Iśvara are also 'symbolized by the letters A, U, M, which combine to form the sacred syllable OM'.[191]

The 'Trimurti' is not explicitly mentioned in the Vedas, but has foundation in them. In the Vedas, Agni (creative heat), Surya (the sun god) and Indra (the storm god) form a triad.[192] Agni became later on the creator god Brahma, Surya became Visnu and Indra merged into Siva. The Upanisads explain Brahma, Rudra (another word for Siva) and Visnu as the manifestations of Brahman.[193] In later texts Trimurti is clearly formulated as Brahma (the world creator), Visnu (the world preserver) and Siva (the world-dissolver).[194] The Bhagavadgita which emphasises the Supreme as the personal God or Isvara regards Him as responsible for the creation, preservation and dissolution of the world. Gita is more interested in the process of redeeming the world and so the Visnu aspect of the Supreme, represented in the human form of Krsna, is emphasised by it.

It was in the mythologies of the Puranas and in the sectarian writings of Vaisnavism and Saivism that stories regarding the members of the Trimurti reached their maximum elaboration.

Trimurti is actually an indispensable factor in popular Hinduism. It is also this notion of the Trimurti that paved way for the development of the doctrine of 'Avatara' (descend of God in tangible form into the midst of men) which we will be considering elaborately in the third chapter of this part of our work. This doctrine has great anthropological and Christological relevance in the Indian context.

a. Brahma

Initially Brahma was considered as a personification of Brahman.[196] In the Puranas his origin is explained variously. 'The primeval essence, or unconditioned self-existent substance, Brahman, created the cosmic waters and deposited in them a seed which became a golden egg, the Hiranyagarbha, in which it was born itself as Brahma, the creator of the universe. The first being was Purusa, the Cosmic Man, one of the names of Brahma'[197]. According to another legend Brahma emerged on a lotus flower from the naval of Visnu. Myths gave Brahma the role of creation that was once given to Purusa, Prajapati and Hiraniyagarbha. He arose from the primeval waters (Narah) to set in motion the creative forces and is therefore called Narayana.[198] The incestous relation of Brahma with his daughter Vac (the uttered Word) is said to be responsible for the birth of mankind.[199] In one of the myths Brahma assumes an androgynous form and converted himself into two persons, the first male, Manu svayambhuva, and the first female, Satarupa.[200]

Brahma's role as the creator of the world is also expressed by his vehicle (vhana), the gander (hamsa). 'Hamsa' stands for the fundamental sound of the universe, the breath: 'ham' is the sound of inhalation and 'sa' that of exhalation. However, the theory of periodic creation and re-creation[201] and development of the cult of Visnu and Siva by the respective sects made Brahma a forgotten god and the mythologies around him did not make further ramifications and he became even philosophically irrelevant and his cult virtually disappeared.[202] Even his title 'Narayana' began to be applied exclusively for Visnu.[203]

b. **Visnu**

The Vedic god Visnu is a solar deity.[204] In the Vedas he is the personified manifestation of solar energy. The root of his name, vis, means to pervade; Visnu can mean the pervader or the one who takes various forms.[205] Many ancient myths and different gods have gradually merged into the majestic figure of Visnu. The sult of Visnu has probably its origin in the non-Aryan cults of Vasudeva, a tribal hero, and of Narayana, a cosmic god. The Aryans identified Vasudeva and Narayana with their solar god Visnu.[206] Visnu is the god of the ocean and the god of the luminous sky, the protector and sustainer of the world.

As the sun-go Visnu has Garuda, the sun-bird, as his vehicle. Garuda is a mythical bird which symbolizes the sun's flight through the sky. In the Vedas Visnu is known for the three steps with which he measures out the extent of the earth and the heavens; these tri-vikrama (three steps) indicate the solar character of Visnu. Visnu is generally represented as a handsome youth of a dark blue colour, in royal clothings. He is shown as having four hands holding a conch shell, a club, a lotus flower and a discus. The discus (cakra) is a solar representation.[207] Visnu as sun-god is credited with the function of pervading the universe.

Visnu is also considered as the cosmic ocean, Nara, which spread everythwere before creation. He is also called the Spirit that moves in the waters (Narayana). In this capacity he is represented in human forms resting on the cosmic serpent Sesa. It floates on the primeval waters. Sesa literally means 'remainder', with the indication that this serpent is shaped out of the remains of the universe after its destruction. It is also called Ananta, the endless or infinite one; it has 1000 heads. This cosmic serpant (Naga) sustains the earth. It coils itself, representing the endless revolution of time, and makes a bed for Visnu, the upholder and preserver of the universe, to recline.[208] It is in this reclining position that Brahma is represented as emerging from his naval, seated on a lotus. The corsort of Visnus is Sri Lakshmi, goddess of good fortune and prosperity.

Visnu is the most popular god of the Hindu pantheon. His power has been manifested to the world in a variety of forms called Avataras (descends), in which his divine essence was incarnated in humanly visible forms. Consequently a lot of myths gathered around him. The most important manifestations or Avatars are considered to be Rama, the hero of Ramayana and Krsna, the hero of Mahabharata and Bhagavadgita. We have to discuss this point further in Chapter III.

c. Siva

The cult of Siva is very ancient in its origin. Long before the arrival of the Aryans the Mahadeva or Mahesvara (great god) was worshipped in India.[209] The term Siva itself is unknown in the ancient scriptures, but Rudra, a tempest-god with his characteristic thunder and lighning, a personification of the powers of destruction is known in the Vedas.[210] In the process of evolution the pre-Vedic Siva absorbed the Vedic Rudra. The characteristics such as suspicious, propitious, gracious, benign etc. (Siva) are applied to the terrible Rudra in the Vedas. [211] Siva represents the natural forces of destruction and fertility. In his auspicious aspect he is also called Sankara.[212]

Siva has various corporeal appearences. Sometimes he has five faces, some times four faces and four arms; he is also represented with one face and three eyes, denoting his insight into the past present and future. The third eye situated in the centre of his forehead possesses a fiery glance which is capable of destroying everything. This eye is represented by three horizontal lines, a mark worn today by his devotees.[213] There is a moon's crescent on his head which shows the measuring of time by months and the serpent coiled around his neck denotes the endless cycle of recurring years.[214] The necklace of skulls and the many serpents about his person also symbolize the eternal revolution of ages and the successive generation and dissolution of mankind. He wears the skin of a tiger and sits alone on Mount Kailasa, high in the Himalaya , as an arch-ascetic or a divine Yogi.[215] He carries the Ganges on his head in his attempt to save the world from the destructive flow of this sacred river, which was sent by god Visnu from heaven to moisture the earth at the intervention of the sage Bhagiratha. In this aspect Siva

is also called Ganga-dhara, 'the upholder of the river Ganges'.[216] He is
also represented in the myths as intervening to save the word by drinking
the poison that emerged from the mouth of the serpent that was used by
the gods to make the 'nectar of immortality' (Amrtam) by churning the
cosmic waters. His throat is blue from the stain of this poison, which was
stopped there by the intervention of his wife Parvati. Thus he is also called
'Nilakhanda', the one with blue throat.

As a learned philosopher and contemplative sage, Siva is said to have revealed
the Sanskrit grammer to Panini. The most known representation of Siva
is as 'Nataraja' (the king of dancers). In his images the Siva Nataraja is
encircled by a ring of flames, the vital processes of universal creation. The
cosmic dancer stands with one leg raised upon a tiny figure, crouching on
a lotus. This is a demon representing human ignorance. In one hand the
Nataraja holds a drum, the sign of speech and the source of revelation and
tradition. His second hand offers sustenance and blessing. A tounge of fire
in the third hand is a reminder of cosmic destruction. The fourth arm points
downward to the uplifted foot, signifying him to be the refuge and salvation
of the devotees.[218]

The creative power of Siva is symbolized by the phallic emblem, the linga
the most widely venerated cult object of Siva worship. Siva's vehicle, a
milk-white bull, Nandi, also typifies his generative energy. The consort of
Siva, as his counterpart and intensification of his creative energy is symbolized
by the female generative organ, Yoni.[219] Siva's consort is called Parvati,
Uma or Sakti, the personification of the active character of Siva. He dances
with his consort the 'Tandava dance', the cosmic dance of creation and
destruction.[220]

The Trimurti : Brahma, Visnu and Siva are the manifestations of the Supreme
spirit in three forms. No one of these takes precendence over the other.
They are equal and their functions are also interchangeable; but with the
sects Visnu and Siva became more prominent. The concept of Trimurti
has, however, helped to some extent to reconcile the sectarian differences
in Hinduism and to develope a monotheistic trend.[221]

The development of a trinitarian theology in India cannot ignore, besides the Saccidananda concept of Brahman, the three modes of divine manifestations as Brahma, Visnu and Siva as understood by the Hindus. It is true that the Saccidananda is easy to assimilate into Christian thinking while the Trimurti theory has serious problems because of its mythological and modalistic overtones, which require substantial corrections and re-interpretations. It is, however, to be mentioned that some interesting, though vague and superficial, parallels could be drawn between God the Father and Brahma, God the Son and Visnu and God the Holy Spirit and Siva. It can easily be noted that Visnu has great Christological relevance because of the 'Avatara' that is related to him as we shall see later. Some Indian theologians have tried, as we shall see in Chapter VI, to find a soteriological correspondence between Siva's stopping of the destructive Ganges or his drinking of the destructive poison and Christ's redemption of mankind from the poison of sin. But the eschatological significance of Siva as the divine power of anihilation and new creation seems to be more attractive for a Christian theologian. We will be evaluating this point from an anthropological, historical and Christological point of view later in Chapter VIII.

Conclusion to Chapter One

Our attempt so far has been to survey the main trends of the Indian man's understanding of God, which indirectly has great anthropological relevance. An academic clear-cut presentation of the concept of God may not be applicable when we come to the individual Hindu. A Hindu feels himself to be at great liberty to determine his 'image' of God; he may ascribe himself to a definite trend, or may take a little from every trend and make a syncretism out of it- which is most often the case- without worrying very much about academic discrepencies or contradictions.

In modern Hinduism there had been also some reformers, influenced very often by Christianity and Islam, who wanted to present a more up-to-date idea of God. Kabir (1440?-1518) is one of them who held to the unity of God which he learned from Islam, but used any name, Rama, Hari, Allah etc., to show the oneness behind apparent diversity.[222] Guru Nanak (1469-1539) and his followers in Punjab (Sikhs) consider God as the formless one dwelling in the realm of truth; yet he is also considered in personal terms as the friend and bridgegroom of the soul. [223] Rammohan Roy (1772-1833), a Bengali Brahmin, maintained that the Upanisads tought pure theism untainted by the later Hindu idolatry. [224] Devendranath Tagore (1817-1905) declared his conviction of the oneness of God behind different names and insisted on apersonal relationship to God.[225] Rabindranath Tagore (1861-1941), the son of Devendranath Tagore, had a very strong theistic approach to God as manifested in his world famous 'Gitanjali' which procured for him the Nobel prize, and in his book 'the Religion of Man'. God for him is the lover and bride groom, the king of kings who appears in a golden chariot, but stoops to ask a beggar for a grain of corn from his bag.[226] Mahatma Gandhi (1869-1948) had probably no very precise notion of God and he, like Hinduism itself, oscillated between monistic Brahman and theistic hari. He considered God as Truth and Love, Ethics and Morality, Fearlessness and Conscience, even the atheism of the atheist, and all things to all men.[227]

Aurobindo Ghose (1872-1950) developed a type of monism considering the Absolute as the 'Supermind', a dynamic concept of God presenting Him as the beginning and end of all creation, to which every thing tends.[228] Sarvepalli Radhakrishnan (1888-1978) aimed at a deliberate synthesis of the best in Hinduism, which is typical of many modern Hindu writers. He tries to re-conciles the different Hindu philosophical schools, especially the advaita of Sankara and the Visista-advaita of Ramanuja. He holds that there cannot be a fundamental contradiction between the philosophical idea of an all-embracing Brahman and the devotional idea of a personal God.[229]

These are some of the new trends in Hinduism regarding the concept of God - to mention only a few - developed from the classical Hinduism. The Christian idea of God based on the Holy Bible has many points in common with the corresponding Vedantic concept inspite of the fact that there are substantial differences. We have already referred to some of these and will be making further evaluations on the same in the course of our work especially in Chapter VII. An adequate understanding of the transcendence and immanence of God without prejudicing each other is vital to the biblical faith and to the proper vision of the God-creature relation which has deep reaching implications on anthropology, history and finally Christology. This exposition is by no means exhaustive; our intention is also not that. We wanted only to outline some of the main trends in the Hindu understanding of God, as a background for the presentation of an Indian Anthropology and a Christology that can be understood in that context. A further elaboration is out of place and does not serve our purpose.

CHAPTER II

MAN AND THE REALITY OF 'ATMAN'

Man's search for God is as we have seen an expression and confirmation of man's attempt at a discovery of himself, the meaning and ground of his existence. The significance of the analysis of the God-concept of a particular people is immense for a anthropological investigation, but it remains an indirect anthropology. A direct attempt to understand the reality of man has also been present in the Indian thinking side by side with a Brahma-vidhya. An analysis of this attempt brings out still more clearly the divine horizon, element or aspect in man as understood by the Indian sages, Vedantic philosophers and ordinary Hindus.

A. The Vedantic Concept of Man

In the Vedic literature man was understood as a 'microcosm' portraying the cosmic order, the 'macrocosm'. The personifications of the powers of nature as gods and the hymns and prayers offered to them as seen in the Rgveda should not be considered as a primitive nature-worship, but as a process of the realization and assimilation of the macrocosmic order into the microcosm, man.[1] 'It is within this religious quest of seeking the corrrelation between the system of sacrifice and the outer world that the ancient seers attempted to penetrate the mystery of the ultimate origin of cosmos and man'.[2]

According to the Rgveda 'Manu' (man) was the ancestor of human race, the first man, 'our father', the representative man and the institutor of sacrifice.[3] 'Yama' is a doublet of 'Manu ' as ancestor of human race: Manu was the first man who lived on earth and Yama the first man who died.[4] The primeval man is called in Rgveda also by the term 'Purusa'. He is conceived as a thousand-headed and thousand-footed giant, who is sacrificed by the gods. The whole universe is formed out of his body cut into various pieces: three-fourths of him are the immortal in heaven, one-fourth of him is all beings on earth. According to the 'Purusa-Sukta', the hymn of man, Purusa's head, when cut off, became the sky, his naval the air, his feet the earth, the moon sprang from his mind, his eyes became the sun and his breath the wind. [5]   According to this concept the whole universe, and the world of gods were made out of the primeval man, the Purusa. The 'Purusa Sukta' also contains elements that justified the development of caste system in India as we shall see later in the course of this Chapter. Some consider the 'Purusa-Sukta' of the Rgveda as the oldest product of pantheistic philosophy in India. [6]   The macrocosmic man (Purusa) is the prototype of the microcosmic man. The human being, therefore, ist the image of the Primeval Man, which in turn means that the individual man is the image of God and of the world, [7]   which together form the macrocosm.

The Rgveda, while speaking of the individual man distinguishes him into two parts: the unborn part and the born part. [8]   The unborn part is the inner man, the immaterial soul, which is the animating principle of the whole body. The animating principle is denoted by two terms: 'asu' which can be translated as life, and 'manas' which means mind. [9]   The 'manas' which is the seat of thought and emotions was regarded as dwelling in the heart (hrd). 'Asu' is the vital force or breath. [11]

In the Brahmanas the Primeval Man's name is 'Prajapati'. [12]   Prajapati is the same as Purusa. In the Taittiriya Brahmana there is an indication that the gods, the plants, etc. are various parts of man, which means that the body of the world is the body of man; [13]   it is an indication of the relation between the macrocosm and the microcosm, man.

The term ' A t m a n ' was used in the Rgveda to denote the unborn part (ajo bhagah) [14]   or the immaterial soul of man. Atman is derived from 'an' to breath, 'at' to move, and 'va' to blow. So the oldest meaning of Atman is 'breath'. [15]   It can also be literally translated as 'vital force'. In the Rgveda Atman is sometimes used to indicate the animating principle or the essence. The sun, for example, is called the Atman of all things moving and non-moving (suryah atma jagatas tastusasca) [16]   and Soma, a plant-juice which was an essential libation of vedic sacrifices and called the celestian dew [17] , is called the Atman (the essence) of sacrifice (atma yajnasya) [18] it is also called the Atma of Indra (atma indrasya). [19]   Atma is the essence or ultimate reality of anything. When we consider the whole universe, its reality or essence is 'Brahman' and therefore the term 'Atman' is applied to Brahman in the sense of cosmic self. As Brahman is the ultimate Reality of everything, He is called Paramatman, to distinguish him from other Atmans which are not'para', ultimate.

Most commonly 'Atman' is used to signify the essence or reality of man, the ultimate self of man, in contrast to his empirical self or Jiva which stands for the totality of man's transient sense faculties. [20] The Atman ist the permanent reality of man: "Unborn, undying, eternal, seated in the cavity (ie. in the deepest recess of man), spiritual, all-pervading". [21] To distinguish from Brahman, the Paramatman, the Atman of man is called generally 'Jivatman' as it occurs in the Bhagavata Purana. [22] The human body and his empirical self are subject to death and destruction; their role is only to support the immortal and incorporeal Self (Atman). On death the Jivatman is destined to rejoin the Paramatman, of which the Jivatman is only a part. [23] To avoid confusion we use the term 'Brahman' for Paramatman and 'Atman' exclusively to mean Jivatman, unless otherwise indicated.

1. The Discovery of 'Atman'

As we have seen, the real nature of man is not a substantial unity of body and soul, but the Atman that ist behind and beyond the visible and sensible aspect of man. The concrete man as he is in this life is constituted of the Atman and various empirical and transient factors. The Atman is the changeless principle behind the changing factors in man. This changeless aspect of man can be discovered only after a process of introspection which helps us to transcross phenomenal aspects to reach the inner reality of Atman.

The analysis of various stages of human consciousness is a method used to reach the ultimate reality of man. In our daily experience we can distinguish in us between a waking state, a stage of dreams and a further situation of dreamless sleep. In the waking state one is conscious of the external gross (sthula) objects of perception, which one is inclined to believe to be the ultimate and only reality. In a sleep of dreams, however, the world of perception disappears and one moves in a world of dreams, which as long as the dreams last is taken by the dreamer as the real world. When the dreamer wakes up he understands that the dreams were his 'fancies' or the creations of his own mind and imagination, which may also be called illusions. When one enjoys a dreamless sleep no external objects can make any impression on the sleeper and all the pains, desires, worries, regrets, anxieties etc. disappear. The state of dreamless sleep is then a state of changelessness, as long as the sleep lasts. This stage of relative changelessness is considered in the Indian anthropology as indicative of the nature of Atman. [24]

The Mandukya Upanisad sees behind these three different states of human consciousness a fourth stage of illumined consciousness. [25] Corresponding to these four grades of consciousness: waking, dream, deep sleep and spiritual consciousness, we may speak of four states of the individual, namely: the gross (sthula), subtle (suksma), causal (karana) and the self of man (Atma). [26] The Mandukya Upanisad maintains that this fourth state or stage of existence called Atman is "neither internally nor externally conscious, nor conscious in both ways; it is neither conscious nor unconscious; it is invisible, intractable, inapprehensible, indistinguishable, indefinable..." [27]

This analysis of the stages of consciousness logically leads us to an analysis of the various spheres which envelope the Atman. The Taittiriya and Maitri Upanisads consider the Atman to be involuted in a succession of concentric material envelopes or Kosas, more and more dense, which constitute its organs, and restrict in different degrees its sphere of action and range of knowledge. [28] Accordingly man is composed of two main factors: the imperishable Atman and its perishable external envelopes. The perishable factor of man may be called 'Jiva' which originally referred to the biological aspect of man. 'Jiva' literally means to breath. The term 'Jiva' is also applied to the five layers or sheaths (Kosas) - according to some tow - encircling the Atman. [29] So the human individual is a complex of five elements. The first two are the material body (anna) and the principle of breath (prana) which regulates the unconscious activities of the individual. The next is the 'Manas', the principle which uses the five sensory organs (indriyas) and the organs of action for conscious activities. All these three are brought to a meaningful organization by Vijnana or Buddhi. It is the intelligence of man. Anna and Prana (matter and life) together constitute the gross physical body of man which is called 'Sthula-śarira', the subtle form of which together with the mind (Manas) constitute the 'Suksma-sarira' or the subtle body. The intelligence (Vijnana or Buddhi) may be called the 'Karana-sarira'. All these four concentric sheaths together constitute the Jiva or the perishable aspect of man.[30] 'Atman' which is the true being of man is in the centre of this concentric structure. This Atman may also well be called 'Purusa' which means that which dwells in the citedal of the heart, derived from 'puri-śaya'. The Katha Upanisad also speaks of this sheath-system of man in clear terms:

> "Higher than the senses are the objects of the sense.
> Higher than the objects of the sense is the mind (manas);
> And higher than the mind is the intellect (buddhi),
> Higher than the intellect is the great Self (atman)." [31]

The ego or Jiva of man is a unity of the physical, biological, psychological and logical aspects of human existence. This ego is in perpetual change; it can move up to the unifying control of the 'Vijnana' or move down to the extremes of selfishness, stupidity and sensuality. The Jiva has also the possiblity of transcending itself to the 'Anandamayatman' or the Atman of bliss hidden within the four sheaths or kosas, which shows that the human being has a transcendental call.[32]

The Atman is the foundational reality underlying the conscious and non-conscious powers of the Jiva. The Atman may be called the inward ground, the ultimate depth and the superreality of the Jiva. The ideal relationship between the psychic faculties of the Jiva and the underlying Atman is explained in picturesque terms by the Katha Upanisad with the metaphor of a chariot:

> "Know thou the self (atman) as riding in a chariot,
> The body as the chariot.
> Know thou the intellect (buddhi) as the chariot-driver,
> And the mind (manas) as the reigns.
> The senses (indriya), they say, are the horses;
> The object of sense, what they range over.
> The self combined with senses and mind
> Wise men call 'the enjoyer' (bhoktr)." [33]

The intellect (buddhi) has a very decisive role to play; it functions as an intermediary between the 'Atman' and the other inferior constituents of man. Its role is that of a chariot driver; whether the Atman reaches his destiny or not depends on it.

The distinction we made above between the gross body of man (Sthula-sarira) and the subtle body (Suksma-sarira) is very important especially when we treat later with the problem of Karma and Samsara. The intellect (Karana-sarira) can also be for all practical purposes considered as belonging to the subtle body. For claritys sake, we may translate Stuhla-sarira as physical body and Suksma-sarira as psychic body. The Atman is within or beyond both.

The method of discovering the inner reality of man (Atman) through an analysis of the various stages of human consciousness and the various layers or kosas enveloping the Atman is as we have seen above a methode typical of the Upanisads. The Bhagavadgita, however, follows another method of understanding the reality of man, which is also very interesting and quite relevant to our topic.

The metaphysical system followed by the Gita with some fundamental modifications is that of Samkhya philosophy.[33a] The Samkhya follows a theory of strict dualism in interpreting the totality of reality. There is no God in Samkhya. Purusa and Prakrti, self and non-self are the basic components of reality. In other words, the Samkhya proposes a matter-spirit dualism avoiding the concept of God. Gita however makes both self and non-self subject to God and subordinate to his power; and further, Purusa and Prakrti are considered to be the very nature of the Supreme Principle God.[34] So Purusa and Prakrti, matter and spirit are not two absolutely independent and sovereign principles but have their source in God.[35] The Purusas, selves or spirits are minute parts of God and are like Him eternal and changeless while Prakrti, matter or nature is dependent on Him and is the source and cause of all change.[36] The Purusa-Prakrti structure is present every where, in God, in the world and in man.

The Purusa-Prakrti structure anthropologically applied considers man as the most concrete example for the interaction of these constituent principles of all existence. The Purusa in man can be understood as the Atman of man as explained above. It is the centre of the whole personality of man, and the principle of his unity and integration. Purusa, Spirit and Atman are almost synonyms.[37]

In the individual man it is the Prakrti (Nature or Matter) and not the Purusa (the Spirit or Atman), that acts through out the whole process of action and change. The Gita says that 'every man is powerless and made to work by the constituents born of Nature'.[38] It is important to know what these constituents of Nature are. These constituents may be called in Sanskrit 'sattva', 'rajas' and 'tamas'. Sattva is goodness and purity, 'rajas' is translated as energy and passion and 'tamas' stands for darkness, dullness and sloth. Prakrti may be compared to a rope made out of the combination of these three strands.[39] The Gita tells us in detail about the salient characteristics of these three constituents:

> "Goodness, Passion, Darkness:
> These are the 'constituents' from Nature sprung.
> They bind the embodied soul
> in the body, though the soul itself is changeless.
>
> Among these Goodness, being immaculate,
> knowing no sickness, dispenses light,
> and yet it binds by causing the soul to cling
> to wisdom and to joy.
>
> Passion is instinct with desire: this know.
> From craving and attachment it wells up:
> It binds the embodied soul
> by causing it to cling to works.
>
> From ignorance is darkness born: mark this well.
> All embodied souls it leads astray.
> With fecklessness and sloth and sleepiness
> it binds.
>
> Goodness causes a man to cling to joy,
> Passion to works;
> but darkness, stifling wisdom,
> attaches to fecklessness." [40]

These three characteristics of Prakrti are actually three irreducible functions of the principle of the evolution of matter. 'There is a function of reflection manifested in thought, which is reduced to sattva, a function of dynamism and creativity termed rajas, and a function of limitation and individuality called tamas'.[41] A proper and ancourageable evolution takes place only if these characteristics are kept within their due proportions. The overaction of one function at the cost of the others distorts the evolution of matter. The physical body, the five senses, the ego, the mind and the soul belong to the Prakrti of man. The function of the three evolutional characteristics

(Gunas) are manifested there. The soul is the one that stands nearest to the Purusa. This soul (buddhi) consists of intellect and will[42] and is subject to the influence of the Gunas. Its function is to integrate the whole Prakrti of man with the Purusa, the immortal self. The senses and the ego (ahamkara - the false centre of personality) can act through the mind [43] and influence the soul. If the constituents of rajas and tamas predominate, the soul (buddhi) will be led astray and if sattva guna predominates the soul can discriminate correctly between Pakrti and Purusa and remain integrated.[44] So the soul has a certain 'responsibility' over the whole Prakrti of man and as the organ of integration it has to bring the whole human Prakrti into subjection to the Purusa or Atman or Spirit that is in man. The soul can do its integrating function only if it keeps the working of the three Gunas in perfect balance, otherwise the Purusa and Prakrti of man can never reach their perfectly integrated stage in the process of evolution.[45]

In the whole process of evolution the Purusa is merely a witness unaffected by the evolution of matter. Its pure consciousness and pure light, however can be obscured by the matter around. 'The ideal condition is when the spirit remains all by itself in isolation, and the matter in itself in a perfect balance of its three functions'[46]

We will be evaluating in Chapter VII the question regarding the discovery of the reality of man, following the thought patterns of Karl Rahner and Wolfhart Pannenberg. A dichotomy of body and soul, as is implied above in the 'Purusa-Prakrti' structure will not be acceptable for Christian faith. Both the active and passive principles of evolution which they represent, however, are quite welcome for Christian theology as we would show in Chapter VII. The reality of man cannot be, acording to the biblical understanding, reduced to his so-called 'soul', which could survive independent of man's 'body'. Its further implications will be interesting for us also when we consider man's eschatology in Chapter VIII and the Christian religious experience in Chapters VI and IX. The 'Sthula sarira' and 'Suksma sarira' structure of man, to which we referred above is very relevant for us in our later discussion on the question of the resurrection especially in Chapters VI and VIII.

2. The Relation between Atman and Brahman

What is the relation of the universal Self to the selves of individuals? There are fundamentally two main approaches to this question: one is advaitic founded mostly on the Upanisads and advocated by Sankara and the other is viśite-advaitic supported by Ramanuja which is more in line with the Bhagavadgita. These are not the only approaches, but they can be called the most representative because of their influence and we limit ourselves to a consideration only of these two as representative samples.

a. Atman-Brahman-Identity

In the early Upanisads Brahman stands for the superpersonal ground of the cosmos and Atman is the principle of individual consciousness.[47] But further thinking about the Unity of the Ultimate Reality, the One without a second, compelled the aupanisadic seers to resume that there cannot be a distinction between the essence or inner reality of the cosmos, the Brahman, and the inner reality of man, the Atman, because Brahman cannot be taken into parts and because the Absolute Consciousness cannot be thought of as being in any way other than the consciousness seen in the individual men as the Brhadaranyaka Upanisad says:

> "He is the unseen seer, the unheard hearer, the
> unthought thinker, the ununderstood understander.
> Other than he there is no seer, other than he
> there is no hearer, other than he there is no
> thinker, other than he there is no understander.
> He is your Self, the Inner Controller, the Immortal."[48]

So the distinction between Brahman, the Paramatman and the Atman of man, the Jivatman, diminished and both were identified. Brahman is not only the basis of the world but also the basis if individual man; Brahman the first principle of the universe is actually known through Atman, the same principle in man. This is emphatically stated by the Chandogya Upanisad: "Verily, this whole world is Brahman...This soul of mine within the heart, this is Brahman."[49] Brhadaranayaka Upanisad also maintains, "that person who is seen in the eye, He is atman, that is Brahman."[50] The aupanisadic seers found within their own interiority the unity, the intelligence and the unlimited thought which they predicated to the Divine. So they were bold enough to say that the Self in man is not merely the divine Self showing itself at one point, but the human Self is divine Self; Atman is not merely a 'part' or diminished form of Brahman but the Brahman Itself, whole and complete. [51] The Brahman and Atman are interchangeable terms; It is the one, simple, eternal, infinite and incomprehensible Reality which assumes every form and name. The human body is the support of this immortal Atman and when the Atman realizes itself to be the Brahman, it overcomes the ignorance caused by the body and merges into its real identity, the Brahman, as the Chandogya Upanisad declares:

> "This self within my heart is smaller than a grain of rice, or wheat or mustard seed, or a grain of millet or the kernel within a grain of millet; and yet this self within my heart is greater than the earth, greater than the mid-region, greater than heaven, greater than all these worlds.... This self within my heart is Brahman itself. When I depart from hence I shall merge into that very self." [52]

The Upanisads give expression to this identity of Brahman and Atman through a number of Great Sayings called 'Mahavakyani'. One of such sayings is that we have already seen to express the transcendence of Brahman and His character of being the consciousness, namely: "Prajnanam Brahma" - Brahman is Consciousness. [53] There are some other Mahavakyani too which bring out clearly the Brahman-Atman identity.

"Ayam Atma Brahma" this Atman is Brahman - affirms the Brhadadaranyaka Upanisad and the Mandukya Upanisad. [54] Everything here is Brahman; this Atman is Brahman. There is nothing in which the Brahman is not the self, ground or the Atman. The Brahman, inspite of His transcendence is therefore immanent. By discovering the identification of Atman and Brahman the individual discovers in his own depths the cosmic plenitude of God. [55]

"Aham Brahmasmi" - I am Brahman. By this statement the Brhadaranyaka Upanisad [56] perceives Brahman as the ultimate ground of man's personal being, the 'Aham'. The Absolute Reality is one with man's intimate self. This underlies even the phenomenal self of man, the 'ahamkara', which man often wrongly understands as the real self.

65

"Tattvam Asi" - That Art Thou, is a Mahavakya of the Chandokya Upanisad.[57] To utter this statement is properly the function of a Guru, a sacred teacher who has realized his identity with Brahman and wants to communicate the same experience to a disciple who has prepared himself for that stage of consciousness. This is a statement of encouragement for the disciple, a reassuring declaration. It is actually a call to correct the false attribution which one may have imposed on one's own self, distancing oneself from Brahman. So this is not merely a statement of indication, but a dynamic call to the understanding of the true Self.

The question, however, remains how one should interpret the aupanisadic Mahavakyani. Its advaidic overtone can by no means be underestimated. Most often they are interpreted in the line of Advaita or non-dualism of Sankara. Even in a non-dualistic interpretation there may be still various shades of emphasis. Some may hold, for example, that the statement 'Ayam Atma Brahma' - Atman is Brahman cannot be interpreted vice versa to mean 'Brahman is Atman'[58] and the statement, 'Aham Brahmasmi' - I am Brahman, does not mean that Brahman is no more than I am.[59] Opinions do differ according to the 'grade' or intensity of the 'advaita' one follows! We will he disenssing this question further while speaking about the Christian position regending the relation between God and man and between the divine and human natures in Jesus Christ.

b. Atman as Part of Brahman

It is true that in the Upanisads and especially in the relatively late Mandukya Upanisad the trend is to a total identity of Atman and Brahman as understood by Sankara and his advaita followers. It cannot, however, be denied that while affirming the divine character of man's Atma some of the Upanisads at least maintain a distinction between Atman and Brahman. The Atman is one with Brahman in so far as, at its deepest level, it is a part of Brahman and has its being outside time, but the Atman is distinct from Brahman in that it does not share Brahman's creative activity in time. The Atman partakes of the Absolute Being but is not for that reason Brahman Himself. The Brhadaranyka Upanisad affirms the origin of Atman from Brahman as his part: "As a spider goes out (of itself) by (means of its) threads, as tiny sparks leap out of the fire, so from this self (Brahman) issue all life-breaths ......"[61] Although the Atman is part of Brahman as a spark is a part of fire, The Katha Upanisad presents Brahman as distinct from the Atman and remaining hidden within the heart of man, who is His creature:

> More subtle than the subtle, greater than the great,
> the Self [Brahman] is hidden in the heart of creatures (here):
> the man without desire, (all) sorrow spent, beholds It,
> the majesty of the Self [Brahman], by the grace of the Ordainer." [62]

According to the Bhagavadgita, since the Atman is a part of Brahman it is beyond the category of time, it is never born, it never dies, it is eternal:

> "Never is it born nor dies; never did it come to be nor will it ever
> come to be again: unborn, eternal, everlasting is this (self), - primeval.
> It is not slain when the body is slain. If a man knows it as
> indestructible, eternal, unborn, never to pass away, how and whom
> can he cause to be slain or slay?" [63]

The characteristic of Atman as part of Brahman is again stated by the Bhagavadgita in a later chapter: "In the world of living things a minute part of Me, eternal (still), becomes a living (self) [Atman]..." [64] So according to Gita, the Atman is a part of Brahman because it shares His mode of being, [65] but at the same time Atman cannot be said to be identical with Brahman because it is only a 'minute part' of Brahman.[66] As a minute part of Brahman enshrined in the body the Atman can be fooled and be in doubt.[67] If Gita admits the distinction between Brahman and Atman, it logically follows that it accepts also a distinction between one Atman and another Atman as G. Feuerstein maintains:

> " The Self is one as well as many The Selves of all beings are inter-
> esting and fully participating in each other's selfhood [as the Gita says],
> (he whose) self is yoked in Yoga (and who) everywhere beholds the
> same, sees the Self abiding in all beings and all beings in the Self."[68]

Ramanuja is one of the greatest supporters of this trend. For him the Atma is one of the modes of the Lord and 'univocal to him as sparks to fire'.[69] Like Brahman, the most important characteristic of Atman is consciousness, but it is not consciousness itself. The Atman like the Brahman is 'someone' who is conscious.[70] The Upanisad passage 'tat tvam asi' means no Atman-

Brahman identity, but that 'God is my self' just as my soul is the self of my body. God and soul are one not because they are identical but because God penetrates the human heart and dwells in it as its 'inner Guide' (Antaryamin). This is the immanence of the Divine Transcendence and not a Divinehuman identity. The realation may be said to be one of whole and part.

In conclusion to a presentation of the above mentioned two approaches to the relation between Brahman and Atman we may say that inspite of the considerable differences, the various Indian philosophical systems agree on these points:

1. The distinction of Atman from Jiva. That means the real self of man is distinct from the aggregate of man's physical and psychic faculties.
2. The Atman is eternal.
3. The Atman as the reality of man is by its very nature divine, either as identical with the Divine or as part of the Divine. So a supernatural elevation of man by 'Grace' is totally foreign to the Vedantic thought.

No modern Indologist is likely to accept the identity of Atman with Brahman in the sense of an identity of man with God. It cannot however be denied that the 'Mahavakyani' and their different Vedantic interpretations contain in them many a great and valuable thought. These put forward in a very emphatic way the divine horizon in man and the Indian seers' understanding of it. They are unequivocal declarations of man's dignity and spiritual grandeur, the immensity of his intellectual faculty, the boundlessness of his desires, man's passion for immortality, his nearness, likeness and kinship to God, God's actual presence in every human heart and the spontaneous and unquenchable desire of the soul for union with God.[71]

Our above discussion regarding the Vedantic understanding of the relation between Atman and Brahman is of great Christological relevance as we shall see in the following Chapters IV and V. The ontological identity of God and man, as proposed by the Vedanta, would contradict the biblical notion o man's creaturely relationship to God. Inspite of the fact that man is only a creature, he has a divine and transcendental horizon, a factor that distinguishes him essentially from the animals. We will have to evaluate this point in greater detail in Chapter VII. We will be dealing also with the question of Christ's divine consciousness (Aham Brahmasmi) as man in Chapter VIII and discussing man's God-experience and God-realization in Chapters VI and IX.

B. Man in Bondage

The ultimate reality of man is, as we have seen, his Atman. In the present state of existence the Atman does not have an independent existence apart from its material embodiment. The Atman is now in a state of 'bondage' to the body, both gross and subtle. Why is man in this bondage? Can man get out of it at least when he dies? These are both existential and escha - tological questions. Every religion tries to answer them.

The soteriology and eschatology of Hinduism is predominated by the notions of Karma and Samsara. Karma-Samsara is a doctrine of reward and punishment in the Hindu system and this forms the corner-stone of Hinduism not only as an eschatological explanation, but also as an explanation of the present life itself. The doctrine of Karma-Samsara is an axiom of Indian thinking. It is accepted as a self-evident first principle which is to be accepted without questioning. Every system of Indian thought, even the heterodox groups like Buddhism and Jainism, adheres to it and seeks after the means of liberating man from its fetters. Both Karma and Samsara are inseparably bound together, but for the sake of clarity we deal first with Karma and then with Samsara.

1. 'Karma' and the Question of Sin

Karma derives from the root 'kr' which means 'to make, to do, to act'. Karma literally means deed, action or cause. Every deed whether good or bad is a cause which is necessarily followed by corresponding effects, good or bad. One who does something must also naturally accept its consequences. So the law of Karma is the law of cause and effect. "As a man sows, so shall he continue to reap", that is the law of Karma in one sentence.[72] 'The law of Karma says that everything that happens, happens only because of the existence of antecedent causes and itself becomes the cause of subsequent effects'. [73] This law is valid in every sphere, physical, psychical and moral. Karma is not a law of predetermination; if there is no sowing there is also no reaping. [74] Each Karma or deed bears its fruit sooner or later and that fruit is called 'Karma-phala'. When we deal with Karma what we intent is not the cause-effect relationship of the physical world.Our concern is anthropological, ie. Karma as it functions in human existence.

The first appearance of Karma theory is not in the Vedas, but in the Brahmanas: "A man is born into the world that he has made."[75] It is the law of retribution and the principle which governs the reality of human becoming. This law by which virtue brings its triumph and evil its retribution is the unfolding of the law that is within man himself. For that there is no need for an external judge. This law is neither merciful nor cruel, it works dispassionately. One cannot escape from the workings of this principle, but it is not a hopeless situation.[76] A man can control his deeds and change the Karma-phala. Even if after one's death one is born into a world of suffering as a result of his evil deeds, one has still the possibility to do better deeds and change one's destiny. In the same way, even if one is born into the company of the blessed because of one's good deeds, that situation is also not definitive, because as a Karma-phala even one's blessed state is in the world of becoming.

The Brhadaranyaka Upanisad presents the law of Karma still more clearly:

"As a man acts, as he behaves, so does he become. Whoso does good, becomes good: whoso does evil, becomes evil. By good works a man becomes holy, by evil (works) he becomes evil.

But some have said: 'This person consists of desire alone. As is his desire, so will his will be; as is his will, so will he act; as he acts, so will he attain."[77]

Even in the epics we can find clear formulations of the law of Karma. We read in the Mahabharata:

"Whatever act a man does by means of his body, he must bear the fruit thereof in a state of physical existence. The body is the place of happiness, as also the place of misery. Whatever act a man does by means of words he must enjoy fully its fruit in a state in which words can be spoken. Similarly whatever act the mind does he must enjoy its fruit in state of the mind. Devoted to the fruits of acts, what ever kind of acts a man covetous of fruits accomplishes, the fruits, good or bad, which he actually enjoys partake of their character. Like a fish follows the current of the stream, so the act of the past life comes to the actor. The embodied creature experiences happiness for his good deeds, and misery for his evil ones." [78]

Brahman is beyond absolutely free from this law of Karma. All actions, whether good or bad, necessarily create Karma. As Brahman cannot be thought of as being within the grip of Karma, he must be inactive or action-less, absolutely cut off from this world of change, or at least not be in any way influenced or determined by this phenomenal world. In the same way the Atman, being essentially divine as identical with Brahman or as part of Brahman, is also free from Karma, eventhough the whole universe is within its domain including the Jiva of man, ie. both his gross and subtle body taken together. It is not the Atman that does the action of affected by the consequences of the actions. Atman is a passive spectator of this world of Karma. The difference between Brahman and Atman as far as Karma is concerned is that Brahman is absolutely free from the limitations caused by Karma, but Atman remains 'imprisoned' within 'Jada', the body, which is held in the hard grip of this remorseless force. [79] Why is it so? This is an irrelevant question for Hinduism. In so far as we are subject to this force, we cannot search outside its dominion and find out an answer for that. It is to be accepted as a given fact!

So, in this world of change what is permanent is Karma. Karma provides the form in which every problem of human destiny is set and answered. Every evil in the world is an outcome of an action, good or bad. To explain the evil in the world we need not, therefore, search for an outside agent. Like any other physical law, which we cannot escape, the Law of Karma is within this world. This law of retribution or justice is described by Edgerton as follows:

"It operates itself, just as much as the law of gravitation. It is there-fore wholly dispassionate neither merciful nor vindictive. It is absolutely inescapable, but at the same time never cuts hope. A man is what he has made himself, by that same token he may make himself what he will. The soul tormented in the lowest hell may raise himself in time to the highest heaven, simply by doing right. Perfect justice is made the basic law of the universe. It is a principle of great grandeur and perfection." [80]

The Law of Karma holds a very commanding position in Hinduism. Its influence has been felt in every aspect of Indian life. As Farquhar observes, it is Karma that has given Hinduism its peculiar flavour and forms the foundation of the Hindu worldvision. [81]

In Hinduism, the problem of evil, both physical and moral - which we call sin -, must be considered within the general framework of Karma. If one suffers physical calamity, that is necessarily due to his past evil actions. Since every evil is ultimately converged to free evil action of man or sin , it is necessary for us to consider the concept of sin in Hinduism, which is also valid for the Vedanta.

In the Rgveda, evil and suffering are considered to be the result of 'sin' and they are even identified with sin. [82] The words used to signify sin in the Rgveda are 'enas' which can be translated as offence, [83] 'agas' which means fault, [84] 'anrta' meaning unrighteousness [85] and 'drughda' misdeed. [86] Sin here means not just an infringement in the moral order, an offence against the gods and their friendship, [87] it is more a ritual error. [88] In the Brahmanas the notion of sin as ritual mistakes and sacrificial impurity is most stressed. Immoral acts imply guilts only in so far as they make a man ritually impure. Therefore sins also can be removed by various sorts of sacrifices and purificatory rituals, as a result of which a man 'even as a snake casts its skin, so does he cast away all his sins; there is not in him even as much sin as there is in a toothless child'. [89]

In the aupanisadic period, sin is no more an offence against gods nor a sacrificial impurity, but it belongs to the sphere of ignorance. Ignorance (Avidhya), desire (Kama) and action (Karma) are sins because they prevent the attainment of right knowledge by man. When one attains the right knowledge of Brahman and Atman all distinctions between good deeds and bad disappear: "He is not followed by good, he is not followed by evil, for then he has passed beyond all sorrows of the heart" [90] . We read further in the Kausitaki Upanisad: "So he who understands me - by no deed whatsoever of his is his world injured, not by stealing, not by killing an embryo, not by the murder of his mother, not by the murder of his father ..."[91] . It is true that such texts have been sometimes interpreted as a free pass for immorality for those who know the Brahman. The true meaning is that the one who has the knowledge of the Brahman cannot do any deed which brings about a consequence whether good or evil. All his deeds are 'absorbed' into Brahman and therefore according to the Brahman! Not the practice, but the theory of sin is reduced to a mere consequence of ignorance. [92]

The concept of sin as the result of ignorance that is to be destroyed by true knowledge, is the main thinking pattern of many of the Upanisads. But sin as a personal offence against a loving personal God is stressed by the Puranas and the Bhakti movements which reach their climax in the Bhagavadgita. For Gita, it is not Karma or deed that is sinful but man's attachment to its fruits. So action without detachment or disinterested action (Niskama karma) can have no consequences which are sinful: "He who works, having given up attachment, resigning his actions to Brahman, is not touched by s i n, even as a lotus leaf (is untouched) by water." [93]

Shortly said, there is a big distinction in Hinduism, including Vedenta, between the metaphysical understanding of sin and the practical and spontaneous moral sense. The root meanings of the words most commonly used to signify sin [94] show that this distinction should not be lightly ignored.

The concept of ' K a m a ', desire, is intimately connected with the idea of sin and Karma. A deed or Karma is always the result of a desire Kama. Karma necessarily presupposes Kama: "In this world no work is seen anywhere of a person having no desire (at all); for whatever one does is the outcome (result) of desire." [95] Kama is a very frequent word in the Upanisads. 'Iccha' is its synonym. As long as one is not free from desire, he remains in sin. The only desire that can bring man out of this world controlled by Karma is the desire for Brahman. Every other desire stems out of egoism (Ahamkara), a false identification of Jiva with Atman, a false process of 'I-making'. [96] By Ahamkara the true centre of one's personality is misplaced; that results in a sense of 'I' and 'mine': "... he whose self is by the ego fooled thinks, 'It is I who do'." [97] Those who are not in union with the Divine are impelled by desire and are attached to the fruits of action and are therefore bound. [98] Those who want to be liberated from this world of bondage must liberate themselves from Karma and its root cause Kama as the

Brahadaranyaka Upanisad says:

> "Now the man without desire:
> he is devoid of desire, free from desire;
> his desires have been fulfilled:
> the Self alone is his desire ...
> When all desires which shelter in the heart
> detach themselves, then does a mortal man
> become immortal: to Brahman he wins through." [99]

Both Karma and its cause Kama are born of Avidhya, ignorance. The ultimate cause of all misery and suffering is Avidhya. Avidhya is false knowledge. It is the lack of right knowledge regarding the ultimate Reality and the true nature of man. It is this ignorance that leads one to Kama and consequent Karma as we read in the Katha Upanisad:

> "Different, opposed, wide separated these, -
> unwisdom (avidhya) and what men as wisdom (vidhya) know:
> wisdom (it is that) Naciketas seeks, I see;
> not thou to be distracted by manifold desire!
> Self-wise, puffed up with learning, some turn round
> and round (imprisoned) in unwisdom's realm;
> hither and thither rushing, they go round, the fools,
> like blind men guided by the blind." [100]

The knowledge (Vidhya) meant here is not any kind of positive knowledge that can be acquired by much learning; it is the liberating wisdom , Jnana, the spiritual knowledge, that is important. Avidhya or Ajnana is the power of Maya, the cosmic deluding power, considered in its application to the consciousness of an individual. Therefore, Ajnana is not a mere absence or privation of knowledge but 'a positive mental state which induces the mind to take a thing for what it is not' [101]. It is a misapprehension of the self, identifying the Jiva with the Atman. As ignorance is the prime cause of all afflictions that lead to bondage, the Bhagavadgita maintains that only by the dawn of true knowledge can ignorance be destroyed. [102]

The Hindu notion of sin determines also its soteriology as we shall see in Chapter III. We will also have to discuss later in Chapter IV the Christian notion of sin especially in its character of being an 'offence' against a personal, loving God and the Vedantic reaction to the Christian soteriological idea of considering man basicly as a sinner who is in need of a gratuitous salvation from God.

In short we may say that according to Hinduism - valid also in the Vedanta the evil in the world, Avidhya, Kama, Karma and the consequent miseries cannot be said to be caused by God. He is not responsible for the evil in the world except in a very indirect way. 'If the universe consists of active choosing individuals who can be influenced but not controlled - for God is not a dictator - conflict is inevitable. S. Radhakrishnan maintains that conflict and evil in the world is the result of the cosmic process which 'is the interaction between the two principles of being and non-being' [103] It does not mean any metaphysical dualism between being and non-being, between good and evil because the principle of non-being is dependent on being. There is no evil in itself; evil can exist only depending on good. Therefore, evil or non-being is a necessary moment in reality for the unfolding of the Supreme. If the world is what it is, writes Radhakrishnan, it is because of the tension, the strife between being and non-being in the process of becoming. This conflict between being and non-being, between evil and good takes place not in the realm of non-being - it does not exist -, nor in the field of being because there is no place for a conflict where there is no tension, but in the world of becoming, which is called 'S a m s a r a'[104].

Why is there the world of becoming? Why is there a precipitation or fall from absolute being to becoming? We cannot, says Radhakrishnan, answer these questions; they are beyond our possibilities. We cannot account for the fact of the world but only can construe its nature, as a given fact![105]

2. 'Samsara'

Samsara is a concept necessarily connected with Karma as its inevitable consequence. [106] What happens if one does not succeed in getting rid of the subtle impressions of Karma before one takes leave of this life? As long as the Karma impressions cling on to the subtle body of man (suksma sarira) the Atman is in bondage! 'Suksma sarira' may also be called 'Linga sarira'. (li=to dissolve; gam=to go out!). The subtle body accompanies the spirit after cremation. The 'Linga sarira' is an essential link in the continuity of life because it is not destroyed by the death of the individual but continues to activate it throughout 'Samsara' until it is merged with the universal 'Atman'. It is something like the 'Ka' of the ancient Egyptians, 'the alter ego or active aspect of the personality that maintains consciousness after death and preceds the deceased and prepares the way to the next phase'[106a]. So it necessarily follows that after this life one gets another chance in another mode of existence to retribute for the evils done in this life and to free oneself from the enslaving impressions caused even by good deeds which bind man to the world of change. If that chance also does not suffice, there has to be still another chance.[107] It is most probably the case that in these succeeding modes of existence one may be accumulating still more and more Karma impressions on oneself instead of getting rid of those of the previous existence! This results in an endless chain of births and deaths. In every new birth one is given a new sthula sarira (physical body) by means of which one can counter balance the deeds of the disintegrated body of the previous existence. The new body need not necessarily be the body of man. Whether the new body one gets is better or worse than the previous one depends also on the Karma. If one had done more good deeds than evil ones one gets a better body and if one had led a very evil life the new body also will be correspondingly inferior! In this succession of births and re-births there can be, therefore, either a process of progressive spiritual evolution or of deterioration[107a] of material enslavement. The Atman can never attain its liberation from the slavery of matter until one's body evolves in this succession of life into a superior body which will have the ability to get rid of even the good subtle impressions of Karma and be integrated in ideal equilibrium with the Atman, so much so that the subtle body of man will be for the Atman no more a factor of enslavement to matter, but becomes an expression of the perfect harmony that exists between God and the world! This cycle of life, death and re-birth dictated by the inexorable law of Karma is called in the Indian terminology "Samsara".[108]

Samsara can be literally translated as stream current[109] and in its most common application it applies to the series of successive lives. The prefix 'sam' indicates 'the wide range of possibilities which lie side by side in this series of rebirths'[110]. It is a cycle of births and deaths. It may also be called transmigration or metempsychosis which is in a perpetual flux.

In the Rgveda there is no reference to rebirth, although some elements of it could be found.[111] The eschatology of the Samhitas and Brahmanas was relatively simple: The righteous dead were considered to be carried off by fire-god to the heavenly world, a replica of earthly pleasures and the evil-doers had their place in the darkness of the abyss.[111a] But the vedic sages kept on asking whether the re-birth in heaven (svarga) was not followed by a redeath. The order (Rta) of nature gave naturally sufficient impetus to such a way of thinking: Every death in the nature is followed by a new beginning and every new beginning followed by death. The change of seasons in the nature was thought to be imitated also in the microcosm, man. The winter is followed by the spring and that by the summer and fall! It is indeed a recurring process of death and rebirth.[112]

The eschatological views of Vedas and Brahmanas developed and received a more articulate expression in the Upanisads.[113] We find the doctrine of rebirth explicitly for the first time in the Brhadaranyaka Upanisad.[114] That is explained with some examples:

> "As a grass-hopper, when it has come to the end of a blade of grass, finds another place of support, and then draws itself towards it, similarly this self, after reaching the end of this body, finds another place of support and then draws himself towards it. As a goldsmith, after taking a piece of gold, gives it another, newer and more beautiful shape, similarly does this self, after having thrown off this body, and dispelled ignorance, take another newer and more beautiful form, whether it be of the manes, or demigods or gods or of Praja-pari or Brahma or of any other beings'."[115]

The Katha Upanisad is still more explicit: "Like corn, man gets ripe, like corn, he is born again."[116] And again: "... Those who think that this world exists and the other world does not exist fall again and again under the sway of death."[117] The Upanisads also maintain that after one's death one has to spent some time in heaven or hell, in the demoniac regions[118] or in the regions which are sorrowless, through the air, sun and moon[119], according to one's good or evil deeds, before one is given a material rebirth. For the new body one has to wait till the present world is completely dissolved and another world comes into existence.[120] The Chandogya Upanisad says that when the time comes for the individuals 'to fall down' from their temperory heaven or hell, they are born again according to their deserts.[121] In this new birth, the Upanisad continues, good characters get covetable births and the vicious ones attain miserable births:

"Those whose conduct on earth has given pleasure, can hope to enter a pleasant womb, that is the womb of a Brahman, or a woman of the princely class, or a woman of the pleasant class; but those whose conduct on earth has been foul can except to enter a foul and stinking womb, that is, the womb of a bitch or a pig or an outcaste."[122]

The theme of Samsara, the transmigrating self, is also very explicit in the Bhagavadgita. The reality of man, the Atman or Purusa is eternal, but in the embodied state it has to strive for liberation through manifold births and deaths: 'Just as in this body the embodied [self] must pass through childhood, youth and old age, so too [at death] will it assume another body: in this a thoughtful man is not perplexed.' [123] The Gita continues: "As a man casts off his worn-out clothes and takes on other new ones, so does the embodied [self] cast off its worn-off bodies and enters other new ones."[124] And the Gita affirms that what is born must die and what dies must be born again as long as it is not liberated. Death is not one for all; there are still more chances to live and die. Therefore the sorrow for the dead ist meaningless:

"And even if you think that it is constantly [re-]born and constantly [re-]dies, even so you grieve for it in vain. For sure is the death of all that dies: so in a matter that no one can prevent you have no cause to grieve. Unmanifest are the beginnings of contingent beings, manifest their middle course, unmanifest again their ends: what cause for mourning here?" [125]

Regardless of the divergent philosophies of Hindu schools and systems Samsara is an unquestionably accepted foundation of Hindu thinking. We conclude this consideration with a sample quotation from the Vedantic philosopher Sankara:

"The deeds (of past existence) produce the link with the (new) body. From the connection with the body (arises the experiences of) pleasure and pain. This is followed by attachment (raga) and aversion (dvesa). Thence (follow further) deeds, from which (are produced) wholesome (dharma) and unwholesome (adharma) consequences . Subsequently the unenlightened (must suffer) renewed connection with the body. Thus the world (samsara) rolls on eternally like a wheel."[126]

How could the Christian theology assimilate this foundation stone of Vedantic thinking, namely, 'Karma-Samsara'? It is a formidable task. But, we will be considering the relevance of the theory of 'Samsara' for Christian eschatology later in Part III. The implications of 'Samsara' are not to be taken

literally, but should be given an anthropological and existential re-interpretation as we shall see in Chapter VIII. We will be referring there also
to the elements which are common to the Catholic faith in the 'Purgatory'
and the 'Karma-Samsara'. In Chapter VII we will also be considering the
Christian notion of 'Original Sin' in relation to the doctrine of 'Karma-
Samsara'.

3. The Important Anthropological Implications

of the Doctrine of 'Karma-Samsara'

Karma-Samsara influences every aspect of Hindu life. Here we consider
some of the most important implications of this doctrine which are relevant
for our investigation of the Vedantic anthropology. They are: (a) the Caste
System, (b) Panpsychism, (c) freedom and fatilism.

a. The Caste System

The caste system in India or more precisely in the Hindu way of life is
philosphically explained as a corollory to the doctrine of Karma-Samsara.
But the fact is that castes existed in India long before the doctrine of Karma-
Samsara found its way into the Indian thinking! Castes are mentioned in
the Rgveda, but Karma-Samsara is explicitly formulated only in the much
later Upanisads. The origin of caste system in India must be traced to sociological backgrounds. [127] It is also certain that later on the religious writings
gave ratification to this as an accomplished fact.

The attempt of one race to subordinate another one which is weaker was
not absent also in the Indian history. The Aryan invaders were conspicuously
different from the natives in their physical apperance, beliefs and customs. [128] The Aryans were warriors and conquerors while the aborigins were
peace loving defenders. The Aryans were the victors and the natives were
the vanquished. Consequently they could not but shrink from close contact
with each other. The difference of colour (V a r n a) also became a basis
of distinction between the two groups. [129] Some kind of a formula of peaceful
co-existence had to be worked out between these two groups in practical
life.   Instead   of   exerminating   the   native,   the   Aryans   admitted

them into their society as servants and they got the name Sudra or servile caste. The Aryans themselves were later on devided into various subgroups on the principle of a certain division of labour forming the three Aryan castes: Brahmin who belonged to the class of priests, Ksatriya caste formed out of the warriors and nobles and the Vaisya who were traders and peasants. The castes were determined necessarily by birth and heredity and so the term ' J a t i ' (condition deriving from birth) were applied to the various castes.[130]   The caste was a system of integration and at the same time isolation. The castes were socially isolated from each other but at the same time all belonged to the wider union of Hinduism. [131]

This attempt to preserve the purity of race and culture and to devide the functions in the society was given religious sanction in the Rgveda. In the Purusa Sukta, a hymn of creation, we see that the macrocosmic man (Purusa) is the prototype of the microcosmic man.[132] The individual man is the image of the Purusa, considered also the super Deity, whose three-fourths are spiritual and one-fourth is material. [133] The creation of human race effected by the sacrificial division of the Purusa is, according to the Rgveda, the theological reason for the division of society into four castes:

"When they divided [offered up] Purusa , into how many parts did they dispose him? What was his mouth? What were his arms? What were called his thighs and feet?
The Brahman was his mouth; the Rajanya was made (of) his arms; that which was the Vaisya was his thighs; the Sudra sprang from his feet." [134]

According to this hymn the human race is not from a single human ancestor, but the whole humanity had separate origins and therefore belong to seperate castes or races. The Brahmans, the Rajanyas (Ksatriyas) and the Vaisyas are the three Aryan classes of priests, nobles and people,[135] and they are a superior creation. They were called 'divija' or twice born, a normal physical birth and another birth into the world of wisdom when they were initiated into the study of the Vedas,[136] as a sign of which they alone could wear the sacred thread.[137]   The aborigins admitted into the Hindu community (Sudras) were considered an inferior creation; they could not be initiated into the Vedas, take part in sacrifices and their function was to serve the other three castes. There was still another group of people who could not be admitted into any of these four castes. They formed a fifth class (Pancamas). They were 'unclean' aborigins and progeny of those who violated the caste rules on mixed marriage. They were considered as out-castes and untouchables. The foreigners (mlechas) also belonged to this group.[138] The peculiar Indian flavour of caste system is that one's caste is fixed automatically by his heredity. One belongs to the caste into which one is born.

In the course of history the spirit of caste, the tendency to subdivide into closed groups, has worked so powerfully that in one and the same caste innumerable sub-castes were formed. It is also a fact that groups of low-caste men have occsionally been able to secure recognition as belonging to higher castes. But, in the main, the system itself has remained unchanged for more than two thousand years.[139]

It cannot be denied that such endogamous groups could be found among a number of ancient peoples and civilizations. The completely unique character of Indian caste system is derived from the theological interpretation given to this social phenomenon based on the formidable doctrine of Karma-Samsara. Accordingly each man is born into that caste for which his Karma or former actions have prepared him. If he is spiritually far advanced he is born as a Brahman; if his state of perfection is a step lower he is born as a Ksatriya, and so on. In short, 'a man's caste is held to be an infallible index of the state of his soul'[140]. The castes mark the stages of the soul's progress toward final liberation.[141]

According to Karma-Samsara all the joys and sorrows of this life are the outcome of the deeds of the past life; ever calamity is the direct result of some evil action in a former life. That explained very conveniently the appallingly degraded and scandalously downtrodden situation of the outcast tribes. There was no reason for compassion towards these wretched people living in the midst of miseries. They were considered to be the criminals of the universe undergoing a life-term of punishment. Their sufferings were the justly measured requital of their past misdeeds, and absolutely no power on earth can liberate them from the revenging clutches of the Karma-Samsara! It was useless to attempt even the slighest improvement in their lot because 'nothing could prevent their Karma from bringing upon them their full tale of misery'[142] . Nobody, therefore, can be saved or redeemed by anybody else. One has to save oneself in the interminable purifying process of Karma-Samsara. Any amount of philanthropy or social development programme can be of no avail before this all-powerful law. This law explained not only the atrocities of the caste system, but also every problem in human relationship, every weakness, defect and calamity.[143] It was not any master organizer who worked out this all-determining law; it slowly evolved from the inner attitudes of the Indian people and their historically conditioned life-situation.

Until a century or so ago the acceptance of the caste system was considered as the criterion to judge whether one is an orthodox Hindu or not. All the differences in beliefs and philosophical divergences did not count. It was the rejection of the caste system and domination of the Brahmans, the priestly caste, - together with the rejection of the divine authority of the Vedas -, and not their philosophical views, that excluded Buddhism from the Hindu fold.[144]

Today the caste system is slowly losing its grip on the Indian mind especially due to the efforts of various reform movements, among which the most powerful has been Gandhism and its understanding of the outcastes as the people of God (Harijan). But its doctrinal support, the Karma-Samsara, is still a formidable axiom in the Hindu and of course the Vedantic thinking. Even educated Hindus still think of this doctrine as a brilliant speculative solution of the problem of misery and inequalities in human existence and as one of the greatest principles ever thought out by human mind! [145]

It cannot be denied that the principle of caste division in India and the idea of man's inequality that is connected with it are formidable problems for the Christian faith that preaches the equality of all human beings as the children of God in Christ. We will have to discuss this question a little more elaborately later in Chapter VI in reference to the liberating aspect of the Christ-experience and also in Chapter IX while considering the unity of the love of God and the love of one's fellow men in Jesus of Nazareth.

b. The Position of Man within the Animal Kingdom: Panpsychism

The belief in the basic equality of all living beings - human beings and animals - is another serious question that Christology and Christian anthropology have to face in the Vedantic context. 'Panpsychism', in general, denotes the theory that all nature has a psychic side. Our reference to the 'Vedantic panpsychism', however, is limited to signify the relation between human beings and the animal kingdom.

The doctrine of Karma-Samsara affects not only the whole human race, but it has its repercussions in the whole animal kingdom. It implies the integration of animals into the same 'cycle' as man which gives the animals a relatively privileged position. [146] If Karma-Samsara is a fact it necessarily follows that all life is akin. The aparent distinction between human and non-human beings cannot be ultimate. [147] Man is just one of the many forms[148] in which the 'Atman' can be embodied in the stream of transmigration and so man does not radically stand apart from the animal world enjoying any place of special privilege which can be considered as resulting from his essential difference from animals. Essentially man is one with all other animals, only accidently is he different. [149] The different realities in the universe are various modalities for the manifestation of the Absolute and the living beings, gods, demons, men, animals and plants have 'life' which is an expression of Atman, which they hold within them. All living beings float in the stream of transmigration (Samsara). Their life is at once retribution for the past and opportunity for the future. All souls are equally eternal and all have the possibility to attain release from the wheel of Samsara or to fall downwards in the ladder of existence. By evil deeds one prepares for oneself a future life as a miserable animal. A man can rise by persistent good conduct to the highest position among men, namely that of a Brahman, or even to the status of a god. But a release from the ever-whirling wheel of birth and death can be won only by stepping out of the common course of existence.

The greatest difference between the soul of an animal and that of a man consists not in their essence but in the possibilities they have to attain an immediate release. Though the soul can receive any species of animal body depending on the merits and demerits acquired in the past, only in the human body can it perform meritorious deeds, or sinful ones for that matter, and work positively for its liberation. In all other life-conditions the soul merely passively expiates an infinitesimal part of its debts. It is therefore necessary, though not enough, to be born as a man before one attains salvation.[150] When through much good Karma the soul is born in a good Hindu family, for example as a Brahman, where it has the possibilities to account for all Karma, it may easily attain emancipation.[151] The gods are themselves transmigrating souls, just like men and animals, but through their good conduct in their past life have they risen to the position of divine beings. Their state too is temporal; they too must get rid of their good Karmaphala or impressions and get out of the chain of Karma-Samsara. If they commit evil deeds they may fall back to a lower position, even that of an animal, and wait indefinitely for the dawn of liberation from Sam - sara![152]

The respect given to animals in India must be understood in this philosophical context. If the soul within me and in the animal is essentially of the same nature, it follows that I have to pay a certain amount of respect even to the animals and that I can by no means do injury to the animals or kill them. Therefore, 'Ahimsa' or non-injury must be practiced not only towards human beings but also towards animals. Hence the prohibition to eat meat!

In this context it is to be mentioned that in the animal world the cow (Go) rose to extraordinary prominence, even that of a special sacredness! The reasons are more economicosocial than theological. Originally what brought cattle its importance was the agriculture of the Aryans which depended on them for ploughing manure etc. In the Aryan society the cow served even as a form of currency. Because of its economical and nutritional importance - milk was one of major nutrient - cow became later identified with the life-giving and life-sustaining mother-earth or the Nature,[153] and it was attributed a heavenly origin.[154] But the cow has never been regarded as a goddess who is to be propitiated by sacrifices. Its sacredness was derived mostly from its relation to other gods. The Satapatha Brahmana, for example, explains that it is a wonder that a red or black cow gives white milk and this whiteness is caused by the fact that milk is the semen of god Agni (fire) who copulated with a cow.[155] Because of its sacredness, a cow could be killed only in sacrifice and it was forbidden to do otherwise any harm to a cow. Cow was generally offered as 'daksina' (present) to a Brahman for a sacrifice. Even when the cow was later on replaced by other sacrificial objects, the prohibition against cow-slaughter survived and cow became a chief character in Puranic myths. [157]

In modern India the relics of the past veneration given to the cow is not totally absent. The Hindu reformers give it another interpretation. Mahatma Gandhi, for example, regarded 'cow-protection' as the central fact of Hinduism. The cow for him is also spiritual in so far as it has life,[158] and the cow symbolizes for Gandhi the entire sub-human world, and cow-protection is an expression of the "brotherhood between man and beast, indeed of man's identity with all that lives"[159] . Go-ology (theory about cow) is, therefore, ultimately anthropology, and anthropology is finally, in the Indian and Vedantic context, theology!

Inspite of the ecological stress and the relation of ecology and theology that are implied in the Hindu attitude towards animals, it has to be mentioned here that panpsychism, a theory that in its exaggerated form postulates a transcendental horizon for subhuman creatures is not acceptable to the Christian anthropology as we shall see in Chapter VII following the arguments of Karl Rahner and Wolfhart Pannenberg. But the notion of the unity and integration of the whole cosmos that is promoted by the above principle points to the recapitulation of all creation under Jesus Christ, a point that will be of interest to us for our evaluation in Chapter IX.

c. **Fatalism and Human Freedom**

There is a general misunderstanding that the doctrine of Karma-Samsara is fatalistic and is opposed to the notion of freedom that is essential for Christian soteriology and spirituality. Man's present existence is all fixed by the past Karma; even man's social situation and the miseries he has to suffer are all its results. One cannot change one's Karma; its consequences must be accepted with resignation. Man cannot fundamentally improve his lot in this life and even what he may do to better his situation may only result in additional Karma and prolonged bondage in lifes to come. This fatalistic understanding of the Indian anthropology is well articulated by Ghosal:

> "(Man) is required to work in full knowledge of the futility of his work - he cannot change his environment. Neither is he an independent agent with free will, and his work in itself can have no value as it comes from his prakrti - the blind forces of nature." 160

This statement is true, but is only a half truth. The doctrine of Karma-Samsara only says that the conditions of one's birth, his place in the society, his position, his family backgrounds, and his inborn tendencies are predetermined. That is our 'fate', that is the givenness of our present situation. But one can in this life cancel by right effort all the debts accumulated in the past and achieve liberation! That can by no means be called fatalism. 161 The conditions of one's birth and the genetic dispositions are conditioned by the law of Karma. They are definitely an impediment on man's possibilities of action, but they do not, as Feuerstein observes, impair man's free will nor relieve him of his obligations and responsibilities. Karma-Samsara is a process of man's spiritual maturation. So, it is not a blind mechanism, but it is teleological. 'The accusation that this doctrine is fatalistic and pessimistic is completely unfounded'. Though the past determines the present, the future is always open.162

The modern Vedantist S. Radhakrishnan emphatically affirms that inspite of the fact that there are many impediments to the human freedom, man is fundamentally the possessor of freedom. 163 The law of Karma-Samsara can be overcome by the affirmation of the freedom of the spirit, because this law holds only in the realm of the not-self. When the self of man affirms itself it achieves liberation. Therefore, Karma is only a condition of human existence, not a destiny or fate.164 Dr. Radhakrishnan continues:

> "There are certain factors in our lifes which are determined for us by forces over which we have not control. We do not choose how or when or where or in what condition we are born. On the theory of rebirth, even these are chosen by us. It is our past Karma that determines our ancestry, heredity and environment. But when we look from the standpoint of this life, we can say that we are not consulted about our nationality, race, parentage and social status. But subject to these limitations, we have freedom of choice. Life is like a game of bridge. We did not invent the game or design the cards. We did not frame

the rules and we cannot control the dealing. The cards are dealt out to us, whether they be good or bad. To that extent determinism rules. But we can play the game well or play it badly. A skillful player may have a poor hand and yet win the game. A bad player may have a good hand and yet make a mess of it. Our life is a mixture of necessity and freedom, chance and choice. By exercising our choice properly, we can control steadily all the elements and eliminate altogether the determinism of nature."[165]

In this view, what we have done in the past has given us certain tendencies and latent dispositions that make us what we are now; but we can alter this situation by our effort. We are our own creators and the future is what we choose to make of it. Karma-Samsara accounts for the conditions of life, but man directs his destiny. 'Centuries of passions and systematized error have built a crust above our souls which light cannot pierce but the spirit when awake can produce miracles'[166]. It is humanity and not the determined factors of Karma-Samsara that shape the future of human history![167]

There are soteriological problems that are implied in the Vedantic approach to the notions of Karma and freedom. The theory of 'Karma-Samsara' points to a freedom that is at the cost of the divine grace. It follows that it is man who liberates himself from his 'bondage' by his own deeds or non-deeds (Karma). A self-salvation, as we shall see in Chapters VI and VIII, would not be compatible with the Christian soteriology God's salvation. Freedom is, according to the Christian faith and unlike the Vedantic approach, a concrete form of grace and they are not opposed to each other. A freedom that excludes grace is not real freedom but tragic fate!

C. The Vedantic Understanding of Human History

An understanding of the Vedantic concept of human history is also of essential importance for our consideration of Jesus Christ as the mystery of human history in the Indian anthropological context. Here our intention is to clarify this point.

The concept of Karma-Samsara shows its influence also on the Indian concept of human history. The human history is not something that began in a far remote past progressing towards a fulfilment in the distant future which is a reflection of the doctrine of Karma-Samsara, the transmigration of the soul. [168] Just as life is given many chances to repeat itself on the way to liberation, so also there are repeated new beginnings for the world-history and the history of humanity. The myths play a very significant role in the Hindu interpretation of history. This interpretation is accepted, in its basic principles at least, by all Hindu systems including the Vedanta.

The Hindu mythology understands universal time as a never-ending cycle of both creation and destruction. Each complete cycle consists of one hundred years in the life of Brahma. [169] Hinduism distinguishes between the years of gods and the years of men. 360 years of men constitute one year of gods. 12000 divine years constitute one yuga. [170] We are living now in the Kali-yuga, the age of Kali. It is an age of deepening decadence and misery. Before this Kali-yuga there had been other three yugas or ages of steady degeneration in the process of retribution. The first yuga was the age of full virtue (krta yuga); [171] it lasted 4000 divine years. [172] During the Krta yuga righteousness reigned supreme and people were virtuous fulfilling their duties without malice, sadness, pride or deceit; there was nothing to disturb the calmness of the age. [173] The Krta yuga passed inevitably into the age of three-fourths of good (Treta-yuga) which lasted 3000 divine years. Changes in relationships began to accur in the Treta yuga. Duties were no longer the spontaneous laws of human behaviour, but they had to be learned. But people devoted themselves to truth and righteousness through ceremonies and sacrifices. It was followed by Dvapara yuga, an age in which only the half of good survived. [174] Its total duration was 2000 divine years. Dvapara yuga witnessed increased imbalance and a steady decline in righteousness. The Rgveda appeared in this period. [175] Diseases, desires and disasters began to harass mankind, some of whom could attain release in austerities and ritual practises. Finally, Kali yuga is the age in which we live. In it only one-fourth of good has survived. Its total duration is 1000 divine years. It is the dark age riven with quarrels, dissension, wars and strife. Here there is a separation between love and sex and few know the truth. It is not righteousness but possessions that confer rank and dignity. Inner religion has deteriorated into external shows. This age might have begun in 3102 BC and it has to run another 427 centuries. [176] So we are living in this last evil age, the age of great depravity, inspite of the fact that there was a past golden age!

The entire cycle of four yugas (ages) and their intervals of twilight extend over 12000 divine years which equals a total of 4,320,000 human years. [177]
All these four yugas together constitute the unit of cosmological time called 'mahayuga' (the great age) and 2000 Mahayugas are reckoned as a 'Kalpa', which is a day and a night in the life of Brahma, which is equivalent to 8,640,000,000 human years. [178] This we read also in the Bhagavadgita:

> "For a thousand ages lasts [one] day of Brahma, and for thousand ages [one such] night ... At the day's dawning all things manifest spring forth from the Unmanifest; and then at nightfall they dissolve [again] in that same thing called 'Unmanifest'. Yes, this whole host of beings comes ever anew to be; at the fall of night it dissolves away all help-less; at dawn of day it rises up again." [179]

Accordingly, Brahma is awake during the day and towards the night he goes to sleep. At the dawn of the 'day' Brahma begins his work of creation and when he goes to sleep, that provokes a long period - 4320 million human years - of cosmic dissolution called Pralaya, [180] and the three worlds, namely heavens, middle and lower regions, disappear into chaos. [181] After the great dissolution the world will be reintegrated into Brahma by involution until it is born again. [182] When Brahma awakes these worlds re-appear and the process starts all over again and all beings that have not obtained liberation must prepare to re-birth according to their Karma (deeds). [183] This process goes on indefinitely, [184] but it does not last for more than a 'Para', a century of Brahma's nights and days, which may be calculated as 36500 Kalpas. According to some Hindu tradition the life of Brahma and the universe lasts for a Para. Our present Kalpa is considered to be at the beginning of the second half of the Para, making Brahma fifty years old. [185] What does happen at the end of the Para? That is uncertain! But anxiety over this cosmic uncertainty is somehow allayed by the knowledge of the fact that it is a long way off, approximately 31,000,000,000,000 years away! [186] One Hindu school of philosophy however denies that the world is finite in time and shares with Jainism the idea of an eternal, uncreated universe. [187]

The accuracy of these countings, which differ from source to source, is not what is of immediate relevance and importance for us. The apparent similarity to the biblical view of history as a glorious beginning, later fall, growing moral depravity and a consequent salvation that culminates in an apocalyptic end are of course interesting for us. But our primary concern in mentioning these complex calculation is only to show the basic historical vision of Hinduism and Vedanta, on which a corresponding anthropology and soteriology are built up. The Indian vision of history is essentially one of cyclic creation and dissolution. [188] At the beginning or a worldaeon being are sent out, and at the end an aeon they pass back into their source as the Gita itself states:

"By applying my own nature I send out again and again All this helpless host of beings." [189]

The ages and aeons follow each other in an endless stream of time. The wheel of Karma-Samsara encompasses the individuals, the species, the social structure, the planets, the gods and the whole universe; it is the time-scale of nature itself. The process of alteration and change are endless, irreversible and unquenchable. 'The cycle of emanation, fruition, dissolution, and re-emanation from the primeval substance, has a vastness incomprehensible to mankind' [190] . The conception of history as an endless series of alternating periods of activity and rest rules out any progress towards an culminating purpose when history is taken in its totality, inspite of the fact that the different periods in this totality represent a teleology because there is a movement towards cosmic dissolution or Pralaya. But that is not the end! There is no evolution towards a fulfilling and liberating end, but there is an end just for the sake of another repetition of the cosmic process and the world is always the same at the beginning of each period of activity. There is no world-purpose to be worked out. [191] The history returns ever again to the point from which it started; its only raison d'etre is retribution. Within this vicious cycle of history there is absolutely no possibility of salvation. History, therefore, in the Hindu understanding can never be a liberating factor. History is a bondage for man. There can be no liberation until one steps out of this endless process of repetition. History is a meaningless passion; historical events are meaningless too. There is no point in registering them in accurate records. [192] These are all irrelevant as far as the ultimate liberation of man is concerned. No event in history, however noble it may be, is unique and irrepeatable and no event can have a salvific character, because every historical event has to be a part of the enslaving vicious circle called history. This is a position that diametrically contradicts the biblical view of human history as we shall see in the course of our work.

For the Greeks too, who placed the emphasis on the immutable cosmic order, the idea of time was cyclic. The Greco-Roman ages of gold, silver, brass and iron [193] are not unlike the four Hindu Yugas or ages. Time for the Greeks was the measurement of movements [194] within the well ordered cosmic system. 'The regular and immutable course of stars gives its image to things and events ' [195]. But true values exist outside of time. Eventhough the Greeks shared the notion of cyclic time, it was never on the vast scale of India. [196] Another important difference between the Indian and Greek understanding of time is that the Indian concept of history tries to combine the cyclic and personal aspects into one.[197] Time is the projection of eternity of God and it falls back into that eternity and therefore at least to some extent history is a self-manifestation of God himself, eventhough not in a soterio-logical sense. The whole history is seen as a drama, with a symbolic and religious value for man. There is a certain divine virtue present in man and in the whole universe, even in stones, water, flowers, trees, ashes, oil and so on. This divine horizon in man and in the whole of cosmos can help man to step out of this Karma-Samsara and its consequent cyclic history to attain liberation in the realization of this Divine.

It must be affirmed here clearly that there is an element of truth in the Vedantic cyclic vision. A cyclic world process in a wide sense is quite plaus-ible from the point of view of the modern cosmic sciences. The beginning of the present world process with a so-called 'Big bang', its evolution in the ever expanding space, its final dissolution preparing ground for another 'Big bang' and such a never ending process of origin, expansion and dissolution are not contrary to the Christian faith. It is only the meaninglessness and purposelessness of history for the destiny of man in a given world process, the denial of the possibility of events with a universally unique character and the repeated appearance of the same 'Atma' in the subsequent 'Yuga' that are implied in the Vedantic cyclic vision of history and the theory of 'Karma-Samsara' that are objectionable as far as the Christian theology is concerned. In this sense the blunt affirmation that the Christian view of history is lineal and thus contrary to the Vedantic vision would not be quite accurate!

The sense of history as a well-ordered plan gradually being carried out

- a linear view of time which is present in the West - was a contribution of the Judeo-Christian conception of salvation. [198] In this vision history has a meaning as it tends 'from creation to eternal consummation through the unique and definitive events of the Crib and the Cross' [199] . In this frame of understanding history can be converted into salvation history. As every event is unique and irrepeatable in this linear vision, people were interested in recording the exact historical dates or at least to invent some dates to give credibility even to some doctrines in the religious field, which are supposed to get an extra scientific corroboration when demonstrated as historical. [200] It cannot, however, also be denied that in the West the Christian conception of history is to some extent rejected by the profane historians who find the meanings of events only in the economic, sociological and cultural laws, inexorable in their course, calculable and foreseeable and therefore c y c l i c in character. [201] From the above considerations it would be more accurate to say that there are both cyclic and lineal elements or aspects in World History!

The Christian understanding of history has had its influence also on modern Hindu and Vedantic reformers. S. Radhakrishnan, for example, is of the opinion that history has a meaning and purpose in its totality, because men determine history as understood by the ancient historians of the Greco-Roman world, Thucydides, Herodotus, Tacitus, Livy, Plutarch and others. [202] But we affirms that any particular event in history taken in itself apart from the totality of humanity cannot have a meaning in itself:

> "Human history is an indivisible whole. It is not a patchwork of un-related episodes. Any fragment of history may not disclose meaning or purpose, but seen as a whole we find sense, meaning." [203]

By this he suggests that one person or one event alone constitute only a part within the march of the whole humanity toward the realization of its highest aspirations and he rules out the Christian notion of history as an inevitable movement towards a spiritual purpose and the unique importance of any particular individual or event of history in respect to other historical epochs. He writes:

"We cannot say that the historical process is a movement towards any spiritual purpose (although mankind bears in itself the seeds of many developments) ... (and) no historical epoch is a station on the road to the ultimate goal of history. In other words each epoch has its own purpose."[204]

While admitting that mankind has made enormous progress in science and technology, a progress of the true self of man and his philosophy is contested by the Vedantic philosopher Radhakrishnan. He repeats the words of Goethe: "World history - the most absurd thing there is!"[205] He continues:

"Belief in the progress of humanity towards a final goal is supported by man's mastery of science and technology. This concerns the external structure of our lifes. The technological progress has no doubt enriched our lifes, but it has also endangered them. But can we say that we have progress in philosophical pursuits? In wrestling with the great riddles posed by human existence, we do not discern much progress. The greatest attempts of philosophers do not go much beyond the thinking of previous centuries. ...
From the way nations are behaving, we do not discern any increase in common sense. ... We cannot minimize the force of evil and believe in automatic progress. Progress is not a basic law of life. (We are fighting one another and the modern weapons threaten us with annihilation) ... It is possible that there may be the death of the old order. We cannot be certain that there will be the birth of the new."[206]

Radhakrishnan contents that it is not the human material progress that helps and developes history but the growth of the 'Spirit' or the divine horizon in man: "Everything ultimately depends upon whether the man who is now such a great master of science and technology is also the master of himself."[207] One who is the master of himself stands outside history and he makes history.[208]

Hinduism is called "Sanatana Dharma", eternal religion. It prides itself of not being a historical religion. Religious truths are supra-historical, not conditioned by time and space, they know no age. Hinduism does not owe its origin to any historical founder or prophet. It is beginningless and endless and authoritative in a non-temporal or supra historical sense.[209] The ultimate release can be attained only by escaping from history , from the wheel of time and action.[210]

Our above discussion on the Vedantic notion of history has its great anthropological and Christological relevance for our work as it becomes evident in the following chapters. We will be referring in Chapter IV to the Vedantic insistence on the metahistorical Christ-principle versus the limitations of a historically bound Jesus of Nazareth. The Vedantic notion of the 'Universal Christ' and its general discard for the historical aspect of human existence and God's self-communication to man will be further dealt with in our evaluation especially in Chapters VII and IX. The contributions of Karl Rahner and Wolfhart Pannenberg will be of immense help to us there. A proper understanding of history has also a great role to play in explaining the Christian eschatology as we shall see in Chapter VIII.

Conclusion to Chapter Two

Our consideration of the Divine horizon in man, who is in bondage to the law of Karma-Samsara manifesting itself in the cyclic history can be concluded with a reference to goals of human existence as it is understood and accepted by Vedanta. We may speak of different aims of human life (Purusartha): Kama (pleasure), Artha (wealth and material prosperity), Dharma (duty and morally sound life) and Moksa (spiritually free life and the consequent liberation). [211] These are the ends of man, the first three referring to man's empirical life and the last to his transcendental life. According to most of the ancient teachers these four ends exclude each other, but the present tendency is to integrate all of them for the pursuit of the Absolute. Artha and Kama are legitimate goals of human life, but they are evil when they are considered in selfish isolation. They must be integrated by Dharma into the higher goal of human existence, which flowers in Moksa. [212] Hinduism itself is 'Santana Dharma', the perennial law of life. 'Dharma' taken in itself is a very complex concept, with which we will deal in the next chapter III.B.1, while considering the ways of liberation. Dharma for the time being may be shortly explained as duty or righteousness, which can be social known as 'Varna Dharma' (the duties of one's own caste) and personal called 'Arama .Dharma', determining the different stages of one's personal life, namely: brahmacarya (Vedic student), garhasthya (householder), vanaprasthya (hermit) and finally sannyasa (wandering ascetic). [213] The ultimate goal of human existence, which is derived from the very divine essential constitution of man is M o k s a. An understanding of the nature of Moksa and the ways leading to it is the concern of our next chapter.

CHAPTER III

THE VEDANTIC SEARCH FOR SALVATION

In the previous chapters we concentrated our attention on the Vedantic Brahma-Vidhya and Manu-Vidhya, the concept of God and man. A theo-logy or an anthropo-logy is not of great relevance for us in our attempt to 'draw' the background for an emerging Indian Christology unless we relate the Vedantic understanding of God and man to a Soteriology or a Yoga-Sastra that necessarily follows from them. In this chapter we try to analyse the Vedantic concept of salvation and some of its important implications. This investigation is very relevant and quite important for us in our discussion about Jesus Christ as the mystery of man's transcendence and its expression in human history. We will be considering this point in greater detail in our evaluative Chapter VII. Our later discussion on the universality of Christ's salvation and the concept of the so-called 'anonymous' Christ and Christians in the sixth Chapter and its evaluation in Chapter IX are to be done in the background of the present study.

A. Salvation as Liberation from Karma-Samsara

The concept of 'Karma-Samsara' is, as we have seen, the corner stone of Indian, and for that fact Vedantic, Metaphysics and Soteriology. If man is by nature or essence divine, the only thing he has to do in his attempt to attain perfect happiness is to get out of the vicious bondage of Samsara. Man attains his inherent harmony not in this world, but beyond it, where he is eternally divinized!

1. The Quest for the Beyond

"Asato ma sad gamaya, Tamaso ma jyotir gamaya, Mrtyor ma amrtam gamaya" - Lead me from the unreal to the real, lead me from darkness to light, lead me from death to immortality: This is the quest of man as we see marvellously presented in an humble prayer of the Brhadaranyaka Upanisad. [1] Man can step out of the world and this proves that he is in some sense beyond the world. As S. Radhakrishnan observes, 'there is the basic human hunger for a world beyond strife and suffering. If there were not a Beyond, we should have been satisfied with the world process' [2]. There is in man a deep rooted feeling of absolute need and as the Katha Upanisad testifies, man cannot be satisfied with perishable things, for example wealth: "Na vittena tarpaniyo manusyah" [3] . Man is seeking after the eternal and this seeking of man is inspired by the eternal in him and it is the presence of the Infinite in him that makes man dissatisfied with the finite. [4] The image of God in man expresses itself in the infinite human capacity for self-transcendence. [5] The unfathomable and invisible impulse to seek God produces the agony that inspires heroic idealism and human fulfilment. The sense of insufficiency, barrenness and void in the heart of man is due to the Infinite Divine Mystery that lurks within man and at the heart of creation. [6]

The history of religions bears witness to man's preoccupation in some form or another with evils of human existence and the ways of eliminating them although the limitation or evils in this life have been variously explained and different solutions have been proposed. Every religion is soteriological in its basic set-up, at least implicitly when not explicitly. Man is in need of salvation, his existence in this world is not the ultimate. Salvation has been proposed by various religions, as M. Dhavamony writes, 'both in the sense of liberation from evil and its consequences, and in the positive sense of reaching a perfect state of happiness and of eternal union with the divine'. [7]

Happiness in this world is not the end of life. Growth to human fulfilment is the real end. The basic principle of this world itself is not to be static, but to grow and every growth includes moments of struggle and pain. The world, observes S. Radhakrishnan, is a process and man is evolving into a higher species where he has to realize new possibilities. 'The future of man is gradual ascent to the divine perfection. The cosmic process will not have finished its long journey until every soul has entered into the blissful realization of its own divinity' [8] and 'the world is the place where human souls grow into spirits' [9] .

a. The Concept of Moksa: 'Heaven' and 'Hell' in the Vedas

The ultimate spiritual goal of Hinduism may be designated as 'Moksa' or 'Mukti'. It may be translated as release, liberation or spiritual freedom.

The Sanskrit-English Dictionary of M. Monier-Williams derives both of these terms from 'moks', 'to free oneself', 'to shake off'. Some trace the root to 'muc' which would mean to let loose, release, liberate, free, deliver[10]. Originally the words 'moksa' or 'mukti' did not have the soteriological significance attributed to them in the late Vedic period.

The Vedic literature uses the word 'muncati' with prefixes like nis-, pravi-, etc. to mean not only the ultimate liberation of man but any kind of freedom or deliverance. For example, "People are deliverd (mucyante) from the sacrificial duties not only by death but also by old age."[11] The Svetasvatara Upanisad speaks of a deliverence from all fetters to which the root 'muc' is used: "After having got knowledge of God he is delivered from all fetters (jnatva devam mucyate sarvapasaih)."[12]

The Bhagavadgita speaks of a liberation or release from the bondage of works [13] , from old age and death [14] , and from material nature itself to which all contingent beings are subject [15] . Liberation is for Gita the way one approaches Brahman [16] and even becomes Brahman[17] . Gita means by liberation the state in which one is never to be born again[18] and once a man reaches liberation he draws near to God himself [19] , participates in his mode of being [20] , and enters into Him [21] . In the Bhagavadgita 'Moksa' and 'Mukti' always mean the final liberation of man.[22] Here are some of the sample texts:

> "With senses, mind and soul restrained, the silent sage, on deliverance intent, who has forever banished fear, anger and desire, is truly liberated."[23]

> "... men who hanker after deliverance perform the various acts of sacrifice, penance, and the gift of aims, having no thought for the fruits (they bring)."[24]

> "Give up all things of law, turn to me, your only refuge, (for) I will deliver you from all evils; have no care."[25]

Bhagavadgita uses the term 'Mukta' for the one who is liberated, [26] and the one who is free from attachments is called 'Muktasanga' [27] . The one who casts off his mortal body becomes 'Muktva'.[28]

Though the terms 'Moksa' and 'Mukti' are the most common in Vedanta to signify salvation, there are also other terms which have a soteriological meaning in the Hindu context. [29] 'Tarana', for example, signifies 'rescuing', 'liberating', 'saving', 'helping over a difficulty', 'enabling to cross' etc. 'Taraka' also means the same. The act of raising, elevating, lifting up, drawing out, pulling up, removal, payment of debt, deliverence, redemption etc. can be expressed by the term "Uddhara". The one who raises or lifts up or saves someone from some difficulty or misfortune is called 'Uddharaka'. The substantive "Uddhanam" means raising up or resurrection. It is interesting to see how the idea of going upwards or resurrection is intimately related with the concept of final liberation of man [30]. There is another soteriological term 'Trana' from the root 'tra' which means 'protector', 'saviour' etc. The act of protecting, guarding, preserving and watching can be expressed by the term "Raksa". The state of salvation or liberation that is finally attained is called 'Sreyas' which literally means welfare, bliss, fortune, happiness, final emancipation, felicity, the better state. 'Sreyaparisrama' is man's striving for this ultimate bliss. The highest goal a man attains in his striving for liberation is known in the theistic context of the devotional works as 'Paramagatih' or 'Paragatih'. "Gatih" literally means 'movement towards something' and in the soteriological context it means 'God-attainment', or the attainment of the sacred feet of God (Isvarapada), the refuge (sarana) of the devotees. The devotional schools understand 'Moksa' also as the Paradise of Visnu (Vaikuntha-dhaman) or 'Svarga' which is the state of existence free from worldly limitations in the company of Lord Visnu.[31] The Advaitic schools on the other hand interpret this state of existence as 'Brahmaloka' [31a] (the world of Brahma) or the attainment of the status of the Absolute Supreme (Brahmabhava or Brahmisthiti) in absolute isolation (Kaivalya) from this world. [32] There is difference in the theistic and non-theistic understanding of 'Moksa' which we will consider in greater detail below. But every school agrees in the understanding of 'Mukti' or 'Moksa' as the ultimate and irrevocable escape from the vicious circle of Karma-Samsara. In reference to the Hindu eschatology we can say in short, following the Rgveda and the Stapatha Brahmana as we have done in Chapter III.B.2, that each man is judged after death according to his good and evil deeds. [32a] One will be rewarded for the good deeds in the heavenly world of gods [32b] and the evil doers will be punished in the abyss of darkness.[32c] In the Upanisads, however, heaven and hell are not considered definitive. They belong to the realm of 'Maya'. [32d] It is the theory of the re-incarnation that gains upper hand in the Upanisads.

b. Moksa as Liberation from Karma-Samsara in the Upanisads

Man is cought up in the wheel of Samsara which is full of desire, anger, delusion, covetousness, fear, depression, envy, hunger, thirst, old age, sorrow, disease, and death. [33] As birth and death are symbols of time, life eternal or Moksa is liberation from births and deaths, from Samsara. It is freedom from subjection to the law of Karma, the root cause of every evil. The material pleasures (Kama), the acquisition of wealth (Artha) and the pursuit of righteousness (Dharma) belong to the realm of this worldly existence and hence they belong to the field of Samsara. Liberation (Moksa) trans-cends all these three goals of human existence. Even Dharma, which should govern this Vyavaharika (empirical) existence or the world of Samsara has no more relevance in the state of liberation which is called the Paramarthika - transcendental and therefore ultimately real - existence.

One who desires salvation should reject the earthly desires and crave only for liberation from Karma-Samsara. The Maitri Upanisad gives an eloquent example for this in the attitude of the ascetic king Brhadratha:

> "Master, foul-smelling, insubstantial, is this body, a compact mass of skin and bones, siniews, marrow, flesh and semen, blood, mucus, tears and rheum, urine and faces, bile and phlegm: what point is there in satisfying one's desires in that? Assailed in this body by desire and anger, greed and delusion, fear, depression and envy, separation from what one wants and close association with what one does not want, hunger and thirst, old age and death, disease, sorrow and the like: what point is there in satisfying one's desires in that?
>
> We see the whole (world) decay: gnats, flies and other (insects), the grass and trees, - they come to be only to be dissolved. But why speak of these? There are other (beings) superior (far to these), great warriors and now and then a world-conqueror ... then there are kings like Marutta and Bharata, to name only the first. With a crowd of relatives looking on they said goodbye to rank and riches and passed on from this world to the next. ... There are others higher yet. ... But why speak of these? Among other things (we see) the drying up of mighty oceans, the crumbling to ruin of lofty peaks, the unfixing of the pole star, the cutting of the ropes (that restrain) the wind, the engulfing of the earth, the fall of the gods from their (high) estate: of such is the round of coming to be and passing away (samsara). What point is there in satis-fying one's desires in that? For once a man has tested of them he is seen to come back to earth ever and again.

Save (me from it), I pray you: in this round of existence I am like a frog in a well without issue, Master, you are our (only) way!" [34]

When one is delivered from this wheel or cycle of transmigration which is characterised by individuality, name and form, one reaches the highest Purusa: "As the flowing rivers disappear in the ocean, quitting name and form, so the knower, delivered from name and form goes to the heavenly Purusa, higher than the high." [35]

The liberation from the law of Karma-Samsara can be generally attained by a Mukta when he dies, when he gets rid of his sarira or deha (body). This type of liberation is called "Videha-mukti". But it is not impossible that one attains such lofty hights of spiritual excellence in this life itself, getting rid of all subtle Karma-impressions of past existence(s). So what is decisive is not our being in the body, but our relation and attitudes towards the body and this empirical world. A deliverance from Samsara during this life itself is characterized as 'Jivan-Mukti'.[36] Death in this case only seals what one has attained in one's life time and a Jivan-Mukta, eventhough he is still within the material limitations of space and time, has attained absolute inner or spiritual freedom! Such a one can attain Samadhi - tranquil and concentrated thought leading to the identification of the contemplator with the object meditated upon - without even the least effort! That is the ultimate and blessed state of mystic union!

Salvation as liberation from Karma-Samsara is in fact only one aspect of the whole truth, the negative aspect. Unlike the 'Nirvana' (extinction) [37] and 'Sunya' (void, nothingness) [38] of the Mahayana Buddhism, the Vedantic Moksa has a positive content. [39] Moksa is not the extinction of man, but his ultimate realization (Saksatkara) through experential and intuitive encounter (Anubhava) with the Supreme Reality. That is our next point.

2. 'Anubhava' and 'Saksatkara'

The union with the Absolute Reality is the positive content of Moksa. Hinduism as a religion of mysticism[40] puts the greatest stress on the experience of Divine as intimate in the self of man. This Divine is considered in various schools of Vedantic philosophy variously; the Divine is sometimes considered as the Supreme, absolute, impersonal or better supra-personal as in the case for example of Advaita, or as the Supreme personal God as in theistic schools. Whatever be the philosophical understanding of the Absolute, in all Vedantic schools the ultimate goal of man and his Moksa is accepted as the communion with this Supreme.[41] Hinduism is mystical through and through and 'its main aspiration and purpose tend toward the Self-realization and/or God-realization in the immediate and direct experience or vision of the Divine in whatever form the religious man would like to choose to experience and possess'[42]. The supreme purpose of Hinduism, Vedanta included, is the realization of the direct experience of the divine, regardless of the fact whatever form this may take. The general notion of mysticism is explained by M. Dhavamony as follows:

> "We can describe it as a direct appreciation of an eternal being, whether this eternal being is conceived of in personal or impersonal terms or simply as a state of consciousness. It is a transcendental experience in the sense that it is above the categories of time and space and change; an intuitive, unitive experience of a timeless, spaceless, immortal and eternal, and unchanging 'something'. It is the realization of oneness with or in something that transcends the empirical self whether this oneness is experienced in total identity or in intimate union with this transcendent being."[43]

Saksatkara or direct perception[44] denotes the various kinds of 'realizations' which are considered as the ultimate in different philosophical schools. If the realization of the spiritual self of man or the pure spirit of man is considered to be the ultimate, such a realization is called "Atmasaksatkara"."Brahmasaksatkara" stands for the realization of the Supreme and supra-personal Brahman and if by realization what is meant is the communion of friendship with the personal God, that is indicated by the term "Isvarasaksatkara". In every type of realization (Saksatkara), whether it is in this bodily existence (Jivan-mukti) or after death (Videha-mukti), the common factor is Anubhava. Anubhasva is experiencial knowledge and it is Anubhava that leads one to Saksatkara or realization.[45]

S. Radhakrishnan translates 'Anubhava' as integral experience.[46] The wisdom attained by Anubhava is far above the knowledge reached through the discursive intellect. 'At the intellectual level we grope with an external vision of things, where objects are extrinsically opposed to one another'[47] causing in us error and incapacity because the intellectual knowledge is rooted in sensations and appetites. Anubhava is intuitive knowledge and therefore immediate, even more immediate than the sensory intuition, 'for it overcomes the distinction between the knower and the known which subsists in sense-intuition. It is the perfect knowledge, while all other knowledge is incomplete and imperfect in so far as it does not bring about an identification between subject and object. All other knowledge is indirect and has only symbolic or representative value. The only generally effective knowledge is that which penetrates into the very nature of things'[48]. Such a penetration of the sub-ject into the object is not possible in lower forms of knowledge such as intellectual (discursive) and sense knowledge. We get close to perceiving the thing as it is by employing the intuitive consciousness or Anubhava and thus we know the object with less distortion. Anubhava is integral knowledge by which we possess the object that is known truly and securely, because to Anubhava nothing is external, nothing is other than itself, nothing is divided or in conflict within its all-comprehensive awareness. Anubhava is the means of knowledge and knowledge itself [49]. It is becoming one with the truth. Here truth is not acquired by the knower, but the truth unveils itself to the knower. It is the self-revelation of the object sought after into the very existence of man and therefore it is an existential knowledge. By Anubhava 'our thought, our life and our being are uplifted in simplicity and we are made one with truth' [50]. We cannot understand it in clear cate-gorial terms nor can we describe it, but we 'taste' the reality and possess it by which we ourselves become new! From the side of the object there is a self-revelation and from the side of the knower there is an intuitive vision in Anubhava, and so Anubhava may be called bi-polar in character.

Empirical objects can be known by sense perception and discursive under-standing, but logical reasoning is incapable of comprehending the living unity of God and man, the Absolute and the relative. God is so co-inherent and co-existent in man that he cannot be externalized or made an 'object' of discursive reason without distorting his real nature and therefore the way of reason to the Ultimate Reality is imperfect ; Anubhava is the most perfect way to the Supreme Reality. Objectivity cannot be the criterion of this Supreme Reality; here the criterion is the Reality itself revealed in our very being [51]. The demand for a criterion of knowledge can be made only on the assumption of a duality between the knowing subject and the known object, which cannot be true in the relation between God and man, which is ratified and eternalized in the state of Mukti or Moksa. 'Those who know the truth become the truth: brahma-vid brahmaiva bhavati. It is not a question of having an idea or a perception of the real. It is just the revelation of the real' [52]. Anubhava is the illumination of being and of life itself. 'It is Satyam, Jnanam. Knowledge and being are the same thing, inseparable aspects of a single reality, being no longer even distinguishable in that sphere where all is without duality' [53].

Anubhava as intuitive knowledge is unimprisoned by the divisions of space, successions of time or sequence of cause and effect. Our intellectual knowledge is in reality only a shadow cast by Anubhava which possesses the object of our striving truly and securely. Anubhava is the activity of the whole reality of man, his Atman and not just his senses or even intellect alone. What one achieves through Anubhava can be communicated to others only in hints and images, suggestions and symbols, because they are not susceptible of adequate expression. [54]

We can know God only by becoming godlike and to become godlike is to reach the divinity in us, become aware of the light that is already in us, and return con sciously to the divine centre within us, where we have always been without our knowing it. This divinity in us, according to the Katha Upanisad cannot be perceived by logical reason but only by spiritual contemplation [55] which leads to Anubhava or to 'becoming-one-with' the Real which cannot be attained by force of intellect or by much learning but is revealed to the aspirant whose will is at rest in Him [56].

The theological knowledge or 'Vidhya' is different from the integral experience or 'Anubhava' of it. Knowledge requires proofs, but in Anubhava the Reality is self evident. The Anubhava, when it is recorded in word of mouth or in writing, becomes the Sacred Word heard, or Sruti. The self-valid certainty or 'svatah-siddha' of the intuitive wisdom or Anubhava should not be confused with occultism, obscurantism or extravagent emotion. 'It is not magical insight or heavenly vision, or special revelation obtained through supernatural powers' [57] . It is the way of knowledge proper to the Atman, it is trans-empirical and supra-rational. Anubhava springs from the Atman of necessity when the necessary pre-conditions are satisfied and preparations are done. The Anubhava in an individual can never be fully destroyed, even though it can be very much obscured.

The fact that Anubhava is supra-rational does not mean that it contradicts reason. Abnubhava goes beyond reason, but not against it.'The dissatisfaction we have in our logical categories is a sign that we are greater than we know, that we can pass beyond our mental confines to a region of truth, though it is a mere beyond to our intellect, which seeks to transcend what it can and will never transcend. The limits which seem to be inevitable and impassable for intellect point to a limitless ground in us higher than logical mind. If thought becomes one with reality, and the individual subject shakes off its individuality and is lifted up into its universal essence, the goal of thought is reached, but it is no more thought. Thought expires in experience. Knowledge is lifted up into wisdom when it knows itself as identical with the known. ... This absolute knowledge is at the same time knowledge of the Absolute' [58] . That is Anubhava or integral experience or direct, immediate and intuitive wisdom. It is also called 'samyagjnana' (perfect knowledge) [59] or 'samyagdarsana' (perfect intuition) [60] . All faith and devotion, all study and meditation, are intended to train us for this experience. Sankara is of the opinion that even though Anubhava is open to all, few attain it [61] because of the hard training it expects from every body who wants to attain it.

Although Anubhava carries with it the highest degree of certitude, it has only a very low degree of conceptual and categorial clearness. Therefore, Anubhava must be interpreted in intellectual terms in this present state of existence and because of its predominantly subjective character, Anubhava's evidence is worthy of credence for others only when it is in conformity with the dictates of reason. [62] So the higher logic of the spirit in Anubhava does not annul the rational endeavours of man. Truth cannot be tied down or limited to conceptual categories or words, but the authenticity of Anubhava cannot be proved to others by any means other than their conformity with knowledge attained by intellectual means. [63]

S. Radhakrishnan describes the essential characteristics of Anubhava: Every man because of his essentially divine nature is capable of Anubhava, although few put forth the preparatory-effort required for it. At the same time it cannot be induced by will or prolonged by effort. It comes when least expected 'with a flash of lightening which suddenly appears in the middle of a dark blue cloud'. This experience is followed by the absolute conviction that by this experience the Reality is revealed. It bears an authority within itself, due to the illumination in one's consciousness. This experience is inexpressible in adequate human categories; the apprehension of the infinite Reality is so overwhelming. It is a revelation of what it normally hidden to man. In Anubhava the Reality is experienced as numinous, clothed in glory, charged with an intensity of being, which is mighty and terrible and yet blissfull, intimate and near. In this state of existence Anubhava is a fore-taste of the glory of man (the Atman) and the divine blissfull end to which he is destined. It is Moksa that comes within the reach of man even in this life and this experience is so absorbing and important that the self is forgotten and everything else becomes quite unimportant! 64

According to the Vedantic thinking Moksa or Mukti, therefore, is something that can be attained not only at the end of one's earthly existence but even when one is in this world. The means to it is ultimately Anubhava. Anubhava can have various grades and intensities and its culmination is called Saksatkara or realization, which denotes the perfect salvific knowledge or wisdom, as Sankara says: "Anubhavavasanam Brahmavijnanam"65 . Integral experience leads to realization. Realization or Saksatkara is the supreme encounter of man with the ultimate reality. In categorial terms it could be variously understood and thematized according to the differing philosophical views regarding the nature of this ultimate reality. The Reality is one in whatever way it is humanly understood or explained.

The Samkhya and Yoga systems of Indian thinking understand Saksatkara in terms of the spiritual self of man which may be designated as "Atmasaksatkara", the realization of one's own Self.66 In the realization of the spiritual self of man or of the pure spirit of man the idea of the existence of God is either denied explicitly or is absent in any expressible form or is admitted but is considered irrelevant to the ultimate experience.67 Here the point of concentration is on one's own self, its spiritual, numinous and

sacred character and the right knowledge about it. One has to try continuously to liberate oneself from desires and acts which bind one to this world
and attain the experience of the transcendent self. By 'yoga' [68] the true
self of man can be dissociated from his body and so one can experience
the undecaying, undying, pure spirit that is in man.

In the Advaita-Vedantic system of Indian thinking, which is considered to
be the most prominent among the various Vedantic schools, Brahman is the
ultimate Reality and the ultimate end of man is the realization of Brahman
(Brahmasaksatkara). "Brahmasaksatkara" is man's experience and realization
of Brahman as the Sat-Cit-Ananda, as we have already mentioned in Chapter
I.B.3. The sages of this school consider the human Self 'to be devoid of
imagination, change or conception, as causing all phenomena to cease, and
as void of non-duality. The Self resident in all beings will be seen to be
One. The mind concentrates on the realization of non-duality: 'I am the
supreme Brahman' .... There is no perception of duality in this state. The
mind gains freedom from illusory assumptions. ... This is the state in which
the mind becomes non-mind. ... The Self becomes self-aware through the
self-nature which is unborn knowledge .... The mind becomes quiescent like
the flame of a lamp kept in windless place; it does not appear in the form
of any imagined object; it is in such a state of consciousness that the Being
of Brahman emerges'. [69]

Many Advaitic thinkers consider the 'Atmasaksatkara' to be a necessary
pre-requisite for the realization of Brahman or even identify Atmasaksatkara as Brahmasaksatkara. According to Ramakrishna (1834-1886), every
man is by nature divine and the goal of life consists precisely in striving
after the realization of this nature of his. Faith in God should be accompanied
by faith in oneself. Faith in oneself signifies faith in one's divine nature
and the human efforts should be concentrated to the realization of the divine
in man and the vision of God (Brahmasaksatkara) dawns in man only when
he has reached his maturity in renunciation and intense aspiration after
self-realization (Atmasaksatkara). [70] Aurobindo Ghose (1872-1950) speaks
of the 'Superman' who has to evolve out of every 'ordinary' man through
integral yoga. Every man is called to become 'the masterman, the superman,
the divinised human being, the Best, not in the sense of any Nietzschean,

any one-sided and lopsided, any Olympian, Apollonian or Dyonysian, any angelic or demoniac supermanhood, but in that of the man whose whole personality has been offered up into the being, nature and consciousness of the one transcendent and universal Divinity and by loss of the smaller self has found its greater self, has been divinised.'[71] S. Radhakrishnan also writes about the integration of personality which reconciles the individual to his own divine nature (Atmasaksatkara), his fellow men and the Supreme Spirit (Brahmasaksatkara). 'Man is destined to realize the divine Spirit in him through release from his sense of individuality and the consequent misunderstanding of his true divine worth'[72]. Radhakrishnan affirms further: "The long record of the development of the human race and the great gifts of spiritual men like the Buddha, Socrates, Jesus make out that man has to be transcendend by God-man."[73]

The Bhakti schools put their emphasis on 'Isvara', God considered in his loving personal relation to man. The Moksa or Mukti for the followers of Bhakti (devotion) consists essentially in Isvarasaksatkara, the realization of Isvara. It is the felt participation of the soul in the total being of God[74] by which one does not lose one's own personality and individuality, but one's person is enriched, elevated and ultimately brought to its divinity through which an integrated man is totally and personally commited to God who though wholly immanent is yet other than himself.[75] Love is regarded here as the central phenomenon.[76] Through love a man comes to know the real nature of God as He is in Himself.[77] According to Bhagavadgita and the most important Bhakti theologian Ramanuja, Isvarasaksatkara leads not to absorption but to association of man with God. 'While in absorption the soul becomes one with God in identity of being, in Isvarasaksatkara the soul becomes one wiht God in love and realizes him as distinct from itself: "I am not lost for him, nor is he lost for me"[78]. In Isvarasaksatkara the salvific knowledge of God is born of love, the more intense the love is, the greater is the God-centredness of man and his union with God and the realization of Isvarda is achieved through union in love between God and man.

In short, Moksa or Mukti, whether it is attained after one's earthly existence or as in the case of a very few even during bodily existence, has as its positive content "Saksatkara". This "Saksatkara" is understood differently by different schools according to their own views regarding the Supreme Reality, as Atmasaksatkara, or as Brahmasaksatkara or as Isverasaksatkara. The ways and means proposed to attain the Saksatkara will be considered by us below under the title of 'Marga'.

As far as the Indian Christology is concerned the concepts of 'Anubhava' and 'Saksatkara' play an essential role as we shall see in the following chapters. It would be interesting for us to see in Chapters IV and IX how we could speak about the uniqueness of the Christ-event in the context of the Vedantic affirmation that God-experience and God-realization, in short, the realization of the metahistorical, are that which constitute the 'Religion' in religions, which is supposed to be represented by the Vedanta as the 'Santana Dharma' (eternal religion). In this context, Jesus' experience and consciousness of God would have great significance for our work as the case is in Chapters V and VIII. We will also have to consider amply and evaluate the liberating aspect of the Christ-experience in Chapters VI und IX. It would be also important for us to see to what extent 'Anubhava' could be considered as the 'Pramana' (source, criterion) of Christology in the Indian context.

3. The Role of Self-Discipline (YOGA) and Spiritual Guide (GURU) on the Way to Saksatkara

Saksatkara or encounter with the Supreme Reality is possible only for those who have attained integration of personality and harmony within themselves by overcoming the various human conflicts within and without. In Hinduism an elaborate system of self discipline (Yoga) helps to free the sleeping forces of the enslaved spirit. A spiritual guide (Guru) is also indispensable for any beginner on the way to Saksatkara. The terms 'Yoga' and 'Guru' are of great Christological importance and relevance for us in the course of our discussion. In the fourth Chapter, for example, we will be considering Jesus Christ as the 'Advaitic Yogi'. In reference to Christ as the great teacher of mankind we will also be using the titel 'Mahaguru' in Chapter VI. The yogic ideals and the role of a Guru are also relevant for anyone who aims at the liberating experience of Jesus Christ as is evident in our discussion in Chapter VI.

Hence the clarification of the concepts of 'Yoga' and 'Guru' here in the context of our presentation of the Vedantic understanding of God-experience.

a. Yoga: Self Discipline

The Indian spirituality is best known by the name 'Yoga'. The word literally means 'the act of yoking (to) another' and is derived from the root 'yui', to unite, to join, to yoke. The word in its origin appears to lack any special religious connotation; the meaning of 'uniting' is implicit in all its derivatives. In the context of psycho-somatic relationships this term was used to denote the yoking of mind and body 'to achieve perfect unity, functioning on the profoundest level to the unconscious, beyond the limits of thought and language, and flowing freely in the currents of the energy that pervades space and time'[79] The practice of 'Yoga' in its embryonic form can be traced to the pre-Aryan civilizations of Harappa and Mohenjodaro long before its development in the Vedic India. Some even maintain that the Aryans borrowed yogic techniques from the Dravidians of India.[80]

The real goal of 'Yoga' is the final concentration of the spirit and escape from the cosmos. As a system of spiritual training 'Yoga' stands first and foremost for the methods of Patanjali who wrote the 'Yoga-Sutra' which includes 194 aphorisms divided into four books.[81] Till his time 'Yoga' could mean simple ascetic practices or even very complicated mystic exercises. In the Upanisads we read such expressions as 'atmayoga'[82] and 'adhyatma-yoga'[83] which can mean disciplines of spiritual life. The Maitri Upanisad[84] speaks of it as the yoking of the whole psychosomatic organism to a single idea. Such ideas gave impetus to philosophical speculations which climaxed in the 'Yoga-Sutra' of Patanjali 'Yoga' however, was not taken to mean man's union with Brahman or God which is now accepted by some as a secondary interpretation given to 'yoga'.[85]

Samkhya Philosophy g ave the philosophical foundations to Patanjali's system. Man is essentially a composition of two principles: Purusa and Prakrti. Purusa is the spiritual self of man which is pure consciousness, changeless and totally self-luminous. Prakrti stands for the outer sphere of man, his empirical reality. It is because of the association of Purusa, which is consciousness itself (citta), with Prakrti, the source of qualities and change, that Purusa, inspite of his being without qualities, experiences himself as having different qualities and inspite of his being active experiences himself as passive and as suffering. To attain Moksa or final liberation the Purusa must be free from his association with the empirical body. Then only Purusa can shine in its own brilliance as unchanging and pure consciousness. This is to be attained, as Patanjali himself writes, through "cittavrtti nirodhah", the restraint of conscious modifications,[86] and as result "the seer stands in his own nature" [87], namely in his own changeless, objectless consciousness.[88]

Patanjali's system is also called 'Raja-yoga', the royal way to reintegration. That stands for the highest form of yoga, all other forms being only preparations for the spiritual efforts of Raja-yoga. The process of Patanjali's Raja-yoga consists of eight limbs (astanga-yoga) or steps of yogic practices.[89]

The goal of the yogic training is the isolation of the spiritual element in man that it may shine in its own spleandour. In Yoga proper the question of God is irrelevant; those who believe in God can use Him as one of the means of spiritual advance. Man remains the centre of his own interests and efforts.[99] God is just "a distinct Purusa, untouched by the hindrances of affliction, action and fruition" [100]. He can be substituted in the place of any other object as a point of concentration to help recollection at the beginning of meditation. So man reaches his own liberation through his own efforts and that liberation consists in a state of absolute and objectless consciousness, a pure spiritual self-awareness. We will have to pay greater attention especially in Chapter VI and the evaluative Chapter VIII to the notion of self-salvation implied in Yoga.

Yoga in the sense of a technique of spiritual training by which all bodily and psychic energies of man are controlled and unified for the purpose of attaining man's highest destiny has been accepted also by various other Hindu sects and philosophical schools regardless of their creed and philosophy. Bhagavadgita, for example, integrates excellently the yogic discipline into its thought pattern. In spite of its predominantly theistic trend, the Gita assumes and accommodates some of the presuppositions of Samkhya-Yoga. Gita means by Yoga spiritual exercises, [101] integration of the soul [102] and any athlete of the spirit is a 'Yogin' [103] . "Thus let the athlet of the spirit (yogin) be constant in integrating himself, his mind restrained; then will he approach that peace which has Nirvana as its end and which subsists in Me." [104] Gita encourages yogic techniques in various passages. [105] But unlike the Yoga-school, Bhagavadgita considers the personal relation with God as the supreme purpose of yogic practices:

> "Higher than the (mere) ascetic is the athlete of the spirit held to be, yes, higher than the man of wisdom, higher than the man of works: be, then, a spiritual athlete Arjuna! But of all athletes of the spirit the man of faith who loves and honours Me, his inmost self absorbed in Me, - he is the most fully integrated: this do I believe." [106]

> "To those men who are ever integrated and commune with Me in Love I give that integration of the soul by which they may draw high to me. " [107]

> "Those I deem to be most integrated who fix their thoughts on Me and serve Me, ever integrated (in themselves), filled with the highest faith." [108]

The Gita even presents the personal aspect of God (Krishna) as the Lord of Yoga (Yogesvara) [109] who helps us in our life to save ourselves. Like the Bhagavadgita many modern interpretations of 'Yoga' tend to give it a more positive outlook and content than the school of Yoga originally meant. [110]

In common parlance 'Yoga' is understood as the system of bodily exercises by which the body and vital energies can be brought under control. That is only one aspect of Yoga and is called 'Hatha Yoga' or 'Bhahiranga Yoga' (external yoga). [110a] The energies of man is thought to be lying latent, like a coiled sleeping serpent (Kundalini), [111] at the base of the spine. When the Kundalini sakti is awakened by yogic practices, it ascends from the base of the spinal column (muladharacakra) through the seven cakras (planes) to the 'Sahasrara-cakra' in the brain, which is represented as a thousand petalled lotus. This is regarded as the transcendental plane where the Yogin emerges from the limitations of time and space and hence from the vicious cycle of Samsara. [111a] The process of 'awakening' the Kundalini sakti through various yogic practices is known as 'Kundalini-Yoga'. [111b] This is very much related to Laya-Yoga.

As a method of self-discipline the term 'Yoga' is also used in reference to the three classical paths or ways (Marga) of spiritual perfection and salvation: The self-reintegration through action, the performance of religious duties and the constant application of oneself to the laws and ordinances pertaining to ordinary religious life, is known by the name 'Karma-Yoga'. 'Jnana-Yoga' stands for the way of self-integration and liberation through knowledge. The way of perfection and salvation through the integrating power of devotion and love to the personal God is called 'Bhakti-Yoga'.[112] These will be considered more elaborately below in the section devoted to the 'Marga' which prepares us conceptually for the notion of Jesus Christ himself as the true "Yogi" and own "Marga"(Way)!

b. Guru: The Spiritual Guide

We read in the Upanisads that a teacher who has attained the goal may help the aspiring soul. [113] The way to Anubhava and Saksatkara are not as a rule within the reach of the spiritually unexperienced. Only a teacher can give it with concrete quality. It is true that the Reality should be experienced and realized by each one through one's own eye of understanding (bodhacaksu) and not through the proxy of any scholar. The experience should be one's own, direct and unmediated; it should not be merely the echo of what another one has felt. But every body needs at least at the initial stage the help of someone who is able to remove the blinkers from the eyes of the aspirant and help him see. [114] Such a spiritual helper is called 'Guru'. Many Hindus have no objection in attributing this title in an eminent way to Jesus Christ as we shall see in Chapter VI.

According to the Advaya taraka Upanisad, the syllable 'Gu' means 'darkness' and 'ru' means 'dispeller'. [115] Hence the word 'guru' may be literally translated as 'dispeller of darkness'. 'Guru' has also the meaning 'the important or the weighty one'. [116] Both of these meanings are applicable to a religious guide or teacher who helps to dispel the spiritual darkness of the aspirant and thus renders a very 'weighty' or important service to the welfare of humanity. He that has a teacher knows: Acaryavan puruso veda! [117] He is the adviser to all those who seek spiritual guidance. [118] It is also to be mentioned that the Sanskrit word 'Guru' originally indicated not only spiritual guides, but also the teacher of any subject in art or science. Any learning in India had traditionally a deep rooted religious bend. One may also distinguish between a 'Siksa-Guru', one who merely imparts instructions and a 'Diksa-Guru', the one who has the additional duty of 'initiating' the aspirant to the path of spiritual growth and final realization. Both of these functions, however, do overlap. [119] In modern times the title of 'Guru' is also applied to the representatives of a particular sect or philosophical school who even if do not claim to teach anything in their own name, transmit faithfully the original doctrine handed down by the first 'Guru' of the school or sect in question through an uninterrupted succession of 'Gurus' and 'Sisyas' (disciples). [120]

The importance of a 'Guru' for anyone who wants to attain the salvific knowledge is stressed by the Upanisads. According to the Katha Upanisad the Supreme Reality cannot be attained by thought and reasoning, but only when revealed by another person of higher attainment, namely by a competent Guru. [121] The Chandogya Upanisad also states that it was already an accepted teaching that the supreme knowledge of Brahman could be best attained only through the help of a qualified Guru. [122]

The spiritual perfection that is demanded from a Guru is very high. He has to embody in himself truth and tradition. Only those who have the flame in them can stir the fire in others. The Vedantic tradition specifies some of the important qualities the Guru should have: He should be versed in scriptures (srotriya), sinless (avrjina) desireless (akamahata) and rooted in Brahman (Brahmanista). [123] The knowledge of the Scriptures that is required from a Guru is not merely theoretical and scientific knowledge, but the knowledge resulting from the integral experience of the sacred writings. Therefore illiterates like Ramakrishna Paramahamsa can also become perfect Gurus, although that is a rare phenomenon. 'The Guru must also be a man who has overcome sin and evil and selfishness, desires and cravings. He must be free from pride and vanity, hypocrisy and jealousy, falsehood, worldly passions and egoism in all its overt and covert manifestations. As a blind man cannot be a reliable guide to another blind man, so too an imperfect and evil person cannot be an efficient guide to seekers after spiritual enlightenment. Only a perfect man can lead others to perfection. A perfect master is a master of himself, is dispassionate and tranquil in all circumstances of life' [124]. The 'Brahmanista' of the Guru manifests itself in his union with the Divine. He must have the immediate and integral experience (anubhava) of the Divine and as a spiritually enlightened person he must have realized (saksatkara) the ultimate goal of his existence, and he must be able to adapt himself to the spiritual needs of the aspirants in various levels of spiritual perfection and that presupposes that he has reached enlightenment. 'If he is not enlightened, he cannot enlighten others; he cannot lead others where he has not been himself; he cannot shed even a glimmer of light beyond his own level of attainment. He illumines others by making available to them the divine light and power, and he will be in a position to do that if only he is one with the Divine; then he draws upon the divine energy' [125].

A Guru without the required Anubhava and Saksatkara may speak in most sublime terms, with imagination and eloquence but he will not be able to transmit the integral God-experience that is expected from a Guru. 'Only a fully illumined Guru will be transparent enough to transmit the uncontaminated wisdom of God and illumine the minds and hearts of others' [126]. The qualities of a true Guru may be shortly put so:

"(He is) capable of destroying the bondage of those who adhere to him. He is an ocean of immutable wisdom. His knowledge is all comprehensive. He is pure as crystal. He has attained victory over desires. He is supreme among the knowers of Brahman. He rests calmly in Brahman (...) He is an endless reservoir of mercy. There is no explanation why he is merciful; it is his very nature. He befriends all sadhus who adhere to him."[127]

Such a Guru will be able to attract also others to his path of God-realization as Sri Ramakrishna says:

"Bees come of themselves to the full-blown flower when the breeze wafts its fragrance all around. Ants come of themselves to the spot where sweets are placed. No one need invite the bee or the ant. So when a man becomes pure and perfect, the sweet influence of his character spreads everywhere and all who seek the truth are naturally drawn towards him." [128]

The role of a Guru in the spiritual progress of a Sisya (disciple) begins with the sacred rite of initiation (Upanayana). By this rite the aspirant is believed to undergo a spiritual re-birth and he becomes a 'Dvija' (twice born). As an external sign of the second birth the Guru gives the sisya the sacred cord made of three strands. The first sacred formula of divine wisdom that is imported by the Guru to the disciple is called 'Gayatri Mantra,[130] also known as 'Savitri Mantra', the sacred formula addressed to the Sun (Savitar) as the supreme generative force. That is found in the Rgveda: "Om! bhur blunvanah suvah, tat Savitur varenyam, bhargo devasya dhimahi, dhiyo yo nah pracodayat" - "Om! He fills the earth, the atmosphere and the heaven; let us meditate on the excellent glory of the divine vivifier Savitr; may he enlighten our understanding."[131] This should be further repeated by the sisya at his morning and evening devotions. Its repetition is denied to menials and to women. [132]

Besides the sacred rite of initiation the Guru has also to initiate a worthy candidate formally into the sacred disciplines. This initiation is called 'Diksa'. Some authors identify 'Diksa' with 'Upanayana'. [133] Diksa originally referred to the early Vedic dedication of the institutor (yajamana) of a sacrifice and in the late Vedic period it began to be applied for the dedication of a student (brahmacarin) by which a teacher (acarya or Guru) accepted him as his pupil. [134]

The most important function of a Guru is to train his Sisya in the "Nitya-nityavastuviveka", [135] ie. in the capacity to discriminate between eternal and impermanent realities, which is a necessary qualification laid down by Sankara for the study of Vedanta. That consists in the disciple's ability "to recognize 'para' from 'apara vidhya' (perfect from imperfect knowledge), 'satya' from 'maya' (truth from illusion), 'sat' from 'asat'. (unchanging from changing being), 'ananta' from 'anta' (infinite from finite reality), 'karana' from 'karya' (cause from effect), 'visayin' from 'visaya' (subject from object), 'atman' from 'deha' (spirit from body), 'bhuman' from 'alpa' (great from small), 'guru' from 'laghu' (important from insignificant), 'sreya' from 'preya' (excellent from pleasant) and, generally, 'mukhya' from 'gauna' (primary from secondary)." [136] Through this means the Guru helps his disciple to go through the way of integral spiritual experience (Anubhava) to the portals of the realization of the Supreme (Saksatkara), ie. to the realization of one's own divine identity! This is a point where we will have to make important reservations, as we shall see later, in applying the title 'Guru' to Jesus Christ!

The relation between Guru and Sisya is very personal, deep and sacred. In ancient India a Sisya was generally incorporated into the family of the Guru, he had to reside continuously with him and suspend all the family ties as long as his education lasted. In the 'Gurukula' (Guru's house) a total submission to the master was demanded from the disciple. The Guru was regarded as the spiritual parent and so there was also a prohibition that a pupil may not marry his Guru's daughter, as she stands in the relation of a sister to him. [137] A code of conduct that is to be observed by the Sisya in his dealings with the Guru is exactly described in 'The Laws of Manu', in the 'Gautama Dharmasutra', and in the 'Apastamba Dharmasutra'. [138] But in the course of time the above mentioned Brahmanic pattern of Gurukula gradually disappeared. Each ascetic and philosophical school had their own Gurus, embodying the highest ideal proposed by each sect.

Because of the all-important role ascribed to a Guru in the spiritual life of the disciple, the scriptures taught that a Guru deserves much more respect than one's own parents. The parents are responsible for one's birth. A disciple is even advised to consider the Guru as the very image of God himself: "He shall approach his teacher with the same reverence as a deity, without telling idle stories, attentive and listening eagerly to his words". [139] The Tantric texts exaggerated even further the 'divinity' of the Guru:

> "To perdition he goes who regards the Guru as human, the mantra as mere letters, and the images as stone. Never look upon the guru as a mortal. Should you do so, then neither mantra nor worship can give you success. Do not associate the holy guru with the ordinary folk either in your remembrance or in talk. Otherwise all the good that is done turns into evil." [140]

The Gurus in their turn were also warned against playing the despot and in any way exploiting the disciple. The Apastamba Dharma-sutra orders the Guru to have paternal affection and attention toward the disciple and not to use him for his own purpose. [141]

Today, it is to be admitted, the title of 'Guru' has undergone great 'inflation'. Many those who present themselves as Gurus are far off from being worthy of that title. Even a well intended usage of the name may not presuppose all the qualities originally expected from a Guru. The title is applied today, at least among the general public, to any venerable person, spiritual master or respectful and influencial teacher! In applying the title 'Guru' to Jesus

Christ, as we do in Chapter VI, a re-interpretation of this title is required without however ignoring its essential characteristics. Further required clarifications could be made in our later discussion.

B. The Paths towards 'Saksatkara'

Jesus Christ is, according to the Christian faith, man's only Way to God. We will be developing this point later in Chapters VI and IX. In the Vedanta also this concept of the 'way' or 'path' has great significance. Before proceeding to explain Christ as the Way, we would try to understand here what 'way' or 'Marga' means in the Indian context.

The supreme goal of human existence, we have seen, consists in the divinization of man or better said, in the realization of the divinity that is already in man, which is known as Saksatkara. In the Vedanta and in every other Hindu school so far is undisputedly accepted. The different philosophical tendencies even in the Vedanta itself, however, understand the nature of this Saksatkara according to their own theologico-anthropological presuppositions and therefore there are considerable and substantial divergences in the paths proposed by the various schools to attain the saving truth.

In the context of salvation the Hindu scriptures use various terms to signify the way or path of liberation. 'Yoga' as we have already seen is the word used to signify this path in so far as what is stressed is the spiritual exercise and discipline. As these paths are only a means to the end, they are also called 'Sadhana', that by which something is performed. [142] 'Marga' is the term most commonly used to signify the path towards integral experience (anubhava) and the ultimate realization (saksatkara). Marga means 'way', 'path', or 'course' and it appears with a religious connotation already in the Upanisads. [143]

As traditionally understood, the ways or Margas to reach the goal of perfection are mainly three: Karma Marga (the path of deeds), Jnana Marga (the path of knowledge) and the Bhakti Marga (the path of adoration and love of the Supreme Person). Karma Marga has been often inaccurately understood by many as the way of the ordinary folk, of popular Hinduism that may find no difficulty in accommodating numerous gods, goddesses and countless superstitions in their spiritual life and pious acts. Jnana Marga has also been falsely represented as the way of those who consider God as the supra-personal Absolute who cannot be worshipped or prayed to but only be correctly understood. It is also not quite accurate to say that Bhakti Marga is the spiritual path for those who are prone to extravagent emotional expressions in religion. These different systems are actually overlapping. There are aspects in Karma Marga which are essential also to Bhakti Marga. No one is born a Jnani. The Jnana Marga, therefore, presupposes the other two at least as preparatory stages.

We will understand better the relation between the various Margas once we have caste some light upon their nature separately. We will be analysing only the aspects that are intimately related to our understanding of man and Christ in the Indian Vedantic background, ie. access to salvation offered by the Margas which is later to be compared with the soteriological role of Christ and the involved problems in the context of an Indian Christology. First we will briefly deal with Karma Marga followed by the Jnana Marga. We will be paying greater attention to Bhakti Marga for the evident and Christologically interesting reason that the concept of the Incarnation of God (Avatara) first originated and developed in the Bhakti circles.

1. Karma Marga: The Path of Deeds

Under this title we understand the path to Moksa which consists in deeds or works. Hinduism embraces every aspect of human life, both individual and social and it lays down laws that are to be observed in every human deed. Hinduism itself is therefore called "the perennial law of life" (Sanatana Dharma). Chandogya Upanisad considers human life as a sequence of deeds which can be compared to a sacrifice:

> "Man is a sacrifice. His first twenty-four years are the morning libation.
> ... In hunger, thirst and abstinence from pleasures consists his initial
> rites. ... In laughter, banquets and other enjoyments he sings a hymn
> of praise. ... Penance, liberality righteousness, kindness, truthfulness,
> these are his offerings. ... His death is the ablution which concludes
> the sacrifice." [144]

That which regulates the totality of human deeds is called 'Dharma'. In modern times Dharma means simply 'religion' but its classical meaning is

'righteousness' or proper ethical conduct according to the age old pre-
scriptions of virtuous ancestors. [145] 'Dhr' is the root from which Dharma
is derived and the root means 'to hold, to remain, to fix, to support, to
make firm etc.' So Dharma may mean the old customs and practices which
hold and support or regulate the human activities and which in the course
of time has become established or settled. [146] The maintenance of Dharma
is of great consequence to human life, physically, economically, psychologically and socially as a stabilizer of human deeds. Dharma is moral law or
principle [147] ; it is the upholder, sustainer and supporter of human existence. [148]

Dharma as the law of the microcosm (man) is a replica of the macrocosmic
law [149] called Rta, the law of seasons - the root rtu means time - which
are eternally fixed and therefore unchangeable, to which even the gods are
subject.[150] It is the divine order of nature established at the time of creation
and 'rta' represents the immanent dynamic order or inner balance of the
cosmic manifestations themselves. It can also mean divine law, truth, right,
duty or custom. The meaning of rta has continuously changed and very often
it has also been identified with Dharma. Dharma is in the words of Taittiriya
Aranyaka that on which every thing else rests:

> "Dharma is the stay of the world; in society people approach the most
> ardent follower of Dharma; by dharma they remove sin; every thing
> rests on dharma; so people declare dharma to be the most excel-
> lent." [151]

Dharma regulates a man's relation to the pleasures (kama) and material
prosperity (artha) of this world and prepares him for his final liberation
(moksa). The source of Dharma is the Vedas: "(The first and foremost kind
of) Dharma has been instructed in every Veda. The second (kind) is what
is declared in the Smrtis; (and) the third is the practice of the Sistas (the
cultured)." [152] Manu also states: "The entire Veda is the source of Dharma;
and the tradition and practice of those who know it; and also the usages
of virtuous men, self-satisfaction." [153] Dharma consists, according to Manu,
essentially in the following of the precepts of sruti and smrti: "It is the
practices declared in the sruti and also those having their origin from Smrti
which are transcendental law; therefore a twice-born man, desiring his own
welfare, should always be engaged in following these."[154] In the Chandogya

Upanisad we see a resume of the Vedantic teaching on the meaning of Dharma. It is a code of conduct:

> "There are three branches of Dharma. The first consists of sacrifice, study of the Veda and the giving of alms. The second is austerity. The third is to dwell as a student of sacred knowledge in the house of a teacher and to behave with utmost control of himself in his house. All these gain the worlds alloted to the virtuous (as their reward). He who stands firm in Brahman wins through to immortality." [155]

Manu distinguishes between two types of Dharma: Varnasrama dharma and Sadharana dharma. Varnasrama dharma consists in the fulfilment of the duties of one's state of life (asrama) and the obligations laid down by one's caste (varna). Asrama dharma is personal in character while Varna dharma is social. Sadharana dharma means the code of conduct or law of deeds that are common to every man, irrespective of his varna (caste) and asrama (state of life). The are the dos and the dont's of Hindu life. These common duties are described in various books variously. Gautama Dharma Sutra speaks of eight good qualities of the soul. [156] According to Manu they are ten. [157] Prshastapada speaks of thirteen fundamental virtues to be practised. [158] The practice of these virtues and the keeping of other laws constitute essentially the Karma Marga to Moksa. However, it is irrelevant for us to quote them in detail. All these regulations can be finally reduced to five in their brief form which is known as 'Samasikam Dharmam'. They are: Ahimsa (non-injury), Satya (truthfulness), Asteya (non-stealing), Brahmacarya (celibacy), Aparigraha (non-attachement). [159] Bhagavadgita presents a more elaborate list of those deeds and virtues that are required of any on the way to Moksa:

> "These are the qualities of one who is born to gain divine estate: fearlessness, rectitude, purity, perseverance in the path of knowledge and discipline, charity, self-control, sacrifice, study of sacred precepts, straight-forwardness, doing no harm, truthfulness, equanimity, detachment, peace and no malice, compassion for all, sobriety, gentleness, modesty, guiltelessness fervour, forgiveness, steadiness, cleanness, freedom from hatred and pride." [160]

The Karma Marga is not only the practice of virtues and keeping the laws of conduct as explained above. It also includes a lot of sacrificial rituals and other religious rites. We deal with a few of them: Yajna (sacrifice), Samskara (rites), and some important observances.

Sacrifice were of extreme importance in the Vedic period. Sacrifices was considered a 'mystical sacrament of redemption'[161] . A sacrificial rite (yajna) was intended as a solemn homage paid to the gods and it is meant to establish communication with the divine world in order to obtain some good or to appease the maleficient gods. Today the great Vedic sacrifices [162] are rare and are mostly replaced by Puja offered to idols which though do not exhaust the being of God are considered by the worshippers as the manifestations of the divine power.[163] Prayer also forms an essential part of Hindu worship; they may consist in supplications, recitation of a 'Mantra' (sacred word or text) or a 'Japa' (repetition or recitation of a mantra in a whispering tone), 'Stuti' (hymn of praise), 'Kirtana' (devotional music), Bhajana (emotional recitations) etc.[164] In reality prayer is not just one of the acts in the life of a Hindu; it is his whole life, whatever be the Marga he may be actually following.

The Karma Marga includes also a good number of sacred rites prescribed in the Vedas and performed on various important occasions in the life of an individual.[165] They are called 'Samskaras'. The word literally means 'purification'.[166] They are meant to cleanse a man from his bodily and spiritual impurities and to prepare him for the salvific knowledge of the Moksa. They can be in a very wide sense compared to the Christian Sacraments. When duly performed, these rites are supposed to possess an infallible efficacy which can be applied even to the dead.[167] There is no agreement as to how many such rites there are; there are forty as most commonly accepted.[168] The most important of them are: Birth rites especially 'Namakarana' (giving the name) and 'Annaprasana' (eating the first rice) applied both to boys and girls, the rite of initiation called 'Upanayana'[169] reserved to the boys of the three upper castes, the marriage rite known as 'Vivaha' and 'Antyesti' or funeral rites.

There are also a number of other observances which are part and parcel of Karma-Marga, for example: keeping of feasts, fasts and auspicious days, pilgrimages (Tirta-Yatra), sacred baths (Snana) etc.[170]

The Karma Marga emphasizes that man is by his very nature divine and that he can attain to the Moksa by his own moral forces and good deeds which enlighten him for the Anubhava (integral experience of God) and for the irrevocable Saksatkara (God-realization).

We will be comparing later in Chapter VII.C.2.a. the 'Karma Marga' with the redemptive sacrifice of Christ. The concept of 'Dharma' which we have explained above has also important points of agreement with the 'Basileia', the reign of God - a point to which we will have to give much attention in the third evaluative part of our work especially in Chapter VIII.B.1. following the theological lines of Wolfhart Pannenberg. The aspect of self-salvation that is implies in the 'Karma-Marga' will also have to be corrected in our later discussions.

2. Jnana Marga: The Path of Knowledge

In the Vedas the way to the saving wisdom is that of sacrifices, rites and other observances which have still great influence among the vast majority of the Hindu masses. In the Upanisads, however, the stress is shifted from Karma (deeds) to Jnana (knowledge) and by Jnana Marga we mean the intellectual pathway to perfection. [171] Initially Jnana appears to have meant the knowledge required by the warrior, herdsman, agriculturalist, craftsman etc., in the performance of their respective duties. Later on Jnana was also applied to the magical knowledge that was expected from a tribal priest by which he is enabled to deal with the mysterious powers of nature. Such a knowledge implied the possession of supernatural power, a power greater than that of the warriors, because by this power one was enabled to enter the region of the gods and influence them for one's advantage. In the Vedanta (Upanisads) knowledge became the criterion of might and it meant not only cognition, 'but the irrefutable intuition of a single, all-including entity, other than which nothing persists' [172]. The Upanisads maintain that it is through the intensification of consciousness that the Ultimate Reality is realized and this approach is called 'the asceticism of knowledge' (Jnanamayam tapah), [173] in other words the intellectual path towards perfection (Jnana Marga).

Jnana, the means (marga) towards Realization, must be distinguished from Jnana as spiritual wisdom, which is the goal of every Hindu school of theology, including the other classical Margas. 'As the same word "jnana" is employed for both the goal of perfection and the way to it, for the recognition of reality as well as the scheme of spiritual knowledge, some are led to think that the intellectual path is superior to the other methods of approach' [174] , although such an absolute superiority at the cost of other Margas will not be admitted by their followers. For the sake of clarity we may distinguish between 'Paroksajnana', that which removes the obstacles towards the salvific wisdom, and 'Aparoksajnana', which is the Anubhava and Saksatkara of the ultimate reality. This wisdom as the goal of human existence can also be called 'Vijnana' [175] . S. Radhakrishnan puts in clear terms the distinction between 'Vijnana' (Wisdom) and 'Jnana' (knowledge):

> "Wisdom, pure and transcendent, is different from scientific knowledge, though it is not discontinous from it. Every science expresses, after its own fashion, within a certain order of things, a reflection of the higher immutable truth of which every thing of any reality necessarily partakes. Scientific or discriminative knowledge prepares us for the higher wisdom. The partial truth of science are different from the whole truth of spirit. Scientific knowledge is useful since it dispels the darkness oppressing the mind, shows up the incompleteness of its own world and prepares the mind for some thing beyond it. For knowing the truth, we require a conversion of the soul, the development of spiritual vision." [176]

Jnana as Marga, however, also does not mean a collection of informations or academic studies which have no immediate reference and relevance to spiritual matters. Jnana in this sense does not stand for the phenomenal knowledge - which can, of course, be remote preparations for the spiritual path - but for the knowledge of all that has immediate relevance for the ultimate destiny, the Saksatkara, of man.

The purpose of Jnana is to remove ignorance (Avidhya). The world is in continuous becoming and what keeps the world going is action or Karma. In the case of man Karma itself is caused by desire (Kama) which originates from human ignorance (Avidhya). In order to achieve liberation from the law of Karma and Samsara one has to get rid of ignorance which is the source of ignorant desires leading to ignorant actions. S. Radhakrishnan observes:

> "At the human level action is caused by desire or attachment, kama. The root cause of desire is avidhya or ignorance of the nature of things. The roots of desire lie in the ignorant belief in the individual's self-sufficiency, in the attribution of reality and permanence to it. So long as ignorance persists, it is not possible to escape from the vicious

circle of becoming. We cannot cure desires by fresh desires; we cannot cure action by more action. The eternal cannot be gained by that which is temporal. Whether we are bound by good desires or bad desires, it is still a question of bondage. It makes little difference whether the chains which bind us are made of gold or iron." [177]

Freedom or Mukti, therefore, results from right knowledge which may be described as 'the illuminating perception which comes as the reward of a life spent in earnest contemplation' or as 'the intuitive apprehension of the divine reality and of the spiritual self of man'[178].

The Upanisad affirms, he who knows Brahman (the Absolute) becomes Brahman: "Yo ha vai tatparamam brahma veda brahmaiva bhavati".[179] It is according to the principle that one becomes what one knows because to know an object is to become one with it (anu+bhava) some how. The greater the knowledge, the more intense is the degree of union between the knower and the object known. As Brahman is the only real and the only one which can fulfil our infinitely oriented desires - and that is because of our fundamentally divine nature - the most efficacious way to attain liberation from the bondage of Karma-Samsara is Jnana: "He who knows Brahman as the real, as knowledge, as the infinite ... he obtains all desires." [180]

This truth which is absolute and which may be called Brahman is within us:

> "More sublte than the subtle, greater than the great,
> The self is hidden within the heart of creatures (here):
> The man without desire all sorrow spent, beholds It,
> The majesty of the Self, by the grace of the Ordainer." [181]

The only way to reach the self's inmost Self (Antaratman) is that of spiritual perception (darsana), introspective contemplation and not the empty and barren religious ritualism! [182] But the criticism levelled against the ritual practices should not be understood as rejection of the whole of Karma Marga. Rites are, of course, inefficient, save perhaps as a remote preparation. Sankara beliefes that Vedic rites are meant for those who are lost in ignorance and desire. [183] But even Sankara admits that even if Karma may not be the immediate cause of liberation, still it is a necessary means for acquiring knowledge. [184] Jnana presupposes the inward concentration of the mind which is impossible without self-discipline, the rejection of evil deeds and the practice of good actions. Jnana includes the moral dispositions and ascetical practices that are conducive to knowledge. 'Karma' in this restricted sense is included in Jnana as it is quite evident in Gita:

"To shun conceit and tricky ways,
To wish none harm, to be long-suffering and upright,
To reverence one's preceptor, purity,
Steadfastness, self-restraint,
(...)
Constant attention to the knowledge that appertains to Self
To see where knowledge of reality must lead,
All this is knowledge, - or so it has been said.
Ignorance is what is otherwise than this." [185]

Sankara is also of the opinion that these actions (Karma) are essential as means for the purification of the mind, but when wisdom is attained action falls away.[186] In the fire of 'Jnana' all works are burnt up! [187]

In Jnana Marga, the process of acquiring right knowledge consists of three steps: Sravana (hearing), Manana (reflection) and Nididhyasana (contemplation). These are the preparatory and Nididhyasana (contemplation). These are the preparatory st ages for Saksatkara. [188] Sravana consists in the acquisition of sacred knowledge by hearing, learning and studying the revealed texts. This hearing is to be accompanied by sraddha or faith in the integrity of the seers who by direct acquaintance and immediate experience (anubhava) knew the ultimate truth that was revealed to them and who formulated these truths in human terms for those who do not yet have the vision of this reality. Manana is the second step. It is the process of the personal assimilation of the revealed Word through thinking, reflection and meditation in order to convince oneself of its veracity. [189] This is the place for logical and philosophical enquiry, inference, analogy etc. which add to faith a know-ledge which increases faith. Faith and reason complement here mutually, lest faith should degenerate into credulity and logical reason into empty speculation. Still the distinction between sravana and manana is to be kept. Sravana is of sruti and they are experiential while manana is the secondary interpretations and formulated conclusions, which are conditioned by the historical situations in which they are produced. [190] 'Logical knowledge ac-quired by a study of the scriptures and reflection on their teaching is only indirect knowledge. It is not a direct grasp of reality'[191]. The Word must pass from the conceptual level into the level of realization through profound meditation and contemplation by which the revealed Word sinks deep into one's existence and simmer before it is re-actualized in life. This stage in Jnana Marga is called Nididhyasana. This is a steady concentration of mind on Truth; it is just holding oneself steadily in front of the truth. This is meditation without the discursive process; it is contemplation. In Nididhyasana we participate in the original truth-experience or Anubhava of the sages who articulated them for the posterity. This participation can have various degree of intensity according to the personal capacity and preparation of each individual. So we can say that though Anubhava in the stage of Mukti or Moksa has to be complete and perfect, it is possible that even those wo have not yet arrived at that sublime stage can still have an experience of the Reality or a God-experience even in a less perfect way, ranging from a simple prayer to advanced illuminations. Jnana Marga, therefore, should not be considered as a path of God-realization reserved for a few elite.

Though Jnana Marga demands great personal efforts to arrive at the sacing wisdom, it would be wrong to interpret Jnana as something that is achieved exclusively by personal efforts. The bi-polar dynamism of 'Anubhava' that is arrived at through Jnana should not be lost sight of. Anubhava is both the achievement of man and the self-gift of Brahman in His self-revelation. Therefore, 'religious experience is by no means subjective. God cannot be known or experienced except through his own act. If we have knowledge of Brahman, it is due to the working of Brahman in us. Prayer is the witness to the spirit of the transcendent divine immanent in the spirit of man'[192].
The all-important role of Prasada (divine grace) in man's knowledge and experience of God is made very clear in the following aupanisadic passage, with which we conclude this section: "This Self cannot be won by instruction, not by sacrifice (or 'intellect') or much lore heard; by him alone can He be won whom He elects; to him this Self reveals his own form."[193] But it has to be mentioned that Jnana as the 'gift' of Brahman does not have here the element of total graduity that is implied in the Christian concept of grace because according to the Vedanta man is essentially divine and the Jnana is only a realization of what one basicly is.

The above discussion on 'Jnana Marga' is of relevance for us especially in the context of our presentation of Christ in Chapter VI as the real Jnana Marga for man. As the Word of God in person and as the definitve self-manifestation of God, as we shall see, Jesus Christ is the true 'Jnana'. It is also appropriate to note here that, as we shall see in the same chapter, some Vedantins consider the resurrection of Christ as the realization of his advaitic illumination or 'Jnana'.

3. Bhakti Marga: The Path of Loving Devotion

The path of rites and observances or the path of knowledge as the essential and most efficacious way to the Absolute is contested by the followers of 'Bhakti Marga', the path of devotion. The Bhagavadgita asks:

> "What were the good practices of Vyadha? What was the age of Dhruva? What was the learning of Gajendra? What was the prowess of Ugrasena? What was the beauty of Kubja? What was the wealth of Sudama? The Lord who is the lover of devotion, is pleased with devotion, and does not bother about (other) qualities." [194]

The verbal root of Bhakti is 'Bhaj' which means, to share, to partake to enjoy and refers to 'the magical partnership of the sacrificer and the chosen deity (Istadevata) to whom oblation is made' [195] . In the religious context it gradually began to mean adoration or loving devotion and as a Marga it is called the path of liberation by faith, in contrast to the Vedic doctrine of liberation by works (Karma Marga) and the mostly aupanisadic doctrine of liberation by knowledge (Jnana Marga). [196] Faith here should not be understood as to exclude the Jnana and Karma but should be taken in the sense of personal devotion and loving relationship with God in His aspect of being a person. For Bhakti, Jnana and Karma are important as preconditions which prepare a soul for the self-dedication in Bhakti.

The earliest allusions to Bhakti can be found in the Rgveda hymns addressed to Varuna in which he is implored to forgive the trespasses of his devotees. [197] But it is also clear that just these two hymns out of 1017 could not have any significant impact on the Vedic understanding of spiritual life. In a few clearly theistically oriented Upanisadic utterances also there is mention about the path of devotion:

"To the great-souled man who has loyal
and great love for his God,
who loves his spiritual master even as his God
the matter of this discourse will with clearest light,
with clearest light will shine."[198]

But such statements are more an exception in the Upanisads than the normal law. Properly speaking the history of Bhakti Marga can be considered to have begun with the Bhagavadgita and its earliest possible period is the 4th or 3rd cen. B.C. Bhakti is taught explicitly by Gita as the way of salvation:

"Whatever you do, whatever you eat,
Whatever you offer up in sacrifice or give away in alms,
Whatever penance you may perform,
Offer it up to me."[199]

"Do works for me, make me your highest goal,
Be loyal in love to me,
Caste off all other attachments,
have no hatred for any beings at all:
For all who do thus shall come to me."[200]

The Bhakti movement further developed through the Pauranic period to the days of the Bhagavata (the 9th or 10th cen.AD).[201] Even the mostly advaitic (non-dualistic) tendency of Vedanta philosophy led by Sankara and his school was corrected and modified by the theistic or qualified non-dualistic Vedantic school of Ramanuja. The theistic sects (eg. Vaisnava and Saiva) contributed substantially to the spread of Bhakti Marga. Two of the most famous basic treatises on Bhakti are the 'Bhakti Sutras' of Sandilya and Narada which were commented and interpreted many times by later Bhakti Gurus. According to Sandilya Bhakti is: "Sa para anuraktir Isvara", supreme attachment to the Lord.[202] Narada understands it similarly: "Sa tv-asmin parama-prema-rupa", the nature of Bhakti is absolute love for him.[203] The 15th and 16th centuries may be considered to be the golden period of Bhakti currents.[204] C.B. Papali remarks about the Bhakti movement, "... of all the forces that worked together to bring Hinduism to its maturity, the Bhakti movement is the foremost."[205]

The Bhakti Marga can be described as 'a specific religious attitude and senti-
ment, the essential features of which are faith in, love for, and trustful surrender, to God. It is an affective participation of the soul in the divine nature;
a most intense love for God; a clinging of heart to the Supreme Lord whose
greatness the religious soul realizes most keenly'[206] . The realization of the
Absolute in this personal aspect is the end of this Marga and 'it is a direct
experience, both within and without, of the personal God'.[207] As Bhakti consists
essentially in the love of God 'it signifies both the highest realization of
God and the highest means of realizing Him' and therefore 'it is both means
and the supreme End, both a method and a goal, both discipline and a realization'. [208] The followers of Bhakti, therefore, consider it to be higher than
either 'karma yoga' (the path of observance and external activity) or 'jnana
yoga' (dry knowledge, philosophical meditation). [209] One can begin with the lower Bhakti and rise gradually to the higher.[210] The lower Bhakti can have
as its object a minor deity. In the higher Bhakti one has to transcend such
elementary forms of devotions and has to concentrate one's loving dedication
on Isvara alone, God conceived as a personal, all-powerful, all-merciful Being,
both immanent and transcendent. In each Bhakti sect Isvara may be identified
with a particular diety, but he will be considered as the supreme. In Bhagavadgita the object of Bhakti, for example, is Krsna, the manifestation of
the all-powerful God in human form.[211] God's saving love [212] for man is the
foundation of Bhakti or the love of man towards God and so 'for him I am
not lost, nor is he lost for Me'.[213] The aspect of love is expressed most
clearly at the end of the 18th Chapter of Gita:

> "Listen again to my supreme word,
> the most secret of all.
> Well beloved art thou to Me,
> I tell thee, therefore, what is good for thee.

> Think of Me, be devoted to Me,
> sacrifice to Me, adore Me;
> thus shalt thou reach Me, I promise thee
> in very truth, for thou art dear to Me." [214]

One speciality of Bhakti Marga is that it is beyond the boundaries of caste
and sex, unlike the ways of Vedic wisdom and Brahmanic sacrifices. What
here matters is only love.[215] In order to express one's love towards the personal God it is not required that one should perform great deeds or complex

sacrifices. Even the least acts, done out of love, is of great value before the Lord.[216] As an essential element of love of God, the Gita demands from the Bhakta a whole hearted self-surrender to God.

The Bhakti Marga does not advocate a complete withdrawal from activity (nivrtti) as the extreme form of Jnana Marga demands, nor an attempt to achieve salvation solely by the merits of one's own good works and active life (pravrtti) as in the exaggerated form of Karma Marga. Salvation cannot be achieved either by works alone or by intellectual contemplation alone; but both are required as preparation, confirmation and proof for the authenticity of Bhakti Marga which consists essentially in Love, devotion and self-surrender to Isvara. "No one can remain inactive", says Bhagavadgita [219], and the Lord Himself is active [220]. Tyaga or detachment from Karma consists not in abstaining from activity, but in renouncing the fruits (phala) of every action. [221] Dharma demands the execution of one's duties, but all actions must be disinterested and unselfish (niskama):

> "Not by leaving works undone does a man win freedom
> from the bond of works, nor by renunciation alone can he win per-
> fection." [222]
> "The man who does the work that is his to do,
> yet covets not its fruits, he it is who at once
> renounces and yet works on, not the man who builds
> no sacrificial fire and does no work." [223]
>
> "However these actions must be done with abandonment
> of attachment to what you do and of fruits of what
> you do; this is my last and definitve word." [224]

So the way of Bhakti rejects the doctrine of 'naiskarmya' (denial of work) and promotes 'karmaphalatyaga' (detachment from the fruits of work) and 'niskamakarma' (selfless and altruistic work). It is by renunciation of reward and by doing all for the Lord that one escapes from the fruits of Karma and the vicious circle of Samsara. Even the Yoga system meant to achieve self-realization (Atmasaksatkara) based on the non-theistic Samkhya philosphy is reformed by Gita. The final goal of yogic-techniques, according to Gita, should not be the selfish, solitary tranquility, but union with the personal God and eternal beatitude in Him. [225]

The Bhakti Marga of Bhagavadgita assimilates also the Jnana Marga as a preparation and means towards Bhakti. The true love of God (Bhakti) should be saturated with wisdom or knowledge: "To them constantly disciplined, who revere Me with love, I give that discipline of the mind whereby they come to me. Out of compassion for them. ... I destroy their darkness born of ignorance with the shining light of knowledge."[226]

The Gita uses the Buddistic expression 'Nirvana' (extinction) to signify the ultimate liberation of man, but in a totally different sense with a positive content. Nirvana for Gita is Brahma-Nirvana,[227] the realization of Brahman. This is a clear indication of Gita's assimilation of terms which are proper to Jnana Marga. But by the realization of Brahman what Gita means is the realization of Isvara, the personal God because Brahma-Nirvana subsists in the personal God, [227a] Krsna. The man who has attained God is in the expression of Gita a man of 'sthithaprajna', steady wisdom.[228] Even Brahma-Nirvana and sthithaprajna are states inferior to real Bhakti because they are only preparation for the loving union between man and God. R.C. Zaehner writes: "This is the real message of Gita: the immortal state of Brahman which is Nirvana is still imperfect unless and until it is filled out with the love of God." [229] So Gita does not support absorption or disappearance of the individual in Brahman even after one has attained liberation, as the extreme form of Jnana Marga may hold. In the loving union of Bhatki the individual soul retains its individuality.

For Gita, the true knowledge, the salvific wisdom consists not in philosophical contemplation but in loving relation. Ramanuja defends this view of Gita, much better than Sankara. For Ramanuja the reality is personal and so the Supreme Reality is the Supreme Person. 'A person cannot be known by mere inquiry and investigation, but only by the relation of love' [230]. That is a justification of the statement of Gita that the Lord imparts knowledge about Himself "to those who are constantly devoted in worship with love." [231] Bhakti, ie. loving devotion, gives the Bhakta a much greater and more valuable knowledge of the Lord than any intellectual process of meditation and reflection. [232]

The Bhakti Marga puts great stress on the importance of God's Grace on the path of Realization following the statement of the Katha Upanisad:

"This Spirit is not to be obtained through study, intellectual acumen or much learning. That very one whom He chooses shall obtain Him, to that one only this Spirit reveals His own nature". [233] Like the Upanisad (theistic) the Gita also maintains that it is through grace that one attains his eternal destiny: "Putting his trust in me, let him then perform all acts, for by my grace he will attain to the eternal, changeless state." [234] The topic of Grace (anugraha, prasada, pusti, krpa) [235] has been elaborately dealt with by the Bhakti theologians like Ramanuja, Madhva, Nimbarka, Caitanya, Vallabha and others. Grace is 'the gracious indwelling of the Lord in the heart of his servant'236. This Grace does not deny the free will of man and therefore the elevating power of Grace requires some collaboration (moral preparation and good works) from the part of the Bhakta which should prove his faith and love. So grace should be 'earned' to some extent. This contradiction of Grace and work was rejected in South India where a notion of 'Prapatti' developed. Grace is absolutely unmerited and therefore the attitude of a Bhakta should be complete reliance upon the Lord, complete quietism and passive surrender. So Prapatti is an exaggerated form of Bhakti and the difference between Bhakti and Prapatti may be symbolized by the monkey-way (markatakisoranyaya) advocated by the northern school and the cat-way (marjarakisoranyaya) of the southern school. The young monkey clings fast to the mother and is safe. A little effort on the part of the young is called for. The mother cat, however, takes the young in her mouth and the young has to do nothing to secure its safety! [237] The notion of Grace in Hinduism, however, is considerably different from that of Christianity due to the difference in the concept regarding the nature of man! We will have to discuss this point further in reference to the Christian soteriology. The goal of Bhakti Marga is described thus by the greatest of Vaisnava theologians, Ramanuja: "It is evident from the scriptures that the Supreme Lord ... permits them (the just) to arrive at the highest beatitude which consists in the direct intuition of His own nature".[238] This supreme beatitude has according to the Bhakti Marga various degrees,[239] depending on the intensity of Bhakti, love of God. The lowest grade is called 'Salokya' which is being in the same sphere, world or kingdom of God. The next is 'Samipya', living in the proximity of God in his presence. 'Sarupya' is the third degree, similitude and conformity to the likeness of God and finally 'Sayujya' which signifies the intimate union with the divine essence. The Bhagavata Purana, an important Bhakti literature adds another stage between Salokya and Samiipya namely 'Sarsti', enjoyment of the same powers of God. [240]

The Bhakti Marga of Bhagavadgita recognizes the importance of ascetic practices, self yogic discipline, works of piety and discerning knowledge but as it is evident especially in the 12th chapter the supremacy of Bhakti Marga is affirmed. 'The ways of knowledge, works and devoting are all valid, but the first two are hard and liable to bring re-birth, whereas devotion [Bhakti] is speedy, open to all, and brings complete salvation' [241]. In this connection it is also to be mentioned that in some Bhakti movements the role of knowledge was too much diminished and devotion became very subjective, sentimental and over emotional even to the point of expressing itself in erotic practices. [242]

As we have so far seen there are substantial differences in the background philosophy and the methods of various Margas. The Gita made an ecletic attempt to co-ordinate all methods under the supremacy of Bhakti. The general tendency today among indologists is to stress the interrelation between the Margas and to leave to each one to follow the Marga that one finds most adapted to one's spiritual constitution. In this regard the opinion of S. Radhakrishnan is worth nothing:

"We can reach the goal of perfection, attain the saving truth in three different ways, by a knowledge of Reality (jnana) or adoration and love (bhakti) of the Supreme Person or by the subjection of the will to the Divine purpose (karma). These are distinguished on account of the distribution of emphasis on the theoretical, emotional and practical aspects. Men are of different types, reflective, emotional or active but they are not exclusively so. At the end knowledge, love and action mingle together. God Himself is sat, cit and ananda, reality, truth and bliss. To those seeking knowledge He is eternal Light ... to those struggling for virtue, He is Eternal Righteousness ... and to those emotionally inclined, He is Eternal Love and Beauty of Holiness. Even as God combines in Himself these features, man aims at the integral life of the spirit. Cognition, will and feeling, though logically distinguishable, are not really separable in the concrete life and unity of mind. They are different aspects of the one movement of the soul." [243]

Unlike the other Margas, the Bhakti school of spirituality has made a very valuable contribution to the Indian scene and that is the concept of 'Avatara', the descent of the personal God in 'incarnate forms'. The Bhakta can therefore worship and love a God who is near to him, who can be seen and touched. Even idolotry is a manifestation of the human desire for a 'God-with-us' and this desire reached its most admirable climax, outside the Judeo-Christian circle, in the 'Avatara' concept of the Bhakti schools, where the moving and pathetic yearning for the God-Man attained its realization.[244] That is our next topic and it is of great relevance and importance in any serious attempt at the search for a plausible Indian Christology! Our above discussion on the notion of 'Bhakti' will also be of great relevance for us later in our exposition of 'love' as the supreme law of Christianity as we shall do especially in Chapters VI and IX.

C. The Quest for a God-Man

The earliest exposition of the Bhakti system of man's attempt to reach the Supreme Personal God is generally considered to be the 'Bhagavadgita'.[245] The teaching of the bodily dwelling of the divinity among men is one of the most important contributions of Bhagavadgita.[246] S.N. Dasgupta observes that Gita is probably the earliest work available to us in which the doctrine of 'incarnation' is found.[247] It cannot, however, be not denied that in the Upanisads there had been hints of man's prayer to the Divinity to appear to him in his kindly form (tanu);[248] that might have paved the way for the incarnational doctrine of Bhagavadgita.[249] In the course of centuries this doctrine acquired many modifications under the title of 'Avatara'. Our discussion of this topic is evidently of great relevance for our work due to its immediate reference to the Christian faith in Jesus Christ as the Incarnation of the Son of God. The Christian implications of this topic will be elaborated especially in Chapters IV, V and VIII.

1. The Concept of 'Avatara'

The word 'Avatara' is derived from the verb 'tri', to cross over, attain, save, together with the prefix 'ava', down. 'Ava-tri' may be translated as descend into, appear, become embodied, incarnate etc.[250] It is generally used to mean a down-coming, a descent, an incarnation of a god into a mortal form. 'Avatara' is listed in Panini's great Sanskrit grammar which dates back to the fourth century B.C.[251] In the sense of the appearance of a deity[252] it occurs in Ramayana, Mahabharata and the Purana tales. In later usage this term began to be applied to any unusual appearance or distinguished person especially in reference to the personification of any virtue or principle that may be found in him.

'Avatar' may be used of any god. Followers of Siva have occasionally spoken of him as appearing in Avatars. Twentyeight Avatars are applied to him.[253] The god Varuna was believed to have appeared out of the point of an arrow and the consorts of Krsna and Rama were also considered as the Avatars of the goddess of the Earth.[254] In the main, however, the Avatar doctrine is reserved for the followers of god Visnu.[255] God Visnu is believed to exist in five different forms:

(1)   as the Supreme Lord (Paratpara),

(2)   his emanations (Vyuha),

(3)   his incarnations (Vibhava or Avatara),

(4)   the Supreme diety as the indweller in all animate beings (Antaryamin),

(5)   the divine presence in consecrated idols (Arca Avatara).

The incarnations (Vibhava) itself can be of various kinds: complete incarnations (Purna Avatara), major partial incarnations (Amsa Avatara), minor partial incarnations (Kala Avatara), incarnations of might as Siva or Brahma who according to some are forms of Visnu (Sakti Avatara), incarnations of power (Vibhuti Avatara) or incarnations for a purpose (Karya Avatara).[256] 'The purpose of these incarnations is to save the world in times of peril and calamity and to preserve it in pressing emergencies, especially when in danger of ruin from some undue acquisition of power on the part of evil demons' and to help souls on the path of final liberation. [257]

The Visnu Purana, compiled probably about the sixth century A.D. and the more popular Bhagavata Purana, compiled abouth the ninth or tenth century A.D. give a lot of details about Avataras.[258] Bhagavata gives three lists of Avatars and also adds that Visnu's Avatars are innumerable, like 'rivulets flowing from an inexhaustible lake'.[259]

The Pancaratra school of Vaisnavaism proposes a list of ten incarnations (Dasavataras) and that is widely accepted with slight modifications. These are taken from Pancaratra Samhita which enumerates thirty-nine incarnatory forms.[260] Although Buddha was later introduced into the list of ten Avatars, the list given in Mahabharata does not include him.[261] But it is generally believed that 'the notion of successive Buddhas and Jainas may have had some influence on the avatara doctrine'[262] . Monier-Williams, in his Sanskrit dictionary, includes also Buddha as one of the main ten Avatars. The 'classic' list of ten Avatars has the following 'embodiments' (tanus) of Visnu:

(1)   Fish (Matsya),

(2)   Tortoise (Kurma),

(3)   Boar (Varaha),

(4)   Man-Lion (Nara-simha),

(5)   Dwarf (Vamana),

(6)   Rama with axe (Parasurama),

(7)   Rama, the prince of Ayodhya, ·

(8)   Balarama, the elder brother of Krsna,

(9)   Krsna, the hero of Mahabharata and Bhagavadgita,

(10) Kalki, the expected liberator. [263]

The exact names and list of these Avatars, however, is of no special relevance for our topic.

Of Visnus' chief Avatars some are animal and some are human. In the Sata-patha Brahmana [264] it is said that the primeval man (Manu) was saved from a destructive flood together with some sages and the seeds of all existing things by a miraculous fish. In the Mahabharata [265] this fish is considered to be an incarnation of Brahma Prajapati. Later the fish was identified with the incarnation of Visnu in the Matsya, Bhagavata and Agni Puranas.[266] This myth is akin to some other ancient eastern tales of a flood and the deliver-ance of mankind from annihilation.In the Satapatha Brahmana[267] it is men-tioned that the god Prajapati assumed the form of a tortoise and created all living beings. [268] Later the Puranas[269] began to consider the tortoise as an Avatar of Visnu who appeared in this amphibious form to help the gods in the churning of the cosmic ocean, the sea of milk, to produce the nectar of immortality and other valuable articles. Regarding the boar incarnation (Varaha) the Bhagavata Purana says that 'with the view to the creation of this (universe), the lord of sacrifice, being desirous to raise up the earth, which had sunk into the lower regions, assumed the form of a boar'[270] . There are also reference to the boar incarnation in other writings.[271] These animal Avatars - some include also the swan - were originally applied to the creator god Prajapati-Brahma and later applied to Visnu, but the human

Avatars are more directly connected with Visnu.

In the Nara-simha Avatara Visnu appears as a man-lion to dethrone Hiranya-kasipu, a demon king, who as result of his austerities had gained enough strength from Brahma to push god Indra out of the heavens. [272] The Vamana Avatara (dwarf) mythology underwent many changes in the process of development. In the later versions Visnu is reported to have taken the form of a dwarf at the behest of other gods, in order to conquer the three worlds from the demon-king Bali with his three miraculous steps and to send the king to Patala (infernal regions). [273] Parasurama (Rama with axe) was the Avatar of Visnu to destroy Kartavirya, the thousand-armed king of Himalayas, who had oppressed gods and men. [274] This myth might have originated in the background of the severe struggle for supremacy between the Brahmana and Ksatriya castes. Parasurama represents the Brahmins. Visnu's incarnation as Rama, the hero of the oldest Sanskrit epic, the Ramayana, is one of the most popular of all Hindu stories. He is also mentioned several times in the Mahabharata. Visnu decided to be born as the son of King Dasaratha of Ayodhya due to the appeal of the gods to deliver them from the misdeeds and menaces of Ravana, the Raksasa king of Lanka, 'who had obtained extraordinary power from Brahma to whom Ravana showed austere devotion and practised severe penances' [275] .M. Dhavamony observes that 'this belief that Rama is a true incarnation of the Highest God Visnu has been one of the fundamental doctrines of the Vaisnavas down to the present day, for this has been one of the cardinal points of the religious system of Ramanuja and Ramananda, and of the great medieval mystics like Tulasidas and Kabir' [276] . The Avatar Balarama, accepted by some, has not been of noteworthy significance. [276a] The great success of Buddha as a religious teacher resulted in his being accepted by the Brahmins as an Avatara, rather than as the adversary which he really was. The motive given to the Buddha incarnation is, however, very interesting: 'Visnu appeared as the Buddha in order to delude Daityas, demons, and wicked men, and lead them to bring destruction on themselves by despising the Veda, rejecting the caste duties and denying the existence of the gods' [277] . The Avatar yet to come is called Kalki. Visnu will appear at the end of this Kali Yuga, seated on a white horse and holding a flaming sword to destroy the wicked and to re-establish righteousness in the world. He comes in the end-time as the future saviour when the world has sunk into total depravity. He will restore order and peace to the world. E.G. Parrinder observes that 'the idea of a future deliverer, at least in later forms, owes something to the Buddhist belief in the coming Maitreya Buddha, or to Zeroastrian faith in the future Saviour Soshyans, if not to Jewish or Christian Messianic eschatology.' [278]

Krsna, the Avatar of the Mahabharata, the Sanskrit epic containing the 'Bhagavadgita', is the most important of divine descents and the most popular deity in India today. Because of the depth and popularity of Bhagavadgita which considers Krsna as the most Supreme God it is quite proper that we deal with the Avatara of Krsna in greater detail. Its relevance for an Indian Christology is also not insignificant.

2. Krsnavatara

Krsna is a hero who probably lived during the period after the fall of the Indus Valley civilization, when the Aryans had not advanced far beyond their first settlements in the North West of the Indian subcontinent. [279] The name 'Krsna' means black and was probably the Sanskrit name for a hero - and later god - of the dark skinned non-Aryans, who after the overthrow of the Indus civilization about 1500 BC, was absorbed into the emerging Vedic religion. [280] A cast mass of legends and fables has been gathered around him in the course of subsequent centuries and he was later raised even to the status of the Supreme as the greatest of Visnu's divine embodiment. [280a]

The name Krsna occurs in the Rgveda, but not as a divine title. [281] Here Krsna is refered to as a 'hymner'. In the Chandogya Upanisad Krsna is presented as the son of Devaki (Devakiputra) to whom the teacher Ghora Angirasa, a priest of the sun, explained the nature of human life as a sacrifice. [282] There is great similarity between the teachings of Ghora Angirasa and that of Krsna later in the Bhagavadgita:

> "When Ghora Angirasa explained this to Krsna , the son of Devaki, he also said, that, in the final hour, one should take refuge in these three thoughts. 'Thou art the indestructible (aksita), thou art the immovable (acyuta), thou art the very essence of life (prana)'." [283]

In the great Indian Epic Mahabharata Krsna is both man and god, the Avatar of Visnu: "Visnu himself, who is worshipped by all the worlds, was born of

Devaki and Vasudeva, for the sake of the three worlds." [284] The epic, the early part of which may date from about 400 BC, [285] makes little reference to Krsna's childhood events. A popular name for Krsna is 'Govinda', herdsman; he is often associated with cow herds. Not knowing his divine origin, Sisupala, king of the Chedi tribe, even insulted Krsna calling him 'that cowboy'. [286] In the epic there are also indications that the supremacy of Krsna was not accepted without challenge. The Mahabharata presents Krsna holding the emblems of Visnu in his four arms. [287] The first book of this epic shows his role as the helper of the five Pandu brothers in their struggle for the throne and he becomes even the charioteer of prince Arjuna against the Kaurava opponents. Krsna also destroyed the demon and various other monsters that had troubled the earth and it is also narrated that he had sixteen thousand wives [288] and numerous children. Inspite of his divine origin his death was fairly simple; he died being shot in the heel by mistake by a hunter called 'Jara' which means old age. [289]

Panini, the Sanskrit grammarian of fourth century BC refers to Krsna as an object of devotion and worship under the title of Vasudeva. [290] The Buddhist work 'Niddesa' dating back to the fourth century BC also refers to the worshippers of Vasudeva. [291] Patanjali in his Mahabhasya gives the title of 'Bhagavat' to him. [292]

There is an opinion among scholars that the Avatar doctrine appears for the first time in the Bhagavadgita since in the development of the Krsna story 'it was made necessary by the identification of Krsna with the supreme deity' [293] . The validity of this statement, however, depends on the scholarly dating of the Gita in which there is no universally accepted position. The Ur Gita, which as opined by Rudolf Otto forms only a section of the present Gita, might have been at least an independent work to which many interpolations were later added. [294] The Bhagavadgita, as it stands now, forms the sixth part (parvan) of the epic Mahabharata. At the close of the unjust exile of the Pandava princes Krsna is presented as taking part in the deliberations which preceded the great war between the Pandavas and their cousins, the Kaurava princes, and he strongly advices a peaceful settlement. As the war broke out in Kuruksetra, the land of Kurus [295] , an extensive plain in central India, Krsna remained non-combatant but became the charioteer and counsellor of the third Pandava prince Arjuna. The Kuruksetra war symbolized for Krsna the struggle to maintain right (Dharma) against the forces of evil. Kuruksetra was for him the Karmaksetra (the field of duty) and he advised Arjuna on the eve of this great eighteen-day battle to have courage and to fight even against his blood-relatives as a Ksatriya for the protection of Dharma. The most highly priced legacy of ancient India, the Bhagavadgita, is placed in this context; it is the advice of Krsna, his song - Bhagavadgita literally means 'the Lord's song' - which is presumed to have been imparted to Arjuna and here Krsna appears and speaks as the 'Avatar' of God.

Eventhough the doctrine of Avatara is expounded in the Gita it is a curious fact that the word 'Avatara' does not occur at all there. [296] The Gita uses various other words to convey this concept: Janman (birth), [296a] Sambhava (come to being), [297] Srjana (creation),[298] Pradurbhava (appearance),[299] Asrita (dwelling),[300] Adhisthaya (I consortwith).[301]

It is a problematic question, according to Gita whose Avatara Krsna is! If Gita is an independent work there is no certainty that he is the embodiment of Visnu, as it is usually supposed because the word 'Visnu' appears only thrice in the whole Gita, once in a list of gods and twice in the narration of a great vision in chapters ten and eleven. The name 'Hari' another title for Visnu, similarly occurs only twice, namely in chapter eleven and in the epilogue of chapter eighteen. [302] Therefore indologists like W.D.P. Hill and Rudolf Otto maintain that Krsna in Gita is not probably the Avatar of Visnu, but of Rudra according to Otto [303] and in the opinion of Hill he is the Avatar of Brahman, the Absolute of the Upanisads.[304] J. Gonda is also of the same view. [305] K. Sharma even denies that Gita is the work of Vaisnavite school and maintains that the teaching of Gita is not the devotion to the personal God but it proposes pure non-dualism of the monistic Upanisads.[306] G. Parrinder has, however, a different opinion: Even if Gita is originally an independent work, it cannot be denied that it is fitted into the context of Mahabharata where Krsna is the Avatar of Visnu. The few references in Gita also point to the identity of Krsna and Visnu.No wonder that the complexity and syncretic character of Gita guarantees many interpretations but the context of the epic suggests that the most plausible explanation is that Krsna according to Gita is the embodiement of Visnu, the all-pervading god. [307]

Inspite of his human form the Krsna of Gita is divine beyond doubt. In chapter four Krsna affirms his divinity:

> "Unborn am I, changeless is my Self, of [all] contingent beings I am the Lord! Yet by my creative energy (maya) I consort with nature - which is mine - and come to be [in time]." [308]

This suggests that Krsna has two natures, one higher and the other lower. The lower is material (prakrti) which is his body and the higher is spiritual (purusa) his divinity which forms the soul; this is to be understood in the context of Smkhya dicotomy as modified by Gita:

> "Earth, water, fire, wind, ether, thought organ (mind), consciousness and the ego: thus is divided my material nature, eight-fold. This is (my) lower (nature). But know my other nature, higher than that. It is the soul by which this world is sustained." [309]

But the critics of Krsna are ignorant of the divine nature that is behind his human form:

> "Foolish people despise me
> When taking a human body (tanu),
> They ignore my higher being
> As the great Lord of beings." [310]

But Krsna who is so condemned is the ground of all beings: "I am the origin and dissolution, and the stable state between ..." [311] Beyond him there is nothing and like 'rows of pearls on a string' everything is threaded on him. [312] No one knows him, but he knows everything that belongs to the past, present and future! [313] Even though unknown by most, he is the source of everything:

> "The multitudes of the gods know not
> My origin, nor do the great sages;
> for I am the source of all the gods
> and of the great sages in every way." [314]

> "I am the origin of all things,
> all things proceed from Me;
> knowing this the wise adore Me
> rapt in deep meditation." [315]

"Whatever is the seed of all things
that I am, O Arjuna;
nor is there aught that can,
movable or immovable, without Me."[316]

Simple affirmation is no proof. Arjuna himself required a proof to be convinced about the divinity of Krsna. In the eleventh chapter the theophany of Bhagavadgita reaches its climax; Krsna was transfigured. To behold his divine power Arjuna was given the divine eye; no human eye can behold the Lord.[317] It was a terrifying and fascinating vision of the Lord filling the universe, his eyes flashing lightning, his voice thundering, the earth - quaking. Arjuna exclaimed in ecstasy:

"If a thousand suns were to burst forth
all at once in the sky,
their brilliance might resemble
the splendour of this Mahatma!"[318]

"I see in thy body, o God, the gods
and all the varied grades of beings,
Brahma the Lord on his lotus throne,
all the sages and celestial serpents."[319]
"By thee alone are filled this space
'Tween heaven and earth, and all the quarters,
seeing this Thy amazing, fearsome form,
the three worlds tremble, O Mahatma."[320]

It was the revelation of Krsna as the Supreme God, who surpasses all the worlds and even all the particular gods who remains at the same time the father, friend and lover of man,[320a] to whom alone the worship of love can be addressed.[321] The divine majesty that has been revealed makes Arjuna suddenly aware that he has been too familiar with Krsna in his human form as Avatar. He begs pardon from Krsna who is really the 'All'.[322]
Arjuna rejoiced at the sight he had never seen before but at the same time he was trembling with fear - 'Mysterium tremendum et fascinans' - and so he requested Krsna to reassume his human form.[324]

In this context it is reasonable to ask how the supreme and unchangeable essence of the unmanifest God [325] can be subject to manifestation in the human form and be subordinate to change? Is not the Avatara doctrine of Gita a contradiction in itself? Das Gupta observes that 'it does not seem to be aware of the philosophical difficulty of combining the concept of God as the unmanifested, differenceless entity with the notion of Him as a super-Person Who incarnates Himself on earth in the human form and behaves in the human manner' [326]. But the opinion of G. Parrinder clarifies this dilemma better. According to him 'the Avatar doctrine is a further illustration of the ability of the Gita to include different conceptions of God without reconciling them'; there are 'logical flaws in every structure of Hindu world-view and the Gita simply takes them over in its syncretism' [327]. I personally find the position of Gita neither as an ignorance of the problem nor as a blunt syncretism; but Gita proposes its own theology regarding the immanence of the transcendent God. The Supreme God is also the Lord of his own nature. Krsna says in chapter four that he consorts with nature by his mysterious power or creative energy (maya).[328] He assumes really a human nature keeping at the same time his higher nature hidden; 'Manusim tanum asritam'[329] : 'Tanu' means form or body!

The assuming of human body does not mean that Krsna is subject to the law of Karma-Samsara. Incarnation is not in any way re-incarnation or re-birth which is the result of Karma. An Avatar is free from Karma-Samsara. That is the difference between Krsna and Arjuna. It is true that Arjuna like every other man, has a spiritual self which is unborn, changeless, eternal and essentially divine. But his self is subject to re-birth which is the result of Karma.The Lord is conscious of His previous incarnations, but Arjuna in his ignorance does not know his chain of re-births:

> "Many births have passed for Me,
> And for you also Arjuna:
> I know all of these
> But you do not know them." [330]

The reason for that is that works do not stain Krsna nor is there in him the longing for the fruits of works and so he is not bound by works. [331] He is in his nature the divine being, not held by the wheel of re-incarnation, and not determined by Karma. His incarnations have a soteriological purpose. [332]

The Gita makes some very clear and important statements regarding the soteriological purpose of the repeated self-manifestation of God:

> "Whenever there appears
> A languishing of Righteousness (dharma)
> When Unrighteousness (adharma) arises
> Then I send forth (generate) Myself.

For protection of the virtuous,
For destruction of the wicked
For the establishment of Right (dharma),
Age after age I come into being." [333]

The Lord comes in human form age after age (yuge-yuge) to establish 'dharma' - the reign of righteousness - by protecting the good and by eliminating the evil. But the Saviour-God Krsna appears not only just to make a happy existence in this world by establishing Dharma, but there is also a transcendental purpose, namely, 'to show and help [people] realize the path of liberation from rebirth, and to reveal the true nature of God, man and religion and thus manifest his love for men' [334]: "He who knows my divine birth and mode of operation as they truly are, his body left behind, is never born again: he comes to me." [335] Therefore we can say that thought Dharma is mainly concerned with this earthly empirical existence, its ultimate goal is liberation from Karma-Samsara, which according to Gita consists in a state of union with God in perpetual and blissful love. So the Avatar is intended to establish the reign of righteousness, Dharma - 'Basileia', the Kingdom of God' - in this world and in the world to come.

The Avatar does not force anyone into salvation. Krsna is God's invitation to man to a union of love with him, which man can accept by becoming integrated in himself (sthitaprajna); that leads one to a relationship of love with Krsna and in him with God. This is according to M. Dhavamony 'the sum and substance of the whole purpose which Krsna has in his incarnation and this also is the sum-total of the message of the Bhagvadagita' [336].

God never spoke to man as person to person in the Vedas and in the philosophical non-dualism of the Upanisads. There was no I-Thou relationship and so there was no room for personal dialogue between God and man. But for the first time in the Indian Scriptures God makes personal conversation with man in the Gita. Here God descends from his mere transcental causal status to a personal relationship with man as his teacher (Guru), Master, Father, Friend and finally as his Lover (priya)! [337]

The aspect of man's loving union with God exemplified in Krsna was later in the course of centuries strongly mythologized by the pauranic literatures like Bhagavata Purana and Visnu Purana. Krsna's Brindaban 'lila' (sport) with the Gopis (cowgirls), his rasa (circular) dance with them and other erotic narrations of frenzied love smybolize man's passionate longing for God. Passionate love (prema) characterizes God-man relationship. 'As the union of love is the highest point of human life, so it is of human-divine relationships. Krsna shows that romantic love is the highest symbol, and that impassionate adoration of God is the best road to salvation'[338].

Inspite of some apparent parallels between the Avatara of Krsna and the Incarnation of Jesus Christ there are significant differences which we will be discussing in greater detail later especially in Chapter V.

3. Avatara in further Reflection

Many authors have tried so far to trace the important characteristics of the Avatar doctrine. The systematization made by G. Parrinder seems to be of great relevance for us too.[339] Some of the implications are also Christologically important. It is better to avoid the term 'incarnation' in reference to Avatars because of their Christian theological overtones. Avatars are incarnations in a wide sense; there are similarities between both but they should not be uncritically identified. 'Embodiment' may be better suited to signify Avatar.

Avatars are theophanies implying the embodiment of the Divine in the animal or human form. Human Avatars are the most important; among these Krsna holds a very popular place in the hearts of millions. What the Avatar assumes is only the body and not the soul or whatever is assumed. The Divinity substitutes the soul. Inspite of occasional miracles the Avatar behaves by and large according to the natural and physiological laws. Because of the peculiar Hindu anthropology, any charge of 'docetism' levelled against Avatar is irrelevant, although it cannot be ignored from the western point of view. The Avatar is not just an illusion or vision, but real for all practical purposes. They have worldly birth, human parents and they are bodily and visible; some of them were of course monsters! There is a mingling of divinity and corporeality in the Avatars and the transitory nature of their body is emphasized by the fact that they were even subject to death.

Most of the incarnations are myths but some sort of historicity cannot be denied at least to figures like Krsna. The Indian notion of time and history is cyclic and history is not given so much prominence in Indian thought as among the Jews, the Greeks or the Chinese. Even myths are realities in the eyes of faith. In the chain of endless repetitions it is quite understandable that any particular history does not deserve any special attention. There is nothing once and for all! Since the history is to be repeated there is also the necessity of repeated Avatars age after age (yuge-yuge). Avatars may be more or less important, but no Avatar is so unique as to exclude the others. There is no Avatar once and for all! Each Avatar has a fixed function in the given situation. This implies the possibility of including the mythical figures of the past, heroes of the present and hopes for the future in the concept of Avatar. There is also a tendency to accept the founders of other religions also as Avatars. A few more in the long list does not make any substantial difference!

Each Avatar comes with a particular purpose, i.e. to establish Dharma and/or to manifest the nature and love of God. They give good examples to edify others and to encourage them to follow suit, they impart deep doctrinal and moral teachings. The Avatar may be a king of righteousness (Dharmaraja) and may share the sufferings in the world. But there is no question of taking upon themselves the sufferings of the world with the purpose of atoning the sins of others by vicarious satisfaction. Each one has to redeem himself from Karma-Samsara. The Avatars are at best good examples, encouragements, helps and grace of God on the way to liberation. Each one has to atone for his Karma, if required by manifold births. No Avatar simply 'takes away the sins of the world' and achieves redemption of mankind 'once and for all'. They only guarantee the divine revelation of the Vedas by their 'special revelations' and make it easier to understand and to follow the path of ultimate realization of God. All religions are true in so far as they do not contradict the eternal religion (Sanatana Dharma) of the Vedas. The Avatara doctrine, especially of the Gita, is an explicit attempt to reconcile the apparently contradicting notion of God as the Suprapersonal Absolute who is beyond manifestation and the notion if Him as the Highest Person who manifests Himself in visible and tangible forms with the purpose of entering into relationship of love with His creatures!

It is interesting to note how the Hindu theologians and especially the Vedantic thinkers down through the centuries have reflected on the question of Avatara. Some of them found this doctrine not quite in accord with their theological presuppositions, others were ardent supporters of Avatara and in the modern times the general trend is to reinterpret Avatara as to suit the different theological currents.

In a logically non-dualistic system there is no room for either Isvara or Avatar. So many consider that Sankara's non-dualism 'breaks on the rocks of the theory of incarnation' [340]. To be consistent with his non-dualistic theory Sankara cannot accept the theory of Avatara as such without re-servations and personal interpretations. If all individuals are Brahman an Avatar cannot be in any way superior to ordinary men! For many non-dualists like Sankara the concept of Avatars is 'an unnecessary complication, if not a betrayal of the non-dualism of the Upanisads' [341]. Non-dualistic Vedanta does away with mythology and crude theological symbols. In the place of a transcendent personal God it proposes a 'universal Mind, with which the human mind is one! In this context an Avatar is simply irrelevant and not in harmony with other philosophical presuppositions. But because of the pres-tige and popularity of Gita Sankara could not but write a commentary on it. He elaborated vastly what could support his non-dualism and greatly watered down the reality of Avatar to the level of an illusion. Commenting on Gita 4.6-9 he writes that God appears to be born, but it is only an illus-ion! [342] In reality Brahman is unborn and indestructible. An Avatar is for Sankara an illusion in a double sense: the phenomenal world itself is the result of Maya and the appearance of God in this illusory world is a further illusion on illusion! [343] While Maya deludes all others into thinking that they are different from God, Krsna has the power of Maya under his control and he is alone conscious of his identity with Brahman. Krsna's embodiment is only something apparent to others and does not touch his true nature. Maya, however, also means that what we see is an illusion only from the absolute point of view; empirically it is real. So also Avatar is real from the empirical point of view but illusory from the absolute viewpoint. [344] Krsna does not in any way exhaust Brahman. Sankara admits Avatar only as a concession to the religious needs of the ignorant: God takes a bodily shape made of Maya in order to gratify his worshippers out of his compassion! [345] Sankara even composed devotional hymns to satisfy the needs of popular Hinduism as means to the ultimate end of realizing the identity with the absolute. Logically there is a great discrepancy between non-dualism and Avatara theory and some authors are of the opinion that Sankara and other Neo-Vedantists misinterpret the theism of the Bhagavadgita. [346]

The Avatar doctrine demands a positive theism. Other Vedantic philosophers like the qualified non-dualist Ramanuja have been more faithful to the message of Gita. This great Vaisnava theologian writes:

> "God ... though He exceeds the capacity of all minds, nevertheless, by reason of His infinite compassion, love and liberality, assumed various forms without giving up His divinity, and repeatedly manifested Himself. ... He descended in this manner not only to relieve the burden of this world, but also to become accessible to men, made like unto us. Thus He reveals Himself to the eyes of all whether high or low." [347]

Ramanuja justified the Bhagavata devotees of Visnu in their teaching that the Highest Brahman becomes manifest in Avatars.[348] The human eyes could see Him and He delightes the world by His looks and language, overflowing with the nectar of friendship and love.[349] The Lord assumes a real body which is no illusion. Ramanuja interprets Maya as the knowledge and creative power of God. The assuming of body however, is not by compulsion as out of Karma, but only due to the free will and compassion of the Lord towards his beloved. By incarnation the Lord also does not lose anything of his essential eternal nature. [350]

The Dvaita (dualistic) Vedantic philosophy of Madhava defends the doctrine of Avatar. He makes a distinction between God, privileged souls and ordinary souls. Ordinary souls are parts of God only in the sense of being reflections of God (pratibimbamsa) and are different from his essential nature. The Avatars are the privileged souls which are parts of the essential nature of God (svarupamsa). This essential identity of Avatar with God does not involve a numerical identity. [351] The purpose of Avatar is to protect the righteous out of his suprem mercy. The theistic and devotional teachings of Madhava made some think that he was influenced by Christian teachings, perhaps by the St. Thomas Christians of South India; [352] that cannot, however, be adequately proved.

Chaitanya, a Vaisnava reformer of Bengal, born in 1486, was a great devotee of Krsna and his consort Radha whom he worshipped with intoxicating kirtan (song-dance). He emphasized the purpose of Krsnavatar as the teaching of Raga-Marga, the path of spontaneous love or prema. Avatar appeared to taste the glory of the love of Radha, to assimilate the sweetness of Radha's love to himself and to know the bliss of this love.[353] Chaitanya himself began to be later regarded as the Avatar of Radha-Krsna and received sacred adoration.[354] Dasgupta points to the symptoms of pathology in the devotional life of Chaitanya.[355]

Kabir, a follower of Sankara's Vedanta, attacked the widespread movements of devotion to Avatars and personal deities. He worshipped Rama, but not as the Avatar of Visnu but as the Supreme Being without qualities, yet who could be spoken of as the Beloved or Guru whom man needs in this life. The followers of Kabir attributed divine honours to him 'in a manner reminiscent of the Avatars themselves'[356] . Similarly Guru Nanak, the founder of Sikhism rejected Avatars, images and all anthropomorphic ways of describing God. God, for him, dwells in the heart of man.[357] A man like Rama or Krsna who is subject to death cannot be the eternal God! Later on Guru Govind was considered the tenth Avatar of Guru Nanak! Tulasi Das (1544-1603), a Hindi Bhakti writer, was, however, a promulgator of the devotion to Rama as the Avatar of God.[358] In reaction to the excessive emotionalism and idol - otry of the Avatara-Bhaktas some of the modern Indian thinkers,inspite of their theistic concept of God, began to deny the Avatar doctrines. Raja Rammohan Roy (1774-1883), 'the morning star of Indian Renaissance and the prophet of Indian nationalism', believed in one God against the idolotry of all religions and refuted the possibility of Avatars branding it as a corruption and degradation of pure Vedism. To promote his ideals he founded in 1830 the movement which was later called Brahmo Samaj, a form of theistic church. Dwarkanath Tagore, Prosonno Kumar Tagore, Debendranath Tagore, Keshub Chunder Sen and P.C. Mozoomdar were the prominent promoters of this movement. This is an eclectic movement. In contrast to it arose the conservative Hindu militant movement Arya Samaj founded by Swami Dayananda Saraswati (1824-1883) in 1875. Its purpose was to revive Hinduism in Vedic purity and defend it against Christianity. It insists on the belief in Karma-Samsara but condemns Avatars as popular corruption.[359] Krsna according to Dayananda Saraswati was not God but a very virtuous human being, who was extremely anxious to further the cause of righteousness.

Many modern Hindus avoid stressing on the exclusiveness and uniqueness of Hinduism and Hindu Scriptures and are willing to recognize the divine inspiration of other sacred books and the divine nature of the founders of other religions, bringing them to the scope of the all-embracing Hinduism. 'The Avatar faith seems ideally suited to include these teachers, who have come age after age, to different peoples and countries' [360]. Sri Ramakrishna Paramahamsa (1834-1886) adopted the Vedantic doctrine together with a certain universalism which accepts what is good and valuable in all religions. For him Avatars are human beings with extraordinary original powers. [361] They are human messengers of God. [362] Buddha, Krsna and many others belong to this category. [363] Whenever there is a special manifestation of God's power there is an Avatar. If a man possesses the love of God that overflows, who lives, moves and has his being in God, who is intoxicated with his love, such a man is God incarnate. Incarnations appear in the world as powerful divine centres of spirituality. They help men in the ways of salvation. The reason why God incarnates in human form is to manifest to man the perfection of divinity. Every man is divine by nature and the realization of this divine nature is the goal of human existence. Incarnations show us the path to this realization. [364] Ramakrishna has been in subsequent years raised to the status of an Avatar and his marble image decorates the main sanctuary (garbha-mandir) of the Belur Math near Calcutta as its 'presiding Deity' [365]. Swami Vivekananda (1863-1902), the most intimate follower of Ramakrishna, follows by and large the avatar concept as laid down by his master. They are Messengers who have a clear idea of their mission from their very birth and consequently can speak with authority. [366] He also must be understood in the general non-dualistic Vedantic context of the divine nature of every man. Further, Aurobindo justifies Avatar in the background of his theory of the spiritual evolution of man to 'Superman'. [367] Incarnations and Gurus are always required in order to release, skillfully and gently, those who dwell in great ignorance, and to lead them up to the path of spiritual evolution. [368] No one incarnation however can figure as the exclusive truth of the Eternal and so we need many of them age after age. The Avatar, according to him, comes as the manifestation of the Divine among men so that the human nature, by moulding its principles, thoughts and feelings may transfigure itself into the Divine and may attain for example Buddahood, Krishnahood and so on.[369]

Mahatma Gandhi (1869-1948), the father of modern India (Rastrapita), dedicated himself to the God of Truth and to the teachings of non-violence (ahimsa) and action without attachment (niskamakarma). He writes in 1921 that he calls himself a sanatani Hindu because he believes in the Vedas, the Upanisads, in the Puranas and all that goes by the name of Hindu scriptures, and therefore in Avatars and re-birth.[370] But, he gave his own interpretation to the Avatar doctrine: "Inscrutable Providence - the unique power of the Lord - is ever at work. This in fact is Avatara (incarnation). Strictly speaking there can be no birth for God."[371] Gandhi maintained that 'in as much as God is omnipresent he dwells within every human being, and all may therefore be said to be incarnations of him. But this leads us nowhere. Rama, Krishna, etc., are called incarnations of God because we attribute divine qualities to them. In truth they are creations of man's imaginations. Whether they actually lived on earth or not does not affect the picture on them in men's minds'[372] . So Gandhi asserts his belief in Avatars with absolute discard for their historicity or uniqueness! As early as 1925 he stated that 'my Krishna has nothing to do with any historical person ... I believe in Krishna of my imagination as a perfect incarnation, spotless in every sense of the word, the inspirer of the Gita and the inspirer of the lives of millions of human beings'[373] . Many followers of Ghandi, however, consider him an Avatar and his grave is a place of pilgrimage.[374]
It has become common in the Hinduism of modern times to call any great personality an Avatar! Vinoba Bhave, the closest disciple of Gandhi encourages devotion to Avatars as we need ' the living warmth of the symbol'[375].

The most well known among the Neo-Vedantists is S. Radhakrishnan, the late President of India (Rastrapati). True to his non-dualistic Vedantic tradition accommodated to the present day thinking with considerable syncretism, he maintains that God can never be born in the ordinary sense. 'Process of birth and incarnation which imply limitation does not apply to him'[376] . God is present everywhere and 'if God is looked upon as the saviour of man, he must manifest himself whenever the forces of evil threaten to destroy human values' and in such manifestations the normal self-manifestation of God 'becomes emphatic' which could be expressed in mythological categories of Avatara. [377] Radhakrishnan distinguishes between two kinds of Avatars: the eternal and the temporal. The eternal incarnation is the essential divinity of each man, the God in man, the divine consciousness ever present in the human being. The embodiment of God - not in the ordinary sense but in reference to finite beings - as seen in the story of Krsna and other Avatars is the temporal incarnation of God. [378] When a saint endowed with spiritual qualities, large insight and charity, sits in judgement on the world and reforms it spiritually, then we say that God is born for the protection of the good, the destruction of the evil and the establishment of righteousness. [379] Every conscious being is a descent of the divine and in this sense every Avatar is a descent of God into men and not just an ascent of man into God.[380] An ordinary man is not fully conscious of his divine reality even though he is as good as an Avatar; when such a man undergoes the process of liberation from his ignorance the ascent of man into God is realized in his case.[381] Radhakrishnan is of the opinion that 'the Avatara is the demonstration of man's spiritual resources and latent divinity. It is not so much the contraction of Divine majesty into the limits of the human frame as the exaltation of the human nature to the level of Godhead by its union with the Divine'[382]. The body of a liberated soul is the vehicle for the manifestation of the eternal and the divinity claimed by Krsna is the common reward of all earnest spiritual seekers.[383] 'The incarnation of Krsna is not so much the conversion of Godhead into flesh as the taking up of manhood into God'[384] and so the incarnations are the realization of human perfection in a deeper sense. [385] What has been achieved by one man, a Buddha or a Krsna must be repeated in the lives of other men. God descends when man ascends and the Avatar shows the condition of being to which human souls should rise, showing their essential divinity; 'the avatara helps us to become what we potentially are'[386]. An Avatar is fully conscious of his divine identity, while an ordinary man has to grow into the perfection of that consciousness. An Avatar is the descent of God into man while the liberated soul is the ascent of man into God.[387] It is consciousness of one's own divine identity that makes the difference. The idea of a unique incarnation and unique revelation is incompatible with this view. It is unthinkable that God is concerned only with one part of one of the smallest planets. Radhakrishnan rejects any type of servitude to any particular historical fact or any exclusive revelation at any unique instant of time. [388] According to Radhakrishnan 'it is of little moment, so far as the validity of the teaching is concerned, whether the author is a figure of history or the very god descended into man, for the realities of spirit are the same now as they were thousands of years ago and differences of race and nationality do not affect them. The essential thing is truth or significance; and the historical fact is nothing more than the image of it'[389].

Conclusion to Chapter Three

In our following chapters IV and V of the second part of our work we will be considering in greater detail the views of the modern Indian thinkers mentioned above regarding the question of 'Avatar' in its reference to the incarnation of God in Jesus Christ. We will have to deal also in Chapter IV more elaborately with the Vedantic position regarding the Christian faith of Jesus' uniqueness as the only and definitive manifestation of God in human history. We also will be discussing in Chapter V among others about the adequacy of applying the term 'Avatar' in reference to Jesus and the approach of Indian theologians to this issue. The soteriological implications of the divine incarnation in contrast to the 'Avatar' will also be of interest to us. In our evaluative part III we will be using the guidance of Karl Rahner and Wolfhart Pannenberg to shed further light on the question of the 'becoming' of God, the importance of the history of Jesus as the Christ, Christ's soteriological function of establishing the Kingdom of God (basileia) in the Indian conceptual background of 'Dharma', the aspect of vicarious substitution that is implied in Christ's salvific work and the value of human body in the process of man's salvation as is shown in the Christian eschatology through the resurrection of Jesus Christ and of the whole human race. In short, our intention is to make clear in the Vedantic context that Jesus Christ is not just one among many possible manifestations of the Divinity, but the unique, definitive and unsurpassable self-giving of God to the transcendentally oriented mankind within the boundaries of the human history.

154

Conclusion to Part I

Our main concern in this part of our work has been to draw an anthropological background to contextualize a possible Christology that is meaningful for India. The person of Christ as the God-Man and His redemptive role in human history or in other words the Christ-event as the key to the mystery of man and human history cannot be adequately interpreted in the Indian context without considering seriously what such terms as God, Man, World and History do mean to the Indian mind.

Our research on these above mentioned categories of thought and expression has been done principally following the direction of Vedanta, with historical differentiation of its manifold forms. We have refered also to non-Vedantic sources in so far as it has been evitable to contextualize the Vedanta. As the Bhagavadgita is a literary piece which has been very seriously taken and commented by such prestigious Vedantic philosophers like Sankaracharya and Ramanuja, we have given considerable attention to its anthropological views. The question of the embodiment of God on earth in human form as understood in India is also of great importance for any Christological interpretation in the Indian context. Gitas contribution in this sphere has been immense. In drawing a background for an Indian Christology it would not be fair to limit ourselves to any single philosophy or theological tendency, for eg. the Advaita Vedanta of Sankara or any single literary work like the Bhagavadgita. Such an approach is possible and useful for a comparative investigation on a particular point, but not enough for a satisfactory contextualization of Christology in India. Vedanta is the general context in which the Indian Christology has to develop.

Our procedure has been thoroughly anthropological concentrating ourselves on the divine horizon in man as understood by the Vedanta. The notion of God which we analysed in the first chapter led us to a proper comprehension of the essential divinity of man as presented in chapter two. We considered further the limitations confronted by man in the realization of his divine character, especially in his relation to the non-human world and the process of history which have an enslaving influence on him. If man is subject to enslavement in his present existence there are also possibilities open to him to get liberated from his bondage. In the third chapter we considered what this liberation means in Vedanta and how it can be attained. Among the various paths (Margas) the way of loving devotion (Bhakti) brings to light very emphatically the picture of a God who becomes man to enter into tangible, loving relation with him to show him the path towards his ultimate destiny. So the authentically Hindu religious aspirations which found their philosophical expression in the Vedanta attained in the Avatar belief (divine embodiment in human form) a new distinctly defined phase in the Indian religious thinking. This belief is the culmination of a series of developments which led the Indian mind progressively to the realization of the mystery of man. Any Indian Christology must be focused in the perspective of this long anthropological development.

By all these we do not intend to say that the Indian mind is an objectionless 'fertile soil' for the acceptance of Christ and his message as the only 'key' to the mystery of man. The Indian or better the Vedantic anthropology implies very serious obstacles for such an ultimate and definitive acknowledgement of Christ. 'Uniqueness', 'historicity' etc. are meaningless jargons in a cyclic vision of world and history. In the context of the essential divine character of every man the divine sonship of a particular Avatar has only a symbolic and exemplary value and the role of any Avatar, especially as the Neo-Vedantins affirm, is to make clear the latent divinity of every man. They also maintain that every Avatar is a revelation of God, but it is for them wrong to believe that the whole divinity could be once and for all incorporated in any single manifestation. The establishment of the Kingdom of Righteousness (Dharma) which is the main purpose of Avatar is in fact only a moral preparation with social implications, for the final self-realization of the Divine in man. No Avatar can 'vicariously' do satisfaction for any one's misdeeds; each one has to atone for his Karma, no matter how long he has to struggle for that. No Avatar can be 'the meritorious cause of man's justification'. In this context the concept of a Redeemer, who takes on himself the evil deeds of the human race to save it from damnation is hard to put through.

In this background of the Vedantic understanding of God, man, world, history, bondage and Avatar we will be examining closely in the next part of our

work the approach of non-Christian thinkers in India towards the question
of Jesus of Nazareth, the Christ, and how the Christian Indologists have
so far confronted the Vedanta challenge!

PART TWO

THE DIVINE IN HUMAN HISTORY

AS VISUALIZED BY THE INDIAN CHRISTOLOGICAL APPROACHES

INTRODUCTION

In the first part of our work our attention had been concentrated on explaining the necessary Vedantic context for an Indian Anthropo-Christology. In this part our concern is to apply these categories to Jesus Christ as the Mystery of Man and of human history. Here we will be discussing various authors, both native and foreign, who have made some contribution towards, the Indian interpretation of the Mystery of the Incarnate Word. It is, however, to be stressed that this part is not meant as an exhaustive 'report' of the various Indian approaches to the mysteries of Man and of Christ. We will rather be trying to make a critical analysis of the salient features and essential thought-patterns of an Indian anthropological Christology. Although we will be referring to the problems and implications of the question discussed, a systematic evaluation is expected only in the third part (Chapter VII).

This Part is divided into three chapters (IV, V, VI) in the dialectics of a thesis-antithesis-synthesis model. In the fourth chapter our stress is on the notion of the Universal Christ. This is situated in the immediate context of the Vedantic approach to other religions which is predominantly dictated by the principle of 'Sarva Dharma Samanatva' (the equality of all religions) and the Vedantic claim to be the 'Sanatana Dharma' (the perennial, all-inclusive Religion behind all other particular religions) that is capable of absorbing and assimilating all permanent aspects of the religious quest of mankind, including thoise that found their expression in Jesus of Nazareth. The historical uniqueness of Christ is the central point in the fifth chapter and that stands in apparent contrariety to the previously discussed notion of Christ's universality. Both of these chapters are methodically concerned with Jesus Christ in himself, as the meta-historical Word of God in history! The sixth chapter aims at synthesizing the opposing poles of the universality of the Christ-Principle and its historical particularity by discussing the universal relevance of the uniqueness of the Christ-Mystery, namely, by clarifying the soteriological aspect of the Christ-event interpreted in the Vedantic context. It has, however, always to be kept in mind that out discussion turns round the central theme of our whole work, namely, the Mystery of Christ as the Mystery of Man and his History.

If the Mystery of the Incarnation is to be made sufficiently intellegible in India it has to be re-formulated in the Indian, more precisely in the Vedantic, categories. That implies not only a Christian assimilation of Hinduism but also its salvific transformation in Christ! There cannot be a realization of the mystery of Incarnation without a consequent actualization of the Paschal Mystery! Here we find a theological application of the dialectics of birth, death and re-birth which is Vedantic as well as Christian!

CHAPTER IV

THE UNIVERSAL, ADVAITIC CHRIST

The person of Jesus Christ has been a great fascination for many an Indian thinker. There had been attempts especially from the side of the neo-Vedantists in the second half of the 19th century and in the 20th century to interpret Christ in the Vedantic categories. Some Christian thinkers have also followed suit. The general trend has been to follow the 'Kevaladvaita' (strict non-dualism) [1] of Sankaracarya with some occasional accommodations based on the 'Visistaadvaita' (qualified non-dualism) [2] of Ramanuja, both being the most prestigious representatives of the Vedantic school.

The universal aspect of the personality of Christ is what is most stressed in the Advaitavedantic approach to the mystery of his person. What we intend in this chapter is to make clear the notion of the "Universal Christ" as understood in the Vedantic categories which makes an 'Advaitin' out of Jesus Christ through a spiritual and mystic approach characterized by a certain discard for his historicity and uniqueness. We also try see how some Christian followers of this thought-pattern react to the Vedantic challence modifying at least some of the extreme but logically derived attitudes of their Hindu counterparts.

A. Jesus Christ within the Context of the Vedantic Question of 'the Religion' in Religions

Beyond the phenomenal diversities of religions and worldviews - so insist the Vedantins - there is a common, fundamental and universal factor of human interiority and mysticism that dissolves the divergences and unites the various religions in the universality of 'the Religion'. As the Hindu Sanatana Dharma [3] represents this 'universal religion' it has no difficulty in accommodating and integrating Jesus Christ in one or another way as a part of its system. Even the category of 'Avatara' interpreted in an advaitic way [4] has been used in this process of the 'hinduisation' [5] of Jesus Christ.

1. The Fundamental Universality of all Religions and the Primacy of Vedanta

India is a land that has given birth to different religions [6] and has accepted gladly into its bosom diverse spiritual doctrines that originated even outside its boundaries. Both Christianity [7] and Islam [8] which are known for their religious exclusivism had also their place on the Indian soil from the very early days of their existence. In such a land where manifold and sometimes conflicting religious currents meet,a national integration would be impossible without religious tolerance, understanding and some kind of mutual accommodation. This fact has been understood by most of the modern Hindu religious leaders.They try to bridge the gap between the various religious differences stressing the elements which are according to them fundamental, common and therefore universal to all religions. The glaring doctrinal differences may be in this process either ignored or explained away. [9] This mentality has come toi its climax in a very widely accepted religious axiom known as "Sarvadharma samantava", which means, all religions are equal!

a. The Equality of all Religions

Sri Ramakrishna Paramahamsa [10] may be indicated as the one who in the history of Vedanta 'expressed in his life to a greater degree than any other teacher the idea of religious universality and harmony' [11]. He underwent the disciplines of divergent sects in Hinduism as a part of his search for God-realization. He practised also Islam and Christianity to some extent and in all religions, as Swami Prabhavananda affirms, he could achieve supreme realization of God and could proclaim with the authority of direct experience: "So many religions, so many paths to reach one and the same goal." [12] He tried to show that the difference between religions is not one of essence but one of forms and names. The essence of religion consists in God-realization [14] and this can be contained in various religious 'vessels'! [16] It cannot be denied that such an approach to cover up religious differences cannot do justice to the doctrinal diversities that lie deep in religions. Each one has the right to give a universal explanation to one's own religious belief but it is not justifiable if one enters another one's religious sphere and tells him what the interpretation of his religion should be! While criticising this element of superficiality in Ramakrishna's approach, we need not also forget his concern for religious tolerance and harmony among peoples.

It goes to the credit of Swami Vivekananda [17], the discipline of Ramakrishna, that later a more doctrinally coherent form of the principle of 'Sarva dharma samanatva' could emerge. Vivekananda advocates this principle with scriptural justification based on the Rgvedic text: "That which exists is one, the sages call it by various names."[18] A statement in the Bhagavadgita also renders support to Vivekananda's position: "Even those who worship other gods, if full of faith in reality, worship Me, though not according to ordinance."[19] Vivekananda is of the opinion that the equality of all religions can be made most beautifully manifest in accepting the worship-forms of other religions:

"... we (Hindus) invite ourselves with every religion, praying in the mosque of the Mohammedan, worshipping before the fire of the Zeroastrian, and kneeling to the cross of the Christian. We know that all religions are alike, from the lowest fetiscism to the highest absolutism, are but so many attempts of the human soul to grasp and realize the Infinite. So we gather all these flowers, and binding them together with the cord of love, make them into a wonderful bouquet of worship." [20]

Vivekananda is convinced that God being the absolute goal of mankind is at the centre of human existence. The individuals' vision of God may be distorted and contradict each other, but this contradiction is only apparent as it belongs only to the sphere of relative perception which in fact affects neither the essence of God nor that of man. The limited visions also help man to God; all the differences of God-visions also vanish when we meet in God:

"We ought to remember that both of us may be true, though apparently contradictory. There may be millions of radii converging towards the same centre in the sun. The further they are from the centre the greater is the distance between any two. But as they all meet at the centre, all difference vanishes. There is such a centre, which is the absolute goal of mankind. It is God. We are the radii. The distances between the radii are the constitutional limitations through which alone we can catch the vision of God." [21]

We can notice considerable sophistication in this approach of Vivekananda. It is, however, a fact that he also falls prey to a general defect that is common in Vedantic arguments, namely, to present an example uncritically as an apodeitic proof for a religious or philosophical statement. Examples, of course, can clarify points, but they are no substitutes for intellectual demonstrations. It is, indeed, not convincing for the modern man to cover up religious cosmopolitanism.

Mahatma Gandhi, as a social leader who dedicated his life to the cause of Indian national integration, also considered 'Sarva dharma samanatva' as a principal doctrine of his socio-religious philosophy. He insisted that there are certain fundamentals that are common to all mankind, which each people have a right to express in their own different ways. For example, a single tree has different branches and many leaves; there may be varieties of attractive flowers in a single garden; so also the thoughts of mankind can be expressed in different languages and philosophical patterns. [22] "All religions", he insisted, "are one at the source". [23] All principal religions are for Gandhi equal in the sense they are all true and they supply 'a felt want in the spiritual progress of humanity' [24]. Gandhiji could not find any reason for any particular religion or religious leader to claim any pre-roragative of uniqueness. Such claims would contradict the universality of man's religious experience and the diversity of their expressions. Gandhi writes:

"We want to reach not the dead level but unity in diversity. Any attempt to root out traditions ... is not only bound to fail but is a sacrilege. The soul of religion is one, but it is encased in a multitude of forms. The latter will persist to the end of time. Wise men will ignore the outward crust and see the same soul living under a variety of crusts."[25]

The ultimate goal of all religions, as understood by Gandhi, is the discovery of truth, which for him is God Himself. [25a] It may not be easy to determine whether what one has found in one's search is the real truth or not. Gandhi adopts the following criterion to distinguish truth from falsehood. Reason and non-violence play there a great role. He writes:

"Truth is superior to everything, and I reject what conflicts with it. Similarly, that which is in conflict with non-violence should be rejected. And, on matters which can be reasoned out, that which conflicts with reason must also be rejected." [25b]

By this Gandhi does not mean that all truth could be comprehended by the limited human mind. Similarly no single human expression can ever claim to exhaust the fullness of truth. Eventhough we are all sparks of truth, we cannot adequately describe how the sum total of all these sparks is like. [25c] Even the different religions in the world possess some degree of truth, but no single religion in the world can possess the whole truth.

Gandhi is also of the conviction that although all religions are fundamentally true, they are also imperfect naturally and necessarily because they 'bear the impress of the imperfections and frailties of human beings' who interpret them. [26] That is why Gandhi insists, that all religions are true 'more or less'. [27] The different religions are like various paths to one and the same God. "If a man reaches the heart of his own religion", says Gandhi , "he has reached the heart of the others too."[28] The presence of truth in all religions demands a pluralistic approach of tolerance to the phenomenon of religious diversity. He writes:

> "If we search we may find as many religions as there are men. Hundreds of men are merely striving to know the Truth. They will put Truth in their own way. No two men will put it in identical terms. ... I do not judge Muslims, Parsis, Christians and Jews. If I am a seeker after Truth, it is quite sufficient for me. I cannot say that because I have seen God in this way the whole world must see Him in that way. All religions are true and equal. ... Another man's religion is true for him, as mine is for me." [28a]

It may not be possible for us to agree with all the points of the Mahatma's religious philosophy. However, we should not forget that Gandhi's main concern is religion in concrete practical life. Religious separatism that promotes fanaticism and intolerance in the name of God cannot be considered as conductive to universal fraternity nor as belonging to the true core of human religiosity. It is also an understandable argument that if the goal of mankind's religious aspirations is the one and the same God, the various expressions of these aspirations also must be understood as leading to that goal. But it is also a fact that Gandhi underestimates very much the undeniable reality of manifold religious opinions that are mutually irreconcilable and contradictory. If all religions are equally true, how is it possible that one truth can be contradicted by another truth? It can be said that viewed in the context of Gandhi's concern for religious toleration and social harmony, his idea of religions' equality deserves sympathetic understanding, if not acceptance.

In his work "Eastern Religions and Western Thought", S. Radhakrishnan also elaborates his notion of the essential oneness of all religions. [30] The religious toleration which, according to Radhakrishnan, characterises the Hindu way of life is due to this conviction of religious equality. This attitude, he says, has helped Hinduism to become itself a 'mosaic of almost all the types and stages of religious aspirations and endeavour' [31]. So Hinduism interprets the different historical forms as modes, emanations or aspects of the Supreme. Radhakrishnan also warns against considering this Hindu attitude as 'the outcome of scepticism which despairs of ever reaching any stable truth' or as 'a mere concession to human imperfection' [32].

In general, it can be said that Hinduism considers the direct realization of the Supreme in one or another way [33] as the ultimate goal of religions and the essence of all religious experience. In other words, God-realization or mystical union with the Supreme is the Religion in religions, no matter how it is explained and understood in various schools of Indian thought. Provided this goal of human existence is reached, it is of no much importance for a Hindu through which way or in which group it is attained. This attitude of 'one goal, many paths ... all religions are equal' is widespread also in the various strata of popular Hinduism. In our opinion, what P.C. Mozoomdar once said about Sri Ramakrishna Paramahamsa could be considered as typical of the general Hindu or Vedantic attitude:

> "He is the worshipper of no particular Hindu god: He is not a Saivite, he is not a Shakta, he is not a Vaishnava, he is not a Vedantist. Yet he is all these. He worships Shiva, he worships Kali, he worships Rama, he worships Krishna, and is a confirmed advocate of Vedantic doctrines. ... He is an idolator, yet is a faithful and most devoted mediator of the perfections of the one formless, infinite Deity whom he terms Akhanda Sachidananda (Indivisible Existence-Knowledge-Bliss). To him each of these deities is a force, an incarnated principle tending to reveal the supreme relation of the soul to that eternal and formless Being who is unchangeable in His blessedness and light of wisdom. ... These incarnations, he says, are but the forces (Shakti) and dispensations (Lila) of the eternally wise and blessed Akhanda Sachidananda who can never be changed or formulated, who is one endless and everlasting ocean of light, truth and joy." [34]

Here the mention is, of course, only about the different Hindu Sadhanas or ways of worshipping God. But, as Swami Nikhilananda comments, a Hindu with the spirit of Ramakrishna has no difficulty to accept that Christ, Buddha and founders of other religions do also belong to this category of 'incarnated principles' revealing the Supreme, in so far as they do not raise any claim of absolute uniqueness, which goes contrary to the notion of universality and equality of all religions. [35]

Here a legitimate question can be asked: If all the religions are more or less the same, why should the advocates of this opinion like Vivekananda and Gandhi have regarded themselves as belonging to the Hindu fold even to the point of criticising the conversion efforts of the Christian mis- sionaries? The answer lies in the theory of 'Ishtam'[36] and the principle of 'Swadeshi'[37] applied to religion.

b. The Theory of 'Ishtam': Personal Religious Preference

According to the theory of 'Ishtam', religion is strictly a matter of personal preference and conviction and not a matter for argument. A strictly organ- ized and institutional religion cannot be called universal. Religion being an indiviual's own concern, a private affair or Ishtam cannot be congre- gational. In the field of religion each one must be free to decide in his own religious experience what is fitting and proper for him. Ishtam being a matter of deep personal religious experience cannot be rationally sub- stantiated. The notion of 'Ishtam' becomes clear in these words of Swami Vivekananda:

> "Your way ist very good for you, but not for me. My way is good for me, but not for you. My way is called in Sanskrit my Ishtam. Mind you, we have no quarrel with any religion in the world. We have each our Ishtam." [38]

Because of this theory a Hindu feels himself to be fully at liberty to chose between the great religious personalities. [39] It helps spiritual growth and a process of assimilation of various religious heritages being fully open to truth without narrow dogmatism. Each one has, of course, the right to preach one's own convictions, but nobody has the right to dictate to others how they should practice their religiosity which is strictly private and personal. [40]

According to this principle, a follower of Jesus Christ is not to become a Hindu or Buddhist, nor the other way about. Each one should respect one's own law of growth in one's own milieu and assimilate as far as possible the spirit of other religions too. [41] "See by your own constitution what you like best, and which is most fitted for you", advices Vivekananda and he adds, "take up that one which suits you best and persevere in it. This is your Ishtam, your special ideal" [42].

According to the conviction of Mahatma Gandhi, equal respect for other religions does not mean that one should have an external membership in them, but it consists in showing respect for other religious views and stressing what unites the different religions rather than exaggerating the differences. [43]

Gandhi is of the opinion that one should remain in one's own religion of birth, as long as one is not compelled to make another decision on the basis of one's own personal religious experience. Here he applies the notion of 'Swadeshi' to religion, according to which he maintains that the culture and religion of the land (Desa) in which one is born is most fitted for one's own spiritual growth and God-realization. The mass conversion of unsophisticated Harijans of India into Christianity, especially for the sake of material benefits, was in the view of Gandhi an exploitation of their disabilities to tear them away from their roots in the ancestral religious community and social structure. [44] So the work of the missionaries should not be aimed at conversions but to reforming social evils and making each man a better man:

> "... our innermost prayer should be that a Hindu should be a better Hindu, a Muslim a better Muslim and a Christian a better Christian. This is the fundamental truth of fellowship. ... Cases of real, honest conversion are quite possible. If some people for their inward satisfaction and growth, change their religion, let them do so." [45]

India's great faiths are, according to Gandhi, sufficient for her. Gandhi remained a Hindu principally because he was born in a Hindu family, [46] and out of personal experience he knew it to be the best for him. [47] He knew that Hinduism is badly in need of reforms [48] especially in the social sphere for which he found it necessary to accept elements from the teachings of other founders of religions, especially from the teachings of Jesus Christ. That would finally make a religious synthesis which for him still will have the name 'Hinduism' although he admits for another one this snythesis could be Christianity. [49] Gandhi saw it quite possible for him to be a sincere follower of Jesus Christ, even while remaining a Hindu:

> "To be a good Hindu also meant that I would be a good Christian. There was no need for me to join your crowd to be a believer in the beauty of the teaching of Jesus or try to follow his example." [50]

It can be said that Gandhi's principle of the universality and equality of all religions was an extension of his political philosophy of 'Ahimsa' (non-violance) to the spiritual sphere. He found that non-aggression actualized in respect for the religious opinions of others was inevitable for the integration of the Indian society. If religion is only the sum total of man's endeavour to attain the absolute, it is easy to understand why the principle of 'Ishtam' should be the supreme to determine the religious allegiance of a man. But when one comes to the religious realization that in Jesus of Nazareth God has definitively manifested His 'Ishtam', then it goes without saying that the 'Ishtam' of God has to be respected above the human 'Ishtam'.'

c. The 'Sanatana Dharma' as 'the Religion' in Religions

It is true that the principle of the fundamental universality and equality of all religions is accepted in one way or another, perhaps, by most of the Hindus and the elite Vedantists. It cannot, however, also be denied that there are some Hindu scholars who do not accept this principle, but claim absolute superiority for the Hindu religion. S. Murthy[51], for example, and D.S. Sarma[52] have published scholarly works defending the primacy and superior character of Hinduism.

Even the statements in the Bhagavadgita[53] which are often explained as supporting the universal equality of all religious worships, could also very well be interpreted as maintaining the supremacy of worship directed to Lord Krishna. If all worships, even the worship of the non-Krishnavaites, are in fact ultimately, even if unknowingly, directed to Krishna, it logically follows that all are 'anonymous'[54] Krishnavites! That would be against the theory of religious equality. Besides, it is also questionable whether the insistence of the Neo-Vedantists on the essential or universal oneness of all religions can be interpreted as supporting without reservations the notion of the equality of all religions. Eventhough Vivekananda, Radhakrishna and the members of the Ramakrishna Mission[55] do make often statements, which as we have seen advocate the equality of religions, it must be said that they are not always logically consistent. Certain statements should in our opinion be understood as accommodations to the western audience.

There are many evidences to show that the theory of 'Sarva dharma sama-natva' is not such an unreserved Hindu offer to religious dialogue as we may be prompted to think. I think, it is also necessary to cast some light on these reservations.

Hinduism is first and foremost the 'Sanatana Dharma', the perennial religion, that can accept and assimilate all possible religious tendencies, even con-tradicting ones.[56] 'Sarva Dharma Samanatva' should be, therefore, understood within this general context of the all-inclusive 'Sanatana Dharma'. All individual religions are one or another temporal expression of this 'eternal' Dharma. The expression 'Sanatana Dharma', it is true, is used for Hinduism in general; but in a strict sense it should be understood as representing the Vedanta, especially in its advaitic form as understood and interpreted by the neo-Vedantists.[57] Advaita, as representing the apex of the experience and realization of the Absolute towards which all other religious experiences lead - not only in the various Hindu Sadhanas but also in other non-Hindu religions - should be considered as the only Universal Religion. This is the position of the disciples of Swami Vivekananda in the Ramakrishna Mission:

> "It must never be forgotten that it was the Swami Vivekananda, who while proclaiming the sovereignty of the Advaita philosophy as including that experience in which all is one without a second, also added to Hinduism the doctrine that Dvaita, Visishtadvaita and Advaita are but three phases or stages in the single development, of which the last-named constitutes the goal."[58]

It is, however, strongly disputed whether the Advaitsa of Sankara or another form of Advaita, for example the Visishtadvaita of Ramanuja, should be considered as the apex in the ladder of religious experiences.[59] Our intention is not to enter into this dispute which is irrelevant for our topic, but only to draw attention to the fact that Vedanta, in one or another of its forms, regards itself to be the all-inclusive religion, a Dharma in whose bosom all other religious convictions can find accommodation. This means that all religious experiences are valid, but they must be understood and interpre-ted within the general frame-work of the Vedanta. The Vedanta can be considered as representing the 'whole' of religious experience, of which the various religions, including that of Jesus Christ, form a part. The whole must be naturally greater than and superior to the parts. The universal religion of the Vedanta is not 'a religion' among many others, but it is 'the Religion' behind all other religions or 'the Religion' of religions. This is based on the assumption that the Vedanta as the 'Sanatana Dharma' rests on eternal (sanatana) principles which are universally valid, and not on temporal and ephemeral historical phenomena, however sublime they may be. This is what Swami Vivekananda has to say on this question:

> "Just as our God is an Impersonal and yet Personal God, so is our religion a most intensely impersonal one, a religion based upon principles; and it has an infinite scope for the play of persons, for what religion gives you more incarnations, more prophets and seers, and still waits for infinitely more?... It is in vain we try to gather all the peoples of the world around a single personality. It is difficult to make them gather together even round eternal and universal principles. If it ever becomes possible the bring the largest portion of humanity to one way of thinking in regard to religion, mark you, it must be always through principles and not through persons." [60]

All historical religions are, therefore, only different forms of the universal religion of the Spirit represented by the Vedanta, which according to Radhakrishnan, is 'not a religion but religion itself in its most universal and deepest significance' [61]. This spiritual religion is universally valid, vital, clearcut and has an understanding of the fresh sense of truth. [62] For Radhakrishnan, neo-Hinduism [63] rightly interpreted, of course within the Advaitic categories, rightly deserves to be regarded as the religion behind the religions, the Sanatana Dharma, which alone can provide a strong basis for an eternal religion 'which, while holding on to the tested values of the past, can also make room for the values of other religions in a spirit of friendliness, tolerance and harmony' [64]. This is because Hinduism as Sanatana Dharma, especially in the form of Vedanta, is allcomprehensive in character, universal in scope, non-historical in nature, tolerant and inner realization, and it represents man's final encounter with the Ultimate Reality. [65]

It may be remarked that what the neo-Vedantists like Swami Vivekananda and Radhakrishnan intend by their concept of the primacy of the Vedanta as the Sanatana Dharma is not a competition of Hinduism with other religions. There is no question of a rivalry with other religions because Hinduism in its sublime form of Vedanta is not 'a religion' among others, but an all-pervading and all-comprehending set of principles. It may be described in the words of S.J. Samartha as 'an ecumenical Hinduism' [66] or as 'Pan-Hinduism', the title preferred by M.M. Thomas. [67]

This attempt of the Hindu reformers to preach the fundamental universal applicability and equality of all religions and to interpret it, especially as the neo-Vedantists do, within the frame-work of the primacy of Vedanta as the most sublime expression of the Hindu Sanatana-Dharma, is understandable especially when we consider the pluriformal religious tradition of the Indian people and their taste for religious syncretism. This attitude has considerably helped to promote an atmosphere of religious tolerance in India. From the rational point of view one also cannot deny that if all religions are at least partially true - no religion being exempt from the limitations that are inevitable in human existence - then the sum total of all these partial truths, as claimed to be accepted and represented by the Sanatana Dharma, must be more than the individual partial truths. But the problem is: Who can decide or has the right to determine what belongs to true religious experience of man and what does not? Can every personal 'Anubhava' be considered as based on truth, objective and therefore normative? What do we say about the question of contradicting 'Anubhavas' in Hinduism itself, not to mention other religions? Can we affirm without reservation that all religions are based on the same presuppositions, inspite of the fact that there is only one God as the source of all truth? To ask more concretely, are both the Vedanta and Christianity based on the same fundamental assumptions regarding the nature of man and his final destiny?

In this context the following question could also be asked:Would it not be more honest to say that the fundamental assumptions of the supporters of Sanatana Dharma and that of Christianity, inspite of the many striking similarities and parallels, are at their core mutually exclusive? [67] The denial of the historical uniqueness of Jesus of Nazareth and God's redemptive plan realized through and in him, as implied in the universalism of the Sanatana Dharma, can by no means be accepted as doing justice to the basic Christian creed. If religion is essentially and fundamentally a matter of personal realization and if creeds and dogmas do have only an instrumental value which can be accepted or rejected by the individual according to his 'Ishtam', it would be difficult to understand why one should be in any way concerned about 'one's neighbour' as Christian fellowship would necessarily demand. [68] At present we do not intend to go deeper into these problems; we would better tackle them in the third part of our work.

Our immediate interest for what has been said so far lies in forming an idea of how the person of Jesus Christ could possibly be understood and interpreted by those modern Hindu reformers who, while stressing the equality of religions as necessary for a peaceful religious-coexistence and Indian national integration, would regarded the reformed Hinduism in the garb of neo-Vedanta as the pre-eminent Sanatana Dharma which is capable of accommodating the various and even conflicting religious currents, but at the same time could discover, unlike in other historical religions, an infinite scope for the play of persons'[69] like Jesus Christ and 'make room for the values'[70] of other beliefs within its all comprehensive universality. This picture of Jesus Christ and especially of his person fitted into the Vedantic frame is not necessarily that of the Christ of the Christians; it is a Hindu view of Christ.[71] This is the 'Universal Christ'[72] who is liberated from the narrow historicism of his so-called followers especially in the west, and made available in his 'unbound'[73] character to the whole of mankind! How the person of Christ is fitted to the context of Sanatana Dharma is our next topic.

2. Christ as Part of Sanatana Dharma

An attempt to mould Christ into Vedantic pattern or Vedantic terms is very characteristic of modern Hindu thinking represented especially by personalities like, as we have seen in the previous section, Swami Vivekananda, Mahatma Gandhi, S. Radhakrishnan and their followers. In the face of the avowed self-sufficiency of Hinduism as Sanatana Dharma it must be considered as a very encouraging development for the cause of Christ in India. This attempt to universalize Christ and to appropriate him to Hinduism from an inclusive standpoint cannot, however, be considered as being loyal to the traditions of the New Testament and the Christian community. Christ is interpreted in the Hindu or more precisely in the Vedantic religio-philosophical categories to show how he can be quite at home in India,[74] especially in the context of the mystic oneness with the Absolute.

a. The Universal Christ-Principle

In the Vedantic Christological approaches, the Vedantic anthropology plays a decisive role. It includes a general disregard for the material world and history as we have seen in the first part of our work. Principles are the most important and not persons of history. There is an attempt even to separate the principles for which Christ stands from his historical person. It may be called the 'Christ-ideal', 'Christ-principle' or 'Christhood'.' Once Christ is freed from his historical limitations it becomes easy to show him as being present everywhere as a principle. Keshub Chunder Sen (1838-1884), a prominent Hindu reformer and leader of the Brahmo Samaj [76], makes the following statement on what he understands by the universal Christ-principle:

> "Scattered in all schools of philosophy and in all religious sects, scattered in all men and women of the East and West, are multitudinous Christ-principles, are fragments of Christ-life, ... Thus all reason in man is Christ-reason, all love is Christ-love, all power is Christ-power .... It exists even where it is not professed." [77]

This statement of Sen echoes the notion of the 'Unknown Christ' that has been recently fully developed by Raymundo Panikkar,[78] not to mention the 'anonymous Christ' of Prof. Karl Rahner. [79] Inspite of the similarity in expressions, I should mention shortly, both of these authors are representing vastly different concepts. We will be dealing with this topic later.[80] For the moment we limit ourselves to the notion of universal Christ-principle as understood in the context of Sanatana Dharma.

Sen explains how Christ is already present in India, in Hinduism, although he is not everywhere fully recognized:

> "In every true Brahmin, in every loyal votary of the Veda on the banks of the sacred Ganges, is Christ, the Son of God. The holy word, the eternal Veda dwells in every one of us. ... Go into the depths of your own consciousness, and you will find this indwelling Logos. ... The real recognition of Christ has taken palce in India. ... Only the nominal recognition remains." [81]

This unconscious presence of Christ in Hinduism manifests itself, according to Sen, in the Vedantic categories of asceticism and Yoga. [82] It must be here noted that inspite of his insistence on the 'unknown Christ' in Hinduism, Sen has never discarded the real historical personality of Jesus Christ. The approach of Swami Vivekananda is, however, characterized by a more onesided insistence on the Christ-principle separated from his person. The possiblity of manifesting a 'Christhood' is open to every human being and is not to be considered as restricted to Jesus of Nazareth:

> "The power is with the silent ones, who only live and love and then withdraw their personality. They never say 'me' and 'mine'; they are only blessed in being instruments. Such men are the makers of Christs ... ever living, fully identified with God, ideal existences, asking nothing, and not consciously doing anything. They are the real movers, the Jivasnmuktas, absolutely selfless, the little personality entirely blown away, ambition non-existent. They are all principles, no personality." [83]

From this passage it is clear how the Vedantic vision considers concrete personality as a limitation of the universal principle. Personality is equated with egoism! When one gets rid of the personal limitations of one's existence one can attain the state of Jivanmukta [84] which is the destiny of every man and which is designated as Buddhahood or Christhood! Jesus and Gautama were only 'instants' in an expression of the universal religion of the Spirit or the religion of Mysticism:

> "Jesus had our nature; he became the Christ; so can we and so must we. Christ and Buddha were the names of a state to be attained. Jesus and Gautama were the persons to manifest it." [85]

For Vivekananda, Buddha had acutally attained a greater mystic realization than Christ. Jesus and Gautama are unimportant 'except as instruments of the manifestation of Buddhahood and Christhood' [86].

This Christ-picture of Vivekananda fits well into his Vedantic pattern. It also becomes clear what a pejorative meaning is attributed to the notion of 'person' in the Vedantic anthropology. We had refered to this problem in our first part. [87] It is also a terminological problem. In Vedanta 'Person' represents a degrading limitation, while in the Christian tradition it stands for the highest expression of the notion of existence as manifested in the communion of persons in the Holy Trinity. It is one of the important tasks of the Indian Christology to make clear the notion of perfection involved in 'person' and to distinguish it from the temporal manifestations of limitations in persons or human individuals that cannot be uncritically applied to the Absolute.

b. The Oriental Jesus

There have also been attempts in Vedanta to orientalize the historical particularity of Jesus of Nazareth even while stressing his larger universality. [88] Pratap Chunder Mozoomdar (1840-1905), a follower of K.C. Sen to the Brahmo Samaj leadership, writes in his interesting Wirk "The Oriental Christ" that 'the celestial figure of the sweet prophet of Nazareth' will be 'illumined with strange and inknown radiance' if 'the light of oriental faith and mystic devotion' are shed on him.[90] Such an attempt according to him makes Jesus of Nazareth more intellegible making him really 'a gain to humanity' [91]. Such an orientalization approach could be detected also in Sen as the presents Jesus in the external features of an oriental mystic:

> "Behold, he cometh to us in his loose flowing garment, his dress and features altogether oriental, a perfect Asiatic in everything. Watch his movements and you will find genuine orientalism in all his habits and manners, in his up-rising and down-sitting, his going forth and his coming in, his preaching and ministry, his very language, style and tone. Indeed, while reading the Gospel, we cannot but feel that we are quite at home when we are with Jesus, and that he is altogether one of us. Surely, Jesus is our Jesus."[92]

Jesus is for the Vedantists an oriental not just because he was born and lived in a geographical region that belongs to Asia but because he was the embodiment of the ideals of spirituality which the people in the Orient cherish and show in their thoughts and actions and because his teachings are completely in harmony with the Hindu view of life and eastern way of simplicity and renunciation. [93] Swami Akhilananda also tries to present an oriental picture of Christ in his book "The Hindu View of Christ". [94]

The zeal to 'orientalize' Christ goes sometimes to the extremes of polemics with the west. "The voice of Asia", argues Vivekananda, "has been the voice of religion and the voice of Europe the voice of politics"[95].

Therefore, he argues that Jesus of Nazareth 'can be better understood by those in the East than those in the western countries' [97]. The eastern Christ, in the view of P.C. Mozoomdar, stands for the incarnation of unbound love and grace while the western Christ represents 'the incarnation of theology, formalism, ethical and physical force' [98]. In Gandhi's opinion the figure of Jesus has been very much distorted by the western Christianity with the backing of political might into 'an imperialistic faith' and he affirms that 'India's contribution to the world is to show this fallacy'[99]. Swami Akhilananda even points out that Jesus and his views can hardly be brought into harmony with the western world-vision:

"The texts of the teachings of Jesus cannot fit in the philosophy of life found in modern Occidental countries, when persons superimpose their own ideas on His and interpret them in His name."[100]

Radhakrishnan sees a possible rebirth of the Christian message in the heritage of India especially because of its original eastern background.[101] He further makes a comparison between western dogmatism and intolerance with the contrary eastern approach to religion as shown in Jesus:

"The difference between the eastern and western approaches and attitudes to religion becomes evident when we compare the life of Jesus, and his teaching as recorded in the Gospels, with the Nicene Creed. It is the difference between a type of personality and a set of dogmas, between a way of life and a scheme of metaphysics. The characteristics of intuitive realization, non-dogmatic toleration, as well as insistence on the non-aggressive virtues and universalist ethics, mark Jesus out as a typical eastern seer. On the other hand, the emphasis on definite creeds and absolutist dogmatism, with its consequences of intolerance, exclusiveness and confusion of piety with patriotism, are the striking features of Western Christianity.
Jesus' religion was one of love and sympathy, tolerance and inwardness. He founded no organization but enjoined only private prayer. He was utterly indifferent to labels and creeds. ... He did not profess to teach a new religion but only deepened spiritual life. He formulated no doctrine and did not sacrifice thinking to believing ...". [102]

There are many interesting points in this process of orientalizing or rather hinduising Christ and making him fit into the frame of Sanatana Dharma. This reaction of the Vedantists against the western figure of Christ is to be understood in the context of the western colonial dominance of India and the arrogant claims of their supposed Christian spiritual superiority. The authors we have mentioned were also ardent Indian nationalists dedicated to the cause of her prestige, identity and socio-political liberation. Besides, it is also to be mentioned that the true Indian mind has an inherited psychological allergy against dogmatic determinations of religious truth which for them is first and foremost a matter of the experience of the Absolute which cannot be limited to human expressions. The quasi political set-up of the institutional church and the juridical formalism of her hierarchy that claims to represent the humble carpenter of Nazareth before the nations could be understood, with an amount of justification, only as a distortion of the true message of Christ. It is also a fact that in the West the figure of Christ was 'westernized' that for all practical purposes it was largely forgotten that Christ is an oriental and that he can be properly understood only in his oriental context.

It must also, however, be said, that the broad generalizations of the Vedantists ignore the centuries of Christian influence on the development of the people in the West. [103] This long Christian experience should not be lightly ignored in the zeal to re-orientalize Jesus Christ. There had also been great spiritual giants in the western history, not to mention the numerous religious reformers who had been quite authentic representatives of the person and message of Christ.

The distortions which we find in the Vedantists' picture of Jesus Christ also do not help very much to understand the true person of Christ. To see in Christ's 'up-rising' and 'down-sitting' an oriental mystic, as Sen does, is more a play of poetic fancy than an objective approach. The claim that a Vedantin can understand Christ better than the Christians themselves is an affirmation that yet has to be proved. It cannot also be admitted that the voice of Asia, as Vivekananda supposes, has been always the voice of religion and that of the West the voice of politics. The historical data contradicts this statement. The Vedantins are also subject to the error of superimposing their own ideas on the person of Christ, an error which the Vedantins like Swami Akhilananda accuse the western Christianity of. S. Radhakrishnan's opinion that Jesus Christ founded no religious group in his name and that he enjoined only private prayer could be understood only as Vedantic projections.

c. The Advaitic Yogi

The orientalization of Christ attains deeper dimensions in the Vedantic attempt to make out of Christ a mystic of the Sanatana Dharma, a true Advaitic Yogi. By this Christ is not only just oriental, but properly Indian, or more precisely Hindu. Swami Vivekananda sees Christ as an 'Advaitin' who realized his essential oneness with God. [104] He is an example for the realization of man's essential divinity.

Vivekananda considers the Gospel of St. John and especially the thirtieth verse in the tenth chapter as a confirmation of his interpretation of the person of Christ in the advaitic and mystic framework:

> "He (Jesus) had no other occupation in life; no other thought except that one, that he was a Spirit. He was a disembodied, unfettered, unbound spirit. And not only so, but he, with his marvellous vision, had found that every man and woman, whether Jew or Greek, whether rich or poor, whether saint or sinner, was the embodiment of the same undying Spirit as himself. Therefore the one work his whole life showed, was calling upon them to realize their own spiritual nature. ... You are all sons of God, Immortal spirit. 'Know' he declared, 'the Kingdom of Heaven is within you'. 'I and my Father are one'." [106]

Vivekananda maintains that Christ as a Yogi realized the reality of his metaphysical unity with God as the Advaita Vedanta understands it and this self-realization of his true identity was revealed by Christ to his disciples only in progressive stages, starting pedagogically from the ordinary God-experience of the masses reaching the climax in the small group of his disciples. [107]

Whether this opinion can be based on objective biblical evidence is no concern for Vivekananda. He is more interested in finding parallels for the aupanishadic statements: 'Aham Brahmasmi' [108] and 'Tat tvam asi' [109], which are meant to prove the advaitic identity of man with the Absolute. [110] J.R. Chandran's remark on this approach is noteworthy:

> "[Vivekananda interprets the Johannine text] with the assumption derived from metaphysics that ultimately there is no distinction between the Self which was in Jesus and the other individual selves, and that whatever is predicted about Jesus is applicable to each individual self. The New Testament on the other hand starts with the conception that Jesus had a unique relationship with the Father.

When the fourth evangelist says, 'I and my Father are one', he is not expounding the nature of the relationship between the Son and the Father, but affirming that 'Jesus is the object of faith and the organ of revelation and salvation, and that the honour which is paid to him is honour paid to the Father'." [111]

Similarly M.M. Thomas considers the Swami's method of using Biblical texts to prove biblical support for the Advaitic philosophy and spirituality as fully out of context. [112]

Manilal Parekh (1885-1967), a disciple K.C. Sen, says in his book "A Hindu's Portrait of Jesus Christ" that the idea of the Kingdom of God preached by Jesus Christ should be understood within the Indian categories of spiritual oneness with God. Although not in advaita Vedantic terms, Parekh considers Jesus a Yogi, whose power to work miracles can be achieved by anyone through the practice of Indian Yoga. [113] But such practices were not necessary for Jesus Christ. Christ was by his very birth already a Yogi. He writes:

"He was certainly a supreme Yogi, though perhaps not such as the Hindu's have in mind. He had neither known nor followed the technique of Hindu Yoga, but by the grace of God and his complete surrender to Him he had attained that communion with Him which is the goal of all Yoga. He passed long hours every night in prayer, which in his case had attained to the level of the highest communion. At such times he came to know the will of God from day to day, and got power, supernatural power to fulfil the same. Herein lay the secret of his miraculous powers." [114]

Here Parekh maintains that Jesus Christ attained the highest state of divine union that is possible for any Yogi. He also believes that the fasting of Jesus had been an integral part of his Yoga. [115] But there is a marked difference between the ideas of Vivekananda and Parekh. Vivekananda, as follower of the strict advaita of Sankara, considers every man to be essentially divine and the yogic practices lead man to the realization of this inherent divinity and metaphysical unity with the Absolute. Parekh on the other hand does not believe in such advaitic unity of man with God. Jesus as a man, according to him, attained only what is within the limit of every man, namely a spiritual union God. Jesus is a mystic and a yogi, but not God. And Parekh considers the realization of the Fatherhood of God as the specific contribution of Jesus to mankind. [116]

S. Radhakrishnan also considers Jesus as a great mystic who through progressive spiritual realization reached the consciousness of his divine status. This approach is different from that of Parekh and in line with the view of Vivekananda with some modifications. He writes:

> "Jesus spent his life in solitary prayer, meditation and service, was tempted like any of us, had spiritual experiences like the great mystics and in a moment of spiritual anguish, when he lost the sense of the presence of God, cried out, 'My God, My God, why hast thou forsaken me?' ... Throughout, he felt his dependence on God. 'The Father is greater than I' (...) Though conscious of his imperfections, Jesus recognized the grace and love of God and willingly submitted himself entirely to Him. Thus delivered from all imperfections and taking refuge in Him, he attained to a divine status. 'I and the Father are one'." [117]

Here we see how Radhakrishnan tries to synthesize both the schools of Sankara and Ramanuja, which he considers, as we have indicated in the first part, as two approaches to the same reality, as two sides of a single coin. [118] The idea of Jesus as a man who through a long process attained to a divine status, vaguely resembles what Wolfhart Pannenberg later developed in his understanding of Christ. We shall consider this question in the third part of our work. Here we limit ourselves to Radhakrishnan's understanding of Christ as 'a mystic who believes in the inner light'[119] and who had a more universal mind than the exclusivistic and militaristic mentality of his fellow Jews[120].

Swami Akhilananda, following the lead of his Vedantic masters but at the same time showing more understanding for the Western view of Christ, tries also to interpret him 'in a manner suited to fit him into the Hindu structure of Yoga' [121] and advaitic mysticism. Jesus Christ was for him a true mystic or yogi 'because he fulfilled in himself all the three well-known pathways to God - Jnana Yoga, the way of knowledge, Bhakti Yoga, the way of loving devotion, and Karma Yoga, the way of responsible action in the world' [122]. Jesus is a Jnana Yogi in the sense that he removed the veil of ignorance in the world which is the basis of multiplicity and duality. Jesus' emphasis on the love and devotion to God as the first commandment and his service to fellow men especially to the poor and the needy, show him as a Bhakti Yogi and Karma Yogi. [123] Akhilananda does not rule out the possibility that Jesus might have learned Yoga in the Middle East which had been in the influence sphere of Hinduism and Buddhism. But it is more probable, he says, that Jesus had the yogic achievements and powers as an innate endowment:

"It does not make much difference where he learned yoga: the fact remains that the expression of the ... yogas were manifested in His personality. In fact .... He knew God directly .... Jesus did not need to learn yoga from anyone. As he was a born teacher, He was intimately aware of all ways of spiritual life and development. [124]

The God-realization of Christ, for Akhilananda Swami, was not something he attained gradually, in a process that involves great yogic efforts. In this point the Swami differs from the view of Radhakrishnan. The Swami's accent is on the divine consciousness of Jesus as a born mystic. [125] From the first moment of Christ's birth, he had transcended the empirical self or ego. He was living in Samadhi. [126] Occasionally Christ referred to himself as 'I'. But his consciousness of 'I' was at the same time a consciousness of the Absolute, whom he called Father. In this sense Jesus was a supernormal being. [127] As there was no darkness or ignorance in the consciousness of Christ, he was no more subject to the law of Karma [128] and the cycle of 'Samsara' [129]. In discussing the basic divine awareness of Christ, Akhilananda also refers to some of the important works by western authors discussing the psychology of Jesus. [130]

The efforts of the Hindu writers, especially belonging to the Vedantic thought, to interpret Jesus Christ in the categories of an Advaitin, Yogi or Mystic have taken, as we have seen, various forms. What is common to all of them is the desire to universalize Christ, to free him from the geographic and sociological boundaries that belong only to the realm of Maya and to make him quite at home in India, not only just as an oriental teacher or spiritual leader, but as a part and parcel of the Sanatana Dharma itself. This achieves a further and still deeper dimension in the attempt of the Vedantins to see in Christ a Hindu divine Incarnation of Avatar. We shall shed further light on this point in the next section.

3. The Vedantic Christ within the Category of Avatara

The concept of Avatar, strictly speaking, was largely developed by the Vaishnavite Bhakti school that is more at home in the Visistadvaitic school of Ramanuja than in the strict Advaita of Sankara. The reason for that is that 'Avatar' as a divine Descent presupposes the doctrine of a personal God who is transcendent to man and this world. The advaita followers felt themselves compelled to accommodate somehow the Avatar theory because of the great influence of the Bhagavadgita, inspite of the fact that they hold a theory of strict non-distinction between God, man and the world. The neo-Vedantists like S. Radhakrishnan try to make a synthesis between Sankara and Ramanuja. We had given sufficient attention to the different implications of this problem in the first part. A further elaboration of it can be, therefore, at present dispensed with.

There have been efforts in the Vedanta to bring Jesus Christ within the category of Avatar and to see him also as an integral part of the Sanatana Dharma. By this Christ could be made universally available. He will be then no more the unique possession of Christianity. In the Vedantic universality Jesus Christ himself becomes just one among many other Avatars of Hinduism, thus losing all his claims to absolute uniqueness as supposed by Christianity.

As we examine the Vedantic category of Avatar as applied to Jesus Christ our research is limited to its universal application. There have been also Hindus who came to the point of accepting some kind of uniqueness in Jesus Christ as the Avatar par excellence. We will be tackling their positions not here but in the chapter that follows this.

a. Jesus Christ as an Example of Man's Potential Divinity

Sri Aurobindo presumes in his "Essays on the Gita" that the idea of Avatar - he identifies Avatar with Incarnation [131] - is a special property of India, which has held to it from ancient times. Europe has never taken the belief in incarnation properly, he maintains, 'because it has been presented through exoteric Christianity as a theological dogma, without any roots in the reason and general consciousness and attitude towards life' [132] . In India, on the contrary, the religious tradition is quite favourable for the doctrine of Incarnation to take root.

The neo-Vedanta tends to interpret the doctrine of Avatar more in terms of the spiritual and mystical ascend of man than as a strict descent of a divinity from heaven into this world. This mystical character is often present also in the recognition of a personality as an Incarnation. Ramakrishna Paramahamsa, for example, reportedly came to the knowledge of the Avatarhood of Jesus Christ in an experience of mystical union with him. [133]

Vivekananda, the disciple of Ramakrishna, stresses also this mystical process when he says that God is manifested in the one who reaches the state of mystical perfection. He holds that Jesus Christ,as a perfect mystic showed us the way 'to become perfect, to become divine, to reach God and see God, and becoming perfect, even as the father in heaven is perfect' [134] we come to the realization that our true nature is in its essence divine. [135] Therefore it can be legitimately inferred that for Vivekananda God becomes man when man becomes divine! It was in this sense that he understood the Incarnation of Jesus Christ and his implied divinity. In a lectures titled 'Christ the Messenger' and delivered at Los Angeles Vivekananda declared:"If I,as an Oriental,have to worship Jesus of Nazareth, there is only one way left to me, that is to worship him as God and nothing else." [136]

This does not, however, mean for Vivekananda that Jesus Christ is essentially different from other men. He makes his position clear: "God became Christ to show man his true nature, that we too are God. We are human coverings over the Divine, but as the divine Man, Christ and we are one." [137] Here it could be legitimately asked: If man is a covering over the Divine, how could the Divinity be understood in his absoluteness and independence from all limitations? How can the Absolute allow Himself to be in any way so 'covered'? The natural response of Vivekananda as an Advaitin would be that this 'covering' is on the phenomenal level of 'Maya' and thus it does not affect the absolute Brahman. Avatar or divine manifestations also belong only to the level of Maya. So what we see in Jesus Christ is not the absolute Nirguna Brahman who is beyond all manifestations, but only the Saguna Brahman. Vivekananda sees in the 'Logos' of St. John's Gospel a parallel for the Saguna Brahman or Iswara. It is not God Himself but only the Word of God who manifests Himself in Jesus Christ through the power of 'Maya',[138] the creative power of God! [139]

S. Radhakrishnan does not deny the aspect of the descent of the Divinity in an Avatar. [140] But in reference to Jesus Christ he puts more accent on the aspect of man's ascent to the divine status to demonstrate the divine potentialities of man which can be attained by everyone through spiritual discipline: He writes:

> "[The Avatara] is the demonstration of man's spiritual resources and latent divinity. It is not so much the contraction of divine majesty into the limits of human frame as the exaltation of human nature to the level of the Godhead. (...) God descends when man rises."[141]

In our first part we had referred to this point. Radhakrishnan applies this principle to the concrete case of Jesus:

> "Jesus is the example of a man who has become God and none can say where His manhood ends and His divinity begins. Man and God are akin. 'That art Thou - Tat tvam asi'."[142]

Just as Jesus did any man can partake of God's nature and can incarnate Him! By this Radhakrishnan means that Jesus of Nazareth is only an exemplification of the universal anthropological principle of the divine horizon in man and so he has no claims to any kind of absolute uniqueness.

Swami Akhilananda also maintains that eventhough every man is potentially divine, there is some difference between ordinary men and Jesus as an Avatar because the divinity has found its fullest and complete expression in his humanity, which is not the case with every man. The fact that all men are potentially divine does not mean that all are equally divine in actuality. [143] Besides, Jesus is not just an illumined soul like anyone else; as an Avatar he belongs to the special category of illumined souls who are even above 'Nitya Siddhas', born Siddhas, who never need any exertion to reach the level of perfection or God-realization.[144] Unlike the Nitya Siddhas, Jesus was never bound by the laws of Karma-Samsara even in his previous or pre-existent life. [145] So he was not just a 'saint' like other liberated human beings. As an Avatar Jesus Christ could help the human

beings understand 'the real purpose of life and the method of its fulfilment' [146]. At present we do not intend to go deeper into the question
of what Jesus Christ could mean for other human beings; we will be tackling
this question in the sixth chapter.

Swami Prabhavananda also refers to Jesus Christ as an Avatar in his book
"The Sermon on the Mount according to Vedanta". He also tries to give
a Vedantic interpretation to the 'Logos' of St. John:

> "According to the Hindus, Brahman conditioned by maya, his creative
> power (which is the basis of mind and matter), is first manifested
> as the eternal undifferentiated Word. But like St. John, Hindus believe
> that in a special sense the Logos is made flesh in the Avatar - the
> Avatar being the descent of God, whereas ordinary man ascends towards
> God." [147]

Jesus' birth, according to Prabhavananda, was not the result of the compel-
ling force of Karma-Samsara, but the result of free choice, unlike in the
case of ordinary men:

> "When an Avatar is born on earth, he assumes the human body with
> certain consequent limitations, such as hunger and thirst, illness and
> death. But his advent differs radically from the birth of ordinary
> embodied souls. In the words of Jesus: 'We are from beneath; I am
> from above'. According to the Hindu view, ordinary souls are born
> in consequence to their karmas ... in a particular environment, with
> particular aptitudes dictated by the desires and tendencies they have
> created in a previous life. They are products of evolution; they are
> tied by the fetters of ignorance and live under the spell of maya, the
> veiling power of Brahman, which makes the absolute reality appear
> as the universe of many names and forms. They are slaves of prakriti,
> of primordial nature." [148]

In this passage Prabhavananda clearly takes the position that Jesus as
an Avatar is a descent of God and not just an ascent of man. This view
is evidently contrary to the opinion held by Radhakrishnan who sees in
Jesus more an ascent than a descent. Here we should be careful not to
confuse this problem with the question of the difference between the ascending Christology and descending Christology as discussed in the West,
because the distinction between God and man as is supposed in this discussion of the western authors is not relevant for the Vedantic thinkers,
who, in one or another way, insist on the fundamentally divine character
of every man. Keeping this point well before mind we would like to point

out that even among the Vedantic thinkers, inspite of their basic agreements, there are differences in nuances, which may appear as logical inconsistency to an ordinary reader. In the quest for universalization, the main concern of the Vedantists is how to reconcile and synthesize the apparently contradicting positions, which they hope to bring about sooner or later. It may, for example, be asked how it is possible to reconcile the Ascent-concept of Radhakrishnan which involves a long strenous process of gradual realization of one's own divinity, with the Descent-concept of Akhilananda and Prabhavananda who speak of a 'free choice' in the birth of Christ as an Avatar! Such logical inconsistencies are sometimes present in the statements of the same Vedantic author. It must be mentioned that Dr. Radhakrishnan's attempt to synthesize both Ascent and Descent in the Incarnation cannot be considered as quite logical and successful in him. As it is common in almost all Neo-Vedantic authors, there is a conscious effort to accommodate his views to suit the 'taste' of his audience; such accommodations need not always necessarily serve the cause of truth! Such expressions as 'the Hindus believe' used by Prabhavananda are actually only rhetorical generalizations. The word 'Hindu' is a very vast concept as we have seen in the first part. So much has been said by way of remark only to point to the fact that in our analysis, of the Vedantic concept of Jesus Christ we should not insist so much on logical distinctions and academic precisions. The Vedantic effort to 'universalize' Christ presupposes a certain amount of free margin!

b. Christ, One among Many Divine Manifestations

We have already mentioned that while Jesus is considered as an Avatar or Incarnation within the framwork of Sanatana Dharma, what is insisted by the Vedantists is the universal principle of Vedantic anthropology, especially the divine character of man, of which the concrete historical figure called Jesus of Nazareth is only an example. The 'Christ-hood' is a universal principle; one of the embodiments of this 'universal Christ' is Jesus. It is also not necessary to call this universal principle 'Christhood'. In the case of Jesus, of course, it is called 'Christhood'; in other cases this principle may very well be indicated as 'Buddhahood' or 'Krishnahood'. What we want to say is that, while the Vedantists are ready to acknowledge

Jesus of Nazareth as an Avatar they are not ready to grant him any so called uniqueness which might distinguish him from other Avatars within the Sanatana Dharma. This insistence on the equality of Jesus as only one of the Avatars is based, as we have seen in the question of the universal equality of all religions, on the Rgvedic statement: "Ekam sat vipra bahuda vadanti" - One is the truth and the wise call it by various names. The difference between the various Avatars is, therefore, not in principle but only in manifestations, according to the needs of various historical epochs and places. We want to shed more light on how the modern Vedantists interpret this idea. Sri Ramakrishna is reported to have said that 'it is one and the same Avatara that, having plunged into the ocean of life, rises up in one place and is known as Krishna, and diving again rises in another place and is known as Christ' [149] . This was his idea about Christ as only one of the Avatars:

> "There are human beings with extraordinary, original powers and entrusted with a Divine commission. Being heirs of Divine powers and glories they form a class of their own. To this class belongs the incarnation of God like Christ, Krishna, Buddha and Chaitanya and their devotees of the highest order." [150]

It is interesting to note that even Ramakrishna is widely recognized by his followers as an Avatar. Swami Vivekananda, the successor of Ramakrishna considers him as 'the foremost of divine Incarnation' [151] . Even Ramakrishna himself is said to have accepted his being included in the list of Avatars and the similarities that were made between Christ and himself. [152] He considered himself as a divine manifestation which is like a 'round hole' in the wall of ignorance through which one could view and experience the infinite reality that is beyond. [153] Ramakrishna places great importance on 'anubhava' (experience); even in determining the fact of an Avatar the feeling or experience is the most decisive; it has more authority than even Scriptures, religious traditions and dogmatic formulations. It is the spiritual experience of the disciple that brings him to the realization that Ramakrishna is in advaitic identity with Jesus Christ and so equal to him. Ramakrishna also comes to the discovery of himself as identical to Christ through spiritual experience or Anubhava. Anubhava leads to Brahmasaksatkara (God-realization) which is the essence of religion. This Brahmasaksatkara is in advaitic terms the same as Atmasaksatkara (self-realization). [154] Here we are dealing with an important question that is very relevant in Indian Christology. Can Anubhava be the pramana (source or criterion) of an Indian Christology? [155] The 'Khristanubhava' or the experience of Christ on the personal level should without doubt play an important role in theologizing in the Indian context. But, if by Anubhava what is meant is an experience of advaitic equality with Christ, it must be clear from the very start that such an approach will naturally be in line with the Vedantic theologico-anthropological presuppositions, but it cannot be unreservedly adopted and brought into harmony with the original experience of Christ, as we find it in the New Testament and the apostolic tradition. We will tackle this question more thoroughly later on. [156]

Another point to which we would like to draw some attention here is the example of the 'hole in the wall' which for Ramakrishna clarifies the idea of an Avatar. As we have indicated earlier, an example takes over very often among the Vedantic thinkers the role of a proof. If an Avatar is a 'hole' in the 'wall of Maya' giving a view of the Infinite and the Absolute behind this wall, then certainly the possibility of having many such 'holes' in the wall with the same function of showing the Infinite cannot be ruled out. Similarly there can be many Avatars. It is also interesting to note that according to this simile of Ramakrishna an Avatar belongs to the realm of Maya which is the cause of multiplicity. Therefore Ramakrishna's idea of many Avatars does not contradict the fundamental oneness postulated by the Advaita.

Vivekananda also finds reason for the multiplicity of Divine Incarnations in the Maya nature of this world which is in an endless cycle of formation and dissolution.[157] In this world of Maya there can be many manifestations of the Absolute: "The Word has two manifestations, the general one of Nature and the special one of the great Incarnations of God - Krishna, Buddha, Jesus and Ramakrishna." [158] He considers it a great mistake to maintain that only Jesus Christ can be an Avatar or manifestation of God:

"The disciple thinks that the Lord can manifest Himself only once. There lies the whole mistake. God manifests Himself to you in man. But throughout Nature, what happens once must have happened before, and must happen in future. There is nothing in Nature, which is not bound by law, and that means that whatever happens once, must go on and must have been going on .... Let us therefore find God not only in Jesus of Nazareth but in all the great Ones that have preceded him, in all that came after him, and all that are yet to come. Our worship is unbound and free. They are all manifestations of the same Infinite God. [159]

So it is clear that Vivekananda bases his idea of the multiplicity of Avatars on the cosmic law of Karma-Samsara, the law of endless repetitions. In the cyclic nature of history, the historical process is repeated. Jesus of Nazareth who lived in a particular historical context as the Christ, is simply not enough to answer the spiritual needs of another world epoch, which is not a continuation and progress of one and the same history towards a fulfilment, but is just a repetition in the cyclic process. The problem of the Vedantic concept of history in reference to Christology will be dealt with later.[160] Now we want to point only to the fact that the Vedantic denial of the uniqueness of Jesus as the only Avatar and the attempt to interpret him as just one of the Divine manifestations among many others is based on the Vedantic anthropology and the cyclic understanding of history. The Incarnations are for Vivekananda like bubbles - they can be small or big - in a kettle of boiling water, Jesus Christ being just one of these bubbles.[161] Vivekananda's idea of small 'bubbles' and bigger 'bubbles', namely, the distinction between Avatars as small divine manifestations and big, does not fit into the concept of Mahatma Gandhi. For him all incarnations are equal.[162] As long as there are material and spiritual needs in this world, says Gandhi, we cannot be satisfied with just a single Christ somewhere in the past. The eternal and universally valid Christ-principle should be born again and again.[163] The question implied in this opinion of Gandhi is the one regarding the universal applicability and relevance of the particular, historical event of Christ. For Christians of course, Jesus of Nazareth is an ever-living and ever-acting reality of salvation, and not just a dead event of the past. That is an affirmation of the universal, salvific relevance of the particular historical fact of Christ's life that culminated in the events of his crucifixion and resurrection. We do not enter into this question here, but reserve it for the third chapter. Now we want only to indicate that once the universal relevance of the particular event of Christ's Incarnation is not sufficiently taken into account, it becomes plausible that the Incarnation must be repeated to meet the needs of each age, as it is indicated in the case of Krishna in Bhagavadgita. [164]

Ghandi's refusal to accept Jesus Christ as the only incarnate Son of God becomes more evident in his following statement:

> "It was more than I could believe that Jesus was the only incarnate son of God, and that only he who believed in him would have everlasting life. If God could have sons, all of us were His sons. If Jesus was like God, or God Himself, then all men were like God and could be God Himself." [165]

He has no objection to call Jesus God in the Vedantic sense, [166] by which we are all gods. He also admits, as we have earlier seen, a certain distinctiveness for Jesus Christ. [167] But it was too much for Gandhi to accept Jesus Christ as the absolutely unique or the only Incarnation of God as held by the Christians. [168] S. Radhakrishnan also finds no justification in defending the uniqueness of Jesus Christ as the only incarnate son of God. He is rather a manifestation or incorporation of the universal principle of the divine sonship of all men: "The divine sonship of Christ is at the same time the divine sonship of every man." [169] This, however, does not mean that Radhakrishnan and Gandhi come to this conclusion from the same philosophical premises. Gandhi cannot be considered an Advaitin to the extend Radhakrishnan is. Gandhi defends the universal divine sonship of all men more in a moral sense, which is also found in the Vedantic tradition of Bhakti, than in the strict Advaitic tradition of essential unity with Brahman: Aham Brahma asmi!

Radhakrishnan gives some reasons why the uniqueness of Jesus Christ cannot be accepted even as a special manifestation of the Divine in man and why there should be many Avatars: In this world of relativity, first of all, there cannot be a complete and full manifestation of the Absolute. As God is infinite his manifestation as Avatar cannot be limited to a particular place or time. According to the needs of places and times it has to be repeated. Further, the striking similarity between the various Incarnations contradicts the claim of any single Avatar to uniqueness. Finally, the Christian claim that Jesus Christ is the only Incarnate Son of God cannot be substantiated by scriptural evidence. [170] He also examines many concrete examples of elements common to the stories of Jesus Christ, Buddha and Krishna. [171] He declares further: "The hopes and fears of men, their desires and aspirations, are the same on the banks of the Ganges as on the shores of the Lake of Galilee." [172] To affirm the uniqueness of Christ and deny the validity of other Avatars of India would make the Almighty a tribal god who could appear only to the Jews on the shores of Galilee and ignored the Hindus on the banks of Ganges. He writes:

"... it is not easy to admit that God has been partial to a fraction of humanity. He cannot be considered to have favourites. If God is Love, he is the creator of all creatures and must have revealed himself to all. So all revelations [or Incarnations] are to be admitted as having validity." [173]

The Christians, of course, interpret the uniqueness of Jesus Christ and the 'once-and-for-all' character of God's final self-manifestation in the Jewish milieu not in an exclusive sense but in an all-inclusive way, as meant for the whole of humanity, of all times and places. This sacramental understanding of Christ's person has to be stressed in any attempt to interpret Christ's person to India. Still it cannot be ignored that the history of Christianity has been no good witness for this universal understanding of Christ's uniqueness. The Christian understandig of Jesus' uniqueness has been the cause of many a blood shed, as Radhakrishnan implies when he quotes a statement of Aldous Huxley with approval:

"Because Christians believed that they had only one Avatar, Christian history has been disgraced by more and bloodlier crusades ... than has the history of Hinduism or Buddhism." [174]

This statement may not be justifiable especially when we cast a look at the religious riots, social problems and caste conflicts marring the Indian History even up to the present day, inspite of the much preached Hindu universality and tolerance! The weakness and misbehaviour of the members of a religion need not necessarily invalidate the world-vision it preaches.

Swami Akhilananda shows readiness in his "Hindu View of Christ" to accept Jesus Christ as one of the divine Incarnations, but not as the only one. He sees the Christian claim of Jesus' uniqueness as a great problem for the Vedantic mind. [175] Swami Prabhavananda also sees Jesus only as one Avatar among others like Krishna and Buddha. They merely choose different dresses to suit the particular needs of successive ages! [176] The great prophets are the aspects of the Godhead worshipped in different faiths and they are the manifestations of the one underlying truth. [177] There is no reason to consider Jesus Christ as the unique historical event especially

when we consider the identical nature of even the teachings of various
Incarnations.[178] He writes:

"A Hindu ... would find it easy to accept Christ as a divine incarnation
and to worship him unreservedly, exactly as he worships Sri Krishna
or another Avatar of his choice. But he cannot accept Christ as the
o n l y Son of God.Those who insist on regarding the life and teachings
of Jesus as unique are bound to have great difficulty in understanding
them. Any Avatar can be far better understood in the light of other
great lives and teachings. No divine incarnation ever came to refuse
the religion taught by another, but to fulfil all religions; because
the truth of God is an eternal truth. ... If in the history of the world,
Jesus had been the sole originator of the truth of God, it would be
no truth; for truth cannot be originated; it exists. But if Jesus simply
unfolded and interpreted that truth, then we can look to others who
did so before him, and will do so after him." [179]

This is a typical statement of the Vedantic or Hindu view of Christ as
a part of Sanatana Dharma. Swami Satprakasananda justifies the Hindu
hesitation to accept Christ as the only incarnation with his personal interpretation of the Gospel of John 1:14! The Word according to him, is not
just Jesus Christ. The Word stands for the 'cosmic ideation' from which
'all incarnations, all human beings, and all material objects' proceed. This
Word cannot be indissolubly linked with a particular historical form that
appeared two thousand years ago. [181] This Word finds expression many
times over the whole course of existence according to the needs of humanity. He writes:

"In the Hindu view this Word finds expression not just in the form
of Jesus Christ but in Sri Krishna, Buddha, and many others in the
past as well as those yet to come." [182]

This view of Satprakasananda comes suprisingly close to some of the statements of Raymundo Panikkar in his "The Unknown Christ of Hinduism"
which we intend to discuss in the next section.

The Vedantic experience of Jesus Christ as a part of its system is evidently
in contrast to the experience of the followers of Christ within the believing
community called the Church, which considers him as a unique historical
event with universal significance. This rules out the possibility of many
Incarnations, not to mention about their equality. The Vedantic approach
to Christ that stresses the primacy of experience and the lack of historical

anchorage has evidently taken wings in flights of fancy. [183] In the Vedantic Christology there are many subjective assertions which cannot be substatiated and cannot be brought into harmony with the biblical evidence. It must also be said that the Vedantic Christ is a docetic Christ beyond historical limitations! A Jeevanmukta or an Avatar is considered the more perfect the more he stands outside the realm of the laws of this material world. An individual in the state of mystical illumination should even be beyond the experience of pain! [184] Since the Vedantic Advaita identifies reality with consciousness, matter and the body are depreciated as belonging to the realm of Maya. So the Vedantic Christ is in his universality a 'spiritual Christ' without historical and material limitations. His reality is the reality of his 'Superconsciousness'. Even his human existence is unnatural and had to sacrifice this level of consciousness as he had to mingle with people for their good. [185] He had not even human desires and was not bound by limitations whatsoever. [186] Jesus could even give up 'the little touch of human element' at any moment as he was not bound by it! [187] He could not have suffered and died actually. [188] This docetic approach is fully in line with the Vedantic anthropology, but is definitely an 'hinduaised' understanding of Christ. The Divine consciousness of Christ finds universal acceptance among the Vedantins; he is called even 'Trikalajnas' [189] , ie. a knower of time in three periods - past, present and future; Christ's bodily reality, however, is very minimized! It is very strange that eventhough the Vedantins criticize the dogmas of the Christian faith, there is already plenty of dogmas in their 'universal Christ'. [190] Inspite of all the defects we find in the 'Universal Christ' of the Vedantins, it has, however, to be recognized with admiration that they have, with their emphasis on the mystical aspect of Anthropology and Christology, drawn our attention to the importance of Christ-Experience in the process of Christologizing in India, which could serve also as a model for others. The question of Christ-experience will be dealt with in greater detail in the sixth and the nineth chapters.

The above discussion on the 'Universal Christ' of the Vedantins should not prompt us to think that the historical Christ and his uniqueness have remained totally without response among the Hindus, especially those belonging to the reform movements. We will be considering those views in the chapters that follow. For the present we would conclude this section with a quotation from Kaj Baago on how Jesus of Nazareth as the 'Universal Christ' is considered in India no more as a monopoly of the organized Church:

> "The name of Christ, the person of Christ and the teachings of Christ are today an ineradicable part of modern Hinduism. ... It is a peculiar fact of our time that Jesus Christ is no longer the monopoly of the organized Christian Church. He has been taken into other religious systems as well, and even if the organized Church for some reason should die in India, which is unlikely, the name of Christ would still be honoured and his teaching still be remembered among Hindus.[191]

B. THE VEDANTIC ISVARA AND THE CHRIST-PRINCIPLE

We have seen that the 'Universal Christ' of the Vedantins is a 'Hinduised Christ' who fits well into the anthropological presuppositions of the Vedanta. There have been attempts also on the side of the Christian theologians in India to follow suit and to interpret Jesus of Nazareth especially in his universality in terms more appealing to the Hindu elite. Dr. Raimundo Panikkar could be considered as one of the most prominent among them. [192] In general it can be said that the universal Christ of these Indian Christian theologians is a christianized version of the Vedantic Isvara.[193] It must be said at the very outset that the theologians in India who prefer to follow the Vedantic tradition do not as a rule deny the uniqueness of Jesus Christ as a historical figure, but they insist that 'Christ' is more than 'Jesus' and he must be liberated from his historico-geographical particularities to facilitate the Hindu-Christian encounter in India. It must, however, not also be misunderstood that all Christian theologians in India follow this universal approach. We concentrate ourselves for the present on this theme for methodological reasons only.

1. The Christ Unknown

Raimundo Panikkar's "The Unknown Christ of Hinduism" is a work widely read and commented. The title may seem to stand in contrast to "The Acknowledged Christ of the Indian Renaissance" by M.M. Thom as.[194] The contradiction between the 'unknown' and the 'acknowledged' is in reality only apparent; they indicate only the difference of concern in both authors. Thomas tries to stress how 'Christ's confrontation with the heart of India' [195] has contributed to the reform of Hinduism especially in the 19th and 20th centuries and how it has helped the social renaissance of India. His concern is socio-political and gives guide-lines on how Christology should be developed in order to contribute to the necessary social revitalization of India, [196] and how Christologization should be 'situational' or 'contextual'. [197] A similar concern is expressed by Stanley J. Samartha in his work "The Hindu Response to the Unbound Christ" especially in his attempt to give historical and personal anchorage to the Advaitic Christ.[198] R. Panikkar's concern is fundamentally one of Hindu-Christian encounter and peaceful coexistence as J.B. Chethimattam observes:

"The fundamental question [for Panikkar] ... is how Christianity, that claims to be 'the Mystery that God has revealed for the whole world' and Hinduism that considers all religions equal and thus denies the unique character of Christianity can coexist and enter into a meaningful dialogue." [199]

To achieve this end of coexistence and dialogue Panikkhar adopts the Vedantic notion of universal Christ and tries to bring this notion a step forward in the Christian sense. Both Hinduism and Christianity, he opines, do really meet in God, the absolute, the ultimate; but this does not mean that they meet 'in their respective conception of God' [200]. Such a meeting on a 'transcendent platform' is however, according to him, not sufficient for us in our concrete situations; here we need a 'concrete meeting-place'[201]. This concrete or immanent platform of Hindu-Christian encounter for Panikkar is 'the one who is already present in the hearts of those who in good faith belong to one or the other of the two religions' [202]. This one who is already present in the hearts of Hindus and Christians can have various names; 'Christ' being the Christian category for this Presence! This is the methodological starting principle of Panikkar's "Unknown Christ of Hinduism".

a. The Universal Divine Mystery

It is a fact that the title "The Unknown Christ o f Hinduism" [203] has been very much misunderstood even by critics and wrongly interpreted. Panikkar himself draws our attention to this uncritical approach of 'many critics' in his Introduction to the new edition (1979). Many had not taken seriouly the subtleties of the genitive form 'o f'! He writes:

"My main concern was not to speak of a) the unknown Christ of Hindus who is 'known' by Christians, nor b) of the unknown Christ of Christians who is 'known' to Hindus, under whatever form and name. In both cases the genitive is objective. But my primary intention was to speak c) about the 'unknown' Christ of Hinduism, which can be either unknown, or known qua Christ, to Christians and Hindus alike. While in the cases a) and b) the genitive is objective, the title of the book intended to stress c), the subjective genitive." [204]

If this distinction is ignored, Panikkar's work is liable to be grossly misinterpreted. Panikkar's intention is not primarily to speak about the historically unique Christ, Jesus of Nazareth, who is known - even if not acknowledged and accepted - to the vast majority of Indians, but rather he speaks about the universal Christ, who is beyond even Jesus of Nazareth as a historically limited person. This universal Christ is the Mystery of God that was present in Hinduism and in all religions even before the appearance of Jesus of Nazareth and is present in all religions, both implicit and explicit, [205] even if Jesus of Nazareth is neither known nor accepted. He calls this universal Christ the 'unknown Christ' because this universal aspect of the Christ-Mystery is not necessarily realized nor understood (known) as such (qua) either by the Hindus or by the Christians! The question is not about a gnoseological possibility, but about the author's intention to shed light on the aspect of the universality of Christ which is not seriously taken nor sufficiently emphasized especially in Christian theological discussion. Panikkar sees that a universal approach to the mystery of Christ is needed in India to face the Vedantic challenge. The emphasis on the universal Mystery makes Hinduism really 'catholic' (universal) and Panikkar affirms that 'the 'catholicity' of Hinduism calls forth the true 'catholicity' of Christianity, while the truth of Christianity calls forth the truth of Hinduism' [206].

Regarding the presence of the divine Mystery in Hinduism Panikkar writes:

"... there is in Hinduism a living Presence of that Mystery which Christians call Christ (...). (Christ) is not only the ontological goal of Hinduism but also its true inspirer, and his grace is the guiding, though hidden, force impelling Hinduism towards its full flowering. He is the 'Principle' that spoke to Men and was already at work before Abraham. He was present in the stone that Moses struck so unbelievingly, and he acted in Moses himself when he chose to share the life of his people. He may have been called by many names, but his presence and activity were always there." [207]

So, according to Panikkar, 'there is in Hinduism a living Presence of the Mystery which Christians call Christ' [208], and he maintains that since Christ is the ultimate and irreducible symbol he can also be shared by others. [209] He writes:

"... Christ is already present in Hinduism. The Spirit of Christ is already at work in Hindu prayer. Christ is already present in every form of worship, to the extent that it is adoration directed to God." [210]

Christ is present in Hinduism not as a stranger, nor as a foreign matter but he is present in the very heart of Hinduism as its principle of life. [211]

The presence of this living universal Christ-principle in Hinduism is further explained as follows:

"The thesis of the unknown Christ is that, whether or not we believe in God or Gods, there is something in every human being that does not alienate Man but rather allows man to reach fullness of being. Whether the way is transformation or some other process, whether the principle is a divine principle or a 'human' effort, or whether we call it by one name or another is not the question here. Our only point is that this cosmotheandric ... principle exists." [212]

Since there cannot be a plurality of 'Christs' as the universal inner principle of human existence and aspirations, it must be the same Christ who is present everywhere and in all religious aspirations, independent of the fact whether this principle is cleary known as such, and to admit the existence of this universal principle is 'to recognize the unknown dimensions of Christ'[213].

Panikkar tries to make his idea of the universal Christ still clearer:

"This, then, is Christ: that reality from whom everything has come, in whom everything subsists, to whom everything that suffers the wear and tear of time shall return[*1]. He is the embodiment of Divine Grace who leads every Man to God; there is no other way but through him [*2]. Is not this what Christians call Christ? It is he who inspires the prayers of Man and makes them 'audible' to the Father; it is he who whispers any divine inspiration and who speaks as God no matter what form a person's faith or thought may have [*3]. Is not he the light that illumines every human being coming into this world? [*4]:"[214]

Such a Christ cannot be limited to the narrow confines of Christianity. He is also in Hinduism. Panikkar goes even to the extent of affirming that a denial of Christ's presence in Hinduism would also deny his presence in Christianity:

"A Christ who could not be present in Hinduism, or a Christ who was not with every least sufferer, a Christ who did not have his tabernacle in the sun, a Christ who did not represent the cosmotheandric reality with one Spirit seeing and recreating all hearts and renewing the face of the earth, surely would not be ... the Christ of the Christians."[215]

Panikkar is of the opinion that it is the consciousness of the universal presence of the Christ-Mystery that makes many Hindus, who even discover Christ as 'the final stage in spiritual evolution' and as 'the most sublime

Epiphany that has ever existed on earth', not to bother about joining the organized Church.[216]

Raimundo Panikkar also warns us against interpreting his expression "the unknown Christ" as "the hidden Christ":

> "The title does not say The Hidden Christ, as though Christians knew the secret and the Hindus did not. I wanted to lay stress on the presence of the one Mystery (not necessarily the 'same' Mystery) in both traditions." [217]

By this he means that although the universal Christ-Mystery is present both in Hinduism and Christianity, it is not necessarily understood in the 'same' way; each way of understanding can enrich and qualify the understanding of that Mystery. In this sense Panikkar quotes with approval the Rgvedic verse: '(God is) One (though) the sages call it by many names'[218].

It mus, however, be mentioned here that Raimundo Panikkar is also, like some Vedantic philosophers, not always consistent in his statements. For example, he has disapproved in the above quotation the expression 'the Hidden Christ' in favour of 'the unknown Christ'. But later in the same work he uses the word 'hidden' without comment:

> "In the wake of St. Paul we believe we may speak not only of the unknown God of the Greeks, but also of the hidden Christ of Hinduism - hidden and unknown and yet present and at work because he is not far from anyone of us." [219]

In another work he states:

> "... the Christ the Christian comes to proclaim is Christ present, active, unknown and hidden within Hinduism. The same Christ who lives and acts in the Hindu is the one whom the Christian recognizes as Jesus of Nazareth." [220]

It is evident that Panikkar makes here no distinction between 'hidden' and 'unknown'! Vague and uncritical generalizations are also not absent in Panikkar. His reference to the 'Gurus' who accept Christ as 'the most sublime Epiphany that has ever existed on earth' [221] is certainly an exception to the general Vedantic attitue, and cannot be taken - exceptions being admitted - as a common Hindu disposition. We have discussed this point earlier. It is true that Panikkar makes an exertion to support his statements biblically; but his biblical exegesis is an accommodated one and not adequately objective and critical; they are very often even irrelevant! Just one example: Panikkar uses the story of the disciples on the way to Emmaus (Lk 24:13-16) and of Mary Magdalene who stood weeping outside the tomb of Jesus (Jn 20:14); they failed to know and recognize the risen Jesus! But these events cannot be accepted as proofs for 'the unknown Christ' as meant by Panikkar. Really it proves the contrary of what Panikkar would have us believe! [224] The Christ they failed to know and identify was not some kind of universal Christ-principle prevading in all religions including Hinduism, but it was precisely Jesus of Nazareth, the concrete figure of history who died and rose from the dead, whom they failed to recognize at first and later with divine help recognized (Lk 24:31) as the Lord (Jn 20:19). There are many more examples in Panikkar for his liberal use of the Gospels. Notwithstanding such deficiencies it can be said without hesitation that Panikkar has been successfull in stressing that aspect of the Divine Mystery that transcends the limited boundaries of the organized Church.

b. The Mystery and its Name

Here arises a very relevant question: If 'Christ' is a universally present Mystery of God, the Divine Principle, why should this universal principle be designated precisely by the term 'Christ' which is so much loaded by the burden of history, identifying this term exclusively with Jesus of Nazareth? Why not use 'Rama' or 'Krishna' or better a neutral word instead? Is not the generalization of the particular term 'Christ' an arbitrary change of the content of his name? [227]

Panikkar goes very deeply into this Problem especially in his article 'The Meaning of Christ's Name in the Universal Economy of Salvation' [228]. A name, says Panikkar, is not just a sign or a label but 'the real symbol of the thing so named' [229]. He continues:

> "It is a symbol, i.e. the very 'thing' as it appears and is, in the world of our experience. The symbol stands for the 'thing', it is the very standing of the thing, it is the thing as it appears, but this appearance is its proper manifestation, so that the symbol reveals what there

is by the same fact that it clothes and expresses it. (...) The name
is neither merely subjective [because as a name a word must necessarily
have a meaning] nor solely objective. A real name is a symbol and
symbols are precisely such because they are "thrown" from the subject
to the object and vice versa remaining - "swinging" - in the middle,
but expressing all that there is."[230]

Inspite of the objective character of a name, it need not necessarily have
a universal validity because a particular world-view which gives rise to
a particular name is relevant only in a definite historical context. But
at the same time, there can be in a particular language names which have
a universal validity in its content; they are 'common' names which unlike
the strictly 'proper' names are translatable 'by having access to the reality
intended by the name through other sources than the name in question,
so as to be able to establish the equivalence'[231]. In the language of religions, this 'common name' stands for the universal Divine Mystery[232] which
can be expressed in different cultural contexts through names 'particular'
to them. To put it more clearly, the name 'Christ' is a 'common' name
standing for a universal divine Mystery, while the name 'Jesus' is a particular name relevant for a particular people as the embodiment of the universal Christ-principle. So it may be said that 'Jesus' cannot be translated,
but 'Christ' can be; the Christ-principle can be embodied and expressed
also in names other than Jesus. The Mystery is One, the sages call it by
various names! These various names also should not be considered as arbitrary because each authentic name is the result of a long spiritual experience and it 'enriches and qualifies that Mystery which is neither purely
transcendent nor purely immanent'[233].

Panikkar refers to Peter's confession to elucidate the problem of translating
expressions and names from one worldvision to another. "You are the Christ,
the Son of the living God" (Mt 16:16). - How can this statement be effectively translated outside the jewish world of St. Peter? Panikkar maintains
that a literal translation cannot convey the original meaning in India while
the Indian tradition considers that everybody is the son of the living
God![234] He continues:

"If the translation is not made and we do not belong to the semitic
cultural world we may well understand that the Jews had a particular
god and were expecting some saviour and that now he has come, but
we will not relate it to us nor will we be able to give any further

or relevant meaning to that revelation, which we will understand only in its own particular terms ...." [236]

The task of Indian Christology is to translate Christ's name in the Indian Vedantic anthropological frame-work without losing its content. The name of Christ stands as the symbol for a universal Mystery, the Mystery of God's self-manifestation in the cave of man's heart, in the deepest recess of reality. [237] The Christians have rightly called this universally present Mystery of God by the name 'Christ' [238]. Panikkar affirms:

"The Christian, in recognizing, believing in and loving Christ as the central Symbol of Life and Ultimate Truth, is being drawn towards that selfsame Mystery that attracts all other human beings who are seeking to overcome their own present condition. The word 'mystery', though it belongs to a certain tradition, stands for that 'thing' which is called by many names and is experienced in many forms; thus it can be called neither one nor many." [239]

Therefore, the name of 'Christ' stands for the One Mystery of God in His universal manifestation. The name 'Christ' is a symbol that points to this Mystery of reality in the midst of the world. 'It is not that this reality has many names as if there were a reality outside the name. This reality is many names and each name is a new aspect, a new manifestation and revelation of it' [240].

This explanation of Panikkar regarding the name 'Christ' is very essential to understand Panikkar's notion of the 'Universal Christ'. Like the Vedantists he also places his argument on the Rgvedic verse that proclaims the Oneness of Truth or Reality in various expressions. [241] But Panikkar, unlike his Vedantic counterparts, maintains that the difference in the 'names' used to express the universal mystery is not merely subjective in character as if they were just arbitrary; each name has some specificity [242] and objectivity that is proper to a symbol. [243]

From such an understanding of the notion of 'symbol' Panikkar proceeds to justify why he uses the name 'Christ' to stand for 'that centre of reality, that crystallization-point around which the human, the divine and the material can grow', eventhough the same Mystery can also be expressed by such names as 'Rama', 'Kr sna ' etc. [244] . One of the reasons for

Panikkar's preference for the name of Christ is the fact that 'Christ has been and still is one of the most powerful symbols of humankind' that has a great historical background.[245] At the same time Panikkar also insists clearly that 'the historical name Christ should not be confined to the thus-named historical Jesus' [246]. It has been the merit of Christianity to lift Jesus Christ from the narrow confines of Judaism and thus setting in motion a process of universalization that should end in a Christ who is not less than a Cosmic, Human and Divine Manifestation. [247] Such a Christ is un-bound; he is even beyond the limits of Christianity; he is present in the Sruti as a Christ whom Hindus could appreciate and he could in this sense be understood as "The Unknown Christ of Christianity" [248], in so far as the Christians are unaware of the implications of such a presence in the Sruti! It is Panikkar's intention to deepen and enlarge the significance of the particular symbol of Christ especially for a Christian readership.[249] 'Christ' is a non-Indian category. Hinduism, according to Panikkar, has no difficulty to apply to itself the occidential category of 'Anonymous Christians' [250], provided Christians are 'anonymous Hindus', eventhough it makes little sense in the context of the Rgvedig saying: 'One is he whom the sages call by many names' [251]. By this Panikkar implies that for a non-Christian readership, another name could be more useful to explain the Mystery behind the name. But for a Christian readership 'Christ is still a living symbol for the totality of reality: human, divine and cosmic' and for them the symbol of Christ is best suited to understand his totality of reality.[252]

Here a relevant referance could be made to "Die anonymen Christen' of Karl Rahner [252a]. To understand all non-Christians as 'anonymous Chris-tians' is an answer to a problem typical of western Christianity, namely: how the 'christian' salvation could also include the non-Christians? The eastern Christians who accept the western categories also have the same problem. Rahner's solution to this question has also not yet found a un-animous acceptance even among Christian theologians. We will discuss this problem later. [252b] Here we want only to point out the fact that the problem of anonymous Christians exists only when one insists that the univer-sal Mystery of Christ is identical to that of Jesus of Nazareth, the historical figure, who is the unique and ultimate self-manifestation of God and the only mediator between God and Man. But if one holds, as the Vedantins, that 'Christ' is the symbol for a Universal Mystery greater than Jesus and standing behind Jesus and that other symbols also could well be used to express this Mystery, then the problem of gathering the whole of humanity, in one or another way - thematically or unthematically, categorically or uncategorically, explicitly or anonymously - under one and the same symbol or name of 'Christ' is no more relevant: Ekam sat vipra bahuda vadanti! This is, in our opinion, the greatest drawback in Panikkar's Christology: The universal dimensions of the Christ-Mystery is stressed at the cost of what is most specific to Christianity, namely, the uniqueness of Jesus of Nazareth as the Christ, the ultimate and irrepeatable manifestation of the theandric Mystery, the Mystery of God and man. How Panikkar understands the relation between Jesus of Nazareth and Christ will be discussed more clearly in one of the following sections. [253]

c. The Christ-Principle in the Trinitarian Context

Panikkar has a special approach to the Mystery of Christ that is not found in other Vedantic thinkers especially of Hinduism in such an expressed way, namely, a trinitarian approach. The God-experience in every religion, according to Panikkar, is in one or another way trinitarian in character. Trinity is all that God has said of Himself to man and all that man could understand about God in his mystical experiences and reflections. [254] This does not mean that all religions understand the 'trinitarian' character of reality in the same way. It can be said that in his understanding of the Trinity, Panikkar follows the Saccidananda tradition of the Vedanta, modified by K.C. Sen, Brahmobandhav Upadhyaya and other more recent Christian Vedantic thinkers like Swami Parama Arubi Ananda (Jules Monchanin) and Swami Abhishiktananda (Henri Le Saux). We will be discussing these authors in   due time. Panikkar himself developes his trinitarian concept especially in relation to the three Margas in Spiritual experience: Karma Marga is refered to as the spirituality of the Father, the Creator and transcendent God of the Old Testament who demands our obedience; the Son stands for the Bhakti Marga and he should be encountered as the divine Person in Love; the Advaitic Jnana Marga is proper to the Holy Spirit who should be discovered through inner realization. [255] In his book, "The Trinity and World Religions", Panikkar ignores the Saccidanan-da interpretation of the Trinity and stresses on the Marga interpretation, and accepts also the Greek Fathers' image of the source, the river and the ocean: Father is the source of Being, the Son is Being and the Holy Spirit is the Ocean of Being.[256] But, in his "The Unknown Christ of Hinduism" Panikkar places the Christ-Mystery within the context of Saccidananda:

> "... there is nothing but God, a God that as the absolute 'I' has an eternal 'Thou', which is equal to him and which is nevertheless not a second, but always a Thou. This Thou which is the Son, is the whole Christ, including the new heavens and the new earth: all beings participate in this Christ, find their place in him and are fully what they are when they become one with him, the Son. All that exists, ie. the whole of reality, is nothing but God: Father, Christ and Holy Spirit. All that exists is nothing but Brahman as sat, cit and ananda, as being consciousness and bliss, ie. sat as the very suppoert of all that in one way or another constitutes 'being'; cit as the spiritual or intellect-ual link that encompasses and penetrates the total reality; and ananda as the perfect fullness that receives into itself and all that is tending towards it. There are not two Brahmans: nirguna Brahman is saguna, precisely when it is, in the same way that sabda-brahman is parabrahman, precisely when it is said."[257]

It must be mentioned here that the 'I-Thou' explanation of the Saccidanan-da is not characteristic of the Vedanta. Here Panikkar tries to 'christianize' the Vedantic Saccidananda and this attempt is encourageable. Here we see, how 'Christ' as the 'Word of God' or 'Sabda' or 'Vac' is a Mystery within the 'Advaita' or unity of God and not apart from Him. Here we also see how the multiplicity of realities lose their duality in their relation with the 'Christ-principle' and how they enter through Him into the unity or Advaita of the Parabrahman, the transcendent absolute, because 'all beings participate in this Christ'[258]. This trinitarian setting of the Christ-Mystery could be considered as a specifically Christian contribution to the Vedantic 'Saccidananda' concept. Panikkar understands the 'Sabda-Brahman' (the transcendental divine Sound[259]) of the Upanisads[260] and of the Vedantic Philosophy as being equivalent to the 'Logos' (the Word of God) in St. John's Gospel, which was in the beginning with God and at the same time universally accessible. This 'Logos' is 'the larger Christ'[261] who as the 'Vac'[262] transcends the historically limited Jesus of Nazareth. The conscience of men of other religious and ideological persuations is 'the voice of Christ' within them.263 Panikkar writes:

> "We believe that Logos himself is speaking in that religion (Hinduism) which for millenia has been leading and inspiring hundreds of millions of people. Vac, the Logos, is the firstborn of truth and was with the Absolute from the beginning." 264

Whatever God does 'ad extra' is done through Christ. Therefore the recognition of the presence of God in other religions like Hinduism is equivalent to the proclamation of 'the presence of Christ in them', the Christ in whom all things subsist.265 Where 'Logos' is present, where 'Vac' is present, there the Christ-Mystery is also present, present as the universal principle that transcends all historical manifestations. In the context of such a universality, all questions regarding uniqueness are out of place. This Christ-Mystery implies uniqueness because it is universal and cannot be compared with a second. Such a concept of universal uniqueness is not in any way exclusive, but all-inclusive. Panikkar interprets the letter to the Hebrews, Chapter I, Verses 1-3 in this sense: "... the Son has inspired not only the prophets of Israel but also the sages of Hinduism..." 266 This of course is an accommodated interpretation. The Hebrews use the term 'Son' in this context by no means as a reference to the universally present divine Principle; it refers to the 'right to inherit' (cf. also: Mt 21:38; Gal 4:7) the whole creation from God, a messianic and eschatological right that is proper to Jesus of Nazareth as the Christ, who 'has gone to take his place in heaven at the right hand of divine Majesty' (Heb 1:3). Panikkar is also not satisfactorily clear on how the universal Christ-principle is different from the all-present and all-penetrating Spirit of God, the Holy Spirit. Can the 'Christ in Jesus' be identified with the 'Spirit of Christ'?269 This is a trinitarian as well as a Christological question. Such questions cannot be ignored in any credible Christian interpretation of the Christ-Mystery. This Problem is also apparently ignored by some other Indian theologians too, who prefer to follow the 'advaitic' path opened by Panikkar. Klaus Klostermaier, a German promoter of the 'Advaitic Christology', 270 refers to the 'Adhyatmic Christ' (spiritual Christ) in his work, "Kristvidhya: a Sketch of an Indian Christology" 271. 'The Christ is a spiritual reality', he says! 272. To prove his point he refers to Rom 8:4-13; Gal 5:16; and 2 Cor 3:17! It is a typical Vedantic mixing up of Christology and Pneumatology! The Uniqueness of Christ is for him the same as the uniqueness of

Brahman, who is unique not by a pre-eminence in comparison, but by his very absoluteness. [273]   The 'adhyatmic Christ' is in the cavity of human hearts. [274] Klostermaier further identifies 'Sabda-Brahman' with the 'Logos' of the fourth Gospel. [275] What I would like to indicate in this context is that in placing the Christ-Mystery within the trinitarian concept of Saccidananda, one should not forget that a confusion between 'Logos' and 'Pneuma' is to be avoided in an attempt to develope a Vedantic Christology.'

2. Isvara, the Christ

Panikkar uses further the difference in the concepts of 'Brahman' and 'Isvara' to elucidate the notion of Christ. As we have already clarified the notions of Brahman and Isvara in our first part, we do not have to elaborate that point here once again. It has been the chief philosophical problem in the Vedanta to explain the question of unity and multiplicity, stability and change: the unity of Reality called the 'Brahman' and the multiplicity of realities we find in this world.' Brahman is absolute, trans-cendent, without qualities, unknown and unknowable. He is Nirguna.' [276] How can this world of qualities and relations have its origin from the Nirguna Brahman? The Vedantic answer was to find out an immanent, knowable aspect in Brahman, a 'sagunic' aspect full of qualities, which is called 'Saguna Brahman' or Brahman with attributes, who is also called the Isvara, the Lord, the Creator, the God with personal attributes. The understanding of Isvara differs in the advaitic and Bhakti schools. [277] As Panikkar follows to a great extent the 'Advaita' of Sankara, he understands Isvara as belonging to the realm of 'maya'. [278] Isvara is the personal God, the revelation of the Nirguna Brahman and He is existence, consciousness and bliss in the relational sense. [279] Isvara is not another Brahman, but only the personal aspect of the supra-personal Brahman [280] and He is respon-sible for the creation of the world of Maya and its liberation from the bonds of Maya. Isvara, for Panikkar, is the connecting link between the Absolute Deity and the creatures.[281] If this 'link' between Brahman and the world is denied, we will have to deny the existence either of Brahman or of the world which is not acceptable because that would be 'a bold statement that the Absolute is the relative and vice versa' [282]. A direct relation between Brahman and the world, avoiding a mediating 'link', would attribute the qualities and limitations of the world to Brahman and the Absoluteness of Brahman to the world, which is a contradiction in itself.[283] It is to escape this dilemma that we need the mediating Isvara, who can even manifest himself in the world of Maya as Avatars in times of need.[284]

Panikkar sees that his interpretation of the 'Link' between the Absolute Brahman and the world as being supported by the verse of the Taittiriya Upanisad which is the scriptural basis of Brahma-Sutra I.1.2:

> "That from which truly all beings are born,
> by which when born they live
> and into which they all return:
> that seek to understand.
> That is the Brahman." [285]

This Upanisadic verse shortened in the Brahma-Sutra's second aphorism (I.1.2) reads: "Janmadyasya yatah" (Janmadi asya yatah). 'Janma' means 'origin'; it is from the root 'jan', to generate, to beget, to create, to cause. 'Asya' means 'of this', being the genitive form of the demonstrative pronoun. The conjunctive particle 'Yatah' can be translated as 'whence'. 'Adi' stands for whatever can be connected with the word preceeding it (here: Janma) and means 'et cetera'. Panikkar translates this Sutra as follows:

> "Brahman is that whence the origination, preservation and transformation of this world come."

> "Or, shorter: Brahman is the sole and ultimate cause of the world." [286]

Panikkar follows the interpretation of Sankara regarding what is meant here by 'Brahman'. He writes:

> "It is well known that in order to defend the absoluteness of Brahman, Sankara's followers were compelled to say that, properly speaking, it is not Brahman but Isvara who is the cause of this world." [287]

Panikkar admits that Sankara himself is not clear on this point, but in the context of Sankara's whole philosophy he sees the distinction between 'Brahman' and 'Isvara' as quite justifiable, Isvara standing for the 'Saguna Brahman'.

In Panikkar's opinion, the Brahma-Sutra verse, which we have just considered can be given an authentically Christological interpretation or 'Bhasya'. It runs as follows:

> "That from which all things proceed and to which all things return and by which all things are (sustained in their being) is God, but we detect two 'moments' in it: the 'first' is the invisible origin whence the source springs forth; the 'second' is primo et per se not a silent Godhead, an inaccessible Brahman, not even God the Father, source of all Divinity, but in a very true sense isvara, God the Son, the Logos, the Christ." [288]

Panikkar affirms that this Absolute from which Christ as Isvara proceeds is the one source and the ultimate reality. Isvara is distinct from this Absolute; He is the expression (Heb 1:3), the image (2 Cor 4:4; Col 1:15), the revealer (Jn 7:16; 12:45; 14:9), the divine person begotten by God (Jn 1:14, 18, 3:18, 6:46); 'he is equal in nature but distinct in his subsistence and personality' [293]. This is how Panikkar explains the equality of Christ-Isvara with the Absolute, the Father, in nature and their distinction as persons. Panikkar interprets the two natures in Christ-Isvara as follows:

> "This beginning and end of all things has two natures, though they are not in the same mode or on the same level. It has two faces, two aspects as it were. One face is turned towards the Divinity and is its full expression and its bearer. The other face is turned towards the external, the World, and is the firstborn, the sustainer, the giver of the World's being. Yet it is not two, but one - one principle, one person." [294]

This 'nature' that is turned towards the world should not be misunderstood as the human nature of Christ as defined by the Council of Chalcedon. We are still speaking not about the 'Incarnate Christ' but only about the universal Christ-Isvara-principle! It emphasizes only that the role of Christ-Isvara is one of mediation as a 'link' between the apparently opposing poles of the Absolute and the relative. The use of the term 'nature' here is, in our opinion, misleading.

Panikkar himself understands that his Christ-Isvara interpretation has problems when applied to the Christian tradition. So he tries to give a Christian twist to the concept of Isvara. He cannot imagine a Godhead (Nirguna Brahman) in Christianity whose transcendence and absoluteness could be understood as a univocal 'relationlessness' to the creation. So Panikkar maintains that the Vedantic Nirguna Brahman is 'the world's cause and Lord <u>in Isvara</u>' [295]. Isvara, therefore, is not merely a Saguna Brahman or a mere 'modality' of the Godhead. The Christological interpretation of the above mentioned Brahma-Sutra should be understood as 'to indicate a way to what the Christian tradition calls God the Father through God the Son' [296]. In short, the Christ-Isvara 'is not just a mere aspect of the Divine' [297]. This is a great difference between the concepts of Saguna Brahman as Isvara and Christ-principle as Isvara! Panikkar makes the point quite clear in the following passage:

> "... I would say that the Isvara of our interpretation points towards the Mystery of Christ, who, being unique in his existence and essence, is as such equal to God. He is not <u>the</u> God, but <u>equal</u> to him, Son of God, God from God. Moreover, he has a double nature, but these two natures are 'without mixture' and 'without change' and yet 'inseperable' and 'indivisible'. He is more than a mediator, he is in a certain sense, as the 'whole Christ', the whole reality of the World, as far as it is <u>real,</u> ie. as it is - or shall be, if we speak in the framework of time - incorporated in him, one with him, forming one Mystical Body. Thus Christ (Isvara), one with the <u>real</u> World is - shall be, if we include time - one with God the Father so that God may be all in all and nothing remain beyond or beside or behind him." [298]

This explanation of Panikkar is clear and satisfactory except in the fact, that his use of the terms of the Chalcedon definition of Christ's two natures in one Divine Person needs further explanation. I have already refered to the problem of 'double nature' [299] as meant by Panikkar. Panikkar's use of the term 'Mystical Body' is with a special meaning; It stands for the 'Cosmic Mystical Body' of Christ-Isvara, that includes the whole of creation. 'The growth of all things in time is nothing but a fuller realization of their being in Isvara, says the Vedanta, and in Christ, as our <u>bhasya</u> discloses. Whatever degree of reality this World may have, it is produced, sustained and attracted by this divine and human mediator, indicated in the Brahma-Sutra' [300] and the whole of reality (all that exists) is nothing but God: Father, Christ and Holy Spirit. [301] Panikkar concludes his 'Christian' Bhasya of Brahma-Sutra with the following statement:

> "Ultimately, we have but one comment to make: <u>that from which</u> <u>this World comes forth and to which it returns and by which it is</u> <u>sustained, that is Isvara, the Christ.</u>" [302]

This is the basic principle of Panikkar's "Fundamental Christology" which according to him 'would make room not only for different theologies but also for different religions' [303]. He is convinced that such a 'universalization of the name of Christ' will serve the cause of mutual understanding and co-existence between Hinduism, especially in the form of Vedanta, and Christianity. The question, however, still remains: What is the relation between the above explained 'Isvara-Christ-Principle' and Jesus Of Nazareth?

3. Jesus of Nazareth and the 'Christ': The Name and the Supername

With Jesus of Nazareth we come to the 'theohistorical' aspect of Christianity. [304] The Vedantists view with respect and tolerance when the Christians call the universal theandric Mystery of Logos, Vac, or Isvara by the name 'Christ'. But the major obstacle for the Vedanta begins when Christianity further identifies, in a very exclusive way, Christ with Jesus, the Son of Mary. [305] Although it is this identification that characterizes the Christian belief, the Hindus cannot share in this Christian interpretation of 'Christ'.

In Panikkar's view 'Christ the Lord and Saviour is, for the Christian, that Mystery which is unveiled in or through Jesus in his act of faith, which extends far beyond an act of historical memory trusting in the testimonies of his elders' [306]. The Christians affirm that Jesus is the Christ. But, this statement, according to Panikkar, cannot be reversed as 'the Christ is Jesus' because 'Jesus, who is the Christ for Christians, is more - but not less - than Jesus of Nazareth, prior to his resurrection' [307]. He makes this point further clear:

"If Jesus Christ were actually only what the tempospatial coordinates yield, no Christian could speak of the real presence of Christ in the sacraments, nor accept that whatever we do to these little ones we do it unto 'him', nor that he is 'yesterday, today and forever' and much less admit that he was before Abraham, not to say anything about the cosmic Christ of the epistles of St. Paul, of many of the sayings of St. John, his Prologue etc.. If Christ were only that, i.e. a mere reality of the temporal and spatial order, which existed at a certain time in history and had a certain place in geography, the whole of the Christian faith would collapse. No Christian will say that the living Christ of his faith is only a being of the past and no Christian will affirm either, on the other hand, that when he receives Christ in the Eucharist, for instance that he is eating the proteins of Jesus of Nazareth who was walking in Palestine twenty centuries ago." [308]

What Panikkar tries to prove by this passage is that Christ is more than the historically limited Jesus. In reality that is by no means a theological problem as Panikkar may suppose it to be. Any Christian can accept the above statement without reserve. But this statement does not in any way substantiate Panikkar's central thesis, namely, Christ is just a 'christian name' for that universal principle or Mystery, the Logos, the Vac or the Isvara, which can be understood variously and expressed with equal validity in history not only just by Jesus of Nazareth [309] but also by Rama, Krishna and other personalities: "The Christ we are speaking of is by no means the monopoly of Christians, or merely Jesus of Nazareth". [310] Christ Jesus is no monopoly of Christians, it is true; otherwise there would not arise the problem of proclaiming him to all the nations (Mt 28:19). [311] It is also true that the person of Jesus Christ being the 'Logos' has a transhistorical existence, an existence 'even before Abraham' (Jn 8:58), and as the one risen from the dead Jesus Christ is not only yesterday, but also 'today and forever' (Heb 13:8 Mt 28:20, Jn 14:18-21, Heb 13:8). But, that all does not justify the assumption that 'Christ' is just a christian equivalent of Vac or Isvara or even of Logos! [314]

An individual cannot be, according to Panikkar, the exclusive possessor of the Universal Mystery. In this case, what could be the role of the 'individual Jesus? He writes:

> "We may exclude the two extreme views as untenable: On the one hand the view of an individual as universal Saviour and on the other hand the diluting of Jesus as a mere abstract on conventional sign for salvation." [315]

Then how should we understand Peter's affirmation that there is no salvation in any name other that that of Jesus? [316] 'Jesus' is a name; but there is another 'Supername' that transcends all other names' Panikkar explains:

> "This name is 'called the Word of God'. The confession of this name is to say that it is 'Lord'. He did not come for his own glory but to make known the Name of Him who had sent him. Jesus is not the revealed name, but he reveals the Supername." [318]

Panikkar continues:

> "The supername is Word and not just a name, it is Logos and not denomination. 'To all who did receive him [The Word] gave power to become children of God, to those who belive in the name of him'." [318]

In short Panikkar's 'Supername' stands for that universal Mystery which can be expressed, as we have seen, in many ways for eg. as Logos, the Word, Vac, Isvara and so on. 'Christ' of course, is the 'christian way' of expressing this Supername. So from the context of what Panikkar says we can interpret him as follows: 'Jesus' is particular and 'Christ' is universal; 'Jesus' is the name that reveals the Supername 'Christ'. [319]

It must be mentioned that Panikkar's use of the Scriptural quotations to explain his 'name-Supername' theory is too far fetched and cannot stand the test of a critical exegesis. The salvation in the name of Jesus actually refers not to a Supername that Jesus might reveal, but to Jesus of Nazareth himself who is the Christ. Our question here in fact is not about salvation - we will deal with this point in the sixth chapter - but about the person of Jesus Christ considered in himself.

In Panikkar's frame of thinking, we would say, it is quite difficult to explain the unity of the person of Jesus Christ. Jesus Christ is not a Jesus plus Christ, an individual revealing a universal Mystery which is apart from him. Jesus Christ of the Christian tradition is at the same time the revealer, the revealed and the revelation. The Chalcedon definition of the 'Hypostatic Union' was one way of explaining the personal unity of the universal and unbound Logos with an individual. The problem raised by Panikkar's Universal Christ is actually a problem that had long been discussed in the patristic period. It is quite interesting to see how even today the same old problems come up when the same old questions are discussed!

The question regarding the distinction and relation between 'Jesus' and 'the Christ' is also not an entirely new problem. What place can Jesus have in a New Testament Christology? Is the 'earthly Jesus' just an occasion or beginning (Anfang) for Christology as the exeget Meinertz understands or even only a prerequisite (Voraussetzung) for the transition to the Christ of faith (Christus des Glaubens) as supposed by Bultmann.[320] There are even authors like Schlier who demand a complete separation of Jesus from Christology. [321] The problem is that of the continuity of the earthly Jesus with the Christ of faith. A Jesuology is no substitute for Christology. There is a discontinuity between the earthly Jesus and the Christ of the Kerygma; but there is also a continuity - a continuity between the 'particular' Jesus-event and the 'universal' Christ-principle.

Both the above mentioned dogmatic and biblical problems are brought to a new light especially for the Indian Christology by Panikkar's concept of the Isvara-Christ-Mystery. This problem could be tackeled better in the third evaluative part of our work. For the moment we would only point to the fact that the development and contextualization of Dogma and Christology should in no way water down what is most specific to the Christian faith, namely: Jesus is the Christ!

C. THE UNIVERSAL CHRIST AND THE PROBLEM OF HISTORICITY

The question of historicity is a problem intimately connected with the notion of the universal Christ of the Vedanta. As we have already given sufficient attention to the idea of the Vedantic Christ as the universal principle, our intention in this section is to concentrate ourselves in a special way on the historical aspect of the issue. Here we have to keep before mind what we have already said about the Vedantic understanding of history in the first part.

1. The Irrelevancy of Jesus' Historicity

The Vedantic affirmation that it is the one and the same truth, the same universal principle, which is expressed in time and space by various illumined souls and founders of religions according to various needs, discourages any special interest for the historicity of any particular religious leader. The universal is what is important and not its particular manifestations. A historical individual is for the Vedanta important only in so far as he is the manifestation of the universal Mystery.

Jesus is the bearer or revealer of the unbound theandric Mystery which Christians call Christ. The historical particularities of this Jesus have no special relevance for others living in other geographic and historical situations. The historical particularities belong to the realm of 'Maya' which bounds; there is no liberation or salvation (Mukti or Moksa) in history. It is the metahistorial Christ-principle that deserves our attention because this transcendental divine horizon is most intimate and relevant to me as the reality of my own Self. So the Vedantic disinterest for the historicity of Jesus should not be confused with the Bultmannian problematic. The Vedantic attitude in this case is based on its particular anthropology and not on the necessity of the historico-critical approach in the interpretation of the Scriptures.

According to Swami Vivekananda 'unhistoricity' is the sign of the perfection of a religion. In 1893 he said in his famous address to the Parliament of Religions in Chicago:

"Vedanta alone, under some form or another, is fit to become the
universal religion of man. For, while all the other great religions
of the world are based on the lives of their founders, Vedanta alone
is based on principles. It is absolutely impersonal. Its authority is
not affected by the historicity of any particular man." [322]

Usually the lack of historicity is considered a serious weakness while what
is based on principles alone is open to the most subjective and distorting
interpretations. But, there is still a point in what Vivekananda says. Historicity cannot be considered as the last word in truth as if in order to
be true something has to be historical. There are also metahistorical,
philosophical and religious truths. Besides, what is based only on the
'shifting sands of the historicity' of a single individual can crumble down
if that historicity is put in doubt. Vivekananda adds further:

"If there is one blow dealt to the historicity of that life, as has been
the case in modern times with the lives of almost all the so-called
founders of religion - we know that half the details of such lives
is not now seriously believed in, and that the other half is seriously
doubted - if this becomes the case, if that rock of historicity, as
they pretend to call it, is shaken and shattered, the whole building
tumbles down broken absolutely, never to regain its lost status." [323]

The historicity of Jesus of Nazareth is for Vivekananda only a non-essential
or accidental part of the Gospel of Christ:

"We are not here to discuss how much of the New Testament is true,
we are not here to discuss how much of that life [of Jesus] is historical. It does not matter at all whether the New Testament was written
within five hundred years of his birth; nor does it matter how much
of that life is true. But there is something behind it [namely, the
universal principle], something we want to imitate." [324]

The Hindu lack of interest for the historicity of the personality of Jesus
Christ should not also be interpreted as to suggest a lack of concern for
those individuals who incorporated in themselves the universal and supreme
ideals. Quoting Swami Ramakrishna, Vivekananda says:

"Whether ... Christ or Krishna lived or not is immaterial; the people
from whose brain the Christ ideal or Krishna ideal has emanated
did actually live as Christ or Krishna for the time being. It requires
a Christ to forge a Christ. Krishna may be a mythical figure, but
the thinkers who contemplated such an idea and conjured up such
an image were as great and noble as [what] ... they conceived." [325]

Mahatma Gandhi also represented a similar position. He expressed his attitude towards the historicity of Jesus in a Christmas sermon he delivered in 1931 on board ship returning from a political conference in London.[326] He repeated the same later in 1940 in his work "The Message of Jesus Christ":

> "I may say that I have never been interested in a historical Jesus. I should not care if it was proved by someone that the man called Jesus never lived, and that what was narrated in the Gospels was a figment of the writer's imaginations. For the sermon on the Mount would still be true for me." [327]

Following the same line of thought Sri Aurobindo also thinks that it is a mistake to insist on the historical character of Jesus Christ. What is historically true also need not necessarily have a theological value. He writes:

> "Such controversies as the one that has raged in Europe over the historicity of Christ, would seem to a spiritually-minded Indian largely a waste of time .... If the Christ ... lives within our spiritual being, it would seem to matter little whether or not a Son of Mary physically lived and suffered and died in Judea."[328]

S. Radhakrishnan remarks that the historical facts regarding the Life of Jesus were soon covered up by accretions of pious imaginations and legends. [329] The historical focus of these imaginations need not be denied.[330] 'Christ' is a historical judgement on this datum of history:

> "For me the person of Jesus is a historical fact. Christ is not a datum of history, but a judgement of history. Jesus' insight is expressive of a timeless spiritual fact; but what the theologians say of it are after-thoughts, interpretations of the fact..." [331]

The historicity of Jesus is of no special importance and the principle of Christhood he represents is not merely something historical but a universal truth which is being continuously accomplished in the lifes of men through out the ages. In their opinions regarding the relevance of the historicity of Jesus, it can be said, the Vedantists are as a whole faithful to their anthropological and cosmical presuppositions. But it is highly questionable whether they apply this historical detachment to all aspects of their religious views; there is an interest even among these above mentioned scholars to discover some kind of an historical anchorage for the narratives and personalities of the Hindu scriptures. [332]

Raimundo Panikkar believes that this Vedantic lack of concern towards historicity should be taken seriously if the Christians want to enter into any kind of Christological dialogue with the Hindu world. He writes:

"If we start with the historicity of Christ, essential though it may be, we are liable to be gravely misunderstood. Not only is the Christian concept of history some what alien to the Indian mind, but such a concept is in fact a posteriori to the incarnation of Christ. To admit the Christian idea of history, indispensable though it may be for an understanding of the historical Christ, is to presuppose the Christian concept of Christ. ... We should not forget that the first philosophical interpretation of Christ begins with a discourse not on the 'flesh', but on the 'Logos' that became 'flesh'. Most philosophical misunderstandings about Christ and the incarnation from the side of the Indian philosophy, would disappear if Christian theology tried to speak of Christ in a way that might make sense to the partner in dialogue."[333]

Panikkar complains that the western world is by and large influenced by an exaggerated historicism, as though historicity were the sole component of reality. [334] In contrast to a narrow historicism which sees Jesus Christ merely as the centre of human history, placing emphasis on the man Jesus [335], Panikkar proposes to stress the aspect of Jesus Christ as the unique Son of God, the second person of the Trinity, the universal theandric Mystery:

"... when the mystical insight into the theandric nature of Christ weakens and is replaced by a merely historical understanding of the human actions of Jesus, this Christian position (of the universality of Christianity as to embrace every people and religion) appears untenable. When the myth of history begins to take hold of western Christianity, Jesus Christ becomes the embodiment of the supreme Imperium. Incarnation becomes just a little slice of history...."[336]

Panikkar's intention to foster Christological dialogue minimizing the historicity of Jesus Christ and stressing the universal and metahistorical 'Christ-Isvara-Principle' revealed or represented in Jesus, may be useful only to encounter the Hindu elite, but not to meet the ordinary unsophisticated Hindus, in whom also Christ is ever present as an unknown reality. K. Dockhorn makes the following pointed remark regarding Panikkar's position:

"This conscious renunciation of the historical basis (historicity) of the Christian faith, which we find here, is based on a predecision, well grounded in western Christian tradition which chooses to make the supra-historical Trinity its starting point rather than the Incarnation. Panikkar's claim to have a truly catholic and universal basis for dialogue, is in fact the narrowing down of the dialogue to the small metaphysical speculation of an elite, where it is no longer necessary to convert, but only to understand each other in depth." [337]

There are other Indian Christian theologians too who like Panikkar think that while admitting the historicity of Jesus Christ one should put more stress on his supra-historical dimensions. The reasons are almost the same as that of Panikkar for those like Klaus Klostermaier and others who have an advaita Vedantic Approach to Christology. Theologians like Pandi-peddi Chenchiah find a historical concern in Christology to be irrelevant because the Christ Jesus who is relevant for today is the one who has transcended historical limiation and has become 'Paramapurusha [338] and Antharyamin, the universal dweller in the human heart, whom men could invoke to whatever religion they might belong' [339] . Paul Sudhakar, one time philosophy student underDr. Radhakrishnan and a Hindu convert to Protestantism, maintains that the Hindus have already known the Logos and so the Christians 'who have preached so much the Christ of History would do well to see the Christ beyond and behind history in the non-Jewish religions prior to the Christian era' [340] . However, there are also Indian Christian thinkers like Samuel Rayan[341] and Stanley J. Samartha[342] who consider that the 'historical anchorage' of Jesus Christ could be a timely contribution to develope a necessary historical consciousness in the Indian mind.

2. The Meta-Historical Christ

Dr. Raimundo Panikkar makes further attempts to clarify why the person of Jesus Christ cannot be determined and described in mere historical categories. The uniqueness of Christ, for him, is not a historical uniqueness and he warns against confounding the historical singularity of Jesus with his uniqueness. The singularity of Jesus is derived from the factors which provide his historical identification, but his personal identity is something that transcends his singularity. For Panikkar, 'singularity' is not equivalent to 'uniqueness' and 'identification' is not the same as 'identity'.

a. Christ's Historical Singularity and His Uniqueness

Singularity is the particular case of a plurality and there is no singularity if not over against a plurality. A thing has singularity when it is 'in se indistinctum', indivisible in itself or 'atomic'. What is single need not necessarily be individual. The elementary particles, for example, in modern physics are single but they have not individuality. To be an individual, a thing must be besides being singular also be different from others (ab aliis distinctum). [343]A man is fully an individual according to this terminology. But, 'individual' is the opposite of 'universal'. Jesus Christ is, according to the traditional theology, not a single individual in the sense in which historical personages are said to be such. Panikkar explains:

> "(Jesus) Christ has human nature indeed, he is Man, but he is not a human person. He is a divine person, the second person of the Trinity having assumed human nature ... following Chalcedon, it could be argued that Christ assumed human nature as a whole, he did it by assuming a human nature, the human nature of the man Jesus whose human person did not even come into being because that person was subsumed by the divine person of the Logos. In this context Christ is man, but not one man, a single individual; he is divine person incarnated, a divine person in hypostatic union with human nature. The Logos is revealed in Christ, and through Christ man comes in contact with the Logos, but Christ's presence for the believer hic et nunc, is the divine presence. [344]

In other words it can be explained that it is the subsistence of a substance [346] that makes a non-subsistent substance an individual 'Supposit', and if this subsistence is 'natura intellectuali' [347] it is called a person. Since in the case of Jesus Christ, the 'Logos', the second person of the Trinity 'supplies' the subsistence, his person is divine. What is divine cannot fall into the category of the individual and singular in the sense explained above. From this Panikkar argues that since the 'who' or person of Jesus Christ is the unbound and the universal Logos - he can also be called Isvara by the Hindus and Christ by the Christans! [348] - he does not belong to the strict category of singularity because the Logos cannot have a plural. To call single that which cannot have a plural is a contradiction in terms. [349] So it is wrong to say that Jesus Christ is historically singular, if we follow Panikkar's interpretation given above! [350] What is singular is necessarily only one among many.

At the same time it is right to say that Jesus Christ is unique; but this uniqueness is not a historical category. This the uniqueness of the universal all-comprising Logos that is not limited to a particular individual, but is shared by everyone. This uniqueness is the negation of singularity and individuality. [351] The Christ of today is the risen and living Christ; he is unique not because he is particular or singular, not because he is a historical individual perhaps as the best among many, but because he is metahistorical and universal as 'the One without a second'. It is in this sense that Klaus Klostermaier also affirms: "... Christ is unique in the sense in which Brahman is unique, not in the sense in which one among many sons of God could claim uniqueness ... Christ is not 'outside' but 'inside' Brahman." [352]

One could wonder whether the problem of singularity versus uniqueness has to be sophisticated to such an extend. It does not also throw much light on that aspect of Christ's historicity which we are discussing. Our question is not whether one can speak about the Logos or Isvara in terms of historical categories, but whether there is any sense in discussing about the historical relevance of Jesus of Nazareth, whose personality was that of the Logos. Panikkar himself asserts that the man Jesus has something peculiar which does not diminish his humanness but transcends it. [353]Otherwise the result would be an unacceptable docetism. Even as the Incarnation of the Logos Jesus was one individual among many in the whole course of history and that makes it possible to compare him with other individuals in history and thus to come to the notion of a historical singularity. Jesus in his human nature was determined by the tempo-spacial categories, even if his person was that of the Logos and whatever that is proper to the human nature of Christ can be validly attributed to the person of the Logos as the notion of the 'hypostatic union' implies. [354] Therefore, we would maintain that we can also validly speak about the historical singularity of Jesus Christ.

b. Historical Identification and Personal Identity

In connection with the question of the uniqueness of Christ Panikkar makes
also an interesting distinction between the notion of historical identification
and personal identity. Panikkar maintains that the word 'Jesus' has 'two
basicly different meanings: one as a historical category and another as
a personal category' [355]. Identification refers to all those empirical
characteristics which properly speaking do not belong to the person[356]
'The personal identification belongs no more to the person than an identification card' [357]. The identification of a person is made up of all that
we expect from an accurate historical information or a physical analysis
of his bodily or psychological diagrams or even a philosophical scrutiny
of his words and doctrines. Such a historical identification of Jesus, says
Panikkar, is interesting but largely irrelevant:

> "The personal identification of Christ will discover him as an undoubt-
> edly interesting and probably great man in history, but it will not
> allow any living relationship with him whatsoever. The historian mis-
> trusts the believer as the judge is suspicious of somebody witnessing
> for some close relative or intimate friend. The thus emerging know-
> ledge of him cannot be called properly personal but only historical.
> Jesus will appear as an historically relevant figure of the past, with
> a still uncommon influence on the present, but the only point of
> referencewill be his historical coordiantes and the impact on the lifes
> of other men. Ultimately this approach does not discover Jesus as
> a person and any kind of belief on such a level would have to be
> catalogued as mere psychological conviction." [358]

What Panikkar wants to insist here is that the life, doctrines and deeds
of a great historical personality in the past can have a more or less influence on the life of an individual who lives today or in a later century;
his influence on his contemporaries is also of course granted. His influence
can alter my attitudes and the external environment in which I live. This
applies naturally differently with regard to those who have done great
contributions to the welfare of humanity and those who were or are guilty
of crimes against humanity, although we discuss for the moment only
about the former. All the historically interesting factors of an individual,
however, cannot bring another person to a living, loving and thoroughly
personal encounter with him. By these we can admire, follow and also
love a personality of the past, but we cannot enter into a living and personal relationship with him, so that we discover him as a 'part' or rather
pole of our personal being, as one of the many traits that make our person. [359]

By identifying a person historically we make only an external discovery of him and no more.[360]

In contrast to identification, the identity of a person 'refers to the core of the human being present to oneself and to others' [361]. It is that which makes the person to be his or her own self. The identity of a person can be reached only through a living relationship with him, 'which enables one to answer the question of 'who', having discovered that who ('him') within oneself also'[362]. In reference to Jesus Panikkar writes:

> "What makes Jesus Jesus is his personal identity and this personal identity can only be said to be real and thus true if we enter into a personal relationship with him. Only then one may discover the living Christ of faith who lives in the interior of oneself." [363]

The living Jesus of the Christians is the risen Lord. It is not the historical Jesus but the Risen One, the Christ universal and unbound, no more limited to time and space, who as a person can enter into the very structure of our personal existence even today. [364] This person of Christ as our 'Thou' cannot be pinpointed by any unequivocal means of historical identification. Any attempt at such an historical identification is 'the freezing of the ineffable Supreme in one particular object of the senses or of the mind' [365]; that is a sin against the Christ who is beyond all such identification. To identify the Unidentifiable is idolatry! [366] It is a sin against the Spirit!

Shortly said, the historical identification of Christ, however accurate it may be, is simply irrelevant for us because it is something in which we cannot participate, and with which we cannot enter into communion; on the other hand we should be concerned with the identity of Christ as the universally present Logos who transcends all identifiability and is really present in the innermost spiritual aspirations of every man. Because of his timeless and spaceless universal presence every man can enter into a living, personal relationship with him. [367] The 'who', person or identity we seek in Jesus, as maintained by Panikkar, is 'the risen one whom men crucified and whom God made both Lord and Anointed'. [368]

Here we could mark a lack of consistency in what Panikkar says. He speaks about the universal availability of Jesus Christ as the Risen Lord. But this Risen Lord is not just the 'Logos' as he was before the Incarnation. The risen Lord is the same crucified one and we would say that the 'Logos' even in this 'risen state' carries with him into his eternity the 'wounds' [369] and marks of His love-adventure in human history. Therefore, 'Christ' cannot be just the Logos or Isvara or that Universal Principle which, though 'unknown', is present in Hinduism.

As Dr. J.B. Chethimattam observes, it can be said both regarding Panikkar's notion of the universal Christ-principle and the implied problem of historicity that Panikkar's 'main endeavour seems to be to shift the Christian emphasis from the humanity of Christ and Jesus of Nazareth to the Logos, the second person of the Trinity, who by his relation to the humanity is the centre of the universe' [371]. In his reaction against the tendency to make Christ merely a man occupying a singular position in history he goes too far to the opposite extreme, 'almost to the point of denying all value to the concrete and historical humanity of Christ' [372]. Chethimattam reacts rightly against Panikkar's assumption that 'the manifestation of the Logos in the concrete historical individual of Nazareth was not anything unique' [373]:

"The central mystery of the Incarnation is not the divinity of Christ but his humanity assumed by the Logos. If the humanity is reduced to a mere 'theophany' of some value only to the Jews of Palestine and the people of the Mediterranean world and of their various colonies, the Incarnation, the advent of the Son of God into concrete human history loses its central meaning." [374]

Conclusion to Chapter Four

In this chapter we have been discussing that aspect of Christ, the Mystery of Man and Human History, which has found great resonance among the Vedantins especially of the Advaitic - kevala, visista or the synthesis of both as in the case of S. Radhakrishnan - schools. They consider 'Christ' as the universal cosmotheandric principle that is present in every man. By this approach they make Jesus Christ an integral part of the Sanatana Dharma. Jesus of Nazareth for them is a mystic, an illumined soul, a Mahayogi (great Yogin) - one among many others India has seen - who incorporated in himself the universal divine Mystery and thus became like other Avatars a great example for the realization and manifestation of the divine horizon in man. In this advaitic approach any question regarding the historicity of Jesus is irrelevant. History belongs only to the realm of Maya. Jesus as one among many manifestations of the Divinity in the repeating cyclic historical process cannot lay claim to any so called historical uniqueness: 'One is the Truth, the sages call it by various names.'

The Christian theologians who see the advaitic approach as the best suited for a Christology in the Indian context try to face his Vedantic challenge. R. Panikkar may be the best known among them. They consider the mystery of Incarnation as exactly the same as that of the Trinity. What is important for them is the encounter with the Logos achieved in Jesus of Nazareth. The Logos can also have various other names. Christ is the name under which the Logos is known to the Christians. The historicity and uniqueness of the Incarnation is watered down. The manifestation of the Logos in the concrete historical individual of Nazareth was not anything unique because every being is a Christophany. These theologians also maintain an attitude of Vedantic detachment towards history; it is the metahistorical principle that matters and is relevant for the whole of humanity in all times and places, and not merely its historical and particular manifestation in one or another place or time.

The notion of the universal, cosmic, unbound and metahistorical Christ serves, of course, to 'liberate' Christ, as they maintain, from the monopoly of Christians. But is must be said that in this Vedantic approach there has been an arbitrary addition and change of connotations in the name 'Christ' which cannot be substantiated by the original Christian tradition based on the direct Christ-experience as transmitted in the New Testament. The Vedantic non-historical and spiritual approach also does not do justice to the humanity of Christ. The arbitrary distinction between Jesus and the Christ-principle points to this unhappy and theologically unhealthy tendency.

What we have seen so far is only one of the tendencies in Indian Christology. There is also another theological current in India which takes seriously Jesus Christ in his totality and historical uniqueness. It must also be said that those theologians who follow the advaitic approach need not by that very fact deny the uniqueness of Jesus of Nazareth as the Christ. It is more a matter of emphasis on a particular aspect. We deal with the other aspect of the historical uniqueness of Jesus considered in himself, in the next chapter. As the above chapter is concentrated on the question of Christ's universal presence, the following one looks at Jesus Christ in the aspect of his being the fulfilment of the transcendental aspirations of humanity in person.

CHAPTER V

JESUS CHRIST FROM THE POINT OF VIEW OF HIS HISTORICAL UNIQUENESS

In this chapter our accent is shifted from the unbound and cosmotheandric principle to its concrete human manifestation, from the metahistorical Trinity to the Incarnation of the Son of God within the limitations of human history, from the universally present and available Isvara-Logos to the personality of Jesus Christ as the unique fulfilment of the spiritual aspirations of mankind and as the tangible and most sublime realization of the transcendental or divine horizon in man. It is a shift from the Universal to the Unique!

The historical uniqueness of Jesus Christ as the incarnate Son of God belongs to the specificity of the Christian Faith (Heb 1:1-4). The word 'unique' is not to be understood in the following discussion as applied to the metahistorical Logos which we have already seen in the previous chapter. R. Panikkar's distinction between 'uniqueness' and 'singularity' is also not applicable in this chapter. Shortly said, we deal now not with a universal principle but with the concrete historical personality of Jesus Christ as understood and interpreted by Indian thinkers, both Hindus and Christians.

An interest for the historical personality [1] of Jesus Christ developed on the Hindu side especially among its theistic reformers of the 19th century. Raja Rammohan Roy [2] who founded the Hindu 'aggiornamento' movement called 'The Brahmo Samaj' [4] can be considered a pioneer in this field. Keshub Chunder Sen [5], and Pratap Chunder Mozoomdar [6] are the most prominent among those reformers who followed the Raja's lead. Brahmabandab Upadhyaya and other later theologians like Aiyadurai Jesudasan Appasamy, Vengal Chakkarai, Pandipeddi Chenchiah and Richard V. de Smet - to mention only a few [7] - have tried to look at the person of Christ from a more Christian point of view. Our intention in this chapter is not to give an exhaustive narration of what the Indian thinkers have so far contributed, but rather to analyse critically the most significant Indian theological approaches towards the historical personality of Jesus Christ.

A. Jesus Christ, the Ultimate within the Bounds of Human History

Here we are encountering a Christological trend that is evidently in contrast with the approaches of the Neo-Vedantins which we have discussed
in the first chapter. Ramakrishna, Vivekananda and Radhakrishnan were
the representatives of a Hindu reform movement which is characterized
by a revitalization of the Hindu orthodoxy, opposition to Christianity
and missionary efforts and an attempt 'to rival and imitate the Christian
Churches in order to bolster up, modernise and propagate Hinduism' [8].
In their concept of 'Sanatana Dharma' and 'Sarva Dharma samanatva'
there could not be absolutely any place for the uniqueness of the historical
personality of Jesus Christ. But, the Neo-Vedanta should be considered
as a kind of 'counter reformation' against the Hindu reformation that
was begun earlier by Rammohan Roy who was predominantly social and
ethical in character.[9] These reform movements owe their inspiration largely
to the Christian values[10] and western secular culture[11] which began to
influence Indian thinking in a more radical way than before towards the
beginning of the 19th century. The monotheistic reformers especially
of the Brahmo Samaj were very positively disposed towards Christ. Many
of them were convinced that the 'person of Christ reveals the ultimate
within the bounds of human history'[12]. The intensity of their response
to Jesus Christ was also different, as we shall shortly see, from person
to person.

1. The Sonship of Jesus Christ

It can be said that among the Hindu reformers of the 19th century it
was Rammohan Roy who for the first time put stress on this particular
aspect of Jesus' personality. By this he does not, however, concede any
divine status to Jesus but considers him as the most sublime among all
the creatures of God. Roy's concern was not so much the person of Jesus
as his moral and ethical relevance for mankind. In this section, however,
we concentrate on the former aspect reserving the latter for the third
chapter. In order to understand properly his approach to Christ it is necessary to cast a look at the theological context which shaped his views.

a. Monotheism and Incarnation

Rammohan Roy was basicly a rationalist. He applied himself to the study of the sacred writings of all major religions and came to the conclusion that these books are to be interpreted solely under the guidance of reason. He insisted that the original teachings of the Sacred Upanisads is not pantheism, monism or polytheism but strict monotheism.[13] In this he seems to be more in line with the Islamic concept of monotheism than the Christian one. [14] He could not accept the Christian trinitarian monotheism and the Incarnation of the Son of God as being conformable to pure monotheism. His rejection of Hindu polytheism made him very suspicious of the doctrine of the Trinity. He was convinced that to include Christ and the Spirit as 'Persons' in the one God-head was a reversion to something primitive and was a yielding to the polytheistic trends of Greece and Rome in the early centuries. It is also clearly a turn from the strict monotheism of Judaism[15] and the original teaching of Jesus Christ. He observes:

> "Disgusted with the puerile and unsociable system of Hindu idolatry, and dissatisfied with the cruelty allowed by Musalmanism against non Musalmans, I, on my searching after the truth of Christianity, felt for a length of time very much perplexed with the different sentiments found among the followers of Christ (I mean the Trinitarians and the Unitarians, the grand division among them) until I met with the explanation of the unity given by the divine Teacher himself as guide to peace and happiness." [16]

Rammohan Roy was in touch with the Unitarians in England and America and like them rejected Trinity as tritheism. [17] He was also against the Hindu doctrine of Avatara and considered it only as mere superstition, mythology and idolatry. To call Jesus an Incarnation of God is to fall into the same error. On this attitude of Rammohan Roy the following observation is made by Kaj Baago:

> "The real reason [for the Raja's rejection of the doctrine of Incarnation] was his aversion to Hindu mythological avatarism. He saw, what the missionaries could not see, that Jesus would simply be understood as another avatar if Christianity was presented in the traditional western garb. A story about a saviour who was born under miraculous circumstances, who performed supernatural deeds, who was put to death, but cheated his enemies and came to life again, - would fit in excellently with the Vishnu Puranas and would be well received on the level of popular Hinduism. However, this would be at the cost of the unique message of Jesus which India needed." [18]

Rammohan Roy himself considers it a great service rendered to human reason if we could root out the imaginary faith in the incarnation. [19] In Roy's monotheistic concept there can be only one God who can receive our worship. He does not deny that the only God can manifest his will to mankind through a messenger or mediator like Jesus Christ and that the title 'Spirit of God' could be applied to His influence. [20] Unlike the Advaita Vedantins, Rammohan Roy practically ignored the fourth Gospel as favouring pantheism by making Jesus Christ equal to God. [21] His preference is for the Synoptic Gospels and the moral teachings contained therein. It is evident from the attitude of Rammohan Roy that the Christian presentation of the doctrine of the Holy Trinity had not been made satisfactorily to the Hindu intelligentia of the 19th century. His theological controversy with the Baptist Missionary of Serampore, Dr. Marshman did not also help very much to clarify the issues. Marshman's arguments were very apologetic and not sufficiently founded. [23] It is quite understandable why Roy in his concern to purge Hinduism of its notorious idolatry and polytheism on the popular level could not tolerate the doctrines of Trinity and Incarnation as being irreconcilable with strict monotheism.

b. The Problem of Christ's Divinity

It is strange to see that Rammohan Roy had no difficulty to accept the elements of miracle in Christ's life. He found that it does not cause much problem in a land that believes already in many miracles. He does not deny the doctrines of the Virgin Birth of Christ and his Resurrection, but insists that they are not to be given much importance and warns against giving personality to the Holy Spirit which would involve 'the Godhead's having had intercourse with a human female' [24]. The miracles are according to Roy no proofs for the divinity of Jesus Christ.

Rammohan Roy denies Christ's divinity on the same ground that he is against the idea of an Incarnation. The very fact that Christ is inferior to the Father shows that he cannot be God. [25] He asks:

> "Is it conformable to the nature of the Supreme Ruler of the universe to take the form of a servant, though only for a season? Is this the true idea of God ...? Even idolators among Hindus have more plausible excuses for their polytheism ... both of them being equally and solely protected by the shield of mystery." [26]

In this controversy with Rammohan Roy, Dr. Marshman had elaborated seven arguments which are supposed to prove the deity of Jesus: Ubiquity, incomprehensibility, authority in forgiving sins, claims to almighty power, status of being the final judge of the world, his acceptance of worship and the fact his name is included in the formula of baptism. [27] Roy had no difficulty in rejecting all these arguments from the authority of the Scripture itself. He gives his own exegesis of Philippians 2:6 and makes a distinction between 'being God' and 'being in the form of God'. The fact that Christ is in the form of God does not mean that he is God. As he takes also the 'form of a servant' the term 'form' cannot be considered as involving the essence because it is impossible to reconcile the concepts of Godhead and servitude in the same essence.[28] The name 'Son' found in the baptismal formula should be, according to Roy, understood as expressing the created nature of Christ, eventhough he is the most exalted of all creatures.[29] Rammohan Roy could understand the relationship between Jesus and God only in terms of subordination and inferiority. He argued to have support for his position in John 5:19., 8:28., 10:17-18., 12:49., 14:31., etc. and ignored John 10:30., 14:10., etc. as incredible.[30] On the basis of the dependence of Jesus on God and his subjection to him Rammohan Roy denies the identity of Christ with God. [31] Roy thought that to apply the term 'God' to Jesus Christ in a literal sense and to consider him as God in human shape would 'acknowledge the same intimate connection of matter with God that exists between matter and the human soul' [32] . To suppose matter in God is tantamount to reducing Godhead to the level of creation. Roy maintains that Jesus himself has never raised any claim of being equal to the almighty God. The statements which may apparently sound so must be interpreted according to him, in the general context of Christ's subordination to God.[33] If Jesus Christ is the Son, he can have only an existence originating subsequently to that of his own father.[34] Rammohan Roy is ready to grant Jesus Christ any degree of pre-eminence among all the creatures, but Christ remains for him always a creature and not the Creator. [35]

234

c. Jesus Christ, the Son of God

To call Jesus Christ by the title 'the Son of God' does not mean for Rammohan Roy that he is God.[36] 'Son' stands for the special and unique relation that existed between God and Jesus. As a creature Jesus is dependent on God and as the first born of every creature he alone deserves to be called 'the Son of God'.[37]

The expression 'the Son of God' refers not to any kind of identity of being. 'I and my Father are one' (John 10:30) is to be understood as describing 'a subsisting concord of will and design'. Whoever saw Jesus 'witnessed proofs of the entire concord of his words and actions with the will and design of the Father'[38]. This should be the interpretation of John 14:9. Any literal interpretation leading to an advaitic conception of the unity of Jesus and God is rejected by Rammohan Roy. Even a trinitarian interpretation of Jesus' Sonship does not, according to Roy, do justice to the monotheistic concept of the One God. The oneness of God and Jesus is the oneness of harmony of will and purpose.[39] It can be asked: If Jesus is only a creature like others why should he be given the exclusive title 'the Son of God'? Jesus is, according to Roy, the Son of God in the sense that he is the 'highest of all the prophets', the Messiah. This title is most suited to Jesus because 'his life declares him to have been, as represented in the Scriptures, pure as light, innocent as a lamb, necessary for eternal life as bread for temporal one, and great as the angels of God or rather greater than they'[40]. Jesus Christ has been the unique among all the creatures, attaining the ultimate within the possibilities of a creature. It is in this sense that Jesus Christ is the first born of all creatures and not in a chronological sense. Rammohan Roy accepts the notion of the pre-existence of Christ but gives it his own interpretation.[41] First of all the pre-existence of Christ is a created pre-existence. Pre-existence does not make him equal to God. Roy argued that the peculiar attributes of God like supremacy, omnipotence and omniscience were never ascribed to Jesus in the Scriptures. He sees an irreconcilable mixing up of natures in Jesus Christ if he had already a divine nature before his earthly appearance:

"Supposing Jesus was of two-fold nature, divine and human ... his divine nature in this case, before his appearance in this world must be acknowledged perfectly pure and unadulterated by humanity. But after he had become incarnate ... was he not made of a mixed nature, God and man, possessing at one time both opposite sorts of consciousness and capacity? Was there not a change of a pure nature into a mixed one?" [42]

The history of the Council of Chalcedon shows that this problem raised by Roy is not something new to Christianity. What Roy wants in the above passage is to criticize a merely literal understanding of pre-existence. The real pre-existence according to Roy belongs not to Christ but to God from whom Jesus Christ has a temporal origin. Jesus himself speaks of his coming from God and going back to God (Jn 5:28., 6:62., 13:36., 16:7). So pre-existence of Christ refers to his origin from and dependance on God as the creator and not to his eternal identity with the deity. In this sense we could also speak of a pre-existence of all creatures in a certain way in the creator but this expression has special relevance in the case of Jesus Christ as he is the first born of all creatures, not in a chronological sense of course, but in the sense of his supremacy above all creatures including the angels. [44]

As we have noticed above Rammohan Roy could never imagine how the eternal and almighty God could be limited to matter; that is the reason why he could not accept the doctrines of Incarnation and the divinity of Jesus Christ. Roy's stress on 'the natural inferiority of the Son to the Father' [45] is clearly an Arian position. The power of Jesus and his pre-eminence among creatures are not intrinsic to Jesus as his right but are delegated from God as gifts. It can still be asked which rational basis can the Raja render in granting Jesus a unique position among all creatures! His answer is clear: the moral sublimity of Jesus' personality and his teachings make his claim to uniqueness credible. [46]

2. Jesus Christ and the Divine Humanity

The positive approach towards the person of Jesus Christ initiated and encouraged among the Hindu elite by Rammohan Roy and the Brahmo Samaj was further developed and brought to greater perfection by Keshub Chunder Sen who joined the Samaj in 1857. But his strongly pro-Christian and anti-Hindu leanings compelled him to leave the original Brahmo Samaj (Adi Brahmo Samaj) and in 1867 he founded his own Samaj under the title 'Brahmo Samaj of India'. The cult of Sen's personality that unhappily developed in this Samaj[48] led to a further split; the dissenters called their Samaj the 'Sadharan Brahmo Samaj' which reverted to the ideals of the Adi Brahmo Samaj.

The Brahmo Samaj of Sen was more Christian than Hindu; it assimilated deep Christian values and laid stress on a more emotional mode of worship.[49] Sen can without doubt be described as a Hindu who came surprisingly very near to the person of Christ. This becomes especially clear in his endeavours to found a new religious group centred on Christ in which he hoped to bring together all the good elements in all religions. This eclectic religious group was given the name 'the Church of the New Dispensation'. He made the ideals of the new Church clear in one of his messages:

> "The Church universal hath he (God) already planted in this land, and therein are all prophets and all scriptures harmonized in beautiful synthesis.... Let Asia, Europe, Africa and America with divine instruments praise the New Dispensation, and sing the Fatherhood of God and Brotherhood of man." [50]

As it is clear, Sen's attempt was to eradicate the abomination of religious differences and sectarianism under the Christian principles of God's Fatherhood and human brotherhood. Therefore, there is a major difference between Radhakrishnan's idea of a universal, eclectic [51] and syncretic [52] religion and the Church of the New Dispensation of Sen. Unlike Radhakrishnan, Sen places the unique personality of Jesus Christ at the centre of his system. The Christological ideas of Sen sometimes appear to be inconsistent; this is mostly due to the progressive growth of his ideas. Towards the end, his ideas were much nearer to that of Christianity than they were in the beginning, so he had to modify later on some of his original views. This background has to be kept in mind in order to understand properly Sen's Christology which had later exercised significant influence on Indian thinkers like Pratap Chunder Mozoomdar, Justice Pandipeddi Chenchiah and others.

a. The 'Pantheism' of the Will

One of the main problems that Sen had to confront in his attempt to reform the Hindu mentality was the Advaitic pantheism of the Vedantins which refused to accept any substantial distinction between God and man.[53] The only form of pantheism Sen could admit consisted not in man's identity of being with God but the surrender and conformity of man's will to the will of God. Against the Advaitins he writes:

> "Let the Indian pantheist behold God everywhere and everything in him, but let him also ... accept the distinct personality of manhood, and by seperating himself from Divinity, learn that the only way to bridge the gulf between God and man is not the total absorption of the human in the divine essence, but to so surrender self that for once and ever, his will may coincide with the Divine will."[54]

Sen finds support for his position in the Gospels and in the person of Jesus Christ. Jesus is essentially man. There is an eternal distinction between man and God which cannot be removed by advaitic fancies.[55] Eventhough pantheism, according to Sen, is very prevalent in India, it does not prevent India from approaching the true person of Christ. For that, however, it is necessary to elevate Indian pantheism to the pantheism of Christ which consists in the union of man's will with that of God which is expressed in obedience, humility and love towards God. This peculiar pantheism purifies man and makes him divine in his humanity - Divine Humanity - without any presumption of equality with God. His words:

> "I do not mean that you should adopt pantheism as it exists in Hindu books. Far from it! ... Christ's pantheism is a pantheism of loftier and more perfect type. It is the conscious union of the human with the Divine Spirit in truth, love and joy. The Hindu sage realizes this union only during meditation, and he seeks unconscious absorption in his God, with all his faults and shortcomings about him. His will is not at one with the will of God. But Christ's communion is active and righteous; it combines purity of character with devotion. Hindu pantheism in its worst form is pride   being based upon the belief that man is God; it is quietism and trance. Christ's pantheism is the active self-surrender of the will. It is the union of the obedient, humble and loving son with God." [57]

It must, however, be said that Sen's conception of pantheism as the common mode of thought in India is a bit exaggerated. Even the Advaita Vedantins interpret often the aupanishadic saying 'Aham Brahma asmi'[58] in the sense of a total dependence of man on God in his being; it is more a stress on the divine horizon in man and cannot be interpreted as to mean: 'God is man'. It cannot also be denied that there is a pantheistic interpretation for 'Aham Brahma asmi', but that is not so predominant as Sen would have us believe.

Self-will (ahankara) is, according to Sen, the greatest obstacle for man to realize his real union of will with God which finally results in the 'Divine Humanity'.[59] It is in this sense that he understands the meaning of John 10:30: 'I and the Father are one'. By this, so maintains Sen, Jesus means his deep communion of will with God and 'he is humanity pure and simple in which Divinity dwells'[60]. His union with God is not metaphysical or material but is moral and spiritual; it is mystical and not hypostatic. It is not a dreamy mysticism that encourages quietism but an active mysticism that consists in doing the will of God:

> "In the midst of activity, Christ was absorbed in God. Eating or drinking, preaching or going about doing good, his spirit always enjoyed serene communion. There was no pride in him, for he was dead to self. There was no dreamy mysticism in him, for he was always engaged in doing the will of the Father."[61]

At this stage of Sen's Christological reflections it is difficult for us to understand why he considers Christ so unique as to invite his countrymen to accept him putting aside their traditional beliefs.[62] If the uniqueness of Jesus Christ consists only in his total and unreserved conformity with the will of God, can it be called unique at all? Every man has the possibility to reach such a stage of human perfection which Sen calls Divine Humanity! Such questions are legitimate especially when we go through the initial lectures of Sen where his stress is on Christ's union of will with God. This is the starting point. In his later lectures, as we shall shortly see, he had greater reasons to maintain Christ's uniqueness.

Pratap Chunder Mozoorndar,[63] a close associate of Sen, also shared his idea of the pantheism of the will especially in reference to Jesus Christ. For him, Christ lived, loved and taught in God and he was 'swimming' in the ocean of Divinity, as this visible universe of ours swims in the might and majesty of God'[64]. But Christ is not God, rather Christ is in God by the submission of his will to the Divine will. If that union can be called 'pantheism' Mozoomdar sees no difficulty in accepting such a pantheism of the will:

"The Divine Spirit permeats every pore of matter and of humanity, and yet is absolutely different from both. (...) There is no beauty, no wisdom, no faithfulness, no purity, no piety and self-sacrifice that is not inspired by him. The goodness of all the good is a ray of reflection from him, the greatness of all the great points to his throne on high. If this is pantheism the Brahmo Samaj is not ashamed of it.... If this be mysticism, the Brahmo Samaj is proud of it. It is eminently the spiritual instinct of India." 65

The person of Christ is also, according to Mozoomdar, to be understood within this concept of the immanence and transcendence of God. Christ is not the almighty God; that would be monistic pantheism! Such a vision of the unity of man's nature with that of God is repudiated by him; the real unity should be that of thoughts, wishes and deeds which are according to the holy will and eternal wisdom of God. 66 Such a unity of the will was realized in Christ's life. 67

Aiyadurai Jesudasan Appasamy, 68 a bishop of the Church of South India, also represents similar views regarding the person of Christ and his relation to God. This relation cannot be explained as 'homoousios', the sameness of substance or nature. The unity between God and Jesus Christ is moral and not metaphysical, 'a completeness of harmony in thought and purpose' 69 as is illustrated in the story of Gethsemane. He surrendered his will entirely to the will of God and that is the essence of his oneness with God 70.

The notion of the 'pantheism of the will' was introduced by Sen and his school with two intentions: it stresses the deep communion that existed between God and Christ on the one hand, and on the other hand it insists that inspite of his greatest possible union, Jesus Christ is not simply equal to God. We should interpret, according to this view, the consciousness of Jesus regarding God as his Father in this background.

b. God, the Father and Christ, the Son

"I and the Father are one" (John 10:30). This statement regarding Christ's consciousness has been interpreted by the Advaita Vedantins in the sense of 'Aham Brahma asmi' as to mean the fundamental divine character of every man of which Christ is presented as an example of realization. Such an interpretation is not acceptable to Sen. For him to present Christ as God is to present him as the Father which is a contradiction. Jesus Christ is not God but the Son of God; because of his total surrender of the will to that of God his relation to God attained the status of Sonship. He is Son not by nature, but by the total conformity of the will. This conformity is so strong and deep that the relationship between God and Jesus Christ can be validly described as Father-Son relationship; 'it is the union of the obedient, humble and loving son with the Father'[71]. To speak of Christ as God is in reality to postulate a second God. In this Sen is fully in line with Rammohan Roy, to whom we have referred in the last section.[72] Sen's reactions are quite understandable especially in the Indian context where he wanted to fight the religious distortions of idolatry and superstition which were prevalent especially among the ordinary people. The idea of Avatar presents God in human form. To say that Jesus is God is to identify him with the Father, the only God, and to make an idol out of this ineffable God.[75] What India needs is not a new avatar, 'the absolute perfection of the divine nature embodied in mortal form' or 'the God of the universe putting on a human body - the infinite becoming finite in space and time' but a true idea of the Incarnation which would mean the true self-manifestation of God in humanity. It is not so much God becoming man as God in man.[76] That is the true meaning of the 'Son of God'. This is the glad tidings that India so badly needs. But on the contrary, if the Christian missionaries 'conceal the truth that Christ is the Son of God, our divine Brother, and present him to our people as an incarnation of the Father, appearing on earth as the Father'[77], they are enemies of Christ and enemies of God and enemies of India. Such a Christ would not be the real Christ, but the anti-Christ.[78]

The understanding of the person of Jesus Christ as the Son subordinated to God the Father through the conformity of his will with that of the Father is common to both Rammohan Roy and Sen. But there is also a difference in the approach of Sen that is not found in Roy. Sen does not stop at the concept of Christ as 'the Son of God'; he proceeds further and nearer to the person of Christ and sees a great influence of the Sonship of Christ on his human existence. Unlike Rammohan Roy Sen goes a step forward and sees the humanity of Christ as 'the Divine Humanity' [79]. We will consider this point in greater detail in the next section.

Sen's idea regarding the subordination of Christ to God as Son to Father is also shared by A.J. Appasamy. Like Roy and Sen he also rejects an Advaitic approach to the person of Christ. Appasamy is very sympathetic towards the philosophy of Ramanuja and the Bhakti tradition. Regarding the Johannine words: 'I and the Father are one', he writes:

"This utterance has appealed to the religious heart of India which, because of the monistic point of view so largely familiar to it, has defied all reasonable laws of exegesis and has interpreted the passage to mean that Jesus, always one with God, realized in a luminous moment this supreme identity. But we must remember that Jesus always lived in whole-hearted trust and faith in the Father. He did not consider Himself as identical with God." [80]

Jesus' Sonship, according to him, 'as set forth in the synoptic Gospels points to the supreme importance of a life lived in close fellowship with God' [81]. He explains the notion of Jesus' Sonship further:

"Jesus ... had no experience of identity in His relation with God. He did say, 'I and the Father are one', but in the light of other statements in the Gospel, we cannot interpret these words to mean identity. They rather indicate a completeness of harmony between Him and God in thought and purpose." [82]

It is clear from the above passages that our authors share the concern of Rammohan Roy to fight polytheism, idolatry and superstition at the popular level and monistic pantheism at the level of the Hindu elite. This concern certainly deserves great respect. Their refusal to acknowledge Christ as equal to God must be understood in this general context of their theological presuppositions. We have seen that Sen accepts Christ as the Son of God and his humanity as the Divine Humanity, without making Him, however, equal to God. He rules out the possibility of a second God. [84] Here we can notice a certain misunderstanding on the part of Sen regarding the Christian position. Christianity does not preach a second God as Sen would suppose. The main concern of the Council of Nicea was precisely to explain the Divinity of Jesus Christ without postulating thereby a second God. [85] The Council of Chalcedon specified the faith further by trying to show how Jesus could be both God and man without diminishing either of the two.[86] Patriapassianism is a position that had long been disapproved by the Church.[87] Inspite of all the disputes and problems regarding the dogmatic formulations within the categories of a particular philosophy and culture, [88] it has to be admitted that the content of those formulations are still normative for the Christian faith.[89] Manilal C. Parekh, [90] a disciple of Sen and later a convert to Christianity points to the confusion of thought and misunderstanding Sen had regarding the Fatherhood of God and the Sonship of Jesus Christ:

> "The Christian Church has never said that Christ is the incarnation of the Father; and to say so has been considered by it a heresy. Unfortunately Keshub made so sharp a distinction between the Father and the Son that he forget that father and son are correlative terms and ... it is the sonship of Christ which makes the Fatherhood of God possible and vice versa. The Christian dispensation was nothing but a fuller revelation of God himself.... The Christian revelation is the revelation of the Fatherhood of God, through the life of sonship of Jesus Christ." [91]

This criticism, however, is not applicable to A.J. Appasamy in the same sense. For him Jesus Christ cannot be equal to God not because he is just a man, whose will is in full conformity with that of God but because he is the incarnation of the 'Logos', who although from all eternity co-exists with God, is inferior to him so much so that the identity betwen God the Father and the Son is not one of nature but one of the will resulting from his obedience and submission to God. [92] Appasamy's view may be roughly categorized as 'Monotheletism' in a semi-Arian sense, while Sen is 'Monotheletist' in an adoptionist way. [93]

c. The Divine Transparency of Christ's Sonship

Every man has the duty to submit his will to that of God. Every man can be considered, especially in the context of Indian philosophy, as a son of God because every man reflects the Divine Light to some extent.[94] A prophet or a religious leader who manifests the spirit of God can, according to Sen, even be considered as an incarnation. [95] Since they combine in themselves the heavenly and the earthly they are certainly above ordinary humanity. [96] If so, it can be asked, in what way can Sen justify the absolute uniqueness he attributes to Jesus as the Son of God? [97] Sen himself gives the answer:

> "Because Christ announced himself as such.... Had he never felt it he would never have said so. Therefore we are bound to believe it.... It seems remarkable that [neither Moses nor Socrates nor Buddha] ever put forth the slightest pretension to sonship. Each was verily a son of God, and a worthy son too, but not the Son of God. That honour was reserved for the prophet of Nazareth. Each had his peculiar and distinctive mission. One interpreted law, another self-knowledge, another tranquility, another love and so on. Christ came to represent sonship. That was his mission - to reveal the harmony of the human and Divine will in the son." [98]

So, according to Sen, the claim of Jesus to Sonship based on his experience and conviction is not just a claim to the sonship that every man has, but it is a claim to his uniqueness as the Son of God. This claim of Jesus to uniqueness as the Son is quite credible because he proved it by his complete self-surrender to the will of God whom he considered as his Father and his example of self-surrender has never been surpassed by anyone in human history so much so that he could say that he who sees him sees God the Father. [99] Sen thinks that the Humanity of Christ underwent a process of 'kenosis' resulting in a 'plerosis' by which the Divinity filled the 'void' in him. His humanity was made divine, without his becoming a second God. Jesus' assertion, 'I and my Father are one', must be understood so. He writes:

> "When I come to analyse this doctrine I find in it nothing but the philosophical principle underlying the popular doctrine of self-abnegation.... Christ ignored and denied his self altogether.... He destroyed self. And as self ebbed away, Heaven came pouring into the soul (because) nature abhores a vacuum, and hence as soon as soul is emptied of self, Divinity fills the void. So it was with Christ. The Spirit of the Lord filled him, and everythin was thus divine within him." [100]

Sen does not accept the doctrine of Christianity which affirms that Christ is God. Christ, for Sen, is divine because his humanity was gradually divinized. His divine humanity, however, does not mean that it makes a 'deity' out of him. [101] Sen recognizes that it is difficult to explain the

relationship that exists between God and Jesus Christ because it is mysterious. [102] The notion of 'Divine Humanity' is, according to him, the best
suited to understand this relation:

> "Christ   truck the keynote of his doctrine when he announced his
> divinity before an astonished and amazed world:' I and my Father
> are one' .... Were it not for this bold assertion ... I would not honour
> Christ as much as I do. Half the beauty of Christianity would be
> marred and obliterated if the principles involved in this important
> doctrine were eliminated from Christian theology." [103]

It is his conviction regarding Christ's divine humanity that prompted
Sen to call upon all Indians to believe in and accept this 'child of God'. [104]
He considers also that Jesus' humanity is worthy of the highest reverence
and worship because it is, unlike in the case of any other man in human
history, touched and inspired by Divinity. [105] As Jesus Christ is due to his
Divine Humanity above every other human being and next only to God
h e is worthy of the maximum reverence after God. This indicates how
high the uniqueness of Christ is for Sen. His view is also shared by P.C.
Mozoomdar who sees Jesus Christ as the perfect embodiment of the
relationship between God and man: "God and man became one, not in
transcendent idealism, but in actual visible reality." [107] Mozoomdar also
does not admit that Christ is equal to God. A.J. Appasamy considers
that the divine transparency of Jesus Christ reached such a climax that
'God revealed Himself to men through the human body of Jesus' [108].
For him Christ's body is fully human, but in this body God dwelt as the
'Antaryamin', inner controller. He considers 'Logos'   as immanent in
all human beings, but only in Jesus Christ he is incarnate. The Incarnation
of the Logos in Christ makes 'unique' his universal immanence. [109] He
maintains,however, that in the historic Christ we do not see all there
is of God; he 'does not exhaust all the infinite grandeur of God' [110].
So the divine transparency of Christ is not an exhausting transparency
but a transparency that indicates the incomprehensibility of the Mystery
called God.   His humanity is divine, but he is not equal to God. Through
him 'we sweep the heavens and realize the inaccessible depths with all
their mystery, stretching to we know not where' [112].

In this section we have seen how K.C. Sen, P.C. Mozoomdar and Appasamy
see and evaluate the uniqueness of Jesus Christ and his personality even

without recognizing his equality with God. Christ stands for what is ultimate within the sphere of man and his history. Christ's human existence reached a divine level through the conformity of his will and desires with that of God. In Christ this was not a ready made conformity, but the result of a process, an evolution that belongs to the level of the Spirit. In the next section we shall consider how some of the Indian theologians see the mystery and person of Jesus Christ within the context of evolution.

3. Christ within the Context of Evolution

The scientific theory of evolution had a significant influence on the Christological views of Keshub Chunder Sen. He maintained that corresponding to the natural evolution there is also an evolution in the whole of nature and especially in man on the level of the Spirit. This concept of evolution in Sen, however, should not be confused with the Advaitic idea regarding man's growth towards the realization of his innate divinity. K.C. Sen is clearly not an Advaitin; he insisted on the theistic transcendence of God and the natural and fundamental distinction of man from God.

In this section we can note a further development in Sen's Christological ideas. In the beginning of his reflections Sen could see Jesus Christ only as an ideal man whose will was fully in conformity with the will of God. Later on he sees Christ as 'the Son of God' even if he is not equal to God and describes his humanity as Divine Humanity. Now we notice a still further development in Sen's views; he attributes even pre-existence to Jesus Christ. This is the pre-existence of a sublime 'Idea' in God regarding the whole of creation. Sen calls this 'idea' in God by the name of the 'Logos' which he places within the mystery of the Holy Trinity! According to the evolutionary view of Sen, this Divine Idea in God regarding the whole of creation undergoes a long process of development in this world of creation and reaches the climax of this evolution in Jesus Christ as the Divine Humanity. Sen's evolutionary approach to Christology has been later shared to some extent by P.C. Mozoomdar and especially by Pandipeddi Chenchiah.

a. The Pre-Existence of the Logos

"Truly, truly, I say to you, before Abraham was, I am" (Jn 8:58)! This claim of Jesus is given serious consideration by Sen. If Jesus's words are worthy of credibility we have also to examine what Jesus means by his claims to an existence even before his earthly appearance. Sen distinguishes an 'uncreated Christ' and a 'created Christ'. The uncreated Christ is an 'idea' in the plan of God and the created Christ is the temporal realization of this supreme idea. He explains:

> "Did he (Jesus) not say distinctly, 'Before Abraham was, I am'? How then, and in what shape, did he exist in heaven? As an Idea, as a plan of life, as a pre-determined dispensation yet to be realized, as purity of character, not concrete but abstract, as light not yet manifested .... In fact Christ was nothing but a manifestation on earth, in human form, of certain ideas and sentiments which lay ahead in the Godhead.... Before the world was, the Eternal God existed, and in His bosom slept Jesus, or rather the ideal Jesus (...) Christ existed in God before he was created. There is an uncreated Christ, and also the created Christ, the idea of the son and the incarnate son drawing all his vitality and inspiration from the Father." [113]

So, according to Sen, there is a beginning for the earthly life of Jesus Christ, but his divine life which consisted in the divine Idea [114] could not have a beginning because 'holiness assuredly has no beginning; wisdom has no beginning; love can have none; truth can never commence to exist ... these existed through all eternity in God Himself. Whatsoever is good and true is co-eternal with God. Though the human Christ was born, all that was divine in him existed eternally in God' [115] .Sen compares the life of Christ to a circular stream that has its beginning and end in the same sea. God is that sea.[116] The eternal idea in God, when manifested, becomes the Word of God, the Logos, that created the universe. Creation is actually 'the wisdom of God going out of its secret chambers and taking a visible shape'; it is God's 'potential energy asserting itself in unending activites' [117]. This Logos becomes fully manifest in the long process of cosmic evolution in Jesus of Nazareth. [118]

For Sen also the Logos is a universal principle [119]; but unlike the Vedantins he maintains that this universal principle attained a unique expression in Jesus Christ. As a universal principle the Logos is present in the whole of creation; not only in human beings and in the depth of their consciousness[120] but even in animals, in all stages of life, instinct and intelligence the uncreated Christ dwells as the Logos. [121] All that is 'true, good and beautiful in the life of humanity' belongs to the Logos. 'Thus all reason in man is Christ-reason, all love is Christ-love, all power is Christ-power' [122]. Thus every human being is a 'partaker of Christ' [123] . We are all little christs as we all participate in the eternal idea of God; we all belong to the process of the evolution of this eternal idea, but this process attained its ultimate perfection and realization only in the Divine Humanity of Jesus Christ! [124]

It is in this context of the pre-existence of Christ as the Logos that K.C. Sen develops his theology of the Holy Trinity which he calls 'the loftiest expression of the world's religious consciousness' [125]. It is clear that Sen does not consider the Trinity as a communion of three persons in one nature; he considers such an idea as tritheism. Trinity, according to him, represents the three functions or aspects of one and the same God. His approach is modalistic. He sees the Vedantic concept of Saccidananda most suited to explain the mystery of the Trinity:

"... the Trinity of the Christian Theology corresponds strikingly with the Sachidananda of Hinduism. You have three conditions, three mani- festations of Divinity. Yet there is one God, one Substance and three phenomena. Not three Gods, but one God. Whether alone, or manifest in the Son, or quickening humanity as the Holy Spirit, it is the same God, the same identical Deity, whose unity continues indivisible amid multiplicity of manifestations.... They shine one into another ... they mingle in synthetic unity, and are lost in the dazling radiance of the Supreme One ... the true Trinity is not three persons, but three functions of the same Person." [126]

Corresponding to the Trinitarian concept of Father-Son-Holy Spirit or Sat-Cit-Ananda, Sen sees also the possibility of other parallels: the Creator- the exemplar-the Sanctifier, the still God-the journeying God-the returning God, 'I am' - 'I love' - 'I save', Force-Wisdom-Holiness, True-Good-Beauti- ful! [127] Sen compares the Holy Trinity to a triangular figure at the apex of which is God the Father whom he calls also Jehova and 'the Supreme Brahma of the Vedas'. From this Divinity the Son or the Cit comes down as an emanation and permeats the whole of creation and especially the humanity. The emanated Divinity carrying up the humanity to the Father is the Holy Spirit.[128] This reminds us of neo-platonic and gnostic theories that influenced the Christian thinking in the first centuries. Although

Keshub Chunder Sen 'had really arrived at a point which is in a way within the compass of Christianity' [129], it must be said that there are certain inconsistencies in the Trinitarian doctrine of Sen. Manilal Parekh, one time disciple of Sen, accuses him of being at times inclined to Arianism and at other times to semi-Arianism. Sen considers the Logos at times as an emanation from the Divinity, at other times as the Father's begotten Son, a child, a creature! He also equates the Son, the Logos to an Idea of God that is co-eternal with God. [130] All these inconsistencies, in our opinion, should be traced to the change of views in Sen due to the development of his Trinitarian and Christological ideas in the course of time.

b. Evolution of the Divine Humanity

In the view of K.C. Sen, creation is not just a single act but it is a continued process. This process has its beginning in the 'Logos', which is the creative Word of God. Every thing originated from 'the one creative fiat'. The Almighty Word, the Logos, took visible shape in creation and as 'the dormant will stirred itself there came forth world after world leaping out of the bosom of God.... That voice, once uttered, has ever since rolled backward and forward ... creating fresh forms of life and light, east, west, north and south'.[131] Sen continues:

> "... a continued evolution of creative force, a ceaseless emanation of power and wisdom from the Divine Mind.... His speech, His Word, a continued breathing of force is creation." [132]

The theory of natural evolution ends in a natural plane; but evolution does not end with this nature. It even goes beyond this nature leading humanity to the realm of Divinity. [133] The ascending scale of creative evolution is also, according to Sen, represented in the Hindu mythology of Avatars. 'The Hindu Avatar rises from the lowest scale of life through the fish, the tortoise and the hog up to the perfection of humanity' [134] ending up in the Divine Humanity of a Purna Avatar. This crude representation of spiritual evolution manifested in the Avatar myths is fully verified in Jesus Christ. As the source and beginning of creation is the Logos, so also the end of the creative process in evolution is also the Logos as a plan fully realized in Jesus Christ:

"Logos was the beginning of creation and its perfection too was the Logos - the culmination of humanity in the Divine Son. We have arrived at the last link in the series of created organism. The last expression of Divinity is Divine Humanity. Having exhibited itself in endless varities of progressive existence the primary creative force at last took the form of the Son in Christ Jesus." [135]

P.C. Mozoomdar also, like Sen, sees the uniqueness of Jesus Christ in the fact that he is the apex on the scale of human progress. He is the 'type of all humanity' [136] and 'he is the human centre and bond of union in the religious organizations of mankind' [137]. Mozoomdar writes:

"He (Jesus Christ) was as no other man ever was or shall be: this is his uniqueness. Christ is unique, not because his flesh was born of a virgin, but because he was the unity of all those who had preceded him in the divine order of humanity ... Christ is unique because in him the unity of all these shapes of divine excellence was first effected. Therefore we call him the Son of Man, and the history of the Christian religion is the history of the progress of humanity." [138]

The deep significance and value of these words regarding the uniqueness of Christ becomes for us all the more evident when we realize that neither Sen nor Mozoomdar ever belonged to a Christian Church. Inspite of the fact that they never accepted Logos' consubstantiality and equality with God, they recognize Jesus Christ as the most perfect manifestation of the divine horizon in man that can ever be realized within the spatio-temporal limits of the human history! It can be affirmed without hesitation, as J.N. Farquhar observes, that the right religious experiences of Sen (and Mozoomdar) came from Christ [139] and S.K. Datta is fully correct when he opines that the nearest approach to a distinctly Indian interpretation of Christ has come (for the first time) from the non-Christians like Sen and Mozoomdar! [140]

c. Jesus Christ, the New Creation

Sen's idea of evolution in explaining the Christ-Mystery is carried a step forward by Justice P. Chenchiah. [140a] He also rejects the application of Avatara categories to Jesus, according to which God assumes the human nature for a limited period for a particular task like a 'Deus ex machina'. For Chenchiah Jesus Christ is first and foremost a man and he finds the title 'Son of Man' most appealing. [141]

He does not accept the pre-existence of a second person in the Holy Trinity. Jesus Christ, for Chenchiah, is not equal to God. [142] In this he agrees with Sen. But unlike Sen Chenchiah affirms that Jesus Christ is also not merely a man; the harmony of God and man in Jesus Christ has resulted in a new phenomenon which is neither God nor man but is an entirely New Creation![143] Chenchiah writes:

> "The fact of Christ is the birth of a new order in creation. It is the emergence of life - not bound by Karma; of man, not tainted by sin, not humbled by death; of man triumphant, glorious, partaking the immortal nature of God; of a new race in creation - sons of God." [144]

Jesus Christ, according to Chenchiah, is a totally new step in the process of evolution. The uniqueness of Jesus Christ consists in this 'Newness'.[145] This is not just a rebirth in God or a perfection and realization of the innate human potentialities. It is the result of a 'new and tremendous creative act of God' [146]. Since Christ is a totally new creation he can very well be called the 'adi-purisha', the original man. [147] In Jesus Christ God 'translated the idea of a new man into a fact of history and projected Him into the arena of life' [148]. Chenchiah explains further the evolutionary 'newness' that is realized in Jesus:

> "Jesus stands to man as man stands to the animal ... [Man] not only fulfils but also transcends the lower creation. Jesus is not God or man, the 'Son' - Son of God or Son of Man - He is the product of God and man, not God-Man. The Spirit of God overshadowed Mary and Jesus was born. He is a new creation - the Lord and Master of a new creative branch of Cosmos. He is the Son of God because the Spirit of God entered Him. He is the Son of Man because He was born out of the Mother of man - the female. He transcends us as we transcend animals. Reason is our differential, the Holy Spirit is His." [149]

Here it must be remarked that the Holy Spirit, according to Chenchiah, is not the third person in of the Blessed Trinity, but he is the 'vital energy' that was in action in the evolutionary process that results in the New Creation. The Holy Spirit is Jesus himself in his universal aspect as the 'indweller' in human hearts who enables every man to share in the 'New Creation' belonging to the species of 'the Sons of God'. [150]

In the new creation that is Jesus, as viewed by Chenchiah, a fusion between God and man takes place resulting in something that is quite different from God and man. He writes:

> "God is God, Man is Man. The twain have met in Jesus: not merely
> met, but fused and mingled into one. Hinduism always longed for
> a state in which we could say, as Jesus did, 'I and my father are
> one' - which was our Lord's affirmation of the Brahma Vakya Aham
> Brahmasmi ... In Jesus it was, for the first time in history, an accom-
> plished reality, not an unrealized aspiration." [151]

It is clear that this view of Chenchiah is not in agreement with the definition of the Chalcedon[152] which explicitly rules out 'confusion and change'
in Jesus Christ who is truly God and truly man. We can also note Arian,
semi-Arian and Apollonarian overtones in Chenchiah,[153] although we cannot
identify the views of Chenchiah with any of the heresies of the first centuries. It is also questionable whether an evaluation of Chenchiah from
the standpoint of a totally different category and frame of thinking is
justifiable! Chenchiah does not 'play' the game of hellenistic theology;
if so how can he be expected to keep its 'rules'? He is faithful to the
rules of 'evolutionary thinking', to the categories of mutation and newness.
But the question still remains whether these notions can be applied to
the totality of the Christ-Mystery without contradicting its basic supposi-
tions, namely, the Divinity of Christ and the graduity of God's salvation
which is realized through him in this world! An evolutionary approach
to Christology is of course not something new. P. Teilhard de Chardin,
Karl Rahner, Wolfhart Pannenberg, J. Moltmann and many other theologians
have differently interpreted the notion of evolution in reference to Christ
- as cosmic, anthropological, historical or eschatological as the case may
be. The evolutionary views of Sen, Mozoomdar and Chenchiah could be
categorized as belonging to one or another of these groups. It is true
that our authors recognize in Jesus Christ a 'Divine Humanity' and a 'New
Creation'; but all that still remains on the level of man, as the realization
of the ultimate human possibilities within the bounds of history. Inspite
of all the qualifications which affirm the absolute uniqueness of Jesus
Christ, he is not God!

In the next section we shall see how some other Indian thinkers approach
this question regarding the person of Christ and his uniqueness as the
God-Man.

B. The Mystery of Divine Incarnation: Jesus - God and Man

In the fourth chapter we have seen how the followers of the Vedantic philosophy interpret the divinity of Jesus Christ in a metahistorical and universal sense. Jesus Christ for them is only one among many possible manifestations of the 'cosmotheandric' principle. As it is clear, this approach does not do justice to the uniqueness of Jesus Christ as the incarnate Son of God. We have also seen how those Indian thinkers who insist on the historical uniqueness of Christ find it difficult to acknowledge his equality with God. In this section we shall analyse those authors who see the uniqueness of Jesus Christ precisely as the historical manifestation of the metahistorical God. They try to explain in the Vedantic categories what it means to say that Jesus is God, that he is man and that he is God-Man!

1. The Divinity of Jesus Christ

Any explanation of the divine character of Jesus Christ in the Indian context has to be done within the frame of thinking that understands God as the trinitarian Saccidananda. [154] A truly Christian interpretation of Saccidananda places also the historical and unique realization of the Christ-Mystery within the mystery of the Holy Trinity.[155] In contrast to the view of Raymundo Panikkar we maintain that the approach to the Mystery of Christ has to be historical as well as trinitarian.

a. 'Saccidananda' and the 'Cit-Logos'

The first serious attempt to give a thoroughly Christian interpretation to the Vedantic notions of 'Brahman' and 'Saccidananda' was made by Brahmabandab Upadhyaya (1861-1907). [156] He holds with the Vedantins that there is only one Essence from which all things proceed and that is Brahman. 'Brahman is Being Itself. He alone is identical with His own Being while creatures have no right of being, but have a merely participated and dependent existence' [157]. He identifies the Vedantic understanding of 'Brahman' with the scholastic definition of God as 'ipsum esse subsistens' and rejects all monistic and pantheistic interpretations. He is a theist and is convinced that the Christian faith of the triune God corresponds exactly to the Vedantic Saccidananda. He writes:

"We can boldly and safely affirm that (the) Vedantic conception of the nature of the supreme Being marks the terminus of the flight of human reason into the eternal regions. The Catholic belief is exactly the same. God is the only eternal being; He is purely positive for the particle 'not' cannot be predicated of Him. He knows Himself and reposes in Himself with supreme complacency." [158]

Brahmabandab's approach to the Holy Trinity is similar to the psychological approach of St. Augustine:

"The differentiation of the Divine Self as subject and object can be served by no other medium than the Undivided, Infinite Substance which is Pure Knowledge.... It is knowledge and nothing but knowledge which can distinguish the Knowing Self of God from His Known Self.... God knows His own Self begotten in Thought and is known in return by that Begotten Self.... God reproduces in knowledge a corresponding, acknowledging Self-Image, and from this colloquy of Reason proceeds His Spirit of Love which sweetens the Divine Bosom with boundless delight." [159]

According to Brahmabandab this 'Known Self' is the Logos and in the Vedantic category it is the 'Cit'. God existing from all eternity has self-knowledge and it is from this self-cognition of God that the 'Cit-Logos' is eternally generated. [160] Brahmabandab clearly identifies Cit-Logos with Jesus Christ as the incarnate Son of God especially in a Sanskrit hymn 'Vande Saccidanandam' which he wrote in adoration of the Supreme Brahman, who according to him, is understood as Father, Son and the Holy Spirit: Saccidananda: Being Awareness-Bliss. [161] It is true that there is no doctrine in Hinduism that is exactly parallel to the Christian faith in the Holy Trinity. Any adaptation of a Vedantic concept into Christian theology needs a Christian re-interpretation. [162] That is exactly what Brahmabandab Upadhyaya tries with his explanation of the Holy Trinity as Saccidananda. This attempt deserves respect although we cannot agree with Brahmabadab that the Christian doctrine of God as Trinity is 'exactly the same' as the Vedantic conception of Brahman as Saccidananda. [163] But it cannot be denied that the doctrine of the Holy Trinity can be to some extent explained to the Hindus in a better way in terms of Saccidananda than in the Greek categories of 'substance', 'subsistence', 'person' etc.. The Christian theology can also draw better insights into the Mystery of the Holy Trinity through the understanding God (Brahman) as Saccidananda, Being-Awareness-Bliss. Robin Boyd holds the same opinion when he writes:

> "Upadhyaya feels that the Vedantic teaching on God as Saccidananda is true and helpful as far as it goes, but that it reaches it completion, its 'finale' only in the full Christian doctrine of the Trinity, which has been given to the Church by revelation. This doctrine, however, must be explained to Hindus in terms with which they are familiar, and in this very process of explaining the Christian faith through concepts drawn from another tradition light will be shed on the inner meaning of Christian truth itself." [164]

Many other Hindu reformers of the 19th century had also seen parallels between Saccidananda and the Holy Trinity. Justice Mahadev Govind Ranade (1842-1906) [165], for example, could find an analogy between Saccidananda and the Holy Trinity. ie. 'Sat corresponding to the absolute existence of the Father, Cit to the Logos, and Ananda to the Holy Comforter' [166]. We have also already discussed K.C. Sen's views regarding the Logos as the Cit of the Vedanta.[166a] The difference between their views and the view of Brahmabandab consists in the fact that only Brahmabandab could, in contrast to the modalistic interpretations of others, understand and interpret the Saccidananda as a Communion of three persons without at the same time falling into the error of polytheism or tritheism as supposed by the Hindu reformers like Rammohan Roy, K.C. Sen, Ranade and others. Without such an interpretation of the Holy Trinity it is impossible to present the correct doctrine of the Divine Incarnation to the Indian mind. If Jesus Christ is God, it is because He is the Incarnation of the 'Cit' who is one in nature with 'Sat' and 'Ananda' being at the same time different from both of them as a person! Here a legitimate question can be raised: Are the terms 'nature' and 'persons' so indispensable in an Indian interpretation of the Holy Trinity as 'Saccidananda'? For the moment we do not intend to go deep into the 'problematic' of this question. We reserve it for our third part. Here we would like only to indicate that inspite of the fact that Brahmabandab uses Sanskrit terms and the category of Saccidananda, he is an orthodox Thomist and Scholastic in his theological thinking. 'Cit' for him is just another term for the Augustinian and Thomistic interpretation of the Johannine Logos. On the 'Logos', for example, he writes:

> "Revelation teaches us ... that the differentiating note in Divine Knowledge is the response of Intelligence. God begets, in thought, His infinite

Self-Image and reposes on it with infinite delight while the begotten Self acknowledges responsively His eternal thought-generation." [167]

We see here a classical, scholastic understanding of the second person of the Holy Trinity. Upadhyaya is quite conscious that the doctrine of the Holy Trinity could be wrongly understood by the Vedantins and the Theosophers in terms of modalism or could be rejected by them as tritheism. It is also too subtle for the common man. Upadhyaya maintains that the problem posed by the doctrine of the Holy Trinity cannot be solved by human reason alone! [168] Upadhyaya finds a solution for this problem only in the Revelation of Jesus Christ who 'has told us that there is a response of knowledge in the God-head ... (and only) this unique revelation gives us a glimpse of the inner life of the Supreme Being' [169]. But actually the setting of the problem and its proposed solution are both in terms of philosophy, more precisely said, scholastic philosophy, than in terms of Revelation to which he refers. The 'response of knowledge' in the Trinity etc. is not something that 'Jesus Christ has told us' [170] in such explicit scholastic terms as Brahmabandab Upadhyaya would have us believe! They are rather later theological explanations - a psychological one - than the words of Jesus himself. Our question here is not whether such an explanation has a universal validity or not, but we want only to indicate that a theological explanation should not be confused with the very words of Jesus himself. A more biblical approach to the doctrine of the Holy Trinity as Saccidananda, rather than a scholastic one, would have perhaps made the theological contribution of Brahmabandab more original and more useful for the Indian context!

Brahmabandab's presentation of the doctrine of the Holy Trinity as Saccidananda looks like 'the stiching of a new Vedanta garb for an already formulated Christian theology' [171]. But as the Father of Indian theology he has succeeded in bringing in the person of Jesus Christ to re-interpret, clarify and affirm the Vedantic concept of Saccidananda as that of the Triune God of the Christian revelation. He does that by equating the relation between Sat and Cit to that of God the Father and Jesus Christ.

b. Jesus Christ, the Self-Manifestation of the Triune God

There are also some others in the Indian theological scene, who, following the lead of Brahmabandab Upadhyaya, have tried to explain the uniqueness of Jesus Christ in the context of 'Saccidananda'. Since Raymundo Panikkar sees the 'Cit' more in terms of the 'Universal Christ' we had discussed his position already in the fourth chapter. [172]

Fr. Jules Monchanin (1895-1957) [173] who changed his name to Swami Parama Arubi Anandam and Fr. Henri le Saux (1910-1973) [174] who prefered to be known as Swami Abhishiktananda are two others who valued the implications of the Vedantic Saccidananda as contributing to a better Indian under-standing of the Mystery of Jesus Christ in the Trinitarian context. Their approach was more spiritual and experiential than purely systematic or dogmatic. Monchanin believes that only in the Mystery of the Holy Trinity can the Vedantic Saccidananda that tends to be interpreted in various erroneous ways be brought to the desired conceptual fulfilment that cannot be reached through philosophical speculations and asceticism of life alone:

> "Only the mystery of the Trinity is capable of resolving the antinomies which cause Hindu thought to swing endlessly between monism and pluralism, between a personal and an impersonal God. India awaits without knowing it the Revelation of the Trinitarian mystery, a Revelation inaccessible both to metaphysical genius and to holiness." [175]

Monachin reacts against the monistic contemplation of the Advaitic mysti-cism and the anthropomorphic personalism of the Bhakti spirituality. The Supreme God is for him neither an 'impersonal Absolute It' nor a mono-personal He or I, but God is rather 'I and I and I. His very existence is identical with tri-personal relationship' [176]. God is for him One 'not despite his Trinity but in very consequence of this Trinity'. God is Sat (Being), Cit (Consciousness) and Ananda (Bliss) 'in such a manner that he constitutes three centres of personality, each one polarized by the other two' [177]. The Unity of God does not make Him less and the Trinity does not make Him more. [178] This is an insight discovered in 'Saccidananda' not by the subtlyties of the Hindu philosophy but by the Self-revelation of God that was fully realized in Jesus Christ. Monchanin observes:

> "More fervently and with greater appreciation than any of his fellow sannyasins, can the Christian monk utter: Sat, when thinking of the

Father, the 'Principleless' Principle, the very source and end of the expansion and 're-collection' of the divine life; Cit, when remembering the eternal Son, the Logos, the intellectual, consubstantial Image of the Existent; Ananda, when meditating on the Paraclete, unifying together the Father and the Son." [179]

In J. Monchanin we note a further development of the Trinitarian approach initiated by Brahmabandab Upadhyaya. A proper theology of the Holy Trinity is indispensable for any faithful interpretation of the person of Jesus Christ as the Son of God. Otherwise we end up with the polytheism of the popular Hinduism or deny the real Divinity of Jesus Christ as we have seen in the theories of Rammohan Roy, K.C. Sen and other Hindu monotheistic reformers or accept the essential divinity of every man in the Vedantic sense!

Following the thought pattern of Brahmabandab and Monchanin, Swami Abhishiktananda (Henri le Saux) also maintains that 'the Hindu experience of 'Saccidananda' should be remoulded to attain the Christian experience of 'Saccidananda' and one that is actualized then the renewed experience of 'Saccidananda' would be the Trinitarian culmination of advaitic experience' [180]. The Vedantic Advaitic experience purified, transformed and elevated by the Trinitarian experience is the genuine Christ-experience. This spiritual approach of Abhishiktananda, when put it in dogmatic terms, would mean that a proper understanding of the divine person of Jesus Christ is possible only in the Trinitarian context. Instead of the word 'Cit', Abhishiktananda prefers to use the words 'Vac' and 'Om' to convey the meaning of the Johannine 'Logos' [181], because the Vedic OM is the primordial utterance, the very Word (Vac) in which all things originate. [182]

Professor Dhanjibhai Fakirbhai (1895-1967) [183], though not a widely known Indian theologian, has made some interesting contributions to the understanding of the divine person of Jesus Christ. In his unpublished manuscript with the title 'Adhyatma Darsana' [184] he avoids 'Cit' and uses 'Prajnana' and 'Sabda-Brahman' to translate the 'Logos' of the fourth Gospel. 'Prajnana' means pre-knowledge or consciousness and 'Sabda-Brahman' stands for Brahman as Word. This Word originates from the Father and becomes incarnate in Jesus Christ. His position is comprised in a few sentences by Robin Boyd:

"Prajnana, primeval intelligence, is the power which creates, maintains and inspires the world and human beings. Prajnana is power and
wisdom, is the Word of God (Sabda-Brahman), is God himself -Brahman.
This Word of God, Prajnana, took a body in the man Jesus. As the
heat of the sun's light, according to the Brahma Sutra, is no different
from the heat of the disc of the sun itself, so this incarnate Prajnana,
the Avatara, is fully God." [185]

This is, of course, an explanation of the divinity of Jesus Christ without
getting once more involved in the Trinitarian and Christological controversies of the first five centuries. It is also questionable whether an Indian
interpretation of the Mystery of Christ should at all repeat and get entangled in those controversies because the Indian philosophical premises
are different from the philosophical categories of those days.

Charles Freer Andrews (1981-1940), [186] a long time friend of Mahatma
Gandhi could not agree with Gandhi's discard for the historical uniqueness
of Jesus Christ as the Incarnate Son of God. [187] Andrews is quite conscious
about the universality of the Christ-principle, but he maintains that Christ's
historical uniqueness does not render him in any way less central and universal and divine. [188] For Andrews, Jesus Christ is the Self-manifestation
of the Triune God, the Son of God who is equal to God. So Jesus' divinity
according to him, is not just the 'metaphyiscal' type of divinity common
to all men as advocated by the neo-Vedantins. [189] He is the unique Son
of God as 'the Eternal Word, the Life and Light of millions who have not
yet consciously known Him', as 'the Divine Head of Humanity' [190]; it was
he who was 'the Light of Buddha and Tulasi Das in their measure, even
as He was, in so much greater a degree, the Light of the Hebrew prophets' [191]. He is the Universal and the Unknown and He is at the same
time the Incarnate and the Acknowledged.

Sadhu Sundar Singh (1889-1929) [192] who places great stress on Anubhava
of Bhakti for the understanding of the Divine Mystery reports one of his
Christ-experiences and contents that even in mystical experiences there
is only one way to the knowledge of God, namely Jesus Christ who is 'the
image of the invisible God' [193]. The Sadhu describes Jesus as God incarnate
and 'the Word of life made flesh' [194]. Jesus Christ as the 'Image of God'
had also been an important theme for Susil Kumar Rudra (1861-1925)[195]. In
his 'Christian Idea of Incarnation'[196] he had maintained that Jesus Christ

is the Incarnation of the Logos who makes the invisible God visible as the Saguna Brahman is the Self-expression of the Nirguna Brahman. 'The knowledge of the invisible God is only possible through Him (Jesus)'. He is the revealer of the Father. 'The Invisible God, the Father, is expressed in and through the Son the Visible Image of the Father'[197].

Richard V. de Smet (*1916), a Belgian Jesuit, an expert in the philosophy of Sankaracharya and Thomistic theology, [198] also sees the uniqueness of Jesus Christ in his being one with the Godhead both in its transcendent and immanent aspects. He explains:

> "To translate (the expression 'Jesus Christ is God') in Hindu terms we must say that Christ is Brahmatman, i.e., the 'One without a second' whose name is equivalently Brahman or Atman. By calling him Brahman we designate him as Absolute, Greatest, self-subsistent Existence, perfect reality (Bhuman, Satya, Mahiman). By calling him Atman or Paramatman we designate him both as the innermost Cause of all beings different from him and as the supreme Spirit whose knowledge consists in perfect self-consciousness and omniscience. Hence, the inner Life of this Being consists in eternal Self-Fruition, i.e., in the absolute Bliss, Ananda." [199]

Here De Smet sees the Divinity of Jesus Christ from the fact of His unity with the Godhead. The difference of trinitarian relations as persons is not made clear. It is evidently an approach from the concept of 'nature' and not from a personal view point. It is true that De Smet considers Brahman as emintently personal, and by no means impersonal. He applies the scholastic definition of 'person' as 'Subsistens distinctum natura intellectuali' to Brahman as the Supreme Intelligence and Consciousness. [200] But this concept of 'person' is a very dry and static one, which by no means brings to light the dynamism of I-Thou relation which is constitutive of persons. De Smet's explanation of the person of Jesus Christ as 'Brahmatman' is a faithful Sanskrit translation of a scholastic theology, which need not necessarily be considered as a genuine contribution to the understanding of the Divinity of Jesus Christ in Vedantic or Indian categories. The approach of Monchanin, Abhishiktananda, Djanjibhai Fakirbhai and Sadhu Sundar Singh may be better suited to explain the Divinity of Christ within the Trinitarian context.

c. The Divine Consciousness of Jesus

Venegal Chakkarai (1880-1958) [201] is an Indian theologian who considers the consciousness of Jesus as decisive in understanding his Divinity. The unique God-consciousness of Jesus Christ, his personal experience of being one with God, is the starting point for every theologizing. [202]   His stress is not so much on the Divinity of Jesus Christ as on 'the Christhood of God'. [203]God the Absolute (Brahman) is 'Avyakta' or unmanifest; He becomes 'Vyakta' (manifest) in Isvara. Isvara is Jesus himself; in him we see the face of the unmanifest God. He writes:

> "Out of the infinite nebulous emerges the face of Jesus. God is the unmanifested and Jesus is the manifested. God is the sat or being, and Jesus is the cit or intelligence, wisdom and love which indicates the nature of the being of God." [204]

Our knowledge of God, therefore, is based on Christ's experience of God, his God-consciousness. Chakkarai considers the God-consciousness of Jesus clearly expressed even in the Synoptic Gospels, for example in Mt. 11:26-27 and its parallel in Luke 10:22. These passages regarding the relation of the Father and the Son, according to Chakkarai, is a clear indication of Jesus' consciousness of his unique relation to God.[205] Chakkarai continues:

> "It is certainly most extraordinary that any man, however exalted he may be, should claim exclusive knowledge of God, and state further that God alone has exclusive knowledge of himself. It is the duty of Christian theology to vindicate this high claim of Jesus of Nazareth .... So far as is known in history, no one else has ever made any such assertion. Not has His assertion been baseless; it has been vindicated by the witness of history and of our experience." [206]

The profound God-consciousness of Jesus had transformed the titles Son, Son of God and Son of Man. This consciousness cannot be considered as dawning upon him just at the time of Jesus' baptism in Jordan: "His Sonship was never learned from any human source. It was the real structure of his deepest consciousness; it was the native endowment of His soul."[207] It points to the uniqueness of Jesus' Divine consciousness that no other religious teacher has ever laid claim to such an 'original and underived consciousness' [208]. Chakkarai maintains that 'the filial consciousness of Jesus was the first and the organic element in His life' and the consciousness of His mission as the Messiah was a derived consciousness, a consciousness derived from His self-realization as the Son of God.[209] His Divine sonship, therefore, is ontological and not just an ethical or eschatological sonship.[210] This is especially clear in Jesus authority to forgive sins and His claim to be the Lord of Sabbath.[211] Jesus is also the Lord of human history because He is the judge to come in the eschatological days 'clad in supernatural power and glory'[212].

"To Jesus alone belongs the attribute of consubstantiality with the Father; and not to others".[213] Although Chakkarai admits the Nicene definition, he maintains that the category of substance cannot be regulative to the Indian thought.[214] In India the divinity of Jesus Christ must be viewed also in the context of the 'divinity' that the Vedanta attributes to every man. Nature and man are, according to Chakkarai, also divine, but only in a derived sense as they 'come from Him (God) and are found in Him (God).[215] Man is rooted in God and he has a consciousness that is 'individuated'; the self-consciousness of the nature reaches its 'crown and climax' in man.[216] In Jesus also there is an 'individuation' of consciousness, but the distinction between Jesus and other men consists in the fact that in Him alone 'the perfect individuation and the perfect unity of mind and heart with God are reached'[217]. The difference is not only in intensity or quality which would imply subordinationism. The difference is specific; Jesus belongs to the realm of God - equal to God:

> "The sonship that He (Jesus) realized is the perfect answer to the quest of God, and the fatherhood is the realization of the fullness of God in relation to His (Jesus') sonship." [218]

This means that God realizes His Fatherhood only in relation to Jesus. That also, however, means that the Fatherhood of God has a temporal beginning! But, Chakkarai does not admit that the Divinity of Jesus has a beginning, because 'Jesus of history is to us the Avatar of God'[219]. This would not rule out that there had been a process of growth in Jesus![220] The growth of Incarnation-process, however, should not be misunderstood as growth in God. The growth is not in the reality of God but in His external manifestation which reached a unique climax in Jesus:

> "God was working in nature and in the lifes of men for the reproduction of His very heart and mind. But in Jesus the image came out perfect and shining, without flaw or mixture." [221]

Jesus as the 'full and final manifestation' cannot be different from God and in Him we come 'face to face with Isvara in a sense which cannot be true of any prophet or saint'[222] . So in the view of Chakkarai, Jesus Christ is the counterpart of the Vedantic Isvara in history. Just an Isvara is the manifested aspect of Nirguna Brahman, so also Jesus Christ is the Image [223]of the Invisible God:

> "We see God with the face of Jesus. To the ordinary and unsophisticated consciousness there is a black veil God would seem to have cast over His face. But now that Jesus has removed that veil, we behold the face of God Himself ... what is vivid and real to us is the face of Jesus with a shadowy background of unknown and infinite potencies into which we strive to penetrate but catch only stray gleams. Whom we call God stands behind Jesus, and it is Jesus who gives, as it were, colour, light and rupa to God." [224]

V. Chakkarai puts stress on the fact that Jesus Christ is the Image of the invisible God; He is God Himself in His visible aspect. He supports Christ's divinity from the divine claims He made and the divine authority He exercised - both based on the divine consciousness of Jesus. Chakkarai considers that the divine claims of Jesus were made credible 'by the witness of history' and by the personal experience we can derive from the narratives of the Christ-experience of His first followers. [225] Chakkarai recognizes that 'Anubhava' should play a great role in Indian Christology and his idea of Christanubhava is not advaitic, but in the tradition of Bhakti. At the same time he maintains that the relation between Jesus and God is not merely one of Bhakti, but that of unity in Being. He understood how useful the Vedantic categories could be in interpreting the Christ-mystery in the Indian context. His Christology did not consist merely in substituting Sanskrit terms for Latin and Greek theological concepts. [226] He made a sincere effort to transform and enrich the Vedantic thinking by the Christ-Mystery and to give expression to this Mystery in genuine Indian categories. However, Chakkarai's theological attempts cannot be considered as all successful. For example, his discard for the concept of 'Person' [226a]makes some of this theological assumptions questionable. We may not find a proper theology of the Trinity in Chakkarai and that gives rise also to Christ-ological and Pneumatological problems. He says: "Jesus Christ is the In-carnation or Avatar of God; the Holy Spirit in human experience is the Incarnation of Jesus Christ." [227] This statement, especially in the context of Chakkarai's comparison of Saguna Brahman (Isvara) with Jesus Christ, would rule out an immanent Trinity. God is eternal, but the Trinity would be only temporal or economical. The distinction between the Father, the Son and the Holy Spirit is not something that is based on the inner life of God, belonging to His very existence, but only realized in the process of God's self-manifestation. Consequently Chakkarai identifies also Jesus Christ with the Holy Spirit; 'the Holy Spirit is Jesus Himself, taking His abode within us' [228]. The Holy Spirit is the 'Antaryamin' (Indweller) or the indwelling aspect of the Paramatman (the Supreme Spirit) as 'Antaratman' (the Inner Spirit). The difference is only of transcendence and immanence: God in His transcendent aspect is called Paramatman, in His historical and visible immanence He is Jesus Christ and finally in His permanent and invisible immanence He is the Holy Spirit. [229] It is evident that such assumptions cannot be brought into harmony with the content of the fundamental faith-propositions of Nicea and Chalcedon, which - if not in formulation, at least in content - is normative for a genuine Christian theology.

2. Jesus, the True Man

If Jesus Christ is truly God, how could we explain his true humanity? This is one of the oldest and most fundamental questions in Christology and this question has a special relevance in the Indian context especially because of the particular Vedantic approach to the problem of creation and the reality of matter.

a. The Humanity of Jesus in the Context of 'Maya'

We have already discussed the Vedantic concept of Maya and also its Neo-Vedantic interpretation. [230] 'Maya' is the key-word used to explain the reality of this material world especially in its relation to God. If Maya means pure illusion, as some extreme monistic Advaitins hold [231], then it follows that the humanity of Jesus Christ is also a mere illusion - an Indian version of Docetism. The understanding of 'Maya' as the creative power of God would, on the contrary, make a Christian approach much easier.

Brahmabandhab Upadhyaya was the first Christian theologian in India who tried to give the concept of Maya a thoroughly Christian interpretation. In the first stages of Upadhyaya's theological thinking he was convinced that 'it was impossible to use Sankara's advaita as an instrument of Christian theology' [232]. Later on he was more and more convinced of its value and began his re-interpretation of the advaitic concepts. An understanding of the nature of this material reality in its relation to God explained in the Vedantic categories is, according to Upadhyaya, indispensable for an Indian Christian interpretation of the matter that was assumed in the incarnation of the Son of God. 'Creation' is the traditional Christian explanation to show the dependence of this world on God without denying its reality and at the same time without postulating any reality other than and independent of God. Upadhyaya maintains that the concept of 'Creation' is equivalent to the Vedantic concept of Maya. He gives his Christian interpretation of Maya which is very similar to the Neo-Vedantic position. He explains:

> "Brahman is Being itself. He alone is identical with his own Being while creatures have no right of being but have a merely participated and dependent existence. They exist by maya, i.e., by the habit of participating in the Divine Being and springing from the Divine Act. Maya is a mysterious divine operation; it is neither real nor unreal.... It cannot be real in the sense of its being essential to the Divine Nature because brahman is self-sufficient and cannot be said to be under the necessity of being related to the finite. Nor is it unreal, for by maya comes to exist the finite which possesses being, though not essentially - the essence of the finite not being identical with its existence. From an unreality nothing can proceed. Maya is neither real or necessary, nor unreal but contingent ..." [233].

Except in the words 'Brahman' and 'Maya' the whole passage above is thoroughly scholastic. In re-interpreting 'Maya' Upadhyaya makes use of the scholastic metaphysical categories of being, necessity and contingence. Only God is necessary (Paramarthika) and all the creatures have no existence by themselves and so they are dependent on God for their existence, which means, they are contingent (Vyavaharika). On the part of the creature 'Maya' refers to its dependence on God and on the part of God it stands for His creative power or Sakti. In another passage Upadhyaya clarifies this point further:

"Maya ... is the fecund Divine Power (Sakti) which gives birth to multiplicity.... It is eternal but its operation is not essential to the being of God. By it, non-being (asat) is made being (sat). By it, that which is nothingness by itself is filled with the richness of being. By it darkness is illumined with the flow of existence. It is Maya indeed." [234]

The paradox of One and many, Being and becoming, Stability and change or Unity and multiplicity is solved in Metaphysics by the concept of the 'Analogy of Being' and in Theodicy by the notion of creation. Upadhyaya sees that the concept of 'Maya', when re-interpreted, can be used both in Metaphysics and Theodicy in a truly Christian sense. He finds justification for his identification of 'Maya' and 'Creation' in the teachings of Thomas Aquinas:

"Maya is what St. Thomas calls 'creation passiva' - passive cration. It is a quality of all that is not Brahman and is defined by the Angelic Doctor as 'the habitude of having being from another and resulting from the operation' of God (see Summa Theologica 1, XLIV.3). The word maya, in its significance of 'abundance' (see Vedanta Sutra, adh. 1, pada 1. 13, 14, and Sankara on the same) is beautifully appropriate and significant, for creation is, as it were, the overflow of the divine Being, knowledge and bliss, and results from the desire of brahman to manifest and impart His own perfections (St. Thomas, Summa Contra Gentiles, Bk. II, Chapter XIV) .... The Vedantins affirm that all that is not Brahman to be 'maya', in the sense of illusion, and they are right, because creatures, in themselves, apart from Brahman, are indeed darkness, falsity and nothingness (tenebrae, falsitas et nihil) as St. Thomas teaches." [235]

Upadhyayas interpretation of 'creatio ex nihilo' in terms of Maya has also been later supported by Pierre Johanns (1882-1955) [236], the author of the work "To Christ through the Vedanta".[237] Independently of God, the world is only privation, absense of being and nothingness. Maya refers to this situation of the world as privation which as creatability is presupposed for the creativity of God and 'if God creates, His creation must be received in that privation' [238]. It is this privation which Upadhyaya means as Maya. Upadhyaya takes the concept of Maya a step further from the Vedantic position. Vedanta applies Maya only to this world in order to explain the reality of matter in relation to Brahman. In the world of Brahman, ie. in the state of liberation there is no more Maysa since everything attains its 'Advaita' with Brahman; the individual beings, according to Sankara, cease to exist. In the school of Ramanuja also there is no more Maya once liberation is attained. [239] According to Upadhyaya, Christian theology could accept Maya even in the liberated state because 'it teaches that individual souls have been blessed by God to live for ever. The Infinite power (ie. Maya as the creative power of God), which has given them life for a day, may give them life for days without end' [240]. In his Vedantic interpretations Upadhyaya rejects any identification of creatures with the Creator [241] which is falsely understood as implied in the doctrine of Maya. Upadhyaya is even of the opinion that 'Maya' rightly interpreted can better express the doctrine of creation than the Latin word 'creare' can do! He reasons:

> "Whenever we speak of creation we should be careful to make explicit three factors implied in the creative act. First: there is not necessity on God's part to create. Second: the coming into being of finite objects with the implication that they did not exist. Third: the finite perfections are contained in the infinite in a pre-eminent way. Now the term 'Creation' expressed only the second significance, while 'maya' conveys ... all the three." [242]

Upadhyaya is quite right in his evaluation. It is true that the strict definition of 'Creation' as 'Productio rei ex nihilo sui et subjecti' does not contain some of the important aspects necessarily implied in the doctrine of creation.

It is indeed a great theological contribution on the part of Upadhyaya to make an important concept in the Vedanta, namely of Maya, relevant and acceptable in the process of interpreting the Christian faith in the Indian context. It does not put any longer the reality of the material world in doubt; it does not also deny the inherent value of matter and this created world which forms an integral part of human existence. 'Maya' in its re-interpreted form liberates Hinduism from its exaggerated and one-sided spiritualism and contempt towards the material aspect of human life. By recognizing 'Maya' even in the state of liberation Upadhyaya underscores the dignity of man's body and its permanent worth. If body and matter were necessarily evil the incarnation of the Son of God would be impossible to explain. It is also noteworthy that docetic interpretations in Christology had their origin in the Manichean and Gnostic circles, where matter and body were considered as intrinsicly evil. The general prejudice against this material world that is prevalent in the Hindu thinking is the main reason for docetic overtones in the doctrine of Avatar. Upadhyaya's understanding of 'Maya' is evidently of extreme importance in explaining the reality of the material body of Jesus Christ, who is not only truly God but also is fully man. Apart from the true humanity of Jesus Christ and the intrinsic value of his body we would not also understand the meaning of Christ's resurrection. Without the reality of Jesus' humanity, the whole doctrine of Incarnation would be a meaningless illusion!

Writers like A. Väth criticize Brahmabandhab Upadhyaya's explanation of 'Maya' as a forced interpretation of the original doctrine and they maintain that Upadhyaya has not even succeeded in purifying the Vedantic thought. [243] This criticism may be a bit exaggerated. Robin Boyd sees in Upadhyaya a great constructive theologian who could 'take common philosophical conceptions and transform them, making them vehicles for quite new theological ideas, as indeed Aquinas did for Aristotle' [244]. It is precisely in this that one could notice the main drawback of Upadhyaya: His theological approach is more based on St. Thomas than on the Sacred Scripture. Instead of leading the Indian theological reflection into new avenues he brought it 'to the point of departure of Aquinas' [245]. These remarks, of course, are not intended to minimize what he has achieved in his own way especially in the initial stages of an Indian Christian theology.

b. Jesus' 'Manusya Svabhava'

A Sanskrit translation of the Thomistic Christology is much more evident in the writings of R.V. de Smet. In this article 'Materials for an Indian Christology'[246] he explains how Christ's human nature is real, complete and at the same time distinct from his Divine nature. [247]

De Smet explains the etymological meaning of 'nature' as 'that basic endowment with which a being is born (natus) and which makes it what it is as distinct from beings of other species (and from God)' [248]. He identifies the notion of nature with that of substance or essence. [249] In God there cannot be any difference between his 'essence' and 'existence' because as pure actuality of Being (esse purum) His essence is existence: Ipsum esse subsistens! The distinction between nature and act of being is a creaturely distinction from which God is free. Since the finite beings do not have have the 'act of being' (esse) from themselves, their nature and their 'act of being' are distinct. They are not 'Nirguna Satya' (esse purum) as God is. So strictly said, the human nature is a mere possible which can be made real by the 'act of being'. Normally the 'act of being' is proportional to the nature, but there is the possibility that the 'pure Act of Being' (esse purum) 'supplies' actualization to the human nature; there is nothing in the human nature that would contradict such an elevation because of its inherent obediential potency (potentia oboedientialis). This possibility was verified in the Incarnation. Eventhough the human nature of Christ could not limit the transcendent Act of Being and it could not exist in virtue of its own 'act of being' as human person, yet the human nature of Jesus remains complete and undestroyed with all its specificities and perfections.

In Indianizing this Scholastic doctrine, De Smet considers it proper to substitute 'nature' by 'svarupa' or 'svabhava'.[250] 'Brahmanya svarupa' or 'daiva svarupa' would then mean divine nature and 'manusya svarupa (or) svabhava' could be used to signify the human nature. He writes:

> "We may ... say that Christ is one brahmanya purusa or jana (divine Person) in two svarupas or svabhavas, namely, His original and independent divine Nature (nisarga svatantra brahmanya scabhava) and His conjoined dependent human nature (samyukta paratantra manusya svabhava)." [251]

This explanation of R.V. de Smet has been well accepted and appreciated by the German Indologist at the university of Münster, the late Dr. Prof. Paul Hacker.[252] It seems, however, that Dr. Hacker, as a Sanskrit scholar, is more interested in the exactitude of the translation than in the theological aspects implied in such a translation. The most important question is whether such theological translations could hope to make any original contribution to the understanding and interpretation of the Christ-event in the Indian context. Are the categories of essence, existence, substance, accident, nature, person etc. so indispensable for an Indian Christology?[253] Is the task of the Indian Christology to spin a Vedantic garb for the Thomistic theology? The Christ-event that was realized in a Jewish milieu can definitely find a genuine expression not only in Greco-Roman terms but also in the Vedantic categories.

c. The 'Sat Purusha': True Man

A genuine effort to understand the humanity of Jesus Christ even in the context of his divinity is made by Vengel Chakkarai without having recourse to the speculative subtleties of a western philosphical system. In his book "Jesus the Avatar", he dedicates an entire chapter to explain his approach to the question of Jesus' humanity. His method is more biblical than philosophical.

Chakkarai maintains that a mere metaphysical analysis of Jesus' person as the Incarnate Logos cannot do justice to the entirety of his mystery. There is no doubt for him that Jesus Christ is the Avatar, the Incarnation, of God in the fullest sense. But what is immediate to us is the humanity of Jesus which mediates the Divinity. So our approach to the Divinity of Christ should be through his humanity. It should be an approach from the known to the unknown, from bottom to the top, from man to God. It is more an ascending approach than a descending one.

Chakkarai, however, does not mean that Jesus's humanity is all evident to us and that only his divinity is beyond the limits of our conceptions. Eventhough the humanity of Jesus mediates to us the unfathomable Divinity, his humanity still remains itself a mystery. That would mean that even Jesus' humanity cannot be understood from mere historical research without the help of revelation.[254] Chakkarai casts a look at the Gospels to understand how the mystery of Jesus' humanity is presented there.[255] The gospel evidences which go beyond the mere datas of his birth, facts concerning his bodily life, sufferings, death etc. point to the fact that Jesus' humanity cannot be explained from the standpoint of our own preconceptions of what humanity is and should be. Jesus should not be considered an 'ideal man' because he fits into our ideas, but on the contrary, our ideas regarding an 'ideal man' should fit into the pattern of what Jesus is. He is not to be judged according to our criterion, but we should be judged according to his criterion. Chakkarai explains:

> "The essential possibilities of humanity are not exhausted by what we see in other men, but we should take the humanity of Jesus into consideration in the determination of human nature. Christ is the interpretation not only of the divine consciousness but of the human

as well, our humanity receives an immeasurable breath in view of the humanity of Jesus."[256]

So, the approach of Chakkarai is not merely an anthropological approach to Christology, even though it is an approach from below, an ascending approach.[257] His starting point is not a philosophical system, but the Bible itself which speaks directly to the basic religious experiences of humanity. These basic experiences are universally relevant and applicable, eventhough their subsequent philosophical formulations are particular, bound by the conditions of space and time.

In reference to Christ's humanity, Chakkarai understands him as the 'Sat Purusha', the true man. Only in this Man of Galilee we see what true humanity is like. He is 'the original pattern in the mind of God Himself after whom all men have been fashioned'[258] Jesus is the spiritual background of all humanity.[259] He as the 'Mulapurusha', the original man, is not just a man among men, but he is the essence of all humanity:

> "... we do not know all about the possibilities of humanity till we have analysed the humanity of Jesus. His humanity lays down the measure and norm of our humanity; our humanity is not to judge the height and depth of His. To use Indian phraseology, He is the Sat purusha; and though we are not asat, we are dominated by maya. We use the term maya in connection with our personality, not in the sense that it is unreal, but in the sense that the true humanity in us has been abscured by some taint, and that its growth is retarded. In Jesus' the maya is cast off and transcendend and His full glory and light have shone on the world ..."[260]

It is interesting to see here how Chakkarai compares Christ to the Purusha in the Vedic creation hymn,[261] without accepting, of course, all its implications and at the same time without bringing in western philosophy to re-interpret, as Brahmabandab Upadhyaya does, this Vedic term in order to apply it to the mystery of Christ. Unlike Upadyaya, Chakkarai uses the concept of 'Maya' to indicate the sinful situation of man which does not belong to the concept of the 'sat purusha' or the 'mulapurusha', and not to give a metaphysical proof for the bodily reality of Jesus Christ. R.V. de Smet's problem for distinguishing and explaining the unity of 'daiva svabhava' and 'manushya svabhava' in Jesus Christ is also not a question that bothers Chakkarai. His concern is more existential and biblical than merely speculative or metaphysical.[262]

Chakkarai considers the sinlessness of Jesus Christ as evidenced by the Gospels in reference to his humanity and not as a proof for his divinity as is usually done. The reason is that, according to him, the concept of a true man excludes the notion of sin. Sinlessness belongs to a perfect humanity, that is fully in union with the creative plan of God. Jesus is sinless, not because he is God incarnate - in which case the notion of sinlessness itself in reference to Jesus would be irrelevant - but because he is the true man, the Sat Purusha:

> "In His (Jesus') presence we stand before the moral miracle of humanity, the true man in whom, as looking into a mirror, we see our own deformities and yet realize what is the inner meaning of our own strivings after a holy and perfect life. He is the magician who has touched with the wand of His person the poor cottage of our humanity, and it has become a domed and pinnacled palace on the banks of time." [263]

Chakkarai maintains that Jesus as a man reached also the highest degrees of human consciousness in his prayer-consciousness or mystic experiences which may be called 'yogic' [264] and 'in the case of Jesus it reaches, so far as is known in history, the highest point' [265]. So Chakkarai distinguishes in Jesus a truly human consciousness that is not to be confused with his divine consciousness, which indicates his disapproval of the Advaita Vedantic approach to the question of consciousness and the relation of man to God. A denial of the reality of Jesus' humanity as distinct from his divinity, according to Chakkarai, is by itself a denial of the Mystery of Incarnation! [266]

It can be said that Chakkarai is successful in interpreting the reality of Christ's humanity without in any way compromising his divinity as the Avatar. His position is really in line with the Pauline thinking which presents Christ as the New Adam (Rom 5:12-21). Jesus Christ, is according to him, not only the Image of God, but he is also the Image of man. But it can be asked whether a narrow 'biblicism' that ignores philosophical and metaphysical achievements of the past can alone answer even the purely Christological questions of the modern man who may not be ready to take the authority of the biblical evidence for granted? A realistic approach to the mystery of Christ must also, we are sure, take into account the philosophical problematics which are indispensable in avoiding a 'Ghetto-Christology', and in promoting a Christology which must also be open to the philosophical demands of the modern world.

3. Jesus Christ, the God-Man

In the previous sections we have examined how some of the Indian theologians try to interpret the true divinity and the true humanity of Jesus Christ in Vedantic terms. The main concern of the Council of Chalcedon had been to 'define' that the two natures are united in one person (prosopon) and one hypostasis of the Word without confusion or change, without division or separation.[268] We shall see here some of the attempts to re-interpret this doctrine of the Hypostatic union in a language that is intellegible to the Indian philosophical context.

a. 'Nari-Hari': God-Man

'God' and 'Man' united into one word by a hyphon stands to signify the Mystery of the hypostatic union. The limitations of human expressions to encompass this ineffable Mystery justifies such a usage. Brahmabandab Upadhyaya considers this usage relevant and especially significant. He translated it into Sankrit by the expression Nara-Hari: Nara means man and Hari signifies Visnu, the God of Avatar.[269] Because of the theological problems involved[270], we cannot identify Hari with the Johannine Logos. But Upadhyaya gives arbitrarily a new interpretation to 'Hari' and uses this word as equivalent to 'Logos'. His dedication to the expression 'Nari-Hari' is especially evident in the fact that he used for himself the name 'Narahari Das', i.e., Servant of the God-Man, as the nom-de-plume. [271]

The expression 'Nari-Hari' is repeatedly used by Upadhyaya in a Sanskrit hymn he wrote - the 'hymn of Incarnation', which he published in the review "The Twentieth Century" in 1901 with his own English translation.[272] Here he follows his tradition of expressing theological thoughts in the form of hymns; but we should not read too much theology into a hymn that is principally devotional in character. Still it is relevant to quote this hymn here; it sheds better light on Upadhyaya's understanding of Jesus Christ as the God-Man:

> "The transcendent Image of Brahman blossomed and mirrored in the full to overflowing (upachita), eternal knowledge: Glory to God, the God-Man (Nara-Hari).

Child of the golden Virgin, director of the universe, absolute, yet charming with relations: Glory to God, the God-Man (Nara-Hari). Ornament of the assembly of the learned, destroyer of fear, chastiser of the spirit of wickedness: Glory to God, the God-Man (Nara-Hari). Dispeller of spiritual and physical infirmities, ministering unto others, one whose actions and doings are sanctifying: Glory to God, the God-Man (Nara-Hari).
One who has offered up his agony, whose life is sacrifice, destroyer of the poison of sin: Glory to God, the God-Man (Nara-Hari).
Tender, beloved charmer of the heart, soothing pigment of eyes, crusher of fierce death: Glory to God, the God-Man (Nara-Hari)." [273]

The last four stanzas are evidently soteriological in character. As our interest in this chapter is primarily on Jesus Christ considered in himself we reserve soteriology for the third chapter. Still the refrain 'Nara-Hari' points to Upadhyaya's insistence on the two natures in Christ and the unity of his person. In the first two stanzas Upadhyaya points to the person of Christ: He is both Nirguna and Saguna! As the 'Ciracit' (Eternal Intelligence), he is 'the transcendent Image of Brahman'; he is Nirguna, infinite in Being and beyond attributes. This refers to Christ's pre-existence in the 'Immanent Trinity' as the Logos. In the 'Economical Trinity' (Saguna Brahman), the Logos fulfils his role as 'the child of the golden Virgin'. In this Upadhyaya rightly rejects an Indian tendency to consider God the Father as the 'Nirguna Brahman' and the 'Logos' as the 'Saguna Brahman'. [274] 'Nirguna' and 'Saguna' should refer to the two aspects - transcendental and immanent - of the same Trinity and to use these expressions in reference to the distinction of Persons cannot be justified from the Vedantic tradition and its Christian understanding.

Upadhyaya's 'Hymn of the Incarnation' is only an exposition of the traditional Christian orthodoxy. Still there is some originality in the way Upadhyaya explains how the transcendent Image of Brahman (Brahmaparatpararupa) becomes incarnate in Jesus Christ. This is especially clear in his adaptation of the Vedantic theory of sheaths (Kosha) to explain the unity of God and Man in Jesus Christ.

274

b. **The Five 'Kosha' (Sheaths) and the 'Ciracit' (Eternal Logos)**

In order to make the doctrine of 'Hypostatic Union' intellegible to the Vedantic mind, Upadhyaya makes use of the Vedantic structure of man in five Koshas, [275] to which we had refered in Chapter two. In an ordinary human being the five constructive and concentric layers of man's bodily and psychic structure are 'governed' by the created human personality (Aham). In the case of Jesus, there is no 'Aham'; the 'Aham' is substituted by the 'Ciracit' (the Eternal Logos) that overtakes in a sublimated way also the function of the 'Aham'. Upadhyaya writes:

> "According to the Vedanta, human nature is composed of five sheats or divisions (kosha). They are: (1) physical (annamaya), which grows by assimilation; (2) vital (pranamaya); (3) mental (manomaya), which are perceived relations of things; (4) intellectual (vijnanmaya), through which is apprehended the origin of being; and (5) spiritual (anandamaya), through which is felt the delight of the Supreme Reality. These five sheaths are presided over by a personality (ahampratyayai) which knows itself. This selfknowing individual (jiva-chaitanya) is but a reflected spark of the Supreme Reason (kutasthachaitanya), Who abides in every man as the prime source of life and light. The time-incarnate Divinity is also composed of five sheaths; but it is presided over by the Person of the Logos Himself and not by any created personality (aham)." [276]

By stating that 'Jiva-chaitanya' is a reflected spark of the 'Kutastha-chaitanya', Upadhyaya does not mean that every man is ontologically divine or one with Got in the advaitic sense. 'Aham' is created reality, whereas the 'Ciracit', the Eternal Intelligence, is one with God as the Logos. Upadhyaya explains further how the Divine Reason unites humanity and divinity in Christ:

> "The five sheaths and the individual agent, enlivened and illumined by Divine Reason, who resides in a special manner in the temple of humanity, make up man. But in the God-man, the five sheaths are acted upon direct by the Logos-God and not through the medium of any individuality. The Incarnation was thus accomplished by uniting humanity with Divinity in the person of the Logos." [277]

So, Upadhyaya distinguishes here the general presence of the 'Cit', the Divine Reason, in all human beings and His special and personal presence in Jesus Christ. So the difference between ordinary human beings and Jesus Christ is not merely one of degree or intensity, but is essential; this difference, however, does not make Jesus Christ in any way deprived of any thing that is essential for his being human, but on the contrary elevates his humanity to a higher plane without destroying it. Since the person of Jesus Christ is the 'Ciracit', He is God 'by the necessity of His being'. Upadhyaya continues:

> "This incarnate God in man we call Jesus Christ. He took flesh from the womb of a spotless, immaculate Virgin for the formation of His body. As the first man (adipurusha) was produced by Divine samkalpa (will), so was the body of Jesus Christ, whom we hold to be the adipurusha of the spiritual world, formed by the power of the Spirit of God and not by the usual process of procreation. Jesus Christ is God by the necessity of His being, but He became man of His own free choice. It was compassion for us which made Him our Brother, like us in sorrow and suffering but without sin. Jesus Christ is perfectly Divine and perfectly human. He is the incarnate Logos." [278]

It seems that Upadhyaya considers 'the virginal Conception' of Jesus Christ as a doctrine inseparably connected with the dogma of the 'Hypostatic Union'. But, besides his reference to Jesus Christ as the 'adipurusha', he does not substantiate his position; perhaps he takes it for granted or as self-evident, which of course it is not! [279] We will be evaluating this question in the third part of our work, Chapter eight.

Upadhyaya's above explanation has been critized as leaning towards Apollinarism. [280] We do not think that this criticism is justifiable. Upadhyaya's idea that the 'Ciracit' (Eternal Intelligence) substitutes the 'Aham' (personal individuality) could give rise to such an impression. But a closer reading of his statement clarifies the point. The Eternal Cit, according to him, does not substitute the three psychic koshas in Christ, namely : the manomaya (mental), vijnanamaya (intellectual) and the anandamya (spiritual) koshas. They remain also in Jesus Christ as in every other human being. So his human intellectual and volitional faculties are not absorbed by the Supreme Cit, as held by Apollinaris. Upadhyaya opines that only the 'Aham' is substituted by the Eternal Cit! On this point, however, we could further dispute the acceptability of the whole approach as is evident in the modern discussions regarding the definition of Chalcedon. [281]

A different Christological interpretation of the Kosha theory of the Taittiriya Upanisad is proposed by R. Antoine (*1914) [282]. He identifies the fifth Kosha in the existential structure of Jesus with the Divine Person. The other Koshas were, according to him, gradually manifested in Jesus in the course of his physical and psychical development. Antoine does not intend by this to substantiate any static doctrine of Hypostatic union as Brahmabandab Upadhyaya does; his approach is more dynamic and practical. Instead of the word 'Kosha' he uses 'atman' as is given in the Taittiriya Upanisad,[283] because the Koshas are actually the progressive and concentric structures belonging to the 'atman', the ultimate reality of man. Referring to Jesus Christ he writes:

> "We first see the little babe drinking his mothers milk: that is the annarasamaya atman, the bodily self of Jesus. Then he appears to us as a boy or a man living among other men: that is the pranamaya atman, the psychic self of Jesus. Further we know him as a person who rejoices and grieves: that is the manomaya atman the psychological self of Jesus. Deeper still we listen to his doctrine and admire his wisdom: that is the vijnanamaya atman, the spiritual self of Jesus. Finally at the very centre of his being, the light of faith reveals to us the anandamaya atman, the divine and blissful Person."[284]

This explanation of R. Antoine is phenomenological and existential, though rudimentary, and avoids the scholastic sophistication of Upadhyaya. Such an approach is, in our opinion, more intellegible to the Vedantic mind than the Sanskrit translation of the philosophical categories belonging to another system of thought.

c. 'Tadatmya' in the 'Brahmanya Purusa'

Like Brahmabandhab Upadhyaya, R.V. de Smet is also concerned with the problem of how to express the Mystery (anirvacaniya)[285] of the 'Hypostatic Union' in Indian terms! [286] Upadhyaya had shown some originality in his adoption of the Kosha-categories; De Smet, however, even dispenses with such attempts and aims at a faithful and practically literal Sanskrit translation of the Scholastic explanation.

Following the Catholic orthodoxy, De Smet writes that 'since the God-man is a single personal being, the unity of His two natures cannot be merely external' nor an internal one that results in a 'tertium quid'; only the notion of Hypostatic union, namely, 'union by the virtue of the personal Supposit (hypostasis) or Person who takes into Himself the human nature' can guarantee the Christian faith regarding the reality of Incarnation.

The Divine Person of the Logos makes the human nature of Jesus Christ exist; the resulting novelty is not on the part of God, but of man. Both the human and the divine natures are united in the same person of the Word [287] - without confusion or change, without division or separation. This is how De Smet sees the Hypostatic Union expressed in Indian terms:

> "If we remember that an atman is an inner principle which transcends with is actuates, we may say that the second Person of the Trinity is the Atman of the manusya svarupa He assumes, and that His divine or brahmanya svarupa is the pratistha (foundation) of His Personality. We may base this latter usage on Bhagavadgita, xiv,27: Brahmano hi pratistha'ham (I-the personal Krsna - am the abode of Brahman), reversing however the purusa-pratistha relationship signified there between the Person (aham) and the Godhead (Brahman)." [288]

De Smet's interpretation of the Bhagavadgita text seems to be forced and a bit irrelevant here. He draws further Vedantic patterns to explain the Hypostatic union from Sankara's concept of the world as dependent (paratantra) on the universal Atman (Sarvatman) for its 'act of being', however restricting Sankara's acosmism to the sole case of Christ. [289] But he does not explain with what justification he can make such a restriction.

The Paramatman, De Smet writes, remains perfectly unaffected by His union with a human nature. This union does not result in total identity, but it is a personal tadatmya, a hypostatic union. [290] The human nature of Christ maintains everything that is proper to man, even the finite soul (Jivatman) and it participates - not by its own right but by appropriation - the attributes of the Paramatman. The human nature of Christ is therefore holy, divinized, enjoying the beatific vision, etc., but it is not Godhead, not immortal. [291]

It is evident that R.V. de Smet attempts at a synthesis between the Thomistic theology and the Sankarite philosophy; his scholarship in both fields makes him quite competent in this effort. It is true that the genius of Sankara and that of Thomas Aquinas meet on very many metaphysical points,[292] but it cannot be ignored that their methods are based on different philosophical categories which are mutually irreducible.

C. The Historical Incarnation in the Context of Mythical Avatars

A Christological investigation in the Indian context cannot be satisfied with a mere Vedantic interpretation of the facts of revelation regarding the 'What' and 'Who' of Jesus Christ. The great influence of Bhagavadgita and the Bhakti tradition in the Vedantic thinking makes it imperative for Christian theology to confront and evaluate the doctrine of Avatar in its relation to the Mystery of Divine Incarnation. Even Sankaracharya, inspite of the doctrinal opposition of his Kevaladvaita (strict non-dualism) to the notion of divine incorporation, had to face this question especially in his Bhasya on the Gita. [293] In the foregone sections of this Chapter we have referred to those Indian thinkers who consider Jesus Christ as an Avatar, in one or another way. In this section our approach is more comparative: the parities, disparities and the problems involved in a proper understanding of Incarnation in the context of the Avatara belief.

1. Incarnation and Avatar

E.G. Parrinder has written a well known book, 'Avatar and Incarnation'.[343] It is irrelevant for our topic in its totality to go into the details of his analysis, especially because of the difference of our concern and method.[344] We will be making, however, occasional references to him as may be required. It may be said that the general approach of Indian Christian theologians to the doctrine of Avatar is positive, although with reservations. But, there are also trends which consider such an approach to be not particularly helpful in facing the Vedanta challenge.

a. The Significant Parallels

The Austrian born Indologist, J. Neuner (*1908), [345] sees important theological points which are common to both the concepts of Avatar and Incarnation. For example, the freedom and initiative of God in entering this world are expressedly emphasized by both. God becomes man not compelled by the run of the cosmic cycle nor by the force of Karma-Samsara. God is beyond the fetters of Karma and the delusions of Samsara; His birth as man is by free choice. The virginity of Mary points first and foremost to this free initiative of God in incarnation. Man is only an humble recipient of the God who comes. 'God's coming is not dependent on the laws of nature, the law of cause and effect which govern all creatures and according to which mortals are born into the world' [346]. As in the case of the birth of Jesus Christ, God's freedom and initiative are safeguarded in all the interpretations of the Avatara doctrine. Eventhough Krsna was not born by a virgin, the spiritual nature of his birth is emphasized in the fact that it was accompanied by special signs which demonstrate symbolically that his entrance into this world was exempt from the laws of natural pro-creation. [347]

Another important parallel Neuner sees between Avatar and Incarnation is that both traditions put stress on the absolute transcendence of God even during his earthly manifestation. The divinity is not mixed up with humanity. The special immanence of God does not deprive God of his transcendence. God is not turned into prakrti nor vice versa. Neuner writes:

> "God's independence of action as manifested by (His) wonderful birth becomes the dominant feature of all.... Avatara representations and herein lies the second parallel to Christ. God is not fused with human nature; he loses none of his transcendence. This 'non-fused' and 'inalterable' condition is expressed not only in the epic descriptions of the Avatars, but also very emphatically in the philosophical interpretations." [348]

There is also similarity between the purpose of Avatar and Incarnation. Both are meant for the salvation of man. Gita refers to the protection of the good [349] and the establishment of the reign of Dharma - the Hindu counterpart for the Kingdom of God! - as the purpose of Krishnavatar. The salvation of man does not end in this world; it takes further dimensions in the self-revelation of God in Krsna as the refuge of men. In the first part of our work we had referred to the theophany that was mediated through the 'transfiguration' of Krsna. [350] Avatar, like Incarnation reveals a personal God, a God of grace, who is concerned with the welfare and salvation of man.

G. Parrinder draws our attention to many more elements that are common to Avatar and Incarnation, although in a reserved sense. [351] The "once-and-for-all" character or the uniqueness of the Incarnation as verified in Christ is, according to him, realized also in some way in the theory of Avatars.

In reference to a particular 'Yuga', world epoch, the Avatar is unique:
Sambhavami yuge yuge. There is no mention of a repeated Avatar in the
same Yuga.[352] The Christian understanding of the world from the beginning
to its consummation can be considered as some way equivalent to a Yuga
as meant by the Bhagavadgita. So at least in terms of the Bhagavadgita
we could speak of a certain uniqueness for the Avatar - eventhough such
an interpretation cannot hold ground in the totality of the Hindu understanding of the nature of the cyclic world and divine manifestations. On
the other hand, we cannot also speak of an unreservedly unique manifestation of God in Jesus Christ, especially in the context of his second
coming! [353] Christ's universal presence in the hearts of all men from the
beginning of history as the Logos, the repeated divine interventions in
the history of salvation. Christ's continuous presence in the life of the
Church and its special realization in the sacramental context etc. correspond at least in a vague way to the Hindu concept of repeated divine
manifestations. [354] So an uncritically generalized statement regarding 'uniqueness' and 'repetition' in the comparison of Avatar and Incarnation is
not quite correct. Similarly it is also not proper to say that the Incarnation
is historical while Avatars are non-historical.It is generally accepted [355]
that at least in some Avatars, for ex. Rama and Krishna, there is some
historicity, however vague it may be, inspite of the fact that mythology
plays undoubtedly the predominant role, as we have indicated in the first
part of our work.

Parrinders description of the twelve characteristics of the Avatar doctrine [356]
points also to many more possible similarities - at least by way of interpretation - between Avatar and Incarnation. The stories regarding the birth,
life and death of Rama and Krsna are so vivid and concrete that they
cannot all be branded as 'docetic'. If we ignore the puranic exaggerations,
the morality and teaching of Krsna could be to some extend compared
with the personality and sublime teachings of Jesus Christ. That is especially
evident in the fact that Bhagavadgita is rightly considered as the Hindu
Gospel. 357

Our discussion regarding the parallels between Avatar and incarnation,
however, should not be interpreted so as to mean that both the terms

are interchangeable. Some of the parallels are well based at least in some aspect, but for the rest it is only a matter of interpretation; some of the above interpretations are evidently forced. But even the possibility for such interpretations can be considered as something positive and helpful in presenting the Mystery of Christ in the Indian context. But, ultimately a Christian approach to the theory of Avatara demands many serious reservations as we shall see below.

b. Jesus Christ, the Avatar par Excellence?

Most of the Indian thinkers, both of the Advaitic and Bhakti traditions, are ready to accept Jesus Christ as one of the Avatars. We had pointed to this fact in our previous sections, both in the Chapters IV and V of this part of our work. We have also discussed their various interpretations which are naturally different in the Advaitic and Bhakti schools. We have seen also that Hindu reformers like Rammohan Roy [357a] reject all Avatar doctrines as superstitions and idolatry while others look upon Jesus Christ as the Avatar par excellence and as the Crown of Hinduism.

Here we look at the question of Avatara from a Christian point of view. There are also Christian theologians who consider that the application of the term 'Avatar' to Jesus Christ is not particularly helpful for the Indian Christology for one or another reason as we shall see. There are, however, many among Christian theologians themselves who would encourage the presentation of Jesus Christ in terms of Avatar. In the following lines we shall discuss the reservations which are necessary for such an approach.

In his work "Khristadvaita - A Theology for India", [358] Robin Boyd discusses the question: Is Jesus an Avatara? [359] He points out many of the problems involved in this question. J. Neuner refers also to some of the important contrasts between Avatar and Incarnation especially in his article "Das Christus-Mysterium und die indische Lehre von den Avatars". [360] In order to apply the notion of Avatar to the Incarnation of Jesus Christ, according to them, some of the implications of 'Avatar' have to be corrected and the term has to be re-interpreted.

The first problem we see in this context is Trinitarian in character. Avatara is a manifestation of the Absolute and not a communication of the Trinitarian Mystery to man. Inspite of the concept of 'Saccidananda' that explains the characteristics of Brahman as 'Being-Consciousness-Bliss' and the idea of 'Trimurthy' as three aspects of Saguna Brahman in his functions of creation, salvation and creative fulfilment manifested in the figures of Brahma, Visnu and Siva, there is no proper theology of the Holy Trinity in the Vedanta or in any form of Hinduism. It is not the Son of God who incarnates in Hinduism, but God Himself. As a result, the salvation of man consists not in becoming 'sons in the Son' sharing the personal communion of the Trinity but in realizing one's own natural divinity.[361]

A radical negation of matter, the created world and the human body is characteristic of the Hindu philosophy. Such an 'angelism' or 'divinism'[362] and a devaluation of the material aspect of human existence is very evident in the theory of Avatar. 'The more a guru or spiritual teacher abstains from food and laughter, the more he rises above human weaknesses and the accidents of life, the more of a master and superior he is considered to be'[363]. That is why there is and has been a tendency in India to raise ascetics and Gurus of extraordinary spiritual character to the position of an Avatar. In this sense the classical Avatars like Rama and Krishna are more theophanies than real incarnations. 'There is an old Hindu tradition that when an Avatara walks his feet do not touch the ground so that he leaves no foot prints'[364]. The Hindu Avatar appears and disappears calmly and passively. He 'withdraws from the phenomenal sphere as calmly, solemnly, and willingly as he descendend. He never becomes the seeming temporary victim of the demon powers (as did Christ nailed to the Cross), but is triumphant in his passage, from beginning to end. The Godhead, in its very aloofness, does not in the least mind assuming temporarily an active role on the phenomenal plane of ever-active nature'[365]. So the Avatara is not really human, there is no real becoming-man because God cannot have anything to do with Prakrti which is deceptive and enslaving. There is in Hinduism no redemption of the Prakrti (natural world), but only out of the Prakrti. There is in Hinduism no Avatar that shares the human Karma, 'who shares in the human situation of kenosis, who labours, suffers and dies'[366]. The resurrection of the body is also therefore out of question.[367] Eventhough some aspects in the life of an

Avatar can be given a non-docetic interpretation, it must be said that the fundamental and predominant set-up of the Avatar doctrine is docetic which is contrary to the Christian faith in the Incarnation. 'The oneness of true God and true man is quite unknown to the Avatara doctrine of India' [368] . The Christian faith in Incarnation 'is concerned not so much with the fact that God came but that he became man' [369] . The Hindu designation of Jesus as an Avatar is most often based on a misunderstanding of the Christian faith. [370] Such misunderstandings of docetism have to be clarified in applying the category of Avatar to Jesus Christ.

The implications of the Avatar doctrine regarding the question of history are also not acceptable from the Christian point of view. As the world-process in the Vedantic thought is cyclic and belongs to the realm of the unredeemable Prakrti, the Avatar does not radically change the world process in order to direct the world history towards a definitve transcendent destiny. [371] The Avatar is a mythological God and not a God who is involved in the real life-process of humanity. We will be discussing this question further below under the title 'Myth and History'. For the moment we would only point out that the Avatar doctrine has a serious lack of the historical sense, eventhough some vague historicity is attributed to the heroes behind the Rama and Krishna stories.

The notion of a repeated and cyclic historical process which is dogmatically held by the Vedantins as a natural consequence of the doctrine of Karma Samsara - there is no positive proof for that - makes it necessary that the Avatars be born again and again in each historical epoch: Sambhavami yuge yuge! This makes it possible for Hinduism to add any number of further Avatars - including Jesus Christ - to its already existing list. In the Christian faith on the contrary, Jesus Christ is not just one of the many incarnations; He is unique, once-and-for all. When applying the word 'avatar' to Jesus Christ, this aspect of uniqueness has to be stressed. A.J. Appasamy, for example, considers Jesus as the only Incarnation, the Avatar par excellence:

> "We believe that Jesus was the Avatara. God lived on the earth as a man only once and that was as Jesus.... It is our firm Christian belief that among all the great religious figures in the world there is no one except Jesus who could be regarded as an Incarnation of God." [372]

V. Chakkarai also points to the uniqueness of Jesus Christ by designating him as 'the Avatar'.[373] The Hindu Avatars appear once and then disappear; their mission is neither permanent nor dynamic. Hence it is necessary for them to repeat this 'appearance' as there are needs. Jesus on the other hand is the incarnation of God; he is God-Man for ever 'and is not simply absorbed into the Godhead with the discarding of his human nature'[374] He is permanent and his mission is ever dynamic in the sense that 'the Spirit of Jesus is incarnated again and again in human hearts'[375].

A major difference can also be pointed out between the purpose of Hindu Avatars and the Incarnation of Jesus Christ. Besides the re-establishment of the Dharma and the protection of the good, the destruction of the evil doers also belongs to the mission of an Avatar: vinasaya ca duskrtam.[376] The Gospels, however, bear ample evidence to the fact that the mission of Jesus Christ was precisely to save the wicked; nobody was excluded from the salvation he offered (Jn 3:16-17., Lk 15:11-32).[377]

A comparison is also often made between the moral character of the Avatars and that of Jesus Christ. The lofty character of Krshna in the Bhagavadgita is blurred in the pruanic stories and later devotions by erotic overtones which 'alienated thoughtful modern writers like Tagore, so that they repudiated Avatar doctrine while holding to the grace and personal revelation of God'[378]. In contrast to the Krshna stories, the moral character of Jesus Christ is 'one of the most attractive elements of the Gospel'[379].

The above discussion regarding the possibility of applying the word 'Avatar' to Jesus Christ shows that such a possibility is accompanied by many reservation. The translation of the Mystery of Incarnation into the Indian terminology requires great care not only because of the above mentioned implications connected with the Avatar theory, but also because the Indian philosophy has no equivalent for terms such as 'nature' and 'person'[380], terms which have origin in a totally different philosophical milieu with entirely different presuppositions. An uncritical application of the Avatar theory to Jesus Christ in the context of the interpretations of Sankara, Ramanuja and Radhakrishnan would result, as J. Neuner opines, in a repetition of docetism, monophysitism and modernism respectively. Some of the modern interpretations, according to him, can be compared to Nestorianism.[381] Neuner further remarks that the Christological heresies show us 'how they deviate from the mysterious divine core of the Christ mystery and how they pass into a sphere in which the non-Christian religions are groping for religious truth'[382].

There are also Indian theologians who think that even with all the reservations the application of the term 'Avatara' for the Incarnation of Jesus Christ is not adviceable because 'Avatara' has a load of unacceptable elements which cannot be simply removed by a mere Christian interpretation. True to his Brahmasamaja tradition, for example, Keshub Chunder Sen is opposed to calling Christ an Avatar; he names it 'the lie of Christian avatarism'[383]. Brahmabandhab Upadhyaya admits the theory of Avatars in its application to the Hindu religious heroes, but he maintains that its application to Christ is inadmissible. Jesus Christ is not Avatar, he is Incarnation! Avatars belong to the realm of Maya - in this he is faithful to Sankar's interpretation -, but Jesus Christ is above Maya because His person is that of the second Person of the Trinity, the Logos, who has existence in Himself. According to him, honour can be paid to the Hindu Avatars, provided we do not deny the uniqueness of Jesus Christ as the only Incarnation.[384] P. Chenchiah also admits the existence of Avatars, but the Incarnation of Jesus Christ radically differs from what is implied by 'Avatar'.[385] Eventhough the theologians who prefer to follow the Bhakti tradition of Hinduism are favourably inclined to consider Christ as an Avatar, those who find Sankara's type of Advaita better suited for the Christian purpose - besides Upadhyaya, we could include here the names of Abhishiktananda, Panikkar, Klostermaier and others - would hesitate to call Christ an Avatar.[386] It cannot, however, be ignored that the word 'Avatar' has been used for generations by the Indian Christians in reference to the Incarnation of Jesus Christ.[387]

2. Jesus Christ, the Mystery of Human History

Myth, reality and history are terms which are intimately related to each other. The mystery of man can be understood and interpreted mythically, metaphysically or historically as far as his ultimate destiny is concerned. Myth, Metaphysics and history are so intimately involved in shaping man's vision of reality that it is difficult to say where one ends and the other begins. This is especially true in the Indian mode of thinking: the metaphysical truths are clothed in primitive myths, the myths are interpreted metaphysically and hardly a line is drawn between what is mythical and what is historical. It is in this context - we have discussed this context elaborately in the first part - that a Christology has to be developed in India. We have also tried to analyse in the fourth chapter how "Christ" is understood as the universal Mystery or incomprehensible principle that pervades and impregnates the reality of man and in the above sections of this chapter we have shown the extent to which the Indian thinkers and other Indologists, both Christian and non-Christian, see this universal mystery of Christ uniquely verified and manifested in the historical figure of Jesus of Nazareth. Before entering into the question of the universal significance of the historical uniqueness of Jesus Christ which we intend to do in the next chapter, it is necessary that we cast a look at the importance and limitations of history in explaining and applying the Mystery of Christ especially in the Indian context.

a. History and Myth

In showing the difference between the Incarnation of Jesus Christ and the Avatara of Sri Krshna, J.N. Farquhar (1861-1929) [388] affirmed emphatically that 'the Krshna of the Gita is a myth, but Jesus Christ is a historical person ... he is a historical person; and he is the only man who ever actually claimed to be the God-man. He called himself the Son of Man and the Son of God, and he was crucified because he would not give up the claim'. [389] The development of form criticism and historical method in biblical exegesis has made such a blunt assertion not fully acceptable today. We have already indicated that a certain amount of historicity cannot be denied to the story of Krshna and the battle of Kruskshetra which supply the context for the religious utterances of the Bhagavadgita. [390] Even the very bare fact of Gita and other Hindu religious works point to the historical milieu which had deeply influenced the formation of the convictions expressed therein. The reality of the historical influence is, of course, one thing and how that historical aspect is understood and interpreted is another thing. So the expressed Vedantic discard of historicity and what is historical [391] cannot make a discussion on the relevance of history, even in the Vedantic context, meaningless. On the other hand, as Stanley J. Samartha (*1920) [392] observes in his "The Hindu response to the Unbound Christ" [393], historicity is not something very special for which the Christians are to be necessarily congratulated. [394] The bold application of the method of historical criticism especially in the protestant circles and the German schools of theology, in contrast to the traditional reservations of the theologians following the Roman line, has brought to light the difference between what is legendary and historical, what is mythical and religious in the understanding of the Sacred Scriptures and especially the New Testament. 'The quest of the historical Jesus', to use the expression of Albert Schweitzer, [395] or the discussion of 'the problem of the historical Jesus', as E. Käsmann would mean, [396] has also encouraged theologians like Rudolf Bultmann, Karl Barth and Emil Brunner - to mention only a few - to liberate Christology from the shifting sands of historicity. Any historical knowledge other than the bare fact of Christ could be dispensed with! This reaction of the western theologians can be compared with the historical distrust of the Vedanta Pundits.

Myths have certainly their importance in conveying the religious vision of a people because of the essentially anthropological character of mythology. But myths will have to be evaluated and interpreted in the context of man's historical experiences, apart from which the myths fall to the category of mere fancies. The task of the historico critical method in the study of a religious scripture is precisely to discover the historical foundations which shed new light upon its mythical expressions. The search for the historical is therefore no threat for the religious and theological elements of the Sacred Scriptures; it is a genuine help for their better understanding, appreciation and practical application. In the concrete case of Jesus Christ, it is in itself a contradiction to accept the bare fact of Christ and at the same time to show no interest to see how this fact had been concretely, in space and time, realized. [397] We will be paying more attention to this point especially in our discussion with Karl Rahner and Wolfhart Pannenberg in the evaluative part III, Chapter VII, Band C.

In the context of the mythical Avatars of Hinduism it is highly necessary for the Indian Christology to keep the distinction between what is historical and what is mythical, both in its encounter with the Vedantic position and in its self-presentation. It does not mean that what is true has to be historical; truth can also be expressed in mythological categories. Myths are the human concretizations of the abstract truths as Bultmann observes:

> "Myths are expression for the insight that man is not himself the master of this world and his life, that the world in which he lives is full of mysteries and secrets and that the human life itself contains many paradoxes. The mythology is an expression for a particular understanding of the human existence. It believes that the world and the life have their foundation and limitations in a power that is outside the field or our calculation and control. One could say that the myths render an immanent and this-worldly objectivity to the transcendental truth. The Myth concretizes the other side in terms of this side." [398]

But the task of separating the truths from their myth forms (genre) is not an easy one. It is here that the Indian Christology has to concentrate itself. The myths of Avatars, for example, is the concretisation of the Hindu desire to see God in a human, visible and tangible form, i.e., in the midst of human history, as a 'key' to history, which is indeed a mystery! The history for the Christians is, however, not a mystery of meaningless repetitions in the bleak eternity of Samsara, as the Hindu mythology might hold, but it has a meaning in so far as it is raised to God's salvific plane in the person of Jesus Christ. A land like India where the religious vision is abundant in myths, what is most required is a historical sense. What is here meant is not a narrow historicism, which again is a myth because it reduces and limits the incomprehensible into the confines of the idol called history. To Hinduism, the eternal Dharma, the implications of the historical nature of the Christian faith are to be conveyed in their eternal and transcendental dimensions.

b. History and Reality

It can be said, as S.J. Samartha remarks, that 'in modern India history is receiving a steadily increasing importance'. [399] The contact of India with the West which resulted in a renaissance of Hinduism especially from the time of Rammohan Roy has helped to promote a historical sense in the Vedantic mind. The Vedantic axiom that the eternal truths are more important than the transient facts of history is understood today in a new light under the influence of the fast developing natural sciences and the international communication systems that have made the world so small that a particular 'fact of history' in one place shows inevitable repurcussions to a considerable extent in the rest of the world. Facts are therefore no monads independent of each other, but each fact is in one or another way involved in the making of other facts which all together are progressing towards a dynamic future.

Not only the facts of history but also the whole vision of reality is today undergoing a dynamic transformation. A static metaphysics is today challenged by a process metaphysics as is seen in the works of Alfred North Withehead [400] and theologians like Charles Hartshorne [401] look for the possibilities of advancing from such a dynamic philosophy to a process theology. [402] This is due to the growing conviction that the facts are in themselves unexplainable and that they receive significance only in relation to other facts which form 'instances' of a dynamic totality. [404] An eschatological fulfilment to this historical dynamism is also foreseen in Wolfhart Pannenberg's historical interpretation of reality, which we will be considering more elaborately in the third part.

History could be described as the progressive revelation of reality and in this sense we could speak of a historical aspect or dimension of reality. In reference to Christology the relevant question would be with regard to the understanding of the Christ-event. The scholastic effort to describe Jesus Christ in terms of his natures and person, as a 'finished product' with a wonderful 'mixture' of this-worldly and the other-worldly, is a static and therefore a sterile metaphysics. Its one or another way of interpreting the Hypostatic union may not have much practical relevance in the lives of men; it can result in a drastic bifurcation between theology and life. The personality of Jesus Christ we find in the New Testament is on the other hand situated in the context of centuries of history of a people. He is born as a part of that history and not as a part of the Greek philosophy or a Roman codex of laws. The fact of Jesus Christ, his reality, cannot be understood apart from the history of the Jewish people. His relevance for any people, of his time or any other time, depends on the possible relevance he can have on their history. The Mystery of Jesus Christ could be meaningfully presented to India only when he is shown as a part and parcel of the integral historical development of India down through the centuries and how he could render the Indian future more meaningful. A mere Sanskrit translation of a metaphysical Christology, as a few have tried to do, would blatantly ignore the historical and incarnational character of the Christ-event.

A credible Christology in India will have to start with the Bible, the historical context of Jesus Christ and not with an imported philosophical system. The historical fact of Christ should preceed the analysis of his ontological status. The history of Jesus Christ as transmitted by the community of his faithful reveals to us what he is. What the single fact of Jesus did for the totality of human history is the key to understand who he is. What is revealed to us first is not the theories regarding Christ's person and his natures; they are only inferences from what he has done for the whole of humanity in its whole process of development which we call history. The progress of history reveals further not only the consequences of the free acts of men in the present and in the past but also the one who is the mystery of the whole historical process, namely, Jesus Christ.

Our insistence on the historical aspect of the reality of Jesus Christ does not mean that 'mere historicity is a matter of final significance' [405]. No Christology can be built upon the bare fact of Jesus Christ. It must also be shown how his history has a decisive and transcendental significance, a significance in terms of the finality and fundamental harmony, for the whole of human history. A fact of history has also to be judged in the context of the totality of history. If, as Samartha writes, 'in the life, death and resurrection of Jesus Christ, there is an authentic disclosure of God's love for man, expressing itself in a single life of concern and compassion for man, then, not only that life but also history itself is invested with a new significance' [406]. The task of any Christology is to make clear this significance.

If the fact or reality of Christ can be significant only in the totality of the whole of history, does it mean that the ontology of Christ is dependent upon the historical process? No! The reality of Christ does not depend on the contingence of history, but the significance of that reality is historically conditioned because the significance of a fact depends upon its conscious acceptance. That means, although the reality is not merely subjective it has an important subjective dimension. The fact of Christ comes down to us through the centuries through an experiencial medium that is subjective. The subjective and personal confrontation of the fact of Christ on the part of the immediate disciples of Christ and the communication of their Christ-experience have a normative value for us today because they have a certain power, intensity and originality based on the objective Christ-event. So, 'subjectivity cannot be regarded as a distortion of reality but as an attempt to penetrate that aspect of reality which manifests itself in subjective forms.... Disclosure is an event of historical mediation through human existence, in which a man's life is embraced by God's meaningful action.... Yet with the subjective initiative in the discernment of who Christ is, Christ remains extra nos' [406]. In the Indian mystic and experiential tradition, both the ontological and subjective (experiential) aspects of the Christ-event are to be stressed without losing sight of their historical dimensions. S.J. Samartha writes:

> "What may be attempted justifiably is to recognize the ontological status of Christ as well as his relation to mystic consciousness, while holding fast to the historic anchorage of the fact of Christ. Without this, any Christology in India is likely to be a leaky boat without moorings in the swirling waters of Indian philosophy and religion."[407]

It must, however, also be made clear that the historical significance and the subjective experience of the Christ-event does not exhaust the Mystery of Christ; on the contrary, the Christ-Mystery gives fulness and fulfilment to history and experience. In Christ 'time no longer means the eternal insignificance of mortal existence; instead, time is divided into the hours

of God, moving towards the end of time. All rhythmic movements of histor-
ical periods are united in this one great movement.' [408] This opinion of
Neuner regarding the fullness of history in Christ is also expressed by
Samartha in the following lines:

> "... it must be said that even though it is recognized that the distinctive
> feature of the New Testament estimate of Christ is historical, it
> must also be noted that one is driven beyond the historical categories
> in looking at the fullness of Christ. Being grasped by Christ through
> faith, experiencing God's grace in him and having the very centre
> of one's life transformed - all this is not the result of just responding
> to a historical teacher in the past. It is much more than that. To
> be in Christ is to be grasped by God who is larger and deeper, who,
> while being active in history, is beyond the categories conditioned
> by time, in his fullness and mystery." [409]

In short, it can be said that Jesus Christ is no God waiting on the other
shore of history; this world and its history have become that shore through
him. But, this world with its history has an end, an end of perfection and
fullness. This historical process will not be destroyed, but transformed
into the fullness of God, the eschatological Kingdom of God. [410]

We shall discuss the soteriological aspect of the universal relevance of
Christ's historical uniqueness in the sixth chapter. In the following section,
however, we shall cast a further look on the person of Christ as the fulfilment of the Vedantic religious aspirations. We have made this distinction
between the 'person' and 'work' of Christ only for the sake of methodological clarity.

3. Jesus Christ, the Historical Fulfilment

In contrast to the theory of Christ's universal presence which we discussed
in the fourth chapter, we have been following in this chapter the line of
thinking that looks upon Jesus Christ as the unique historical fulfilment
of the Indian philosophical and religious aspirations. Before ending this
chapter we shall concentrate here in a more explicit way on the Indian
approach to Christ as the historical fulfilment of the religious aspirations
of mankind.

The conviction that Christ is not only the fulfilment of the law of Moses
but also of the religious aspirations of all "pagan" (!) religions and especially
of Hinduism had been the theme of the well known book "The Crown of

Hinduism" written by J.N. Farquhar (1861-1929) and published in the year 1913. The approach of Farquhar had been highly apologetic and negative to Hinduism.[412] Still he was convinced that all the elements of pagan religions, including Hinduism, spring from the religious need of man. What is true in Hinduism, i.e. the fundamental religious aspiration, is not to be destroyed, but is to be fulfilled in Christ. He writes:

> "Christ's own declaration, 'I came not to destroy but to fulfil', has cleared up for us completely all our difficulties with regard to the Old Testament.... Can it be that Christ Himself was thinking of pagan faiths as well as Judaism? ... If Christ is able to satisfy all the religious needs of the human heart, then all the elements of pagan religions, since they spring from these needs, will be found reproduced in perfect form, completely fulfilled, consumated in Christ." [413]

Our concern here is not with 'pagan religions' in general but Hinduism in particular: How Christ is understood in India as the fulfilment of the Advaitic and the Avataric quest?

a. The Fulfilment of the Vedantic Aspirations

In presenting Jesus Christ as the fulfilment of Hinduism J.N. Farquhar observes that 'in Him is focussed every ray of light that shines in Hinduism. He is the Crown of the faith of India.' [414] This line of thought is further explicited by Acarya R.C. Das:

> "He (Jesus Christ) is the Maitreyi of Buddhism, the concrete realization of its Dharma. He is the full historical manifestation of the Rita (moral order and cosmic law) of the Vedas, the perfect Incarnation satisfying the fundamental longing of the Vaishnava Hindu as expressed in the Gita (IV:7-8). He is the true Kalki of popular Hinduism satisfying the demans for final justice, and the true Hari who takes away the sin and sorrow of the world. He is the Sadguru of the ignorant and sinful, the Jivanmukta of popular idealism, the Perfect Man of the Unitarian and the Brahmo, the Purushottama of the Gita, the Purusha or Prajapati of the Rigveda." [415]

Christ, the meeting point of the diverse spiritual ideals of Hinduism, is the concretisation of the Advaitic aspiration of identity with Brahman: 'Aham Brahma asmi'; I am Brahman! Jesus Christ is in reality the only human being who could, according to the Christian faith, claim to be one with Brahman in a pure advaitic sense, both from the ontological and experiencial point of view. The reality of Christ as truly God and man makes of him an 'Advaitin' in the fullest sense of the term.

Even Indian thinkers like K.C. Sen and P.C. Mozoomdar, who do not accept Christ as equal to God, consider him to be the fulfilment of the Indian Advaitic and Yogic aspirations. Sen's following observation goes in this line:

> "He (Jesus Christ) comes to fulfil and perfect that religion of communion for which India has been panting as the heart panteth after the waterbrook.... For Christ is a true Yogi, and he will surely help us to realize our national ideal of a Yogi." [416]

P.C. Mozoomdar similarly observes that 'so far as God's nature and relation could be shown within the limits of finite humanity, at a distant age and in imperfect human society, Christ showed it.... From the mystic depths of Father's eternal reason, the Son sprang into personality as a fitting consummation here on earth of created things in the fullness of time becoming flesh ... the divine humanity of Christ only crowns (the) marvellous structure of man.' [417]

Brahmabandhab Upadhyaya was also convinced of the fact that Christ as the God-Man is the fulfilment of the genuine Vedantic tradition of India:

> "The more strictly we practice our universal faith [in Christ], the better do we grow as Hindus. All that is noblest and best in Hindu Character is developed in us by the genial inspiration of the perfect Narahari (God-Man) our pattern and guide. The more we love Him, the more we love our country, the prouder we become of our past glory." [418]

In his article "To Christ through the Vedanta"[419] P. Johanns presents Christ as the fulfilment of the Vedantic systems and expresses his opinion that 'we can reconstruct our catholic philosophy with the materials borrowed from various Vedantic systems' [420]. His review "The Light of the East" followed a policy of accepting from the Vedanta all that could be assimilated into the Christian faith and to show that 'the best thought of the East is a bud that, fully expanded, blossoms into Christian thought'. His intention was not to lead India to something that is foreign to her heart but to assist her to 'become fully herself by pointing out to her true ideals, showing her the way to realize them' [421] . Regarding the Vedantic 'thirst' after Christ; Johanns writes:

"The Indian heart is after Christ. India wants a human God either in Brahman or in Krshna... We have to offer them something: the realization of their own ideal..." [422]

Sadhu Sundar Singh similarly maintains that 'Christianity is the fulfilment of Hinduism. Hinduism has been digging channels. Christ is the water to flow through these channels' [423] Sudhakar, however, prefers to call Christ as 'the Answer' to the question called 'Hinduism':

> Hinduism is a hunger and Christ comes to satisfy it. So I emphasise Christ 'the Answer' rather than Christ 'the fulfilment'. God puts the hunger and provides the food for the hunger in Christ." [424]

Swami Abhishiktananda sees in Christ the 'eschatological fulfilment' of Hinduism. [425] The deep and permanent values of Hinduism and of the Upanisads are not cancelled but fulfilled in Christ: "Bible is the Crown of the Upanisads." [426] "All that is said in the upanisads is said of Christ, they find fulfilment in Christ." [427] The idea that Jesus Christ is the fulfilment of Vedanta is also held by Bede Griffiths. [428] Both of them see the idea of Christ as fulfilment not merely in a doctrinal plane, but on the level of spiritual experiences. [429]

b. The Fulfilment of the Avataric Quest

Many Indian theologians consider that the 'Avatar' mythology of Hinduism is an expression of the human quest or search to see and touch God in human form. The Incarnation of Jesus Christ is the fulfilment in history of this mythological search. Nehemiah Goreh, for example, sees the Avatar stories as a 'praeparatio evangelica'. Regarding his conversion from Hinduism to Christianity he writes:

> "I gave up the Hindu religion because I came to see that it was not a religion given by God. The errors of it I condemn. But I never found fault in idea with its teaching that God becomes Incarnate. Indeed, many stories of Krshna and Rama, whom the Hindu religion teaches to be incarnations of God, used to be very affecting to us.... And thus our countrymen have been prepared to some extent, to appreciate and accept the truths of Christianity." [430]

It is evident that he considers the Avatar myths as prefiguration of the true Incarnation of God in Jesus Christ. This is similar to the view held by Prof. R.C. Zaehner:

"... wonderful though the myth of the Incarnate Krshna is, it is still only a myth, though a myth full of meaning and prefiguration of the historical Incarnation of the God who is at the same time love."[431]

In his work "Jesus the Avatar", V. Chakkarai maintains that the Hindu Sastras and Darsanas formed the precondition for the true Avatar, Jesus Christ.[432] The divine Avatars formed in India 'the background' for the preaching of the Incarnate Word, Jesus Christ. Christ is the fulfilment for the quest we find in the Bhagavadgita for a God in human form. It is quite reasonable to think that had the author of the Gita encountered the person of Jesus Christ he would have unreservedly accepted him! 'The need of man is for a central figure, a universal model, one who includes in himself all (the) various embodiments of God's manifestation. The need of man is for an incarnation in whom all other incarnations will be completed. Such an incarnation was Christ.'[433]

The Hindu Avatar mythology can very well be considered as dreams in the religious sphere of man that look towards their realization as N. Goreh observes:

"He (Jesus Christ) showed the meaning of those anticipations and gave the answer to those doubtings, and satisfied those yearnings and shadowy foretastes of truth, which expressed themselves in the imagery incarnations dreamed of by poets and philosophers. He proved the truth of the anticipations, not only by his preaching, but also by his history. He was and is substantially and in fact all that they had dreamed and infinitely more."[434]

J. Neuner also speaks of Avatars as the 'dreams' that should find their realization in Jesus Christ. The words of Neuner on the dream-character of Avatar myths:

"Just as in the natural life of the human soul a desired object is perceived as real through dreams, the spiritual destiny helps to create a myth in which man's hope takes visible shape. Dreams are not history, and yet they have a real bearing on the psychological reality of man. In the same way the [Avatar] myths, insubstantial though they are in a historical sense, reflect a real human inclination towards Christ. Thus we find in the myths, motives that are similar to those of Christianity. They speak of the miraculous coming, of the unfolding of limitless power, of the bliss of love in the kingdom of God made manifest. But all these analogies only help to set off the fundamental difference: Christ is history, the Avataras are myths."[435]

Like dreams, so opines Neuner, the myths are also blurred and confused; they t end to aberrations. 'Yet the myths spun around the incarnate God testify mankind's eternal longing for Christ, and particularly where the joyful tidings of his actual arrival have not been heard.' [436] The Avatar myths are not 'truths of a tangible kind, but they bear the truth of prophecy' [437], because they are 'the profoundest expression of man's desire and destiny to meet God not only in his transcendence but in the closeness of human contacts'. [438] J.N. Farquhar had also written in his "Crown of Hinduism" about the Incarnation of Christ as the realization of the Hindu dreamy imaginations expressed in the Avatar stories:

> "The Indian religious instinct divined that God would become man, but did not realize the depths of the divine humility. The main idea is right, but the detailed outworking is a failure.... Thus, Jesus fulfils the Indian thought. He is the realization of the Indian ideal; but in this case, as in every other, the reality sent by God is far better and more wonderful than the imagination of man." [439]

Farquhar also sees a special relationship between the worship of idols that is prevalent in popular Hinduism with the Incarnation of the Son of God. Idols are for the ordinary Hindus partial Avatars (Amsavatara). Idol worship, according to Farquhar, is a pitiable distortion of the basic human need and search for the transcendental God in visible and tangible forms. Jesus Christ as the true Image of God purifies this transcendental orientation of man: "Jesus actually takes in the Christian life, the place which is held by idols in idolatrous systems. He is effectively the image of God." [440] This interpretation and approach to the Christ-Mystery especially in the Indian context is warmly welcomed also by J. Neuner. The image worship in India , according to him, achieves a greater meaning in the background of the mystery of the Incarnation. As in an image or idol, a believer 'sees' and 'touches' God himself in the person of Jesus Christ. [441] The instinct of idolatry found in most of the religions like Hinduism finds its fulfilment in Jesus Christ, the Eternal Born Personal Image of God. [442] Neuner maintains that those who worship the Avatars and similarly the stone images are worshipping the Unknown God; Avatars and idols are really images of Christ himself, 'not, to be sure, of the historical Christ', but 'of the Saviour who is written into the hearts of all men as the promised Messiah' [443].

Jesus Christ is the fulfilment of the Vedantic longing and the historical realization of the Avataric quest. This longing for the fulfilment is both anthropological and transcendental in character. The fulfilment theories proposed and supported by the Indian theologians - excepting of course those who hang exclusively to a theory of universal presence in a fanatic attempt to ape at all costs the supposed preeminence of pure Advaita which with a gnostic air is mostly concerned with the Nirguna Brahman and the Jnana Marga - are very much in harmony with the transcendental anthropology and the anthropological Christology of Karl Rahner, who insists on the Christward orientation of man and the right of man to search for the concrete realization of this transcendental orientation in human history. We will be discussing this point more elaborately in the third part.

Conclusion to Chapter Five

Our consideration of Jesus Christ from the stand-point of his historical
uniqueness and especially as the fulfilment of the Vedantic aspirations
is of no much value if a doctrinal confrontation is intended by it. Fulfilment is ultimately a matter of experience and religious experience cannot
be 'injected' by doctrinal arguments and counter arguments. It must not
also be forgotten that the Neo-Vedantins propose a theory of religious
fulfilment in the 'Santana Dharma', i.e. reformed Hinduism as the Eternal
Religion! Dr. D.S. Sarma, for example, writes:

> "India's need is not ... any fresh imported religion as   Christians
> missionaries want to make us believe. On the contrary, the rest of
> the world is in need of India's Vedanta for making its religion more
> liberal and broadminded." [444]

The convinced followers of the Vedanta or the popular Hinduism should
not also be considered as 'inferior' in their religious experiences. It is
a fact, as V. Chakkarai observes, that Hinduism perfectly satisfies its
votaries. [445] They do not as a rule experience any 'quest' or 'aspiration'
or 'religious want' in favour of Christianity on the subjective, experiental
level. They are also, certainly, not far from salvation! The religious
depth and sincerity of the Hindu brothers are beyond doubt. Therefore,
it must be evident from the very start that the theory of fulfilment is
a 'Christian answer' to a 'Christian question'. There is also another question
that is involved in the notion of fulfilment: What is fulfilled? Hinduism
as a religion or the religious aspirations of man for which Hinduism is
an expression? The theological opinions in this regard are manifold [446]
and this question involves also the notion of 'anonymous Christians' and
'anonymous Christianity', a notion directly connected with the soteriological
aspect of the Christ-Mystery which we will discuss in the third part. [447] Fulfilment also should not be understood as a total acceptance and assimilation of all elements found in non-Christian religions. Samartha asks
whether'what Christ said about fulfilling the law of Moses can be extended
to all systems of religion, particularly when some of the crucial aspirations
of men are not fulfilled by Christ, but, on the contrary, are shattered
in order to rekindle the new life in them' [448]. The Old Testament has
certainly an immediacy to the Christ-Mystery which the other religions

and holy scriptures cannot validly claim. So there is a difference in the notion of fulfilment when it is applied to Judaism and other religions. The question regarding the 'how' of fulfilment is also very important.[449] We cannot think of any Christian fulfilment except in terms of the Paschal Mystery, the Mystery of death and resurrection. Christ's fulfilment is necessarily a death to the old and a birth into the new. That is why the person of Christ cannot be understood except in the framework of his deeds, namely, in the context of his life, teaching, death and resurrection, i.e., in reference to the soteriological relevance of Jesus Christ for the whole of mankind. That is our concern in the next chapter![450]

CHAPTER VI

THE UNIVERSAL RELEVANCE OF CHRIST'S UNIQUENESS IN HISTORY

"The announcement of Christ and his Gospel", writes Duraisamy Simon Amalorpavadass, [1] "... will not be a revelation of God, unless it is first and foremost a revelation of man, an interpretation of his human existence and an answer to his problems and aspirations."[2] The concern of our work is not merely to tell the story of an uniquely interesting historical personality called Jesus Christ, nor just to analyse the make-up of his ontological and psychological 'structure' for its own sake, but to have a look at the universal significance and relevance this person may have in relation to the whole of human history and how to interpret this relevance especially from the Indian point of view. In the last chapter we have refered to Jesus Christ as the Mystery of human history.[3] That was a consideration restricted to the reality of his historical person as the fulfilment of the Vedantic aspirations and the avataric quest. Now we concentrate on the other aspect of the problem: the 'how' of it! The anthropological approach which we have been so far following in considering the Christ-Mystery takes a decisive turn in this chapter - a soteriological turn. Soteriology is not merely a 'theo-logical' question; it is through and through anthropological too. God cannot be called 'Saviour' in Himself; He is Saviour only in relation to man and his history. The Christ-Mystery is relevant for man only in so far as it is anthropological, i.e. in so far as it interprets the human existence and answers credibly the problems and aspirations of man. An understanding of the 'who' and 'what' of Christ is necessary, of course, to realize the deep implications of the 'work' he did, but 'it is more important to ask what is the Reality that one encounters in Jesus Christ as the living and the risen Lord, in the totality of his life, death and resurrection, and how, through him, a renewal of human life is possible' [4]. Only from a proper answer to this question can we actually derive the 'who' (person) and 'what' (natures) of Christ. The reality of salvation, as interpreted by the New Testament tradition, is inseparably connected with the Christ-event and that is manifested to us, according to the apostolic witness, through what Jesus did (Acts 1:22)[5]. The 'deeds' of Jesus are a 'key' to the interpretation of his person, and his person in turn throws further light on the 'deeds' themselves! In other words, the relevance of Jesus for the rest of mankind alone can ultimately explain his person.

In the fourth chapter we discussed the question of Christ in himself under the aspect of his universal and unbound presence. It has, however, to be rememberd that this presence is invariably salvific in character, inspite of the fact that we reflect more systematically on the relevance of this presence from the soteriological point of view especially in this chapter. As an apparent 'antithesis' to the notion of Christ's universal presence we considered Jesus Christ in the fifth chapter from the stand-point of his historical uniqueness. It must again be stressed that the uniqueness of Christ is not merely the singularity of an interesting chapter in history, but his uniqueness is essentially a salvific uniqueness as we want to explain in this chapter. The aim of this chapter is to dissolve the apparent 'contrarity' of the two poles, namely the universal and the unique, in a 'salvific' synthesis. The historical uniqueness of Jesus Christ consists primarily in his universal relevance and the universality of the Christ-Mystery is based on its uniqueness. As P.D. Devanandan observes, there is no uniqueness for Christ without his universality and vice versa:

> "[Our conviction is] that what God has done in Jesus Christ has been done for all men. So that the claim for uniqueness is only an affirmation of its universality ... Christians believe that with the coming of Christ, God Almighty identified Himself for a while with man in all man's struggles for perfection and the realisation of his true nature. Such identification initiates a new era in creation. It marked the beginning of a redemptive movement which takes in humanity in its entirety, that is the whole community of mankind inclusive of all peoples, whatever their beliefs, language and race. So that, far from wanting to shut others from participation (which would be being exclusive) the Christian wants the world of men to share his faith in this all-inclusive cosmic process of new creation." [6]

In short, the universality of Christ means the all-inclusive uniqueness of Christ; his uniqueness is by no means a narrow and exclusive uniqueness. This point is especially important to tackling the question of salvation in non-Christian religions.

It will be evident in the following sections that there are substantial differences in the Vedantic and Christian approaches to the question of Christ's relevance for the rest of mankind and for the whole of history. The Vedantins consider his importance in his showing the way to the realization of man's innate divinity, while the Hindu reformers see in him a great ethical teacher of mankind. In both cases the role of Christ is not considered as that of a Saviour in the Christian sense; he is not for them the 'final', 'efficient', 'meritorious', 'instrumental' and 'formal' cause of our justification. [7] In the context of the fundamental divine character of each man and the notion of Karma-Samsara, no one can 'merit' salvation for the sake of another one through a process of 'satisfaction'. The doctrine of Karma-Samsara demands that each one should merit and satisfy for himself; the Avatars, for example, can only help in this process; the great Gurus and liberated souls cannot work out the salvation for others, but they can only be examples for others: In the Bhakti tradition, of course, the notion of grace plays a significant role[8] and similar to the Christian concept of grace this notion also has a certain element of gratuity, but this gratuity is largely superficial because of the innate divine character of every man! The Hindu reformers who reject this Vedantic trend and insist on the theistic understanding of the cosmic reality also do not admit any 'vicarious' character to the role of Christ; his importance for them is also one of a universally valid example. It is the task of Christology in India to make clear the universal liberating significance and the saving role of the Christ-mystery for the whole of human history.

A. Christ, the Mahaguru: the Great Teacher of Mankind

The concept of the 'Guru' which we analysed in the first part of our work[9] is especially relevant here in reference to Jesus Christ. A 'Guru' is, as we have seen, a spiritual teacher and the adjective prefix 'Maha' (great) conveys an idea of comparative excellence. For the Indian Christians Jesus Christ is the 'Daivya' Guru' (Divine Master). ' A 'Guru', in the Indian tradition, stands in the place of God as his representative. The addition of 'daivya' to 'Guru' is meant as a further stress on his ontological divinity which, of necessity, gives him a unique place among all Gurus. The use of the same expression is also normal among non-Christians, even if all its implications in the Christian usage are not accepted.

A 'Guru' is first and foremost a great example for his disciples both in ethics and on the path to God-realization. It must be said that it is in this sense that the name of Christ is most popular among the Hindus. His relevance for them is that of a great teacher and not that of a saviour as the Christians would mean.

The Hindu religious reformers of the 19th and the 20th centuries who were concerned not only with the spiritual aspect of religion but also its social and political repercussions, found in the New Testament and in the teachings of Jesus a rich source of ethical renewal for India. - According to them, the relevance of Jesus for India lies first and foremost in his ethical teachings especially as contained in the Sermon on the Mount.

1. The Sermon on the Mount

"Of all the teachings of Jesus Christ or of the entire Bible", writes Manilal C. Parekh in his "A Hindu's Portrait of Jesus Christ", "nothing has made so deep an appeal to the Hindu heart as the Sermon on the Mount."[10] Raja Rammohan Roy, K.C. Sen, P.C. Mozoomdar and Mahatma Gandhi belong to the great number of prominent Indians who valued the deep implications of the Sermon for social transformation in India. M.C. Parekh sees in it the core, the sum and substance of Jesus teachings and attributes to it 'a charm of its own which no other teaching in the entire religious literature of the world ... is found to possess'[11]. Gandhi also considers the Sermon on the Mount as the most essential aspect of Christ's message;[12] but, unlike Parekh, he does not see in the Sermon anything that is absolutely unique or not present in other religions and religious literatures. He thinks that the Sermon on the Mount and the teachings in the Bhagavadgita stand on the same footing. He writes: "The spirit of the Sermon on the Mount competes almost on equal terms with the Bhagvadgita for the domination of my heart. It is the Sermon which endeared Jesus to me."[13] Gandhi's natural preferance, however, is for the Gita. Inspite of that he maintains: "Today, supposing I was deprived of the Gita and forgot all its contents but had a copy of the Sermon, I would derive the same joy from it as I do from the Gita."[14] Swami

Prabhavananda [15] and D.S. Ramachandra Rao [16] , like many other Hindu elites, hold a similar view regarding the teachings of Jesus as contained in the Sermon on the Mount.

It is evident that there is a general tendency among the elites in India to identify the essence of Christianity and Christ's Gospel with the Sermon on the Mount. It must, however, be remembered that for reformers like Gandhi, what is important is not the person of Christ but the universally applicable principles contained in his teachings. [17] It is certainly true that the Sermon on the Mount contains valuable religious teachings. But to reduce Christianity and the message of Christ to a number of good teachings, as the above authors do, does not do justice to Christ in his entirety. As far as the Christians are concerned, Christ is not merely a religious teacher, nor the Gospels only a code of principles, as we shall see later. But it is understandable that those who see Jesus Christ only as a 'Guru' may not find anything more than mere 'teachings' in the New Testament! In the following section we shall pay special attention to the 'ethical' aspect of Jesus' teachings as understood by the Hindu reformers.

2. Jesus Christ, the Ethical Teacher

It was Raja Rammohan Roy who, among the Hindu reformers of the last century, put the greatest stress on the ethical teachings of Jesus to help the renaissance of India. He considered the questions regarding the nature of Christ's person simply irrelevant for India; his moral teachings are more important. [19] Roy's insistence on the ethical teachings of Jesus is most evident in the fact that he made a collection of the main ethical sayings of Jesus as found in the synoptic Gospels and published them in 1820 under the title, "The Precepts of Jesus: The Guide of Peace and Happiness". [20] In this work Roy makes a real effort to elucidate and commend the teachings of Christ to his fellow countrymen. His concern cannot be considered as primarily religious, but social. The ethics of Jesus, according to him, are well suited to regulate the human conduct in reference to the individuals and society and to promote peace and happiness in human existence beyond the limitations of religious differences. [21] By this book Roy hoped to withdraw man from his imaginary faiths, rituals and observances and to encourage him to lead a better ethical life manifested in good works. [22] Rammohan Roy was convinced that 'there is nothing so sublime as the precepts taught by Christ and there is nothing equal to the simple doctrines he inculcated' [24] . His insistence on the moral principles of Jesus in contrast to the dogmatic religious truths of Christianity becomes all the more evident in the fact that unlike many other Indian thinkers 'he is attracted more by the Synoptic Gospels with their emphasis on Jesus' teachings than by the Gospel of St. John with its meditations on Jesus and similarity to traditional Bhakti or mystic religious experience' [25] . Only in a few pages towards the end of his collection "Precepts of Jesus" there are references to John! This shows that his use of the Gospels had been highly selective and accommodated. Still it cannot be forgotten that unlike many Indian thinkers Rammohan Roy was considering the moral teachings of Jesus even as superior to the teachings of all other religions: "No other religion can produce anything that may stand in competition with the precepts of Jesus, much less can be pretended to be superior to them." [26]

Roy's selective use of the New Testament passages brought him heavy criticism from the part of the Baptist missionaries at Serampore. In an editorial written in their magazine "Friend of India", Dr. Joshua Marshman blamed 'the intelligent heathen', Rammohan Roy, for ignoring Jesus' divinity in accepting only his precepts.[27] It must be remarked that the apologetic approach of Marshman was also not very conducive to truth. In the discussions that followed, Roy had no difficulty in defending his position from a rational point of view and from the sayings of the New Testament. [28] The use of the expression 'heathen' in reference to him greatly offended Roy. He reacted against it by writing "An Appeal to the Christian Public" in which he observed that the editorial treated him in an 'unchristian-like manner' violating the essential principles of Christianity, namely, of truth, charity and liberality! [29] The precepts of Jesus, he maintained, do not justify any retaliation even upon enemies. [30]

Following the line of thinking of Raja Rammohan Roy, P.C. Mozoomdar also finds in Jesus' ethical teachings a great contribution to mankind especially in establishing the moral principles and universal brotherhood of all men. He writes:

"That men who looked upon each other as aliens, strangers, not unoften enemies, who disliked, distrusted, deluded by each other, feared, illtrea- ted, made tools of, made toys of each other, should forsake such attitudes and look upon each other as members of the same household, brothers, equals, friends, children of the same Father, bound to cherish, help edify, elevate, sanctify each other by the overmastering impulse of love, mutual interest and common earning, an intense feeling of oneness, of ownness, is the principle which Jesus Christ came to establish." [31]

What attracted Gandhi most in the moral teachings of Jesus was his principle of non-resistance to evil as enunciated in the Sermon on the Mount. For Gandhi Jesus was the representation of the principle of non-violence[32] which is a door towards the infinite possibilities of universal love. Non-resistance to evil is, according to Gandhi, the new law given by Jesus.[33] Evil can produce only further evil, violence only further violence. Eye for eye can only make the world blind. To see the truth underlying human existence, to 'grasp' and realize truth (Satyagraha), the only way is that of non-violence (Ahimsa). 'Ahimsa is the means and Satya is the end'. [34] He promoted a way of life (Ashram) of which the ideal is 'seeking truth through the exclusive means of Ahimsa' [35] . In his autobiography, "My Experiments with Truth", Gandhi writes about his conviction that 'Ahimsa' is the only way to truth[36] Ahimsa, as understood by Gandhi, is not a passive and cowardous submission before insolent might; on the contrary, Ahimsa requires great courage and self-control; Ahimsa is a non-attachment to every thing, including one's own body, which makes one spiritually free. So Ahimsa necessarily pre- supposes detachment and selflessness, which make all other beings feel safe before us. [37] Where there is no Ahimsa, there reigns the law of the jungle and man is degraded to the level of animals: "Though we have the human form, without the attainment of the virtue of non-violence we still share the qualities of our remote, reputed ancestors - the urangutang." [38] Ahimsa, according to Gandhi, should include the whole of creation, and not only human beings.[39] Ahimsa is just another aspect of the eternal Law of Love.

Gandhi finds the relevance of Jesus Christ for the whole of humanity in his being a supreme example of Ahimsa and Satyagraha. Regarding Jesus' influence on his life Gandhi writes:

"Though I cannot claim to be a Christian in the sectarian sense, the example of Jesus' suffering is a factor in the composition of my under- lying faith in non-violence, which rules all my actions, worldly and temporal. Jesus lived and died in vain, if he did not teach us to regulate the whole of life by the eternal Law of Love." [40]

In the preface of the same work Gandhiji points to Jesus Christ as the perfect man whose example of non-violence should be a challenge for every body. [41] Jesus Christ rendered credibility to his teachings on Ahimsa in a very special way by his martyrdom on the Cross which indeed is 'a great example to the world' [42]. Jesus' life and ethical teachings confirmed by his death makes him a great teacher of mankind. Gandhi writes: "I do not need either the prophecies or the miracles to establish Jesus' greatness as a teacher. Nothing can be more miraculous than the three years of his ministry." [43] Even if Gandhi could not sincerely look upon Jesus as the unique saviour of mankind, he was convinced that Jesus is ever relevant as one among the mighty teachers in human history. [44] He maintains that Jesus is a great source of spiritual strength not only for himself but for the entire world regardless of the distinction of races and religions:

"I refuse to believe that there now exists or has ever existed a person that has not made use of his example to lessen his sins.... The lives of all have, in some greater or lesser degree, been changed by his presence, his actions, and the words spoken by his divine voice." [45]

The reference to sin and the word 'divine' in the above passage should not be understood in the traditional Christian sense. We had already refered to Gandhi's idea regarding Christ's divinity. [46] We will be discussing the question of 'sin' in one of the following sections.

Inspite of Gandhi's great respect and veneration for the teachings of Jesus Christ, it must be remembered that 'the basic inspiration for Gandhiji's life and work came not from Christianity but from his own religion, viz. Hinduism' [47]. The opinion of V. Chakkarai that Hinduism satisfies its votaries is clearly verified in the life of Mahatma Gandhi. His attitude towards the Christian scriptures was very selective. Gandhiji was, indeed, 'essentially a religious person endowed with the highest and most human qualities' [48], and there are many points in his life and even in his death that are comparable with the life and death of Jesus Christ, but it has to be admitted with all respect that he never grasped the centre of the Christian faith regarding the salvific relevance of the person and teachings of Christ, not to mention his redeeming death in the light of the resurrection. But Gandhi's religious sincerity and dedication to Truth is beyond all doubts.[49] The life and teachings of Christ constituted a 'supporting plank' for the political, ethical and religious vision of Gandhi, even if they were not 'the main pillar of his life'[50]. But it can be assumed that Gandhi has done more to make the message of Jesus Christ feel at home in India, perhaps, than any other Christian missionary. This assumption can be corroborated by the following remark of a well known disciple of Mahatmaji, namely, of the late Vinoba Bhave, the Sarvodaya leader:

"I, for myself, can say on behalf of the whole of Indian culture that Christ is acceptable to India.... It is my claim that, to my knowledge, nowhere else has a collective experiment of Christ's teaching carried out on so extensive a scale as in India under the leadership of Mahatma Gandhi. It is proved to be in our interest that God gave us the wisdom to accept the message of Christ." [51]

3. 'Ahimsa' in Practice

The principle of non-violence (Ahimsa) contained in the teachings of Jesus Christ has been a source of inspiration not only for Mahatma Gandhi; he was actually only a representative of the whole Indian 'mood'. The reason for that lies in the fact that Christ not only preached an attractive doctrine, but also lived accordingly. For many Indian thinkers Jesus is the personification of the agonized humanity and its thirst for righteousness even in the face of injustice and persecution. Swami Aseshananda writes:

"The grandeur of Christ, the Man of sorrows, who knew not where to lay his head, making the sky his roof and the earth his bed, cannot even be conceived of by a selfish mind. A vulgar soul can never visualize such an image of perfect endurance admidst fiery ordeals and inhuman persecution of a tremendous magnitude.... The overflowing milk of human love and heartfelt sympathy for the poor, the afflicted and the down-trodden, will earn for Christ the homage of an agonized humanity for all time and in all climes. 'Blessed are they which are persecuted for righteousness' sake, for theirs is the Kingdom of heaven' is his message of hope to the suffering, drooping and dejected souls. Washing the feet of his disciples with his own hand he said: 'I call you not servants but friends. He that is greatest amongst you, let him be as the younger and he that wants to be the chief, be he the servant of all.... The best temple of the most High is the body of man. 'He who serves man, serves God', was the precept he preached and practised." [51a]

The Indian leaders could not find in the followers of Christ a sincere practice of what they preached. The colonial domination to which India was subject and the foreign exploitation to which it was a victim also did not help in any way the Christians from the imperial West to witness the teachings of Christ in their lives. There were seven missionaries who considered that the 'Christian' colonial domination was a providentially arranged blessing for India. [51b] This, of course, cannot be considered representative of the whole missionary attitude. There had been Europeans, and not a few, who were really conscious of the cultural heritage of India; many had even directly promoted the struggle for Independence and contributed a lot to the socio-political development of India. Still Christianity as a religion of the colonial power was in general considered to have lost all credibility as the true following of Christ and especially his teachings of service for the fellow men and denunciation of all methods of violence (Himsa) in settling disputes or in establishing one's own views. The two World Wars fought mainly in the Christian West within the short span of thirty years substantiated the Indian doubts regarding the credibility of the preaching of the principles of Christ by the Western Christianity. Manilal Parekh observes even that Christ's Ahisma is practised better in India than in the Christian West. [51c] Swami Aseshananda was also convinced that the Hindus were much better in following Christ's teachings than the Christians themselves as a whole. The principle of non-violence and love for the enemies belongs, according to him, to the age old tradition of India. He makes the following relevant observation:

> "The spirit of Christ has sunk deep into their (Hindus') heart even before Christ came to the earth. 'Love thine enemies, bless them that curse thee, do good to them that hate thee, and pray for them that despite-fully use and persecute thee' has been the message voiced by all the Hindu sages and seers. The picture of Jesus preaching his Gospel of the brotherhood of man and the Fatherhood of God - wandering from place to place, knowing no fixed shelter, a supremely gentle being, a consoler of troubled hearts and a healer of aggrieved souls - is most appealing to the Hindu mind." [51d]

'Practice what you preach', is a warning often levelled by Hindu thinkers against the professional followers of Christ! Undoubtedly there is much truth in this and this warning is a challenge. On the other hand, it would not be also fair to ignore the communal riots, bloodshed and social inequality plaguing the Indian society even up to the present day!

4. The Vedantic Sadguru

The Vedantins see the relevance of Jesus Christ for India and for the rest of the world not primarily in his role as an ethical teacher but as a spiritual master on the path to Vedantic God-realization. In the fourth chapter we had discussed the Vedantic consideration of the person of Christ as the 'Advaitic Yogi'.[52] If Jesus Christ is first and foremost a Yogi, it follows that his relevance for humanity also consists in leading men to the yogic ideal of realizing God within one's own inner consciousness. As there is not fundamental distinction, as the Vedantins hold, between the self which was in Jesus and the other individual selves, whatever that was proper to Jesus, is applicable to each individual self!

Swami Vivekananda once observed: "If I, as an Oriental, have to worship Jesus of Nazareth there is only one way left for me, that is to worship him as God and nothing else."[53] Just as Jesus is God or the Son of God, in the Advaitic sense, every human being is by right the Son of God and each one has to realize in one's own life what Jesus attained in his advaitic consciousness. This consciousness can be attained only through a process of internal yogic purification. This is what Jesus means, according to Vivekananda, when he teaches us about the Kingdom of God that is within us![54] The verse in St.John: "Behold the Lamb of God, who takes away the sins of the world" (Jn 1:29)[55] is to be understood, as the one who saves the world from its sins would be incorrect. Jesus is not the one who takes on himself our sins, but he is the one who shows us the way to become perfect by our efforts. Jesus Christ shows us our true human nature, that we too are God.[56] Christ, who is the incarnation of God, i.e. who has not forgotten his divinity, can help us in our own divine self-realization.

In the opinion of Vivekananda, Jesus Christ teaches us the true path of God-realization through three progressive stages which he himself had experienced:

> "... three stages are taught by the Great Teacher in the New Testament. Note the Common Prayer he taught: 'Our Father which art in heaven, hallowed be Thy name', and so on; a simple prayer, a child's prayer, mark you, it is the 'Common Prayer' because it is intended for the uneducated masses. To a higher circle, those who have advanced a little more, he gave a more elevated teaching. 'I am in my Father, and he in me, and I in you'. Do you remember that? And then, when the Jews

asked him who he was, he declared that he and his Father were one; and the Jews thought that that was blasphemy. What did he mean by that? That has been also told by your old prophets: 'Ye are gods and all of you are children of the Most High'. Mark the same three stages; you will find that it is easier for you to begin with the first and end with the last." [57]

Radhakrishnan similarly sees in Jesus Christ the Vedantic Sadguru whose life was a teaching and illustration of the Advaitic principle that is universally valid: "That God may be all in all." [58] This, of course, is an advaitic version of the Pauline soteriology. Even before Radhakrishnan there had been attempts among some Vedantins to follow the line of Vivekananda in interpreting the Gospels and the salvation preached therein in the Vedantic categories. Some examples could be given from the writings of Sri Parananda, even though he is not so well known as the above two. He interprets Matthew 6:12 which speaks about forgiving debts in an advaitic way. He maintains that what Jesus intends by the idea of forgiving debts is, that our communion with God should be so complete that there does not exist any distinction between 'I' and 'Thou'. When there is no distinction between the one and the other the obligations left undone are effaced. In the Advaitic unity there is not debtor-creditor relation or distinction! [59] Similarly, Jesus indication of his life as a ransom for many in Matthew 20:28 is not a reference to any vicarious substitution. Jesus is using here a figurative language:

"This figure employed by Jesus is, that he taught the soul its condition of captivity and awakened in it a desire for freedom, and then gave his own body to the captor as a consideration for the release of the soul. All this figurative language means that in order that 'lost' souls may regain the Kingdom of God, he had to teach them objectively (by sanctifying his life) the subjective truth that self-effacement, or forsaking all the rudiments of the flesh, was essential to obtain God." [60]

'Forsaking all the rudements of the flesh' stands for the practice of self-discipline or Yoga which is necessary for ultimate self-realization. A Guru himself cannot transmit to us the divine self-illumination if we are not prepared for it by subjective efforts. This view is also expressed by Swami Prabhavananda:

"A truly illumined teacher can transmit to us the power which unfolds the divine consciousness latent within us. But the field must be fertile and the soil ready before the seed can be sown." [61]

He sees the role of Jesus in the life of man as that of a master who 'teaches us how to become absorbed in the consciousness of God and find eternal joy and freedom' [62].

Swami Akhilananda also sees in Jesus a teacher of God-realization as understood in the Vedanta. The attainment of the Kingdom of God, as preached by Jesus, is nothing else than the Vedantic realization of God. [63] 'Jesus as a teacher of mankind demonstrated the idea (of God-realization) in His life through actual spiritual practices.' [64] He also helped mankind to reach the same realization which he himself attained. Akhilananda clarifies this view with the help of an example borrowed from Sri Ramakrishna: Jesus as an incarnation was a ship which carries innumerable persons to the infinite ocean of God. When a mighty log of wood floats down the stream, it carries on it hundreds of birds and does not sink. So also innumerable men can find salvation by taking refuge in him! [65]

By helping the human society to spiritual illumination, Akhilananda maintains, Jesus Christ also helps the process of social transformation and thus helps the progress of human civilization. Through his consciousness of unity of existence and God, Jesus Christ could re-establish the spirit of religion and transform groups of people to a higher plane of existence which results in starting a new civilization.[66] The reason for that is, when the individuals are spiritually stabilized a strong basis is laid for the reconstruction of society at large.[67] Akhilananda writes:

> "(Jesus came) to show the people that their methods of obtaining joy and satisfaction are wrong and he (revealed) ways to get them directly by becoming aware of God. This does not mean, however, that divine incarnations prohibit enjoyment of the objective world. (Jesus showed) us the background of the world is divine. In other words, the subject and object of experience are basicly one. (Jesus demonstrated) how to live on the basis of this knowledge." [68]

The social tranformation that is effected by the divine illumination taught by Jesus Christ is also emphasized by Swami Satprakasananda. Jesus as an incarnation inaugurated a new order of things and his influence increases as the years pass by.[69] Jesus Christ infused new life into the inner spirit of religion when it was most needed. The result was a renaissance of cultural development. The spiritual tidal wave set in motion by the illumined souls like Jesus Christ works at the root of human existence and that helps the development of the spiritual faculties of man even in the fields of architecture, art, music, literature and politics. [70] Satprakasananda explains with an example:

> "If you water the root of a tree, the whole tree is taken care of. But if you forget the root and care only for the branches, you cannot keep the tree alive. Similarly the spiritual principle in man is the root of his life. Whether you wish economic, political, social, or cultural development, the inner spirit has to be cared for. Life's fulfilment is in none of these outward forms, but in inner spiritual development." [71]

Such social application of Vedantic principles are, of course, relatively new. But it shows a healthy change of trend among the Vedantins. The world, for them is no longer merely a matter of delusion. They see positive values not only in the 'spirituality' of man but also in his so-called 'materiality'. This trend, especially among the Neo-Vedantins, is surely the result of their encounter with the Christian world-vision. Akhilananda and Satprakasananda are quite right in their evaluation that the spiritual principles constitute the basis of all human life and development. But the question remains whether human existence can be made meaningful just through self-attained spiritual illumination. In the Vedantic world-vision that insists on the fundamental divine nature of every man, such a vision becomes quite intelligible. In this case the role of Jesus Christ and his relevance for the whole of mankind could be restricted to that of a Vedantic Sadguru (true teacher) who points to the true meaning of life and points out an approach to the absolute values of human existence. [72] This approach is surely positive, but is far away from the Christian understanding of Jesus Christ as the Saviour of mankind.

The Vedantic concept of 'Guru' has been also adopted into by Indian Christian theologians. Brahmabandhab Upadhyaya was the first 'who made the concept of Guru applied to Christ the corner stone of Indian Christian theology' [73]. Jesus Christ as Guru, according to the Christian understanding, is not just a mystic who by his example and teaching helps others also to God-realization through the realization of their own proper identity as basicly one with God. In the Christian theological understanding, Jesus Christ is, as J.B. Chethimattam observes, 'the one saving Guru for all men since in his death and resurrection all can discover their own final glory and self-fulfilment. Christ is God's decisive, eschatological and soteriological presence to the individual' [74]. Every human being can find his authenticity in Jesus Christ as the Sisya (disciple) discovers his own authenticity in the Guru. We could conclude this section with a quotation from J.B. Chethimattam who sees Jesus as a true Guru because he is to us the supreme revealer of the Father:

"The most significant aspect of the Guru as applied to Christ is the effective divine presence it implies. Guru is a presence, an intensely energizing personal presence, or rather supra-personal presence. For the sisya the Guru is identical in function with God, because he opens up a personal relationship that embraces all persons in a single mystery of the supra-personal Absolute. Guru is the actual presentation to the individual of the Isvara, the cosmic Logos. Christ is the unique Teacher who through his Spirit reveals to us the Father." [75]

B. The Saving Role of Jesus Christ in Human History

The relevance of Jesus Crhsit for the whole of mankind and human history cannot be explained only be recognizing his role as a universal teacher (Guru) of ethical principles and the path to God-realization as we have seen in the previous section. The Christian theology in India tries to interpret the redemptional or soteriological aspect of the Christ-Mystery in Vedantic categories. The phenomenon of Sin, the redeeming work of Christ as realized in his Cross and Resurrection and fulfilled in the mystery of the Pentecost and the interpretation of Christ's salvation in the predominantly Hindu context in India need to be given here special consideration. Our intention in this section is to examine critically what the Indian Christology has to contribute in this regard.

1. The Question of Sin and the Vedantic Problematic

The Vedanta is concerned more with the problem of achieving release from Karma-Samsara than with the question of redemption from sin. [76] Here it is very relevant and highly important to keep in mind what we have already said in the first part of our work regarding the Vedantic notions of 'Avidhya', 'Kama', 'Karma' and 'Samsara' under the title "Man in Bondage". [77] It is indeed a challenge to Christian theology to explain the problem of sin and the consequent need for redemption especially in the above mentioned context. The Vedantic anthropology makes an explanation of the Christian notion of sin very problematic. If man is essentially one with God or if he is in his inner reality a part of God, he is no more in need of a 'gratuitous redemption' or liberation from a state of sin; he is already divine by right. The only question that remains is of realizing his true identity and achieving Brahma-Saksatkara or Isvara-Saksatkara as the case may be.[78] We do not, of course, ignore the fact that in the system of Ramanuja where a personal God is accepted, the idea of 'bondage' is different from that held by the followers of the system of Sankaracharya. But it cannot be denied that in both of these important systems, what we call 'sin' belongs only to the phenomenal level of reality, and so does not enter into the fundamental reality of man. In the first part we have also referred to the fact that if not in theory, at least in practice, the consciousness of human sinfulness is very prevalent among the Hindus. [79] But, a theological confrontation with the Vedanta necessitates an analysis of the question also on the theoretical level.

a. The Vedantic Reaction

The Vedantic thinkers have often criticized the Christian notion of sin as rediculous. Vivekananda, for example, observes:

> "The greatest error is to call man a weak and miserable sinner. Every time a person thinks in this mistaken manner, he rivets one more link in the chain of <u>avidya</u>, that binds him, adds one more layer to the 'self-hypnotism' that lies heavy over his mind." [80]

Sin-consciousness, according to this view, is an illusion and what man needs is not actually a salvation from sin but a 'de-hypnotism' on the level of man's consciousness. This implies that to call man a sinner, is to deny his reality of being divine, i.e. to deny his Atman: "Essentially all ideas of imperfection and sinfulness are hallucinations since man is of the substance of God himself." [81] In considering sin as mere ignorance and caused by the Mayahypnosis, Vivekananda follows the view of his spiritual master Ramakrishna Paramahamsa, who was of the firm opinion: "He who says day and night, I am a sinner, I am a sinner, verily becomes a sinner." [82] This would mean that sin belongs essentially to the psychological level, to man's thoughts and imagination, i.e. to the Gnoseology of man as an epistomological factor rather than to man's ontology, his very reality! Consequently what man has to correct in himself is not radically a sinful existence that is supposed to be away from God or opposed to God, but the wrong assumption that he is different and consequently in duality with God! Such a wrong knowledge

(Avidhya) can be corrected not by a 'Saviour' who takes upon himself the sins of the world, but by Advaitic Jnana: 'Aham Brahma asmi! Tat tvam asi: I am Brahman! That thou art!' [83] When one realizes one's identity with Brahman, one is fully detached from oneself and from this world and there cannot be anymore reason for wrong doing. So in the practical life the true Jnana will be the governing principle of all man's actions. That would mean, the Advaitic Jnana is no blank cheque for an 'as-you-please' life or immorality. One has to prove in one's practical life whether one is a true Jnani (wise man). To look for a so-called 'gratuitous salvation' from a representative figure in history is a sheer neglect of one's own responsibilities. Besides, a constant preoccupation with sin can weaken a man psychologically and that through Avidhya can promote evil tendencies which blind one's existence. Ramakrishna is of the opinion that the Christian concern with sin could be the result of a certain lack of faith in God:

> "With you it is always sin and sin! That is the Christian view, isn't it? Once a man gave me a Bible. A part of it was read to me, and it was full of that one thing - sin and sin! One must have such faith that one can say, I haved uttered the name of God; I have repeated the name of God; I have repeated the name of Rama and Hari. How can I be a sinner? One must have faith in the glory of God's name." [84]

So, in the Vedantic understanding unlike in the Christian view, the question of evil rotates around the basic doctrine of Karma-Samsara. Swami Prabhavananda interprets the reference to sin in the Lord's Prayer, 'And forgive us our debts, as we forgive our debtors', as debts of 'Karma'. 'By our actions and reactions we are always contracting debts, obligations that must be paid off. We alone are responsible for these obligations. We are even responsible for our own character, which has resulted from our habits of thougth and action. When we recognize our debts, when we realize that every thing, good or bad, that comes to us, has been previously earned by ourselves alone, then we know that we must not hold anybody else responsible for anything that we suffer' [85].

b. The 'Original Sin' and the 'Actual Sin'

The traditional Christian distinction between the Original sin and actual sin is also irrelevant in the Vedantic pattern of thinking. Consequently the notions of 'Peccatum originale originans' and 'Peccatum originale originatum' are also out of place. We cannot accuse our ancient ancestors for the evils we suffer today in our present existence. Each one is individually responsible for the misery one has to face. Man has prepared for himself the evils of this life by the evil deeds of his previous existence resulting from his slavery to 'Avidhya' (ignorance) and 'Kama' (evil attachments and desires). It is up to each man to get out of this vicious circle of Karma-Samsara. So man's present day misery is his own making. The Vedantins understand the Biblical reference to the Original Fall and the story of Adam and Eve in strictly anthropologico-existential terms. It is not a 'report' of what happened somewhere in the distant past, but an explanation of the concrete life-situation in which man finds himself. It is an illustration of the present, namely, how man is subject to existential ignorance. Swami Prabhavananda explains:

"The Vedantists see an allegory of the temptation of maya in the story of the Garden of Eden. Adam smybolizes the Atman, the divine Self; Eve, the intellect of Adam; the serpent, maya. As Eve (the intellect) yields to temptation, Adam also succumbs: he too eats of the forbidden fruit. He forgets his divine nature, recognizes good and evil, and experiences instead of Paradise, the universe of time, space and relativity." 86

Although this explanation of 'Original Sin' is in Vedantic categories, it is surprisingly in line with the modern Christian interpretations of original sin. We will be elaborating this point further in the third part. For the moment we would only like point to the possibility of understanding the Vedantic idea of Karma-Samsara in terms of the Christian doctrine of Original Sin.

It is, however, true that in the Vedanta there is no idea of the essential sinfulness of man. The Atman, which alone constitutes the fundamental reality of man is divine and therefore pure, without sin. All impurities belong to the phenomenal and apparent levels or transient sheaths of man's external structure.[87] This should not, however, be understood as a denial of the distinction between good and evil. Contrary to the common misunderstanding, Vedanta is not indifferent to immorality and the problem of evil. Its difference to the Christian view consists in the analysis of the root cause of evil and the extend to which it affects man in his present existence. For the Vedanta, man is not God's fallen creature, who is in need of a Saviour in the person of Jesus Christ. Sin exists only in the relative plane of existence and in the absolute state all distinctions (Dvaita) vanish.[88] God will be all in all! So the emphasis of the Vedanta is not on the moral evil but on the metaphysical evil, namely, 'of the one becoming involved in the many and of the soul immersed in the material world of maya' [89].

The Hindu reformers, especially of the Brahmo Samaj, found the theoretical denial of sin by the Vedantins not acceptable. As their concern was mainly on improving the ethical life of the people, they had an approach to the question of sin that is nearer to the Christian understanding. Still they protested against a mere legal understanding of sin; it is first and foremost a moral disease.[90] It belongs not only to the phenomenal level in man, but affects his existence radically. K.C. Sen writes:

> "Man through infatuation does something wrong, and becomes a sinner. If he performs some kind of atonement and goes through certain penances and mortifications, there is no longer any sin left in the heart.... But sin is not accidental it is radical." [91]

Here also the insistence is not on any gratuitous reception of justification, but a self-purification on the moral level. Sen also does not accept an inherited sinfulness of man, which from the time of his birth results in a radical separation from God even without his free decision. But he admits that man from his birth is 'liable to go wrong' because of his existential situation of being weak as 'a slave to sense'. [92] This 'liability to go wrong' could be interpreted as being inseparably connected with man's existential situation from the time of his origin, i.e. as original sin, but this does not, according to Sen, radically distort the human existence as is done by the actual and free evil deeds of man. He insists that man is not born a criminal, he 'is not born a murderer or robber', he is not yet born into sin, but yet to be born. [93] It seems that Sen misunderstands and identifies the Christian concept of original sin with that of actual sin:

> "Man is not naturally a sinner. He is not born in sin. If it be otherwise, why did Jesus Christ vindicate little children? ... The little infant just ushered into the world is perfectly innocent and immaculate.... Do not say that man comes into the world as a born sinner with a vicious constitution. There is no original iniquity in man." [94]

It is evident that a traditional interpretation of the doctrine of Original Sin as formulated by St. Augustine and followed in the classical theology of the Scholastics is not credible in the Indian context. Manilal C. Parekh, the disciple of Sen whose sympathy for the doctrine of Christ led him even to the point of receiving baptism as an external sign of accepting Christ, also is very critical of the notion of Original Sin:

> "According to it (original sin), all human beings are sinful from their very birth, not because they have done anything wrong in their past birth as the Hindus believe, but simply because they inherit the flesh of Adam and Eve, the first supposed parents of humanity. Because Adam committed the sin ... all his posterity, millions and billions of men and women and children, share his sin and consequently are cursed by God.... It reduces every human being to nothing but a stinking mass of sin until he or she is re-generated or re-born by faith in Christ.... This is a fantastic doctrine, wholly untrue, and what is worse, extremely unfair to God. Surely God must be a capricious and cruel person if He could condemn billions of his creatures to perdition for the sin of only one person." [95]

Parekh also refers to St. Paul as the one who made the belief in such an Original Sin 'the corner-stone of his theology' [96]. Parekh's reaction against an ungodly understanding of the doctrine of sin is justifiable, but he may not be right in criticizing St. Paul for supporting it. It is true that for centuries St. Paul has been wrongly interpreted by theologians on the basis of Jerome's translation of the Greek word "eph'ho" into the Latin as "in quo" (Rom 5:12), which could result in a theory of 'peccatum originale originans' that interpreted the sinful situation of man 'a priori', as if a supposed human being 'Adam' were responsible for the present calamity of mankind! The present day exegesis has proved his interpretation to be wrong. We shall elaborate this question further in the third part. For the moment we confine ourselve to the remark that even Christian theologians in India like P. Chenchiah found the traditional presentation of the doctrine of original sin not acceptable as is evident in his following observation:

> "The view of life which would implicate men in tragic fall, hardly had they commenced their existence, and leave them in the wanderings in the wilderness all through history appals the imagination." [98]

Inspite of his negative attitude towards Original Sin, Chenchiah like Sen, does not deny the reality of sin as the Advaitins do. The reality of salvation in Jesus Christ, the True Man without Karma, is for him, however, more important. This attitude stands also in harmony with his evolutionary approach to Christology.

It must be remembered that both K.C. Sen and P. Chenchiah are accused of not giving sufficient importance to the supreme tragedy of sin and failing 'to see the great gap in (the) process of evolution', namely, 'the awful abyss between man and God caused by sin, an abyss which can only be bridged by the love of God suffering on behalf of sinful man' [99]. It is doubtful whether such a criticism can be substantiated. Sin for our authors is not just a 'lacuna' in the otherwise perfect process of evolution, but on the contrary it refers to the 'lesser humanity' which is in need of a growth towards the perfect humanity realized in Jesus Christ!

c. The 'Maya' of the Will

We have seen that .Brahmabandhab Upadhyaya had used the Vedantic concept of 'Maya' to explain the reality of the created material world against the exaggerated illusionism of some Vedantins, which consequently has relevance in explaining the reality of Christ's humanity. This metaphysical explanation of Maya can also be given a moral application in considering the question of sin. Regarding sin Upadhyaya writes:

"By sin we allienate ourselves from God. By choosing the finite (anatma) as our goal we incur spiritual death and darken our understanding (viveka) ... Sin leads to bondage and darkness from which there can be no escape notwithstanding the hardest struggle on our part." [100]

Upadhyaya does not use the term 'Maya' as a synonym for 'sin', but the notion of finiteness, bondage and darkness which are involved in his notion of sin are intimately related to his interpretation of 'Maya'. Sin is to make the relative reality (Maya) of this world as the absolute goal of human endeavours. St. Paul's reference to this world as subject to vanity (in Greek: 'mataiotes', Rom 8:20), can be considered as equivalent to the neo-Vedantic notion of 'Maya'. What is true in the metaphysical realm has relevance also on the spiritual plane. When our heart and will are subject to the vanities of this world contrary to the divine purpose of creation, then we call it sin. The interpretation of sin as the transference of 'Maya' from 'the realm of being to that of will or purpose' is supported by P.D. Devanandan and Robin Boyd. This natural world accquires meaning only when it is 'shot through with a reality which is supernatural' and when 'the phenomenal is conditioned by the nouminal' [102]. It is sin to deny the total dependence of the natural on the supernatural and the phenomenal on the nouminal. By this man falls into the sphere of the flesh (sarx) as against the realm of the Spirit (Pneuma), to use the expression of St. Paul (Rom 8:5) 'Man himself, in his state of sin - in all his violence, hatred, greed and lack of love - is in the realm of flesh, of sin, of Maya.'[104] The idea that sin is 'Maya' is also indirectly advocated by Sadhu Sundar Singh when he denies an independent existence to sin:

> "Sin has no independent existence: no one can say ... that it is something ... It is only a name for a state of mind or a disposition.... Satan can only injure that which has already been created; he has no power to create ... Sin or evil ... has no independent existence; it is merely the absence or negation of good." [105]

It is, indeed, a positive approach to present the Christian doctrine of sin to the Vedantic mind in the categories of Maya and Avidhya as pertaining not only to ontology, but also to the realm of the will. The notion of 'Karma' with the implications of personal responsibility is also a good starting point. But 'Samsara' with its stress on automatic or self-achieved retribution in the cosmic process still remains a stumbling block! In the context of 'Samsara' it is difficult to put through the redemptive role of Jesus Christ as the sole mediator between God and man (1 Tim 2:5) and the fully gratuitous character of God's salvation in and through Jesus Christ. In this regard, it must be pointed out that the role of Christology in India is not merely to confirm all the Vedantic pre-suppositions, but also to correct and re-interpret what hinders in India the proclamation of Christ as the Mystery of man and human history.

2. The Saving Fact of Christ

We have seen in the fourth chapter that the Vedantic approach to the Mystery of Christ essentially consists in considering Jesus as an example for the Advaitic God-realization that is open to every man. [107] 'Christ' stands for the universal divine principle of which one of the historical concretisations was Jesus of Nazareth! This approach, of course, is not acceptable to Christian theology as it ignores the basic distinction between the person of Jesus Christ and other human individuals in the course of history. Still, we would say that with some reservations this approach could be used as a starting point for the Indian explanation of the universal relevance of the person of Jesus Christ for the rest of mankind. The Vedanta asserts that salvation consists in the Brahmasaksatkara or God-realization which is bas icly Atmasaksatkara (self-realization) for the school of Sankara and Isvarasaksatkara (realization of Isvara) for those who follow the personalistic school of Ramanuja. [108] In both cases Jesus of Nazareth is recognized as a representative figure for the rest of mankind, even if not as the only one, nor in the sense of 'salvific cause'. The Vedanta admits a cosmic implication for the event realized in Jesus of Nazareth. Even if Christ did not bring salvation to the whole of humanity, he has become his own saviour as a man realizing all the divine potentialities that are already in man! This fact of salvation he realized, in this context, is not attributed to the intervention of a God 'ex machina', but is placed in the general frame-work of man's growth towards his supreme destiny. The idea of an original 'Fall' has no place here; but the reality of evil and immoral deeds is not negated but they are understood in the context of growth from a state of lesser perfection to that of a greater perfection. We find no substantial theological problem in this approach if we could limit this Vedantic theory to the Christ-event alone and not apply to every individual. This reservation is inevitable for Christian theology if it has to be faithful to its basic belief that Jesus Christ 'is the image of the invisible God, the first-born of all creation; for in him all things hold together' (Col 1:15-17) and that he is the Son of God who was appointed the heir of all things because the world was created through him (Hebr 1:1-3). This approach would also be in harmony with the recapitulation theory of salvation as proposed by St. Paul (Col 1:20) and warmly promoted by the Church Fathers especially St. Ireneus [111] and by Gregory of Nyza.[112] Such an approach would avoid a narrow separation of the fact of Christ as a salvific reality for mankind and the act of Christ, namely, the Crucifixion and the Ressurrection of the Lord which constitute the climax of the salvific Christ-event. A onesided and juridical approach to the question of Salvation as a moral event of satisfaction and ransom on the other hand cannot bring to light the beauty of God's salvific plan and the depth of his love. God's plan of salvation has to be understood in the whole context of his creation. Salvation is not the destruction of the plan of creation but its final realization which has entered a definitive phase in the Christ-event already beginning with his redemptive incarnation (Heb 2:14-18., 4:14-15).

K.C.Sen's stress on the Divine Sonship of Christ which we have seen in the fifth chapter [114] should be understood in this context. The Divine Sonship of Christ refers to the Divine Humanity that was realized in Christ as a result of man's evolution in the spiritual plane. Jesus Christ is the end result of the creative flow of existence; in him the whole of mankind is represented. He has realized the Divine Humanity as an eminent member of mankind; every human individual participates in his achievement. The atonement worked out by Christ consists essentially in the unity or 'reconciliation of humanity with divinity' [115]. By Jesus' Sonship we are accepted by the Father.[116] Jesus Christ is the Saviour of mankind not just because of some acts of moral satisfaction he did but by the very fact of his being the Divine Humanity:

> "Behind the function lies the fact; behind the Saviour stands the Son. In seeking the elucidation of Jesus in terms of his function, we miss the deeper meaning of the fact of Jesus ... Jesus saves, but He does this by virtue of the status and constitution of His being, i.e., by his Sonship." [117]

In the reconciliation, effected by the fact of Jesus Christ, achieved not only an at-one-ment[118] of man with God but also a unity of men among themselves which was destroyed be the duality of sin: "He (Jesus Christ) is the reconciliation of man with man and of all men with God, the harmony of humanity with humanity and of all humanity with Divinity." [119]

Vengel Chakkarai also finds in 'the fact of Christ' the key to the mystery of existence. [120] Jesus claimed to be the Son of God and the Son of Man; that would mean that he sums up and focuses the two mysteries of God and man or rather to use the language of the Indian thought, the one mystery of the Sat (the Real) [121]. In Jesus the true Advaita has been realized and 'this advaita has been wrought on the anvil of the life of Jesus. Thus the incarnation is our inheritence and we in our measure are invited to participate in it' [122]. Thus the Incarnation of Christ is the realization of the dreams of the sages.[123] "Binding the two centres of consciousness into an indissoluble whole, the Incarnation has raised human nature to the very height of God, as it has enriched the Divine mind with the very texture and hues of man's life on earth." [124] Chakkarai explains further the redemptive value of the very fact of Incarnation:

"... till Jesus appeared God was in the world and as the Logos, the Eternal Word, He was in the Life of man. Contingency was known to Him as he knows that the human mind is. But in the Incarnation, instead of merely watching, sympathizing with and helping man in his struggle, He plunged into the ocean and felt the waves and billows rolling over His head. In other words, not only man entered a new phase of life but God, too, did so in the Incarnation. Thus ... the metaphysics of God is not the key to the Incarnation, as in Hindu thought, but the life of Jesus is the explanation of the working of the mind of God and His adaptation to the needs of man." [125]

This insistence on the redemptive fact of Christ rather than on what he does is also evident in the theology of P. Chenchiah. Viewing the Christ-event in the context of cosmic evolution Chenchiah writes: "Today we have to realize Jesus as the head of a new world order; or as the creative expression of God's higher purposes with regard to man." [126]

By Jesus' Incarnation, Chenchiah maintains, God's energy is released for the transformation of the world, which cannot be attained merely by the God-realization of individual human beings. [127] Jesus Christ is the manifestation of a new creative effort of God; Jesus Christ himself is this new creation and the Kingdom of God is this new life-order realized in him. [128]
He explains:

"The fact of Christ is the birth of a new order in creation. It is the emergence of life - not bound by Karma of man, not tainted by sin, not humbled by death, of man triumphant, glorious, partaking the immortal nature of God, of the birth of a new race in the creation of the Sons of God." [129]

For Chenchiah 'Christianity is not primarily a doctrine of salvation but the announcement of the advent of a new creative order in Jesus' which he considers as a thrilling discovery imparted to mankind. [130]

The idea that the very fact of Jesus Christ is redemptive is also shared by P.d. Devanandan. He sees in Christ 'a forecast of what God intends man to be from the beginning of creation' and 'of what God is making of man when he totally surrenders himself to the creative purpose of God's design for mankind' [131]. He writes: "The Incarnation is the beginning of a new Creation. This new world is already present here and now." [132]

The totality of the Christ-event as the saving fact is given an additional stress by D. Amalorpavadas in his following explanation:

"In taking our nature, in making himself one of us, in coming to save mankind, Christ has assumed, redeemed and integrated all that is human, not only the individuals but also the whole material reality, every civilization and cultures, every form of thought, all religions, all that go to make up man and all that man makes, all human existence and all human activity, every creation of God, particularly every expectation of and search for God and for salvation. Christ has restored everything, saved everything, has marked everything with the sign of the Cross, has brought everything to its fulfilment by integrating everything in the march of the redeemed humanity towards the Father, through the Spirit in the current of the trinitarian charity." [133]

Though Amalorpavadas makes this statement in substantiating the need of missionary adaptations, it equally casts light on his view on the redeeming fact of Christ. As it is evident, he does not set aside the mysteries of the Cross and the events marking the last moments of Christ's earthly life. This stands in evident contrast to the view of Chenchiah namely, that the salvation of Jesus Christ is realized not by an act of his, but 'by virtue of his existence and being' because 'Christ does not save us by suffering on the Cross. Just as animal is saved in man by the animal nature being sublimated by the entry of mind and reason, men are saved by attaining Christhood' [134] : Chenchiah, in his zeal for his evolutionary Christology forgets the deep significance of the Cross of Christ in the redemption of mankind. This attitude of Chenchiah is not fortunately followed by the other Indian theologians we mentioned, who at the same time could see and appreciate the saving role of the very fact of Christ. The saving fact of Christ is no fact at all apart from the mysteries of the Cross and Resurrection. The Cross and the Resurrection are the crowning of the fact of Christ as we shall see in the following section. The events of the Cross and Resurrection are especially important in the Indian context to explain the human tragedy of persecution and suffering [135] and the value of the material reality [136] which belongs to the salvific plan of God.

It is also important in the context of the Vedantic insistence on universal principles as against concrete facts of history to show that the essence of religion does not consist in mere moral or ethical betterment of society, but it is an initiative and work of God which transcends the limitations of human possibilities. The historical person of Jesus Christ is the self-disclosure of God as righteous, merciful, just, forgiving and above all loving [137]. Therefore it is not the Sermon on the Mount that is the essence of the

Christian faith but the initiative of God in the person of Jesus Christ. Salvation is not a human achievement as the Vedantins may hold nor a movement of asceticism from the body to the soul behind which an element of self-deception and self-righteousness could lurk. [138] Salvation is not man's achievement, but it is purely a gift of God; an unmerited gift, a grace! The Christian message is that of a Saviour, of a Good News that is identical with the very fact of Christ. To accept Jesus Christ as the Saving Fact in human history is to realize the gratuitous character of salvation that is beyond man. This is what M.M. Thomas means when he writes: "In secular anthropological terms this faith in human salvation through God in Christ means the recognition of the ultimacy of the pattern of Jesus' humanity for existence." [139] Thomas similarly maintains that in the new humanity of Christ the distinction between nature, history, culture and religion is not absolutized but transcended in the awareness of the solidarity of all mankind. [140] Therefore, the recapitulation of all things is realized in the historical personality of Christ, the whole Christ-event is the Saving Fact for mankind. All the redemptive actions of Christ are necessarily to be understood in the background of this given Fact.

In the anthropological Christology of Karl Rahner this approach to the person of Christ as the Saving Fact in human history is especially important. Without such a fact there would not be any justification for the search of man in human history for the verification of the anthropologically undeniable desire for an absolute Saviour. Similarly, Wolfhart Pannenberg's insistence on the necessity and possibility of 'going back behind the apostolic kerygma to the historical Jesus' [141] and his idea regarding 'the summation of humanity in Jesus Christ' [142] also point to the Salvific Fact of Jesus Christ which was crowned in the mystery of the Resurrection. We will be discussing these questions in greater detail in the third part.

3. The Redemptive Act of Christ

Jesus Christ as the Saving Fact in the history of mankind reaches a visible point of climax in the Mystery of his Passover - his death on the Cross, Resurrection and the sending of the Holy Spirit. In the following lines we shall investigate how the Paschal Mystery has been accepted and interpreted among the Indian thinkers.

a. The Mystery of the Cross

Vengel Chakkarai, speaking on his conversion from Hinduism to Christianity, refers to the Mystery of Christ's suffering and death as 'the central thing in the life of Christ, which he studied with the greatest interest and care before he became His humble bhakta' [143] . He found the significance of the Cross 'more interesting than the philosophies of his own ancestral religion, and more profound than even the deepest experiences of the rishis and yogis of India' [144]. He saw that 'the summit of the cross towered beyond human vision (even the yogic) into the very mysteries of the Divine essence and of humanity' [145] . The death of Christ was intimately connected with the accomplishment of the purpose of his life, namely, the establishment of the Kingdom of God. "Jesus without his death", writes Chakkarai, "would be a tree magnificent in its growth and foliage, but without its flower and fruit." [145] In our comparison between Avatar and incarnation we had indicated[146] that the 'Christian faith in the Incarnation is not simply guarenteed by birth but by death, by the whole of human life, and this makes for its distinctiveness' [147] . Eventhough the redemptive Cross of Christ is not something completely apart from his person as a kind of priestly technique, it must all the same be affirmed that Christ cannot be understood apart from his Cross. [148] 'The human life of Christ not only ended on the Cross, but it is in the ligth of the Crucifixion that all the life before it takes on new meaning' [149] .

i. The Scandal of the Cross

G. Parrinder writes about a Buddist author, D.T. Suzuki, who feels revulsion at the sight of the naked body of Christ hanging on the Cross:

> " 'I cannot help thinking of the gap that lies deep between Christianity and Buddhism.' The symbol of Crucifixion is one of the most difficult things to comprehend. 'The crucified Christ is a terrible sight and I cannot help associating it with the sadistic impulse of a psychically affected brain.' How can such an object of devotion conduce to calm and spiritual elevation? This is called a morbid preoccupation with death, which makes Christians negative and neurotic, instead of finding the detached calm that comes from discovering that there is no self and following the Middle Way between extremes." [150]

Parrinder points out that such an attitude that depreciates 'the harsh reality of the Crucifixion and its centrality to Christian faith may be linked with

an underestimate of the reality and power of evil in the world'[151] . Such
an attitude is seen also in Islam which even denies the reality of the event
of the Cross itself. This is especially evident in the attitude of a Moslem
author similarly quoted by Parrinder:

> "From them (disciples of Christ) came that sadness which is a ruling
> element in the character of the greatest adherents of Christianity,
> their fear of sin, their love of self-reproach and abasement, their sense
> of the importance of the sin of Adam and their belief that it had to
> do with the anguish that Christ underwent that mankind might be saved
> from its consequences.... Such a psychological stress could not be without
> effect on their psyche. Is it not just possible that such effects can
> be inherited? The best Christian in his most sublime moments is a
> sad man."[152]

It is true that the Cross of Christ crucified is a stumbling block not only
to the Jews and a folly not only to the Greeks (1 Cor 1:23). Man finds
something folly in the level of the Spirit especially when he does not understand it (1 Cor 2:14). If can be affirmed with a certain amount of consolation
that the Hindu attitude towards the Cross has not been so negative or pessimistic as we have seen in the above quotations from the Buddhistic and
Islamic milieu even though the Hindu brothren at large have not been able
to accept the salvific or redemptive value of the Cross as all-sufficient
and indispensable for salvation.

Raja Rammohan Roy maintains that pardon for evil deeds is obtained not
gratis by the suffering of a third person, but only through real personal
repentance.[155] He finds the notion of atonement implied in presenting Jesus
on the Cross as a sacrificial victim as unacceptable:

> "Would it be consistent with common notions of justice to afflict an
> innocent man with the death of the cross, for sins committed by others,
> even supposing the innocent man should voluntarily offer his life in
> behalf of those others?"[156]

Roy thinks that the use of the categories of sacrificial system by the
followers of Christ was only an accomodation to the Jewish thought patterns.
'These were modes of speech made use of in allusion to the sacrifices and
blood-offerings which the Jews and their high priest used to make for the
remission of sins'[157] . The task today should be to translate the Cross of
Christ in a language that is understandable to the modern man, namely,
in a spiritual sense.

Such a spiritual interpretation has been attempted especially by the Vedantins as we shall see in one of the following sections. True to the Advaitic tradition, Vivekananda could not find much meaning in the Cross which was only an illusion: "Christ was God incarnate; they could not kill him. That which was crucified was only a semblance, a mirage." [158] It is quite understandable that where there is no value for historical events, the Cross also loses its significance. Similarly Dr. Radhakrishnan was also of the opinion that 'a suffering God, the deity with a crown of thorns, cannot satisfy the religious soul' [159].

The Cross remains a scandal and a paradox because life itself is a paradox, a mystery that cannot be explained only by the rational method. The Cross of Christ is a key to the paradox of human existence: those who mourn are comforted (Mt 5:4); those sow in tears reap with joy (Ps 126:5)! Joys and sorrows form the two inseparable sides of existence and the ultimate joy is in the Lord of Resurrection: "So it is with you: you are sad now, but I shall see you again, and your hearts will be full of joy, and that joy no one shall take from you" (Jn 16:22).

The opinion that the insistence of Christianity on the Cross of Christ is responsible for the melancholy in the world is by no means justifiable. The Cross of Christ offers the great consolation to millions in their darkest moments of existence; it enables this world not to lose heart before the unexplainable drama of evil played on the world stage. The Cross of Christ which may be a scandal before this world is the wisdom of God: 'The language of the cross may be illogical to those who are not on the way to salvation, but those of us who are on the way see it as God's power to save.... God has shown up the foolishness of human wisdom.... God wanted to save those who have faith through the foolishness of the message that we preach ... here we are preaching a crucified Christ, ... a Christ who is the power and wisdom of God. For God's foolishness is wiser than human wisdom, and God's weakness is stronger than human strength' (1 Cor 1:18-25).

In the following lines we shall see some of the aspects of the positive approach of the Indian thinkers to the event of the crucifixion of Christ.

ii. The Supreme Example of the Cross

Rammohan Roy, who insists on the ethical teachings of Jesus Christ as a guide to peace and happiness, finds a supreme example of faithfulness to duties of his mission in Christ's willing submission to the cross. [164] This example of Christ, however, does not support any doctrine of atonement because, as Roy writes, 'not even a single passage (is) pronounced by Jesus, enjoining refuge in such a doctrine of the Cross as all-sufficient or indispensable for salvation' [165] . Even though there is no atoning value for the Cross of Christ, still it has an intercessory value before God for the rest of mankind:

> "... for God is represented in the sacred books to have often shown mercy to mankind for righteous men's sake. How much more, then, would he naturally manifest his favour towards those who might petition him in the name of one whom he anointed and exalted over all creatures and prophets?" [166]

Similar to Rammohan Roy, Satprakasananda also sees in the crucifixion of Christ the very perfection of the spiritual principles he taught. [167] But unlike Roy, the Vedantins consider the Cross chiefly from another point of view: as an example of self-purification and self-denial on the way to God-realization. 'Ahamkara' (egoism and pride) is the basis of wrong doings which are results of 'Maya' and 'Avidhya'. Divine illumination is not possible without overcoming the duality of I and Thou caused by man's bondage to this material world including his own body. Self-denial is the only path to God-realization and is the denial of every thing that is transient and therefore illusory. By his Cross Jesus Christ shows us the radical way of self-abandonment and liberation from the Ahamkara. This self-purificatory example of Christ is stressed by Sen when he says that 'in (Christ) we see human nature perfected by true affiliation to the Divine nature.... He shows us not how God can become man nor how man can become God, but how we can exalt our humanity by making it more and more divine' [169] . Even though Sen cannot be counted as an Advaitin, he agrees with them in accepting the spiritual and exemplary value of the Cross as the perfection of the 'kenosis' that is required for any spiritual progress. [170]

The Neo-Vedantin Dr. S. Radhakrishnan says that the secret of the Cross lies in the abandonment of the ego which 'is the identification with a fuller life and consciousness. The soul is raised to a sense of universality.... In Gethsemane, Christ as an individual felt that the cup should pass away. That was his personal desire. The secret of the Cross is the crucifixion of the ego and the yielding to the will of God'[171]. Jesus' mission was to do the will of God, to attain the spiritual perfection that was expected of him and to be an example of the same for others. In the accomplishment of a spiritual mission a lot of self-sacrifice is involved. The heroic example of a religious leader has a certain intercessory and expiatory value for the world, even if not a redemptive one as in the Christian sense. This is evident in Jesus Christ as well as in other religious leaders.[172] The Cross of Christ is for Radhakrishnan first and foremost an inspiration towards personal asceticism on the way to Self-realization. Some Vedantins who had thought that Christ on his part did not need any self-purification have ventured even to say that 'when Jesus was crucified, He withdrew His mind completely from His body; He was in another state altogether, a state of samadhi or superconsciousness. The nails pierced through His body but the mind was unaffected'[173]. Swami Akhilananda attributes to the Cross a demonstrative value of 'crucifying the flesh' in the process of advaitic purification to be freed from the empirical self and to be established in immortality:

> "Jesus demonstrated on Good Friday that we must allow our empirical selves to be crucified in order to conquer the flesh and its cravings. Then alone is there a possibility of changeless immortal life."[174]

The Christians cannot, of course, deny that in the Cross of Christ there is an aspect of Christ's Kenosis reaching its perfection and that has the value of a great example for the whole of mankind. But the question is whether we have to understand this self-renunciation of Christ as a denial of his empirical ego and as an active withdrawal from the values present in this world or should it be considered 'as an intensified interest in the world based on God's loving will'[175]. The interpretation of the Cross as an example of contempt for this world created by God is not acceptable to Christian faith. Christ took upon himself the miseries of this world in one of their most brutal forms not to negate this world but to affirm it in the plan of God by saving it. That is the reason why withdrawal from this world and practices of asceticism are for the Christians no virtues in themselves;

they have value only in the general frame-work of God's salvation. The Hindu understanding of the Cross of Christ as the supreme example of dedication to moral principles and self-purification on the way of salvation contains in it important positive points; but that is not the whole of the significance of the mystery of the Cross.

iii. Suffering for the Sake of Love

The Cross of Christ and the suffering involved therein attain a deeper dimension when the event of the Crucifixion is considered in the context of love and human solidarity. Jesus Crhist shares the fate of mankind and assumed the human limitations to show us how they can be overcome in love. Suffering attains a special and transcendental [176] excellence when it is faced not just for the sake of a 'self-centred' spiritual purification or ethical perfection but out of love towards and solidarity with mankind. The cruciform humanity of Christ is the demonstration of the ultimate destiny of mankind [176] and it is in the Cross, that we see his solidarity with the anguish and sufferings of this world and its history. Love is the root of all solidarity. There are many Indian thinkers who see the Cross of Christ also as an excellent example of suffering for the sake of love.

Manilar Parekh, for example, makes love the key to the interpretation of the Cross of Christ:

> "Love is the last term in the moral and religious vocabulary of man, and all true love logically ends (in) or is synonymous with sacrifice, and it is by this that the death of Jesus Christ has to be interpreted and understood. The cross is the consummation of the life of Jesus, and it is by that, that his whole life is to be understood and not vice versa as that would be explaining the higher by the lower." [177]

Parekh's identification of love with sacrifice shows a very positive approach to the mystery of the Cross and sufferings. It is love that gives dynamism even to the precepts of Christ. Jesus 'sealed the Precepts with his blood and through the love that he thus showed invested them with not only that authority but even divine power, without which they would have been but a dead letter or what is worse an infinitude of burden which no human being could bear for a moment' [178]. The fact that Christ has sealed his precepts with his blood shows that love and the self-sacrifice involved therein are the supreme precepts that are meant for the benefit of mankind. Parekh opines that 'the cross, which was in ancient times a symbol of shame, has become to-day the greatest symbol of self-sacrifice and even glory. Self-sacrifice and forgiveness have to be recognized as the noblest virtues of mankind'[179].

Parekh's theme of love and self-sacrifice in explaining the Cross of Christ had been developed also by K.C. Sen: "(Jesus') death on the cross affords the highest practical illustration of self-sacrifice ... (for) the benefit of the world." [180] Sen maintains that the love of Christ manifested in his self-sacrifice is a great moral influence that animates all beneficial movements in human society. [181] Sen sees the contagious character of Christ's love verified in self-sacrifice admirably manifested in the heroic dedication and sufferings of the early Christians and their following of Christ has 'conferred lasting benefits on the world'[182]. The sacrificing love of Christ should be, according to Sen, also an inspiration for India in facing its problems. There is no human progress without love and self-sacrifice.[183] Nothing short of self-sacrifice, eradication of selfishness, can regenerate India, and in this process of Indian renaissance, the example of Christ is a guide line. [184] Regarding the relevance of Christ's self-sacrificing love for India K.C. Sen writes:

> Jesus is identical with self-sacrifice, and as he lived and preached in the fullness of time, so must he be in time preached in the fullness of time. The more is sacrifice needed in India, and the more it is made, the more will Jesus find a home in this land. I am, therefore, patiently waiting that I may grow with the age and the nation, and the spirit of Christ's sacrifice may grow therewith." [185]

The self-sacrificing aspect of Christ's love manifested in the event of the Cross had also greatly attracted the attention of Mahatma Gandhi. Even-though he could not believe literally that Jesus redeemed the world from its sins by his blood and that there is any miraculous virtue in his death on the Cross [186] he was convinced that love and joy can be established in this world only through the Way of the Cross tread by Christ. His remark regarding the impression he had before an image of the crucified Christ:

> "I saw there at once that nations, like individuals, could only be made through the agony of the Cross and in no other way. Joy comes not

by the infliction of pain on others, but of pain voluntarily borne by oneself." 187

From this it is evident what an influence the Cross of Christ had on the principle of 'Ahimsa' preached and above all practised by Gandhi. 'Ahimsa' in its positive aspect is nothing else than suffering for the sake of love towards others. Gandhi's socio-political method was quite in line with the message of love implied in the Cross. E. Stanley Jones remarks:

> "Never in human history has so much light been shed on the Cross, as has been through this one man and that man not even called a Christian. Had not our Christianity been vitiated by our identification with un-Christian attitudes and policies in public and private life, we would have seen at once the kinship between Gandhi's method and the Cross."

The assassination of Gandhi was the consequence of his efforts to establish love and fraternity between the mutually fighting fanatical elements of the Hindu and Moslem communities in India. Gandhi's martyrdom crowned his life, in close parallel to the Cross of Jesus Christ. He lived to the end the Cross of Christ:

> "You may certainly experience peace in the midst of strife, but that happens only when to remove strife you destroy your whole life, you crucify yourself... the Cross (is) an eternal event in this stormy life... Living Christ means a living Cross, without it life is a living death."

To live the Cross of Christ in the present world means for Gandhi a loving self-dedication, especially to the cause of the poor and the oppressed in todays society. The crucified Christ bearing only a loin cloth is a representative figure for millions of underprivileged men, women and children of today's so-called advanced human society! 190 The Cross of Christ, in order to be meaningful, has to be confronted even today repeatedly in the life of indiduals and nations. The challenge of the Cross is, indeed, to suffer for the sake of love! "The Cross of Christ is not an offence or a stumbling-block to the Hindu" - remark of S. Radhakrishnan - " It shows how love is rooted in self-sacrifice." 191

iv. **The Redemptive Sacrifice**

It has to be admitted that the Indian non-Christian approach to the event of Christ's crucifixion comes surprisingly near to the Christian understanding of the mystery of the Cross. In the above sections we have seen how the Cross of Christ is interpreted in India as a supreme example of self-purification on the way of perfection, of fidelity to one's own moral principles and suffering and self-sacrifice for the sake of altruistic love. It has still to be admitted that all these do not make in themselves the Cross of Christ substantially different from the persecution and even martyrdom undergone by any just man. In this section, our intention is to concentrate on the specificity that is in the Cross of Christ, namely, its redemptive character.

Our concern, however,is not to discuss whether the term 'redemption' is suitable to express this specificity or we should use some other expressions like 'expiation', 'liberation', 'reconciliation' or 'salvation'. We also do not intend, per se, to analyse the implications of the word 'sacrifice'. We intend only to discuss how the Indian theologians interpret the significance of the Cross and its universal relevance being faithful to the central Christian faith that 'God in Christ was reconciling the world to himself, not holding men's fault against them, and he has entrusted to us the news that they are reconciled' (2 Cor 5:19). God's initiative and the gratuitous character of his salvation belong to the essentials of Christian faith. It is this what M.M. Thomas means when he writes:

> "For Christian orthodoxy, the Cross is the revelation not only of the Divine Humanity of Jesus, as the goal of history, but also of the spiritual evil which is present in the best of human institutions of religion, society and state leading to their rejection of that goal and revealing the need of their redemption by God's initiative." 193

A look at the initiative of God in the salvation of man is not meant merely to interpret the Cross of Christ in juridical terms inherited from imperial Rome, namelly, 'in terms of sacrifice and propitiation in law, offence and punishment'[194] but to accept the unfathomable depth of God's love for man manifested in the Christ-event: "Yes, God loved the world so much that he gave his only Son, so that everyone who believes in him may not be lost but may have eternal life" (Jn 3:16). 195

While speaking about the redemption of mankind achieved in Jesus Christ it need not be forgotten that eventhough in the Vedantic thought there is no 'redemption' from the Karma as is implied in the Christian Soteriology, still we have seen that the Avatars and Jeevanmuktas can help an individual entangled in Karma-Samsara to get liberated by accelerating the process. Ramakrishna Paramahamsa even had been of the opinion that even if the Avatara cannot set aside the rigid working of Karma-Samsara, he can rescue the devotee by taking the inexorable effects of the devotees' Karma on himself. [196] The strict Jnana schools may not find it easy to subscribe to this opinion, but it is one of the basic assumptions in the Bhakti schools. This 'help' rendered by the Avatar to his Bhakta could be considered as a vague prototype of the unreserved and gratuitous help that flows to mankind through Christ, the only mediator between God and men (Tim 2:5). Similarly the sacrifice of Prajapati or Purusha to which we had referred in the first part [198] could also be legitimately considered as an image of Christ's self-sacrifice on the Cross. Salvation from sin by the death of a Saviour, therefore, is not fully strange to the Indian ears. [199] K.M. Banerji even calls Jesus Christ the true Prajapati:

"It was in fact a fragment of a great scheme of salvation which was at first partially revealed and has since appeared in its integrity in the person of Jesus Christ - the true Prajapati of the world." [200]

The Prajapati of the Vedic Yajna (sacrifice) was, according to the vedic mythology, both the priest and victim of the original sacrifice. [201] 'The pure faith to which the Vedas testify is found in its fulness in Christ, the true Person, the Agent of Creation, the true Self-sacrificing Prajapati' [202]. There is also a story of god Siva drinking poison to save the world [203] which also resembles the redeeming act of Christ who destroys the poison of sin, 'himself drinking that bitter cup to the dregs in order that he may win the victory over death, destroy fear, and overcome Satan, the spirit of evil' [204]. What we intend to say by this reference to Hindu mythology, is only that the redeeming act of Christ is pre-figured not only in the Hebrew scriptures but there are also at least vague indications of it in the Hindu sacred writings. The sacrificial character of the Crucifixion is a point stressed by K.C.Sen. He refers to it as a 'sacrifice for the redemption of the world'. 'In Christ's death more than in his life was the saving economy of providence fulfilled'. Jesus Christ cleansed the world of sin and sorrow by his blood. 'He gave his life, that we sinners may gain life eternal and get reconciled to God' [205]. Similarly, H.A. Krishna Pillai (1827-1900), a Tamil Christian Bhakti poet, compares the blood of Christ to the Hindu belief in the saving water of Ganga, the sacred River. [208] These considerations of the crucifixion as a bloody sacrifice that definitively brings divine salvation to the world are fully in harmony with the New Testament presentation of Christ as the Pascal lamb (1 Cor 5:7), whose sacrificial blood (Rom 3:25) has bought us as if by ransom (1 Pt 1:8) from the power of the evil one. The understanding of Christ in the Letter to the Hebrews as the High Priest and Holy victim, who seals the new covenant with his blood,[212] is well expressed in the Indian explanation of Christ's Cross as a redemptive sacrifice foreshadowed in the Vedic Yajna and symbolized in the water of Ganga.

Divine justice, satisfaction and expiation are the categories preferred by Brahmabandhab Upadhyaya in explaining the mystery of the Cross. The sufferings of Jesus Christ offered adequate satisfaction for human transgressions.[213] But this theory of vicarious satisfaction, we would maintain, should not be pressed so far as to make out of God a caricature of a merciless tyrant! [214] The vicarious character of Christ's obedience to the will of God should be presented in the context of human solidarity both in good and evil. It is true that God did condescend to the level of the suffering humanity [214a], but this divine condescence should be understood as God's solidarity with mankind in freely accepting his fate. In God, man's tragic fate enters into a salvific and divine sphere. As Sadhu Sundar Singh observes, Christ's surrender of life has brought us eternal life.[215] V. Chakkarai does not accept the vicarious character of suffering, but he stresses 'the factual, qualitative and causal importance of the Cross as something without which man's redemption couldnot have reached its fruition and assurance' [216]. The important question is not, however, whether we use the expression 'vicarious satisfaction' but the content of it. It does not seem that Chakkarai denies that Christ's Cross is the meritorious cause of our justification. A.J. Appasamy sees sufferings as a consequence of sin and so it was necessary that Christ should undergo sufferings in order to save mankind from its transgressions. The Cross of Christ is a reminder of the gravity of sin and how difficult it is to re-establish righteousness in this world:

"The Cross is the revelation of the tremendous cost which God has to pay for the redemption of man. It is not as if without any effort on His part He forgives men whatever they may do.... The moral law is not set aside, in any sense; whereever there is sin there is suffering. The sin of men has brought about the suffering and death of Jesus on the Cross. If God forgave without the Cross, He would be laying aside his own moral law which He has established among men.... So the experience of the Cross is absolutely necessary. After the Cross no one can say that God forgives men because it is easy for Him or because he does not care to uphold the law that righteousness should prevail in the world." 217

This statement of Appasamy should not be understood merely in terms of penal substitution. He makes clear the intimate relation between sin and suffering. Even the suffering of the innocent can often be traced to the malice and wickedness of other individuals in the society. This is not do deny the presence of evil in this world which is beyond all human control and which points to the fundamental limitation of human existence. Still, it cannot be ignored that harmony and mutual love in the society based on the indispensable demands of existence and co-existence - sin is really an infringement of these fundamental demands - can make this world a better place of live! Therefore, the Cross has also a deep anthropological significance. It is a sign raised in the midst of the nations - a sign of man's inhumanity to man. It is a warning that God is not indifferent towards human injustice which is a radical violation of God's creation. It is an incorporation of the problem of human existence and God's answer to this problem; the answer is love!

The Cross is therefore not only a sign of man's suffering for the sake of this fellowmen as many of our Hindu brothren may accept. It is ultimately a proof of God's suffering for the sake of his love towards men and consequently towards the whole of his creation. God loved the world not because the world had merited it: "... what proves that God loves us is that Christ died for us while we were still sinners" (Rom 5:8). St. Paul declares further: "For our sake God made the sinless one into sin, so that in him we might become the goodness of God" (2 Cor 5:21). Paul seems to say that by a kind of legal fiction God identified Jesus with sin so that he might bear on behalf of humanity the curse incurred by sin. Still, what underlies the thoughts of Paul is the fact of God's immeasurable love towards humanity. It is in the supreme love, expressed radically in the unimaginable sufferings of his Son on the Cross, that God shows the magnitude of his gratuitous initiative in reconciling the human beings among themselves and through that, definitively with himself. Love does not accept defeat even in front of sufferings. As M.C. Parekh observes, it is God's love that will supply

us the key to open the mystery of Christ's death on the Cross. [220] V. Chakkarai similarly writes that Christ 'redeemed the hated symbol of His suffering
into the glory of the children of God and the sign manual of God's love
for the world of sin and suffering' [221]. The real novelty of the Christian
message consists in the radicality of love that is revealed on the Cross;
a radicality which can never be found in any other religion. It is this novelty
that is to be presented to the Hindu conscience and that is what A.J. Appasamy means when he says that the Hindu 'should be first helped to understand
the wonder and the depth of God's love, particularly as revealed on Calvary' [222]
because 'the sacrifice on Calvary is the uttermost expression of the love
of God (and it is through this sacrifices that) God has fulfilled Himself and
(in a certain sense) has realized to the full the riches of His love' [223].
Christianity has to be in India a real challenge to the Vedanta, to the whole
Hindu vision of salvation. Hinduism has to 'die' and has to be transformed
into the body of Christ. There is no transformation without death and no
full acknowledgement of Christ without this transformation. The question
is not whether Hinduism accepts one or another aspect of the mystery that
is revealed in Jesus Christ, but whether it is ready to acknowledge Christ
in his totality. We shall conclude this section with a relevant quotation
from D.S. Amalorpavadass:

> "Hinduism needs a deeper metanoia; it is not simply one of purification
> and fulfilment, but also one of rejection and rupture. There is no possi-
> bility of new life without real death. Christ will then be a sign of contra-
> diction, whether we like it or not: the scandal of the cross cannot be
> avoided in any case. Perhaps Hinduism needs to be provoked and chal-
> lenged; this may serve as a better way to discover Christ as the ful-
> filment and Saviour." [224]

b. The Relevance of Christ's Resurrection for the Human History

The Cross is not the last word in the Gospel of Jesus Christ. It is only a
pre-condition - and a necessary one of course - for the final and definitive
realization of man's salvation. The goal of human existence and of the whole
of creation is the eschatological glorification already begun with the resurrection of Jesus Christ; we share this glory through Christ's sharing of
his Spirit with us as was manifested in the event of the Pentecost. First
we shall examine how the mystery of the resurrection could be interpreted
in the Vedantic background.

i. The Resurrection and the Advaitic Illumination

The resurrection of the whole person, both body and soul, is also a faith that distinguishes Christianity from other religions. It is something that is very diffictult to put through to the Vedantic mind as J. Neuner observes:

> "Indian philosophy never considered the possibility of a salvation of nature itself, of a transfiguration of the Prakrti. There is no resurrection of the flesh; the body is shed like an old garment and the world left behind. Just as there is no [real] human incarnation of God, there is no Apotheosis of man. The spiritual core of man has, after all, always been considered divine; it is divine even beneath its earthly guise which, in the end, is shed. Man's earthly nature is but an outer shell: it always remains outside divine life." [225]

Since the innermost reality of man, the Atman, is by nature divine there is nothing very extraordinary about its salvation or God-realization. The Vedantic mind that holds this view finds the salvation of the body as something utterly mysterious'[226]. How can body and matter which belong to the realm of the unreal, which are the factors constituting the entanglement of Karma-Samsara, be themselves elevated to the divine milieu? The events of the bodily resurrection of Christ and the empty tomb as recorded by the New Testament as taking place at the margin of human history are, according to Dr. S. Radhakrishnan, the result of a misinterpretation of the spiritual experience of Christ's disciples. He holds that 'the simple story of the life and activity of Jesus was transformed with an epiphany of a heavenly being who had descended to earth and concealed Himself in robes of flesh. The picture of Jesus of the later Christology blurred the contours of the spiritual God. The Risen Lord takes the place of God...'[227]. Even if a literal understanding of bodily resurrection is meaningless, it could be given a meaning when interpreted in a mystical sense as a symbol of spiritual illumination and the realization of the union with God. He contends that 'the resurrection is not the rise of the dead from their tombs, but the passage from the death of self-absorption to the life of unselfish love, the transition from the darkness of selfish individualism to the light of universal spirit, from falsehood to truth, from slavery to the world to the liberty of the eternal'[228]. Swami Akhilananda is also of the same opinion. The Easter can be understood, according to him, only in the context of the Vedantic God-realization: "Death can be defied only when we have that realization of the abiding presence of God in us. So we learn from Jesus at Easter that we can defy death only be realizing the truth." [229]

ii. The Eschatological Matter-Spirit Integration

K.C.Sen has a different approach to the question of Christ's resurrection. Unlike the Vedantins, he sees in the resurrection not only a mystical meaning but also a corporeal one. Resurrection suggests a very important idea, namely, the continuitiy of Christ's humanity even after his death. It is a repudiation of the Vedantic absorption of man into the Divinity and the Buddhistic Nirvana. Even today Christ 'retains his humanity in the fullest measure' [230]. This, however, does not mean that the resurrection had been bodily or physical; it was essentially spiritual. In the Resurrection the humanity of Christ was fully transformed into Divine Humanity. In his transformed state Christ has not destroyed his humanity; it was only elevated. But, if we interpret the Resurrection of Christ as a bodily resuscitation, that would be contradicting all scientific evidence. He explains:

> "... Science tells me that the body is altogether decomposed in a few days after death. Surely the body cannot rise up; yet my Christ is there (in heaven). Oh! it is the Spirit of Christ who is there, reclining on the bosom of the Lord. But the man Christ, they say, was cruelly and ignominiously persecuted and crucified unto death by his enemies.... But there was such a thing as Resurrection subsequently.... I do verily believe and am prepared to testify that Christ has risen from his earthly grave.... If you think Christ is in the grave, you are certainly dreaming ... Christ dead and decayed is a deception. Christ risen is Christ indeed. The Spirit of Christ has risen and returned to the Father." [231]

So, even if the physical body of Christ is dead and decayed he lives in his Spirit even today in complete integration with his humanity. The Resurrection spiritualizes or universalizes the concrete Jesus of Nazareth for all humanity and for all eternity. It is through the Resurrection that the historical uniqueness of Jesus Christ achieves a universal relevance. Through the Resurrection Christ has become a life giving factor in the life of all believers even today. [232] 'He is living in all Christian lives, and in all Christian influences at work around us' . He asks: "Of what use is a dead Christ to us or to our nation?" He continues: "It is the living spirit of Christ which you should put into your hearts and affections, your daily life and character." [233]

K.C. Sen's idea regarding the resurrection is also shared by his disciple M.C. Parekh. He maintains that resurrection cannot be accepted as physical resuscitation. The physical body of Christ remained in its grave. Nevertheless, the humanity of Christ was transformed to a divine milieu. The Sthula Sarira (cross body) of Christ - to use the Vedantic terminology - did decay in the tomb; but his Sukshma Sharira (subtle body) did rise to life ever-lasting.[234] Such a distinction between 'Sukshma Sharira' and 'Sthula Sharira' or between body and soul was quite foreign to the Jewish anthropology. They 'could not think of a soul without a material body; with them both these go together. These people had no idea of there being other bodies than the pyhsical one, and this is why they had and have such a queer idea as that of the resurrection of the body with the soul...'[235]. Like Sen and Parekh, P.C. Mozoomdar also holds that the resurrection of Christ is not material, but substantial; 'its substance is the same as the composition of the Spirit of God with whom we commune every day'[236] He writes:

> "He (Jesus Christ) was spiritualized entirely; he was the Spirit made flesh. The glory of his transfiguration was spiritual glory.... The glory of his resurrection was spiritual glory: it was no flesh and blood, but the spirit ascended with the Kingdom above. We materialize him because we have so little of Spirit. We know nothing higher than flesh and blood. The Spirit of God glorifies himself in the Son." [237]

The message of the Easter Sunday, according to Mozoomdar, is one of the consummation of Creation as against its complete annihilaton The relevance of Christ's resurrection for us consists in the fact that we too will be sharing the fulfilment of existence which Christ has already realized. Therefore, the second coming of Christ should also be understood in the context of his resurrection. 'The past prefigured him, the future shall illustrate him, from him the present shall draw its inspiration.... The world does not hold out a prospect of speedy annihilation but of steady progress and prosperity; and if Christ's second advent is to take place, he shall come as the expected guest of the world's bridal chamber, not the avenging angel of its grave-yard'[238].

iii. Love as Life Conquering Death

Vengal Chakkarai sees the Resurrection as the realization of the Nava Sakti (new energy) that was established in the world with the Incarnation. This Nava Sakti is the Sakti (force, energy) of Love. It is love that fulfils the process of the spiritualization of nature. Eventhough man stands at the very apex of creation his inner aspiration towards the realization of his divine horizon is 'mocked by the indifferent forces of nature and laid in the dust by death'[239]. This challenge of the nature levelled against the dignity of man had been successfully confronted by humanity in Christ's Resurrection:

> "In the history of the Lord culminating in the death and resurrection, a great and terrible experiment was made by Him, resulting in the moralization and spiritualization of nature. This is the beginning of a new step in evolution." [240]

In Christ's Resurrection, the nature has 'become responsive to man's needs and his highest moral ideals. That is to say, love should dominate law; faith should control force; morality should defeat mortality. In the death and resurrection of the Lord, the first phase of the nava sakti emerged. Jesus died because of the weakness of the flesh and the sinfulness of man and rose again from the dead in newness of power because of the Atman or Spirit in Him'[241]. Love is the greatest reality (Parama Sattva) in the world; it hopes and suffers; it appears to be weak in 'the gladiatorial arena of cosmic forces, rolling on relentlessly, regardless of the good and bad alike, producing the terrors of day and the horrors of night'[242]. In the Resurrection of Christ the cosmic power (sakti) was overcome by the power of God(divine sakti) which is essentially love and holiness:

> "It is the spirit of holiness, the atman of Jesus, that reanimated the bruised and dead body lying in the grave of the Arimathaen Joseph. The first Easter joined together energy and l o v e, laying the foundations of the Christian view of the Avatar of God in Jesus Christ." [242]

The resurrection of Christ, therefore, was a 'logical and psychological necessity in the process of Incarnation' [243]. V. Chakkarai connects inseparably the mysteries of Incarnation and Resurrection by the 'Nava Sakti' of love. Unlike K.C. Sen and P.C. Mozoomdar, however, he insists on the physical reality of the Resurrection of Christ. He lays great importance on the Gospel narratives of the Empty Tomb. He writes that he 'is convinced on purely legal and psychological grounds that there was a physical resurrection of the very body that was consigned to the tomb and that the various hypotheses ranging from obvious imposture to subjective hallucinations and Ghost appearances of Jesus (including telepathic communications) are utterly unsatisfactory. The greates obstacle to the recognition of any of these theories in the empty tomb of Jesus, which in our opinion is simply impossible to explain away' [244]. Chakkarai's insistence on physical Resurrection, however, does not mean that he accepts some kind of bodily resuscitation again back to an historical existence as for example in the case of the 'reanimation' of the body of Lazarus. Chakkarai also uses the categories of 'Sukshma Sarira' and 'Sthula Sarira' [245]as done by Sen. So the risen body of the Lord was not just a repetition of his earthly body; on the contrary, his earthly body was sublimated to a heavenly one. [246] But Chakkarai's view of the Empty Tomb evidently stands in contrast to the view of Sen on this point.

In the evolutionary Christological view of P. Chenchiah, the mystery of the Resurrection is presented as the culmination of the progress of man from the sphere of matter to that of the spirit. This progress is characterized by the victory of love, of the Spirit and of truth over hatred, injustice and passions:

> "In the moving tragedy of the Cross, for the first time in history, all power, all might, arrogant aggression of imperialism allying itself with fanaticism, conservatism, obscurantism of the priest, was arrayed against a single man facing life with no other armour than love. Both in the incidents that led to the Cross and the Cross itself, we are presented with history in which the powers of the world grappled with the reserves of love and the power of the flesh with the power of the spirit. The Resurrection of Jesus is no happy ending which a sense of justice has invented for a tragedy of woe. It is the triumph of Spirit over flesh, of the new world order over the present, the triumph of satyagraha over the passion of the warrior and the ruler." [247]

The relevance of the Resurrection of Jesus Christ for the world lies precisely in the power of love and non-violent realization of truth (Satyagraha). The Resurrection was not, therefore, just a compensation for the injustice done towards a particular man in history, but it was a triumph in human solidarity - a triumph of love over hatred, injustice and all kinds of evil. Those who remain in solidarity with Christ participate also his triumph over death!

Jesus Christ is for Chenchiah, as we have seen, [248] the New Creation which was realized ultimately in his Resurrection. The task of the Christians is, as P.D. Devanandan observes, to witness the significance of this event before the world history:

> "Christian witness is to the reality of New Creation in the risen Christ, as the one determining factor in world history which gives it significance and meaning, despite the confusion and disorder produced by man's endeavour to direct its destiny towards ends of his own devices." [249]

S.J. Samartha also stresses this aspect of newness realized in Christ's Resurrection when he affirms that 'the cross and resurrection of Christ manifest the power to overcome evil and tragedy in human life and the hope of reaching a consummation which is not a return to the old but a bringing in of the new' [250].

In facing the emerging secular ideologies of India, M.M. Thomas thinks that the Resurrection of Christ should be presented as love becoming victorious in human history. He writes that 'the meaning of every historical action directed to love and justice in history and every fragmentary realization of truth, goodness and beauty in life, is protected, redeemed and fulfilled in the End ... our guarantee is the Risen Jesus Christ' [251]. Therefore, it is important to stress the historical aspect of Resurrection as the unique act of divine salvation for man, lest it should evaporate in subjective interpretations. [252] This historical approach is extremely important in a secular society because 'the question whether the ultimate spiritual destiny of man involves a redemption and consummation of Jesus being a bodily one - being a happenedness with some deposit in the chronological history, and not only in some primal salvation history known only to God or faith or only in the history of the internal soul of individual believers' [253]. In other words, todays secular society needs a concrete and historical proof for the victory of Suffering for the sake of love. If Jesus Christ's resurrection is that victory then he becomes 'the prototype of true manhood in history and the source of ultimate humanisation of human nature and mankind' [254].

In conclusion to our discussion on the question of the universal relevance which the Christ-event reached through the mystery of the Resurrection we would remark that even in this specifically Christian point the Hindu thinkers have shown great broadness and accommodation of mentality in their theological thinking. A mystical interpretation of Resurrection as the realization of the goal of one's spiritual striving is quite positive. But in this case the problem will be to explain the unique character of the Resurrection of Christ and its unique relevance for the rest of mankind. The Vedantins are not interested in this Christian problem especially due to the standpoint that stresses the universality in all religions as against the uniqueness of any particular one. A merely mystical interpretation of the Resurrection, however, will make it impossible for Christian theology to explain why the Resurrection of Christ should be different from the continuing spiritual existence and influence of a Guru, for example, among his disciples! So even in the theology of the Resurrection, the uniqueness of Christ cannot be set aside for some kind of mystical universality. Even in his resurrected universality, the uniqueness of Christ continues. This, of course, is not an exclusive uniqueness. This is what S.J. Samartha means when he writes that the 'affirmation of the lordschip of the crucified and risen Christ over all life does not involve any exclusiveness'; it is rather 'the declaration of the universality of the unbound Christ[255].

It is quite understandable that true to their anthropology, the Vedantins cannot accept any integration of matter or body with the spirit; there is no salvation for the body in the Hindu thinking. But the Hindu reformers K.C. Sen and P.C. Mozoomdar come surprisingly near to the Christian position in accepting the matter-spirit integration that was effected in the Resurrection of Christ. Even on the mere material plane there cannot be any development or improvement of the earthly existence as long as this corporeal aspect of salvation is ignored. An exaggerated and puritanical 'spiritualism' has been also one of the reasons for the stagnation of Indian economy. An attitude which is impressed in the subconscious by centuries of tradition cannot be changed with a few 'five-year plans'! The theology of the resurrection could be a contribution to foster the value of this creation and material reality in the Indian mind. This aspect had been dis-covered both by Sen and Mozoomdar, even though they were not sympathetic with the 'Empty Tomb' theory.

The introduction of the Vedantic notions of 'Sthula Sarira' and 'Sukshma

Sarira' into the theology of the Resurrection could be considered an authentic Indian contribution derived from the Vedantic anthropology. The Christian theologian V. Chakkarai follows Parekh in accepting these categories; but unlike Parekh, Chakkarai derives from this the possibility of the Empty Tomb, which for him is indispensable for a proper Christian understanding of the Resurrection. In this respect he has much in common with Wolfhart Pannenberg's view of the Resurrection. P. Chenchiah's interpretation of the Resurrection-event as the eschatological fulfilment in anticipation is also a view shared by Pannenberg.

In our systematic evaluation in the third part we will have to discuss the implications of the problems of the Empty Tomb especially as could be raised in an Indian interpretation of the Resurrection. The Resurrection theology will have to work out a healthy synthesis between matter and spirit, concrete fact and eternal truth, history and eternity, unique and universal and ultimately a Christian Advaita of man and God in the communion of love, that is life in the Holy Trinity!

c. Towards an Indian Pneumatology

The redemptive act of Christ enters a particular phase in the sending of the Holy Spirit; it is in the event of the Pentecost that the universal relevance of the salvation realized in Christ was concretely manifested by visible signs of transformation among Christ's disciples and those who came to hear their message. The sending of the Spirit was necessary to make the disciples experiences in a tangible way the power of Christ's Resurrection. So, any discussion on the universal relevance of Christ's unique redemptive act logically leads to a consideration of the role of the Holy Spirit in universalizing the uniqueness of the Christ-event. But it must be clear, that our concern here is not, per se, to make a research in Indian-Pneumatology, but only to cast some light on points which stand in immediate relation - what I mean is methodological immediacy - to an Indian interpretation of Jesus Christ which would give some lines of approach towards an Indian Pneumatology.

i. The Non-Personal Spirit

Just as in the case of Christology, a truly Christian Pneumatology in India presupposes a proper theology of the Trinity.[256] A Vedantic concept of Saccidananda can easily assimilate and accommodate a Holy Spirit as the 'Ananda' aspect of Brahman; but that would not be a Spirit truly and personally different from the Father and the Son in the Unity of their Being! The Hindu renaissance reformer, Raja Rammohan Roy, also accepts the 'Holy Spirit' but in strictly impersonal terms. In his 'Second Appeal' he devotes a chapter to defend 'the impersonality of the Holy Spirit'[257]. The Holy Spirit is for him only a representation of the influence and power of God and not any distinct or self-existent personality. To make a person out of him would be to fall into the sphere of Hindu idolatry and mythology. "If we believe that the Spirit, in the form of a dove, or in any other bodily shape was really the third person of the Godhead," he asks, "how can we justly charge with absurdity the Hindoo legends of the divinity having the form of a fish or any other animal."[258] It is evident from this that Rammohan Roy had grossly misunderstood the Christian Pneumatology! Still his concern for the eradication of superstitions is quite admirable.

ii. Jesus Christ and His Redemptive Universality

Like Rammohan Roy, Keshub Chunder Sen is also a strict monotheist. In his zeal to refute Tritheism, he prefers a modalistic approach to the Trinitarian Mystery. We had discussed this question sufficiently earlier.[259] Sen uses the term 'Person' in reference to the Father, Son and the Spirit of the Holy Trinity.[260] This should not mislead us because Sen does not accept a personal difference in the Trinity as understood in Christian theology. God the Father is for him the only God; the Son and the Spirit are only functional and so conventional differentiations in one and the same God: "Though there is a fundamental unity in the Trinity, we must recognize and demarcate functional differences. The Holy Spirit has a functional peculiarity of His own...."[261] If we do not keep in mind Sen's basic modalistic understanding of the Trinitarian theology, we would find his pneumatology especially in relation to Christology highly confusing and even inconsistent!

Sen uses the word 'Spirit' very uncritically and often without sufficient clarifications. 'Spirit' is for him first of all a synonym for God, whether he be the Brahma of the Vedas, the Jehova of the Old Testament or the Param Atman of the Vedanta.[262] There are also cases in which he sees Jesus Christ as the Incarnation of the Holy Spirit. The Wisdom of God (Logos) is the same as the Holy Spirit.[263] He also identifies the Risen Christ as the Holy Spirit: "... the body cannot rise up ... it is the Spirit of Christ (who has risen) ... The Spirit of Christ has risen and returned to the Father..."[264]. The Holy Spirit is the power of Christ, or the Spirit of Christ or to use an expression proper to Sen 'the Christ-force[265].

The peculiarity of Sen's understanding of the Holy spirit consists in the fact that for him the Holy Spirit, apart from the use of the term as indicated above, is identified with the soteriological aspect of the Christ-event. Jesus Christ, all by himself, is only a particular individual in the course of history. He is indeed a good example for the whole of mankind; but without the Holy Spirit he remains only an example It is the Holy Spirit who gives power to or enables every individual in every epoch to follow the example of Christ. In other words, it is the Holy Spirit who makes the historical uniqueness of Jesus Christ universally relevant. Christ teaches, reveals and shows us the way; he cannot give us the power to overcome sin; this power is given by the Spirit. Christ is the Way and the Spirit is the power to follow this Way. Sanctification or salvation belongs only to the Holy Spirit.[266] Regarding the universalization of the salvation of Christ through the Holy Spirit Sen writes:

> "It is the Spirit that makes the Christ, otherwise a mere historical character, a sanctifying power within us... (Only when) the Holy Ghost quickens the heart, even the most degraded and wicked sinner accepts Christ and is saved."[267]

Sen's idea that the Holy Spirit universalizes the Christ-event is acceptable. Since Sen accepts the redeeming value of the work of Christ, we should not interpret Sen's statement so as to mean that Jesus Christ cannot save at all! Jesus Christ is for him the Saviour, eventhough it is the Spirit that universalizes the effects of Christ's salvation. Still it cannot be denied that there is a certain amount of discrepancy in Sen's statements. In the context of 'Perichoresis'[268] and its implication regarding the essential unity and equality of the three persons in God it must be made clear that the application of the term 'Sanctifier' to the Holy Spirit is only a matter of essential appropriation, namely, the predication of a particular essential attribute of God to a particular divine person rather than to others due to a comparison and a certain relationship that exists between the attribute and the property (-ies) of that person. In our case the procession (spiratio passiva) of the Holy Spirit in the Trinitarian Communion is the basis of the essential appropriation of 'sanctification' to the Holy Spirit. It does not imply by any means that the Father and the Son have no role in the sanctification or salvation of man! As this question belongs to the fundamentals of the Trinitarian theology, it is unnecessary that we elaborate this point further. A lack of theological precision in Sen could be traced to the fact that he is not a systematical theologian; he is interested only in the practical applications of the faith in Christ. But it cannot be denied that without a systematic foundation, the practical aspect of the Christian faith cannot be sufficiently substantiated!

iii. Holy Spirit, The 'Antaryamin'

Vengel Chakkarai, for whom Jesus Christ is the Avatar or Incarnation of God, considers the Holy Spirit as the Incarnation of Jesus Christ in the human experience.[269] The Holy Spirit is the 'Antaryamin' or indweller God. Chakkarai maintains that it is through the Resurrection that Christ becomes our Indweller as the Holy Spirit: "The Holy Spirit is Jesus Christ Himself, taking his abode within us."[270] We had already indicated the fact that Chakkarai's Trinitarian theology is modalistic.[271] Only in this context can his pneumatology be understood. Chakkarai is of the opinion that the specifically Indian Christological contribution could be in the sphere of Pneumatology. The Vedantic Paramatman (Supreme Spirit) becomes for a Christian Bhakta the Antaratman (the Inner Spirit) in the form of the Holy Spirit.[272] He explains:

"The orientation of Indian thought in respect of the Incarnation would be set on the Holy Spirit and the significance of His indwelling in human lives. The Holy Spirit is the starting point; not that the historical Jesus goes out in the Indian consciousness; He takes His place and functions in the perspective furnished by the Holy Spirit. In other words, while the historical is the primary element in the Western interpretation, the spiritual is or will be the primary element in the Indian conception."[273]

Chakkarai says that this insistence on the universalized Christ in the form of the Holy Spirit is not 'a concession to the Indian neglect of history'[274]; it is only a matter of emphasis. The Holy Spirit being the resurrected Lord, he carries us 'beyond the historical Jesus to the continuation of His life-work after his earthly ministry'[275]. 'In the historical Jesus we have the specialised consciousness conditioned by time and space, but in the Christian life the same becomes universalized'.[276] The spirit of Jesus is the Holy Spirit.[277] It is this Spirit that gives us the Anubhava or experience of Christ. The Spirit takes us beyond itself and there is no injunction in the New Testament that we should pray to or worship the Holy Spirit.[277a] Still 'we adore and glorify the Spirit along with the Father and the Son but we do not worship and love Him as we worship the Father and the Son'[278].

It is clear that Chakkarai's view of the Holy Spirit as the one who 'universalizes' the salvation of Christ is acceptable, but for the rest his pneumatology is very defective and even inconsistent. The Indwelling God is the Trinitarian God and not just the Holy Spirit; the Christian life is essentially a participation in the life of the Holy Trinity. Chakkarai has also not reasonably explained why we cannot pray to and worship the Holy Spirit if, as he himself maintains, Jesus Christ is the Incarnation or Avatar of God; the Holy Spirit in human experience is the Incarnation of Jesus Christ'[279]. Unlike Sen, Chakkarai maintains that Christ is the 'Avatar' of God; but his ideas of the resurrected Christ and Holy Spirit are very similar and equally unfounded as those of Sen.

P. Chenchiah places his pneumatology within the general context of evolutionary Christology. The function of the Spirit is to realize the advent of a new creative order in Jesus. The New Creation is not just a question of being born again, but it is a further stage in the evolution of mankind 'brought about by the release of fresh energy through a new and tremendous creative act of God'[280] which results in a 'biological mutation of the whole species'[281].

The Holy Spirit is this New Cosmic Energy working in this evolutionary process:

> "The Holy Spirit is the new cosmic energy; the Kingdom of God the new order; the children of God the new type that Christ has inaugurated .... God in Jesus has made a new creation.... The children of God are the next step in evolution and the Kingdom of God the next stage in cosmos." [282]

He explains further the nature of this cosmic energy that is identified with the Holy Spirit:

> "The Holy Spirit is the energy beyond creation, which in Christ has flowed into the world.... The Holy Spirit is the energy through and by which Jesus is going to re-create a new heaven and new earth...." [283]

The cosmic energy of P. Chenchiah, however, cannot be considered as a new contribution. It is actually not much different from the 'vital energy' of Bergson and 'the within of cosmic matter' found in P. Teilhard de Chardin's Christology. We had already seen that, according to Chenchiah, Jesus Christ is neither God nor man but a New Creation between God and man, a new stage in the process of evolution which through the Holy Spirit will be realized in the whole of mankind. [284] Chenchiah does not seem to be interested in determining the nature and relation of the Holy Spirit to the Godhead. The understanding of the Holy Spirit as the 'Mahasakti' (the great power, the cosmic energy) in the process of biological mutation cannot be also satisfactorily harmonized with the biblical revelation. Chenchiah also discards the Church, the Christian dogmas, and the Sacraments leaving the whole spiritual life to the working of the 'Amrita Yoga' (the Yoga of everlasting life) which he calls also the 'Parisuddha Atma Yoga' (Yoga of the Holy Spirit) which consists in an inner personal surrender allowing the Spirit to work. [284] The communitarian aspect of Christian life and salvation seems to be rather neglected in this approach.

The Holy Spirit is indeed intimately related to the redemptive work of Jesus Christ and the Indian Christology could give special attention to the working of the Holy Spirit especially in realizing the salvation of those who have not yet heard of or accepted Christ. This, however, should not result in a reduction of Soteriology to Pneumatology as we have seen in the case of K.C. Sen, V. Chakkarai and P. Chenchiah. Salvation worked out by Christ should be considered as essentially Trinitarian; it is the union of man with God the Father, through the Son in the Holy Spirit. At the same time the notions of the Universal Christ and the Holy Spirit are no substitutes for Jesus of Nazareth, 'the only mediator between God and mankind' (1 Tim 2:5).

4. The Universality of Christ's Salvation in the Indian Context

The problem here is regarding the real catholicity or universality of the Christian faith. This question is especially relevant in India, a land where only less than three percent of the whole population have accepted Jesus Christ as their sole Saviour! If Jesus Christ alone can be recognized as the mediator between God and man, it must be also explained how his salvation could be accessible to the millions of non-Christians. Our interest here, however, is limited to the presence of Christ's salvation in Hinduism.

It must be clear from the outset, that we do not intend to develop here a theology of Hindu-Christian dialogue. A lot has been written already on this point.[286] The question of the 'Universal Christ' that we developed in the first chapter need not be repeated here, but its implications are to be kept in mind.

a. The Salvific Value of Hinduism

"It is inconceivable that the Supreme is concerned only with one part of one of the smallest of planets."[287] This is the remark made by S. Radhakrishnan regarding the Christian claim that the salvation of mankind was definitively realized only in Jesus of Nazareth. This is a just reaction against an all exclusivistic understanding of the uniqueness of Christ's salvation and the arrogant claim that at least in practice maintains without qualification that there is no salvation outside the Church.[288] This had led the Christians to ignore the presence of salvific elements in other religions and to blacken the practices of non-Christian worship as the work of devil. Robert de Nobili, an Italian Jesuit missionary in India who did a lot in the way of adapting the Hindu culture into the Christian way of life and worship in the beginning of the 17th century had the following opinion about the Hindu religious practices:

"(The Hindu) prescription for the removal of sin is from the Devil. He teaches them that repeating the name 'Siva' thrice will remove all the sins of the past and present... [and that] repeating the names 'Rama' and 'Krishna, worshipping in their temples, taking bath in Kaveri, wearing sacred ash in the forehead, and Rudraksha around the neck will remove...sins."[289]

This is evidently a very negative approach that denies all salvific value to the Hindu religious practices. Such an attitude is emphatically negated by the Second Vatican Council that sees also in other religious practices something that is 'true and holy' and a 'ray of that Truth which enlightens all men'[290].

On the other side there is also a tendency that sees the Christian faith on equal footing with the Hindu one; just as one of the possible means of attaining salvation. Even though not explicitly, at least implicitly, the soteriological view of Dr. Raimundo Panikkar is in this direction. First of all his stress on the so-called 'Christ-Principle' at the cost of the historical Christ and his trinitarian approach to theology rather than an incarnational one defends the presence of salvation in Hinduism, but by that justice is not done to the specificity of the Christian faith nor to the uniqueness of Salvation realized definitively in Jesus of Nazareth. We do not intend to elaborate this point here further; it has been considered sufficiently in the first chapter. [292]Still it is relevant here to cast a brief look at Panikkar's view of Hindu-Christian relation-ship.

Raimundo Panikkar is quite right in holding that the relation-ship between Christianity and Hinduism cannot be expressed by such correlatives as Sin and Sanctity, Error and Truth, Natural and Supernatural. All that is in Hinduism cannot be merely natural, sinful or erroneous.[292] It is indeed a monstrosity to think that God leaves the vast majority of mankind simply in error or sin limiting his favour to a selected few. If there is in Hinduism that is 'true and holy' and that is a 'ray of that Truth which enlightens all men', then Hinduism cannot be denied an element of the Supernatural in it, because these elements cannot be a mere production of the human genius. In the practical sphere of life a so-called Christian superiority is also doubtful. There are sufficient parallels in Hinduism for doctrinal sublimity, mysticism, miracles, and goodness of life.[293]

Panikkar accepts that there is salvation only in and through Christ both for Christians and Hindus. But this 'Christ', according to him, need not necessarily be identical with Jesus of Nazareth - we had refered to it in the first chapter. He writes:

"... because the human person is not just an individual, but also has a sociological, historical and cosmological dimension, salvation, though an inner and personal process, is prepared and normally carried out by external and visible means which we call sacraments. The good and <u>bona fide</u> Hindu as well as the good and <u>bona fide</u> Christian are saved by Christ - not by Hinduism or Christianity <u>per se</u>, but through their sacraments and ultimately, through the <u>mysterion</u> active within the two religions. This amounts to saying that Hinduism also has a place in the universal saving providence of God and cannot therefore be considered as negative in relation to Christianity." [294]

So salvation is through the 'Christ-mysterion' that is equally but differently present in both religions. Here Panikkar proposes a relation between Hinduism and Christianity on the basis of this equalitiy and difference on the model of the equality and difference in the Trinitarian relationship. [295] So the Hindu Christian relationship should be based on the principle of mutual fecundation or mutual enrichment and not on a desire-fulfilment model that characterises the relationship of Hinduism to Christianity as 'potential-actual; seed-fruit; forerunner-real presence; allegory-thing in itself; desire-accomplishment; symbol-reality; or the specifically Christian dynamism of death-resurrection' [296]. As Hinduism, according to Panikkar, is a full religion, he denies all kinds of special fullness of God's revelation and salvation ot Christianity.[297] He is of the opinion that both Hinduism and Christianity are different expressions of the same theandrical 'Christ-Mystery' and therefore equally important for mankind! [298] The difference is only one of cultural and temporal backgrounds and it is the duty of each religion to strive for its own fullness. [299] Hinduism and Christianity are equal partners in the question of human salvation! Hinduism is fuller or more perfect not when it moves in the direction of Christianity, but when it is composed of more and more people who mystically realize the theandrical mystery of the fullness of man.[300] A true religious transformation should be to the fullness of what each religion is, not what another religion is - a transformation to a better form of itself.[301] Each person should be helped to find and live his own deep reality. So the relation between Hinduism and Christianity is not one of 'towards' nor one of 'versus', but one of mutual fecundation from the fullness proper to each.[302] He explains:

> "... each religion is a dimension of the other in a <u>sui generis</u> co-inherence or co-involvement just as each human is potentially the whole of Mankind, though each one develops and actualizes only a finite number of possibilities in a limited way." [303]

Therefore, each religion is complementary; each reveals a different aspect of reality. Christianity stresses the historical aspect of man, while Hinduism the a-historical. [304] The meaning of Christian Mission is also to be understood in this background: "Human solidarity must impel people to share experiences, and both material and spiritual goods; and this mutual interpenetration may guide us towards building a true family of man!" [305] In this sense, Hinduism also has a mission just as Christianity.

Panikkar is of the opinion that the mutual fecundation based on the equality of both Hinduism and Christianity could bring about a transformation and a growth to fullness in both of these religions. A death to the old and a resurrection to the new is required in both. So when we apply the death-resurrection analogy to Hinduism 'the real intention behind the analogy is not to say that Hinduism should become Christianity, but to point out that there is within Hinduism itself a dynamism which leads it towards that peculiar movement of death and resurrection in which we detect the work of the antaryamin, the inner guide, which Christians call Christ. The individual must die to himself, to his previous limiting beliefs concerning the nature of Man, and be 'resurrected' in true knowledge of the cosmotheandric reality [306]. In this context it must be said that some presentations and interpretations of the ideas of Panikkar based on the first edition (1964) of his 'The Unknown Christ of Hinduism' may not be acceptable after a critical reading of its latest 'revised and enlarged edition' of 1981. For example, the statement that Hinduism will have to suffer a transformation and a radical change by a certain process of crucifixion and death into a 'better form of Hinduism' [307], that means 'as a risen Hinduism, as Christianity' [308]! In the light of the above given re-interpretation of death-resurrection analogy (made by Panikkar himself) [309], the death or radical transformation of Hinduism and its resurrection to the fullness of Christianity seems to be no more acceptable to Panikkar!

In our personal opinion, both of the above positions regarding the presence of Christ's salvation in Hinduism seem not to be acceptable in a true understanding of the universal salvific value of the redemption realized in Jesus Christ. Both Robert de Nobili and Raimundo Panikkar stand on extreme theological positions which are not easy to accept. On the one hand it is wrong to say that the Hindu practices and rituals are absolutely the work of devil and on the other hand it is equally a misinterpretation of the Gospel message to maintain that both Hinduism and Christianity are equally valid as means of salvation, the difference being only one of 'Ishta' or personal preference.[310] This position of Panikkar has much in common with the notion of the 'Universal Religion' proposed by S. Radhakrishnan and the principle of the equality of all religions advocated by the Vedantins,[311] but it is contrary to the New Testament affirmations regarding the uniqueness of Christ's salvific mediation.[312]

It must also be stated that Panikkar indulges in using an ambivalent language, that wants to be all things to all men! The terms he uses may help more to conceal his theological intentions rather than to clarifiy his ideas. In discussing the question of the universal presence of salvation in mankind he seems to make unnecessary confusions between the so-called theandrical Christ-principle and the historical individual called Jesus Christ. To express the 'theandrical principle' it would have been better to use some term other than that of 'Christ'; his justification for its use [313] may not be sufficently convincing. It would have been also better to clarify the distinction between the Church as mere religious institution which necessarily includes many human failures and in this sense need not necessarily be better than other religious organizations, and the Church, which in its basic reality is the Sacrament of Salvation for the whole of mankind as recently emphasized especially by the Vatican II.[314] It is inconceivable how the Church, as the continuation of the Christ-event in the rest of history, could be placed in its salvific significance on equal footing with Hinduism! We are of the opinion that the question of the salvific value of Hinduism should be approached from a more 'Christian' stand-point.

b. The 'Anonymous Christians' and the 'Anonymous Christianity'

"It is acceptable to Hindus to be 'anonymous Christians', provided one also admits that Christians are 'anonymous Hindus'."[315] This remark of Raimundo Panikkar clarifies sufficiently the Vedantic attitude towards the Christian concern to see everything that is good in other religions as belonging to Christ and Christianity, if not explicitly at least implicitly! It must be said that the idea of the anonymous Christians as stressed by Karl Rahner,[315] does not have much in common with the 'the unknown Christ of Hinduism' as understood by Dr. Panikkar. Both of them are speaking on different topics inspite of the generally misleading word-similarity between 'anonymous' and 'unknown'.[316]The question of anonymous Christians is a typically Western problem 'that makes little sense in (the Vedantic) tradition which takes polynomy for granted, ever since the famous Revedig saying: One is he whom the sages call by many names'[317]. What Panikkar wants to affirm by this explanation is that once the principle of the fundamental equality of all religions is accepted as held by the Vedantins, it is simply irrelevant to say that one religion is anonymously or unthematically another religion. Panikkar's frame of thinking is this Vedantic one; but Rahner's theological procedure is from totally different Christological and Ecclesiological presuppositions. The historical uniqueness of the Christ event as realized in Jesus of Nazareth and the unique role of the Church in the subsequent economy of salvation belong in Rahner's theology - unlike in the case of Panikkar - to the essentials of the Christian faith. Further it must also be said that even in the Western theological categories the expression 'anonymous Christians' is not without problems. We shall be discussing this question more elaborately in the third part, Chapter IX.B.

In his article, "The Salvific Value of Non-Christian Religions",[318]the Belgian Jesuit theologian James Dupuis (*1923), at present teaching in India, tries to sort out the problem of anonymity of salvation that is highly relevant in the Indian context. He mentions two contrasting views based on the theories of fulfilment [319] and universal presence [320] of Christ. R. Panikkar, K. Rahner and H. R. Schlette are presented by Depuis as the protagonists of the 'theory of the presence of Christ in the world-religions'. According to this theory, he maintains, it is not only that the salvific power of Christ reaches individuals belonging to other religious convictions personally and in a hidden way, but salvific value must also be attributed to other religions as such. Non-Christians are saved by Christ because his power is hiddenly at work in the world religions. They are saved in their own religions.[321] This would mean that Christianity as an institution has monopoly of the means of salvation. The means of salvation are present in other religions even if in a lesser degree than in Christianity and millions are saved normally through this means. 'It is therefore legitimate to speak not only of "Anonymous Christians", but also of "anonymous Christianity", for the salvific power of Christ does not merely attain men in the recess of their hearts;

it reaches them in the practice of their religion'[322]. According to the theory of fulfilment, which Depuis sees as being advocated by N. J. Farquhar, P. Johanns, H. de Lubac and H. Urs von Balthasar, every sincere man is saved by Christ, but 'it does not follow that the religions of the world can be called salvific'[323]. To attribute salvific value to non-Christian religions would be tantamount 'to obscuring the unique value of the decisive means of salvation established by Christ Himself'[324]. Since its institution by Christ, Christianity is the only valid means of salvation and the other religions must die to themselves and find life in Christianity. The false elements are to be eliminated and they have to reach fulfilment in Christ. In the plan of salvation, the Church is the unique axis on which all other religions have to converge. Still, it cannot be denied that Christ has 'his hidden ways of reaching down personally to souls' and such souls or individuals can be called "anonymous Christians", in so far as unknowingly they have been touched by the power of Christ. But there is no "anonymous Christianity" or "implicit Christianity" in the world religions'[325]. All religions do not play an equal role as ways of salvation.

The author does not seem to consider 'anonymous Christian' as problematic, but he does not agree with the expression 'anonymous Christianity'[326]. There is no salvation other than in and through Jesus Christ. The Church as the universal sacrament of salvation[327] realizes the personal presence of God to man in Jesus Christ in its highest sacramental visibility. Other religions cannot be put on a level with Christianity; yet a certain mediation of God's grace cannot be denied to them. The salvation of Christ operates in Christianity and other religions in diverse manners. But Christianity is different not only in degree but also in nature and so 'the uniqueness of Christianity cannot be reduced to the mere awareness of a mystery of salvation that would be found else where in the same manner'[328]. The newness of Christianity implies 'more than the simple unveiling of a mystery already fully though unknowingly experienced; it brings with it the full sacramental realization of God's presence to men'[329]. Hinduism's transformation to Christianity is not merely a process of gnosis, i. e. awareness (from unknown to the known) nor one of explicitation (from the hidden to the acknowledged). It involves a radical conversion, a death to itself and a resurrection into the unique newness of Christ.

It is true that the Hindu symbols and religious practices do help its adherents on the way to salvation; but it cannot be denied that all rituals need not be conducive to salvation; in his ignorance one could also be misled. The guarantee of infallibly encountering God in Christ through the Christian sacraments cannot be claimed by the Hindu rituals. Besides there is a great difference between an unending search for a valuable treasure and its definitive and realized possession - in this case God's self-giving to man in the humanity of Jesus Christ and his historical and sacramental contin- uation in the Church. There is a uniqueness for the Christian experience of God and that uniqueness is the person of Jesus Christ. In short, the 'more' or the 'newness' of explicit Christianity consists in Jesus of Nazareth himself, who is the Christ!

Depuis does not deny the possibility that certain aspects of the mystery (of Christ) are more deeply experienced by many Hindus. A Hindu who lives according to his conscience is surely nearer to Christ than a Christian who ignores the challenge of his privileged situation. Considering the great majority of non-Christians it could be said that those religions are the ordinary means - but not the normative means - of salvation for many, and the Church the extraordinary means. Christianity as the means of salvation is extraordinary because it 'is the select, the exemplary, the perfect means of salvation, ideally destined by God for all, even if in reality it is not granted to all. The Christian lives in a privileged situation as to the signification of the mystery of Christ'[330].

We personally find most of Depuis's conclusions quite convincing and accept- able. Hinduism with its rituals and practices, its search for truth and deep mysticism mediates divine grace, though not in the same manner or at the same level as Christianity. [331] Man being a social being is saved in and through his immediate milieu because it is the will of God that all be saved. [332] Eventhough the Church is the Sacrament of Christ (Ursakrament) and consequently Christ's salvation 'subsists' in the Church, [333] the Church does not and cannot exhaust the mystery of Christ. Jesus Christ transcends the Church, so the salvation realized through him is 'open to different orders of mediation' [334] without being equal or constituting a challenge to the speci- fically Christian mediation. Jesus Christ is the only Saviour of mankind; so a Hindu believer is saved not on account of his religion and also not inspite of it, but in and through his own religion of sincere conviction.[334] This could be a reasonable interpretation of the universality of Christ's salvation in the Indian context. So the statement 'extra ecclesiam nulla salus' is to be understood as 'extra Christum nulla salus'.

It must also be stated, as a matter of critical observation, that Depuis' division of salvation theories into two, as we have seen above, may not be fully acceptable. Even from the purely logical point of view, the division is not mutually exclusive. It may not be correct to assume that those who accept the universal salvific presence of Christ reject the aspect of fulfilment of Hinduism in Christ and his Church, nor vice versa. Unlike what Depuis holds,[335] there is substantial difference between Rahner's and Panikkar's views regarding the question of anonymous Christians; we have already referred to this point. Depuis should have also clarified the difference between the essential nature of the Church as the Sacrament of Christ and the historically and culturally conditioned external and institutional structure through which the fundamental nature of the Church is expressed. If there can be bad or imperfect Christians there can also be imperfect structures which could hinder the Church's transparency of the face of Christ. The Church requires a ceaseless reformation to make its privileged position in the salvific plan of God credible to the Hindus: Ecclesia semper reformanda!

In conclusion we would like also to mention that the expressions such as 'anonymous Christ', 'anonymous Christians' and 'anonymous Christianity' are even liguistically problematic. Depuis finds only the application of 'anonymity' to other religions ('anonymous Christianity') as not acceptable. He proposes 'latent Christianity' as a possible alternative while he rejects 'implicit Christianity' and 'subjectively implicit Christianity', as these expressions do not 'state what exactly differentiates the non-christian religions from Christianity'[336]. We would say that the very usage of terms such as 'anonymous', 'latent' and 'implicit' in reference to Christ, Christians and Christianity is a self-contradiction. Christ, Christians and Christianity are the visible signs or perceptible symbols of God's salvation in the midst of mankind. It is a contradiction in terms to speak of an 'invisible sign'. A sign or a symbol has to be visible, somehow perceptible, manifest - or it is no sign at all! This view is substantiated also by the principle of Incarnation and the theology of Sacraments. We will be coming back to this point again in our evaluative part!

We are conscious that the connotations of a term or expression is also a matter of convention and personal interpretation. This is especially valid for theological terms. Sometimes we have to adopt apparently illogical expressions to convey the Christian faith. But where it is possible one has to avoid expressions which run the risk of being misunderstood. It is true that in order to explain the universality of Christ's salvation in the Indian context we have to take inevitably into account the salvific value of Hinduism. But the question is whether just the mysterious and providential presence of Christ and his Spirit in Hinduism could be a sufficient justification to describe Hinduism as Christianity without name! We will be shedding more light on this problematic in our evaluative part, Chapter IX.B., with the help of the corresponding theological views of Karl Rahner and Wolfhart Pannenberg.

C. Khristanubhava: The Liberating Experience of Christ

The salvation accomplished by Jesus Christ remains merely as an objective reality if it is not assimilated and appropriated into personal existence in one or another way. The redemption of Christ is universally available, but this universal availability can be realized only when it enters the sphere of individuals. In the preceeding sections we have discussed the question of the universality of salvation in Christ. Here we consider the question from the side of human co-operation and acceptance. In this respect we intend to develop the theme around the notion of 'Anubhava' or experience. It is through Christ-experience (Khristanubhava) that the salvation is subjectively realized in us.

This discussion on 'Anubhava' is of great relevance for a Christology in the Indian context especially because of the importance attributed to it as the 'Pramana' (source, means, criterion) of Christology as is evident, for example, in an article on this topic by T.M. Manickam. [337] We are of the opinion that a differentiated approach to this question is very important in order to avoid unhealthy theological generalizations. We will have to deal with this problem also in our evaluative Part III. Ch. IX.C.

1. The Nature of Christ-Experience

For this discussion it is necessary to keep in mind what we have already said regarding the question of Vedantic Anubhava and Saksatkara in chapter three. The Khristanubhava in the Indian context will have to be built up in the context of the corresponding Vedantic experience. I would like also to warn against a simplistic understanding of 'Anubhava' or experience as a matter of mere individual fancies or personal and psychological emotions. 'Anhubhava' in our usage is the sum total of the whole of spiritual life that leads one to the realization (Saksatkara) of the goal of existence. In Christian life Jesus Christ is the axis or the centre around which man's existence turns. The centrality of Christ could be considered as the specific characteristic of the Christian experience. Thus 'Khristanubhava' is the synonym for Christian ascetism, spirituality and mysticism. It is this, that brings one to one's ultimate liberation. Hence the title: Khristanubhava, the Liberating Experience of Christ.

a. Christ-Experience and God-Experience

"In Christian experience", writes V. Chakkarai, "the most central thing is Christ Himself."[337a] The supreme object of Christian devotion also is, according to him, Christ Himself.[338] He writes:

> "The peculiar trait in Christian experience that raises, purifies, and gives men and women, otherwise insignificant, sublimity of character and daring is the consciousness that Jesus Christ has placed them in a secure place in the world. They are not solitary atoms in this bewildering world, nor units for whom God does not care, nor are they left to their own devices to find their way through life to the ultimate destiny. To find Christ is to find the harmonizing principle that will reduce the chaos of facts into a cosmos. He is the liberator...."[339]

Jesus Christ is for us the human face of God. We encounter God and experience him in and through Jesus Christ. 'We can no more think of God without Jesus Christ (nor can we) think of Jesus Christ without God'[340]. The experience of Jesus Christ is, therefore, the experience of God. Jesus as the final and full revelation of God 'has contributed some vital elements to our experience (of God)'[341]. He has altered and perfected our knowledge of God so much so that 'we can no more think of God without Jesus than we can conceive the world without the sun'[342]. An examination of the Christ-event and what Jesus is in human experience gives us new ideas of God which could be transferred to the reservoir of all our God-experiences. As Jesus is the very image of God and God himself, our knowledge and experience of God cannot be seperated from Jesus. We are privileged to define the unknown God by the known Jesus.[343] In Christian life there is not knowledge and experience of God other than what is known and experienced in Jesus Christ.

Such an experience is not a scientific achievement, nor a matter of much learning. Chakkarai explains:

> "We worship God, not as a bloodless category of thought as He is regarded by pure metaphysics, but as He was and is revealed to Christian experience in Jesus Christ. When we speak of Christian experience, it is not that of man in relation to God alone but includes also that of God in relation to man." [344]

So Christian experience is fundamentally a matter of God-man relationship of which the concrete model is the Incarnation of Jesus Christ. A perfect relationship is based on the total and mutual acceptance of two persons. It is personal in character. A personal relation with God in Jesus Christ cannot be reached through merely scientific analysis and exegesis of the Bible. The Bible itself is in fact the book of God-experience.[345] The authors of the sacred books reflected on their spiritual experience and articulated it as far as they could in a language of the intellegible to other men. The God-experience of the Old Testament reaches its culmination in the Christ-experience of the New Testament. We can appropriate this redeeming experience only through a face to face confrontation with God in Christ. Acarya R.C. Das of Benares observes:

> "[The Christ-experience] is not just an intellectual notion, a logical conclusion, a formal and professional statement nor an evangelistic slogan. ... It is the result of the meeting of the soul face to face with God in Christ." [346]

More than intellectual intuition, what is most required in Christ-experience is faith-intuition. Without faith the Christ-event has no more any redeeming significance. In his time many had seen Christ and witnessed also the different stages of his life; but only in the community of his believers the Christ-event aquired a salvific meaning.[347] This is not a denial of the objective value of the redemption realized by Christ; but what is objective has to be subjectively realized. Religious experience belongs necessarily to the subjective realm of individuals; but this subjectivity is based on the objective foundation of the ultimate reality and so it does not distort that reality. The Christ-experience is a subjective participation of the Christ-mystery. S.J. Samarthas explains:

> "It is necessary for the Church also to acknowledge and to participate in the Christ-event so that the meaning of the incarnation might manifest in the Church's life with renewed power. Here subjectivity cannot be regarded as a distortion of reality but as an attempt to penetrate that aspect of reality which manifests itself in subjective forms."

The experiential participation of the Christ-mystery is also a matter of consciousness and awareness. The mere fact of being in the state of 'grace' does not constitute Khristanubhava; but when one is aware of this state of union with God in Christ, one is encountering in one's level of experience the supreme destiny of one's existence in Christ and that is Khristanubhava. Every human being has the obligation to transcend from time to time to the awareness or consciousness of his own reality in God and to establish a communion of personal friendship with him in loving 'conversation'. That is what we call 'Prayer'! The intensity of prayer depends on the depth of this 'anubhava'.

The divine worship, the participation of the holy sacraments and the fulfilment of the personal and communitarian acts of prayer are by their very nature oriented towards the 'Khristanubhava'. It must also be clear that a merely material or automatic fulfilment of these religious practices, without any real and personal involvement have nothing in common with what we call Christ-experience. The experience being the result of consciousness and awareness it needs a certain amount of personal reflection at least in the remote sense of the term. But an intellectual reflection in itself - even of a religious fact - is not a religious experience. The intensity of the Christ-experience therefore has nothing to do with the 'intelligence quotient' (IQ) of an individual. The Christ-experience is essentially not so much a matter of thinking much, as of loving much.

There is a general misunderstanding that 'Khristanubhava' or any religious experience should be considered in terms of tranquility of mind, peace, and joy - in short, a certain amount of psycho-spiritual well-being. It is possible that Christ-experience is transmitted also to the emotional aspects of man and in most cases a certain amount of spiritual satisfaction could be experienced also on the emotional level; but emotional and psychic reactions do not belong to the essence of Christ-experience. One can have a 'Khristanubhava' and at the same time one could feel total 'dryness' from the emotional point of view. The emotional aspect of God-experience is sometimes not only 'neutral', it could even take a negative turn namely in the anguishing experience of God's absence from the sphere of human emotions. It is, to use the terminology of St. John of the Cross, the dark night of the soul which was experienced by Jesus himself on the Cross especially in his experience of being forsaken by the Father. In human existence the dark night of the soul is the experience of the absence of the beloved. Inspite of its pain and anguish this experience also belongs to the reality of love that is the basis of personal and mutual self-giving. Therefore, suffering for the sake of Christ's love is an indispensable aspect of 'Khristanubhava'.

b. 'Khrista-Sayujya'

Love tends towards unity. The love towards Jesus Christ also reaches its climax and fulfilment only in an experience of union with Christ which we may call 'Khristasayujya'.[349] It is not a question of being 'lost' in Christ or 'absorbed' into Christ as the Vedantins may hold. The free and personal communion with Christ and a participation of his very same life are what is implied in Khristasayujya. To be united with Christ is in a way to become 'Christs' as K.C. Sen observes:

> "God sent His only begotten Son in order to make all His children, one and all, sons and heirs of God.... The problem of creation was not how to produce one Christ, but how to make every man Christ." [350]

Sen advices every man to realize this destiny of human existence:

> "Be Christ. Do not rest satisfied with anything short of this.... Incorporate him into your being; import him bodily into your own consciousness. Make him your flesh and blood. Let us all be many Christs, each a small Christ...."[351]

Faith in Christ, for Sen, is life in Christ. To eat Christ's body and to drink his blood means to be spiritually identified with him in truth, love, wisdom and purity. And it is in Christ that we are also one with God.[352]

Mark Sundar Rao understands the spiritual union with Christ in terms of non-alterity to which he gives the name 'Ananyatva' (not-being-another). It is according to him a Christian version of 'Advaita' (non-dualism) that does not result in ontological absorption, but is a mystical union.[353] It is not merely an I-Thou relationship; it is rather an 'I-in-Thee and Thou-in-Me'. This special type of our spiritual union with God in Christ is based on the 'Perichoresis' (co-inherence) of the Trinitarian relationship, eventhough it is not in the same order. [354]

c. The Trinitarian and Communitarian Dimensions of Christ-Experience

Indian Christian theologians insist also on the Trinitarian aspect of Khrista-nubhava. Our 'Sayujya' with God in Christ is not merely a 'union', but it is rather a 'communion' which presupposes the personal difference of those involved in the union. There is no Christ-experience that is not related also to the Father and the Holy Spirit; it is the experience of communion with the Father through the Son in the Holy Spirit. Therefore, the Holy Trinity is not just a 'Mystery for thought' in Christian life; it is rather the Mystery of Salvation. The Trinitarian life is the goal and ultimate destiny of human existence and therefore it is also the model of man's existence in this world, both in the material and the spiritual sphere. The Trinitarian aspect of Khrista-nubhava is a point that is to be stressed especially in the 'Saccidananda' background of the Vedantic mysticism. Swami Parama-arupya-ananda (Jules Monchanin) maintains that 'through acknowledging in the "Indwelling God" the mystery of the universal and deifying presence of the Holy Ghost, India, in rising towards the "One without a second", ekam eva advitiyam (Chand. Up.6.2.2) will find at length the mystery of the Father's love overflowing into the Plenitude of His Incarnate Son...' [355]. He believes that through the concept of the 'Saccidananda' India has been specially prepared for the Trini-tarian aspect of the Khristanubhava:

"Is not India destined in a very special way to contemplate the mystery of the blesses Trinity? To begin with, to the contemplation of the Divine Spirit, the 'uncircumscribed' Person, who appears only under the fluid forms, breath, water ... fire..., the Person who is not perceived through the visible like the Word, but through spiritual realities, the charisms, and above all, the agape, the charity, the communion of saints, the mysterious immanence of all in every one and of every one in all.... From Him, she (India) will pass on to the Word of glory, to the Risen One ... then to the Word of sorrow assuming every pain to transmute it into the paschal bliss - finally to the Word in His terrestrial life,

not an illusory one as the avatara's but a 'realizing reality' in which
(all things have their consistency). The contemplation of India will
end in the abyss of the Father, the Person unmanifest in Himself, whom
the two others manifest...." [356]

Swami Abhishiktananda also stresses the Trinitarian dimension of Khristanubhava: "Apart from the Trinitarian revelation there is no possible alternative to the Advaita of the Upanisads." [357] He continues:

"At the very source of Being, the one without a second of the Chandogya
Upanisad (6,2) there is koinona, co-esse, 'being-with', 'being-together',
community of being, mutual love and communication of life, and eternal
call to each other. In its most impenetrable core of non-duality Being
is threefold movement within Itself towards Itself, the tripple achievement of itself in itself." [358]

It is to this 'Advaitic anhubhava' of the Trinitarian life that the Khristanubhava is oriented because 'in the mystery of God, at the very heart of
Being, the Son and the Spirit proceed from the Father, alike in the non-duality
(advaita) of nature and in the threefold communion (koinonia) of persons' [359] .
Khristanubhava, in short, is the personal communion with the Holy Trinity
through Jesus Christ in the 'cave of the heart' [360] . The Advaita that lies
at the root of Christian experience, according to him, means 'neither God
alone, nor the creatures alone, nor God plus the creature, but an undefinable
non-duality which transcends at once all separation and all confusion' [361].
This would mean that the Khristanubhava or Christian Advaita comprises
the totality of reality; it is not just an 'I-and-my-God-affair'; it has an indispensable social and cosmic dimension too. In the Trinitarian and social
dimensions of religious experience, the Khristanubhava has to act as a corrective for the Vedantic experience of Saccidananda. In this sense the Vedantic God-experience has to 'die and rise' into the experience of Christ. [362]

An important question regarding Khristanubhava is how to make the profound
spiritual experience in and through Christ, i.e. a spiritual immediacy with
Christ, compatible with the mediatory role claimed by the institutional
Church! Does not the structure hinder and harm the free movement of the
Spirit? A Vedantin finds it impossible to compromise the religious experience
with the religious structure. The structure belongs to the realm of 'Maya'
and bondage, while it is the Spirit that liberates. Inspite of his very positive
attitude towards Christ, Keshub Chunder Sen could not get reconciled with
the idea of the institutional Church as he found it in his days. He wanted

a 'broader Church' in which 'whatsoever is true and good and beautiful' in different religions could be integrated into the centrality of Jesus Christ.[363] His 'New Dispensation Church' was intended to be such a broader Church against all Christian sectarianism.[364] It was an effort to unify 'all that is Christian in other creeds'[365]. By this he hoped to universalize the Khristanubhava. Similarly P. Chenchiah also, in his insistence on the direct experience of Christ, criticizes the organized Church, Dogmas and Sacraments; even the New Testament has for him only a role inferior to the direct and personal experience of Christ:

> "Why do churches and books intervene and bring Him to us like water from a distant fountainhead? ... If there could be direct contact with Jesus, why should we seek it through bread and wine? If God speaks to us today, why hear his words through a book written about twenty centuries ago?"[366]

What we have already mentioned regarding the social aspect of the Trinitarian experience in Christ would be important here in facing the criticism of Chenchiah. No man is an island. Even in the salvation economy man remains a social being, who has to continue his pilgrimage to salvation in the company of his fellowmen. The Church being such a gathering of Christ's believers is an indispensable factor in the process of salvation. The Hindu spiritual individualism is nothing else than egoism in a 'divine' clad and that has been the reason for the surprising lack of social concern in Hinduism. The experience of Christ stands in contradiction to this basic Hindu tendency; Khristanubhava has to correct it. Apart from the solidarity of the whole of mankind, the universal relevance of Christ's salvation cannot also be explained. On the other hand, Chenchiah is fully right when he observes that in the commonplace Christianity, the Hindu 'does not find ... anything corresponding to the deeper levels of Hindu spiritual experience' and that we have told the Hindus not much of 'living with Christ and in Christ'[367].Eventhough this statement cannot be accepted as such in view of the numerous Christian mystics, it cannot be denied that 'the face of the Church' is for a Hindu observer more institutional than mystical.

In short we would say, Khristanubhava is the liberating experience of Jesus Christ. This is the experience of the God-Man unity in Jesus Christ which invites every man to fellowship and communion with the Trinitarian life.

Our Fellowship with Christ is in itself fellowship with God. There is no approach to God other than through the God-Man, Jesus Christ - whether this fact is acknowledged or it remains unknown in subjective good faith is a different question. The Khristahubhava is by its very nature not only Trinitarian, but also social in character because just as the life of the Holy Trinity is communitarian, so also in an analogical way man has to come to his salvation or the ultimate destiny in and through the society, of which the Church is a God-given symbol - Sacrament! In the following section we shall discuss the three possible ways of giving concrete expression to Khristanubhava in the Vedantic categories of the three Margas or Ways: Karma Marga, Jnana Marga and Bhakti Marga - the ways of action, contemplation and love!

2. **The Pluriformal Dimension of Khristanubhava: Jesus Christ, Our 'Brahma-Marga'**

In the third chapter we had discussed in detail the Vedantic notion of 'Marga' which leads one to the Brahmasaksatkara or God-realization. [368] What we intend here is to give a Christological interpretation to the category of 'Marga'. 'Marga', as we had seen, literally means 'way' and in theology it is used to indicate the Way(s) to God-realization. The universal relevance of Jesus Christ's uniqueness in history is especially emphasized in considering him as the Way to God: "I am the Way, the Truth and the Life. No one can come to the Father except through me" (Jn 14:6). Jesus is our Way, the Marga, because we have in him our access to God; it is he who makes the Father known to us (Jn 14:9). [370] In the sections A and B above we have shed light on this aspect of Christology especially in presenting Christ as the Saviour of mankind. Here our approach is more subjective: not just how Jesus Christ is in himself the Way to God, but how he could be practically assimilated and appropriated as 'our Way' in the context of Khristanubhava and Brahmasaksatkara, i.e. in the context of personal religious experience.

In considering Jesus Christ as the Way, Keshub Chunder Sen limits the role of Christ to indicating to us the Way to the end that is God [371] as an eminent example in human history [372] and refuses to acknowledge him as the end: "Christ was only a means, not the end. He was the 'way'." [373] The end is God the Father, who for Sen is the only God. [374] This position of Sen is in conformity with his understanding of the person of Christ as inferior to God. But, the properly Christian understanding of Christ identifies in him both the way and the end as Prema-arupya-ananda writes:

> "Through Christ full man and full God - the way - to the abyss of fathomless Godhead ... Christ as man is the starting point. The same Christ as God, is the final goal. And at this ultimate stage, God is meditated upon as He is..." [375]

Jesus Christ does not merely show us the way as any other religious teacher, but he is in himself the Way and the Goal. [376] We do not 'touch' God except through Christ. [377] In his God-Man reality, Christ is both our 'Marga' and our 'Saksatkara' - the Way to God-realization and God-realization itself!

Here we shall see how an experience and realization of God in Christ could be interpreted through the Vedantic categories of 'Karma' (action), 'Jnana' (knowledge) and 'Bhakti' (loving devotion).

a. Karma Marga: The Way of Action

The Marga of Karma must be, as we have seen earlier, understood in the context of the Vedic Vajna or sacrifices which were performed especially in the early Vedic period to appease the gods and to obtain favours from them. [378] Properly speaking, 'Karma' in this context stands for the vedic 'yajna-mantra' complex. [379] Refering to the Cross of Christ we have already indicated that Christ's sufferings and death on the Cross are a sacrifice that fulfils the transcendental aspirations of man foreshadowed in the Vedic Vajna especially as narrated in the sacrifice of the Purusha or Manu, the original Man. [380] In the light of Christ's ministry and death on the Cross, he can well be interpreted to the Vedantic mind as the Supreme Karma Yogi. [381] In this frame-work we can speak of the salvific role of Karma or of deeds of religion by which we faithful try to do and contribute their share in the process of salvation. The salvific work of Christ does not become automatically effective in an individual's life. In so far as one has personal freedom one is placed before the possibility of personally accepting the salvation in Christ or of rejecting it. Man's free deeds reflect his fundamental option and further confirm it. No one who is capable of exercising one's freedom can escape from the Way of Action (Karma Marga) towards God-realization.

The external practice of religion should be understood properly in this context. Since man is also a body, his deeds or Karma are indispensable on the Way of salvation. Personal and communitarian acts of asceticism and prayer, deeds of charity and reception of sacraments belong to the Karma Marga. The 'Via Purgativa' of the classical Christian spiritual theology could be compared to the Vedantic Karma Marga.

The religious practices of non-Christians should also be seen in the general context of Karma-Marga. Their rituals, forms of worship, samskaras (counterparts of Christian sacraments in Hinduism), pilgrimages, observances for the removal of sin, pilgrimages and even image worship on the popular level have a certain subjective value and at least an indirect role to play in the process of salvation. Jesus Christ, the Incarnate Word of God, satisfies the primitive religious instinct of man that searches after idols. Jesus being 'the Image of the invisible God' (Col 1:15., 2 Cor 4:4), he has taken the place of idols in primitive religions. Regarding the worship of images in popular Hinduism, J.N. Faquhar observes that 'the man who has been used to the accessibility of the idols and the joy and passion of their worship finds in Him (Christ), in purest spiritual form, more than all the emotions and stimulus to reverent adoration which their vividness used to bring him'[383]. He continues:

> "there is a great truth behind all idolatry, the truth that at any moment, in any place, we may have access to the Father's heart, but it is pitiably distorted by idols and mixed up with the most degrading and polluting superstitions. Christ by His life and teaching reveals the Father in His holiness, His self-sacrificing love, and His readiness to answer prayer, thus making idolatry impossible, and enabling us to worship the Father in spirit and in truth." [384]

The idol-worship is a desparate attempt to represent the mystery of Christ and inspite of all its aberrations it cannot be denied that it reveals a sincere desire to love and serve God. In line with M. Eliade we can maintain that the idol worshipper, despised by philosophic schools as a publican, is perhaps [385] less distant from the kingdom of God than Plato. J. Neuner considers it quite plausible to think that 'some of the abundance of God's grace and his promise of eternal life for all who believe in Christ would come to those who worship the (idols)'[386]. He gives the reason:

"For they open their pious hearts not to some superstition but to Christ the Saviour, whose message of salvation is to some degree still contained in their limited and humanized, and all too often, distorted imagery." 387

A proper understanding of the Christian 'Karma Marga', therefore, demands a certain sympathetic understanding for the religious practices, especially on the popular Hindu level. It is quite unchristian to expel Christianity, as P. Chenchiah does, from the realm of deeds or actions, from the 'region of nama and rupa [name and form]' to the realm of spirit. 388 The Karma Marga reminds us to take the material and cosmic aspects of human existence more seriously in the process of reaching God-realization. It is an affirmation of the Mystery of Incarnation itself!

Karma or action in the form of disinterested service for the material and spiritual welfare of mankind is a consequence of love and so we deal with it under the title of 'Bhakti Marga' later.

b. Jnana Marga: The Way of Knowledge

Our detailed exposition of the Vedantic Jnana Marga in the third chapter 389 could be supplemented here with a Christian interpretation of the same in the light of Jesus' statement in the Gospel of St. John: "If you make my word your home you will indeed be my disciples, you will learn the truth and the truth will make you free" (Jn 8:31).

Man's search for ultimate liberation or definitive freedom through the knowledge of truth is what is stressed in Jnana Marga. What is meant here is not scientific truths which could be attained by research; the liberating truth is the truth of one's own identity in relation to the totality of existence which could be discovered only through a process of interiorization in the cave of one's heart and in the unity of one's consciousness. The adequate method here is that of intuitive contemplation and inner experience. This could be roughly compared to the 'Via Illuminativa' of the traditional Christian spiritual theology.

The 'Jnana' and the 'Jnana-Marga', according to the Christian understanding, is Jesus Christ himself. 390 The identification of Jesus with the Truth is a main concern in the Gospel and letters of St. John. The application of 'Logos' to Jesus indicates that in Jesus Christ we meet with the fullness of the grace of Truth. [391] "The Word was made flesh, he lived among us, and we saw his glory, the glory that is his as the only Son of the Father, full of grace and truth" (Jn 1:14). But one could still ask with Pontius Pilate: "Truth? ... What is that?" (Jn 18:38). We find the answer in Jesus' own identification of himself with the Truth: "I am ... the Truth" (Jn 14:6). And Jesus' words before Pilate is equally definitive: "... I am came into the world for this: to bear witness to the truth; and all who are on the side of truth listen to my voice" (Jn 18:37).

Jesus Christ is the Truth or the saving knowledge in Person because the self-manifestation or revelation of God is fully realized in Jesus Christ and only in him! [392] The words, deeds and the very person of Jesus Christ manifest to us the reality of God, man and the world, fully and definitively. Jesus' advaitic experience (experience of non-duality) of God, as testified by St. John (Jn 10:30., 14:10ff), confirms further his claim to be the liberating truth or Jnana in person.

To be a Christian would mean to share the inner experience and consciousness of Jesus and his communion with God through personal intuitive awareness and advaitic experience. Man's consciousness is nothing but a reflection of the divine consciousness itself. Abhishiktananda writes:

> "In (the) most secret centre of man's being the only means of illumination is the purest awareness of the self; and this self-awareness is in fact nothing else than the reflection, mirror of the unique 'I am'..." [394]

But there is a fundamental difference between the Adavaitic experience of Jesus and the experience of union with God to which every man is called. Here the Christian position is in sharp contrast to that of the Vedantic understanding: The divine nature realized in man is not one of natural identity, but one of participation by Grace - an unmerited gift of God beyond the spheres of human endeavours. It would be better, therefore, to use a word other than 'Advaita' to denote the liberating knowledge of unity with God. Mark Sundar Rao, for example, proposes 'Ananyatva' (Non-Alterity) as a plausible alternative. [395] But S.J. Samartha criticizes this term for its lack of social dimension. [396] Whatever be the word that is used, it could be affirmed with Abhisiktananda that the 'Advaita' (non-duality) 'lies at the root of the Christian experience. It is simply the mystery that God and the world are not two. It is this mystery of unity, ekatvam, that characterizes the Spirit in God, and in the whole work of God' [397]. This, however, should not be interpreted in the strict Vedantic sense!

The Christian participation in the 'Jnana' or inner experience of Christ is in fact the realization of one's own existence; it is the ultimate salvation. That is why the 'Jnana' of Christ the liberating 'Jnana'. 'Knowledge' in the biblical sense is not a stale assimilation of truths; it is rather an encounter of persons in deep mutual unity: "You will understand that I am in may Father and you in me and I in you" (Jn 14:20). The meaning of Christian Advaita is further clarified in Jesus words according to John: "May they all be one. Father, may they be one in us, as you are in me and I am in you..." (Jn 17:21). The unity between the Father and the Son is an existing ontological fact; the unity between God and other human beings is not based on such ontological identity, but it is a matter to be realized by accepting the Truth in Christ Jesus in one or another way.

What does it mean to accept the Truth (Jnana) in Christ? It is to live the truth as stated by the letter of St. John: "It was a great joy to me ... [to be informed] of your faithfulness to the truth, and of your life in the truth ... to hear that my children are living according to the truth" (3 Jn 1:3-4). [399] One's life is, of course, manifested in what one does. Hence John's insistence on doing the truth or deeds of light: "... everybody who does wrong hates the light and avoids it, ... but the man who lives by the truth (literally: does the truth) comes out into the light, so that it may be plainly seen that what he does is done in God" (Jn 3:20-21). Here we find a true answer to the deep human questions and searches after the mystery and meaning of one's existence; it is the Truth that is identical with and revealed in Jesus Christ; it is this that confers fullness and meaning to the human existence and leads man to his ultimate realization; it is the realization of our existence in Christ - the Christian existence! It is the Truth of Christ that confers man the definitive freedom (Jn 8:31), which we call salvation.

There is a major difference between the Vedantic Jnana Marga and the Jnana Marga of Christ: the latter insists that it is not enough to know the

Truth and become aware of it in the cave of one's heart, but the Truth must be realized in deeds; every one is called to be co-operators in the realization of Truth which finds its climax in the realization of Love. It is in Love that one proves oneself to be the child of truth, the true Jnani, as we read in the letter of St. John: "... our love is not to be just words or mere talk, but something real and active; only by this we can be certain that we are children of truth..." (Jn 3:18-19). In the Way of Christ there is an indispensable relation of dependence between deed (Karma), knowledge (Jnana) and love. We shall discuss further the Way of love and devotion (Bhakti Marga) in the following section.

c. Bhakti Marga: The Way of Loving Devotion

We would like to insist here once again, as done above, that a Christian inter-pretation of the Bhakti Marga should keep well in mind what we have already mentioned in chapter three,[400] regarding the Vedantic Bhakti Marga especially as it is developed in the Bhagavadgita. It is our conviction that Hinduism comes nearest to the Christian spirituality in the Bhakti Marga; this position is, of course, contented by such Christian Advaitins like Abhishiktananda, Raimundo Panikkar, Klaus Klostermaier and others whose primary concern is to establish a Hindu-Christian dialogue on the level of the elite, the Jnanis! We do not deny that the Jnana Marga is generally considered to be the most prestigious Marga in India, as it has the theological support of the Vedantic genius, Sankaracharya. But, what is most prestigious need not necessarily be, by that fact, nearest to the Christian position. The centre of the Christian message is not the Advaita of Jnana, but the Advaita of Prema (Love), i.e. non-duality in Love! The ultimate state of divine union (Via Unitiva!) that brings man his final existential realization is in the trini-tarian Grace, Love and Fellowship (2 Cor 13:13). The true Jnana or know-ledge, as we have already mentioned, which the Bible considers as salvific, is not what results from an intellectual process; the salvific knowledge - in the biblical sense - is the fruit of an inner experience that follows a personal contact, a contact of Love between God and man. [401] The true knowledge necessarily results in Love: "I have made your name known to them and will continue to make it known, so that the love with which you loved me may be in them, and so that I may be in them" (Jn 17:26). This is the Christian Bhakti Marga, the Way of loving union. As A.J. Appasamy observes, the Indian soul has been prepared by the doctrine of bhakti to recognize the truth and supreme grandeur of the message of Jesus' [402] .

Bhakti, in the words of Appasamy, is 'the deep, unselfish love of the whole man for God, finding its highest bliss in union with Him' [403] This insistence of Appasamy on love should not make us think that he ignores the aspect of 'Grace' which forms an integral part of the Vedantic Bhakti Marga that follows the guide lines on Grace given by the Bhagavadgita. We had amply elaborated the question of Grace in the third chapter. [404] Since we have also discussed the question of God's Grace realized in the universal salvific act of Christ, we would concentrate here rather on the point of love, that is important both in the Vedantic and Christian Bhakti Marga. Bhakti, as Appasamy writes, 'is the path of love, not merely of love of God, though that is its supreme passion , but also of love to man' [405].

As the first letter of St. John states, God is in His nature love (1 Jn 4:8,16). The Indian theologian of love, Dhanjibhai Fakirbhai (1895-1967) maintains that God can best be described as 'Prema', love and that the whole of creation should be interpreted in terms of love:

> "The origin and development of creation took place out of the very nature of God, which is love. In creation there is nothing like ignorance (ajnana), illusion or fall. Rather it is the spontaneous expansion of God's love. Creation is the revelation of Absolute Love (Parama Prema, Parabrahman)." [406]

Far above creation, Jesus Christ himself is the supreme manifestation and personification of God's love towards man (Jn 13:1., 17:23). K.C. Sen writes:

> "He (Jesus) who says that the only way to eternal life is the love of God and the love of man, also says, 'I am the Way'. Jesus Christ, then truly analysed, means love of God and love of man.In him we see a heavenly embodiment of this love of God as the Father and the love of man as the brother...." [407]

Manilal C. Parekh writes that 'in the New Testament as well as in much of the highest Christian literature of later times, while the love of God for man has found perhaps more expression than in any other religious literature, love of man for God has not been emphasized so much as it is in the Bhakti literature of the Hindus' [408] . This statement has to be re-

pudiated as fully false in the light of the New Testament evidences.[409]
Considering the supremacy of man's love towards God in the Christian
spirituality Dhanjirbhai Fakirbhai maintains that the Way of love in divine
worship integrates in itself all other ways:

> "... it is that the complete yoga of Action, Worship and Knowledge,
> (karma, bhakti and jnana) is attained through the Way of Love (prema
> yoga). To love God with all our hearts, with all our mind, with all
> our understanding, with all our powers, with all our soul - with our
> whole personality - that is the Way of Love." [410]

It seems to me unnecessary to counterpose Bhakti Marga and Prema Marga,
as our author does. Prema is an integral part of Bhakti!

The greatest law of Christian existence is without doubt the law of Prema,
love. Our love towards God is, as we see in the first letter of St. John,
manifested by keeping His Commandments (Jn 14:21., 1 Jn 2:3-4). Obedience
to God's Word is a tribute of love. The Commandments of God become
meaningful only in the context of love. Sadhu Sundar Singh writes:

> "Gos is love and in every living creature He has set this faculty of
> love, but especially in man. It is therefore nothing but right that the
> Lover who has given us life and reason and love itself should receive
> His due tribute of love." [411]

Love is fellowship with God [412] and it is the highest worship man can offer
to God.[413] The letter of St. John maintains that since God is love and since
love comes from God, every man is obliged to love his fellowmen (1 Jn
4:7-5:4). Every love is a participation in God's universal love. "Any one
who says, 'I love God', and hates his brother, is a liar, since a man who
does not love the brother that he can see cannot love God, whom he has
never seen. So this is the commandment he has given us, that any one who
loves God must also love his brother" (1 Jn 4:20).
Jesus Christ is not only the manifestation of God's love towards man but
also the supreme concretisation of the most perfect form of man's love
towards God and to other men: "... the world must be brought to know that
I love the Father ..." (Jn 14:30). And further: "As the Father has loved me,
so I have loved you. Remain in my love" (Jn 15:10). In his Commandment
of love Jesus Christ offers himself as the model of man's love for one
another (Jn 15:9-17): "A man can have no greater love than to lay down

his life for his friends" (Jn 15:13). The law of Christ comprises, however, not only friends, but even enemies (Mt 5:44). It is, finally, love that serves as the criterion of man's definitive salvation (Mt 25:31-46). The first letter to the Corinthians extolls love above all other spiritual gifts, and even above faith and hope (1 Cor 13:1-13). The Christian spirituality is eminently the Marga of Love!

The last discourse of Jesus as is narrated in St. John's Gospel clarifies the "remaining in love" as the supreme mystical union: "May they all be one. Father, may they be one in us, as you are in me and I am in you..." (Jn 17:21). So, the goal of Christian existence is to remain in Jesus and through him in God an interpersonal communion. The human person is not absorbed into the divine, as the purest form of Vedantic Advaita may hold, but the human individual retains his personality even in the most perfect form of mystical union. Appasamy writes:

> The fundamental idea which lies at the basis of all bhakti religion is that of the seperateness of man from God. Bhakti whether Christian or Hindu, does not resolve God and man into one; but maintains that there is always a difference between God and man..." [414]

But Appasamy puts the relation between Christ and the Father on the same plane as that of man's relation to God, i.e. not of identity in nature, but of mystical union in faith and love! [415] This position is influenced by his understanding of the person of Christ which may not be acceptable because it implies subordinationism, which deprives Christ of his true divine nature! Sadhu Sundar Singh, however, understands Christian mysticism as Christ living in man to make him Christ-like:

> "If Christ lives in us, our whole life will become Christ-like. Salt which has been disolved in water may disappear, but it does not cease to exist.... Even so the indwelling Christ, although He is unseen, will become visible to others through the love which he shares with us". [416]

In short, the essence of Bhakti Marga in its Christian interpretation is the union with God and fellow-men in love (the whole of cosmos is not ignored here as it is a essential factor of human existence!) that is realized in and through Jesus Christ, who in Christian faith is the key to the mystery of human existence!

In conclusion to our Christian interpretation of the 'Marga' categories of Indian thinking, we would maintain that the Christian view prefers an integral view of all the Margas, not excluding any of them. Bhakti Marga understood as the Way of Grace and Love is the most important aspect of Christian existence; the Ways of Karma and Jnana necessarily lead one to Bhakti - the Way of Love! It need not, of course, be ignored that according to individuals' personal and temporal dispositions one or another of the Margas may play a predominant role in the realization of the Christian existence in each one. But the goal of every Christian effort and Knowledge is ultimately LOVE!

Dr. Raimundo Panikkar makes an attempt to integrate the Margas in his theology of the Trinity.[417] Karma Marga, according to him, represents the spirituality of God the Father, who is unseen and so has to be depicted by icons and images as in the case of Hindu Karma Marga. God the Son being like the personal Isvara of the Vedanta, the personal manifestation of God, could well be approached as a Person[418], and as he is the 'visibility of the invisible'[419] God, could well be responded to by love, prayer and praise[420] as indicated in the Bhakti Marga. The Jnana Marga, according to Panikkar, is the spirituality of the Holy Spirit, who is God beyond person, who is immanent and could only be reached through personal realization. What is predominant in this spirituality of the Holy Spirit is not personal dialogue as in the case of Bhakti Marga, but the response of knowledge, awareness and realization.[421] It is evident that Panikkar's preference is for the 'Jnana Marga', although he considers the other two as also important. This is understandable in the general context of his concern for dialogue with Hinduism on the level of the Advaita, which has to begin with the all-pervading Spirit of God. We do not personally find the argument of Panikkar either as substantiated nor as being faithful to the specificity of the Christian faith. The specificity of Christianity is Christ himself (not the unknown one!) and the supreme love God has manifested to the mankind in the radicality of Christ's Cross and the confirmation of the Resurrection. This love is God's challenge to mankind.

The Bhakti Marga as the Way of Love does not limit itself to a theoretical love of God and neighbour. The Christian Bhakti Marga is also a call to action, a call to the concrete realization of love in man's social existence. That is our next point.

3. The Christian 'Prema Marga' (Love as the Way)
and the Call to Social Concern

The Christian social concern is a necessary consequence of Christ's commandment of love that is universal and does not allow to exclude even the enemies
(Mt 5:44). The parable of the Good Samaritan was intended by Christ as
a challenge to his disciples to put love into action for the benefit and well-
being of mankind: "... Go, and do the same yourself" (Lk 10:37). In this
section we shall consider the practical and social aspects of putting Christ's
commandment of universal love into action in today's Indian situation. This
is the practical aspect and necessary conclusion of a relevant Indian Anthropo-
Christology.

a. The Indian Problematic

The Hindu world vision has down through the centuries impregnated the
Indian mentality and has determined the sociological consciousness of the
Indian people of whom more than 82 percent are Hindus. It can be asserted
without hesitation, especially in the light of our discussions in the first
part of our work, that Hinduism is first and last an individualistic religion.
The Hindu doctrine of Karma-Samsara, the principle of individual retribution,
can be considered as primarily responsible for this unhappy situation. Religion
is a private affair; each one should be concerned with his own 'Mukti' or
liberation. If one is socially and economically well situated it is the merit
of his past life; if one is, on the contrary, in a miserable and subhuman
situation, that is his Karma. It is useless to undertake anything against
the rigorous working of Karma. Each one has to come out on his own. Every
deed can only entangle man further in the process of Karma-Samsara. Even
the inevitable duties and deeds required by life should be done without any
desire (Kama) for their results or fruits (Phala). It is Kama that binds man
to his works and keeps him slave to his Karma (deeds). As we have seen
in the first part, the Bhagavadgita promotes 'Nishkamakarma' (fulfilment
of one's duties without being attached to the results of one's deeds) as
a better alternative to the inactivity of the strict Jnanis. Even the idea
of 'Nishkamakarma' was not a sufficient solution for centuries of inherited
social lethargy and utter indifference towards the misery of the lower castes
and of those who were at the margin of the society. Nishkamakarma was
applied only to caste duties and the duties that are strictly related to one's

state of life. And finally, it is the individuals Karma that determines every-thing in one's present existence. One can expect, of course, a better ex-istence in the 'Punarjanma' (Re-birth)! We are of the conviction that Hin-duism, with its beliefs and traditions, with its philosophies and superstitions, has been primarily responsible for the lack of social concern and the wide-spread social injustice and utter insensitivity to the miseries of the fellow-men that are prevalent even up to the present day - although in a very diminished way - among the masses of India.

We do not intend to ignore the social upliftment programmes conducted by various Hindu charitable institutions. Such institutions, however, have actually no doctrinal foundations for social activities in their own religious philosophies, although this fact may not be so accepted today by their members. They are rather imitations of the social undertakings of the Chris-tian missionaries. It need not also be forgotten, that the Hindu renaissance beginning in the 19th century, from the time of Rammohan Roy, owes its inspiration to the Christian world-vision. It was undeniably the result of Hinduism's unavoidable contact with the teachings of Christ and an educa-tional system that was at least indirectly based on Christian principles.

It could still be asked, why the Gospel of Christ which was brought to India even in the apostolic times (according to reasonable traditions)[422] or speaking from the point of historical evidence as early as the fourth century, did remain dormant in a small corner of India - todays State of Kerala - for so many centuries till the arrival of the Portugese in 1498? The search for an answer could be a doctoral dissertation by itself! The caste mentality and the inherited passivity of the 'Thomas Christians' [423], however, could be indicated as the most important reasons for this unhappy development. Hence, the original Christians of India have also not made any significant contribution to the social consciousness of the Indian people!

In the wake of the new Indian theology, the concentration is directed mostly towards a dialogical understanding on the level of the elite. This also has not helped much to solve the situation of social stagnation in India. Authors like P.D. Devanandan, M.M. Thomas and Samuel Rayan who try to interpret the Gospel to a secularized Indian society are rather exceptions to the norm!

b. The Social Dimension of Indian Christology

This heading could be easily misunderstood. Our intention here, however, is not to reduce Christology to sociology nor to consider it as a substitute for Missiology or for the theology of socio-political development and liberation. But a proper understanding of Christ and his mission in the world and the human response to Christ in the community of the believers must have its necessary social consequences. The Christian social teaching is first and foremost based on the mystery of Christ, in whom God has said His irrevocable and definitive 'Yes' to the world. So a proper Indian Christology must have an aspect of social orientation, which may be called Christology in action. A Christology, in order to be meaningful for India, cannot ignore its dimension of transforming the Indian society according to the principles taught and lived by Christ. It is not enough to preach a 'theoretical Christ'; what India needs is a living Christ who is revealed in the deeds of his followers as Sadhu Sundar Singh writes:

> "We Indian do not want a doctrine, not even a religious doctrine; we have enough and more than enough of that kind of thing; we are tired of doctrines. We need the Living Christ. India wants people who will not only preach and teach, but workers whose whole life and temper is a revelation of Jesus Christ." [424]

We may not be able to agree with the Singh's discard for doctrines because doctrines will have to supply ultimately the foundation for any deed. But his concern for an Indian Christianity in action is admirable. This witness of Christ in deeds of social development on the part of Christians is stressed by Ashok Mehta, the former minister for Planning in the Central Government of India:

> "We must recalim 900 million people of the world who are today [i.e. in 1967] in a state of abject depression. This human reclamation requires a peculiar type of social engineering. This is ... the big challenge that all people, all men of religion, all men of God have to face. And if it is the pround claim of the Christian churches that they have the spiritual understanding, the spiritual agony, and that their spiritual outflow is going to be greater than that of other men of God, well, it has got to be proved in the crucible of life itself. If it is the claim of the Christians that even to this day they feel the agony of Christ on the Cross whenever humanity suffers as it were, it has to be proved in action, not by any statement." [425]

This could be understood as a criticism against the exaggerated divinism or spiritualism of some of the Indian Christian theologians, whose main concern is to meet Hinduism at the level of the Vedantic Advaita, 'in the cave of the heart'. That is necessary, but not enough! A Christology that is needed for India today is one that can inspire a radical social awareness too among the people, a Christology that takes earnestly into consideration the concrete Indian social situation and not a Christology that hopes to go back to the upanishadic period. The task of Indian Christology today - if it is serious about its anthropological claims - is to re-interpret the upanishadic God-experience in the light of Christian faith which is necessarily social and communitarian in character. Regarding this point Samuel Rayan writes:

> "... the India to which we want to interpret Christ cannot be the India of the past, of the Rishis and the Upanisads, but the India of today, of the factories, five year plans and atomic reactors, the India which finds itself today in a ferment of change under the impact of forces like western technology, revolutionary Marxism, the Christian message, political independence and the new sense of dignity and hope that is sweeping through the masses. The past needs to be taken into account only in the measure in which it is present, is alive now, and affects and qualifies life today." [426]

This call to integrate Christology fully into the actual Indian situation re-volts against all forms of abstract Christology.[427] We need a Christ 'who came to feed and to heal and to liberate', a liberation that is directed also to the political and socio-economical spheres. [428] A certain liberation is also required from a perverted understanding of the 'ancient spiritual heritage', in so far as it does not foster but even hinders the building of a new India. [429] M.M. Thomas also warns against an unhealthy and unsocial understanding of spirituality and mysticism:

> "The peril inherent in all mystic consciousness is that it tends increasing-ly to isolate itself from society, and to revert back into an experience of undifferentiated consciousness which cannot make moral distinctions. The (Hindu-Christian) dialogue should make spirituality more rele-vantly social and moral ... it is not the ontic Christ or the mystic Christ but the historical Jesus who has made the deepest impact on Hinduism." [430]

The God of the Bible being the God of history, Thomas maintains, the Chris-tian saving-knowledge of God has its central emphasis on doing the will of God and responding to God's purpose in the historical realm rather than on gnostic or ontic union. [431] The insights of our faith in Christ, writes

Samartha, should work as a corrective by supplying a 'sense of the personal, the historical and the social, in the structure of the Hindu spirituality'[432]. Only such an approach can have a transforming effect on the Indian society as is maintained by Samuel Rayan:

> "Emphasis on the historical should be made meaningful by showing in relief the significance of Jesus for society and social change. Otherwise situating Jesus in history becomes unimportant, and history fails to enter truly into the heart of religion." [433]

The historical is meaningful in Christology especially because of its social and communitarian consequences. In the uniqueness of Jesus' historicity, God has affirmed the human and the earthly which calls for 'community awareness in a sense of service and of responsibility for the social situation' [434] because the theology of corporate personality is an essential dimension of Christology.

A sense of service and responsibility for the social situation implies necessarily a theology of the Cross, a theology of suffering for the sake of love; and that is the true spirituality in action. These words of the well known poet of India, Rabindranath Tagore, are quite relevant:

> "However unpleasant it may be, we must admit that neither the capacity nor the effort to bear the sorrows of others, intrinsic in the love of God, is widely evident in our country.... We have sought the delights of divine love to the exclusion of its pain.... There is no spirituality in the cultivation of suffering for some ultimate gain; true spirituality lies in suffering for the sake of love..." [435]

The Indian spirituality has always insisted that it is by losing one's self that one comes to one's true Self. But this principle has been understood and applied in India in a very individualistic way as is implied in the above critical remark of Tagore. But one has to lose one's self also in bearing the sorrows of others, in the imitation of the Suffering Servant and his Redemptive Cross, in service and toil, in sweat and blood; only these can uplift and build up an India that will be impregnated by the mystery of Christ. As Samuel Rayan again observes, 'only work can produce new values, only service can bring relief to the masses, only through the death of much that is old can the new India come to birth' [436]. The practical or social aspect of Indian Christology is aimed at India's integral re-generation in Christ. Christ is the only foundation [437], the centre and the dynamism [438] that uplifts and unifies the Indian society; he is the only and perfect remedy for all her ills.[439]

He is the mystery of man and human history!

Conclusion to Chapter Six

Our intention in the sixth chapter has been to draw a synthesis between the apparently conflicting thesis (the universal Christ) and the antithesis (Christ, the unique) of the fourth and the fifth chapters respectively. Here we have tried to explain how Christ could be universal without ceasing to be unique and how he could be unique without abandoning his universality. This has been an attempt to present the soteriological dimensions of an anthropological Christology in Vedantic categories. In this we have taken earnestly the material and historical aspects of man in the process of his salvation in and through Christ, as is implied in the 'materiality' and 'historicity' of the Incarnation.

Eventhough Jesus Christ as a man is limited to a particular place and time, his uniqueness as the manifestation of the God of Salvation makes him relevant beyond all the historical limits. This universal relevance of Christ is not merely that of a 'Mahaguru' (a great teacher) of mankind as in the case of other ethical teachers, but above all as the Saviour who redeemed mankind from the tragedy of Sin and its consequences by his very fact of existence, his Death on the Cross and the recapitulation of the whole universe in him by his Resurrection and the confering of his Spirit. The explanation of these fundamental truths of Christian faith by some of the Indian theologians has also prompted us to cast a view on the salvific value of Hinduism itself in the context of Christ's universal salvation. Faithful to the Vedantic mystic tradition we have emphasized the paramount role of Khrista-Anubhava (Christ-experience) in deciding the course of a relevant Indian Christology. But the specificity of the Christian message, we have insisted, lies in the mysticism of radical love (Prema) that finds its necessary expression in the social concern for the integral development of India's underprivileged millions!

A Christology that is required for today's India, therefore, is not merely a theoretical Christology, not also a onesided mystical Christology, but a Christology which, not ignoring the necessary and fundamental doctrinal explanations in the relevant Vedantic categories, is also practically oriented in order to face the problems of a modern India in their integrity. 'Suffering for the sake of Love' - that is Christ's answer to India's search for liberation; and there is no better answer!

389

Conclusion to Part II

In the preceeding three chapters we have been discussing the question of the Divine in human history as visualized by the Indian Christological approaches. The thesis-antithesis-synthesis dialectic has been used to explain in Vedantic categories the reality and universal relevance of Jesus Christ from an anthropological standpoint. The problems connected with the question of historicity have played an important role in our analysis. The meta-historical saving principle, the historical redemptive event and the pan-historical applicability of the salvation that is achieved in Jesus Christ were the necessary aspects that had to be explained for a proper anthropological exposition of the Christ-Mystery in the Indian context.

The Indian attempt to 'hinduise' Jesus Christ is quite understandable especially in the background of the principle of 'Sarva Dharma Samanatva' and the Vedantic self-evaluation as the 'Sanatana Dharma'. Here we perceive a Vedantic concern to see every man as an 'anonymous Hindu'! Inspite of the Vedanta's claims of antidogmatism, we see already a dogmatic attitude implied in this approach. The Hindu view of Christ, shortly said, is a Vedantic projection. In the context of the essential divinity of every man held by the Vedanta it is the task of the Indian Christology to clarify, as we have tried to do to some extent, the difference between the divine horizon or the transcendental dimension of every man and the Divine Sonship of Jesus Christ. Similarly, the 'unknown Christ' of Raimundo Panikkar, inspite of all its apparently appealing aspects, cannot be considered as an authentic interpretation of the Christ-Mystery because of its discard for the incarnational aspect of human salvation and the historical specificity and uniqueness that are inseparably connected with the Christ-event. Panikkar is also not convincingly clear how the universally present Christ-principle is to be distinguished from the all-pervading Spirit of God! It is, indeed, a trinitarian problem which must be tackled on the basis of the Christian Revelation rather than from the stand-point of the unverifiable postulates of a particular philosophy!

It is, indeed, interesting to see how the Hindu reformers of the 19th and the 20th centuries came very near to the personality of Jesus of Nazareth eventhough they stopped short of acknowledging fully his divine person. It is, however, to be mentioned that their selective approach to the Bible and especially to the Gospels has been quite arbitrary and prejudical in ignoring the long tradition of the community of Christ's believers. Some Christian theologians who apply the Vedantic categories in interpreting the Mystery of Christ confine themselves to the translation of the scholastic theology into Sanskrit terms, while others, whose approach is more biblical and genuinely Indian, stray into the quagmire of Christological errors which were typical of the controversies in the early centuries. We have also insisted that a proper presentation of Christ to the Hindus requires a thorough 'dehinduisation' and that important reservations are necessary in applying categories like 'Avatar' to the mystery of the Incarnation. Jesus Christ is not only the fulfiller of the Vedantic aspirations but also the 'destroyer' of many of Hinduism's anthropological and theological positions and pre-suppositions which we had discussed in the first part!

The attraction of Christ's moral teachings in modern Hinduism is beyond doubt. It is also, as we have seen, an undeniable fact that some Hindu leaders have done more to make Christ and his moral challenge credible and at home in India than the organized efforts of many missionaries. But, in their preference for the moral principles in Christ's message, the reforming leaders of Hinduism have at large missed not only the historical person of Christ, but also the gratuity of God's salvation that was realized in him. The sinfullness of man and his natural incapacity to liberate himself from the entanglements of the mundance existence will have to be made clear in any interpretation of the Christ-Mystery in India. The principle of the essential divinity of every man and the doctrine of Karma-Samsara present considerable obstacles in presenting the person and the salvific function of Christ to the Vedantic audience. The radicality of God's love towards man, which necessarily implies suffering as is manifested in the event of the Cross, is not just a matter of good example or the symbol of a persecuted just man, but it is the manifestation of God's saving and transforming love that became victorious in the Resurrection of Christ. The Resurrection is, indeed, not a negation of the material world and the created realities, but an affirmation and salvific 'recapitulation' of man and the entire cosmic reality in Christ. The Christian faith sees no salvation except in and through Jesus Christ!

The Indian Christological approaches are keen to insist on the important role of 'Anubhava' (personal experience) in the process of theologizing. This attitude could work as a corrective and counterbalance the general tendency in the West to ignore the aspect of personal experience in the theological method. This does not mean that 'Anubhava' could be the sole 'Pramana' (criterion, norm or source) of Christology, as some Indian theologians would suggest! Anubhava apart from the scriptural tradition and the believing community is only a matter of individual fancy! The Indian Christology cannot also afford to fall into the temptation of an individualistic mysticism of the Vedantic type that ignores the necessary social challenge that is involved in the following of Christ.

It is evident that there are formidable obstacles in presenting an authentic picture of Jesus Christ, the Mystery of Man and human History, in Vedantic categories. Our attempt in the preceeding chapters has been only to show that it is not impossible, although much is still to be done in this direction. We have already indicated some necessary precautions and possible suggestions. The further evaluative reflection, which we intend to make in the next part especially from the anthropological, historical and Christological view-points of Karl Rahner and Wolfhart Pannenberg, is aimed at giving a more penetrating and systematic clarification of some of the relevant questions involved in the discussion of our topic!

PART THREE

AN EVALUATION FROM THE THEOLOGICAL PERSPECTIVES

ESPECIALLY OF KARL RAHNER AND WOLFHART PANNENBERG

INTRODUCTION

No theology can afford to close itself up in its own self-sufficiency. The universality of the Christian faith makes it necessary for a particular trend in theology to encounter other theological traditions and to enrich itself by complementation and corrections of others while contributing on its part to the diversity and richness of theology as a whole. What we intend in the following three chapters is to bring the Indian anthropo-Christological approaches to an encounter, by way of evaluation, with the theological positions primarily of Karl Rahner and Wolfhart Pannenberg. It must be mentioned at the very outset that we are not aiming at an exhaustive evaluation either of Rahner or of Pannenberg; there is, any way, no scarcity of such works as our bibliography whould show. We will also be referring of other authors in so far as they may shed further light on the views of Rahner and Pannenberg. An exhaustive evaluation of the Indian anthropo-Christological approaches is also not undertaken here. Our evaluative approach is not to be understood as a negative criticism; nor is it meant only to set limits for dialogue possibilities. We will, of course, be interested in pointing out the problems confronting Christology in the Indian anthropological context. But we will also be paying attention to suggest positively the possibilities of dialogue between Christology and the Vedantic anthropology, even though at every instant it is not labelled as such! Since our sections and sub-sections are thematically arranged, we deal in each section with the problems, the dialogue possibilities and break-throughs without considering it necessary to schematize our contributions artificially once again. It is also not our intention to go into the minute details of every dialogue possibility in each topic. What we say is meant only as indicative of further possible theological discussions on a much vaster plain. We concentrate ourselves more on the possibilities of mutual complementations, corrections and clarifications of certain aspects of Indian anthropology and Christology as far as we judge them to be relevant for our topic. In short, what we are aiming at in this part of our work is a limited Indo-German theological encounter, that is critically concentrated on the anthropo-Christological questions of bilateral interest.

The method of thesis, antithesis and synthesis will be followed also here.

The metahistorical universality of the Christ-Principle (Chapter VII) leads us to the question of the historical uniqueness of Jesus of Nazareth as the Christ (Chapter VIII) and both of these apparently contrasting positions will be elevated to an "Advaitic" (non-dual) synthesis in the final chapter (IX). By this method we intend to clarify, in theological conversation especially with Karl Rahner and Wolfhart Pannenberg, how Jesus Christ could be credibly presented as the God-given clue to the mystery of man and of the human history. In this way we try to show the necessary relationship between what is transcendentally necessary and what is historically and concretely contingent as far as both anthropology and Christology are concerned.

Attention could also be drawn to the fact that, as in the previous parts of our work, we do not limit ourselves to the theoretical plain of thinking, but try to bring our theological consideration finally to the level of concrete life to bear fruit in God-experience and God-realization in Jesus of Nazareth, the Christ.

CHAPTER VII

CHRIST, THE UNIVERSAL MYSTERY OF MAN

In Chapter IV we have discussed the notion of the universal advaitic Christ as developed by the Neo-Vedantins and the Indian Christian thinkers like Raimundo Panikkar. Here our intention is to evaluate this concept from the apparently corresponding views of Karl Rahner and Wolfhart Pannenberg. Needless to say, we also will be necessarily referring to the anthropological background of this concept which we had developed in the first part of our work. It cannot be overemphasized that the necessary differentiations we had made between various Indian authors and concepts in preceeding chapters should be kept in mind to maintain the necessary clarity and precision in our following investigation. Here our emphasis is on the question of anthropological transcendence which could have a certain demythologizing effect on Christology, which would make the recognition and acceptance of Jesus of Nazareth as the Christ less problematic and more meaningful for the modern man.

A. Man's Transcendental Horizon: The Mystery of 'Atman' before the Mystery of 'Brahman'

Here we try to make three approaches to the essentially transcendent aspect of human existence. Although not exhaustive in character, these approaches could examine man's transcendence from the side of day-to-day experience that is common to every man, from the side of that possible reality, which could be the foundation of this experience and the ontological determinations that are indispensible, even to talk about a transcendental factor in the midst of human existence.

1. The Transcendental Aspect of Human Experience

Here we are not dealing with the question of God-experience as such which, of course, is necessary in any meaningful talk about Indian Christology. We will be dedicating ourselves to this task in the ninth chapter. Here we concentrate ourselves on the question of daily experiences which do not have any explicit religious reference, as is evident in the notion of human existence as a radical questioning arising from the deep existential experience of finiteness, the self-transcending experience resulting from human knowledge and I-Thou relations. With the help especially of K. Rahner and W. Pannenberg, we shall see how much the Vedantic anthropological context is prepared to encounter the Christian proclamation in a positive way.

a. The Human Existence as a Radical Question

The history of any philosophy is the history of man's questioning about the ultimate whats, whys, hows and wherefores of human existence. The Vedantic philosophy is no exception to this general principle. That is what we have seen in the first three chapters that constitute the first part of our work. Here we pay our attention mostly to the question of the existential finiteness and bondage as experienced by the Vedantins.[1] We do not have to repeat all what we have already written to clarify the Vedantic notion of life in this world as a bondage. The concept of 'Maya' which we elaborated in the first chapter is of special relevance here.[2] It is the expression of the fact, that this world taken in itself is absolutely meaningless because what we find here is nothing more than non-reality, death and darkness as affirmed by the Brhadaranyaka Upanisad.[3] It is implied in this view, even if not in explicit terms, that the experience of this existence as a limitation, i.e. as non-real, death and darkness, presupposes in some way or other a basic human experience transcending the experience of finiteness itself.

The theological method of Karl Rahner, known as 'the transcendental and anthropolocial method in theology'[4], draws our attention precisely to the a priori structure in human existence that makes the experience of limitation as limitation possible at all! There is in man a reality, something that belongs to humanity as such which is the presupposition or 'the condition of the possibility' (Bedingung der Möglichkeit)[5] of identifying a limitation as a limitation. This a priori structure that is necessarily present in every man is what is known in Rahnerian Anthropology as the 'transcendental'.[6] Man encounters his transcendentality in and through his experiences of existential finiteness; but it is never the direct object of one's experience; it is always anonymous and implicit.[7] It is always present as a given fact and is knowable in experience through reflection, but is not acquired as a consequence of experience. It is 'a priori' and not 'a posteriori'. It cannot be reduced to words and concepts; its depths are unfathomable; it is in every man, but not limited to any man; it is beyond particular individuals definite concepts and therefore, this given structure of human existence is called 'transcendental'. It is an inexpressible reality that does not belong to this world. It is neither the result nor the sum total of man's categorial [8] experiences, but transcends all of them. Rahner's concept of human transcendence becomes much more expressed and clearer in his analysis of the process of human knowledge as we shall see below.

W. Pannenberg too sheds light on the Vedantic insistence on human transcendence that is experienced in and through the experience of human limitations. Man's capacity to disclose the questionableness of the realities he encounters and thus to disclose his own questionableness (die Fraglichkeit des Daseins)[9] is very much emphasized in Pannenberg's anthropology and this capacity, like the 'transcendental' of Rahner, distinguishes man from the rest of the animal kingdom.[10] The unique capacity of man 'to enquire and to move beyond every given regulation of his existence' [11] underlines, according to Pannenberg, the structure of man's being as a question, a question that pushes man continuously into the open which he names as man's 'openness to the world' (Weltoffenheit) [12], a terminology that Pannenberg adopts from Max Scheler and shares with other anthropologists like Adolf Portmann, Arnold Gehlen and Michael Landmann. [13] This 'Weltoffenheit', for Pannenberg, is not just an openness of man to the world, but it is much more an openness beyond the world. [14] It is transcendent! This would mean that man in his experience of the questionability and finiteness of the world is himself essentially a question open into the infinite. This question is not immediately directed to any specific object. So this experience of questionableness, to repeat the word of Rahner, is the experience of human transcendence or 'the experience of infinite longings, of radical optimism, of unquenchable discontent, of the torment of the insufficiency of everything attainable, of the radical protest against death' against the non-real and darkness as we have seen in the aupanishadic verse. [15]

b. The Humans Transcendence in 'Jnana': The Gnoseological Aspect

'Jnana' is an important concept in the Vedantic system that stresses the transcendence of man. Jnana is the true knowledge that dispels darkness and ignorance (Avidhya) from the human mind through spiritual illumination as we have seen especially in the first part of our work.[16] Through 'Jnana' man transcends the phenomenal world that is by itself illusory and misleading (Maya) to the numenal world which is permanently real. 'Anubhava' or conscious experience which is nothing else than becoming-one-with the object on the level of consciousness is the 'Pramana', i.e. criterion or source of true knowledge.[17] The Vedanta, as we have seen, further identifies consciousness with Brahman[18] who is 'the Real of the real' and 'the Truth of the true'.[19] The Vedantic identification of the Brahman with the Atman[20]—we will have to deal with this question more elaborately later[21]—makes Brahman or Consciousness the inner principle of every man, that makes true knowledge possible at all. In this context it is quite understandable why the Vedanta identifies Consciousness with Reality and maintains that the levels of consciousness are indicative of the levels of reality.[22] In short, the 'Prajnana' or the consciousness of man has a transcendental dimension which is intrinsic to it, to the point of being identified with it, which alone makes out of 'Prajnana' a 'Jnana' or true knowledge. We do not have to discuss here the notion of Brahman-Atman identification in various Vedantic schools as we had paid sufficient attention to it in the first part;[23] what is important for us for the moment is the idea of transcendentality that is, according to the Vedanta, necessarily connected with the process of knowledge. It is interesting to examine how Karl Rahner, although preceeding from different premises, establishes similarly the transcendentality of man from the process of human knowledge!

Rahner's masterly work 'Geist in Welt' is an elaborate exposition of his theory of knowledge.[23] In his argument he proceeds from the doctrine of human metaphysical knowledge as developed by St. Thomas Aquinas[24] and formulates an epistomology based on man's nature that is adequate for the foundation of a theology. In his later work 'Hörer des Wortes' Rahner applies his findings in the 'Geist in Welt' to base a philosophy of religion, that justifies the possibility of Divine Revelation in human history.[25] As many scholarly studies are available on both of these works, we do not intend here any repetition of the same.[26] We will be limiting ourselves to some basic points regarding the transcendence of man as seen in the process of knowledge. More is also not required for our limited purpose of evaluating the Vedantic anthropology.

An understanding of Rahner's theory of knowledge necessarily presupposes an elucidation of his philosophical affinities not only with Thomas Aquinas, but among others also with Emmanuel Kant, J.G. Fichte, G.W.F. Hegel and especially with the transcendental Thomism of J. Maréchal.[27] The different studies in this line show us that, as Rahner himself affirms, as opposed to Kant, there is in Rahner 'always a question of a noetic hylomorphism, to which there corresponds an ontological hylomorphism in the objects, in the sense of a thoroughgoing determination of knowing by being'[28]. The human being, as Rahner affirms, is a 'Spirit in the World' and spirit in this context means for him 'a power which reaches out beyond the world and knows the metaphysical'[29] or the 'Real of the real' as Vedanta may put it. This spirit is in the world and 'the world' stands according to Rahner for 'the name of the reality which is accessible to the immediate experience of man'[30]. Man faces the world of sense-data which is called finite cognition and due to the unity between being and knowing, the former determining the latter, in every finite cognition man implicitly faces the ultimate ground of his knowledge of these sense-data, namely, Being itself. Since the concept of Being, for Rahner, cannot be separated from the concept of the knowability of Being, the definition of Being itself could be stated as 'present to itself' (Beisichsein). Since the human cognition is not such a simple 'Beisichsein' but rather a process towards 'Beisichsein', it cannot be grounded on itself but on Being as such.[31] Since Being is not immediately available to man, but only through sense-data, there follows logically the need of 'abstracting' Being from sense-data. Rahner seeks after the condition for the possibility (Bedingung der Möglichkeit) of this abstraction and this for him is the anticipatory and implicit awareness of Being on the part of the knower which he calls 'Vorgriff ad esse'. This would mean that all knowledge is carried out within a horizon in man which is infinite and that may be called 'Sein überhaupt' or 'esse in generali'.[32] An indirect intuition of Being is the condition of the possibility of knowing any sense-data.[33] This may be called 'Pre-apprehension' (Vorgriff) or to use the Thomastic term, 'Intellectus agens'.[34] It is that which permits the knower to grasp the concrete particular in its universal aspect.

Rahner bases his argument for the transcendence of man on the fact that all human knowledge and conscious activity are necessarily grounded on the 'pre-grasp' or anticipation or pre-apprehension of Being (Vorgriff). This 'Vorgriff' however, is unthematic; it is the ever present - not acquired - knowledge of the infinity of reality. [35] It is this that constitutes the human being as a person, a spiritual being. [36] The 'Vorgriff' as the 'a priori' structure of human knowing makes all categorial and particular knowledge possible; 'the individually and specifically and objectively known thing is always grasped in a broader, unnamed, implicitly present horizon of possible knowledge and possible freedom, even if the reflective mind, only with difficulty and only subsequently, succeeds in making this implicitly present fragment or aspect of consciousness a really specific object of consciousness, and thus objectively verbalizes it' [37].

There is, indeed, a fundamental difference between the Vedantic concept of human transcendence and Rahner's approach to the same question. Human transcendence, for Rahner, does not consist in any identification of man with the absolute Being or Being as such, but the transcendentality, which is the basic constitution of man, consists in his absolute openness to being in general. [38]

Similar to Rahner, W. Pannenberg also bases the human transcendence on the cognitive capacity of man. 'The human mind represents an intensified form of self-transcendence' and he affirms that 'the experience of freedom, the capacity for abstract cognition, the particular ecstacy of imaginative inspiration - all this seems closely related to the distinctive structure of the mind to his reflective nature, to his ability to look at himself from a distance and therefore to take the position of something else in distinction from himself' [39]. 'Spirit' (Geist) is the name which Pannenberg gives to this ecstatic element of the life of the mind. [40]

The basic distinction between the notion of the transcendence of human spirit, or better of man as such, as seen in Rahner and Pannenberg, and the same as understood by the Vedanta, must be kept in mind especially when we speak later about the existential relation that exists between man and the Absolute Being!

c. Transcendence in Freedom and Love

The fact that man in the process of his knowledge experiences himself as transcendent, as open to the infinite and indetermined and as the subject who is given over to himself would mean, according to Rahner, that man is at the same time responsible for himself.[41] In his self-reflection, in his Being-Present-to-Self (Beisichsein) 'the knower is present to himself as different from the other', i.e. the object of knowledge, and 'he elevates himself above the other'. This transcendence beyond the other of sensibility, which is the return of the spirit to itself can be called Thomistically the freedom of the spirit'[42]. This is the absolute breadth or universality of the human spirit. The freedom of the spirit is 'only another name for the possibility of the pre-apprehension of being in its totality'.[43] So freedom, for Rahner, is the transcending (Überspringen) of the human spirit.[44] In his freedom man can remain closed to himself - a static person - or he can also exercise his basic transcendence in committing himself in trust to another person in different ways and intensities. Trusting in another one is an event of self-transcendence (Selbsüberbietung).[45] Whether it is realized or not, the very nature of man can exist only in its continuous attempt to leave himself and to give himself up fully to the other.[46] If one does not achieve this self-transcendence in Trust and commitment, one remains closed up in one's own finitude, stifled by one's own loneliness which in its definitive character is named hell! Where the human transcendence in self-commitment really takes place or at least where it is tried, there we can speak of love.[47] Trust in freedom is also a central concept in the theology of Pannenberg. Freedom, for him, is the realization of man's self-transcendence, the freedom of choice being only its formal expression.[48] In free trust one leaves oneself to the constancy (Beständigkeit) of the other and it is a daring step towards the unknown.[49]

The aspect of hazard or venture (Wagnis) that is implied in trust and love is not ignored also in the thinking of Rahner. Rahner calls love a venture towards the other without reservations (bedingungslos)! But how can another human being in his finitude (Endlichkeit), fragility (Brüchigkeit) and unreliability (Unzuverlässigkeit), in short as a sinner, justify such an unreserved act of self-commitment, without allowing this venture to end up irresponsibly with the danger of falling into the destructive abyss of the other or face the tragedy of the other's faithlessness? Therefore, Rahner is convinced that no other human being, no other finite thing in this world, can justify a love which is the expression of human transcendence. Every particular act of love must have a transcendent basis, which is the condition of its possibility. [50] So as in the case of the process of knowledge the reality of trust, love, freedom and responsibility presuppose an 'a priori' transcendent structure in man.

In the 'Jnana Marga' of the Vedanta this aspect of transcendence in love and trust is, indeed, not brought to light. This weakness however, is compensated, as we have seen in the first part, by the Bhagavadgita, the Puranas and by the Vedantic Bhakti schools, [51] although not so systematized as by Rahner and Pannenberg!

2. The Whither (Woraufhin) of Human Transcendence

In the last section we discussed the question of man's transcendence on the basis of human experiences of finiteness, cognition and interpersonal relationship in freedom, trust and love. Inspite of some hints, our discussion so far has left open the finality or the destination of man's transcendental openness. Here we shall try to evaluate the Vedantic position regarding the question of the Absolute Being in a more systematic way. Here what we intend to say is that in the objective knowledge of man an unobjective knowledge of his own personal reality and of the personal reality of the infinitive creative source of being are also included. [52] Our problem is not primarily how this source of being can be called; we accept that this Reality can have various names as the Vedanta would insist [53] ; our question is how the Being that is the condition of the possibility of being is to be understood. Is man's ability to transcend himself and the categorial world 'no more than a subjective ability, an idea, demand, wish or illusion present in the mind and not corresponding to any objective reality, with the result that man is bound to remain in his ability to know within the realm of the finite and also that nothing but the finite exists' [54] ? Or is the Infinite that is the basis of human transcendence identical with man himself and his world in the sense of monistic pantheism?

a. The Incomprehensible Mystery

Man is a mystery! On the one hand man is greater than the reality he confronts because he can transcend them by questioning, by thinking and by willing; on the other hand the reality is greater than man himself because it is beyond human control. Man stands before an incomprehensible Mystery.[55] The ability in man to transcend what is finite cannot be based on man himself who is finite, nor on his finite power of imagination because a finite system cannot know by itself its own finiteness. [56] As Karl Rahner observes, man's transcendental experience is basicly an experience of being borne by an incomprehensible ground. [57]

S. Radhakrishnan calls this incomprehensible ground the Supreme. The Supreme, according to him, is not an object presented to our knowledge but is the condition of the knowledge. [58] This expression used by Dr. Radhakrishnan in 1932 is quite reminiscent of what Rahner later developed under the expression 'Bedingung der Möglichkeit' following the Kantian line! Radhakrishnan follows, of course, the aupanishadic tradition which maintains that the way to the Supreme is first of all the way of negations: Neti, Neti - Not this, Not that! We have elaborated this point in the first part. [59] Following the Brhadaranyaka Upanisad and the Vedantins like Sankara we can say, in short, that the Supreme that is the condition of the possibility of man's transcendence is 'Nirguna' (without qualities), 'Nirakara' (without form), 'Nirvisesa' (without particularity) and 'Nirupadhika' (without limitations)! [60]

It is such a 'Neti, Neti' approach that we find in Rahner as he presents the whither (Woraufhin) of human transcendence as the Mystery (Geheimnis).[61] God, according to him is the name that simply stands for this unfathomable mystery which lies behind all accessible and definable reality, the nameless and the remote Mystery. [62] The most proper object of human reason, so insists Rahner, is that sovereign and all-embracing exigence ,which cannot be mastered, comprehended or challenged, in a word, the Mystery. It is the goal where reason arrives when it attains its perfection by becoming love. [63] This Mystery is the Nameless and the Infinite and the Indefinable; it is the horizon of human transcendence and the condition of the possibility of any distinction between God and all finite beings and it is just because of that, this Mystery is indefinable. Since it is the condition of the possibility of all categorized distinctions and divisions, it cannot itself be distinguished from other things by the same modes of distinction. 'The horizon cannot be comprehended within the horizon, the whither of transcendence cannot really as such, be brought within the range of transcendence itself to be distinguished from other things. The ultimate measure cannot be measured; the boundary which delimits all things cannot itself be bounded by a still more distant limit'.[64] The Mystery as the Whither of human transcendence is absolutely beyond all determination; it is at no one's disposal, 'it is that which disposes of us silently and ceaselessly at the very moment when we begin to dispose of anything, when we make a judgment on something and try to submit to the 'a priori' laws of our understanding'[65]. This Whither of human tran - scendence, Rahner continues, 'is not experienced in itself, but only in the subjective transcendence and it is known only unobjectively. Its presence in transcendence is the presence of a transcendence which is there merely as a condition of possibility for a categorized knowledge and not of itself and by itself alone. Thus the Whither of transcendence is only there in the form of a distant aloofness. It can never be approached directly or experi- enced immediately. It is there only by referring us to something else, some- thing finite, which is the object of direct regard.'[66] To this infinite Whither of transcendence Rahner gives the name 'Holy Mystery':[67] 'Man in accepting himself as being and infinite emptiness accepts him who has decided to fill this emptiness that is the mystery of man with the infinite mystery that is God.'[68]

This incomprehensible but luminous aspect of the Whither of human tran - scendence is asserted also by W. Pannenberg when he states that man 'already stands in the experience of the reality about which he is concerned in his question - the experience of a non-objective depth of reality, which underlies all exis tert objects and supports his own life'[69]. Against Feuerbach, Marx, Fichte and Freud, Pannenberg would insist that the development of an idea of God is of the essence of man's being and not just a misunderstanding on the part of man,namely, an error of projection. Similarly, he would also not consider God, as Nietzsche, Nicolai, Hartmann and Sartre do, as the one whose existence is a contradiction to freedom; on the contrary God, as the reality beyond man and all finite things, sustains man in the very act of freedom.[70] Man's openness to the world (Weltoffenheit), according to Pannenberg, presupposes man's openness to God (Gottoffenheit)[71] or in

other words a God-relatedness (Gottbezogenheit) [72] . Instead of Rahner's designation of God as the 'Whither of transcendence' (Woraufhin der Transzendenz) [73] , Pannenberg uses for this mystery the expression 'das Gegenüber
der grenzenlosen Angewiesenheit des Menschen' (that which faces man in
his boundless dependence).[74] In content, we would maintain, both expressions
are the same and they stand, like the Neti, Neti approach of the Vedanta,
to express the incomprehensible, qualityless, formless, indefinable and the
limitless Mystery!

b. The Mystery of Fullness: 'Purnam'

The incomprehensibility of the Mystery we call God, as Karl Rahner explains,
is not just a blank unintelligibility, nor the mere absence of a reality; the
incomprehensibility of God is of course a positive side. [75] This positive approach, however, does not cancel the Mystery of God; on the contrary, the
Absolute is grasped precisely as the incomprehensible. Rahner distinguishes
between knowledge as clarity, sight and perception and knowledge as the
possession of the incomprehensible. [76] In the latter, the Absolute is contemplated as the divine incomprehensibility. Following the tradition of the
Christian thinkers of the past like the Areopagite, Maximus the Confessor,
St. Gregory of Nyssa, St. Thomas Aquinas and others, Rahner tries to reconcile
'radical creaturehood with absolute immediacy to God, making God's incomprehensibility the blessedness of man and not the limit of his happiness,
and seeing man as made for the one abiding mystery' [77]. As Thomas Aquinas
teaches, the supreme knowledge we can have of God is to know that we
do not know God, in so far as we know that what God is surpasses all what
we can understand of him.[78] Even the beatific vision, Rahner contends,
does not remove God's incomprehensibility; the supreme knowledge is the
knowledge of God as the Mystery!

We do not deal here, per se, with the question of God-knowing and God-
talk; we will come back to this point in one of the following sections.[79]
What we want to insist here is that Rahner's concept of God as the Mystery
is not just a negative concept, but similar to the 'Sat' or 'Asti' concept
of the Vedanta it has a rich and positive content! It is the bright incomprehensibility of God that is self-sufficient, self-evident and self-explanatory .
'If the Whither of transcendence', reasons Rahner, 'is that which by disclosing

itself gives transcendence its reality; if transcendence is the condition of the possibility of all spiritual understanding and insight; and if the Whither of transcendence is the holy Mystery: then the holy Mystery is the one thing that is its own self-sufficient reason, even in our eyes (...) there is nothing man knows better than that his knowledge, ordinarily so called, is only a tiny island in the immense ocean of the unexplored. He knows better than anything else that the existential question facing him in knowledge is whether he loves the little island of his so-called knowledge better than the ocean of the infinite mystery' [80].

Rahner's concept of the 'Mystery' we would say, gives a 'Christian' confirmation, to what the neo-Vedantin Dr. Radhakrishnan opines regarding the 'Neti' approach to the Absolute; 'Neti' means only man's consciousness of the Divine Transcendence; God is not a negative vacuity, but Being in the positive sense. [81] As we have seen in the first part, 'Brahman' is the term used by the Vedanta for the Absolute Mystery. [82] This Mystery we have also mentioned is the Mystery of Fullness (Purnam) according to the Brahadaranyaka Upanisad: 'That One is Fullness, and this one also is fullness; from the Fullness fullness does proceed; when the fullness is drawn from the Fullness, what remains is again Fullness.' [83] It must be seen also, as we have already indicated in the first part, in the context of the Atharva Veda's explanation of the 'Brahman' as the highest principle and basis of the world, self-existent, eternal, desireless, but it animating the cosmos and being the source of all changes, [84] i.e. the stability that is the condition of the possibility of all changes, the One (Ekam) [85] that is the condition of the possibility of multiplicity and which is named by the wise sages in different ways, the unity underlying the so-called polytheism, or better and more correctly 'henotheism' [86], on the level of the popular Hinduism!

Both in the Vedanta and in Rahner, we would say, there is a minor defect in considering the 'Mystery' or the 'Brahman' only from one side of the question, namely, as the source or foundation of knowing and consequently of being. W. Pannenberg, however, proposes an approach from the 'End', an eschatological approach to the Mystery of Fullness, which he names as 'The Power over everything' (Macht über alles). [87] This we would consider as a valuable corrective or complimentation to the above two views! It is more a matter of explication or emphasis.

What we mean by the word 'God', contends Pannenberg, 'is the power that is powerful over everything that has being' [88]. Pannenberg identifies the deity of God with his rule. The true God is the one who proves himself master over all. This view does not make the existence of God dependent on finite things on which He could exercise his power; it means only that 'if there are finite beings, then to have power over them is intrinsic to God's nature' [89]. It could further be asked why the description of the deity of God as his rule, should be considered an eschatological one. That is because Pannenberg's concept of the 'all' or the totality of reality is an eschatological one. No individual fact or event is adequately understandable exept in the 'totality' to which it belongs and the totality is realized only at the 'end'! This futuristic dimension of the totality of reality gives also a futuristic or eschatological stress to the concept of god. 'Whether an alleged deity', reasons Pannenberg, 'is God, i.e. powerful over all things, is a matter that can only be demonstrated in the event in which ... he is supposed to be powerful. It can finally be demonstrated only in the totality of all events, in so far as what we mean by the word 'God' is the power that is powerful over everything that has being' [90]. There is no fullness (Purnam) without the end; God 'becomes' the master over all only in the end of the process towards the fullness. 'The futurity of God's rule implies that in some sense the existence of God himself is yet future' [91]; 'in a restricted but important sense God does not yet exist ... God's being is still in the process of coming to be'[92]!

This eschatological dimension of God in Pannenberg's theology should not be understood in the sense of the Process Theology of Whitehead and Heartshorne, as to imply any kind of development or process in God because, as Pannenberg explains, 'what turns out to be true in the future will then be evident as having been true all along' [93]. As the power of the future, God dominates the remotest past! So the futurity of God is an essential aspect of his eternity. God is the future of even the most distant past events; so he existed before every present as the pledge of the future. 'He existed as the future that has been powerful in every present. Thus, the futurity of God implies his eternity' [94]! He is eternal because he is not only the future of our present but has been also the future of every past age. Each present was assigned its own historical future which in turn has become a past for us. God can release to each single event its actual historical future because he is the power of the ultimate future. 'In relation to past and present, God is constantly bringing himself back into his own eschatological futurity. [95]

The eschatological vision of Pannenberg is, as we shall see later, of great importance in his Christology, especially in reference to the resurrection of Jesus as the definitive manifestation of God as the power of the future, as the power over all things, in an anticipatory or proleptic way. We should, however, also indicate here that Pannenberg's identification of the divinity of God more explicitly with his power that with his love, has also its problems! He insists that if the love of God were powerless, then it would not be God![96] We would just turn the question: If the power of God were loveless, would it then be God? A bifurcation of power and love in God would not be quite acceptable! The power of God, we would maintain, is precisely the power of love. Pannenberg has fortunately clarified this point in another place by harmonizing both the power and the love of God. [96a]

c. 'Prajnanam Brahman': Consciousness and Person

A positive understanding of the absolute Mystery as the 'Purnam' (Fullness) or as the power over all things does not necesssarily bring one to the understanding of God as person. The neuter form of 'Brahman' that is used in the Vedanta to stand for the Absolute would indicate apparently an a-personal God![97] J.G. Fichte also follows a similar line when he considers the 'person' as applied to God is a contradiction to his infinity and it is a projection of man's finite anthropomorphic notions on the Infinite. [98] Though the pantheism of Spinoza also rules out the concept of a personal God, G.W.F. Hegel succeeded in developing a trinitarian structure of God, i.e. a personal one, from the concept of God as Spirit, as Subject and as Self-Consciousness.[99] The absolute Being is as Spirit Self-Consciousness; as Self-Consciousness he is open to himself, transparent to himself. He himself -not something outside him - is the object of his consciousness.[100] Hegel's understanding of God as the pure unity of thought [101] within itself corresponds to the Vedantic explanation of Brahman as Prajnanam (Consciousness), although the Hegelian element of necessity that is implied in the self-realization of the Spirit (Selbstwerdung des Geistes) [102] is foreign to the concept of Brahman. To deduce God's personality from his consciousness and subjectivity is as old as St. Augustine himself [103] and has been stressed in the modern times by Karl Barth [104] as well as by Karl Rahner, [105] without however falling into the hegelians necessity! Consciousness according to Rahner following the theory of Thomas Aquinas, is proportionate to the intensity of being of an existent being; the intensity of being is determined by the degree of possibility of being able to be present to itself (reditio super seipsum). God being the Supreme Being is, therefore, Consciousness itself, Prajnanam Brahman - to use the corresponding Vedantic category! As Karl Barth identifies 'person' with consciousness and liberty and postulates only one person in God with three modes of its being [106], so also Karl Rahner would prefer to attribute only one personality to God with three modes of its subsistence. [107] Although in expression this could sound as something new, in content it is not different from the traditional trinitarian concept of one nature and three persons in God! What is new in Rahner may be the theology of symbol which he applies to the concept of person in God. Rahner insists on the necessity of an internal self-expression in God, as the Supreme Being; 'all beings are by their nature symbolic, because they necesssarily express themselves in order to attain their own natures' [108]. Similar to Hegel, Rahner postulates an internal necessity in God; but, unlike Hegel, this necessity would not be seen in God in his relation to the created world! The creation is not a necessary moment in the self-realization of God as person. God as the perfect being is perfect consciousness and as such is personal. God in himself (immanent trinity) is person without necessarily supposing thereby an extra trinitarian relation (economic trinity). [109]

If the concept of person is determined by the notion of consciousness, then the Vedantic Brahman, even in its character of being qualityless (Nirguna) is person as observed by R.de Smet - we have referred to that in the first part [110] - because according to the Vedanta, Brahman is consciousness and consciousness is Brahman! [111] Dr. Radhakrishnan maintains that we cannot know anything about the immanent reality of God, as he is in himself, but only in so far as he is related to the world, i.e. in his economical aspect. [112] God as the Absolute (Nirguna) and God in his personal aspect (Saguna) are for him only two ways of considering the same reality. [113] Radhakrishnan justifies the validity of applying the human concept of person also to the reality of the Absolute. We are persons (Purusas) and God is perfect personality (Uttama Purusa). Some of the highest and richest manifestations which religion has produced, he maintains, require a personal God. 'There is a rational compulsion to postulate the personality of the Divine' [114]. 'If we analyse the concept of personality, we find that it includes cognition, emotion and will, and God is viewed as the supreme knower, the great lover and the perfect will. Brahman, Visnu, Siva. These are not three independent centres of consciousness, as popular theology represents, but three sides of one complex personality' [115]. Unlike Radhakrishnan, Dr. Raimundo Panikkar does not limit the personality of God to his Saguna aspect and to His manifestation as Brahma, Visnu and Siva. As we have already seen in the fourth chapter, Panikkar sees quite rightly the personal character of the Absolute in His very inner nature as the 'Saccidananda', [116] i.e. in the innertrinitarian relationship. As far as the Indian Christian theology is concerned, we opine, there are vast possibilities of research on the notion of 'person' in terms of relations rather than as mere consciousness. Personal relation is not a matter of imperfection in being but the summit of its perfection.

Pannenberg too approaches the personality of God not just from the fact of his reality as consciousness, but from the notion of the identity of I and Self (Ich und Selbst), i.e. ego and subject. The person is neither ego nor subject taken separately. Person is realized only through the presence of the Subject in Ego (Gegenwart des Selbst im Ich) [117], i.e. through the identity of Ego and Subject. The Subject of human beings is a reality that is in process and it is realized or made definitive only at the end of man's historical process, while the identity of Ego and Subject is a permanent reality in God. It is not right to apply the human experiences and concept of person to God, but on the other hand through the experience of God as person, the human concept of person attains a new and specific weight. 'Person' in God is the totality of existence realized through relations. [118] Person is not just the Subject (Selbst) nor the consciousness of the Subject (Ich) alone, but both together with the specifying relation Contrary to the views of both Karl Barth and Karl Rahner, Pannenberg reasons that if God could be person in the unity of his being as consciousness, then a trinitarian differentiation in God would be inconsistent and superfluous. [118] Only in the trinitarian context God could be understood as person. The one God apart from the three persons cannot be person at all, because God can be person not just as consciousness, but only as the Father, as the Son and as the Holy Spirit. [119] One divine Person confronts the other persons not as a multiplication of the divine subject or divine consciousness; each divine person realizes his divine subject and divine consciousness not in himself but only in his relation to the other two! [120]

It could well be said that Pannenberg's criticism of Rahner and Barth sheds much light also on the Vedantic understanding of the Brahman as a-personal or supra personal. Consciousness (Prajnanam) alone is no proof for the personality of God. In its encounter with the Vedanta the Christian theology has to stress and make clear its specific contribution to the concept of Brahman as community of persons based on relations. The Brahman, as Saccidananda, is not just a single person in his splendid isolation of infinite consciousness. The reality of 'Sat' cannot be independent of 'Cit' and 'Ananda'. But 'Sat' is 'Sat' and consequently Brahman only in relation to 'Cit' and 'Ananda'; what is true of 'Sat' as far as the relations are concerned is also true of 'Cit' and 'Ananda', without implying thereby any multiplicity in the reality of the Brahman as Subject (Selbst) or as Consciousness, Prajnanam (Ich). Man's experience of himself as person is dependent on his experience of God as person; [121] man participates in the personal character of the divine power; [122] this personal divine power is the ground and support in the openness of man's freedom and personality. [123] We will be further dealing with the notion of 'person' in Chapter VIII.A.2 in reference to the Chalcedon formula and the Indian problematic.

3. Man as the Event of God's Self-Giving

In reference to the transcendental horizon of man we have discussed in the preceeding sections man's concrete experience of transcendence, especially in the activities of his spiritual faculties and the basis of the human transcendence which we call God. Here we consider mostly that basic reality in man that justifies his being called transcendental.

a. Man, the 'Rational Animal' - 'Zoon logikon'?

The scholastic philosophy, following the thought patterns of Aristotle, defines man as 'animal rationale' (zoon logikon). That which distinguishes man, according to this definition, from the rest of God's creation is his spiritual character as evidenced in his rational capacity. In the Vedantic understanding of man, as we have seen in the first part, [124] the Atman is the reality of man. The Vedanta does not accept any specific difference between the basic reality of human beings and those of other animals; Atman is present in varying degrees of consciousness in different living beings following the cosmic

laws of Karma and Samsara. So both animals and human beings have a transcendental horizon in so far as the Atman is identical with Brahman in one
or another way, as the different interpretations suggest. This difference
in the scholastic and Vedantic understanding of man is caused by their varying
interpretations regarding the relation between God and this world. The doctrine
of creation from nothing (ex nihilo sui et subjecti) rules out any concept
of emanation as in the gnostic sense and emphasizes the infinite difference
between God as creator and the world as creation. The doctrine of 'Maya',
on the other hand, gives a monistic or pantheistic turn to the Vedantic
understandig of this world while insisting on the absolute dependence of
the world on God. [125] Both 'creation' and 'maya' could agree on the notion
of dependence, but not on the nature of God-world relationship.

The Vedantic interpretations regarding the Atman-Brahman relationship rules
out all notions of creator-creature difference. [126] Man is by nature divine;
the task of human life is to realize this essential divinity. Man is not only
transcendentally oriented; he is transcendence itself! Such an identification
of man and God would not be acceptable to the Christian faith. Man is spiritual
in character, but that does not by itself make him divine. Man is an animal,
but his spiritual dimensions make him specifically different from animals.
We will be dealing later more elaborately with the question of the Vedantic
panpsychism[127] and pantheism [128] in their reference to the Christian faith,
but for the present we limit ourselves to that spiritual reality in man that
makes him different from animals though it does not make him equal to
God.

The reality of man presupposes, in the Christian faith, an intimate relation
between the order of creation and the divine order without mixing up or
identifying them. The traditional christian theology distinguishes, consequently,
in man a supernatural order of grace and an order of nature that is presupposed
and perfected by the supernatural order ('Gratia non destruit naturam, sed
supponit et perficit eam'). [129] The capacity (potentia) of man as a creature
to accept obediently the disposition and action of God, in such a way that
this is not his due, is called in the traditional theology as 'Potentia obo -
edientialis'. [130] Accordingly, nature is a 'potentia oboedientialis' for the supernatural grace, which as self-communication of God, is in no way owed
to man. The obediential potency can be considered as 'simply identical with
nature as personal and spiritual; its reality is the tremendous reality of the

spiritual nature' [131]. Man as a spiritual being is open to God's self-communication, but he must accept it as a grace and not as something that is his
due! It could be compared to the experience of gratuitous love between two
persons. [132] By reason of the potentia oboedientialis man is capable of receiving
the self-communication of God without being elimi nated thereby and ceasing
to be a human and creaturely being. But a very static definition of man
as 'animal rationale' could make a caricature of the 'potentia oboedientialis'!
If the natural reality of man is nothing more than that of a rational animal
then the divine self-communication would be nothing more than a superstructure on an otherwise complete hypostasis! The human nature would be in
this case only non-resistent and indifferent to Grace - a negative non-repug-
nance towards God's self-communication. [133] This interpretation of the relation
between nature and grace is clearly far from the Vedantic position; but
it is also criticized by Karl Rahner as very negative and static, as an approach
that makes grace extrinsic to the being of man. [134] Contrary to the Vedantic
position, however, Rahner stresses the gratuitous character of grace; he
contends that 'the fulfilment of a nature and the gratuitousness of that
fulfilment are not contradictory concepts in the case of spiritual beings' [135].
Man, according to him, is not just negatively disposed to salvation, but
positively open to it. Rahner develops further the scholastic concept of 'potentia oboediantialis' in a more positive, dynamic and existential way by
his idea of the 'Supernatural Existential' as we shall see below. [136]

b. Man as Orientation to the Mystery of Fullness

The aupanishadic Mahavakyani 'Aham Brahmasmi' (I am Brahman) and 'Tat
tvam asi' (That art Thou) [137] as interpreted by the Vedanta confer on man
a divinity that is innate to him, to the conscious realization of which man
has a right. Dr. Radhakrishnan borrows even the term 'consubstantiality'
from Christian theology and applies it to show the intimate relation between
the spirit in man and God. [138] There is in the self of man, according to him,
at the very centre of man's being, something deeper than the intellect,
which is akin to the Supreme! He sees the biblical narration regarding the
creation of man in God's image (Gen 1:27) and Jesus' declaration of his
identity with God (Jn 10:30) as further support for the Vedantic teaching
regarding man's intrinsic and natural divinity! The divine in man, thinks
Radhakrishnan, is the source and perfection of his nature. [139] Although this
position is as such not acceptable to the Christian faith, it cannot be denied

that valuable truths regarding the transcendental nature of man are contained therein. Karl Rahner's theory of the supernatural existential (Übernatürliches Existential) is, in our opinion, a valuable contribution to confront the Vedanta precisely in this point.

The orientation (Verwiesenheit) of man to the Mystery of Fullness, as Rahner insists, belongs to the very nature of man. [140] Man's nature is not a static one that is already determined; man's nature and existence are determined by the acceptance or rejection of this orientation to God. [141] In this sense we can speak of man as an 'indefinability which is conscious of itself' [142]. Man's transcendental orientation, therefore, is not just something arbitrary or external to man but it is an element in man's ontological constitution precisely as human being, an element which is constitutive of his existence as man, prior to his exercise of freedom; in other words, this orientation to the Divine or the Supernatural is existential [143] to man. Hence his use of the expression 'Supernatural Existential' (Übernatürliches Existential) for this basic reality or 'a priori' structure of man, that is oriented to divine realization. Man is not only negatively disposed for salvation but positively open to it. Man's unlimited reference to the infinite fullness of the mystery [144] must have, according to Rahner, a real ontological effect in every man from the first moment of existence. If God gives man a supernatural end, then man is by that very fact always and everywhere inwardly other in structure than he would be, if he did not have this end and hence other as well, before he has reached it partially in sanctifying grace or fully in the beatific vision. In this case, what Rahner means is not a theoretically possible 'natura pura' but the 'concrete quiddity' of man. [145]

The 'Supernatural Existential' thus understood is nothing else than God's continuous offer of salvation to every man prior to man's free decision. In this sense this 'a priori' ontological determination of man is a gift of God, a Grace! [146] As Grace it is nothing else than the continuous offer of God's self-communication (die der menschlichen Freiheit immer angebotene Selbstmitteilung Gottes [147]); it is God's continuous offer of salvation to man! 'God's self-communication must be present in every man as the condition which makes its personal acceptance possible' [148]. So the mystery of man can be called a 'call to God' and a salvation that comes from God. [149]

We will be discussing the question of God's universal will of salvation that is intimately connected with the notion of the supernatural esistential in greater detail in the final chapter.[150] Here he would pay some more attention to the problem of the gratuity of grace in the context of supernatural existential as an 'a priori', interior, ontological constituent of man. Rahner's theory does not make grace man's due, to which he has a right.[151] The 'existential' itself is gratuitous; the supernatural existential - to put it in scholastic categories - is not of the essence or nature of man, but with the essence it makes up the 'quiddity', that is the existent reality which is man.[152] Man cannot merit grace for the very fact that he is a finite creature and a sinner.[153] In the light of what we have said so far we can say that God's will to save man, the supernatural existential, the dynamic finalization of every one in the direction of God's grace, i.e., God's self-communication, in the innermost depth of man's being, the supernatural a-priori disposition from which man cannot escape is an unmerited, gratuitous gift of God.

The notion of the 'Supernatural Existential' has brought to light not only the essential transcendence of man - an aspect which the Vedanta considers as its basic tenent - but also the basic differences between the Vedantic and the Christian anthropology especially regarding the divine aspect of man and the gratuity of salvation.[154] We will be evaluating later its Christological implications. The Supernatural Existential can also be named as the 'Christ-Principle' or the 'Idea of Christ' in every   man as we shall see soon.

W. Pannenberg uses the biblical category of the 'image of God' (Gottebenbildlichkeit) as the essential reference and orientation of man to God's self-giving.[155] Pannenberg stresses especially the operative, eschatological, communitarian and ecological implications of this image of God in man. This image confers man the lordship over the whole of creation as God's representative in this world.[156] The task to conquer and subdue the world, Pannenberg observes, has been misunderstood by man and that has led to the senseless exploitation of nature leading to the consequent ecological problems. The power over nature implied in the understanding of man as God's image, maintains Pannenberg, is not a licence to the arbitrary plundering of the nature, but a commission to keep and protect it.[157] Such an ecological concern is evidently lacking in the anthropology of Karl Rahner and in the Vedantic vision (Darsana) of man!

c. The Anthropological Turn in Theology

As it is implied in our exposition of the Vedantic anthropology in the first part of our work, the Vedanta does not recognize any significant difference between anthropology and theology. This attitude is a logical consequence of the basic tenet of the Vedanta that every man is by nature divine. In the Vedanta, theology and anthropology become one! In scholastic theology the position of philosophy and consequently of metaphysics and philosophical anthropology is only that of 'ancilla theologiae'. This too is quite understandable in the context of the strict distinction between nature and grace, between the order of creation and the order of salvation! Karl Rahner, however, as a necessary consequence of his notion of the 'supernatural existential' in man, sees an intimate unity between theology and anthropology. [158] He sees an element of truth even in the pantheistic anthropological approaches - as could be the case with the Vedanta - because they express a sensibility to man's transcendental dimension. [159]

Anthropology is for Rahner only a framework to locate his theology because the order of creation is intimately related to the order of salvation. Man is so created, that he can transcend beyond the limits of space and time, that in every act of cognition he perceives the absolute being itself as the condition of the possibility of the former. [160] Anthropology as transcendental philosophy and theology are, consequently, inseparably united. [161] If every philosophy, that deserves to be called metaphysical, has to be transcendental in its character, then one could say that every theology that is more than a mere report of the salvation history, i.e., the theology that truly reflects, has to be philosophical in character, that means, it has to be a transcendental philosophical theology, a transcendental theology! [162] The transcendental theology, in short, is that theology which makes use of the transcendental philosophy as its method of investigation. [163] A transcendental anthropological approach to theology tries to demythologize faith by interpreting it from the self-understanding of man as having the condition of the possibility of God's action in him and in his history; that implies an anthropological turn in theology. [164] 'Only knowledge of God attained by a transcendental method', Rahner argues, 'prevents God being regarded as a part within the all, or a demiurge whose action on the world is merely from without' [165]. The transcendental theology however, concedes Rahner, is only one element in theology;

it cannot and does not try to be the whole of theology. [166] In short we could say that eventhough Rahner's transcendental method stresses - like the Vedanta - the transcendental horizon in man, it avoids - unlike the Vedanta - making God pantheistically a part of the immanent system and the other extreme of deistically making the world function totally independent of God. God is immanent in the created reality, not as a part of its system, but as its transcendental cause.

Hans Urs von Balthasar sees and criticizes an anthropological reduction in Rahner's transcendental approach to theology from an anthropological stand point. [167] But Rahner defends his position insisting that the approach of a transcendental theology is genuinely theological in character, transcendental philosophy being only a point of departure. [168]

We would agree with Rahner that every theology in order to be meaningful for man has to be in some way anthropology. [169] Atman is the mystery that is oriented towards the fullness of the mystery called Brahman. Man by his essence has a centre outside himself, in God. That is what we mean by the transcendental horizon in man!

Rahner's attempt to bring theology and anthropology into a mutually complementing dialogue has been followed in a much broader scale by W. Pannenberg. He advocates a vast interdisciplinary approach to theology and insists on using the findings not only of anthropology but of all extra-theological and natural sciences to reflect on the implications of faith. [169a] What comes to light in such an approach is the intimate relation between the divine and the human, the supernatural and the natural and finally the transcendental and the historical, a relation which would be irreconcilable with the Vedantic vision of God, man and the world!

B. Transcendence in Process

In the first part of our work we had discussed the Vedantic understanding of history. [170] The Indian Darsanas see an irreconcilable opposition between man's transcendence and his being involved in history which also belongs to the realm of 'Maya' and consequently of bondage. The never ending cyclic character of history as taught by the Vedanta also underlines the spirit-world contrast. The world of changes and becoming has no participation in the fullness of transcendence. Karl Rahner, on the other hand, has a different approach in explaining the relation between human transcendence and world history. Transcendence, according to him, is not some kind of a human business alongside the world history, but the human transcendence is lived and realized only in concrete history. [171] Transcendentality is first and foremost that which results from the experience of the historical process. [172] In this section we shall evaluate the Indian notion of human transcendence in face of its necessary historical dimension which is necessary for a proper understanding of the Christian faith in the Incarnation of God.

1. History as the Event of Transcendence

What is the role of 'matter' in the self-realization of the human spirit? How can we relate the scientific theory of evolution to the notion of transcendence? What does distinguish the human being from the rest of the animal kingdom of which he is a member? A clarification of these questions is important in facing the Vedantic anthropology.

a. Spirit in the World

The Christian faith recognizes as Pannenberg observes, no dichotomy - whether it is platonic or Vedantic - between the body and soul of man. Man is body and man is soul. There is a substantial unity between body and soul, between matter and spirit in man. [173] Man precisely as spirit lives in this material world. Matter is the metaphysical principle of individuation (principium individuationis) [174], while the soul of man, the spirit, is the substantial form of the body, the matter (forma substantialis). [175] In line with the scholastic philosophy, Rahner also maintains that the 'materia prima' - to distinguish the material principle from the concrete matter which is called 'materia secunda' - as the empty, non specific but real possibility of having being, is as such the cause of the manifold actualization of being in space and time, i.e. in history. [176] The materiality of man determines not only his history, but also his social character because man as essentially 'material' is one among many - matter is the principle of individuation - and so a part of humanity, because only in its totality the essence given to each man is realizable and manifestable. [177] It is quite understandable that a depreciation of the material aspect of human existence in the Vedanta has been responsible for the historical and social disinterest that belongs to the tradition of Hinduism. The unrepeatable uniqueness of history that is lacking in the Vedantic view is also the result of the negation of matter from the reality of man. Since matter is the 'principium individuationis', i.e., cause of a particular realization of a thing, it is also the reason for the unrepeatable uniqueness of that thing. [178]

Spirit and matter, Rahner asserts, have necessarily an intrinsic connection with one another 'because both of them derive from the one infinite spirit which is God as their Creator' [179]. Rahner continues: "Things created by him are not _maya_, the veil, which dissolves like mist before the sun the more one recognizes the Absolute, i.e. the more religious one becomes."[180] Under the dynamic impulse of God's creative power the development of biologically organized materiality is oriented in terms of an ever-increasing complexity and interiority towards spirit until, finally, matter becomes spirit through a process of self-transcendence. [181] Here Rahner follows the line of thinking of Teilhard de Chardin.[182] Every becoming, Rahner argues, is not only becoming 'different', but it is becoming 'more'; in real becoming of matter something is not just added from outside, but the result of becoming is the effect of what was already there before as a participation in the fullness of being; it is a real self-transcendence; it is the evolution of the matter towards the spirit. [183] The autotranscendence of matter proceeds in the direction of man and in the human spirit matter, the cosmos, becomes conscious of itself. [184] So the history of the cosmos becomes the history of man's autotranscendence which progresses further in a lineal way - as against the cyclic vision of the Vedanta - towards a unique 'Point Omega'. [185] Rahner does not see any contradiction between the notions of creation and evolution; the latter is the continuation of God's dynamic creative power. [186] In the opinion of Rahner, man is the being in whom the basic tendency of matter to find itself in the Spirit by self-transcendence arrives at the point where it definitely breaks through. Such a view places man within the basic and total conception of the world. The transcendental character of man serves further as the condition of the possibility quite gratuitously by God, and by God's communication of himself' [187]. Thus, 'the end is the absolute beginning'[188].

Rahner uses also the 'theology of the symbol' to explain the unity of spirit and matter, soul and body. The body is the symbol of the human spirit in space and time. The body is the way man, as Spirit, becomes in the world..[189] This argument is evidently Hegelian in character, because matter is here seen as created essentially for the sake of spirit and oriented towards it; it must partake of the same fundament as does spirit;[190]they are two corelated and inseparable elements which cannot be reduced to each other; [191] what is material, is nothing but a limited and as it were 'solidified' spirit.[192] Man is spirit in the world or cosmic spirit, and the material world is something like a raw material for the spirit.[193] In explicit reference to Hegel, Karl Rahner affirms that becoming or self-expression of the spirit in matter, even in its application to the Infinite Spirit, God, - here the immediate reference is to the possibility of the incarnation of God - should not be considered as a sign of deficiency but as the height of perfection to be able to become less than what one is.[194] This does not mean that Rahner agrees with Hegel's dialectical pantheism which insists on the necessity of the process of self-expression in God. [195]

As Prof. A. Ganoczy remarks, the notion of the intimate unity of matter and spirit has also its reflections in the Indian thinking. He sees quite rightly the cosmic dance of Siva as a concrete expression of the creative, destructive and re-creative dimensions of matter and spirit.[196] Dance is actually the symbol of matter in its evolutive motion, a movement into the realm of the spirit! The theological content of the 'Nataraja' symbol could be well considered as a good starting point for further investigations into the possibility of developing a more integrated vision of matter and spirit in the Vedantic context. It must also be remarked that in the 'Purusa-Prakrti' concept of the world, which is prevalent especially in the Samkhya-Yoga schools and the Bhagavadgita, the constitutive principles of 'Prakrti', namely, Sattva, Rajas and Tamas are really principles of the evolution of matter.[197] But in the strict Vedanta thinking 'Maya' predominates and the reality of the material world is either denied or considered as a merely illusive self-projection or play (Lila) of the Brahman! It is, however, also worth mentioning that Indian Christian theologians like Brahmabandhab Upadhyaya give a positive interpretation to 'Maya' as the absolute dependence of the material world on the Absolute Spirit. [198]

b. The Historical Mediation of Transcendence

The Hegelian dialectic philosophy sees transcendent Spirit, and consequently truth as such, as essentially historical because the historical process is a necessary moment in the self-expression of the Spirit. This understanding of truth as history is found also by W. Pannenberg as a unique opportunity to interpret the biblical faith. [199] Historicness of truth, he declares, is not against the unity of truth. Pannenberg's insistence on the historical character of truth does not prejudice against the immutability of the divine reality, but what he means is that the divine truth is experienced and understood by man not diving beyond the process of the world history, but in and through it. In short, as far as man is concerned, the transcendental truth must be historically mediated. The Vedantic philosophy, on the contrary, insists on the non-historical and immediate (i.e. not mediated) character of the transcendental truth. Truth is 'apaurusheya'; [200] the truth reveals itself to the Atman and even the Rsis, through whom the eternal truth may be communicated, do not have any personal role to play; they function like impersonal reflectors! What is important is 'anubhava' (experience), introspection and a-historical reflection. Knowledge is essentially realization. The more man frees himself from the 'Sthula' and 'Sukshma Sarira' (gross and subtle body) and the more he penetrates beyond the five sheaths enveloping the Atman, the more will he be nearer to true knowledge, Jnana.[201] According to Rahner, however, such an independence from matter and history in the process of the realization of human transcendence is absolutely impossible!

History is the event of man's transcendence because, as Rahner says, independently of history human transcendentality cannot be understood. [202] The ultimate thing about history itself is that it is the history of man's transcendentality. Man's dependence on matter and consequently on history for the realization of his transcendence is expressed by Rahner through the expression 'conversio ad phantasma', an expression taken from the Thomistic philosophy. [203] Although Rahner's work 'Geist in Welt' makes contributions to epistomology and natural theology, it could very well be re-titled 'Conversio ad phantasma', because it is a long reflection on the need of the human spirit to incarnate itself in matter i.e. in history, in order to be itself, to act at all, to know and to love. Rahner establishes a metaphysics of human incarnate spirit, whose mode of knowing is but a way in which spirit is and shows its openness to all being, including God as absolute Being! [204] Man has no escape from history; the human spirit comes into its own reality only in the turning to history (conversio ad phantasma) and man's place of encounter, therefore, even with God 'lies necessarily within human history' [205]. 'Man knows about being in general only through sense perception' and so there is for man 'an approach to being in general only in the materially existent things. There is access to God only in a penetration of the world' [206] . Every knowledge in man is received through sense perception; every knowledge is receptive; there is no innate categorical (objective and concrete) ideas in man.[207] Contrary to the Vedantic position, Rahner rejects all metaphysical intuitions in man,[208] an intuition that could be free from the sense faculties of man. God who cannot be subject to man's sense-perception cannot also be known as an object of man's categorial knowledge, but he can be understood only transcendentally as the principle of human knowledge and reality. [209]

Rahner bases his argument for the dignity of the human body on the fact that man realizes his transcendentality precisely through his corporeality. 'The bodily nature of man', Rahner explains, 'is necessarily a factor in man's spiritual becoming; it is not something alien to the spirit; but a limited moment in the achievement of the spirit itself ... the finite spirit reaches for and finds itself through the fulfilment of the material itself' [210] . A Vedantic depreciation of the bodily aspect of man - something that Vedanta shares with Platonism, Manichaeism and Gnosticism [211] - has no place in the anthropology of Karl Rahner. This is important to understand properly the mystery of God's Incarnation in Jesus of Nazareth in contrast to the practically docetic type of Avatara myths.

c. The Question of the Vedantic Panpsychism

The Vedanta does not recognize any essential difference between human beings and other animals. The Atman is present in all living beings in various degrees of consciousness. The Hindu principle of 'Ahimsa' (non-violence) even to animals is based, first and foremost, on the panpsychic assumption: 'All life is akin'! This in turn finds its justification in the theory of 'Karma-Samsara'. We had elaborated this Vedantic position sufficiently in the first part. [212]

Rahner does not recognize any such equality between human beings and other animals. Animals are not spiritual or transcendental beings; they are sub-spiritual. Like Thomas Aquinas, Rahner sees the specific difference between animals and human beings in the subjects ability to return to oneself as subject in a self-luminous antithesis of the sensibly experienced object (reditio completa subjecti in seipsum), which is the distinctive attribute of the spirit in contrast to all that is sub-spiritual. [213] The Vedantic anthropo-zoology is untenable because a transcendental horizon as in man is not detectable in animals, especially as manifested in the spiritual activities of knowing, willing and questioning. There is not transcendental 'a priori' openness to being in animals to which they can refer the particular data of sense perception, thus universalizing and spiritualizing them under the notion of 'being'. [214] So man is essentially and radically different from other animals. An animal is not just an undeveloped man. The qualitative 'more' that creation has achieved in man, is evidently not present in animals. The essence of this qualitative 'more' is, as we have mentioned, the ability to return to one's own horizon of knowing, i.e. the 'reditio in seipsum'! Although for a western mind the distinction between human beings and animals could be self-evident, it is not so evident for the Indian mind. Hence our dealing with this question!

Wolfhart Pannenberg sees man's openness to the world (Weltoffenheit) as the basic factor that makes a human being and differs him from other animals. [215] Animal behaviour, on the other hand, is bound by the nature and the environment (umweltgebunden) with automatic reaction according to innate tendencies, instincts and impulses. [216] In contrast to animals man is open to various possibilities as far as his environment is concerned; he can see the one and the same fact from different points of view and can freely choose according to his experience, experiments, comparison and research. Man is not pre-determined like animals, but he is open to new things and possibilities; he can search endlessly because he transcends beyond the world which he confronts. [217] Man's imaginative power, creativity, openness to the future (Zukunftsoffenheit), human confrontation with the question of death, man's never ending needs, the phenomenon of human expression in languages, the question of God - all these are significant points in which one can, according to Pannenberg, clearly observe the irradicable difference between human beings and animals. [218]

Pannenberg also levels his criticism against the notion of the 'immortality of the soul'. In the absense of a dualism of body and soul in man, a dichotomy, - theory of Greek origin - we cannot speak of a 'part' in man, namely, his 'soul' that could survive death! [219] The theory of the immortality of the soul must be understood as a popular way of expressing man's openness to and beyond the world. It is primarily the 'Weltoffenheit', and not the immortality of the soul which distinguishes human beings from other animals. We will have to deal with this question later when we consider the human eschatology in relation to Jesus' resurrection. [220] The Vedantic question of panpsychism has also great relevance in reference to the transmigration of souls that is implied in the theory of 'Samsara'. [221]

2. Revelation as History

In one of the former sections we discussed the question of the necessarily historical mediation of human transcendence, namely, man's dependence on the 'sensibles' of this world of becoming for the realization of his transcendental orientation. [222] Here we would like to go deeper into the same question concentrating our attention mostly on God's self-communication to man, which we call revelation, especially in reference to the 'apaurusheya' (impersonal) character of the same as insisted in the Vedanta.

a. Unity of Truth as the History of Truth

In the second part of our work we had referred to the accusation of narrow mindedness that is levelled against the Christian claim of uniqueness as far as the truth is concerned. [223] The Vedanta insists that truth cannot be limited and particular; it is universal; it is the whole! Different religious views represent different approaches to the same truth; and all these approaches together make the whole truth. No particular religion can, in this sense, be above any other religion; all religions are equal (Sarva Dharma Samanatva)! Vedanta alone as the religion of universal principles, without any particular historical founder or historically defined dogmas, can lay claims to be the Religion of religions or the Religion in religions! Although such a religious 'socialization' or equalization may not be acceptable for the Christian faith that is based on the historical tangibility of the transcending and universal Word of God, still it cannot be denied that there

is some truth in the Vedantic accusation of narrow mindedness in the traditional Christian approach to truth.

W. Pannenberg too, like the Vedanta, stresses the unity of truth and its
wholeness. Truth for him is not just one event in a particular time; it is
the totality or wholeness of all events. Pannenberg also warns against 'narrow-
mindedly substituting a particular perspective for the whole truth' [224]. Truth
consists not in any kind of narrow exclusivism, but in a wide-hearted all
inclusivism! There is still a fundamental difference between the Vedantic
- in this case Vedanta shares the Greek static ontology - and Pannenberg's
approach to truth. For Pannenberg, truth is not a static, non-historical and
impersonal principle, but the unity and wholeness of truth, as far as man
is concerned, is strictly historical and eschatological in character.

As Pannenberg observes, 'the unity of truth can ... only be thought of as
the history of truth, meaning in effect that truth itself has a history and
that its essence is the process of the history. Historical change itself must
be thought of as the essence of truth'[225] and this view is necessary to maintain
the unity of truth without substituting the particular for the whole. The
concept of 'whole' for Pannenberg is historical and eschatological, based
on the reality of process and fulfilment at the End! Here it is to be mentioned
that Pannenberg's understanding of truth - and consequently his understanding
of man and Christ - is from the background of the problematic of history
as raised by Hegel. [226] Pannenberg agrees with Hegel in the assumption that
truth is the whole and the whole emerges only at the end of the historical
process. [227] History is truth in its wholeness ('Geschichte ist die Wirklichkeit in ihrer Totalität').[228] Pannenberg considers this view as fully biblical.[229]
The Bible does not understand truth as timelessly unchangeable, but as a
process that runs its course and maintains itself through change; it has a
divine beginning and an apocalyptic end. The unity of the process 'which
is full of contradictions while it is under way, will become visible along
with the true meaning of every individual moment in it, only from the stand-
point of its end. What a thing is, is first decided by its future, by what
it becomes of it' [230]. Truth is that which will show itself in the future. [230a]
Such a lineal vision of history as a process towards an 'End' of fulfilment
stands evidently in contrast to the historical concept of the Vedanta which
is essentially cyclic. [230b]

The historical and eschatological character of truth, Pannenberg argues, is also evident in the experience of reason. It is through an 'imaginative fore-conception'[231] that we understand the truth and wholeness of a particular event. The reason understands individual events in the context of the 'whole' and in the context of the 'end'. Similar to the gnoseological 'Vorgriff' (pre-concept) of Rahner, Pannenberg speaks about a historical 'Vorgriff' as the condition of the possibility of understanding particular events. This may be called the historical and eschatological 'a-priori' structure of the reason 'which permits faith to speak of an eschatological future for the whole of reality without appearing irrational as such' [232]. In other words, there is already in the particular events of history a subtle, intrinsic indication towards the 'whole' and the 'end' of which it is only a part, just an in-stant! Not only the 'part' is contained in the whole, but also the 'whole' is contained somehow in the 'part'. Pannenberg refers also to Heidegger who maintains that the life of man is a 'whole' only at his death, but argues further and contends that as a member of the whole human race man remains as the part of a whole (Glied eines Ganzen) even at his death, thus binding the individual eschatology with the universal eschatology. [233] We can say without hesitation that comparable to the anthropological turn ('Anthropologische Wende') of Karl Rahner there is in Pannenberg a theological turn to the future ('Eschatologische Wende'). [234]

In Pannenberg's theology, however, there is a substantial correction of Hegel's historico-eschatological view! As Frank E. Tupper observes, Hegel considers his own position as the end of the history of thought and consequently he denies the horizon of a still open future, namely, an eschatology in the Christian sense. Besides, Hegel also devaluates the contingency of events and slightens the uniqueness of the particular. [235] For Pannenberg, on the contrary, the eschatology is still an open fact and the importance of the particular, contingent events lies precisely in the fact, that they have a proleptic or anticipatory function in reference to the whole and to the future. This is very important - as we shall see later [236] - especially in understanding the unique value of the particular event of Jesus' resurrection!

b. The Historico-Eschatological Character of Revelation

The lineal and eschatological vision of history has also its logical and necessary repercussion on Pannenberg's concept of revelation or God's self-manifestaton. If the deity of God is his rule (Basileia) [237] , then God manifests his deity only when he establishes his Lordship (Basileia) over all things. When Pannenberg describes the deity of God or the essence of God as 'Power over all things' (Macht über alles), he speaks of God strictly in terms of his relationship to creation. [238] The revelation (Offenbarung) in its strict sense, the full self-manifestation of God in His essence, is the establishment of His Lordship over all things at the Eschaton, which is the fulfilment of history, the event from which history receives its unifying meaning. This manifestation of God at the Eschaton is not something that takes place all of a sudden at the end of times. It is a process that has begun with the creation itself and extends all over history till the Eschaton. The transcendental nature of man enables him to recognize this self-manifestation of God. But the mere fact that man is transcendentally oriented, does not mean that man necessarily meets God in His Lordship, because 'even the claim that by his questioning concerning himself and the meaning of his existence and of everything that has being, man is questioning toward God, can, strictly speaking, only be justified if the reality on which man turns out to be dependent in the openness of his questioning, meets him personally and hence as "God"; speaking of God as a self-revealing person is an affirmation 'of the infinity of the freedom of God[239]. The important question regarding revelation is whether God in His freeedom really encounters man and offers 'to bear him to the unknown fulfilment for which he longs' [240] . An answer for it can be found only in man's concrete experience, i.e. his history.

If the historical process towards an end of fulfilment is so important in understanding the revelation, then it logically follows that every aspect of truth in this world of experience and every branch of knowledge - even non-theological science - is oriented to, and enters into, the concept of revelation, because only in such a way God could be understood as the Beginning and End, as the creator and fulfiller of all things, i.e. of the 'whole'. [241] Pannenberg's seven dogmatic theses on the doctrine of revelation are very important in clarifying his understanding of the historico-eschatological character of revelation. [242]

In contrast to the Vedantic position, we have seen that Pannenberg insists on the value of the historical process in the divine self-manifestation and that this process progresses towards a future of definitive fulfilment. The material world and the historical events are not excluded from the process of man's realization of his transcendental orientation; on the contrary, man has to reach his salvific goal in and through this world and its history, which are elevated by God as the means of His self-manifestation by establishing his Lordship (Basileia) over them!

The Vedantic view that it is in the cave of man's heart, within the Kosa (sheath) superstructure of one's existence that the Atman encounters the Absolute (Brahman) is also to some extent held by Karl Rahner when he denies that the event of revelation could be understood as an intervention of God purely from without, an act that is fully extrinsic to the nature of man.[243] But without falling into the Vedantic and modernistic immanentism on the one hand and the scholastic extrinsicism on the other hand, Rahner represents a middle position between the two,[244] a position that insists on history as the place of encounter between the immanent and transcendent mysteries of man and God. Rahner's insistence on the receptive character of human knowledge - whether acquired or infused - as against the gnostic and Vedantic type of innate knowledge, is also valid with regard to revelation. Man is not in possession of the Whither of his transcendence by virtue of his very nature. Man as spirit in the world realizes his transcendence 'only through an outgoing to another existent thing that is different from him'[245]. The Absolute Being as personal knowledge, i.e. self-possession in consciousness (Bei-sich-sein), and as freedom can open himself and give himself to man who is transcendently oriented. The fact that God has revealed himself does not mean that it was done out of necessity.[245a] But if the Being reveals himself to the being-in-matter-and-history, man, then this revelation can take place only in and through matter, space, time and history. Man is indeed spirit; but as finite spirit in the world, he depends on sense intuition (conversio ad phantasma) — as we have already mentioned in one of the previous sections in reference to the process of natural knowledge [246] for all objective or categorial knowledge which takes place by transcending all objects toward the infinite horizon of being. It is that which makes metaphysics (knowing of being) and revelation (Being communicating Himself to man) possible. Since man as spirit in the world can know 'being' only by 'Vorgriff' and not by intellectual introspection or sense intuition as an object of cognition and since this being can be known only through sense perception, the Being (God) if He wants to reveal himself at all to man, has to do that necessarily by entering space and time, i.e. history and thus making himself 'available' to man's sphere of perception.[247] So the place of encounter between man and God who may possibly reveal himself 'is the transcendence of man in its specifically human character'[248], i.e. in human history! Man as spirit in the world is possible hearer of the possible Word of God;[249] the actualization of this possibility being possible only in and through history. This is clearly a counter-Vedantic position that, basing itself like the Vedanta on transcendental-anthropological reflection, points to the necessarily historical character of revelation! [250]

If man is 'that existent being who necessarily stands in freedom before the God of a possible revelation'[251] in the reality of human history, then man, as a being oriented to the mystery of Fullness and as such essentially a potential hearer of a word from God or at leat his silence,[252] has also an existentiell obligation to 'hear' the Word. Hearing is 'to attend' to Being; 'hearing' defines the essence of man as existence, as the place where Being is manifested. In this view Rahner is very much influenced by the Phenomenological existentialism of Martin Heidegger, [253] although Rahner himself is of the view that to call him a Heideggerian would be a slight exaggeration! [254] It is true that like Heidegger, Rahner affirms that man is able to raise the question about being and that man's pre-apprehension (Vorgriff) of being is distinct from 'beings', but unlike Heidegger, Rahner holds that the ultimate sense of being is not nothingness, but rather the fullness of being i.e. God because the 'limited' is grasped by man as 'limited' in terms of the absolute being, within the horizon of a 'more' which is the source of being. The problematic of both, Rahner and Heidegger are also different; Heidegger is concerned with the meaning of being (Dasein) - 'being' is what appears, phenomena, and time is the horizon for the understanding of being [255] - and raises no question about transcendence and consequently also no answer for nor against God; but Rahner is concerned with the source of cause of being, implying a question of transcendence to Being, God! So, according to Rahner, if hearing defines the essence of man as existence, then man as a body-spirit existent has the potentiality to receive a revelation from God, if such a one is given![255] Since revelation as a necessarily 'historical event' must be 'expected to be an event fixed in time and space, within the total history of mankind', man cannot afford, following the Vedantic example, to have an attitude of indifference towards history.[257] Making use of an 'historical memory', man has to search and enquire in his own history and as a social being also in the history of the whole human society to see whether somewhere or in someone the revelation has been already made available in a partial way at least or even in its definitive, unique and unsurpassable realization.[258] We will have to deal further with the question of the 'historical search' in a later section especially in reference to a 'Searching Christology'[259] and in the context of the problem of Jesus' historical uniqueness as understood by the Vedantic anthropology and the Indian Christology.[260]

c. God-Knowing and God-Talk

In the context of God's self-manifestation, the question of our knowledge and language about God is also important. This topic is of great relevance for the Vedantic thinking and consequently also for the Indian Christology especially because of the strict Vedantic distinction between the 'Nirguna Brahman' (God in Himself or God in His transcendence) and the 'Saguna Brahman' (God in relation to us or God in his immanence in the world).[261] Besides, the Indian attitude towards mythology in speaking about God and the idols in representing Him makes this discussion especially interesting. We will also have to refer to the Vedantic discard for Dogmas - an important point that distinguishes Hinduism from Christianity - which are supposed to 'fix' (definire) and to 'clarify' our knowledge of and language about the 'Whither' of human transcendence.

According to Rahner there is an intimate relation between God's revelation of himself to us (economical aspect, i.e. as is seen in the plan and realization of human salvation) and what He is in Himself in His own intrinsic reality (the immanent aspect). This vision is intimately related to Rahner's theology of symbols by which he maintains that 'being is of itself symbolic because it necessarily expresses itself'[262]. We had referred to this point earlier.[263] Being has to express itself necessarily in order to attain its own nature. This is a Hegelian position which Rahner adopts. In God as the Supreme Being there must be necessarily an immanent self-donation, a point which

Rahner insists in his theology of the immanent Trinity. But unlike Hegel who maintains 'that the world is not other than God in an ultimate sense but is contained in him as a necessary moment or stage in his life; since he must go out to himself into his other in order to attain self-consciousness', [264] Rahner refuses to accept such an intrinsic divine necessity 'ad extra' in the sense of a Hegelian dialectical panentheism. But if God, in his freedom, makes a self-utterance outside himself - this is the point important for us now in this discussion - then it has to correspond necessarily to his immanent self-utterance in his eternal fullness. [265] According to the theology of 'symbol' the 'immanent trinity' is the condition of the possibility of the 'economic trinity', which is a continuation of the former. The reason why God can utter Himself 'ad extra' is that he must express Himself 'ad intra'. It is the inner reality of the immanent trinity that is expressed in a finite way through the economic trinity. The immanent trinity is the economic trinity and vice versa! [266] When we translate this trinitarian principle to the question of our knowledge about God, it would mean that the God we know from revelation is the same God as He is in Himself. Otherwise revelation would not be God's self-expression and hence reliable. If the reality of God is revealed in human history as trinity, then he has to be trinity in His internal life; if God espresses Himself to us as Father, Son and the Holy Spirit, then God has to be in reality so. This is what Pannenberg also affirms when he declares, 'if Father, Son and Spirit are distinct but coordinate moments in the accomplishment of God's revelation, then they are so in God's eternal essence as well' [267]. This view of both Rahner and Pannenberg stands in clear contrast to the Vedantic position as is clearly expressed by Dr. Radhakrishnan when he says that we do not know 'what God is in himself but only what he is to us' [268]. The 'Saguna Brahman' does not correspond necessarily to the 'Nirguna Brahman' [270]. The former belongs to the realm of 'Maya', while the latter alone is the reality as Saccidananda! The manifestation of 'Brahma', 'Visnu' and 'Siva' [271] do not reveal us anything about the inner reality of God! These are just anthropomorphic conceptions of the Divine relative to our needs! They are determined by our needs and not by the reality of God as He is in Himself! This is also similar to the opinion of P. Schoonenberg who considers the Son and the Holy Spirit as only modes in God becoming persons only in time, in the economy of salvation! [269] Such a position would strongly devalue the reality of revelation as God's self-manifestation and self-giving and would reduce all God-knowing and God-talk to mere nominalism without a corresponding reality!

It must also be mentioned in this context, as we had already done in the first two parts of our work, [272] that the Hindu God-knowing and God-talk, especially on the popular level, are expressed in the forms of myths and idols. It could very well be said that the Hindu mythology is richer, purer and nobler than most mythologies known to us and that 'even more than in philosophical speculations of the Hindu sages do we find expressed in these ancient and manifold myths the deep religiosity of the Hindu soul'[273]. A positive understanding of myths not merely as false and infantile stories, illusions, fables, fictions, inventions or falsifications, but as perfect, realistic and meaningful anthropological expressions of the primordial experience of man, expressions of profound truths which in those given situations could not be better expressed in any other way, would also make it possible to apply a theology of the symbols applicable to myths: They interpret the reality symbolically. [274] So what is important in demythologization is not a negative approach of elimination, but a positive approach of interpretation in an existential way not dissolving them but freeing them from time con-ditioned clothing! [275] What is true of myths is also true of religious images or the so-called idols. It is difficult to understand why on the one side we develops a 'theology of the sacred image' in Christianity, [276] but on the other hand speak with depreciation on the idols of the so-called pagans! By this, however, we do not underestimate the possibility that both myths and images could be misused considering them as the ultimate - as is the case in idolatry - and thus depriving the transcendent Mystery of its transcendence. Any absolutisation of immanent and finite realities is, for that fact, idolatry!

What is true of myths and idols is also true of religious dogmas, if falsely understood. As Rahner observes, a dogmatic formula that is composed of human concepts does not only make the approach to the divine truth possible, but it can also - if misunderstood - make this approach difficult! [277] Rahner defends, however, the use of precisely formulated statements in God-talk, because 'in no other way is it possible to mark the boundary of error and the misunderstanding of divine truth' [278] . In a certain sense a dogmatic formula is an end, an acquisition and a victory which helps us with clarity, security and facility in instruction, but 'if this victory is to be a true one, the end must also be a beginning' [279]. The historical character of human truths, which God uses as medium in revelation, also shows that 'neither the abandonment of a formula nor its preservation in a petrified form does justice to human understanding' [280]. Faithful to his eschatological approach to reality as such, Pannenberg would give only a provisional value to all God-talk, because the reality is not fixed now but it will be manifested to us only in the eschaton. So all our expressions and languages about God are only provisional anticipation of what we will definitively know at the eschatological self-manifestation of God. [281] We cannot today, Pannenberg contends, even speak of God in terms of the scholastic analogy of being; what we could use is only a Kantian type of analogy of language. [282] Even this analogy should be understood as 'doxology' because the use of analogy and anthropomorphy even in the Bible, so argues Pannenberg, is meant not as a definition of God but is 'rooted in adoration and is in this sense doxological' [283]; they are not attempts to comprehend God in human concepts, but a recognition of His infinity and transcendence. This argument of Pannenberg, we would maintain, could also be applied in the Indian context by giving a doxological interpretation also to myths and idols! We do not challenge Pannenberg's contribution to the doxological character of our language about God, but, it has to be mentioned that his preference for the analogy of language at the cost of the analogy of being - even in the context of his eschatological vision seems not to be justifiable because by that revelation itself falls into nominalism! A proper solution to this question would be neither an 'analogia entis' alone, nor an 'analogia fidei' alone as meant by Karl Barth, nor a Pannenbergan type of doxology based only on the analogy of language, but, as Hans Urs von Balthasar thinks, an analogy of being within an analogy of faith or doxology! [284]

3. The Tragedy of History

Our discussion on the transcendental nature of man and history as the event of the transcendental process would be quite one-sided and unrealistic if we were to omit from our consideration another important aspect, namely, of sin and brokenness in human history. This fact stands also in blatant contrast to the Vedantic claim of the essential divinity of man. An expulsion of finiteness, evil and suffering from the inner reality of man to the illusory

436

realm of 'Maya' would be no convincing solution to this problem.

a.   **The Limitedness of Human Transcendence: The question of Man's Divinity**

We have already referred time and again to the pantheistic character that
is essentially implied in the Vedantic thinking, in one or another of its forms.
The interpretations given to the auphanishadic Mahavakyani, 'Aham Brahmasmi'
(I am Brahman) and 'Tat tvam asi' (That Thou art) by the Vedantins, especially
Sankaracharya, Ramanuja and by the neo-Vedantins in the most recent times
point to this direction. [285] By asserting the essential divinity of man the
Vedantins deny all the need and possibility of a gradual growth for the human
nature, but similar to the ideas of the Platonists and Gnostics they maintain
that what is required is not a 'pilgrimage' of man in history to the Whither
or goal of his transcendence, but rather a recognition and realization of
the divine nature that one already has, through a process of interiorization
or introspection and experience (Anubhava). By insisting on the notion of
creation, the Christian faith contends that God is the origin, ground and
goal of man and this world and that God cannot be ontologically identified
with them. The Creator-creature relation is the free relation of the Absolute
communicating Himself. There is no question of necessity or the relation
of identity. This fact is evidenced by man's experience of contingence and
finitude. As Karl Rahner reasons, 'the true and complete relation of the
Absolute and of what we experience as ourselves and our world and know
to be finite and contingent is not a relation of identity or of necessary connection in which the Absolute unfolds and attains its own plenitude as in the
various forms of pantheism' [286]. The pantheistic view of man is a rejection
of the essential finiteness of the human spirit. Such a view also makes the
revelation of God as His self-giving superfluous, because what is then required,
is not an acceptance of what one is not, but a becoming aware of what
one already is! One of the basic principles of the Christian faith, on the
contrary, is that man even as spirit and transcendent is essentially finite.
As man is finite and contingent, 'Being' does not lie at the disposal of man.
He cannot push himself into the centre of the infinitude of Being. [287] The
fact that man enquires into being shows the transcendence of man; but that
man _must_ enquire, affirms that he is not 'Being'. The human being 'through
his transcendence and in the specifically human mode of this transcendence
is not simply placed before the absolute being of god as semper quiescens,

but before that God who may possibly still undertake free action towards man, and for knowledge of whom there is still room left in man's cognition'[288]. By his transcendence man does not become identical with God in any sense of its interpretations, but he is just 'a standing before the mysterium inperscrutabile whose ways are unfathomable and whose decrees are incalculable'[289].

Pannenberg too considers it necessary to counterbalance the one-sided emphasis often placed upon the active, creative aspect of man's transcendence. The 'lack' and 'dependence' experienced in man's 'question', 'desire' and 'drive' in his world-openness (Weltoffenheit) points, according to Pannenberg, to the recipient - as against the already possessive - character of human transcendence. The unending orientation of man is understandable only as a search for God who is not in his free disposal and control.[290] Even in his transcendence man is essentially finite!

Some of the tragic elements in human history are understandable only in the background of the essential finiteness of human transcendence. The role played by sin, evil, suffering, destruction and brokenness[291] belong to the tragic aspect of human history!

b. The Hard Realities of Sin and Suffering

The Bible sees an immediate relation between sin and suffering.[291]Similarly , the Vedanta sees also an intimate connection - a cause and effect relation- between 'Karma' (free previous actions of man) and his sufferings in this world, as we have already explained in the first part. [292]The theory of Karma puts all blame for the human sufferings on man himself, his 'Avidhya' (existential ignorance), 'Kama' (desire) and the deeds ('Karma') which follow them, and not on Brahman to whose reality man belongs by his very nature. So sin and suffering do not touch the true reality of man, but only his peripheral aspects of existence which belongs to the field of 'Maya'. Eventhough the Christian faith too sees an immediate relation between sin and sufferings, a relation on the model of cause and effect, as implied in the Karma-theory, may not be acceptable. Following St. Paul, St. Augustine, the traditional Church teaching and even Martin Luther we could say that evil is the consequence of sin, but what implied therein is not a 'Karma-theory', but the affirmation that evil and suffering in this world have a theological significance, namely, the fact that sin deserves only suffering and death. Suffering is an indication of the godlessness of man; but that would be only one side of the reality of suffering. Suffering, as the Augustinian concept of evil as 'privatio essendi et boni'[293] shows, can be understood not in its negativity, but only in relation to being and perfection.[294] In contrast to Luther, this positive approach to suffering and evil is seen in Hegel in his consideration of evil as a normal and necessary antithesis in the dialectic process.[295] This positive approach to suffering has become prevalent also in the neo-Vedanta of Dr. Radhakrishnan.[296] Suffering is not necessarily an evil, opine similarly modern theologians like Sertillanges; in certain circumstances it can even be good.[297] Against the opinion of Ch. Journet who holds that suffering is by nature a detestable evil,[298] Jean Galot maintains that suffering belongs to the very nature of man and it contributes to human development.[299] If suffering were intrinsicly an evil, a theology of the suffering of God would be inconceivable.[300] We will have to come back to this point later in reference to the historical destiny of Jesus.[301]

Wolfhart Pannenberg acknowledges the criticism usually levelled against him that, 'the role played by sin, evil, suffering, destruction and brokenness in human history has not received very extensive treatment in my writings'[302]. The fact that Pannenberg has by and large concentrated his attention on the positive structure of human destiny, history and salvation is mainly due to the fact, as he himself explains, that the positive nature of things is to be presupposed in order to describe their perversion. At the same time he asserts that 'a convincing interpretation of the human situation has to take into account also the negative aspects of human experience and behaviour. Otherwise no balanced evaluation of the reality of man would be achieved'[303].

The moral aspect of sin is that which distinguishes it from other sufferings and evils in this world. Although the Upanishads as a whole waters down the moral aspect of sin as offence against a personal God, reducing it to gnostic ignorance, and although in the Vedas sin is identified with ritual error, still it must be mentioned that in the Puranas and especially in the Bhagavadgita the personal, moral character of sin as offence against a personal God, is not absent.[304] According ot the Vedantic thinking what we call 'sin', could be identified with 'Ahamkara' or self-centredness, i.e. putting one's own self (Atman) against the Supreme Self (Pasramatman). A similar approach could be detected also in Pannenberg's explanation of sin as 'Ichhaftigkeit' (self-centredness). 'Ichhaftigkeit' is, according to him, what comes into conflict with man's 'Weltoffenheit', 'Zukunftsoffenheit' and 'Gottoffenheit', in short what conflicts with the transcendental openness of man. It is the self-centredness that closes one to oneself.[305] The 'Ichhaftigkeit' as such need not be a moral evil in so far as it is in harmony with the whole of God's creation; but becomes a sin when man opposes his infinite destiny and falls back into his own narrow confinements.[306]

Karl Rahner also insists that his evolutionary view of the world should not be misunderstood to mean 'that freedom, guilt and possibility of ultimate perdition by final self-willed self-closure to the meaning of the world and of its history have no place' in his theology.[307] Sin is not rendered harmless; it is not just a kind of unavoidable difficulty which is all part of the development, included dialectically from the outset as one of the factors of the evolutionary process. Sin is the closing of oneself against God in freedom. It is the rejection of the self-communication of God addressed to the free history of the human race.[308] Although the whole of creation could participate in suffering as a necessary stage in the process of evolution, still sin as the moral evil can be contracted only by human beings, because 'the essence of sin is an actualization of the transcendental freedom in rejection of God'[309]; it is the closing up of oneself into the absolute, deadly and final loneliness of saying 'no' to God.[310]

The hard realities of sin and sufferings are undeniable in the otherwise positive vision of evolution as the event of transcendence; while the latter is inevitable in this process, the former is directed against the very roots of human transcendence.

c. 'Karma-Samsara' and 'Original Sin'

The theory of 'Karma' in Hinduism teaches that those effects of one's deeds (Karmaphala) from which one is not liberated completely in the given life-span will follow one even after one's death into a re-incarnated life and the cycle of life, death and re-birth continues until one's complete liberation from all Karma elements is achieved. We had sufficiently elaborated this doctrina of 'Karma-Samsara' in our first part. [311] It seems to us that this faith has some important elements in common with the traditional Christian faith in original sin. [312] Both 'Karma-Samsara' and original sin are supposed to explain the apparently hereditary character and the real universality of the phenomenon of evil in this world. Both put the blame for the origin of evil on man himself, and not on the Absolute. An important point of difference consists, however, in the fact that the original sin is not a personal sin for which one is in any way responsible;it is sin only analogically; but, the doctrine of 'Karma-Samsara' affirms that everybody is personally responsible for the miserable situation in which one may find oneself and the responsibility lies of not in this life in one's own previous life! Another point of essential difference is that the faith in the original sin presupposes the solidarity of the whole mankind from the very beginning; Karma-Samsara rules out any such solidarity in human existence; each one is responsible fully and only for one's own past deeds. From the soteriological point of view it may be said that the original sin affirms the radical incapacity of man to attain his transcendental goal all by himself; he needs a divine Saviour! But, Karma-Samsara implies that each one has to work out one's own salvation; each one is his own saviour; even the role of an Avatar is only to give some valuable help especially be means of example! We have indicated a few points of comparison and contrast between the two doctrines; a further elaboration is not the intention of our work. We shall turn our attention to how Rahner and Pannenberg see this problem.

Rahner maintains that man lives and exercises his transcendence and freedom in a situation that is determined by history and other persons. The guilt of others constitute a permanent factor of his situation. The human nature bears the stamp of the guild of others, in one and the same history, in a universal, permanent and ineradicable way, i.e. in a way that is original to the very nature of man, although one is not responsible for this situation.[313] The original sin, Rahner explains, is 'nothing but the historical origin of the present, universal and ineradicable situation of our freedom as co-determined by guilt, and this in so far as this situation has a history in which, because of the universal determination of this history by guilt, God's self-communication in grace comes to man not from 'Adam', not from the beginning of the human race, but from the goal of this history' [314] . It is the historical situation for which - unlike what is held by the theory of Karma-

Samsara - man is not originally responsible! Rahner's idea of situated or co-determined freedom finds its echo also in Pannenberg. Freedom, according to Pannenberg, is 'identity with being oneself' [315]. A sinner is one who is remote from his identity, which he has to realize as the goal of his transcendence. The goal is reached only at the end; that would mean that every one is born as the 'first man' (Adam), not yet in identity with one's destiny. This situation of not being in possession of one's goal or perfection or identity to which one is destined, i.e. the situation of self-alienation and lack of freedom into which one is born, may be called original sin. Only the 'Second man' (the Saviour) can set man free, bring him to the identity of being oneself. So the original sin would teach us - in contrast to the Vedantic position - that we are fully dependent on a divine saviour to reach the destiny of our transcendence! So 'Adam' is not merely the chronologically first man, but every man. The outline of God's image is present in every 'Adam', but we need a 'Second Adam' to carve it out as no man can carve himself into the likeness that is his destiny! [316]

Pannenberg develops further the notion of lack of freedom that is implied in the original sin. It reduces the radius of human transcendence, although the freedom of choice is not radically abrogated. This lack of freedom is not just the result of one's own deeds, but previous to them as the basic or original structure of motivation (Motivationsstruktur) which is the source of the failures in man. [317]

A mere mythological presentation of the doctrine of original sin cannot be imposed upon the modern man. The mythology of Adam, as Pannenberg observes, is the story of every man. [318] It is not just a man at the dawn of history who is responsible for the situation of godlessness, the dynamic incapability of entering into dialogue with God, the basic need to be divinely saved, into which every man is born. A theory of imputation as taught by St. Augustine, the old scholastics and the old protestantism, and the view, which following St. Augustine, holds that original sin is inherited through physical procreation and the concupiscence of sexual delight implied therein, makes a caricature of the original sin. [319] It is impossible to understand that a God who forgives even the personal sins of man can be thought of as 'imputing' the sins of others on him! [320] This is one of the reasons why K.C.

Sen, as we have seen in Part II, [320a] finds the doctrine of original sin unacceptable. The new understanding of the Sacrament of Baptism more as
an incorporation into the Church by grace than as a cancellation of original
sin, as Prof. A. Ganoczy observes, [321] is an example for the necessary corrections that could be undertaken in a critical appropriation of the post-
biblical traditions. This is also important in understanding better the Christian
faith expecially in the context of the salvation of non-Christians, who do
not undergo such a rite that cancels the original sin! In conclusion, it is
interesting to observe that both in Hinduism and in the Judeo-Christian faith
an explanation is sought after - whether in the form of an original fall
or through the doctrine of Karma-Samsara - to explain the existential helplessness in which man finds himself, without, however, attributing the responsibility for this situation to the Supreme Being!

C. The Mystery of Christ as the Mystery of Man

As the heading itself shows, our intention here in this section is to draw
the Christological conclusions from the transcendental approach to the mystery
of man and his history which we have so far evaluated in reference to the
Vedanta, Karl Rahner and Wolfhart Pannenberg. Here we will be paying
special attention to the intimate relation between Anthropology and Christology.

1. 'Transzendentale Christologie'

Here we must keep in mind what we have elaborated in our fourth chapter
which deals with the universal, advaitic Christ-principle. The Vedantins prefer
to speak more of a universal Christ-principle that is present in every man[322]
and the destiny of every man as the realization of the 'Christhood' which
one already possesses, [323] a principle that leads every man to the fullness
of being. [324] This principle of anthropological fulfilment need not necessarily
be called 'Christ-principle' or 'Christhood'; other indications like 'Buddahood'
or 'Krishnahood' are equally possible and valid alternatives, 'Christ' however
being a significant 'Christian' name for this universal anthropological principle! [325]
Dr. Raimundo Panikkar also declares his solidarity with this Vedantic position
in considering 'Christ' as the universal principle that is present everywhere
and in every man and, as he maintains, this universal divine principle is
the 'Isvara'. As this anthropo-theological, universal principle is not often

known and recognized as such - this is the case especially in identifying this universal principle with any particular historical individual - one can speak of the 'unknown Christ of Hinduism' or equally well of the unknown Isvara of Christianity! In the transcendental anthropological approach of the Vedanta in short, there is a strong anti-historical bias. The necessarily historical aspect of the human transcendence - a fact that is very much emphasized by Karl Rahner and Wolfhart Pannenberg - is by and large ignored and the possibility of a unique, unsurpassable and concrete realization of this universal divine principle in human history is discarded as narrow particularism! The universal Christ-principle is so identified with every man that to speak of any historical uniqueness in this case becomes superfluous!

As we have already seen, there are many elements that are common to the Indian and Rahnerian vision of human transcendentality. [326] But Rahner does not accept that the anthropological transcendental possibility in its absolute, unique and unsurpassable way could be realized by every man, as in the case of Jesus of Nazareth. The transcendental approach of Rahner seeks after the possible verification of the Christ-principle in the human history itself, in an absolute and irrepeatable way! It is in this sense that Rahner speaks of a 'transzendentale Christologie', or better said, a transcendentally deduced Christology, because 'transcendence' in this context refers not to the divine 'Logos', but to the basic transcendental nature of man, as orientation to the Mystery of Fullness. So Rahner's transcendental Christology stresses the 'a priori' possibilities in man for the reception of the free self-giving of God, which is the same as the Mystery of Christ! [327]

It is in the background of a universal Christ-experience that Rahner proceeds to speak of a historical Christ-realization. [328] The transcendental Christology is an attempt to counteract any mythological misinterpretation of the divine Incarnation by preparing a conceptual background (Verstehenshintergrund) for this mystery in the very nature of man. [329] The historical fact of Christ is based on the very existential nature of man, as Christ is the definitive realization of this nature. [330] According to Rahner, a preconcept, anticipatory understanding - a 'Vorverständnis' that is similar to the 'Vorgriff' in Rahners epistomology - about the transcendental nature of man is the condition of the possibility (Bedingung der Möglichkeit) to understand the Christ-event.

The idea of Christ (Idee Christ) is gained from the a priori structure of man, from Man's understanding of himself, not as a contingent idea, but as an idea that is necessarily present with man. [331] The task of a transcendental Christology is to show that man expects with an inner transcendental necessity his own ultimate fulfilment in history, a fulfilment which he himself cannot be. [332] So the faith in Christ is not something to be merely added from outside, but he is found in the innermost centre of human existence. [333] A historically contingent event is related to and harmonized with an anthropological transcendental necessity! The transcendental Christology shows that creation, in the centre of which man himself figures, and redemption are in harmony with each other and that they fit each other without any illegal, mythological and ancillary structures. [334] Man is the anticipatory design (Vorentwurf), and not just a passive neutrality, of his supernatural destiny and fulfilment. The 'Idea of Christ' (Idee Christi) is in fact only the 'correlate' of the transcendental structure of man; he is the subjective precondition for the objective realization of the Christ-principle. [335] An understanding of the transcendental orientation of man, man as the reality (Wesen) of 'desiderium naturale in visionem beatificiam', liberate incarnation from mythological conceptions and understands it as the possible realization of the very nature of man through a free act on the part of God. [336] By his transcendental approach, Rahner prepares man to acknowledge the worldly and historical presence of God in Jesus Christ and to accept him as the gratuitous fulfilment of man's own ultimate possibilities. [337] The transcendental Christology is by its very nature directed towards a possible 'absolute bringer of salvation' (absoluter Heilbringer) somewhere in history, [338] which we ourselves cannot be as is evident from our concrete historical and existential experience. This 'absoluter Heilbringer' has to be God himself, his self-giving, in order to be 'absolute' at all, even in the historical realization of man's transcendental nature. The human transcendence makes it possible that the absolute bringer of salvation can really become one with the human reality as its ultimate realization, instead of using it only as an instrument or covering, with all its miraculous or even mythological aspects, without really having anything to do with it. [339] The transcendental Christology understands the mystery of the Incarnation as the ultimate realization of the very human reality in Jesus (Existenzvollzug des Menschen). [340] That would mean that the divinity of Jesus is not just a superaddition to his humanity, but the very realization of the transcendental orientation of the human nature by the ultimate and free self-communication of God Himself.

It is because of this fact that the humanity of Christ is the self-manifestation of God just because of his humanity, and not merely inspite of it! [341] It is, however, evident from the history of God's self-manifestation and from our own experience that there are different grades of self-realization of man through the self-giving of God inspite of the fact that every body is transcendentally oriented. [342] This would mean that the fact of human transcendence does not imply that man is already in possession of his ultimate reality, but it is something yet to be realized and - in contrast to the Vedantic position - it is not merely a matter of becoming aware of what one already is!

Rahner considers the human transcendental experience of love as a particularly appropriate point of departure towards a transcendental Christology. Every act of human love, that is directed to another human being, if it is to be called love at all in the proper sense, has a character of absoluteness. It belongs to the very nature of man to abandon himself completely and commit himself radically (radikales Sichanvertrauen) to another person, to leave one's own closedness to find oneself as person in the communion of another person. One can speak of love only where such a radical self-commitment takes place or is at least attempted. Without that a human being cannot exist as a human person. [343] A human being is not merely an occasion to love God; that would depersonalize and reduce him to the level of an instrument! But, how can our love towards another human person be so absolute if he as a finite and unreliable man cannot legitimate it? The condition of the possibility of such an unreserved love, Rahner maintains, cannot be any human being, but only that man who can legitimately accept such a love, without allowing it to fall into the bottomlessness of another finite creature. This human person who can be object of unreserved love must stay in unity with the whole humanity, besides his absoluteness which justifies his love. So every venture of human love is a confident assertion that there is a human being who can be unreservedly loved. [344] That is a conscious or unconscious declaration of the unity of the love towards God and towards human beings that takes place in the God-Man. [345] With him love cannot become any more disappointed. [346] This reality of the God-Man could be a given fact or a reality of the future. So in every act of unreserved self-commitment of love, that absolute person who alone can legitimate it and make it possible, is affirmed. In this affirmation the one who is implicitly or explicitly accepted is Jesus Christ himself who declared that what is done to the brothren is done to him. [347] such a claim of absolute love can be made only by the one who is in union with God in a unique and radical way as his promise (Selbstzusage) and self-expression (Selbstaussage). [348] So every authentic act of the love of one's neighbour is thematically or unthematically an act of faith in Christ. [349] Rahner dismisses the objection, how a natural act of love could get such a supernatural dimension, with the argument that in the concrete reality there cannot be a moral act of freedom which could be only 'natural'. The dynamism and courage that is implied in one's radical self-commitment to another one is possible only by the power of God's own absolute self-giving, the culmination of which is the mystery of Christ, [350] which is nothing else than the mystery of the God-Man. [351]

The approach to the mystery of Christ from the transcendental character of man's love is only one among many other possible approaches, for example, from the phenomenon of death that does not make life an absurdity and the experience of hope for an absolute future. [352]

Summing up what we have discussed so far about the universal, advaitic Christ-principle in its conceptual encounter with Rahner's transcendental Christology, we could say that like the Vedantins Rahner also maintains that there is in every man a 'Christ-principle', an 'Idee Christi' and that 'Christ' is the fulfilment of man's own ultimate possibilities. But, unlike the Vedantins, Rahner insists that this human realization, if it takes place in history, implies the self-giving of God in an absolute, unique and consequently in an irrepeatable way. Such a historical and unreserved self-giving of God has, of course, no convincing place within the Vedantic anthropology which has the ontological unity of man with God - in whatever way it may be interpreted - as one of its fundamental tenets: 'Aham Brahmasmi.'

2. 'Suchende Christologie'

The transcendental approach in Christology alone does not make the faith in Jesus of Nazareth, as the Christ, very convincing. It is the task of Christology to make clear that the God-Man whom we implicitly or explicitly affirm in the historico-transcendental experience, for eg. of love as we have just seen, is precisely Jesus of Nazareth and no one else. [353] The transcendental Christology does not say that the 'absoluter Heilbringer' in his concrete historical realization can be deduced from a transcendental anthropology. [354] Only the experience of history can tell us that. So the search in history for the absolute bringer of salvation should necessarily follow the transcendental reflection. Hence the importance of a 'searching Christology' (suchende Christologie)! Here we will also have to refer to the element of 'search' that is implied in the 'Avatar' myths of Hinduism, which we had discussed in our first two parts. [355]

a. Anthropological Reduction?

Karl Rahner has been often criticized, even by knowledgeable theologians, for the danger of reducing the mystery of Christ to ready made cosmological anthropological or historical schemes. Hans Urs von Balthasar is one of the prominent critics who see such a danger in Rahner's transcendental Christology. [356] A. Gerken observes that Rahner's Christology is so 'anthropological' that it is not sufficiently 'Christological' (zu wenig christologisch). In avoiding the mythological interpretations of the divine Incarnation, he alleges, Rahner falls into the other problem of presenting Christology as being legitimated by anthropology, i.e., Christ being legitimated by man, instead of the other way round! [357] According to the apprehensions of Pannenberg, a Christology that is based on anthropology could degenerate into a Christology of projection, with the necessary consequence, that as anthropological views change, Christology must also be subjected to change! He maintains that Christological views should be guaranteed not by human existence, but by the history of that one man, Jesus of Nazareth. So, in fact, it is not that anthropology is the foundation of Christology, but Christology should be the foundation of anthropology! That means, it is not anthropology that is the starting point of Christological reflections, but Jesus of History. [358]

It is, however, to be mentioned that what Rahner means by the transcendentally deduced Christology is not an anthropological reduction, although is has to be admitted that such a reduction, that is avoided by Rahner, has been unfortunately realized by other theologians like F. Buri, Sch. Ogden, D. Sölle, P.M. van Buren, H. Braun and others. [359] Rahner does not hold that Jesus as the Christ can be deduced from the transcendental experience. It only means that the existential longing for the absolute bringer of salvation has the possibility of being fulfilled. [360] So it does not mean that the transcendence would lose all meaning if it did not find its fulfilment, and it means 'being immeasurably open with regard to the freedom of the mystery, and being utterly abandoned to the necessity of allowing oneself to be disposed of. We can therefore deduce from the transcendence no exigency of such fulfilment'[361]. Transcendental Christology shall not presume that the absolute bringer of salvation is Jesus of Nazareth because that is something to be derived from historical experience.[362] Rahner protests against all such theological rationalism.[363] The 'Idea of Christ' is a correlative object of the transcendental structure of man and his knowledge, but that 'could never decide the question as to where and in whom this 'Idea' is reality.[364] But a transcendental approach, he contends, is necessary to avoid the historical message concerning Jesus being dismissed by the modern man as a mere piece of mythology.[365]

b. Search in History

As we have mentioned, a 'seeking Christology' is indispensable to avoid an anthropological reduction of the mystery of Christ. Rahner's principle of the historical mediation of the human transcendence[366] - a question we have discussed earlier[367] - has its applications also in Christology. The 'conversio ad historiam' which Rahner stresses in his 'Hörer des Wortes' could function as a Christological foundation.[368]

Corresponding to the unity of transcendentality and historicity in human existence, the hope for a self-communication of God is historically mediated and, therefore, expected also in history.[369] Man, as the one who cannot escape from his history, will inevitably look within the history for the ultimate realization of his transcendence.[370] The transcendental orientation (desiderium naturale in visionem beatificiam), 'since it is that of man who experiences and realizes his deepest essence in history, must find historical manifestation, must await and seek God's promise in this dimension if it is to achieve its valid realization through God's free action'[371]. The personal and absolute saving event and the one who is this salvation, instead of merely being the one who teaches it, as God's irreversible self-giving to mankind must be historical, 'because nothing purely 'transcendental' can be definitive, unless it is already the vision of God or unless it were possible for man's transcendent character to be fulfilled without affecting his history'[372]. So the man who responsibly seeks after his salvation searches in the human history to which he belongs for a man, in whom this event of salvation as the self-giving of God, has been or will be realized and become concretely tangible beyond all merely abstract possibilities.[373]

Rahner sees such an anthropological search for the absolute bringer of salvation beyond all the boundaries of particular religions. Rahner suggests that dogmatic Christology should also pay a little attention to the general history of religions, especially for the doctrine of incarnation in other religions in all its parallels and contrasts. The history of other religions is an unconscious seeking for the Word of God who was to come in human flesh. Our knowledge of the historical incarnation in Jesus of Nazareth gives, according to Rahner, a really illuminating interpretation of the history of religions. That would show the 'seeking' of man as it is in the depth of his concrete nature. It shows man as a being 'who in the course of history looks out for the presence of God himself'[374] . This suggestion of Rahner, as we would evidently agree, has special relevance in the context of the Indian faith in the 'Avatara'. N. Goreh, R.C. Zaehner and V. Chakkarai, as we have indicated, consider the Avatara myths as 'praeparatio evangelica' for the preaching of the real mystery of God's incarnation. According to J. Neuner and Farquahr 'Avataras' are dreams which point to the reality of the Word of God in flesh. These views which we had mentioned in the fifth chapter confirm Rahner's position!

c. 'Fides ex auditu'

We have discussed so far about man's right and duty to look out in history for a concrete encounter with the decisive answer made by God about the question of man's existence, inspite of the theoretical possibility that this answer may not yet be given! This implies an encounter with the claims of various personalities in human history to verify whether these claims are founded and substantiated. Transcendental theology cannot undertake to prove that a particular person - for that matter Jesus of Nazareth - is the absolute bringer of salvation, the Incarnation of the Word of God, that is sought after. This verification cannot come 'a priori', but only from historical experience. Jesus of Nazareth, as the one who has raised absolute claims regarding his person and function[375], deserves to be taken earnestly in his claims at least for the sake of identification and verification.[376] It is not difficult, so opines

Rahner, to find the one whom we are seeking in Jesus of Nazareth as the final and unsurpassable realization and culmination of humanity's encounter with God. Rahner finds no other person in human history other than Jesus, who has made such substantiated claims legitimating us to commit ourselves fully to him in absolute and unreserved trust! The absolute bringer of salvation after whom man seeks in his transcendence is historically verified in Jesus of the Bible.[377]

Karl Rahner, however, is not so naive to think that such a historical verification could solve all the problems of anthropology and Christology! A historical knowledge as such could be interpreted and accepted variously as the history itself shows! What is required is not merely an encounter in knowledge, but an existential encounter with Jesus of Nazareth which leads to absolute trust in him by assimilating and appropriating him into our existence. This is what we mean by 'faith in Jesus as the Christ'. This faith is subsequent to our encounter with the historical reality of Christ, subsequent to our 'hearing' - here the Heideggerian interpretation of 'hearing' as paying attention to being is very relevant[378]- of the claims of Jesus: 'Fides ex auditu'! [378]

Though theoretically speaking transcendental experience could be the starting point of Christology, for all practical purposes, speaking in terms of chronological priority, the transcendental deduction of the 'Idee Christi' is always subsequent reflection on the concrete faith received from historical experience. [379] Christology as such begins with faith in Jesus as the Christ. The task of the transcendental Christology is only to show that man is oriented towards Jesus Christ and that he can find in Christ what he has always been looking for. [380] It leaves man to seek and to understand, while seeking, what he has already found in Jesus of Nazareth through faith.[381] The accomplishment of the human transcendentality is concretly bound up with the historical Christ-event. The transcendental anthropology shows the fact (Daß) of human transcendence, but it is Jesus of Nazareth who shows how (Wie) it is realized.[382] According to Rahner, an aprioristic design of the transcendental Christology is possible only because there is already the 'de facto' faith in Christ, because the mankind has already made the historical experience of the realization of the transcendental idea. The insight into the transcendental possibility can be gained only in the reflection of the experienced Christ-fact. [383] 'Ab esse ad posse valet illatio'! Faith, therefore, has to preceed every theology.

In short, following the transcendental Christological method of Karl Rahner we could say that - to use the words of Walter Kasper [384] - the Christology is not merely the self-transcending anthropology. Christology is the determination of the content of an open anthropology. Using the classical theory of analogy one could say that although there is great similarity (eadem secundum quid), the dissimilarity between anthropology and Christology is still greater (simpliciter diversa)!

In conclusion to our discussion of the 'Searching Christology' (Suchende Christologie) we would observe that there is a radical irreconcilability between the universal, advaitic, transcendental Christology of the Vedantic thinkers including Dr. Raimundo Panikkar - we considered it in the fourth chapter - and the transcendental Christology of Karl Rahner precisely on the point of the necessity of the historical seeking after the possible ultimate realization of the human transcendence in history and its verification in, and only in, Jesus of Nazareth who is the Christ.

3. Christological 'Historiophobia'?

In the second part of our work we had discussed the Vedantic problem of historicity in reference to Christology. [385] Since historical process belongs to the realm of 'Maya' no salvation is realizable in history, but only beyond its enslaving boundaries. The Vedantins even maintain, as we have seen, that unhistoricity is the sign of the perfection of a religion because it 'is not affected by the historicity of any particular man' [386] which could be shaken and shattered. What is important is the universal principle that lies behind particular historical manifestations. As far as Christology is concerned, Vedantins like Radhakrishnan maintain that 'Christ' is not a datum of history but a judgement, after-thought of the timeless spiritual fact represented by Jesus. In order to avoid an unnecessary repetition here we would rather refer back to what we have said in the second and the fourth chapters regarding the Vedantic approach to history and the historicity of Christ. We have detected in the Vedantic position a very strong indifference, or even a certain aversion and fear (Phobos), towards the fact of history. This Christologically morbid and unhealthy fear towards history could be named 'Christological Historiophobia'.

The discussion regarding Jesus of history and Christ of faith in the western theology [386a]could be also traced to a similar fear towards the role of history in human salvation. Martin Kähler, for example, maintains that faith should not depend on scholarly historical investigation. [387] The real Christ is the Christ who is preached! Such an insistence on the Christ of the Kerygma, rather than on the historical Jesus, is evident also in Paul Althaus. Not historical reflection - Althaus thinks - but only faith can show us the revelatory character of Jesus' history. Faith does not deal primarily with what Jesus was, but what he is as he encounters us in the proclamation (Kerygma). [389] This follows the line of thought earlier proposed by D.F. Strauß in which he distinguishes between the Jesus of history and Christ of faith, between the historical 'Kern' and the mythological, as he says, interpretation of it. One projects, Strauß complains, the ideal picture of a man on Jesus, making the religion of Christ to a humanity religion. [390] Such an idea of 'projection' is also hinted by A. Schweitzer when he says that what is given in the Gospels as the historical Jesus in only the reflection of the ideas of each author. [391] In this context Rudolf Bultmann protests against giving legitimation to faith through history. [392] The investigations on the development of Christological titles by Oscar Cullmann and F. Hahn also point to the gradual growth of Christological consciousness through the faith of the community. [393] Since the resurrected Lord is effective in faith, so argues Walter Künneth, the certainty of our faith is not established by historical research but by the immediate experience of the exalted Lord! [393a]

A discard for the historical 'Kern' of the Gospel message can, as observed by W. Pannenberg, reduce Christology to a not indispensable wishful thinking or human projection.[393b]Such a wishful thinking - Joachim Jeremias also refers to its various appearances [393c] - is also not rare in the Indian interpretation of Jesus Christ as an 'Advaitic Yogi', an 'Avatara', the 'Vedantic Sadguru', the 'Bhagvan' etc. as we have indicated in chapters four, five and six. Such dangerous subjectivization of the mystery of Christ has prompted theologians like Herman Diem to change their pure Kerygmatic position admitting the opposite, namely, the necessity of seeking Jesus himself behind the evangelists' testimony as the source of their proclamation. [394] E. Käsemann also thinks in this line when he says that the only way to know whether really Jesus Christ stands behind the word of his Church (faithful) or the Kerygma is only a myth, is the search for the historical Jesus. [395] Gerhard Ebeling also contends that unless the proclamation (Kerygma) of Christ has a strong support in the historical Jesus, this proclamation would be pure myth.[395a] Kerygma being only the product of faith, as Wilhelm Hermann had long before observed, it cannot at the same time justify faith.[395b] Since Christ of the Kerygma and Jesus of the history in isolation are meaningless, a complementation of both is advocated by E. Fuchs.[395c]

In this context Wolfhart Pannenberg strongly affirms that the antithesis between Jesus and the primitive Christian Kerygma about him, i.e. Jesus of history and the Christ of faith, remains unsatisfying from a historical point of view.[396] 'It is possible to go back, beyond the apostolic kerygma, to the historical Jesus', Pannenberg contends, and it is 'not only possible, but also necessary'[397]. The fact that Israel's faith is fundamentally established in a 'theology of history' should be taken as a corrective to the historylessness of the kerygmatic theology.[398] Pannenberg sees the theological depreciation of history as an escape from the historico-critical flood tide into supra-history (Übergeschichte) or to pre-history (Urgeschichte) on the false supposition that historico-critical research as the scientific verification of events does not seem to leave any room for redemptive events![399] In order to make the Christian faith credible[400] the Christian faith must be historically based. The Christian has no escape to a 'safe area' (Sturmfreies Gebiet), so maintains Pannenberg, in front of the historical questions. If we avoid the historico-critical questions from our faith, we denounce the historical event that bases our faith. Faith has nothing to fear before the historical research.[401] The sensational denials will disappear if we investigate objectively the disputed historical questions essential to faith.[402] All theological questions and answers are meaningful only within the framework of the history which God has with humanity, and through humanity with his whole creation.[403] True to his method, Pannenberg rejects all untested claims of intuition and immediate religious experience which try to separate themselves from the historical existence to the realm of subjectivitiy, as we know is the case in the Vedantic position, Personal religious experience, according to him, cannot substitute but only corroborate the confirmation of revelation through history.[404]

Pannenberg's criticism against fleeing into subjective realm in the face of historical criticism is especially understandable when we consider that he sees Revelation as the inherent significance of history.[405] So revelation is acceptable to us not by faith but by means of historical criticism. Historical significance is the revelatory significance. Faith is not an intrinsic moment in the knowledge of revelation. Faith is essentially our trust in God, and this trust of course is based on the knowledge of god's revelation through historical reason. For eg., we know historically, that in the Christ-event which culminates in his resurrection, God has revealed himself proleptically (as an anticipatory reality) as the Divinity who establishes his Lordship (Basileia) over all things in the Eschaton. This historical knowledge is the basis of our faith that we too shall be taken up similarly by resurrection into the realm of God's ultimate Kingdom! [406] So faith is our trust in God's future. Thus he hopes to preserve the extra-subjective foundation of faith. The function of theology is to confirm the historical truth which is presupposed for faith and for this, theology has to use even extra-theological sciences in an interdisciplinary way. [407] Historical study of the bible, rational approach and dialogue with positive sciences - these constitute, according to Pannenberg, the essentials of systematic theology! The Christian theologian, therefore, is a historian whose area of specialization is the Christ event.[408] One can and must get back to Jesus himself from the witness of the apostles and it is quite possible to distinguish 'the figure of Jesus himself, as well as the outlines of his message, from the particular perspective in which it is transmitted'[409]. This knowledge of Jesus leads to faith, and the more exact it is, the more certainly it does so. [410]

It cannot be denied that Pannenberg has restored historical study and historical research to a place of honour in theology. It is indeed relieving to know that, as he maintains, critical study does not only raise problems in systematic theology, but also provides it with answers. [411] At the same time, it cannot also be ignored -- and we join also to this criticism - that the distinction he makes between the knowledge of revelation (notitia) and faith (fiducia)[412] is at least for the first sight very artificial![413] Pannenberg, of course, defends his position by his theory of the 'provisional anticipation' (Vorgriff) which faith-trust (fiducia) does in reference to faith-knowledge (notitia). He declares that 'the process of knowledge in which faith makes sure of its foundation is usually directed and held in progress by faith - by a trust which to some extent anticipates the results of a cognitive process' [414]. In fact it can be that one has first faith-trust - it cannot be denied that faith often has reasons which the reason does not know - and then one searches for the knowledge that is sufficient to base it. So eventhough the moments of 'fiducia' and 'notitia' may be distinguished from one another, they cannot be isolated from each other! If our faith in Jesus as the Christ is not based on 'notitia', this 'faith would be blind gullibility, credulity or even superstition'[415].

It could be remarked without hesitation that Pannenberg's notion of the anticipatory character of faith is substantially the same as what Karl Rahner means by the primacy of faith - our attention could be drawn to the previous section - in his approach to Christology from transcendental anthropology. At the same time it must be mentioned that Rahner also does not accept an escape into the subjectivity of personal experience in front of historical criticism, as done by the Vedantins and their western counterparts, however, on different reasons as we have indicated earlier. Rahner stresses the importance of faith in understanding the Scriptures, because they are documents of faith. But faith cannot create or posit deliberately the historical event which is its basis. So it is the function of fundamental theology to establish the presuppositions of faith in Christ by determining historically the claims of Jesus (as the eschatological prophet, absolute and definitive saviour) and by examining the credibility of his claims (as shown by his miracles and mighty works and finally by his resurrection). It can also finally be mentioned that Rahner's enumeration of those facts which could be taken as historically indisputable as far as Jesus is concerned, is a very significant indication of Rahner's conviction regarding the necessity of going beyond the Christ of kerygmatic faith to the Jesus of history.[416]

Conclusion to Chapter Seven

In our above discussion we tried to come to a dialogue with the Vedantic position that stresses the universal aspect of the Christ-Mystery. We have accepted the Indian emphasis on the transcendental horizon of man without, however, falling into the consequent 'Pantheism' that identifies the 'Whither' of human transcendence with the reality of man himself. The goal of this transcendence or Brahman, we insisted, is not a mere 'Consciousness', nor the 'Brahma-Visnu-Siva' or 'Sat-Cit-Ananada' in the modalistic sense, but a community of persons as Father, Son and the Holy Spirit, whose 'personality' is constituted not by merely being 'Consciousness' itself, but in the mutual relationship of knowledge and love. We have also tried to discuss the positive elements that are contained in the Vedantic notion of 'Maya' comparing it with the act of God's free creation. We also stressed the dynamic aspect of creation, as is mirrored in the Indian mythology representing the cosmic dance of Siva (Nataraja), and the auto-transcendence of the created reality that attains a stage of spiritual transcendence in man which opens him, as the unity of matter and spirit, into the infinite mystery of God, which enables him to be accepted into God's trinitarian fellowship. Here we have also made the necessary distinction between man and the subhuman world, showing the unacceptability of the Vedantic 'Panpsychism' for the Christian faith. In hearing and accepting the possible Word of God addressed to the transcendence of man, we pointed out, man depends on the sensible factors of his knowledge. In this connection we also mentioned the doxological value of the Hindu idols and myths! As we have further tried to show, the history of man's transcendence is marred by the reality of sin which is the self-closure of man to his ultimate destiny. We found also possibilities of dialogue regarding the notion of 'Original Sin' and the implications of the 'Karma-Samsara'. The question of suffering in this world, we have stressed, should not be considered merely in its negative aspects but as necessary steps in the dynamism of progress. In emphasizing the value of the human history we pointed to the need of searching for the possible, ultimate realization of the human transcendence in the human history itself, which could be discovered, under the guidance of faith, in Jesus of Nazareth, opening up the possibility for all men to accept him as the Christ!

The following statement of Karl Rahner could serve as a conclusion to this chapter and could also be very well directed as a criticism against those who reduce Christology in India to a mere anthropo-theandric, universal, advaitic principle at the cost of Christ's historical concreteness: 'Christianity has never been merely a doctrinal system of eternal ideas', he writes, 'pointing on to realities with an eternal validity and prescribing a mere mystical sinking into God which involves a withdrawal from history.' Rahner continues further: 'On the contrary Christianity is the proclamation of a saving history in which the true absolute which is significant for man is the historically concrete.'[417]

CHAPTER VIII

JESUS OF NAZARETH, THE UNIQUE MYSTERY OF HUMAN HISTORY

In the light of the theological views especially of Karl Rahner and Wolfhart Pannenberg, we evaluated in the last chapter the 'Christ-Principle' as is understood in the Indian Christological thinking. There we came to the conclusion that since man is essentially an historical being, the reality of his transcendence seeks after its concrete historical actualization. Here in this chapter we deal more concretely with the 'Christ-Fact', i.e. with that historical fact which according to the Christian faith is the ultimate historical realization of man's transcendence, namely, Jesus of Nazareth, and how he in his historical particularity could be understood as the ultimate meaning of human existence.

A. The 'Jesus is God' - Problematic

In this section it is very important to keep in mind especially the principles we have discussed previously in reference to the 'transcendental' and 'seeking' Christology.[1] Here we try to examine critically how Jesus of Nazareth could be considered in a meaningful way in his uniqueness as the God-Man.

1. Jesus of Nazareth as the Image of Man and as the Image of God

Here we intend to deal with three intimately related points which are immediately derived from the transcendental and seeking Christology: Jesus as the ultimate realization of the human nature, Jesus as the unique event of God's definitive and irrevocable self-communication to man and finally the mystery of the God-Man unity in Jesus.

a. Jesus, the Image of Man

In the fourth and the fifth chapters we had referred to the Vedantic vision of Jesus of Nazareth as an example of the realization of the divine, transcendental possibilities of man. The concept of 'Yoga' as the means to the realization of the innate theandrical possibilities have given ground to call Jesus of Nazareth as an 'Advaitic Yogi', namely, as the one who gradually became aware of his innate divinity, or perhaps in difference to other ordinary men, as the one who from his very birth was already in the state of divine consciousness.[2] Dr. Radhakrishnan, viewing Jesus as an example of man's potential divinity, maintains that man becomes God in Christ.[3] Similar to the view of Akhilananda who considers Jesus as a born mystic[4], Radhakrishnan also speaks of Jesus as a born Avatar (descend) of the Divinity while other ordinary men have to 'ascend' towards the divinity through the progressive realization of the divine consciousness.[5] In the view of other Indian thinkers like K.C. Sen, P.C. Mozoomdar and P. Chenchiah, this progressive realization is not merely a matter of advancing consciousness, but it is conceived more in line with an evolutionary view of the world. For them Jesus is not God himself, but the perfect evolutionary realization of the anthropological reality, the very summit of the creative process, the New Creation.[6] V. Chakkarai even speaks of Jesus as the 'Image of man' as he is the criterion or goal of what humanity is supposed to be.[7] As we have clarified these points sufficiently in the previous chapters, an indication of them would suffice for our present purpose of evaluation.

It is well known that Karl Rahner too supports 'Christology within an evolutionary view of the world'[8] although he does not, unlike the Vedantins, limit the sphere of evolution merely to the level of 'conscientization'. As we have already noted in the previous chapter[9], the evolution that is brought to climax in Jesus of Nazareth is intimately related to the auto-transcendence of the material world and the transcendental nature of man. Chakkarai's idea of Jesus as the 'image of man' is especially clear also in the theology of Rahner when he affirms that the basis and the norm of what man is has appeared in history through Jesus Christ.[10] Rahner adds further that Christ is the unsurpassable climax of history.[11] According to him, Christ is the guarentee and historically tangible demonstration that man's destiny is attained and 'in Christ man's highest dignity and ultimate nature as radical openness to God is manifest'[12]. The 'idea' of the God-Man takes flesh and blood in Jesus of Nazareth and thus he is the best design of the highest possibility of man and in reference to him only we can understand what it means to be 'man' at all.[13] The truth of Christ is the summit and the conclusion of God's work in creation[14], the most sublime event of the realization of what man is[15] and the radical and unique actualization of the ultimate possibilities of the human nature.[16]

A similar view of Jesus Christ as 'the image of man' is found also in Pannenberg especially in his consideration of Jesus' communion with God as the manifestation of what man really is (In-die-Wahrheit-Bringen des Menschseins) [17]. As God's revelation, Pannenberg observes, 'Jesus is at the same time the revelation of the human nature and the destiny of man' [18] and so we can say that the idea of Christ is not merely a projection of the human wish, but the real fulfilment of man's hopes and longings. [19] Pannenberg, however, insists very much also on the difference between us and Jesus Christ. Every one of us is the 'first man' (Adam) and Jesus is the 'second Adam'; the second Adam is not simply a 'living being', but also a 'life-giving spirit', as St. Paul writes (1 Cor 15:45 f). The first man (every man) is earthly and mortal, but the second man (Jesus Christ) is heavenly and immortal. The latter is the perfection of the former and 'the idea that the first man was created in the likeness of God and that this likeness was perfected by Jesus Christ is seen as a bracket enclosing the beginning and the end of (the) road to unity in the history of man and thus avoiding the danger of a gnostic dualism between the first, earthly man and the second, heavenly man' [20].

It must, however, be mentioned that v. Chakkarai's understanding of Jesus Christ as the 'image of man' can be also misunderstood. In common parlance, an image is naturally lesser than the reality. To call Jesus as the image of man could give the impression that man is greater than Jesus Christ, although what is meant by the expression is just the opposite of it! Pannenberg's comparison of the first man and the second man, following St. Paul, contributes to the elimination of this possible misunderstanding. Jesus is the image of God that is meant for man as the ultimate 'model' for the realization of God's image that is, in the language of J.G. Herder, to be carved out of every human being. [21] So Jesus is man's image as the unique and perfect image of God that is manifested by God himself to the mankind. The first man is man only in so far as he is related to the second man in whom God's image in man reaches its perfect realization. Thus the Christology within an evolutionary view of the world ends up not with an ascending process on the side of the auto-transcending creation, but only by the free, unexacted and unsurpassable self-communication of God to the reception of which humanity as such, as the crown of creation in the process of evolution, is destined!

b. Jesus, the Image of God

Jesus is the summit of the natural evolution of spirit from matter, but, for some Indian anti-Vedantic thinkers like R. Mohan Roy, K.C. Sen, P.C. Mozoom-dar, and P. Chenchiah, Jesus is not the Son of God, inspite of all exceptionalities.[22] Such a view could also be found in many of the modern western theologians like A. Hulsbosch.[23] But it is an indispensable component of the Christian faith that Jesus is not only a true man, even the image of man, but he is the true image of God as the Logos, the Word of God, the Son of God become man.[24] It is extremely important for Christology to try to understand the humanity of Jesus Christ without minimalizing his divinity.

The theology of Rahner does not recognize any contra-position between Jesus' humanity and his divinity, because like Duns Scotus,[25] Rahner asserts that creation is for the sake of incarnation and according to Rahner's evolutionary world-view Christ culminates and defines the convergence of spirit and matter. So according to Rahner, the evolutionary process of the cosmos has a twofold dynamic, namely, the self-transcendence of man and the self-giving of God. Creation and Incarnation are not two disparate, adjacent acts of God 'ad extra', but they are 'two moments and phases in the real world of the unique, eventhough internally differentiated, process of God's self-communication and self-expression into what is other than himself'[26]. God 'has creatively brought the world into existence as the recipient of his self-communication in such a way that this self-communication is God's fundamental purpose, but is not something to which the finite creature has a right' and it remains a free grace of God's love.[27] God's supreme self-communication is the communication of His own Logos and this accepted by the creation in Jesus Christ - that is the mystery of Incarnation - means that the world has in principle entered into the realm of God. This is the cosmic 'Omega Point'[27a]- an expression common to both Teilhard de Chardin and K. Rahner - towards which the world moves. So incarnation is not seen as an isolate matter - a mythology, a 'deus ex machina', a God who comes down to this world to put in order what he could not possibly do from above.[27b] - but as the God-given climax of the whole creative process. The history of the cosmic self-transcendence is directed by God towards a subject called man who is capable of accepting a self-bestowal on the part of God and this acceptance of God's unsurpassable self-communication achieves an unsurpassable, and hence unique, historical manifestation in Jesus of Nazareth. The incarnation is 'nothing else than the historical event of that transcendental self-bestowal of God and the acceptance of it in the dimension of human freedom'[28]. It is in this sense that the incarnation is the uniquely highest event of the realization of the human reality.[29] So Rahner comes to the conclusion that the reality of man is not understandable in a static way as the 'zoon logikon' (animal rationale)[30], i.e. in isolation from the mystery of incarnation. Only the mystery of incarnation can manifest to us the nature of man and its ultimate possibilities. Therefore according to Rahner, 'Christology is the self-transcending Anthropology and Anthropology is nothing but a deficient Christology'[31], or in other words 'Christology is at once beginning and end of anthropology, and ... for all eternity such an anthropology is really theo-logy'[32].

c. Jesus, the Mystery of the God-Man

We have seen that, according to Rahner, man is a mystery.[33] Man is a mystery not only because he is open to the mystery of the incomprehensible fullness of God, but 'because God uttered this mystery as his own'[34]. The fact that the self-utterance of God and its acceptance takes place is itself a mystery and that this obviously absolute mystery has taken place precisely in Jesus of Nazareth is also a mystery.[35] Together with the mystery of the Holy Trinity this mystery of the divine Incarnation belongs to the foundation of Christian faith.[36] This mystery tells us that man is the place where God has accepted the world and its history into his own destiny.[37]

Rahner tries to understand the mystery of Jesus as the God-Man with the help of the theology of creation. The concept of creation, as we have previously seen,[38] understood essentially as 'ex nihilo sui et subjecti' tells us that God can constitute something in a state of distinction from himself without denying the radical dependence of all created things on him - as against pantheism and deism. God is immanent in his creation as its transcendent cause and not as a part of its system! Rahner applies this basic truth concerning the creator-creature relationship, radical dependence and distinction, also to the mystery of unity of God-Man in Jesus of Nazareth.[39] Accordingly, Jesus Christ is 'most radically man, and his humanity is the freest and the most independent, not inspite of, but because of its being taken up, by being constituted as the self-utterance of God'[40]. The genuine self-coherence and independence of Christ's humanity, consequently, increases in direct and not in inverse proportion with its radical dependence upon the divinity. The relation between the Logos-Person and his human nature must be conceived in such a way that 'here independence and radical proximity equally reach unique and qualitatively incommensurable perfection' and this perfection in the God-Man is the perfection of a relation between Creator and creature.[41] This understanding evidently goes beyond the traditional 'Two-natures-one-Person' formula, without, however, contradicting it in any way. Here the truth that is involved in the mystery of the God-Man is that the history of Jesus of Nazareth, 'by the very fact of being God's own pure and radical revelation, is the most living of all, the most free before God from the world towards God, and thus mediatorial, because it is the history of God himself and because it is supremely creaturely and free' [42]. Here the Christ-mystery is seen not as an after-thought of God, but in a perspective in which it appears as peak and conclusion, as the mysterious goal of God's plans and activity for his creation from all eternity.   Here Jesus Christ is seen as 'the first-born of all creation' (Col 1:15) and as the point of the cosmos where God's rule (Basileia) is established over every thing because 'Christ is all, and in all' (Col 3:11). It is evident that such a cosmic and historical understanding in God-Man relationship cannot be derived from the mythology of the 'Avatars'[43] as is developed in Hinduism! It must, however, also be mentioned that, as we had indicated in the fifth chapter, the approach of Brahmabandab Upadhyaya to the Vedantic doctrine of 'Maya' is a valid way of explaining in Indian theological categories the Creator-creature relationship, the reality of matter and the dignity of the human body,[44] eventhough Brahmabandhab does not come to an interpretation of the mystery of Jesus Christ as the God-Man in terms of Creator-creature relationship.

As far as the Vedantic thinking is concerned, it must further be added here, that kind of an unsurpassble and free self-communication of God to his creation which we have just discussed does not make any sense because every human being is in reality already divine which makes a further self-communication of God superfluous. The cyclic vision of history according to the law of endless repetition (Samsara) does not also logically recognize any final and unique concentration and climax of the process of transcendence in any particular historical event. It is evident that an Indian theology, that could be called Christian at all, cannot dispense with both of these aspects - i.e. God's self-communication and the uniqueness of Christ - in Christology. The question of Jesus' uniqueness in the Indian conceptual context will have to be discussed further later on. [45] Now we turn our attention to the question regarding theological expression of the truth of the God-Man unity in Jesus of Nazareth, namely, the Christological formula of the 'Hypostatic union'.

2. The Christological Formula of Chalcedon and the Indian Problematic

The ecumenical council of Chalcedon (451) teaches,[46] in conclusion to centuries of Christological controversies, that the man Jesus did not have the ground of existence in himself in so far as he is a man, but in the person of the 'Logos' (en-hypostasis). Jesus Christ is one and the same in two natures ('en duo physeon' and not 'ek duo physesin' as seen in some early less critical Greek editions [47]). Jesus has a true human nature and a true divine nature. His human nature is ontologically so dependent on the 'Logos' that it has no human subsistence or human person. The human nature is 'personalized' in a pre-eminent way by the person of the 'Logos', i.e. the human nature of Jesus subsists in the second person of the Holy Trinity. In the light of the past controversies and toward of further heresies, the Council Fathers defined the unity of the two natures in one person - generally known in theology as the 'Hypostatic Union' - as unmixed (asynchytōs), unchanged (atreptos), indivisible (adiairetōs) and inseparable (achōristōs). [48] A Christology that is based on the Greek philosophical categories and frame of thinking that form the back-ground of the Chalcedonian definition, and which with necessary consequence tries to investigate, deepen and explain it within the same categories is called a 'Chalcedonian Christology'. The Chalcedonial Christology should by no means be devalued as a hellenization of faith because the Greek categories are used. Using the Greek categories themselves, what the Council Fathers intended, was actually a de-hellenization of faith; the concept of the two separate natures in one person is quite foreign to the Greek thinking and that is a modifying contribution to the hellenistic way of thinking, a contribution that is derived exclusively from the faith in Jesus of Nazareth as the Son of God!

In reference to the Indian problematic, however, it has to be mentioned that even the awareness about the dehellenizing function of the Chalcedon Christology does not make it easy to explain the Chalcedonian Christology in a meaningful way and with the expected clarity in the Indian Vedantic context. The problems which the Chalcedonian formula tries to solve are those which are peculiar to the Greek categories of thinking at least in its expression. It is true, thought is universal, but its expressing categories are different. The questions and solutions that are peculiar to a particular philosophy or category of thinking are not adequately translatable to another philosophical category with other presuppositions and consequently with other problems. Does the faith in Jesus as the Son of God demand from other peoples with their own proud philosophical traditions also an acceptance, at the cost of their own God-given heritage, of the Greek categories in the expression of their Christian faith? The answer is evidently 'No' and the consequence is the possibility of non-Chalcedonian Christologies, without being anti-Chalcedonian.

If one has to remain true to the Vedantic categories of thinking which we have elaborated in the first part of our works as the necessary anthropologico-theological context for the Indian Christology, it has to be remembered once again that adequate equivalents for 'person' and 'nature' are simply not available in the Vedanta because they are irrelevant and meaningless for the Vedantic anthropology. Dr. Joseph Neuner, as we have seen, has sufficiently clarified this point.[49] If one wants to introduce these categories by all means into the Indian thinking, as De Smet does,[50] then the result is a Sanskrit translation of a scholastic theology which cannot claim to be Indian in its proper sense. 'Tadatmya' in the 'Brahmanya Purusha', for example, does not say to a Vedantin what the 'Hypostatic Union' is supposed to explain to a Scholastic.

We had also mentioned in the fifth chapter the various attempts by Indian theologians to explain Jesus' union with God. K.C. Sen in line with the mono-theistic thinking of Raja Rammohan Roy rejects any ontological union between Jesus and God; he admits only a mystical union.[51] Vengel Chakkarai sees Jesus as the 'manifestation of God' and identifies his person with that of God the Father.[52] The theology of 'New Creation' according to P. Chenchiah comes to the conclusion that Jesus is neither man nor God in the purest sense, but a creation, something new, between God and man, a mixture of the human and the divine![53] P.C. Mozoomdar and J. Appasamy attribute a divine humanity to Jesus, but like Sen they also maintain that Jesus is not

God.[54] It is unfortunately evident that these positions, though non-chalcedonian, are not much different from the Christological heresies of the first centuries. Brahmabandhab Upadhyaya's interpretation of the God-Man unity in Jesus Christ, using the Vedantic categories of the five sheath anthropological system,[55] sounds original and looks properly Indian, but unfortunately it betrays a static ontology he had inherited from scholastic philosophy. This defect in the vision of Upadhyaya, we think, is corrected by R. Antoine, as we have seen,[56] by introducing an aspect of progressive growth into the five-sheath (Kosa) concept. His approach, we would maintain, is Indian as well as orthodox and it has also an element of originality.

The anthropo-christological works of Karl Rahner and Wolfhart Pannenberg also show that a non-Chalcedonian approach to Christology - in contrast to the anti-Chalcedonian positions of some modern theologians[57] - is required not only in the Indian context, but anywhere. A Chalcedonian Christology that is based on Greek static ontology could be misunderstood as mythology or even could be falsely understood leading to cryptogamous heresies[58] in the popular faith, inspite of the professed orthodoxy!

Karl Rahner is of the opinion that the Chalcedonian formula is valid and binding even today because Christianity has confessed it for almost two millenia and lived according to it.[59] Still he does not consider it, as Jean Galot and other opponents of a non-Chalcedonian Christology do, as an inalienable foundation of all Christological researches.[60] Inspite of the fact that the classical Christology is still understandable sufficiently, it is legitimate to codify the faith today in a way and language that is _more_ understandable and _more_ appropriate to the modern man _than_ the Chalcedonian faith-formulation.[61] The most urgent task of Christology today, so argues Rahner, is to formulate the Christological faith in such a way that what is understood by this formula could be better understood avoiding all the possibilities of mythological interpretations,[62] which is the case in many of the Christian heresies from Apollinarism to Monothelitism which still live on in the picture which many Christians who confess the Chalcedon faith-formula have of the 'Incarnation'.[63] A mythological presentation of the Christian faith is the reason for the fact that many an average non-Christian - here special mention could be made of the modern Hindu reformers like Raja Rammohan Roy and Keshub Chunder Sen - 'feels called upon to protest in his unbelief, refusing to admit that God has become man 'like this' and thus believing that he must reject the Christian doctrine of the Incarnation as a myth[64].

According to Rahner, the Chalcedon formula is a legitimate end of a long Christological controversy and 'we shall never cease to return to this formula because whenever it is necessary to say briefly what it is that we encounter in the ineffable truth which is our salvation, we shall always have recourse to the modest, sober clarity of the Chalcedonian formula'[65], but in order to make it meaningful it is not sufficient to repeat it. It is not only our end, but also our beginning and the point of departure for new creative thinking,[66] which is not meant to reject or replace the Chalcedon formula, but to supplement it through other formulations which perhaps are better understandable for the modern man.[67] Rahner proposes to use in such new formulations existential categories rather than the ontic substantial concepts. It is with this intention that Rahner developes a Christology based on transcendental anthropology.[68] The 'Hypostatic Union' expressed in existential terms would say that Jesus Christ is the man who receives the 'human essence from God in such absolute purity and integrity and so actualizes this relationship with God that he becomes God's self-expression and once-for-all pledge of himself to the world he calls into existence'[69]. That would make the Incarnation neither a myth nor a fairy-tale, but shows it as the unique occasion which saw the radical achievement, by the free decision of God, of the ultimate possibility of man's existence.

Such an understanding of the 'Unio hypostatica' based on the transcendental understanding of man would not only affirm the uniqueness of Jesus Christ in difference to all other human beings, but would also bring to light what the other mortals have in common with him. Then Christ's uniqueness - we will have to tackle the question of uniqueness later on - will be understood not as an exclusive uniqueness, a stumbling block for the Vedantic mind, but as an all-inclusive uniqueness which is the ultimate realization of the transcendental orientation of the entire humanity. 'What' Jesus is, is the same in him and in us, the human nature, although there is between us and him an unbridgeable difference in his 'Who' as the self-expression of God.[70] According to the transcendental and evolutionary view of Karl Rahner, the God-Man unity as is realized in Jesus of Nazareth exists as a real possibility for all human beings. Everybody has the 'potentia oboedientialis' for the hypostatic union. [71] So Jesus' hypostatic union should not be considered as something that distinguishes him from us, 'but rather as something which must happen once, and only once, at the point where the world begins to enter into its final phase in which it is to realize its final concentration, its final climax and its radical nearness to the absolute mystery called God'[72]. The hypostatic union is the absolute guarentee that the ultimate and unsurpassable self-transcendence will succeed and that it has already begun. As far as the humanity of Jesus is concerned, Rahner maintains, it does not realize anything more than what 'theology prescribes for all men as their goal and consummation, viz. the direct vision of God enjoyed by Christ's created human soul'[73]. Grace and glory as the direct self-communication of God belong to all men and the hypostatic union is a peculiar moment in the process of the granting of grace which cannot be conceived without the Hypostatic Union taking place on account of it.[74] The Incarnation (Hypostatic Union) occured for the sake of our salvation; 'it does not give any real increase in reality and life to the divine nature of the Logos'[75]. Besides, 'the prerogatives which accrued interiorly to the human reality of Jesus on account of the Hypostatic Union are of the same essential kind as those intended by grace also for other spiritual subjects'[76]. The Hypostatic Union of the humanity of Christ with the Logos necessarily results in the intrinsic divinization of this human nature, although this divinization is distinct from the union itself. This intrinsic divinization of humanity is exactly that which is to be bestowed on every human being as grace of justification.[77] So the unique event of the Hypostatic Union is 'an intrinsic factor of the whole process of the bestowal of grace on the spiritual creature in general' as its irrevocable consummation.[78] Rahner clarifies further that 'the Hypostatic Union does not differ from our grace by what is pledged in it, for this is grace in both cases (even in the case of Jesus). But it differs from our grace by the fact that Jesus is our pledge, and we ourselves are not the pledge but the recipients of God's pledge to us'[79]. The fact that we receive grace does not say that it is possible even without a hypostatic union which in fact does not take place in us. The fact that we have grace in divine self-communication is made possible and effected precisely by God's unsurpassable self-giving and its definitive acceptance as are realized in the Hypostatic Union. Grace and Hypostatic union can be thought of only together. What has taken place in Jesus of Nazareth is meant for all human beings as the condition of the possibility of their participation in the divine life, i.e. grace.[80]

Rahner's existential approach to the understanding of the God-Man union (Hypostatic Union) in Jesus of Nazareth, brings to light more clearly the solidarity that exists between him and the whole mankind.

Wolfhart Pannenberg's approach to the Christological formula of Chalcedon is also similar to that of Karl Rahner, although there is difference in the content of the solutions they propose. Pannenberg also maintains that 'when a conciliar formula becomes liable to misunderstanding, unintelligible or inadequate to a new necessity, the demand for a new approach to the doctrine of faith must prevail' [81]. On the basis of Pannenberg's theology of revelation, he speaks of the 'Revelatory Unity' as a possible alternative to explain the God-Man unity in Jesus Christ.[82] That would mean that the self-manifestation of God as the power over every thing, i.e. the realization of the Kingdom of God, His Lordship (Basileia) is realized in Jesus Christ, a realization which in a definitive way, although proleptically (in anticipation as far as the whole creation is concerned) comes to its culmination in Jesus' resurrection - a point which we reserve for a later discussion. [83] If revelation is in a strict sense, as we have already seen, the revelation of God's own self, the medium of revelation cannot finally be distinguished or separated from God himself. We can speak of a self-revelation only if the revealer and the content of the revelation are identical. Jesus as the medium through which God reveals himself cannot be something alien to him; otherwise this revelation would not be unsurpassable. The distinction between God and his revealing medium, Jesus Christ, disappears. Jesus of Nazareth as the self-revelation of God belongs to the essence of God. This creaturely medium of revelation is raised up in his distinction from God and is received into the unity with God himself. [83a] Jesus of Nazareth is truly man and truly God!

In reference to the 'Person' of Jesus Christ, Pannenberg has the same approach which he uses in his explanation of the mystery of the three persons in the Holy Trinity. We have discussed this point earlier.[84] It is an approach based on 'I - Thou' relationship and is similar to the view of Friedrich Gogarten, according to whom, Jesus existed entirely from God's 'Thou'. It is the 'Thou' that makes the 'I' a person. Man's being as person is fully realized in Jesus of Nazareth. Jesus is the Son of God precisely in his humanity as the realization of his human personality entirely from the 'Thou' of God. By being fully human, in virtue of the absoluteness of his relation to God, Christ's

person is divine! [85] Similarly Pannenberg too maintains that the ego or 'I'
of Jesus comes not from himself, but from beyond himself, from a Thou;
it is the divine Thou that constitutes the 'I' of Jesus as a person and Jesus
received his destiny - unlike we do - unconditionally from the 'Thou' of his
Father, who established in Jesus His Lordship over all things in a definitive
but anticipatory way. The future of the Father is the destiny of Jesus. God
can become present to the I through the human Thou and constitute that I
as a person - as in the case of Jesus - only where the human Thou is distinguished from God and, by his being there, points to that God who is different
from him.   By his absolute trust in God's future, the complete likeness of
God appeared in Jesus Christ in the unity of God and man. [86] Jesus, therefore,
is a concrete human person with the speciality that through his special relation
to the Father he is the eternal Son. In other words, Jesus as man is not
evidently the Son of God from all eternity, but he gets his identity as Son
of God through his special relation to God. The fact that this identity is
the person (Personsein) of the eternal Son, is the unique mystery of his individuality. [87] Jesus' divinity is not a second 'substance' in addition to his humanity
which results in a synthesis, an absorption or in a third thing. Jesus is the
Son of God precisely in his particular humanity. The uniqueness of Jesus'
humanity in his path of dedication to the Father has established the confession
of Jesus as the Son of God. [88] Only his personal community, I-Thou relation
with the Father, demonstrates that Jesus is the Son of God. [89]

It cannot, however, be denied that this explanation of Pannenberg regarding
the God-Man unity in Jesus of Nazareth is not only non-Chalcedonian, but
at least for the first sight it also looks like adoptionism! But that is not
what is intended by him. Unlike the Chalcedon, Pannenberg does not make
the difference of the two natures as the starting point of his Christological
investigations, but the unity of Jesus' person as man. This one and the same
person, the man Jesus of Nazareth, can be described from different points
of view as divine and human. The unity of the concrete person is given in
Jesus of Nazareth and true divinity and true humanity are to be said about
this one person. He is God and he is man! In this context it must be mentioned
that it would be wrong to identify this concept of 'person' with that which
is presupposed in the Chalcedonian formula. So it would be completely wrong
to criticize Pannenberg's categories from the point of view of the categories
which are different from his. The criterion of judgement here should be

adapted to the pattern of thought in question. The time of conceptual monopoly is gone! It may be required that an ontico-static understanding of 'person' should, according to today's needs, make room for a more dynamic and existential vision with the possibility of a different interpretation of the Christian faith!

As far as the Indian Christology is concerned, we would maintain, that the Chalcedonian Christology will have to be accepted as valid and binding within its own categories, as is advocated by Karl Rahner. But that should not forbid us to re-think the Christian faith in the Vedantic categories which are more appropriate to the Indian context. The starting point for such a creative re-thinking should not be any particular philosophical system that is foreign to the Indian mind, but the Holy Bible itself that is understood through the proper exegesis based on the modern and proved methods of investigation. That is necessary to avoid the prolific subjective interpretations for which the Indian mind is second to none. The Holy Gospel according to St. John will have great relevance in the development of an Indian Christology, which true to the Vedantic traditions should not be an ontolocial one, but one that is based on consciousness. The Vedantins have traditionally given great importance to the Johannine texts which show Jesus' consciousness of his identity with God. We had discussed this point sufficiently in the fifth chapter. In adopting a 'Consciousness-Christology', however, great attention is to be given to a certain 'de-hinduisation' of the Vedantic concepts with a consequent and necessasry 'Christianisation' of the same, similar to what was done by the Council of Chalcedon in adopting the Greek categories into the Christian faith. That implies inevitable modifications. For example, the concept of 'person' must be developed in the Indian context in terms of relationship, as we have mentioned in Chapter VII.A.2.c., and not merely as consciousness. Another example for such a modification would be to distinguish the consciousness of Jesus' divine identity from the consciousness of all Christians who also have participation in the divine life, and consequently are truly Sons of God! An excellent contribution to the notion of 'the divine sonship of Christians in the Johannine writings' has been already made by Dr. Matthew Vellanickal.[90] Although this work has not an explicit Indian contextual concern, its findings could be considered as a point of departure for further Indian Christological developments. The divinization of the human reality - as is stressed by Karl Rahner's view of the Hypostatic union - as a destiny which we will have to share with Jesus, is also an important point that is to be stressed in the context of the Vedantic devaluation of body and the material reality. The Vedantic 'historiophobia' must also be counteracted as we have suggested in the last chapter. The solidarity of all humanity in the salvific process is also a point that is to be stressed in front of the Vedantic spiritual individualism with all its consequences on the social structure. It is the task of the Indian Christology to make clear that the true and definitive 'Advaita' (non-duality) of the whole cosmic reality with the Creator has realized proleptically but unsurpassably in the Christ-event!

3. Can God 'become'?

The answer to this question, according to the Vedantic thinking, is a categorial 'No'. God, the absolute Brahman cannot become. We had discussed the question of the immutability of 'Brahman' sufficiently in the first part. [91] The 'becoming' that appears in the 'Saguna Brahman' in reference to the 'Trimurthy' and especially in connection with the theory of 'Avatars' is not a 'becoming' in the reality of God, but it belongs to the realm of 'Maya', cosmic illusion. The docetic understanding of 'Avatar' that is based on a dualistic anthropology makes any 'becoming' on the part of God superfluous. [92] In this context, the question of God's becoming that is implied in the mystery of the Incarnation is quite relevant for our evaluative discussion. We will also have to deal here with the problematic of traditional Christological faith in the virgin birth (ante partum, in partu!) and the nature of Jesus' divine consciousness in connection with the Vedantic denial of any 'becoming' in God.

a. 'Pre-Existence' or 'Mission'?

The question of a 'becoming' in the mystery of Incarnation involves also the question of the 'pre-existence' of that which becomes prior to its becoming. Some Indian theologians like K.C. Sen and J. Appasamy find no problem in accepting 'becoming' and 'pre-existence' in the Incarnation because they deny the reality of Incarnation to the very reality of God! The 'CIT' that incarnates, according to Sen, is not identical with God, but only the 'Idea' that pre-existed with God and was fully realized in Jesus Christ. [93] So Jesus is the Son of God, not in his identity with God but in the perfect surrender of his will to the will of God. [94] Appasamy also maintain that what incarnates is the 'Logos' or 'Cit' of God which is really inferior to God.[95] The incarnation of this pre-existent 'Logos', therefore, is not a becoming in God!

Such a subordinationism is certainly not in accord with the Christian faith. But the interpretation of Upadhyaya in this context is quite orthodox. He places the mystery of the 'Logos', whom he calls also 'Cit', 'Vac', 'Om' and 'Prajnana', in a trinitarian context, in perfect equality with the other persons, and explains Jesus as the true incarnation of this 'Vac' (Word) of God.[96] His explanation however is not much different from that of the Scholastics.

The 'becoming' in God that is involved in the theology of Incarnation is also an important theme in Karl Rahner's Christology. According to Rahner, if somebody says: 'I cannot really believe that a man is God and that God has become a man', that does not necessarily mean a rejection of the basic Christian dogma; it could be a rejection of the particular interpretation that is given to the copula 'is' and to the verb 'become' which are contained in this statement.[97] Unlike in a universal affirmative proposition the 'is' in this proposition of faith, 'Jesus in God', is, as we have mentioned in the previous section, necessarily characterized by the qualifications of 'adiairetos', 'achoristos', 'asygchytos' and 'atreptos' (indivisible, inseparable, unmixed and unchanged). These characteristics are important also in understanding the question of 'becoming' that is involved in the incarnation. God became man! If there cannot be anything that God is not, then how can God 'become'? The traditional answer to this question is that 'the change and transition takes place in the created reality which is assumed' and not in the eternal immutable 'Logos'.[98] Rahner is not satisfied with this solution and he affirms that 'it still remains true that the Logos became man, that the changing history of this human reality is his own history: our time became the time of the eternal'[99]. Our concept of the immutability of God should not distort the fact that 'what happened to Jesus on earth is precisely the history of the Word of God himself, and a process which he underwent'[100]. So God can 'become', Rahner affirms, and he can be subject to change in something else. But this 'changing in another' should not be reduced to a changement of the other; i.e. as something that takes place in the region of the creature alone! As God can be at the same time unity and trinity without prejudicing each other, in the same way in spite of his immutability he can truly become something. This anylogy of the mystery of the Holy Trinity and that of the divine Incarnation would avoid a mere Hegelian interpretation of this becoming, although it is to be admitted that Hegel is an inspiration to think in a positive way about the 'becoming' in God! The possibility of 'becoming' in God, Rahner continues, is not a sign of deficiency as the Vedantins would argue. It is the height of his perfection because God would be less if in addition to his immutability and infinity, he could not become less than what he always is! [101]

According to the classical post-Augustinian tradition, any one of the persons of the Holy Trinity could become man in principle, and only the Revelation can show us that it is the Logos, the Word of God, that became man. This position is quite unacceptable according to Rahner's theory of the identity between the economical trinity and the immanent trinity. [102] The establishment of something different from the inner necessary reality of God is the work of God without the distinction of persons as is in the case of creation. Even in the case of creation, we could argue with Bernhard Philberth basing on the structure of the microcosmos, macrocosmos, the cosmic history, the theories of relativity and quantumphysics, [103] it is a fact that cannot be denied that the whole world contains an analogy, reflection and likeness of the Trinity of God. Although Rahner does not take into account these findings of the modern physics regarding the 'tri-une' structure of the cosmic reality, we can say that these findings corroborate his theory that the economical trinity is the immanent trinity and vice versa. The trinitarian reflection becomes especially evident in human sexuality and partnership. [104]

If there is a 'trinitarian reflection' in the order of creation, it must be 'a fortiori' valid in the order of salvation, i.e. God's self-communication to his creation that is realized in man. God expresses his own Self in the divine Incarnation, unlike in the creation which is the establishment of something different from God (ex nihilo sui et subjecti). If God expresses his very own Self, his own Image, his own Word into the emptiness of what is not God, then this expression has necessarily to be the 'ad extra' expression of the immanent Word, the Logos, and not something arbitrary! [105] So only the Logos can incarnate, not the Trinity, nor the Father, nor the Holy Spirit; 'it must be the Logos, who is the personal fidelity of self-utterance displaying itself historically, who reveals the Father in the flesh and in doing so reveals the propriety of the Logos himself' [106]. The immanent self-utterance of God in his eternal fullness is necessarily the condition of the possibility of the self-utterance of God 'ad extra' and the latter continues the former. When God utters himself - again we distinguish this utterance from the creation which is not God himself - then this expression speaks out his immanent Word and not something which could be true of another divine person! [107] This theology stands evidently in contrast to the concept of the 'Avatar', according to which it is the 'Visnu', [108]who is just a 'mode' in the appearance of Brahman, who mascarades in an illusory body. This implies neither a true Trinity nor a true Incarnation!

The faith in the 'becoming' or Incarnation of the Logos is necessarily followed by the question of the pre-existence. The basis for the Christological faith in the pre-existence is the judeo-hellenistic speculation about the personified and pre-existent Wisdom. It is quite logical, Rahner maintains, that if Jesus Christ is the self-expression and the self-giving of God, then he who is giving himself or expressing himself, i.e. God, has to be pre-existent. [109] The 'Son' to which Jesus refers in reference to himself is pre-existent in so far this 'Son' is identical with the God who expresses himself in time. [110] This faith in pre-existence also safeguards very well the uniqueness of Jesus as the Son of God. But, it cannot be ignored that 'pre-existence' is a concept in the temporal realm, a concept which cannot be applied to the realm of God. The 'pre-existence' can also be easily misunderstood making out of the mystery of the Divine Incarnation a 'mythery' in the docetic line. Rahner proposes the term 'mission' - and we also find it right - as a better substitute for 'pre-existence'. The Son's mission would not mean that the one who was to be sent existed as such before he was sent! [111] This also could allay the fears of theologicans like Pannenberg for a mythological interpretation of pre-existence [111a] and for a revival of the 'Logos-Christology' like that of the apologets in the patristic period, who maintained that the 'Logos',[112] the divine plan of being, shared by every man appeared fully for the first time in the history of Jesus Christ, thus making Jesus the first fully rational being and thus the first full man. [113] The use of 'mission' instead of 'pre-existence', we think, would understand the Logos not as the original divine idea regarding the static world order (urbildliches Weltgesetz) but as a personal address of God to man in the 'I-Thou' categories as suggested by Pannenberg [114] in line with Emil Brunner, F. Ebner and Martin Buber. In conclusion we would also observe that the expression 'mission' would be better suited for a Indian Christology too, because that helps the Indian Christology to differentiate and distance itself from the 'pre-existence' that is postulated by the Vedanta for all living beings according to formidable law of Karma-Samsara!

b. Incarnation and the Virgin Birth: 'Hieros gamos'?

The 'becoming' of the pre-existent Logos, the Incarnation of the Second Person of the Holy Trinity, leads to the notion of the 'virgin birth' apparently as a necessary consequence. In the Indian theory of 'Avatara', however, there is no much relevance for a virgin birth as is understood in the Christian tradition. The body that is assumed by Visnu does not enter the realm of the reality of God. It belongs to the world of appearances.[115] This approach is similar to that of the Gnostics, Docetists and the Ebionits who also denied any concept of a virgin birth in the early centuries of Christianity. [116] A general disdain for the bodily in relation to the divine is the reason why even a 'virginal conception' cannot make it fit to enter the divine realm. Still as Joseph Neuner observes, there are certain factors in the concept of 'Avatar' which are comparable to what the virginal conception is supposed to express in the Christian faith, namely, the free initiative of God in the incarnation, God's transcendence and the freedom of the 'Avatar' from the enslaving and binding law of Karma-Samsara. [117] Still the differences between the concepts of Incarnation and Avatar are so great that theologians like K.C. Sen, Brahmabadhab Upadhyaya, P. Chenchiah and R. Panikkar are of the opinion that 'Avatar' as an alternative expression for 'Incarnation' is not acceptable.[118] But it is surprising to note that among the Indian theologians of the past, as we have indicated in the fifth chapter, there is wide acceptance for the idea of Jesus' virginal conception. Inspite of all his aversion to mythologies, Rammohan Roy maintains that the Spirit overshadowed Mary and thus Jesus was born without a human father. [119] A similar view is also held by Chenchiah. Upadhyaya considers the virginal conception of Jesus as one of the essentials of Christian faith. [120] It could even be doubted whether this view is not very much influenced by a strong depreciation of human sexuality at least in an unconscious level rather than by any serious Christological concern!

We do not intend here to make an elaborate discussion of the question of Jesus' virgin birth with all its traditional implications of 'ante partum', 'in partu' and 'post partum'. Attention, however, could be drawn to a previous work of ours in this line.[121] Here our intention is only to examine very briefly how important the virginal conception of Jesus should be considered for an Indian Christology. The views of K. Rahner and W. Pannenberg are of great help in this regard.

The Christian faith in the Virgin Birth, according to Pannenberg, originated probably in the hellenistic and jewish circles as an historical expression for the divinity of Jesus, who could not be considered inferior to Samson, Jeremiah, and the Servant of God in whose birth there was a special divine intervention.[122] The prophecy of Isaiah 7:14 in its Septuagint translation 'parthenos' (virgin) for the Hebrew 'álmāh' (young girl) is taken as normative in the infancy narrative according to Matthew (1:23) which affirms the virgin birth. The spurious historical character of the infancy narrative according to Luke cannot be ignored in this context.[123] John 1:13 speaks of the virgin birth of all Christians because they are born of God.[124] Besides these, there is a very conspicuous silence in the New Testament regarding the question of the virgin birth. Pannenberg opines that the Egyptian tradition of 'Hieros gamos' (Holy marriage) between gods and virgins might have had a strong influence in the development of this Christian faith,[125] which is strongly anchored in the patristic tradition and the ordinary magisterium of the Church.[126] The present day approach to this question is very divided and many knowledgable theologians consider it only as a matter of secondary importance for the faith or only as a 'theologoumenon - an historicization of faith.[127] For Karl Barth, however, the virgin birth is an important theme; he considers it as a 'sign' of the 'secret' of the divine Incarnation.[128] Pannenberg, on the other hand, maintains that 'one cannot and may not say that in the reality of the divine work of revelation the masculine must be eliminated'[129]. The 'virgin birth', according to him, is significant only as a preliminary expression of the basic Christian truth that Jesus was the Son of God from the beginning and that he is the Son of God in person.[130] In his opinion, the virgin birth does not actually point to Incarnation, but even contradicts its conceptual structure. The content of the story of the virgin birth - Jesus became God's Son through Mary's conception - irreconcilably contradicts the Christology of the Incarnation of the pre-existent Son of

God who only bound himself to the man Jesus as is suggested by Paul and John (Jn 1., Rom 8:3., Gal 4:4., Phil 2:6-11). [131] The faith in the virgin birth, according to him, can however be tolerated only because of the anti-adoptionistic and anti-docetic tendencies which the virgin birth has historically represented. [132] But, following Paul Althaus, [133] Pannenberg contends that it is 'absolutely forbidden to conceive the human fatherhood as competition for the divine' and that it is not to be 'treated as the condition for the sinlessness of Jesus' following the conceptual patterns of St. Ambrose and St. Augustine regarding the doctrine of the original sin.' [134] Here it is to be mentioned that Pannenberg's argument regarding the contradiciton between the pre-existence and the virgin birth may not be quite convincing because for the early Church fathers and for the general Christian attitude even today the virginal conception is rather a confirmation of the pre-existence! [135] But we would also maintain in line with Paul Althaus and W. Pannenberg that the virgin birth is not to be placed on the same level, nor to be considered so fundamental or essential for the Christian faith, for example, as the resurrection. [136] The greatest problem, we would suggest, is actually in reconciling the virginal conception with the true humanity of Jesus who is similar to us in all things except sin (Heb 4:15., Phil 2:7 etc.)! Jesus would still have been God's Son even if his humanity took its origin from two human parents instead of one as in the case of any other human being, because in the Christian faith the 'Annunciation' was never considered as a biological substitute for the role of a human father. Could we, one could ask further, sincerely maintain, especially in the light of the modern discoveries regarding the chromosome structure of the reproductive cell - not to mention other basic discoveries in embryology which replaced former clumsy presuppositions - that Jesus could be truly the Son of Man if he had only one parent? The Christian faith teaches us the fact that Jesus is the Son of God. Is it the task of theology to determine the 'biological how' of this fact in the way of a 'deus ex machina'?

We think that Karl Rahner makes a very reasonable approach to the question of the virgin birth without falling into rationalism. [137] Rahner does not deny the virgin birth; he also does not limit himself to a biological virginity (biologisches Vorkommnis), but deals with it as a deed of the whole person (ganzmenschlicher Akt), especially the person of the Virgin Mary, the mother of Jesus. Mary is virgin in her totality. She is in her whole nature (Wesen), in her whole person, radically different from us (Anderssein) because she belongs to the economy of salvation especially as the one in whom the salvation-event was accepted by humanity which makes her a proto-type of salvation, of a new beginning in spirit and flesh. Mary gave birth to her uniqueness as a person in the history of salvation.[138] Accordingly, Rahner argues, 'Virgin' in reference to Mary's giving birth to Jesus would mean the whole person of Mary in her 'being different' (Anderssein) from others by the wonder of the grace which gave her a unique role in the event of salvation. The 'Anderssein' of Mary can be deduced only from the 'Anderssein' of the one to whom she gave birth.[139] Although Rahner expresses this view in reference to the 'virginitas in partu', it is equally applicable in our reflection of the same as 'ante partum' and 'post partum'. Rahner hints that the traditions which give the concrete content or biological details of Mary's giving birth to Jesus are not logically and sufficiently based.[140] Instead of concentrating on the physical details, Rahner suggests, we have to pay attention to the 'Kern' of the tradition regarding the virgin birth, as indicated above, without making absolute statements regarding the biological details as something obligatory for every body to believe.[141]

It is the personal self-surrender of Mary to God in the economy of salvation, her uniqueness in giving birth to the Son of God (Theotokos !), that must be stressed also in the Indian Christology while explaining the virgin birth. Otherwise this mystery also degenerates into another 'mythery' disappearing gradually in the vast ocean of Indian Mythology!

c. The Divine Consciousness of Jesus: 'Visio immediata'?

The question regarding the divine consciousness of Jesus belongs also to the 'Jesus is God'-problematic. The notion of 'becoming' that is implied in the Incarnation is also important here: Was Jesus aware of his divinity from the first moment of his earthly existence or was there a growth in his consciousness as in the case of any other human being? The question here is about the self-consciousness of Jesus Christ. Self-consciousness could be explained as the act of the cognitive faculty by which the subject through self-reflection comes to the knowledge of himself as the proper subject. As true man and true God Christ must be having a true human and a true divine intellect or cognitive faculty. But there is only one subject in Christ, the divine person. The question: how can the human consciousness of Christ terminate in a divine person? In other words: How can the man Jesus know about his Hypostatic Union?

We have already seen in the fourth and fifth chapters that for the Vedantic thinkers this question regarding the divine consciousness is not a serious problem. Every man being essentially divine, it is only natural that his consciousness terminates in the divinity! Ordinary men have to work out this awareness through a long process of inner purification, The 'Jnani's who are at the climax of their self-awareness through yogic practices and especially the 'Avatars' who are born in the perfection of this awareness are in reality enjoining the divine consciousness. The Vedantins find it not difficult to accept Jesus also like Lord Krsna, as a 'Yogesware'. [142] This does not, however, make the task of the Indian Christology in any way easier, but only more complicated. The myth of a God disguised in human appearance is not what the Christian faith in the Incarnation of God in Jesus Christ wants to proclaim! A consciousness-Christology in India should not be developed at the cost of Christ's true humanity!

The traditional theological solution to the question of Jesus' divine consciousness is that since the divine consciousness is essential and necessary for the mission of Christ as the Saviour, the knowledge of his divine identity was given by God to the human cognitive faculty of Jesus as an extraordinary grace. [143] Accordingly, Jesus' human consciousness could know of its hypostatic union with the Logos not as a datum of human self-consciousness, but in virtue of an objective communication by God which is said to depend on the 'visio beatificia' of this human consciousness. [144] Some theologians like Jean Galot, however, maintain that there is no foundation either in the Holy Scripture nor in the patristic tradition to attribute a so-called 'visio beatificia' to the earthly Jesus. [145] Karl Rahner also denies that the earthly Jesus enjoyed the beatitude of the blessed (visio beatificia); it cannot be reconciled with the true humanity of Christ especially as shown by the historical sources regarding his death-agony and the feeling of being forsaken by God in his death on the cross. [146] But Rahner considers that we 'are not permitted to doubt the binding, although not defined, doctrine of the Church's magisterium which states that the human soul of Jesus enjoyed the direct vision of God during his life on earth' [147]. He attributes to Jesus a direct union of his consciousness with God, a 'visio immediata' without finding it necessary to qualify this 'visio immediata' as 'beatific'.[148] A purely ontic 'Unio Hy-postatica', without its intrinsic element of 'visio immediata' is, according to Rahner, impossible to conceive.[149]

The originality of Rahner consists not in his use of the expression 'visio immediata', but in the explanation he gives to it. This explanation is similar to his interpretation of 'Vorgriff', which we have already discussed in connection with his theory of knowledge. It is not the categorial or thematic object of Jesus' consciousness, but the condition of the possibility, the horizon, of all his knowledge and activity! How? According to Rahner, Jesus' knowledge had a multi-layered structure or different dimensions of consciousness and knowledge that something may be known and not known at the same time.[150] There is conceptual consciousness and transcendental consciousness, reflected and unreflected consciousness, permitted and suppressed consciousness and there is an 'a priori' condition for knowledge and an 'a posteriori' object of knowledge! So there is a multiplicity of possible forms in which something may be present to the consciousness. The 'a priori' structure of consciousness is not known objectively and concretely although this horizon-consciousness is actually more immediate to the subject than the concrete objects of consciousness which follow it! The human consciousness of the historical Jesus as we know him from the Gospels is that of the one who questions, doubts, learns, is surprised, is deeply moved and even of the one who is overwhelmed by the deadly feeling of being forsaken by God! It is also questionable whether even those 'ipsissima verba' of Jesus like 'Abba', 'ego eimi', 'Amen' which are traditionally taken to prove the objective divine consciousness of Jesus could be taken in that sense even if it is proved that they are not merely post-resurrectional projections on the pre-surrectional Jesus. Rahner maintains that Jesus' divine consciousness or his awareness of divine Sonship 'must not be conceived as being-faced-with an object-like God to which the intentionality of the human consciousness of Jesus would then be referred as to the 'other', the 'object' facing it'[151]. The divine consciousness was not the objective but the subjective pole of the Lord's consciousness. It is possible that this subjective pole may never be reflected upon, or even be given a false conceptual interpretation or attained only very in-adequately and never completely. The divine consciousness was the unembraceable ground, the permanent condition of the possibility of all other knowledge in Jesus as its law, gauge and ultimate form. This all-pervading basic condition could be present as an unthematic, uncategorial consciousness - all the same real and immediate without ever being noticed and conceptually declared. So Jesus' direct and conscious presence to God must not be understood in the sense of the vision of an object. What the 'visio immediata' in Jesus means is this direct presence, that excludes the element of 'standing opposite' to an object. It is clear but inexplicable. Such an approach to Jesus' divine consciousness avoids the danger of 'Monotheletism' (at least of the hidden, practical type as a crypto-gamic heresy) and safeguards the true humanity of Jesus and is reconcilable with a genuinely human spiritual history and development of the man Jesus.

Jesus learned to express to himself what he is, and what he has already seen in the self-consciousness of his basic condition, only in the course of his long experience.[152] Christ realized his thematic, categorial divine consciousness only gradually. Jesus had the 'visio immediata' without having a 'visio objec-tiva', the latter being the result of a long spiritual and religious development in Jesus. This does not mean that Jesus discovered something which he did by no means know beforehand, but it means that he grasped more and more what he already was and what he already knew in the basic way. This would explain how true nescience in Jesus could be reconciled with his divine nature (Mk 9:1., 13:32., Mt 10:23., 16:28., Lk 2:52., 9:27).[153] Jesus knowledge of every thing that is connected with his mission and soteriological task was implicit in the beginning and it became gradually explicit. The 'visio immediata' of Jesus is not an extrinsic and supplementary addition to his 'Hypostatic Union', but this visio is an intrinsic and inalienable element of this union. It is not, as Galtier maintains, that Christ knows about his hypostatic union because he has the visio, but as Rahner explains, Jesus has the visio because he has the hypostatic union.[154]

Rahner's understanding of the 'infused knowledge' in Christ is also in line with his concept of the 'visio immediata' and his theory of knowledge in general. Rahner admits that the 'visio immediata' in Christ was an infused, i.e. a priori, knowledge![155] But unlike many other theologians[156] he denies any 'species infusa' to the human knowledge of Christ, quite in accordance with his principle that every human knowledge is one that is received through the sensibles: 'Nihil est in intellectu quod non prius erat in sensu'! The infused knowledge ignores the historical character of knowledge and the principle of 'Conversio ad phantasma'! Rahner opines that Jesus 'eschatological pronouncements and his knowledge of the future should not be referred to any 'species infusae'; Jesus' knowledge of the future was derived from his deep vision of the empirical realities of the present.[157] As Rahner derives the possibility of miracles from the inner transcendental and dynamic potentialities of the nature, so also he maintains that vision regarding the future can be derived by some from a deep and accurate vision of the present. What is ultimately decisive for Rahner in this case is the understanding of the relation between the 'natural' and the 'supernatural', to which we have referred in the last chapter.[158] We are also aware of the fact that Rahner's explanation regarding the knowledge of the future (prophecy)[159] has been subject to theological criticism,[160] but we think that this could be led back to a certain transposition of thought patterns or categories due to a lack of vision into the Rahnerian hermeneutics.

Wolfhart Pannenberg also insists very like Karl Rahner on the progressive character of Jesus 'divine consciousness. He suggests even that Jesus' explicit identification of himself with the Father: "I and the Father are one" (Jn 10:30), cannot be judged with accuracy whether it is of the Johannine Jesus or of the pre-Easter Jesus.[161] Jesus' consciousness was more directed to the Father than to the Logos and 'it is certain that Jesus' self-consciousness was decisively stamped by his message of the nearness of God and his Kingdom'[162] Jesus' oneness with God demands that he must be one with himself in his self-understanding which must be somehow even if not explicitly, related to his unity with God.[163] Jesus knew himself functionally to be one with God's will in the realization of the Kingdom of God and through this function to be one with God himself.[164] Just as there was a progress in the divinization of Jesus' humanity and in the manifestation of his ontological unity with God that culminated in Jesus' resurrection, so too it was only in his resurrection, according to Pannenberg, that Jesus attained the perfect objective clarity in his consciousness of the divine identity.[165] We have to deal with this point further in one of the following sections that deals with the question of resurrection.[166]

In reference to the Vedantic Christology we can observe that the Vedantins attribute to every human being a progressive divine consciousness which Rahner and Pannenberg reserve exclusively for Jesus Christ, because of his unity of being with God. The Vedantins attribute to the 'Avatars' a clarity in divine consciousness, as we have seen especially in the third and the fourth chapters of our work, from the very first moment of their birth. This is evidently due to the docetic and monotheleic overtones in the Avatara concept. The Vedantic emphasis on those passages from the Gospels, especially that of St. John, which testify Jesus' consciousness of his divine identity is therefore - it must be clearly mentioned - based on false and unacceptable Christological pre-suppositions. The Christian faith in God's becoming man, becoming a part of history and its progressive process, has the task of encouraging man not to seek his salvation in some historically independent idea or eternal principle as the Vedantins do, but in history and 'to encounter God in man and ultimately in the man in whom God definitively exists and historically appears in the world, that is to say, in Jesus Christ' [167].

B. The Historical Destiny of Jesus

So far we have concentrated our attention on the person of Jesus Christ as the mystery of man and of the human history. Now we turn our discussion to his salvific function. By that, however, we do not mean to support the classical distinction between ontological Christology and soteriological Christology. In the light of our discussion so far we would maintain that the very 'fact' of Jesus Christ is salvific. This is a point that is to be stressed very much in the Indian context in order to make clear the permanent and intrinsic value of the human reality of the Word become flesh. A soteriology that is concentrated only on death and resurrection of Christ could possibly serve as a confirmation for the Vedantic depreciation of the bodily and historical aspects of human existence. P. Chenchiah's theory of Jesus Christ as the 'New Creation' also stresses the redemptive aspect of the very fact of Christ.[168] Karl Rahner also sees both Christology and Soteriology as intimately related to each other. The Incarnation, according to him, is not merely an ontological event, but it is first and foremost a salvific event.[169] Similarly, W. Pannenberg opines that even though the soteriological interest cannot be the principle of Christological doctrine - the human soteriological interest can change according to the changing sociological situations and that can lead to a Christology of projection that considers Christ as a mere social revolutionary, political liberator and so on - still, 'the confession of faith in Jesus is not to be separated from Jesus' saving significance for us' [170]. The divinity of Jesus, Pannenberg continues, is the presupposition for his saving significance for us and it is also conversely true that the saving significance of his divinity is the reason why we take interest in the question of his divinity. It is because the 'fact' of Christ is the basis of his salvific 'act' that the 'Christological research finds in the reality of Jesus the criterion for the critical examination of the Christological tradition and also the various soteriological concerns that have determined Christological presentations'[171]. In other words, 'Jesus possesses significance for us only to the extent that this significance is inherent in himself, in his history, and in his person constituted by this history'[172]. Following our discussion so far on the redemptive 'fact' of Christ, what we intend in the following pages is to reflect more on his redemptive 'act', namely his eschatological claims as is reflected in his teachings and the consequences which he had to draw from these claims, especially with critical reference to the Indian soteriological problematic.

1. 'Dharma' and 'Basileia': The Message of the Kingdom

The great interest especially of the renascent Hinduism, as we have seen in the sixth chapter of our work, is predominantly ethical. Jesus is for most of the Indians a 'G u r u'[173], a master or teacher who can lead others to God-realization. In this regard what is most often stressed is the ethical teachings of Jesus. The 'Sermon on the Mount' and especially the teaching on 'Ahimsa' (non-violence) that is contained therein is for many Hindu thinkers like Raja Rammohan Roy, M.C. Parekh and Mahatma Gandhi the very essence of Christ's Gospel.[174] Those who take earnestly the doctrine of 'Avatar' do not find it difficult to attribute also to Jesus Christ the avataric goal of re-establishing the 'Dharma' (righteousness).[175] In short, Jesus is for the Indian mind the ideal of moral perfection!

The ideals of ethics and morality are not new. According to Plato, for example, the good is which is truly divine,[176] and becoming good one can become divine. The good man is similar to God (homoiosis theoi). The ethical striving of becoming 'good' and Jesus as the great example of this human striving are emphasized by the early Christian thinkers like Origen[177] and Gregory of Nyssa[178]. The Kantian morality of 'duty for duty's sake' also finds its confirmation in Jesus as the ideal of moral perfection. It identifies the Kingdom of God with the spreading of good through morally perfect men and the foundation of community according to the laws of virtues.[179] A. Ritschl also sees the special function of Jesus as the founding of the universal, moral community of human beings. [180]

The ethical teachings of Jesus Christ are, of course, of great importance and are absolutely indispensable for the Christian life. But, the reality of Jesus Christ and his saving significance imply much more than ethics and morality. The 'Kingdom of God' (Basileia) is to be understood, according to Wolfhart Pannenberg, not merely ethically but eschatologically. [181] He warns against robbing 'the eschatology of Jesus of its relation to time and to convert his passion for God's future into the presence of eternity, into the momentary now' [182] of human ethics and achievements. The futurity of the Reign of God becomes in the ministry of Jesus a power that determines the present. [183] The single, pulsating reality of Jesus' existence was the coming Kingdom of God. [184] This Kingdom is not the ethical or moral achievement of human beings, but it is worked out by God. [185] It is not a mere internalized 'Reign of God', but it embraces the whole of reality. [186] But, according to Pannenberg, the futurity of God preached by Jesus Christ should not be considered as having no relevance for the present. The uniqueness of Jesus' message of the future consists in its anticipation (prolepsis) in the present. The future, eschatological Kingdom has its impact on the present as the future of God is already dawning. [187] Jesus further identified the message of the nearing, dawning Kingdom of God with his own person so much so that he claimed that where he is accepted, God's nearness and salvation are also accepted. The Kingdom of God, the eschatological Lordship of God as power over everything, has appeared with him and Jesus was certain that in his activity the future salvation of God's Kingdom had broken into the present time, and this distinguished him basicly from other prophets and religious teachers. [188] Jesus' identification of the 'Basileia' with his person, according to Pannenberg, should be understood on the general background of Jewish apocalypsis. As a result of this identification, Jesus also expected the apocalyptic End (Eschaton) to be imminent. [189]

Jesus' identification of his person with the Kingdom of God was also the basis of his claim to absolute authority which implied the consciousness of a personal unity with God. So his claim was the claim of an authority that belongs only to God. [190] But Jesus expected the definitive divine confirmation of his claims only from the future of God where the resurrection of the dead and the judgement of the Son of Man, according to the Jewish apocalyptic hope, actually took place. And this future of God is imminent. According to Pannenberg, even though Jesus does not identify himself with the apocalyptic imagery of the 'Son of Man', still he was convinced that the coming judgement of mankind depends on man's present attitude towards him (Luke 12:8).[191] This claim of Jesus to divine authority, as suggested by Pannenberg, has a proleptic structure. It is true that Jesus expected a confirmation of his authority from God only in the realization of the Eschaton, but still the claim of Jesus implies the expectation of some kind of a divine confirmation in anticipation.[192] A partial confirmation of Jesus' claim can be seen in the 'saving deeds' of the Endtime that were already happening in his ministry. So Jesus' activity is already the beginning of God's definitive rule.[193] The forgiveness of sins Jesus preached and his actual pronouncement of forgiveness of sins upon those who opened themselves to his message of the nearness of God or even upon those who only trusted in him personally are, according to Pannenberg, a clear evidence of Jesus' claim to divine authority and the identification of the message of the Kingdom with his own person.[194]

Pannenberg also thinks that Jesus was aware of the possibility that he would have to pay dearly for his claims and that he even reckoned with the possibility of his death as a price for his claims. It was, however, not of great importance for Jesus even if he died before the apocalyptic coming of the Kingdom he preached, because Jesus was convinced that God would justify his claims in the establishment of the 'Basileia' that was any way imminent![195] The apparent tension between the present and the future that we find in the message of Jesus could be definitively reconciled, according to the Pannenbergan thinking, only in the later event of Jesus' resurrection!

So the speciality in the message of Jesus, as Karl Rahner also affirms in agreement to what we have seen in reference to Pannenberg, is not in some 'ideas' or ethical principles which could not be conceived or attained in other times and places. His uniqueness is in his eschatological message of the Kingdom of God (Basileia) that has come in him, in his person in a quite new, radical and demanding way and a Kingdom which is meant for every body.[196] In the light of what we have said so far, we have to affirm against the Vedantic 'idea-ism' that the very historical person of Jesus Christ and the identification of God's salvation with himself are more important than the ethical principles he preached. This is especially important in our approach to the modern Hindu ethical reformers like Rammohan Roy, K.C. Sen and M.C. Parekh. The ethics of Jesus are only a logical and necessary conclusion to the acceptance of his person. 'Dharma', the reign of righteousness according to the Indian 'Darsana' will have to be brought in an Indian Christology into harmony with the 'Basileia' with all its necessary implications regarding the person of Christ!

2. Jesus' Crucifixion: A Suffering God?

In the sixth chapter we had referred to the possibility of the cross of Jesus being considered as a scandal, that is associated 'with the sadistic impulse of a psychically affected brain', a morbid and neurotic preoccupation with death which is not conducive to calm and spiritual elevation![197] A suffering God, as S. Radhakrishnan observes, the deity with a crown of thorns, cannot satisfy the Indian religious soul![198] But Radhakrishnan himself admits that growth and development include moments of pain and suffering.[199] The Vedantins also stress very much the point that there cannot be a progress towards inner illumination (jnana) without arduous asceticism which consists in the practice of the integral Yoga and the 'crucifixion' of the 'Aham' (ego).[200] But the need for such a progressive purification and the endurance of suffering is ruled out in the case of an 'Avatar' who is born in perfect 'Jnana'. This is in line with the docetic approach of the Vedantins towards the mystery of Incarnation. This is reflected also in their approach to the question of Jesus' crucifixion: 'Christ was God incarnate; they could not kill him. That which was crucified was only a semblance, a mirage' - to quote Vivekananda.[201] The Vedantins deny to God a real identification with the human destiny, the reality of the human body and the tragedy of human history. We had also indicated that many thinking Hindus, on the other hand, were enamoured of the mystery of Christ's suffering and death which led some of them like Vengel Chakkarai even to the point of conversion from Hinduism to Christianity![202] The death of Christ, according to Chakkarai, crowns the whole life and teachings of Jesus.

Both in the theologies of Karl Rahner and Wolfhart Pannenberg, there is an intimate relation between the life, claims and teachings of Christ and his crucifixion. But, Pannenberg makes a distinction between the nature of

Christ's teaching and his death. In his teaching and giving the message of the nearness of God's Kingdom Jesus was the acting agent; that was his mission. But his death by crucifixion was not something he actively chose. Though he was not taken by surprise, it was something that 'befell' him, something that 'happened' to him as his destiny and as the consequence of his mission. The passion-predictions are, therefore, to be understood as 'Vaticinia ex eventu' and the idea that Jesus offered himself deliberately to the crucifixion must be interpreted as a retrospective sacrificial interpretation of the event. [203]

Pannenberg maintains that Jesus understood his imminent crucifixion as a great blow to his mission. It radically called into question all his claims! He preached the nearness of God and now he experiences his own destruction in the name of the same God of Israel! He finds it as a personal disaster to be excluded from God's nearness inspite of clear consciousness of it. That is hell! [204] Jesus died the death of one rejected especially as manifested in his cry of dereliction. He experienced the terrible 'dark night' with all its implications, which has nothing to do with the so-called Vedantic tranquility! For his disciples too the crucifixion was a disaster and they deserted him because the cause of Jesus, until the contrary was proved, was negatively decided; after the crucifixion the question of the legitimacy of Jesus' mission was no longer open. But inspite of his disappointment, Jesus trusted in the future of God without having any idea of what it would be! [205]

Pannenberg opines that the crucifixion of Jesus was the immediate result of his conflict with the jewish authorities. The accusation of blasphemy they levelled against him was well based and made 'bona fide'. To question the jewish law that was absolutized as the supreme norm of salvation was to question God himself. [206] The jewish authorities were not particularly malicious because the law of blasphemy (Ex 22:28) and its punishment by stoning (Lev 24:16) were broadly interpreted in the time of Jesus and this law could be 'justly' applied to him. Jesus was for them 'evidently' a messianic pretender who made himself equal to God by claiming authority above the law and the temple. That was blasphemy (Mk 14:64). [207] The charge of state subversion and sedition, of course, was false and malicious; still it was made because the Jewish authorities found it inopportune, in the face of his popularity, to stone him and so the task of eliminating him was put on the Romans by fabricating political motives in his activities. [208]

Jesus' execution, which was in itself unjust but justified by the law of Israel, repudiates, according to Pannenberg, the positive legal tradition which had become calcified as the 'the law' after the exile.[209] This repudiation was more an invalidation of the absolutisation of the law as the criterion of salvation than an inevitable consequence of the jewish tradition as such. Jesus showed that the God of Jewish history stands above the law.[210] So Jesus' death at the hands of the self-justifying and self-saving law is a repudiation, we would maintain, not only of the jewish law, but of all human pretensions and world visions which consider that the ultimate goal of human existence is attainable by one's own spiritual and moral efforts. This is especially valid for the Vedantic thinking; in particular for the exclusively 'Jnana' and 'Karma' paths towards salvation, which we have explained in the first part of our work.[211]

The aspect of disaster that is implied in Jesus' execution, Pannenberg observes, should not also be exaggerated. Jesus never lost his absolute trust in the future of God. Jesus encountered the power of evil, but his death cannot be identified 'as the simple victory of that power'.[212] There is a meaning that is already implied in the Cross, a significance that is intrinsic to the death of Jesus which would be fulfilled and established by God's vindication of Jesus' claims through the resurrection - a point we will be discussing elaborately later. This resurrection, we would just mention here shortly, is not a later addition of a significance to the death of Jesus and, as Pannenberg asserts, 'one cannot say that the resurrection signified a reversal of the most radical significance of Jesus' death, unless one postulates that Jesus' humanity, his being in history, meant that he too was a partisan of basic sin in such a way that he had to die the death of a sinner'[213]. We can declare without doubt that death, in all its destructive aspects, was the immediate preparation for the irrevocable and unquestionable vindication of Jesus' claims.

The Cross of Christ which is a stumbling block for the jews and a folly for the nations [213a] plays a central role also in the transcendental Christology of Karl Rahner, as it is central to the New Testament Kerygma. Jesus, according to him, accepted the fate of the Cross as the fate of a prophet and as the consequence of his mission.[214] Besides the aspect of Jesus' faithfullness to his mission, we can also say that according to the transcendental Christology of Rahner, the Cross shows the radicality of Jesus' obedience as a man in accepting god's self-communication and Jesus' sharing the fate of mankind in all its implications. Rahner sees a great and indispensably positive value in the fact of death. It is more than a mere biological or medical event in its anthropological implications. It is the ultimate, irrevocable realization of human freedom in one's decision for or against God. Only through death can man freely and definitively accept God's self-communication. In this sense the death of Jesus is a constitutive, inward aspect of God's eschatological self-promise to the world. [215]

In the context of a 'superficial and fashionable death of God theology' Rahner thinks it meaningful also to reflect more closely on Jesus' death in itself as the death of God. [216] Rahner warns against even tacitly understanding that Jesus' death did not affect God who is immutable and hence cannot die and against maintaining that the incarnate Logos died only in his human reality. The full and real Christian truth is that God _himself_ - and not just what is other than he - has in what is other than himself a destiny, through the incarnation, and hence a death too. Jesus' death belongs to God's self-utterance. [217]

The mystery of God's suffering that is manifested in the Cross of Christ, we would maintain with D. Amalorpavadas, [218] is a very healthy and necessary provocation that could be directed against Hinduism in general and the sublime and tranquil Vedantic advaita in particular. Stoic tranquility need not necessarily be a perfection, nor suffering necessarily an evil. The God who gives himself to man in love and in his free creative generosity is perfect enough to be affected by the destiny of his creation and generous enough to suffer for the sake of love. We would just indicate here that the pain of God has been subject to serious studies in the recent times especially by theologians like K. Kitamori, H. Mühlen, J. Moltmann, H. Küng, and J. Galot, - to mention only a few. [219] Our topic does not require an elaboration of their theologies; still we would briefly mention a few points which should not be lost sight of in developing a 'pain of God theology' in the Indian context. It must be first of all mentioned that the suffering of God must be understood in the general context of God's 'becoming' which we have discussed in one of the previous sections. [220] We do not have to repeat those fundamental notions here. Further, we have to distinguish between the problem of suffering and the problem of evil, both physical and moral. Suffering can be called even a physical evil, we would suggest, only when it is _meaningless_. Even humanly speaking, suffering has a very positive value in the nature and development of man physically, psychologically and spiritually. We can boldly say that Jesus has not removed suffering from the world, but made it _meaningful_ and bearable.[221] The pang of birth suffered both by the mother and the child, for example, or the so-called 'sweet pain of love' may not be considered as evil eventhough it is suffering in the real sense of the term. The fact that God has by his Incarnation shared everything with us, except sin, would mean that our suffering was also not shun by him. Here the notion of analogy is also very important. The suffering of God is not conceivable as man's suffering in univocal terms, nor in equivocal terms, but analogically. There is similarity; there is also difference! We know _that_ God suffers, that God is involved in our destiny out of free love - a fact that is revealed ultimately by the mystery of the Incarnation and the Cross. But, _how_ can God suffer? - That we do not know! But the suffering is real, because God's personal involvement in the human destiny by love is also real. God's immutability and impassibility are different from our concept of them.[222] God's sovereign freedom implies also that he is free to love and out of love to suffer. Love expressed in suffering cannot be an imperfection. We would also hold that a God who is _not able_ to be affected by the sufferings of his creatures, whom he has created out of free love, cannot be the loving God and hence he cannot be the true God! The reality of numerous sufferings in this world cannot cast so much doubt on the existence of God as the wrong concept of a God who cannot suffer! The concept of a relationless, impassible Brahman is a full absurdity. Finally we would also point to the trinitarian aspect of the suffering of God. If God is 'personally' involved in the suffering destiny of man, then he is involved as Father, Son and the Holy Spirit because there is no person in God other than that of these three. Hence the theology of the suffering of God is not satisfied by a mere transference of the human sufferings of Christ to the self of the Logos based on the fact that the properties of both natures are possessed by the same subject according to the principles of 'communicatio idiomatum' (cross predication), [222a] thus leaving the Father and the Holy Spirit totally unaffected by the whole event of the Cross! The question of the basic unity of the economic and immanent trinity is also important here. The 'Dramatik' on Calvary is necessarily a 'Theodramatik'[223] and not just a 'Logodramatik'. If the Father and the Holy Spirit are 'related' to the Son in the community of love, this relation cannot remain suspended or bracketed in the suffering of the Son. What we mean here is not 'patri-passianism', which identifies the suffering of the Father with that of the Son on the basis of a trinitarian modalism, but that the other persons cannot remain 'neutral' in the face of the Son's suffering. The Cross was a trinitarian event and in the words of J. Moltmann it can even be described as the 'sacrifice' of the Son by the Father in the Holy Spirit.[224]

Such a theology of the suffering God is, of course, not easy to put through in India especially in the context of the Vedantic impossibility and the absolute tranquility of the Nirvana, but it is indispensable if Christology has to be true to the mystery of the divine intervention in human history. The Cross is not a sign of the contempt of matter and history, but it is the most striking manifestation of God's intensified interest in this world!

3. Vicarious Substitution?

'Christ died for our sins in accordance with the scriptures' (1Cor 15:3). This statement belongs to the earliest Christian tradition and, as Paul himself mentions, it is of first importance for the Christian faith. This evidently refers to the soteriological aspect of Christ's death by crucifixion. In theological terms it would mean that Christ is the 'final', 'efficient', 'meritorious', 'instrumental' and 'forma' c a u s e of our justification, according to the decree on justification issued by the Concil of Trent (DS 1529). It will be further clarified how Christ has 'merited' our justification: "... Dominus noster Jesus Christus, qui 'cum essemus inimici' (cf. Rom 5,10), 'propter nimiam caritatem, qua dilexit nos' (Eph 2,4), sua sanctissima passione in ligno crucis nobis iustificationem meruit (can. 10), et pro nobis Deo Patri satisfecit...'[225]. The Cross of Christ is the 'cause' that 'merited' our justification. It must be mentioned at the very outset that our intention here is not the presentation of an elaborate soteriology, but just to evaluate briefly how this statement could satisfactorily confront - here also using especially the guidelines of Rahner and Pannenberg - some of the problematics raised by the Indian Christology.

We have mentioned time and again that in the context of the principle of Karma-Samsara, the automatic cosmic law of retribution, there is no place for a 'Saviour' in the strict sense of the term. Each one is responsible for himself and has to work out one's liberation all by oneself. [226] This principle of 'self-retribution is valid also in the 'Bhakti' school of spirituality, although some faint similarities to the Christian 'Soteriology' and 'Grace' are not absent in some of the Bhakti interpretations as we had mentioned in the first part. [227] It is the principle of the essential divinity of man which makes the role of a divine saviour superfluous. Even the role of an 'Avatar' is to function as an 'example' for others and as a 'helper' towards liberation, which of course is not indispensable! The goal of 'Avatar', namely to save the good and to destroy the wicked, is also irreconcilable with Christian soteriology. [228] The Vedantins do not recognize any redeeming role for the Cross of Christ, but they value it as an important example of self-denial, progressive withdrawal from this world and faithfulness to duty. Rammohan Roy recognized some intercessory power to the Cross, while M.C. Parekh sees it as sign of Christ's solidarity with human destiny and misery. We had also referred in the sixth chapter to Gandhi's veneration for the Cross as a sign of altruistic love and self-sacrifice for others, without, however, acknowledging any universal and indispensable redemptive value to it. [229] We had also indicated that K.C. Sen sees in the blood of Christ a sacrificial power to reconcile us with God and the Christian theologians, of course, stress that the Cross of Christ is more than a mere sign of altruistic love; it is, indeed, central to the mystery of divine redemption. [230]

The universal saving significance of Jesus 'death has been interpreted in the history of theology in different ways. The understanding of Jesus' death as a ransom paid to the devil for the sins of mankind originated in the palastine community and was later adopted by the Greeks (Mk 10:45., Rom 3:24 etc.). [231] It was elaborated by Irenaeus,Tertullian, Origen, Augustine, Ignatius of Antioch, Gregory of Nyssa, Gregory the Great and others. [232] Anselm of Canterbury, however, rejects such a ransom theory as he could not accept any power of the devil over humanity and proposes in line with the doctrine of penance in the middle ages a theory of judicial vicarious satisfaction according to which the infinite offence against God's honour by sin is removed by the infinite worth of Jesus death. [233] The letter to the Hebrews designates Jesus as the High Priest whose death is understood in the categories of the jewish expiatory sacrifice (Heb 9:11-14). [234] The sufferings of Christ were also not rarely interpreted in terms of penal substitution, an idea especially accepted by Martin Luther, according to which the punishment for human sins were arbitrarily imposed upon the innocent Christ as a representative of mankind which was an expression of the wrath of God and his compensating justice (Gal 3:13., Rom 8:3., 2 Cpr 5:21).[235]

In the Indian Christology, the idea of the sufferings of Christ as an adequate satisfaction for the sins of mankind had been accepted by Brahmabhandab Upadhyaya, but M.M. Thomas warns against interpreting the divine redemption in judicial terms inherited from imperial Rome. The idea of an 'avenging God' in the sense of a penal substitution finds no sympathy among the Indian thinkers, as we have explained in the sixth chapter.[236]

According to the opinion of Karl Rahner, an ontic Christology necessarily leads to a soteriology that is abstractly formal, juridical and moral which is interested only in 'merit' and 'satisfaction'.[237] A 'satisfaction theory' is not adequate to explain the mystery of man's salvation in Christ.[238] According to the transcendental Christology of Rahner, the death of Christ is not a mere 'accidental' which could also be substituted by a positive juridical decree of God.[239] Human decisions and free acts are made definitive and irrevocable only by death and it was only the death of Jesus that made the free acceptance of God's salvation by humanity as such definitive and irrevocable.[240] The definitive human acceptance of God's self-giving to mankind is realized by the irrevocable human decision implied in Jesus' death; what Jesus achieved is the achievement of humanity as such.[241] The Cross of Christ adds a unique dimension to the death of Christ, which, as we have explained in the previous section, manifests the radicality of Jesus' faithfulness to his mission and self-surrender to the will of the Father as in the case of the fate of a prophet and the death of a just man.[242] The salvific 'mediatory' role of Jesus Christ should not be understood as if he were a 'third' inserted between the two spheres of God and man. Jesus does not come between God and man, but he is the mediator of the immediacy of God to man. He makes it possible for God to be experienced directly by man and also for man to have an intimate eschatological community with God.[243] Rahner opposes the misunderstanding of interpreting Christ's salvic action as changing the mind of and appeasing an angry God. Rahner is quite correct in affirming that 'it is not Christ's action which causes God's will to forgiveness, but vice versa, and this redemption in Christ... was already effective from the beginning of humanity'[244]. The redemption or destruction of sin is not merely a moral or legal transaction, acquittal from guilt or non reckoning of guilt. Redemption is 'the communication of divine grace and takes place in the ontological reality of God's self-communication' and it is 'the continuation and accomplishment of that existential process which consisted from the very beginning in the supernatural pardoning and divinization of humanity'[245]. The Christian redemption follows, according to Rahner, of itself from a Christological evolutionary conception of the world. The redemption is the victory over sin, which is the obstacle of God's self-communication to mankind, and thus to the whole of creation!

Wolfhart Pannenberg too stresses the universal vicarious character of Jesus' death, but he considers the 'ransom theory' only as a symbolic designation and popular illustration of its universal character. If stretched too far, it is nothing more than a myth.[246] Like F. Schleiermacher[247] he rejects also the 'grotesque idea' of penal substitution.[248] The cultic substitution is also only a symbolic representation of the vicarious character of Jesus death in the Hebrew context of expiatory sacrifice.[249] Pannenberg sees the soteriological, universal significance of Jesus' death, which is the 'Kern' of the various imageries used in the scriptures (Is 53:1-12 esp. 4,5., Mk 14:26 and parallels),[250] in terms of a vicarious substitution.[251]

The idea of a vicarious substitution is unimaginable within the context of a moral individualism as seen in the Indian theory of 'Karma' and self-retribution. If a moral deed is strictly individual and personal, it is fully unjust to impose it arbitrarily on another one. The God who forgives even the most wicked cannot be thought of committing the injustice of punishing the innocent to quench his wrath! But, unlike that the theory of 'Karma' suggests, every evil deed has an intrinsic social aspect, because the consequences of an evil deed affect not only the individual, but the whole society in which an individual lives. In the history of Israel a single word was used to signify both the evil deed and its consequence, thus forming a unity between the two: "awon" or "hattat".[252] The doctrine of Karma, we have seen in the first part, also implies such a unity; 'Karma' means both the evil deed and its consequence! But unlike the Vedanta, the tradition in Israel does not limit the 'consequences' of evil deeds to the doer, but as is evident from life experience it is to be borne by the whole society more or less. In this sense, the 'consequence' of sin has a certain independence from the doer which makes its 'trans-

ferability' on others by substition possible.[253] As man is essentially a social
being, one may have to carry sometimes the 'Cross' made by another. In
social life a participation both in the good and evil done by others is a universal reality. The vicarious character of the fate of Jesus can be understood
only in the background of this universal phenomenon of substitution in the
social structure of man.

Considered in this sense, the death of Christ, so contends Pannenberg, should
not be understood as an arbitrary punitive suffering in the line of a forensic
or criminal substitution, but only in the context of a relationship between
men which entails modes of substitution and vicariousness.[254] For Pannenberg
the death of Christ has a vicarious character as expiation for the sins of
the whole mankind, not only because of the miraculous supernatural uniqueness
of Jesus as the Son of God with infinite merits for his doings, but also because
of the basic social character of human existence which affirms the social
relationships of individual behaviour. Every human deed is a deed in and
on behalf of the society, which makes 'vicarious substitution' a universal
phenomenon in human social relationships.[255] Jesus Christ represents the
whole humanity not as one who stands outside it, but as he is himself that
what is in all individuals and by his death (in the light of the resurrection)
he overcame what is alike in all individuals.[256] Jesus died for jews and non-
jews, in their stead, taking upon himself the consequences of the blasphemous
existence of mankind and this is what is meant in 2 Cor 5:21: "For our sake
God made the sinless one (Christ) into sin, so that in him we might become
the goodness of God." This would mean that the 'death' of Christ as a punishment for blasphemy was authorized by the law given by God. So in a certain
sense, God himself laid on Jesus the tragic misfortune inherent in blasphemy,
which rightly belonged to the jewish authorities in particular and the humanity
in general as is signified in the sinful involvement (blasphemy) of Pilate in
the death of Jesus.[257] As a true member of the human race Jesus takes upon
himself the tragic consequences of sin - here we have to keep in mind the
notion of 'awon' and 'hattat' - by a vicarious substitution on the basis of
human solidarity. As Jesus' death gathers up our dying into his own, the
character of our dying changes.[258] Jesus' death on the cross is a vicarious
death, a death suffered in the place of humanity for its blasphemous existence.[259] The theories of ransom, satisfaction and penal suffering may be
employed only within this horizon - and not in their mythological exaggerations

of God expiating history through the altruism of Jesus. [260] In Jesus we experience the fact that 'the mystery of man, which it is not for man himself
to control, and which is bound up with the absurdity of guilt and death, is,
nevertheless, hidden in the love of God' [261].

It is clear to us that the above given interpretation of 'vicarious substitution'
is unexplainable in the moral individualism of the Vedanta. Here the Vedanta
itself will have to undergo a correction, a 'death', before being raised up
to the possibility of conveying Christological truths in the Indian context.
As A.J. Appasamy observes, the Cross is for us a reminder of the seriousness
of sin and how difficult it is to re-establish divine righteousness. [262] It is
not just a matter of achieving advaitic awareness. Even in Indian mythological
terms it can be said, as is done by K.M. Banerji, that Jesus is the true 'Prajapati' who as in the 'Purusha Sukta' [263] is sacrificed for the entire humanity,
the true Siva who drank the destructive poison of shin, whose blood is, as
opined by H.A. Krishnapillai, the saving water of Ganga! [264] Of course, both
the Indian philosophy and mythology require re-interpretation before they
could be applied to the mystery of Christ as the mystery of man and of
the human history!

C. The Eschatological Saviour

We have already mentioned that the resurrection of Jesus is the explicitation
of the soteriological significance that is intrinsic to the historical 'fact'
of Christ that manifested the radicality of Christ's obedience to the will
of the Father in the event of the Cross. The Resurrection is not a reversal
of Jesus' destiny nor a correction of something that went wrong in Jesus'
preaching of the Kingdom. This point is especially important in the Indian
context where some of the Vedantins brush aside the event of the crucifixion
as a 'mirage' that did not affect the reality of Jesus, but belonged to the
realm of illusion. Here in the following lines we intend to evaluate further
the Indian approach to the fact of the Resurrection, the question of its historicity and its reference to the 'end' of every man, as we have done so far
with the help of the corresponding views especially of Karl Rahner and Wolfhart Pannenberg.

1. Jesus' Resurrection: Eschatology versus History?

The Vedantins in general, it goes without saying, are not particularly interested in the historical aspect of the resurrection of Christ. After all there can be no salvation or liberation from the bonds of 'Samsara' with the body and in history. Both the human body and the human history are factors that enslave the 'Atman'. In this context the Vedantins re-interpret the Resurrection to suit the Vedantic philosophy, for example, as the ultimate advaitic illumination, as we have already seen in the sixth chapter. We will evaluate this point further in the following section. In the Vedantic context, it can be mentioned shortly, the 'resurrection of the body' is absurd! The Indian Christian theologians evidently accept the mystery of the Resurrection as also some non-Christians like K.C. Sen. The interpretations, however, differ from person to person as we have already indicated in the sixth chapter. M.C. Parekh and P.C. Mozoomdar accept the Vedantic differentiation of the human body as 'Sthula sarira' (gross body) and 'Sukshma sarira' (subtle body). The 'Sthula sarira' of Jesus, according to them, decayed in the tomb, while the 'Sukshma sarira' rose up gloriously from the dead. [265] Accordingly, Sen, Parekh and Mozoomdar affirm that resurrection is not the 'resuscitation' of a dead body and hence the tradition of the 'Empty Tomb' is not acceptable. This, however, does not rule out the apparitions of the risen Lord to his disciples. Vengel Chakkarai, on the other hand, considers the 'Empty tomb' as an essential and indispensable part of the faith in the Resurrection! [266]

Wolfhart Pannenberg's theology is based on the historicity of the resurrection of Jesus as the anticipated realization of the 'Kingdom of God' within history. We will consider this point more intensively in the next section. The historicity of the Resurrection, according to Pannenberg, is based on the apparition narratives especially of 1Cor 15:1-11 and the tradition of the 'Empty Tomb' especially as given in Mk 16:1-8. [267] But we think that the question of the historicity of the Resurrection is not as simple as that. We will have to differentiate between the truth of Jesus' resurrection from the language in which it is expressed. [268] There are numerous passages in the New Testament which bear witness to the mystery of Jesus' resurrection: the short formulas (Acts 17:31 ff., Rom 4:24 etc.), [269] the long formula found in Paul which is comparatively the most reliable as the repetition of a very old tradition (1Cor 15:3-8), [270] and the various Gospel witnesses. It cannot be denied that there are many contradictions in the Gospel narratives concerning the sequence of the apparitions. [271] If we concentrate, for example, on the appearance to the twelve who are the official witnesses of the Resurrection we find that in three accounts (Luke, John 20 and the Markan Appendix) that Jesus appears to the Twelve gathered together in a room in Jerusalem. In two accounts (Matthew and John 21) Jesus appears to them in Galilee. As far as the Ascension after the Resurrection is concerned, in Luke's Gospel it takes place on Easter Sunday night; in Acts it happens after forty days. In John 20:22 the risen Lord confers the Holy Spirit on the occasion of his first appearance to the disciples on the Easter Sunday night. The angel's directive in Mark 16:7 and Matthew 28:7 bids the disciples to go to Galilee to see Jesus - a command that would make little sense were they to see him first in Jerusalem!

In the face of such apparent divergences the theologians have taken various attitudes towards the Resurrection, [272] from denial to qualified affirmation. For some the Resurrection is a 'falsification', a primitive mythology to express the truth of Jesus' victory over death. Some others taken an 'agnostic attitude'; they affirm that Jesus is risen from the dead, Jesus lives and the cause of Jesus continues, but they hold that the 'how' of it cannot be determined with certainty. Most of the theologians avoid both of the above mentioned extreme attitudes and take an 'affirmatory attitude': Jesus' body did not corrupt in the tomb, it was also not resuscitated to the physical existence as in the case of Lazarus! The Resurrection was an eschatological transformation of the physical, historical body of Jesus (1 Cor 15:35 ff.). [273] The physical body that is described in some of the accounts of the appearances were only apologetic developments to counter the argument of the opponents that it was only a hallucination (Lk 24:39., Jn 20:27., 21:10-13). [274] 'Flesh and blood cannot inherit the Kingdom of God' (1 Cor 15:50)!

Pannenberg rejects first of all a positivistic conception of history which would exclude 'a priori' the possibility of the bodily resurrection of Jesus. [275] Pannenberg considers the Resurrection as historical on the basis of the essential historicity, as we have mentioned, of the tradition of the appearances and that of the 'Empty Tomb'. He maintains that both of these are independent traditions and they prove in a complementary way the historicity of Jesus' resurrection. [276] Pannenberg is also convinced that the reports regarding a 'physical' or 'corporeal' Jesus encountered by the disciples in the appearances cannot be true.But the report of Paul in 1 Cor: 1-11 regarding the appearances, he argues, has good historical foundation. It involves concrete witnesses who could still be interrogated. Paul's own personal vision of the Lord corroborates the report of those who first saw him. The interpretation of the 'appearances' as an imaginative projection of the disciples, Pannenberg declares, cannot hold ground. The appearances result in the Easter faith and it was not vice versa. [277] Karl Rahner is also of the opinion that the Resurrection experience of the disciples was not a merely subjective one; it was given from without. It was different from experiences of religious enthusiasm or mysticism or some other emotional phenomena which could be stimulated and repeated.[278] Like Pannenberg and Rahner we also prefer to maintain that the appearance of the risen Lord was not an hallucination. At the same time it could not also be a physical vision as that of a body resuscitated and brought back once again to the realm of space and time. The Greek word 'ōphthē', appeared to (1Cor 15:5ff), which is repeated does not refer to a physical vision; but what is meant by that is also not mere internal experience nor synchronized ecstacy. We also do think that the discrepencies in the sequence of the apparition narratives are simply irrelevant; what is important is that the Lord appeared. [279] Even in the modern journalism, we know from daily experience, the details differ from report to report!

Regarding the 'Empty tomb', various hypotheses are proposed by those who deny it. [280] Some opine that according to the custom the body of Jesus, as that of a criminal, was dumped into a common burial place (Deut 21:23; Gal 3:13). But the story of Joseph of Arimathea who is mentioned in reference to the burial in all four Gospels would prove that the burial place of Jesus was not a mass grave. Pannenbergs thinks that the story of the 'Empty Tomb' is presupposed in the Pauline statement even though it is not explicitly mentioned by him. It was a tradition of the Jerusalem community and as such it must be reliable; if not true, it could be immediately refuted by those who lived in immediate vicinity to the scene. This is especially relevant in reference to the Jews who spoke of a 'grave robbery'. Pannenberg also suggests that the empty tomb tradition developed independently of the appearance traditions. [281] Pannenberg's insistence on the 'Empty Tomb' would imply that Jesus' body did not corrupt in the tomb. The historicity of the 'Empty Tomb' as proposed by Pannenberg is questioned by Christian Duquoc. [282]

It could also be asked if the resurrection of Christ is our resurrection as Paul himself asserts, then why should we expect his to take place in a way different from ours which does not presuppose an empty tomb![283] Why should Christ's resurrection be of a different order from our resurrection? By becoming man Christ entered fully into that human condition which entails physical corruption after death. If so, why should a transformation of Christ's body be not in harmony with the process of corruption?[284] At the same time we have also to recognize that if Jesus' resurrection were just like our resurrection it would not make an event that had radical consequences in the life and faith of the first Christian community. As the event of God's self-manifestation and as the revelation of his power over creation - a point which we will discuss in the following section - it is quite understandable that the resurrection of Jesus took place in a way extraordinarily different from ours. Otherwise it would not have that revelatory value which we give it today. It would no more be a guarantee for us of our resurrection!

We have referred to the appearance traditions and the 'Empty Tomb' as two factors which independently of each other point to the fact of the Resurrection as an historical event. But what kind of a history is that after all? Karl Rahner warns against understanding the Resurrection as if the resurrected Lord were still within the dimensions of space and time, history![285] The Resurrection is first and foremost an eschatological event, an event that took place beyond the categories of space and time. It was not a physical resuscitation. In the Resurrection event we cannot also play eschatology versus history or vice versa! It is true nobody has seen the 'Resurrection' as such and that in this event the limits of history yields to God's freedom from space and time. Resurrection lies outside the public domain in which the general ministry of Jesus was set. Still there is an interaction between history and eschatology in the event of Jesus' resurrection. What happened beyond the limits of time and space, i.e. in the eschatological sphere touches human beings who are still within the bounds of space and time.[286] The consequences and effects of the eschatological event of Jesus' resurrection has bearing on history, eventhough we do not accept the disasterous principle that what is not historical is therefore unreal![287] We would also maintain that the language that is used to explain the Resurrection should be understood as an analogous language or as a metaphorical language which is only some way approximate to the event, for example, speaking with the risen

Lord, touching him etc. The language of the Resurrection, as Pannenberg himself concedes is a metaphorical one and the incomprehensible reality of Jesus' resurrection and his eschatological destiny can be expressed in no way other than the one that is historically conditioned for us.[288]

Admitting the eschatological character of the Resurrection as a radical transformation of the physical body to a realm that is free of space and time, i.e. history, Pannenberg argues that Resurrection is still to be considered as an historical event. It is more a matter of words than of substance, so asserts Pannenberg, whether 'historicity' can be applied to Jesus' Resurrection. The Resurrection does not dissolve into the subjective impressions of the witnesses; it refers to an event that really happened at a definite time and in a place that can be specified.[289] The event of the Resurrection can be subject to historical verification as far as it is deduced from the real death of Jesus, the appearances and the empty tomb which are all events in space and time.[290] From beyond the history, from the eschatological plane, the Resurrection leaves its effects on history. The history guards the mystery of Resurrection. The destiny of Jesus in the Resurrection must be open to historical research, says Pannenberg; otherwise the faith in the Resurrection rests on caprice and illusion.[291] It has however, also to be remembered that Pannenberg does not consider the historical proof of the Resurrection as a proof that is incontrovertible in a scientific historical sense. The non-historical and strictly eschatological aspects that are involved in this event make such a proof impossible. So strictly speaking, the Resurrection is to be considered 'historically very probable' and valid until the contrary is proved.[292] What we have is a provisional but reliable knowledge; the Resurrection is made 'credible' and 'tenable' but not 'incontrovertible'. An absolute verification is possible only in the Eschaton![293] Karl Rahner's understanding of the Resurrection as a 'miracle', a 'semeion' (sign) or call, directed to us, could also complement the above mentioned view of Pannenberg.[293a] The Resurrection is not contradictory to the nature, but it is a qualitative leap from the realm of the history into that of eschatology![294]

In reference to the Indian Christology, we think that the categories of 'Sthula sarira' and 'Sukshma sarira' which are used to explain the Resurrection could be further enriched by the theology of the Resurrection both of Karl Rahner and Wolfhart Pannenberg. We would also maintain that the lower is eminently contained and fundamentally possible in the higher. Eschatology is not versus history, but history is contained in the eschatology. Although there are apologetic elements that are contained in the scriptural descriptions of the event of the Resurrection, the faith in the 'bodily resurrection' of Jesus, as the guarantee of our resurrection is true. The traditions regarding the appearances and the 'Empty Tomb' are also to be taken basicly, although not in all details, as reliable. We would conclude this section with the remark that even though Jesus is removed from the tangible dimensions of space and time with his resurrection, he is still the master and Lord of all realities both tangible and non-tangible, sensible and non-sensible and therefore it would be quite appropriate for the risen Jesus to show to his disciples his freedom not only from tangibility, but also from non-tangibility, his freedom not only from sensibility, but also from non-sensibility, i.e., his freedom to be tangible and sensible as well as to be non-tangible and non-sensible. In his eschatological state the Lord still retains his capability to be historically tangible and sensible, if he prefers so for some adequate reasons - for example to guarantee and strengthen the faith of Jesus' disciples in a situation of delusion that followed his Crucifixion.

2. The 'Basileia' in 'Prolepsis'

In the sixth chapter of our work we indicated that the Vedantins consider the Resurrection as a symbol of 'Advaitic illumination' for Christ, the ultimate realization of his divinity - something that is expected from every body- and as Christ's final realization of truth by his defiance of death. These views are held especially by S. Radhakrishnan and Akhilananda.[295] The Indian Christian theologians like P. Chenchiah and P.D. Devanandan, however, see the Resurrection as the realization of the 'New Creation' and as the victorious integration of matter and spirit by Christ. For V. Chakkarai, as we have mentioned, the resurrection is Christ's overcoming the 'Sakti' (force) of death by the 'Navasakti' (new force) of love. S.J. Samartha thinks that Resurrection is the event by which the historical uniqueness of Jesus reaches universality as the 'unbound Christ'.[296] It is to be mentioned that the position of the Vedantins which implies a depreciation of the human body does not do justice to the aspect of 'corporeality' that is an essential element of the Resurrection faith. The material world and its history are still excluded from the sphere of salvation. God does not become all in all! The universal and eschatological salvific aspect of the Resurrection, on the other hand, is stressed in the concepts of 'Navasakti' and 'New Creation', although not to the point of a thorough systematisation as we find, for example, in the theology of Pannenberg.

In the view of Pannenberg, the resurrection of Christ is to be understood in the context of the jewish apocalyptic hopes which linked the revelation of God's glory at the end with the general resurrection of the dead.[297] Much has been written so far on the apocalyptic tradition that was prevalent during the time of Jesus.[298] Jesus also shared this tradition of eschatological expectation and his teachings cannot be understood if not in the horizon of this apocalypsis.[299] Jesus preached the imminent Kingdom of God. According to Pannenberg, this resounding motif of Jesus' message must be recovered as a key to the whole of Christian theology.[300] The 'end-time' (Eschaton) in which God's glory and Lordship would be established over the whole creation, however, did not come as Jesus and his contemporaries expected; the Kingdom of God (Basileia) is apparently not realized; Jesus is executed; the Son of Man has not appeared; neither the last judgement nor the resurrection of the dead took place! In such a situation of delusion Jesus appeared to his disciples and 'evidently something had happened to the witnessess of the appearances of the Risen One for which their language had no other word than that used to characterize the eschatological espectation, i.e. resurrection from the dead'[301]. The apocalyptic expectation is verified, but not exactly in the way it was expected. Only Jesus is risen! But that would mean the end time (Eschaton) has begun definitively with this resurrection. The final establishment of God's Lordship has already begun in principle and its completion is imminent! Jesus' identification of his message of the Kingdom of God with his person and the claim to divine authority that was implied in this identification,[302] hence, became intelligible for his disciples within the tradition of the Old Testament promise of the 'apocalypsis' (revelation of God's glory) at the 'Eschaton'. God's glory is manifested in Jesus resurrection; God has revealed himself to be the power over all things (Macht über alles) including the final destiny of man called death! The Reign of God (Basileia) has occured in the personal fate of Jesus and thus his preaching over the immanence of this Reign is vindicated. In the resurrection of Jesus God manifests himself in anticipation (Prolepsis) as the eschatological Lord. If God has Himself revealed in Jesus' resurrection as the Lord over all things, then, according to Pannenberg, revelation which is the manifestation of the deity of God and the establishment of his power over all things - we had explained this point in one of the previous sections[303] - in the strict sense has occured in Jesus.

It is evident, according to Pannenberg, that we cannot share the apocalyptic eschatological expectation in its imminent form for the whole of creation in all its details as was held by the first disciples of Jesus. Still he maintains that 'if the apocalyptic expectation should be totally excluded from the realm of possibility for us, then the early Christian faith in Christ is also excluded'; then there would be no continuation between the Jesus preached by the apostles and the one in whom we believe. The apocalyptic expectation of a future judgement and the resurrection of the dead, therefore, belong to the basis of the Christian faith. Apart from the horizon of the eschatological expectation, Pannenberg declares, it remains incomprehensible 'why the man Jesus can be the ultimate revelation of God, why in him and only in him God is supposed to have appeared'[304].

The resurrection of Jesus as of the one crucified is the eschatological self-demonstration of God; but no one can comprehend what is specifically contained in this self-demonstration.[305] The self-manifestation of God has not abolished his own mystery. We do not know how that which happened to Jesus in his resurrection is going to be realized in the whole of God's creation because 'Christian knowledge stands under the sign of the same 'already' and 'not yet' that marks every aspect of the life of Christians between the resurrection and the second coming of Jesus'[306]. In the resurrection of Jesus we see the end (Eschaton) of history within history. In the destiny of Jesus God reveals himself 'as the God who is powerful over all events, because the one who controls the end of all things is likewise the One powerful over everything'[308].

From the resurrection of Jesus Christ, according to Pannenberg, the human history achieves a new dimension. The former is a clue, a 'key', to the understanding of the latter. As we have seen in the seventh chapter, man in his characteristic of being open to the future (Zukunftsoffenheit) hopes for a fulfilment beyond death, a fulfilment which involves not only himself, but also the society and the history as a whole. So the eschatology proposed by Pannenberg is fully in accord with his anthropology. It is not an uncritical acceptance of the attitude and conceptions of the primitive Christians. The anthropological hope for a fulfilment is corroborated and confirmed by Jesus' resurrection. Pannenberg's hypothesis regarding the course of history as progressing towards a future of fulfilment in the Eschaton is not an arbitrary one. It is not just a hypothesis which is verifiable only at the end and hence cannot be taken for certain until the End comes. The proleptic character of the fulfilment at the Eschaton that is manifested in the resurrection of Jesus is the clue, according to Pannenberg, to understand how it will be more or less with the human history at the end of times. We have a ground and paradigm for the destiny of History in Jesus himself because the destiny of history has been manifested in the resurrection of Jesus. It is a concrete 'Prolepsis' (anticipation) of the Eschaton. The first Christians were also in a certain sense right in their imminent expectation because there is an essential unity between the event of Jesus' resurrection and the final fulfilment of history; the time separating these events does not cancel this essential oneness. [309] What can be fully verified only at the end of history is already verified in anticipation in the resurrection of Jesus. It is the guarantee of our hope. As the anticipated expression of the end of history, resurrection enables the meaning of the universal history to be deciphered from this moment.[310] The difference between Jesus' resurrection and of others is only one of precedence, anticipation and unsurpassability; qualitatively it is the same. The anticipation of the end is not the end itself, but the beginning of the end.[311] Because in the destiny of Jesus the end had been anticipatorily realized without qualitative difference, the first Christians could proclaim him as the eschatological revealer of God, and the anticipatory structure of his destiny functions as a clue to explain the whole of history.[312] The fact that Jesus is the ultimate revelation of God as 'Macht über alles' does not prejudice the openness of the future. Hence the importance of understanding the event of the Resurrection proleptically. [313] Though the end remains outstanding on the horizon of the future, as Frank Trupper observes explaining the view of Pannenberg, it has occured provisionally in Jesus Christ, making, in contrast to the view of Hegel, a conception of the unity of history possible without sacrificing its openness. [314] So the anticipatory appearance of the end of history does not mean that history itself is now abolished and the human endeavours to bu ild up a better future is senseless. The opposite is true! Since the end of history is already present, it is made possible for the first time to understand the history and human endeavours in a unitary and meaningful whole! [315] It is this concern for the 'whole' of history that distinguishes the eschatology of Pannenberg from that, for example, of Moltmann. Pannenberg does not begin with the category of the future, but with a concern for the wholeness, truth of the whole and meaning of the history. There is no 'eschaton' independently of the history, because it is the truth of the history that is realized in the eschaton.[316] The fact that the truth of God's revelation that is realized definitively in the resurrection of Jesus is a key to the understanding of history would mean that Jesus is the revelatioin of the nature of man, the human destiny [317] and of the whole of reality because 'as long as the whole of reality can be understood more deeply and more convincingly through Jesus than without him, it proves true in our everyday and personal knowledge that in Jesus the creative origin of all reality stands revealed' [318]. This view of Pannenberg corroborates our thesis that Christ is the mystery of man and of the human history!

The resurrection of Christ as the revelation of God throws light not only on the mystery of man and his history, but above all on His own mystery of Incarnation. Resurrection is also the clue or the key to understand the theology of the Incarnation. The theology of Incarnation has to be derived from the theology of resurrection ('Christologie von vorn'!), because 'the acknowledgement of the incarnation is a final résumé of the revelatory history of the God of Israel' [319]. The Incarnation is an interpretation, according to Pannenberg, 'of the historical self-demonstration of God in the destiny of Jesus of Nazareth - in his earthly works, in his cross, and decisively in his resurrection' [320]. According to the historico-eschatological Christology of Pannenberg, Jesus can be understood as with God and thus is himself God only starting from the perspective of his resurrection from the dead [321] and the key to the central theme of Incarnation is the eschatological function of Jesus as the anticipation of God's future.[322] That means 'apart from the resurrection from the dead Jesus would not be God, eventhough from the perspective of the Resurrection, he is retrospectively one with God in his whole pre-Easter life' [323]. Before the Easter event Jesus was not only unrecognizable as God, but he would not have been who he was, without this event [324] because 'apart from Jesus' resurrection, it would not be true that from the very beginning of his earthly way God was one with this man. This is true from all eternity because of Jesus' resurrection. Until his resurrection, Jesus' unity with God was hidden not only to other men but above all.... for Jesus himself also ... because the ultimate decision about it had not been given' [325] . This view of Pannenberg has nothing to do with the heresy of 'Adoptionism', as is often misunderstood. Pannenberg asserts that 'Jesus' unity with God, established in the Easter event, does not begin only with this event - it comes into force retroactively from the perspective of this event for the claim to authority in the activity of the earthly Jesus. Conversely, the pre-Easter Jesus' claim to authority is to be understood as an anticipation of his unity with God that was shown by the Easter event'[326]. Jesus Resurrection establishes retroactively that Jesus' person is not to be separated from God in any way or at any time. Jesus was what he is before he concretely knew about it. [327] What we have explained in the previous sections regarding the divine consciousness of Jesus and his virgin birth should be understood in the context of this eschatological vision of Pannenberg's Christology. Pannenberg considers as most probable that for the primitive Christianity the starting point of all Christological confessions was the resurrection of Jesus. [328]

We think it unnecessary to consider here in reference to Karl Rahner those points which he has in common with those we have discussed. But, we would mention that just as Pannenberg, Rahner also bases the faith in the Resurrection on anthropological considerations. We have mentioned that according to Pannenberg, the jewish apocalyptic expectation, that forms the context of the Resurrection faith of the disciples, is based on man's basic experience of hope for a future of fulfilment (Zukunftsoffenheit). Similarly, Rahner also argues that the apostolic witness of Jesus' resurrection would be simply unintelligible and unacceptable - unlike secular testimony this cannot be positively verified - unless in the context of our transcendental hope in the Resurrection. [329]The affirmation of one's own existence is an affirmation that one's existence is permanently valid and redeemable. The platonic misunderstanding of an anthropological dualism is to be avoided here. This is our transcendental hope and this eschatological hope necessarily seeks the historical mediation and confirmation in which it can become explicit.[330] Man's transcendental hope is the condition of the possibility of the faith in Jesus' resurrection. This has to be understood in the background of what we have already explained in the preceeding sections regarding Rahner's concept of transcendentality and categoriality. The transcendental hope beyond death is an a priori datum of existence; to deny it is to deny the full dimension of one's own existence. Still Rahner admits, true to his line of thinking,

that even without guilt, in certain situations, one may not bring one's transcendental affirmation of the Resurrection into categorial or thematic explicitation by acknowledging the Resurrection of Jesus as the guarentee and
historical confirmation of the resurrection of every man. [331] According to
Rahner, man finds his death not absurd and he derives his readiness to die
only on the basis of this anthropological transcendental hope. [332]

Here it is also worth mentioning that there is a major difference between
Rahner and Pannenberg in their approach to the question of Jesus' resurrection. True to his historico-eschatological Christology, as we have mentioned,
Pannenberg sees that the theology of Incarnation is something that is implied
in the Resurrection and hence to be derived from the Resurrection. Pannenberg's Christology from below is also a Christology from the end (Christologie
von vorn). On the contrary, true to his anthropo-transcendental approach,
Rahner's Christology from below is a Christology from the beginning, based
on the ultimate God-given possibilities already implied in the reality of man.
So, for Rahner, in apparent contradiction to the position of Pannenberg,
the theology of the Resurrection is something that is implied in the theology
of the Incarnation and hence to be derived from the Incarnation. [333] We would,
however, maintain that this difference is only one of approach and not one
of substance; they are mutually complementary and not contradictory! A
synthesis of both would be also a rich contribution to make explicit the notions
implied in the 'Navasakti' of V. Chakkarai, the 'New Creation' of P. Chenchiah,
the 'matter-spirit-integration' proposed by P.D. Devanandan and the concept
of the 'unbound Christ' that is suggested by the resurrection theology of
S.J. Samartha. It is also important to stress in the Indian theological context,
as we had mentioned in the sixth chapter, God's manifestation of the supremacy of love that is implied in the event of the Resurrection. Love is life
conquering death [334] because love is mightier than death! [335]

3. The Resurrection and the Re-incarnation

In the above sections we dealt with the question of Jesus' resurrection as
the vindication of Jesus' eschatological claims and as the explicitation of
the meaning that is intrinsic to his death. Now we consider the question
of the eschatology in reference to all human beings with special regard for
the Indian Christological problematics.

a. Death and Immortality

In the first part of our work we discussed sufficiently the Vedantic quest for immortality. [336] Death, according to the Vedantic thinking, is followed by re-birth until the Atman is completely liberated from all Karma particles. The body is like a shell that is to be shed; it has no permanent value; it has no part in immortality. Such a body-soul dualism and a consequent so-called immortality of the soul would not be reconcilable with the Christian vision of man as the substantial unity of body and soul. [336a] Man has no soul that could be separated from the body, as Karl Rahner argues. [337] Body and soul are not separate realities that could exist independently of each other. Death 'definifies' the human existence in its totality as body and soul. The human immortality, Rahner, contends, does not mean just the continuity of a human soul after death, in a platonic way. [338] The death of man means the end of both body and soul! The history of man comes to an end with his death. [339] Pannenberg also affirms that death is the end of all what we are at present, both in body and soul. The Greek concept of 'soul' as a permanent 'kern' within man, similar to that of the Vedantic view, is according to Pannenberg not acceptable. [340] Death is a radical event that affects the whole of human existence and the seriousness of this radicality is watered down by the expression 'immortality of the soul'. The inner life of our consciousness or the so-called soul, Pannenberg reasons, is 'so tied to our corporeal functions that it is impossible for it to be able to continue by itself alone. This seriousness of death must be recognized by every conception of a life-beyond-death that is to be regarded as being meaningful for us today' [341]. No element of human existence can outlast death. What follows death is not the continuation of a part of the former existence, but a totally new existence of the whole man that results from a radical transformation. It is another mode of existence of the whole man. [342] An 'immortality theory' is not required to defend the eternal aspect of human existence. The jewish apocalyptic conception of the resurrection of the dead was understood as a totally new beginning; a new creation. [343] It is this seriousness and irrevocability of death that is also meant in the concept of transformation advocated by Paul (1 Cor 15:51ff). Inspite of the radicality of death, so opines Pannenberg, it is inherent to man to hope beyond death [344] and this hope beyond death is that which makes all human hopes meaningful because 'whether or not hope is a meaningful attitude in life at all is decided for the individual in the final analysis in the question of whether there is anything to be hoped for beyond death' [345] . Pannenberg prefers the expression 'resurrection of the dead' to the expression 'immortality of the soul' to clarify the human destiny beyond death because it preserves the positive impulses of the idea of immortality, it implies a radical transformation or new creation and it is eminently concretized through its association with the destiny of Jesus.[346]

According to Rahner also, what continues after death is not just the 'soul' of man, but the totality of man in a radically different way. The human existence cannot be reduced to a biologico-sensitive sphere. Man is more than the mere interplay of elementary particles of physics and biochemistry.[347] The identiy of man in his totality that continues after death means man as the being of transcendence (Wesen der Transzendenz) which comes to its definitiveness before God. It would not be just an 'immortal soul' that identifies a man after his death.[348] In the order of salvation both the body and the soul have to participate; body as the concrete historicity of man (konkrete Geschichtlichkeit des Menschen) and soul as the subject of timeless human transcendence (Subjekt unbegrenzter Transzendentalität). [349] Unlike the Vedanta, the Christian theology stresses the abiding value of the whole of human existence even after death, without devaluating the totality of the phenomenon of death and the radicality of the new beginning in a divinely transformed existence, similar to the existence of the risen Lord.

b. 'Re-Incarnation' and 'Purgatory'?

Here we are dealing with a question of great importance for the Indian Anthropology and Christology, namely, that of Transmigration, also known as Metempsychosis, Palingenese, Metensomatose or simply re-incarnation. [350] In the first part of our work we had sufficiently discussed the question of re-incarnation in conncetion with the doctrine of 'Karma-Samsara'. [351] In the Vedas, as we had indicated, we see 'heaven' and 'hell' as the possible alternatives for man in his life after death. But in the Upanisads the doctrine of re-incarnation or transmigration appears and even 'heaven' and 'hell' are relegated to the realm of change and non-permanence. Salvation cannot be in this changing and cyclic history, but only beyond it. [352] The body's function in the long process of life, death and re-birth is as an instrument of purification of the Karma particles of the previous life. If one succeeds in self-purification already before death he attains liberation inspite of his still continuing bodily existence (Jeevanmukti) unlike those who may have to wait till the separation of the soul (Atman) from the body at the moment of death (Videhamukti). [353]

It must be mentioned without reservation that what lies as a basis for the theory of 'Karma-Samsara' and the consequent belief in transmigration of the soul is the Vedantic postulate of the basic and essential divinity of every man which further leads to the faith in the self-salvation of man. Through births, deaths and re-births one has to develope interiorly until one becomes illumined and a single life span is considered too short for this process of self-realization which ends only with the unification of one's own consciousness with the divine consciousness. [354] So we would say, the re-incarnation is a bi-product of the theory of self-salvation. In the Bhakti schools were a certain notion of salvation by grace gains upper hand the hold of the concept of transmigration is also proportionately reduced.

The essential aspect of the re-incarnation theory is that it is relative in character; it is not the absolute destiny of man; it belongs to the realm of 'Maya'. Some western supporters of the re-incarnation theory like Hans Tor-westen refer even to biblical passages which would point to such a 'relative situation' of man even after his death: Mt 17:10-13; Mt 27:52-53; Jn 9:1-3 etc.! [355] For those who find the concept of an 'eternal hell' as monstrous, the theory of transmigration looks like a reasonable alternative! [356] Prof. Norbert Klaes points to the aspect of 'relativity' even in the Christian eschatology especially in reference to the faith in the second coming of Christ, last judgement, the concept of a 'purgatory' that is limited in time, and the non-simultaneousness (Nicht-Gleichzeitigkeit) of the individual and collective eschatology. He rightly suggests that these points of Christian faith have elements that are in common with the Indian theories of 'Karma', 'Maya' and their implied place-time relativity! [357] Prof. Klaes refers especially to the faith in the 'purgatory' as a very good example for the presence of a certain re-birth theory (Wiedergeburtslehre) among some Christians; it points to the fact that an imperfectly lived life is not sufficient for the ultimate human fulfilment; hence the need for a state of purification after death and before the final judgement. [358] But contrary to the theory of Samsara and re-birth and its parallel elements in Christian faith Prof. Klaes stresses that the definitiveness (Endgültigkeit) of the human life before God is realized here and now in this world and in this life; it happens in a single span of human life.[359] This is also, we would note, what is implied in Hebr 9:27. The biblical evidences which are often cited to support a re-incarnation theory are interpretations out of text and context. Inspite of the fact that there are some faint similarities between the theory of re-incarnation (Seelenwanderung) and the Christian eschatology, there is a fundamental irreconciliability between the two because the transmigration contradicts the basic and substantial unity (Wesenseinheit) of man's body and soul which is indispensable for the Christian anthropology.[360] The question of salvation by 'Grace' and not by 'human deeds' which is central to Christian soteriology cannot also be reconciled with the notion of self-salvation in repeated births and deaths!

We have mentioned that there is no place for an eternal Hell in the context of the theory of re-incarnation. According to Pannenberg, 'eternity' means 'judgement'; after death there is no more possibility of changing the option that has been made for or against God; the personal decision or judgement is made definitive and irrevocable and man's 'exclusion from God and from his destiny is the pain of eternity'[361]. This would imply one life and only one death without a further chance. This position is also similar to that of Karl Rahner who considers 'eternity' as the finalization and definitivization of the spiritual freedom which has been exercised in time. There is no more becoming or 'Samsara' after death.[362] Eternity is in every day life; it comes to be out of time; eternity is not a time-span after death, but time made definitive through death.[363] The eternity is already at work in the present and the eschatological statements are only transposition into the future of something which a Christian experiences in grace at present.[364] The present basic disposition of a human being for or against God acquires a final and definitive validity through death.[365] In reference to the question of an eternal hell, Rahner maintains that the 'whole humanity' will have to reach a positive conclusion, according to the very plan of God's self-communication to the creation. Although that is the case with the 'whole', the seriousness of human freedom demands that the possibility of individual eternal loss due to the abuse of freedom must be seriously reckoned with. This 'possibility' of eternal hell, according to Rahner, however does not assert its actuality, i.e. the actual loss of certain people cannot be asserted.[366] In reference to the 'purgatory' Rahner conceeds that there is a possibility of a process of maturation 'after' death in which man's basic decision permeates the whole length and breadth of his reality. Due to the multiple structure and unequal phases of man, a complete integration of the total reality of the subject into his basic decision has to take place. But this should by no means be understood as a process of becoming in temporal categories after death in a purifying place or state or fire which do not belong to the essence of the dogma of 'Purgatory'. [367] These above mentioned clarifications are important in avoiding an superficial parallelization of 'Re-Incarnation' and 'Purgatory'.

c. 'Eschaton' Now

The notion of 'eternity' in reference to the present which we have just discussed is very important in this section: eternity is not the continuation of time without end, nor the incalculable long lasting mode of pure time; eternity comes to be in the present time as its mature fruit, as Rahner himself affirms. [368] Eternity is, according to W. Pannenberg, time itself, freed from its relativity. In time man already lives and determines his eternity. Our eternal life in the resurrection is the same life and reality that we are today in time; our future resurrection is nothing else than the eternal depth of time which we already have, and which for God's creative eyes is already present. As the depth of eternity is already with us in the present, in the present we are already living the eternity to which we will be raised by resurrection. [369] So the question of a time of waiting between death and the final resurrection at the end of the world is simply irrelevant; so also the problem of a body decaying in the tomb or being cremated! Just as this life is already eternity, so also after death there is no need to wait for the beginning of eternity till the rest of the world comes to its end. Beyond the flow of time everything is eternal present. [370] There is a continuity between the resurrection life and the life lived historically; man's historical life is eternalized through a radical transformation of the resurrection which discloses 'that which already constitutes the depth of time now and which is already present for God's eyes' [371].

Pannenberg maintains that the 'general resurrection' which is the destiny of humanity and of the whole creation has already occurred in Jesus Christ. [371a] So we do no have to wait still for another collective resurrection.

In the moment of death each one of us shares in this fundamental and general resurrection initiated by Christ. Still there is point in speaking about a 'general resurrection' in the future because 'if the social and individual destinies of men condition each other so that they can only be realized together, then the totality of human individuals is required for the realization of the social destiny of man'[372]. The categories of the 'final resurrection' and a waiting for the end are only indications of the communitarian, social and cosmic aspects of the ultimate human realization.[373]

Karl Rahner also rejects the idea of a 'state-in-between' (Zwischenzustand) from individual death to universal resurrection. He argues that to express the intimate relation between individual fulfilment and the universal fulfilment, the temporal category of a 'state-in-between' is not required.[374] It is only a conceptual model (Vorstellungsmodell) to understand the universal solidarity in the order of salvation, by uniting the individual destiny with the collective destiny of mankind. The 'State-in-between' (Zwischenzustand) in its mythological form, according to Rahner, is also not a binding dogma and so one is free to keep it or not.[375] This would imply that every human being faces the reality of his resurrection at the time of his death regardless of the fact whether the dead body is buried or cremated or something else happens to it. Even the Catholic dogma of the 'Assumption of the Blessed Virgin Mary' does not say that it is a reality that is reserved only for her.[376] In this sense we can say that even if the custom in Palestine were to cremate the dead instead of burying them, still we can validly speak of a 'bodily' resurrection and ascension of Jesus and a 'bodily' assumption of Mary and the reality of the 'bodily' resurrection of the dead in this pattern. The fate of those who died before the Christ-event, we would opine, and the fate of those who die without ever having known or heard of Christ must also be understood according to the same pattern with special consideration of the whole of cosmic history as an eternal presence before God. This does not, however, cancel the fundamental difference between the resurrection of Jesus and of the rest of humanity because, as Rahner observes, unlike the others Jesus was made Lord and the Messiah by the resurrection, he becomes the divine norm for the rest of creation and as the culmination of creation Jesus' resurrection manifested God's definitive self-communication to the creation in and through Jesus' 'Hypostatic Union' which ultimately is the cause of God's self-communication to every man in Grace!.[377]

There is, therefore, we would argue, an intimate relation between the 'Eschaton' and 'Now'. The eschatological interpretations are not anticipated reports of the future; they are actually the interpretations of man's present existence now; they explicate the deep and eternal dimensions of life now. In this sense the Vedantic concept of Karma-Samsara and re-incarnation could also be given; as Norbert Klaes suggests, a positive Christian interpretation. They need not necessarily be considered as informations about the future situation after death but as the present existential experience of man that his life is inseparably bound up with the world, that he is now a 'prisoner' of the changeables and that a liberation from this situation, by one's own efforts and without the Grace of God, is not an easily realizable one. [378] Even in this interpretation, the idea of a 'saving God' will have to be introduced as a necessary Christian corrective!

Conclusion to Chapter Eight

In complementation to our evaluation on the Mystery of Christ as the universal principle that lies at the root of the mystery of man and the human history which we did in the seventh chapter, we tried here in the eighth chapter to concentrate our evaluative discussion on the historical fact of Jesus of Nazareth as the centre and summit of Creation and as the realization of the transcendental destiny of man as is manifested in the mysteries of the Incarnation, the Life, the Cross and the Resurrection of Christ. We have indicated especially the possibilities of a Hindu-Christian dialogue through a process of re-interpretation of the Vedantic categories. For example, we made use of the notion of the 'Advaitic Unity' to understand the concept that is implied in the doctrine of the 'Hypostatic Union' in a less ontico-static and in a more dynamic way. Similarly, we have put the 'becoming' of God that is implied in the event of the Incarnation in a new light to make it not repugnant to the Vedantic mind. The substitution of 'Mission' for 'Pre-existence' was meant to avoid an uncritical and superficial dialogical parallelization of the notions of 'Avatar' and Incarnation. We have also tried to clarify the questions of the virginal conception and the divine consciousness of Christ with the purpose of avoiding the misunderstanding in a Hindu-Christian discussion on the Christ-Mystery that could arise from a dualistic Vedantic anthropology. In drawing a harmony between the 'Dharma' and the 'Basileia' we have insisted on the Reign of Dharma as integrally united with Jesus

Christ, thus putting the person of Christ himself above his ethical teachings. We have also tried to counteract the Vedantic depreciation of the material reality and the human body by stressing God's intensified interest in man's material history as is manifested in the events of the Cross and the Resurrection, bringing to light thereby how salvation is to be understood as a gratuitous gift of God through Christ and not as man's personal achievement. We have found the Vedantic categories of 'Sthula' and 'Suksma Sarira' as a possible starting-point for a reasonable dialogue regarding the question of man's resurrection, arguing thereby that the 'end' of the human history is not a 'dissolution' leading to a new cosmic process, but a definitive fulfilment realized through the divine transformation. It was also considered important for us to clarify the notion of the 'immortality of the soul' in reference to the Vedantic notion of 'Karma-Samsara' and how dialogue possibilities could be opened regarding the concepts of the 'Purgatory' and the 'General Judgement' stressing the present, existential character of all futuristic, eschatological statements. In short, in an earnest attempt at a search for the possibilities of dialogue with the Indian picture of Christ, we have indicated how the mystery of Christ, as realized in Jesus of Nazareth, is ultimately the mystery of man himself and his history. Our consideration of the 'Christ-Principle' and the 'Christ-Fact' leads logically to an evaluation of the 'Christ-Sharing' in the Indian context. That is our concern in the next, final, chapter of our Indian Anthropo-Christological investigation.

CHAPTER IX

JESUS CHRIST, THE MYSTERY OF MAN AND OF THE HUMAN HISTORY

It must mentioned here at the very outset that this final chapter is a synthesis of the anthropological, historical and Christological issues we have evaluated in the two preceding chapters. The title of this chapter also shows this intention clearly. In other words, we are recapitulating in this chapter the problem of the 'unique' and the 'universal', which is the most fundamental problem of the Indian Christology.[1] If Jesus of Nazareth is according to the Christian faith 'the Christ', then it is the task of the Indian Christology to make clear how Jesus' historical uniqueness does not contradict his universal relevance for the salvation of the whole creation as consummated in man and his history. We shall evaluate here this problematic as done so far especially in the light of the corresponding views of Karl Rahner and Wolfhart Pannenberg and draw the necessary conclusion as far as the salvation of the non Christians and the universality of the God-experience are concerned.

A. The Universality of the Unique

Here we shall consider the interrelation between the 'unique' and the 'universal' which would further serve as a basis for an 'Advaitic' (non-dual) synthesis of the apparently contrasting polarities in anthropology, history and Christology.

1. Jesus' Uniqueness in Question

The problem that underlies the question of the uniqueness of Jesus of Nazareth is that of the relationship between the transcendence and history: the historicisation of the transcendence and the transcendentalisation of the history. In the Indian context of a thorough dualism between the transcendence and history, this problem is immensely acute. We shall recapitulate in a more systematic way what we have already mentioned in the course of our evaluation.

Ontologically speaking, according to the predominent Vedantic thinking, 'oneness' or 'unity' (Ekam, Advaitam) is the reality; change and multiplicity belong to the realm of non-reality: 'Ekam sat vipra bahuda vadanti!" The One is seen in various ways; only the 'One' is unique and what belongs to the multiplicity of appearance is particular and that cannot be unique.[2] This ontological principle, when applied to history, means that as history belongs to the realm of change, no historical event can have a unique and permanent validity. Each epoch, as Radhakrishnan would maintain, may have its purpose, but history as such in its cyclic and never ending character according to the law of 'Karma-Samsara' is outside any salvific goal. There is no salvation in history, but only outside its enslaving boundaries.[3] When this ontological and historical principle is applied to the concept of 'Avatar' (God's so-called descend into history) the necessray conclusion follows that as the history is cyclicly repeated, the 'Avatar' also will have to be repeated: 'Sambhavami yuge yuge!' There are many 'Avatars'; they are basicly equal. As limited manifestations of the Infinite, 'Avatar' has to be repeated according to the needs and necessities of each age! It is absurd, as Radhakrishnan himself argues, to think that God could be 'partial' and be manifested and be born only for example, in the Judeo-Christian context! Although as Vivekananda maintains, there can be 'bigger' and 'smaller' Avatars as there are bigger and smaller bubbles in a boiling pot of water, still, as M.K. Gandhi would argue, all the Avatars are basicly the same. Most of the Hindu thinkers do not find it difficult to add Jesus of Nazareth also to the long list of 'Avatars', after all, a few more or less do not make any fundamental difference.[4] Even Avatars belong only to the sphere of changing 'Maya'![5] And finally what distinguishes an 'Avatar' from another 'ordinary' man is only a relative uniqueness as examples and guides for others.[6] No religious teacher or 'Avatar' could considered as superior to any other teacher.[7] According to each one's spiritual taste and ambience each one is free to accept one or another 'Avatar' as one's 'Ishtadeva';[8] the eternal principles incorporated and preached by the 'Avatars' are the supreme and not any of its particular historical manifestations.[9] In this Vedantic approach, to speak of the uniqueness of Jesus of Nazareth as the Incarnation of God has no point. What is historically unique is contingent and particular; it cannot have any 'per se' absolute and universal validity! Such a Vedantic approach of stressing the universal principle at the cost of the uniqueness of Jesus Christ is also followed, as we have already seen, by some Indian theologians like Raimundo Panikkar. Jesus of Nazareth, for him, is only just one possible manifestation of the universal 'Christ-principle'; 'Christ' is more than Jesus of Nazareth and so the affirmation 'Jesus is the Christ' may not be acceptable for him especially in the Indian context! It is not the historical particularity of Jesus, but the universally valid 'Christ-principle' that is to be preached to the nations. Panikkar ignores the mystery of the Incarnation as the unique historicisation of God and prefers a universally valid theology of the 'Logos', 'Isvara' or 'Christ'. There is no place, as we have indicated already in our evaluation, for a historical synthesis of the universal and the unique, according to the theology of Panikkar.[10] So far: only a recapitulation of the problematic of Jesus' uniqueness in the Vedantic context! The details given in the previous chapters are to be kept here in mind!

Karl Rahner is also aware of the complexity of the problem that is involved in clarifying the universal salvific relevance of a historically particular individual called Jesus of Nazareth! His questions arise from anthropological and historical considerations. How can we affirm, he asks, that the one who is thematically or unthematically affirmed in the act of one's absolute self-commitment to another is precisely Jesus of Nazareth and not anyone else in the history?[11] Why precisely he and only he?[12] These questions are to be understood in the context of Rahner's transcendental anthropology which we have sufficiently discussed especially in the seventh chapter. The question is how a 'contingent' and 'casual' event in a particular place and time can have an ultimate significance for the existence of all human beings in all places and times![13] Would it be sufficiently convincing simply to appeal to 'God's decree' to explain why there is and will be only one Christ? Why should, for example, the 'Unio Hypostatica' as the ultimate realization of the transcendental nature of man be realized only once?[14] In reference to history Rahner asks how the history of Jesus should be considered as something more that what simply happened somewhere in the past, perhaps, with an exemplary value for us today and so very little to do with the basic existence of man as such.[15] How can a finite history claim an absolute character before the Infinity of God? Is not everything that is in history actually only of a provisional character before God who is beyond all history? If so, what has the history of a particular individual, Jesus of Nazareth, to do in reference to the basic existential realization of the whole mankind?[16] As an historical event of a foregone age we do not know even the full details regarding the life of this individual! How can we then make an absolute commitment to the salvific relevance of an historical event that is so to say 'non-absolutely', i.e. only relatively known?[17] If we emphasize, on the other hand, that aspect of man's being that transcends time and history, then history becomes nothing more than a series of cases in which nothing really new happens and every historical event is simply an interpretation of the transcendental reality which is authentic, while the historical reality is not, in which case history simply becomes something of secondary importance in the world! If so, how should it have reached a unique and unrepeatable climax in the particular historical event of Jesus of Nazareth? This is the acute problem of the relationship between transcendence and history of which Karl Rahner is quite conscious. [18]

Similar to the problems which arise from Rahner's anthropological and tran-scendental approach to Christology which we have just mentioned, there are also questions which are caused by the historico-eschatological Christology of Wolfhart Pannenberg regarding the historical uniqueness of Jesus Christ. If the totality of history constitutes God's self-revelation, then it can be asked, how could the historical particularity of Jesus of Nazareth, one event within the whole of history, possibly be the final revelation of God? Or to put the question in an eschatolgical way: if only the End of history illuminates God's revelation in the whole of history, how could a past historical figure be considered as constituting the whole of revelation in the on-going process of history?

These are, of course, no new questions for us; we have discussed them all through our work. In this section, what we wanted is only to recapitulate these questions with special reference to the question of the historical unique-ness of Jesus of Nazareth! We wanted only to put in clearer light the great contrast between the 'universal' and the 'unique' and between the 'transcenden-tal' and the 'historical'!

2. The All-Inclusive Uniqueness

As the last section is a recapitulation of the question of the 'transcendentality' and 'categoriality' which we have been all through discussing, especially with special reference to the historical uniqueness of Jesus Christ, so also this section intends to deal with the same problem of the 'universal' and the 'unique' synthesising our previous anthropological, historical and Chris-tological discussions. What we intend to indicate here is that the uniqueness which the Christian faith claims for Jesus of Nazareth is not some kind of an exclusive uniqueness which would keep him outside the boundaries of the whole humanity and its history, but an all-inclusive uniqueness, a uniqueness which would explain the totality of the created reality because, as W. Pannenberg affirms, 'as long as the whole of reality can be understood more deeply and more convincingly through Jesus than without him, it proves true in our everyday experience and personal knowledge that in Jesus the creative origin of all reality stands revealed' [19]: The uniqueness of Jesus is his universal validity and his universality is based on his uniqueness! There can be no contrast between a 'universal presence theory' and a 'fulfilment theory' as some would like to have it! [19a]

a. Jesus' Anthropological Uniqueness

We have already seen, especially in the seventh chapter, that Karl Rahner attempts to solve the dilemma of the relationship between transcendence and history with his transcendental and anthropological method. [20] We do not have to repeat here the apparatus he uses, his battery of ideas based on his method; we have already discussed them sufficiently. Some points, still, could be stressed here once again, but with special reference to the question of Jesus' uniqueness.

Anthropologically speaking, the uniqueness of Christ can be explained meaningfully only when we offer, as Rahner does, a picture of the world in which the one Christ, the one Christ as man, seems meaningful. That is possible only by demythologizing Christology from an evolutionary view of the world.[21] Jesus Christ, accordingly, stands for the climax of the whole of creation; it is in him that the creation reaches its peak of being united with God, without confusion and mutation, without division and separation, [22] and this fact makes a repetition of the same unnecessary, absurd and even contradictory! The evolutionary realization that is concretized in Jesus belongs to the whole of creation. This evolutionary vision is also, as we have already seen, intimately related to the very transcendental nature of man. Jesus Christ is God's answer to the transcendental question which is man. Since God is the incomprehensible term of human transcendence, God communicates himself in forgiving love to man both existentielly and historically as man's own fulfillment in Jesus Christ. If such a self-communication of God to the human transcendence is real, it is also irreversible and irrepeatable.[23] Jesus in his human lot is the (not a!) address of God to man and is as such unsurpassable. [24] This is also what W. Pannenberg means when he says that Jesus is the unique fulfilment of human destiny.[25] In other words, 'the being-human' of man is realized only in Jesus of Nazareth. [26]The destiny of man is dependent on Jesus because it is not already given in every individual human being, but it comes to every man from the future of God that is realized in Jesus of Nazareth. [27] A similar anthropological affirmation of Jesus' uniqueness is also, as we have already mentioned, evident in V. Chakkarai according to whom, man finds his real being only in Christ and that it is not our humanity that is the criterion to judge his, but Christ's humanity is the norm for what our humanity has to be. P. Chenchiah's concept of Jesus as the 'image of man' also points to the same conceptual direction.

We had also made it clear that an anthropo-transcendental approach does not all by itself prove that the transcendental scheme of a possible and irrevocable self giving of God as the ultimate answer to human transcendence is actualized precisely in Jesus of Nazareth. Only a searching Christology can identify in faith that Jesus of Nazareth is the realization of the 'idea' of the God-man, and nobody else. We do not have to repeat its implications here as we have done it already in the seventh chapter. It is not the 'idea' of Christ that saves and is eternally valid - Christianity is after all not an 'idealism' as the Vedantins and Raimundo Panikkar would like to have it - but 'one is a Christian only once one has grasped the uniquely concrete fact of this particular man' [28], Jesus of Nazareth!

b. Jesus' Historical Uniqueness

Here we turn more explicitly to the question how the Christ-event as a particular fact in history could be of relevance for the whole of history. The universal significance of a particular historical event can be explained only in reference to the historical significance of particular events.[29] According to Rahner, there are facts in history which are not of immediate existential relevance of every man, but there are also historical facts which radically affect a man's existence. If history, for example, can provide us with a definitive and reliable answer to our questions about truth, love, hope etc., then those historical facts are also of great importance and sometimes they can even be of decisive importance for human life. [30] In reference to the particular historical event of Christ we could say that if it is a convincing answer in history to the basic transcendental, a priori or suprahistorical question of the very existence of man, then this particur historical event has of course a supra-historical aspect which makes it relevant and meaningful for the whole of human history. Since man's transcendental question is for him of ultimate importance, so also its anwer. So the Christ-event, even in its historical relativity contains a transhistorical and absolute value as far as the fulfil ment of man's existential goal is concerned. This argument of Rahner is evidently based on his anthropological view of Jesus Christ as the climax of the human existential transcendence.

The concept of 'Saviour', according to Rahner, implies the irreversibility of God's self-communication in history. The title of Saviour is applicable only to 'that historical person who, coming in space and time, signifies that beginning of God's absolute self-communication for all men as something happening irrevocably and which shows this to be happening'[31]. The Saviour is the irrevocable climax of God's self-communication in history. It could very well be said that 'the whole movement of this history lives only for the moment of arrival at its goal and climax - it lives only for its entry into the event which makes it irreversible - in short, it lives for the one whom we call Saviour'[32]. This historical salvific event in Christ is insurpassable because the summit of all 'evolution', the eruption of God into the world and the radical opening of the world to the free infinity of God in Christ, has already been realized for the whole world, however true it may be that what has already taken place definitively in this event must still reveal itself within the world in the reflection and image of all history still to come, in an eschatological climax'[33].

Pannenberg bridges the historical particularity of the Christ-event with the whole of human history with his idea of 'Prolepsis' (anticipation). History reaches its fulfilling destiny only at the 'End' of history; but 'in the destiny of Jesus the 'End' of all history has happened in advance, as prolepsis[34]. Jesus is the anticipated 'End' and not just the middle of history.[35] It is this proleptic character of the Christ-event that makes it unique in history with its universal relevance. Its content cannot be fundamentally revised by new events in history; it is unsurpassable and thus unique.[36] Therefore, the universal meaning of the dogmatic statements about Jesus is grounded and confirmed by 'the historical particularity of the message, way and figure of Jesus'[37] which attains unsurpassability (Unüberholbarkeit) in Jesus' resurrection.[38] The notion of Jesus' historical uniqueness, which we have indicated recapitulating the views of both Rahner and Pannenberg, is reflected also in the Christological vision of S.J. Samartha who maintains that Jesus' history becomes relevant and significant for the whole mankind because in Jesus Christ history is transformed to the fullness of God.[39]

c. Jesus' Revelational Uniqueness

In the previous chapters we discussed the notion of divine revelation and here we would stress more clearly Christ's uniqueness as the ultimate manifestation of God. As the Vedantins may consider, Jesus is not just a religious genius, a prophet or a 'Guru' among many others. As Rahner observes, Jesus Christ is qualitatively more than any other prophet! Jesus is unique and indispensable for mankind unlike any other prophet.[40] This assertion of Rahner must be understood in the context of his transcendental anthropo-Christology. No prophet or religious genius, in short, anything else that is other than God can in principle be the last, uttermost, ultimate, unsurpassable and definitive.[41] It is Jesus' essential unity with God - a unity which is realized in Jesus and Jesus alone - which makes him qualitatively different from all other prophets. The transcendental revelation of God is 'categorized' in every culture and religion by specially gifted men of God. But Jesus Christ is the unsurpassable climax of all divine revelation because, as Karl Rahner affirms, revelation reaches its absolute climax only when God's self-communication reaches its unsurpassable high point through the hypostatic union and in the incarnation of God in the created, spiritual reality of Jesus for his own sake, and hence for the sake of all of us. But this takes place in the incarnation of the Logos because here what is expressed and communicated, namely, God himself, and secondly the mode of expression, that is the human reality of Christ in his life and in his final state, and, thirdly, the recipient Jesus in grace and in the vision of God, all three have become absolutely one. In Jesus God's communication to men in grace and at the same time its categorial self-interpretation in the corporeal, tangible and social dimension have reached their climax, have become revelation in an absolute sense[42]. So Jesus Christ is not an arbitrary end of revelation, but its end by his very reality. If Jesus is God's full expression and self-giving in human form there is nothing more to be said or to be given. In Jesus God's self-revelation in its fullness is irrevocable because in Jesus God can never again cease to be man! Jesus is not simply something brought about by God; he is God himself and that is the basis for his unsurpassability and uniqueness. [43]   Rahner is quite right in declaring that the 'faith in Jesus does not acknowledge merely a religious genius or the prophet of a passing phase in the history of religions, but the absolute Mediator of Salvation now and always[44].

According to Wolfhart Pannenberg, the revelational uniqueness of Jesus consists in the fact that he 'not only issued a call to repentence, but with full authority he granted to the men he met the salvation expected in the future. He was certain that in his activity the future salvation of God's Kingdom had broken into the present time. This distinguishes Jesus basicly from the Baptist as well as from all the prophets'[45]. This statement of Pannenberg should be understood in the context of his historico-eschatological Christology, which we have discussed sufficiently earlier. It was the history of Jesus, according to Pannenberg, that shows that in him God is definitively revealed.[46] Pannenberg does not deny that there can be many anticipations of revelation as is evident in the history of the nations; but these partial revelations are only preparations for the Revelation in the strict sense, namely the manifestation of Lordship of God over all things, that was realized in Jesus' resurrection in an anticipatory way.[47] Jesus is the fulfilment of all revelations and the Revelation in person. [48] It is the concrete, historical person of Jesus Christ that justifies the uniqueness of the Christian faith! [49]

A further question still remains: how can one make an a absolute commitment to the Revelation that is realized in the historical Christ-event that is known, so to say, not absolutely, but only relatively especially because of our great temporal distance from him? It is true, as Rahner admits, that our historical certainty regarding many aspects of the Christ-event is only a relative certainty. Rahner argues that in human existence it is most often so; our knowledge which should justify our decisions are relative, not fully certain. But our decisions, by their nature, are absolute; it is either 'Yes' or 'No'! Eventhough the knowledge is relative we cannot abstain from absolute decisions. Therefore Rahner argues, if the reasones to say 'No' to the revelation in Christ are weaker that those to say 'Yes', then the only alternative that is left to us is to say 'Yes'! An abstention in decision itself will be a 'No' with its indispensably absolute character. [50]

In opposition to the Vedantic position what we wanted to insist in this section is that the uniqueness that is claimed for Jesus of Nazareth is not an all-exclusive uniqueness, but an all-inclusive one! What Jesus is, is on behalf of the whole of God's creation with man at its top! It is true, as Prof.Alexandre Ganoczy observes, that this uniqueness of Christ that belongs to the substantial content of the Christian faith is a matter of offence for most of the non-Christians, but for the Christians it is precisely this unique and definitive character of Jesus, Christ that makes him the recapitulation of all human beings and the whole of creation. [51] In the light of our discussion so far, S. Radhakrishnan's accusation that according to the Christian faith God is partial to a particular people [52] does not hold true. God is in Jesus of Nazareth the Lord of the whole creation and of all the nations. That is the sum and substance of the short Christian confession: "Jesus is the Christ"! [53]

3. The Advaitic Synthesis of Polarities

Here in this section our intention is to go deeper into the problems of relation (Verhältnisprobleme) between the universality and the uniqueness, between the transcendentality and the historicity and between spirit and matter which we were discussing all through. This is of immense importance in the Advaitic (non dual) context of Indian Christology. The Vedantic philosophical system as a whole - and the 'Advaita' in particular - is an attempt at reconciling the contrasting realities that confront human existence. In the previous section we have tried to synthesize the contrast between the 'universal' and the 'unique' in Jesus Christ. For this synthesis, the pattern of the unity between the divinity and humanity in Jesus Christ, i.e. without confusion and mutation, without division and separation, has been followed. The same pattern of synthesis is applicable further for all the inevitable polarities of human existence.

In the mystery of the divine Incarnation in Jesus Christ the Absolute enters history without compromising its absoluteness and the divinity enters humanity without undergoing any change or negation of itself. The 'Advaitic' synthesis that is to be adapted into Christology similarly has to avoid any negation of what is synthesized. The unity of both polarities is to be affirmed without devaluing each other. Both contrasts are to be assumed and elevated to a new and dynamic synthesis. Such a synthesis would solve, in the pattern of the mystery of the Incarnation, the contrasts and the problems of relation between the Creator and the creature, the Infinity and the finite, the Necessary and the contingent, the Transcendental and the historical, the Unthematic and the thematic, the Metacategorical and the categorical, the Anonymous and the known, the Implicit and the explicit, the Principle and the fact, the General and the particular, the Spirit and the matter, the Numenon and the phenomenon, the Universal and the unique, the Eternity and time, the Unity and multiplicity, the One and the many, the Stability and change, the 'Advaita' and the 'dvaita' and ultimately between God and man in Jesus the Christ! Finally the Salvation is nothing else than such a divinely initiated synthesis of the basicly divergent and mutually contrasting polarities of creation with God himself!

Rahner's transcendental Christology is an attempt similarly to mediate between the transcendentally necessary and the historically contingent. According to Rahner, both these aspects of human existence combine together for the whole of humanity in an unsurpassable way in Jesus of Nazareth, which justifies the name 'Christ' for him in a definitive and irrepeatable way. [54] The world history becomes in Jesus Christ the history of God himself. [55] The Absolute does not merely hover over history and finite frailty, but in Jesus Christ - a point that is to be stressed against the Vedanta - the Absolute enters into history and thus time must now be taken as seriously as eternity because a salvific synthesis between time and eternity is definitively and irrevocably reached in Jesus Christ. [56] In such a synthesis the helplessness of time, cyclic and non-salvific history and of the law of self-retribution (Karma-Samsara) are cancelled and the creation is assumed into God himself by the gratuity of salvation in Jesus Christ, because in him God becomes a piece of this cosmic history (ein Stück der Geschichte des Kosmos) [57]. Here we see the importance of the reality of the divine Incarnation by assuming the real matter, the real body, as against the docetic type of 'Avatara' theory. The mystery of Christ's death and the consequent 'bodily' resurrection are also to be understood in the context of this ultimate matter-spirit integration or synthesis as M.C. Parekh and P.C. Mozoomdar have very well pointed out. [58]

Wolfhart Pannenberg's concept of the 'Prolepsis' is also aimed at a similar synthesis of polarities. Like Hegel, Pannenberg also affirms the biblical view that truth has a history and the unity of this history is seen in Jesus Christ. But unlike Hegel, Pannenberg does not eliminate the historical openness to the future. The realization of the dialectic synthesis in Jesus Christ is a synthesis in anticipation (Prolepsis) of the End of history within history. The End remains outstanding on the horizon of the future, but it has occured provisionally in Jesus Christ. That makes the conception of the unity of history possible without sacrificing its openness.[59] Hence a synthesis between actuality and futurity, between realization and further dynamism! True being, as Pannenberg explains, is thought of not as timeless but instead as historical, and it proves its stability through a history whose future is always open.[60] It is possible to find in the history of Jesus, Pannenberg contends, 'an answer to the question of how 'the whole' of reality in its meaning can be conceived without compromising the provisionality and historical relativity of all thought, as well as openness to the future on the part of the thinker who knows himself to be only on the way and not yet at the goal'[61]. Eternity, according to him, is not the opposite or the cancellation of time, but its foundation. Remaining eternal and changeless, God is the source of time, change, history and their meaning in Jesus Christ,[62] who is the synthesis of the question of man and the question of God is one![63]

We can say without hesitation in the light of the previous discussions, that God in Christ really became world and by recapitulating and synthesizing everything in a salvific way in himself, God is All in all (Col 1:15) and so as Rahner insists, 'we can make use of the general categories of the God-creature relation (distance-proximity; image-concealment; time-eternity; dependence-independence) in their radical, sharply differentiated form in order to make fundamental statements about Christ, and regard all other realities in this field of what is distinct from God as deficient modes of this primary Christological relation'[64]. As human beings plunged into history our task is to discover the salvific synthesis of the Universal in the unique, God in man, Salvation in history, Eternity in time, Spirit in matter, Truth in facts and the Mystery in the evident.[65] This approach, however, does not cancel the Mystery, but makes it credible!

B. Salvation: A Christian Monopoly?

Here also our intention is not to discuss something fully new, but only to recapitulate some of the points which we have considered, now especially from the point of view of the salvation of non-Christians. This theme is of great relevance for the Indian Christology especially because the Christians in India constitute a very small minority of its vast population that is likely to grow beyond a milliard in a not distant future! It is of course not an easy task to explain to the millions in India, who have perhaps never heard of Christ, or even if heard, never came into contact with the depth of the mystery he incorporates in his historical person, that Jesus Christ is the only mediator between God and man and that there is no eternal salvation possible except in and through him! This is predominantly a missiological problem and we have been discussing all through our work a credible explanation of Jesus Christ as the mystery of man and of the human history from the point of view of systematic theology especially stressing the issues related with the dogmatic and fundamental theology. In this section, therefore, what we have discussed so far has to be kept in mind. Our intention here is also not to consider the question of the 'Anonymous Christians' as developed by Karl Rahner, nor the issues connected with 'the unknown Christ of Hinduism' in an elaborate way. It would be superfluous because already a lot has been written on the issue raised by Rahner[66] and we ourselves have sufficiently discussed the latter question as understood by Raimundo Panikkar.[67] Our aim here is only to indicate some of the issues which are intimately connected with and implied in the problematic of an Indian anthropo-Christology which we have been dealing with so far.

1. The Universality of Salvation

This is one of the principles, we have seen, very much stressed by the Vedantic thinkers. It is on this presupposition that the principles of 'Ekam sat vipra bahuda vadanti', 'Sarva dharma samanatva' and the notion of 'Ishtadeva' are based.[68] These principles, as the Vedantins understand, have nothing to do with Jesus of Nazareth in any unique way. Our anthropological approach to an Indian Christology basing on the transcendental method of K. Rahner and the historico-eschatological method of W. Pannenberg has been aiming to explain the universality of salvation as a reality that is founded on God's self-manifestation and self-giving that has reached its definitiveness, irreversibility and irrevocability for the whole of mankind in Jesus of Nazareth.

According to Rahner, the university of divine salvation is gua renteed by the fact of the 'Supernatural existential' that constitutes the transcendental reality of man as we have explained in the seventh chapter.[69] The 'Supernatural existential' may be considered as the heart of Rahner's theology.[70] God's universal will to save (1Tim 2:4), a fact very much stressed by the Vatican II (AG 7; GS 22), is an effective will of God and it is this will that is reflected in the transcendental constitution of man. Salvation of man is nothing else than the realization of the 'Supernatural existential', which may also be called the 'Christ-Principle' or the 'Idea of Christ' that is in every man, which is the self-communication of God that is offered to every man and fulfilled in the highest way in Jesus of Nazareth as the goal of all creation.[71]

Rahner's concepts of the 'transcendental' and the 'categorial' revelation is also important in clarifying the universal salvific will of God. Man's fundamental openness to the Word of God (Hörer des Wortes!) is the condition of the possibility of a definitive Christian revelation. As Rahner asserts, 'the express revelation of the Word in Christ is not something which comes to us from without as entirely strange, but only the explicitation of what we already are by grace and what we experience at least incoherently in the limitlessness of our transcendence. The expressly Christian revelation becomes the explicit statement of the revelation of grace which man always experiences implicitly in the depths of his being'[72]. Prior to the explicit acceptance of the Christian faith the acceptance of the transcendental revelation can be present 'in an implicit form whereby a person undertakes and lives the duty of each day in the quiet sincerity of patience, in devotion to his material duties and the demands made upon him by the persons under his care'[73]. By the acceptance of his own existence one is accepting God's revelation in Christ as the absolute perfection and guarentee of his own anonymous movement towards God by grace.[74] It must also be mentioned that the notion of 'transcendental revelation' is derived from the idea of the 'supernatural existential'[75].

The concept of 'transcendental revelation' as understood by Rahner is also important to explain the universal salvific will of God. The question is, how can revelation be always and everywhere, in order that the salvation could also be present always and everywhere? [76] The transcendental revelation is the universal presence of God to the whole of mankind [77], which is the result of the universality of the salvific will of God [78] which preceds every existentiell decision of man. [79] On the basis of the transcendental revelation we can affirm that there is 'no religion of any kind in which the grace of God is not present, however suppressed or depraved it may be in its expression' [80]. This fact must be understood in the context of the original transcendental constitution of man. [81]

The transcendental revelation is the condition of the possibility of the categorial revelation, the revelation as it is articulated in history; the latter is the interpretation of the former. Rahner distinguishes between a more or less successful interpretation of the transcendental revelation as is seen in non-Christian religions and philosophies and the absolute, irrevocable, irreversible and historical interpretation in Jesus of Nazareth, the God-man. [82] Every man in his social and philosophical environment attempts to objectivize the transcendental revelation; but there are gifted men or prophets in every epoch who are inspired by a special and more intense experience of God and are able to put into words and actions the transcendental revelation with the result that certain religious impulses originate from them and unlike ordinary mortals they can express their transcendental experience in such a way that it becomes an objectivization or categorialization of others' own transcendental experience of God and can be recognized by them as correct and convincing. In every non-Christian religion, therefore, we can detect at least some aspects which must be traced back to God and this is especially true of Hinduism. Judaism has, however, a unique position in the history of religions as the categorization of the transcendental revelation. It is not the historic content of Judaism that makes it unique; nothing happens in it that does not happen in one or another way in the history of other peoples. It is the interpretation (Word) of this history (Deed) as a partnership in dialogue with God as the immediate preparation for God's own definitive and irrevocable self-manifestation and self-giving to the world in Jesus of Nazareth which makes the Old Testament and the history of Israel unique. Christ makes the difference! [83]

The universal transcendental revelation, according to Rahner, attains its definitive and correct interpretation (richtige Auslegung) in the categorial

revelation of Jesus Christ. [84] Christ's explanation of the transcendental revelation without any misinterpretation (Auslegung ohne Mißdeutung) [85] is the
explicitation of that which is already present in the very depth of man and
it is the illumining (Sich-Lichten) and awakening (Das Zu-sich-kommen) of
the human transcendentality. [86] It is evident that in this perspective Rahner's
position is surprisingly near to the Vedantic one. We do not have to repeat
here their fundamental differences as we have done already the required
elaboration of the reasons why Rahner considers Jesus of Nazareth as the
absolute and definitive revelation of God in an unsurpassable way. [87]

In the light of what we have said above we can speak, as Rahner does, of
a transcendental history of salvation and an official history of salvation.
The former is the interpretation of man's transcendental experience not firstly
by means of an explicit anthropology or Christology, but in the history, culture,
society, art, religion and the external technical and economic mastery of
nature. The official history of salvation or the history of revelation, on the
other hand, is a historical self-interpretation of the transcendental experience
which is constituted by God's self-communication. [88] In this sense we can
say that the history of salvation is coexistent with the whole of human history
(i.e. everybody who does not close himself to God finds salvation) eventhough
it is not identical with the world history which is also marked by sin, rejection
of God and opposition to salvation. The history of salvation or its opposite,
in other words, is the history of God's universal offer of Himself to mankind,
an offer made in freedom and accepted or rejected in freedom! [89] So to understand the universal salvific will of God, an explicitation of the transcendental
character of divine revelation is indispensable.

The universal salvific will of God as expressed in the universality of God's
revelation is also stressed by W. Pannenberg. We have discussed already Pannenberg's notion of revelation. [90] As Rahner, Pannenberg also considers the salvation
history as coextensive with the world history although not identical with
it and he affirms that 'the conception of a redemptive history severed from
ordinary history ... is hardly acceptable on theological grounds .... It belongs
to the full meaning of the Incarnation that God's redemptive deed took place
within the universal correlative connections of human history and not in a
ghetto of redemptive history, or in a primal history belonging to a dimension

which is 'oblique' to ordinary history...'[91]. So, according to Pannenberg, thre revelation has a universal character and the historical revelation is open to anyone who has eyes to see.[92] The events in which God demonstrates his deity are self-evident in their historical context.[93] All truth lies before the eyes and its appropriation is a natural consequence of the facts and there is no need for any additional perfection of man as though he could not focus on the supernatural truth with the normal equipment of knowing.[94] These considerations justify and substantiate theologically the fact that God's salvation is not the monopoly of a particular group of people, but is open to every human being in whatever concrete historical situation he may be situated. Therefore, even from the Christian point of view, a Hindu is also on the way to salvation as a Christian is, and so Radhakrishnan's charges of Christian intolerance do not hold ground from a theological point of view.

On the one hand there is no salvation except in and through Jesus the Christ[95] and on the other hand salvation is open in principle and in fact to every human being, even to those who may never have heard of Christ, as is affirmed by the Vatican II.[96] Grace works in an unseen way in the hearts of all men of good will (GS 222, LG 16)! Rahner's concept of the 'Anonymous Christians' is an attempt to explain theologically the 'unseen' or implicit work of God's grace and salvation beyond the visible boundaries of the Church, which can be explained only in the context of the transcendentality of revelation and the universality of salvation that is conceptually derived from the transcendental nature of man.[96a] The notion of the 'anonymous Christians' implies that 'in achieving his salvation in faith, hope and love, man does not do this in explicit religiosity. He achieves salvation primarily by expressing his acceptance of his transcendental experience and living his every day life in the light of that acceptance and by loving trusting, hoping, working, caring and persisting in thanksgiving'[97]. Rahner admits that the theological virtue of faith is essential for salvation, but this faith according to him is basicly 'the obedient acceptance of man's supernaturally elevated self-transcendence, the obedient acceptance of his transcendental orientation to the God of eternal life'[98]. Such a saving faith is present even where there is a lack of an explicit dogmatic faith-formula or there is a formula that is conceptually false.[99] Rahner sees everywhere an anonymous Christianity because the explicit Christianity is not just an opinion among many others, but the concrete realization (Zusichselbergekommensein) of that what is lived everywhere as truth and love.[100] The implicit or anonymous Christianity is the situation of those human beings who on the one hand live in grace and justification and on the other hand are not yet in contact with the explicit preaching of the Gospel and hence are not in a position to call themselves 'Christian'.[101] These 'Christians' are 'anonymous' because, as Prof. Elmar Klinger observes, their participation in the salvation of Christ is supra-historical and unreflected, i.e., transcendental, as constitutive of human existence.[102] As Rahner himself declares, one who says 'yes' to existence, says 'yes' to Christ without consciously knowing it or reflecting over it.[103] Anyone, Rahner clarifies, no matter how remote from any Christian revelation formulated in words, who accepts his existence, i.e. his humanity 'in quiet patience, or better, in faith, hope and love - no matter what he calls them, and accepts it as the mystery which hides itself in the mystery of eternal love and bears life in the womb of death; such a one says yes to something which really is such as his boundless confidence hopes it to be, because God has in fact filled it with the infinite, that is, with himself, since the Word was made flesh. He says yes to Christ, even when he does not know that he does'[104]: This implies, according to Rahner, that there are degrees of membership of the Church not only in ascending order, 'but also in descending order from the explicitness of baptism into a non-official and anonymous Christianity'[105]. It would be highly relevant for the Indian Christology to examine how the concept of the anonymous Christians could find its application in the Hindu context. Before going into this point we would rather investigate further in the next section the problematic that is implied in the expression 'anonymous Christians'

2. 'Anonymous Christians' - the Indian Problematic

The greatest problem that Christianity faces in the Indian context is that of relativization. We had referred to this point especially in the seventh chapter. If all religions are equal and if the different religions are only different paths to the same goal called God or salvation - a point that is very much stressed by the Vedanta - then Christianity cannot naturally raise any claim of priority or uniqueness in the history of religions. It will be just a phase in the phenomenology of religions. Dr. Raimundo Panikkar's 'Logos-Isvara-Christology' also seems, as we have already observed, to support such an approach. Karl Rahner's notion of the 'Anonymous Christians' is also accused of relativizing Christianity in a similar way. Hans Urs von Balthasar is the most prominent representative of such a criticism. A univocal application of the term 'Christian' to Christians and non-Christians, Balthasar protests, could mean that the explicit confession of the faith in Christ would not make any substantial difference from its non confession. The same logic could also justify the atheists calling the Christians as 'anonymous atheists'.[106] The same applied to the Indian context, we could think of the vast majority of Hindus calling the Christian minority in India in a very generous way as 'Anonymous Hindus'. James Dupuis also, as we have see in Chapter VI, considers the expression 'anonymous Christianity' applied to the cosmic religions like Hinduism as open to criticism because 'it is liable to be understood as unduly reducing the newness of Christianity to a process of gnosis. It may seem to suggest that a non-Christian is already a Christian, though still remaining unaware of his true identity'[107]. But the difference between Hinduism and Christianity, Dupuis contends, is not only one of degree but of nature. Christianity is not just a mere 'awareness' of a mystery of salvation which would be found elsewhere in the same manner, as if what is required is just an unveiling of what is contained hidden in Hinduism. There is a great difference between Hinduism and Christianity, that is watered down by the expression 'Anonymous Christians' and that is the confession of Jesus of Nazareth as the Christ.[108] While in non-Christian religions like Hinduism the mystery of Christ is imperfectly revealed and his grace imperfectly mediated, Dupuis declares, 'Christianity is the full disclosure of the mystery and the perfect mediation of grace. It's newness implies more than the simple unveiling of a mystery already fully though unknowingly experienced; it brings with it the full sacramental realization of God's presence to men'[109]. A Hindu can become a Christian not by a process of 'awareness' but only through 'an intrinsic transformation which consists in entering into a new order in the mediation of Christ's grace'[110]. We had given sufficient attention to the aspect of 'newness' or the 'more' of explicit Christianity in Chapter VI.B.4.b. Here a repetition of it could be dispensed with.

In a mission land like India a certain missionary problem is also connected with the expression of 'anonymous Christians' - a problem that is derived from the relativization of Christianity of which 'the underlying assumption would be the denial of the unique character of God's historical manifestation in Jesus Christ'[111]. As Walter Kasper observes, when one isolates and absolutizes the catchword of anonymous Christians, then it leads logically to the assertion that mission has no other concern than 'that the Hindu becomes a better Hindu, the Buddist a better Buddist, the Moslem a better Moslem' (H. Halbfas).[111a] Kasper points to the provocative remarkt of J. Ratzinger: "Then one also has to say a cannibal ought to be a 'good cannibal' and a convinced SS-man ought to be a thorough-going SS-man (!)" Kasper agrees with the opinion of Y. Congar that God cannot choose the incognito of hate, of hedenistic egoism and of pride. The Vedantic position that all religions are equal, a position that would rule out the logic of all missionary works in the name of tolerance 'sounds very humanitarian, big-hearted and progressive; in reality it actually betrays a conservative philosophy. It does not know how to overcome the specific system critically for the sake of a deeper and more all-embracing truth'[112].

There are some theologians like Jüngel who see in the doctrine of anonymous Christians an offensive taking over of non Christians.[113] To call a Hindu, for example, as an 'anonymous Christian' is to impose something on him which he does not like; it looks like an attempt to convince the Hindu that he is what he does not believe to be! This attitude seems to violate the human dignity and the religious freedom of another individual!

In reference to this optic it is also to be mentioned, in order to stress once again what we have said in Chapter VI.B.4.b, that the very expression 'anonymous Christianity' as well as 'anonymous Christ' is problematic. We have argued that there is a substantial contradiction of terms in using 'anonymous' in this context! We based our argument especially on the theology of symbols of even that of the revelation. 'Christ' is the revelation, the ultimate self-manifestation of God to man. Since 'Christ' is revelation itself, it would be contradictory to speak of an 'anonymous Christ', an 'unmanifested manifestation', an 'unrevealed revelation' or of an 'unapparent symbol'. The terms 'Christ' and 'anonymous' are by their very meaning mutually exclusive. The contradiction that comes to light in such a linguistic analysis is also similarly evident in the expressions of anonymous Christians and anonymous Christianity. Our position is also corroborated by the views of Jüngel and Hans Küng who consider that the expression 'anonymous Christians' does not suit the matter that Rahner intends to cover.[114] James Dupuis also, as we have mentioned, points to the inadequacy of the term and suggests that 'latent Christianity' seems to be less inadequate - nobody has succeeded till now in proposing a fully adequate term! - and considers other expressions like 'implicit Christianity', 'non-Christian' etc. as not suitable. [115]

In reference to the above and similar other objections raised against the use of the expression 'anonymous Christians', it must be mentioned that what is important for Karl Rahner is not the terminology, but its content.[116] He would have no objections to accept another more suitable terminology if such a one were to be proposed. What Rahner wants to bring to light by this expression is the basic Christian understanding about the salvation of a non-baptized human being who follows sincerely the voice of his conscience. [117] Rahner's point of view has to be evaluated only in the context of the transcendental anthropology he accepts as the starting point of his theology and the consequent notion regarding the universal salvific will of God that is made philosophically credible on the basis of Rahner's 'Supernatural existential'.

The objection that the expression of anonymous Christians is an offensive taking over of non-Christians does not seem to hold ground. It is not an intolerant attempt to convince a non-Christian that he is what he does not believe to be. This term does not impose anything on non-Christians. It is a Christian answer to a Christian question - a question each Christian asks himself about the salvation of many around him, who are no worse than himself. [118] Prof. Elmar Klinger also points to the subjective and experiential aspect of the expression 'anonymous Christians'. Anonymous Christianity, he argues, indicates not so much an historical fact as a fact of life in one's own experience. It is a subjective experience and attitude of the Christians in front of the world of non-Christians; it is not to be misunderstood as an 'object' confronting us. [119] The concept of the anonymous Christians belongs to the world-vision of the Christians who consider themselves obliged to a transcendental anthropology. [120] A lack of differentiation in understanding the concept of the anonymous Christians and an objectifying application of this notion are, according to Prof. Klinger, the reasons for the objections raised against this expression by critics especially like Hans Urs von Balthasar and Hans Küng. The basic problematic of the question (Konstitutionsproblematik), complains Klinger, is not sufficiently respected by them! [121] We also think that most of the criticism against Rahner are levelled against points which he himself does not mean to support!

A so-called relativization of Christianity is also not what is intended by Rahner's concept of the anonymous Christians. The point discussed in this concept is by no means the question of the essential contrasts (Gegensätzlichkeiten) and the basic differences between the Christian and the non-Christian religions like Hinduism. [122] It is evident that there are unacceptable elements in other religions and that a radical human transformation is required in order to share the salvation of Christ. Hence the ironical remark of J. Ratzinger regarding the cannibal and the SS-man simply misses the point! Without making any relativization, Rahner is also aware of the ecumenical implications of the expression he advocates. He does not exclude the possibility, for example, of Hindus calling Christians as anonymous Hindus and, vice versa. So also it need to be denied that the Catholics are for the Lutherans 'anonymous Lutherans' as they themselves are for Catholics 'anonymous Catholics'. Naturally, who is right and who is wrong - that is another question! [123] It would also be against the intention of Rahner to draw the unwarranted conclusion from the concept of the anonymous Christians that it is no longer necessary to preach, convert and missionize! We will be discussing this missiological point in the next section.

3. 'Extra Christum nulla salus' - and the Salvific Value of Hinduism

Our intention here is not to go into the details of the ecclesiological axiom 'extra ecclesiam nulla salus' [124] which is to be interpreted as 'extra Christum nulla salus' [125] implying thereby the tautological statement that there is no salvation outside God, 'außer Gott kein Heil' - to use the title of an article by Prof. Alexander Ganoczy. [126] What Karl Rahner really means by his 'anonymous Christians' is nothing else than what is implied in the above expressions. This must be understood also in the context of the absoluteness of Christ as the unique mediator between God and man (1 Tim 2:4f) - a point which we have sufficiently discussed in one of the previous sections. [127] We have stressed that Christ's and consequently the Christian claim to uniqueness is not contrary to religious tolerance. [128] Rahner's notion of anonymous Christians is actually a theologically substantiated exercise of tolerance. [129] This does not mean that Christianity compromises its claim of being 'the absolute religion, intended for all men, which cannot recognize any other religion beside itself as of equal right' and the recognition of itself as God's own interpretation in his word of the relationship of God to man and so as the true and lawful religion for all men and therefore as the religion which binds man to God. [130] While admitting as Paul does in his speech on the Areopagus the positive value of non-Christian religions (Acts 17:23) a Christian confesses that there is salvation in no other name except in the name of Jesus Christ (Acts 4:12) and so 'Christianity can never understand itself as a religion among other religions. It is the god-willed religion' [131]. The essential difference between Christianity and Hinduism or in other words the uniqueness of Christianity in relation to Hinduism is based on the fact that there is no salvation outside Christ - extra Christum nulla salus! [132]

Wolfhart Pannenberg sees the axiom 'extra Christum nulla salus' and consequently the question of the anonymous Christians in reference to Christ's descend into hell (1 Peter 3:19f; 4:6). The symbolic language of the descend into hell, according Pannenberg, points to the universal significance of Christ's death and the possibility of salvation for those who had died before Christ and for those who are to die outside the visible Church without ever having heard of Christ. The Kingdom of God is already at work even where Christ is not explicitly recognized (Lk 6:20ff; Mt 5:3ff); by their behaviour itself many are related to the content of Christ's message. [133]

The salvific value of non-Christian religions, in our case that of Hinduism, has also to be explained within the context of the axiom, 'extra Christum nulla salus'! It may not be proper to make a distinction between the subjective religiosity of the Hindus where the grace of Christ may be at work and its objective socio-historical expression in the symbols, rites and other charac teristics of Hinduism. Anthropologically speaking, the external and social aspects which are intimately related with the Hindu religiosity, in other words Hinduism as a religion, has also, as Dupuis observes, an objective salvific value. [134] Christologically speaking, it has to be affirmed that if the Hindus have the possibility of being saved in Hinduism - neither inspite of Hinduism nor on account of it - then it is necessary to admit that they are somehow related to the mystery of Christ through whom alone there is salvation. The Church which explicitly confesses Christ is, of course, the unique eschatological sign of the mystery of Christ, but we cannot deny that there can also be other incomplete signs.[135] Hinduism may be recognized as a lesser mode of the signification of the mystery of Christ or as its imperfect and dimmer expression. [136] The grace of God manifested through Jesus Christ is present also in Hinduism, however suppressed or depraved it may be in its expression! Hinduism can, according to the terminology and conceptual background of Rahner, be rightly called as anonymous Christianity even if it were to be in explicit opposition to the Church and has not come to Christ reflectively and this 'is a profound admission of the fact that God is greater than man and the Church' and this fact calls upon the Christians to 'be tolerant, humble and yet firm towards all non-Christian religions' [137] like Hinduism!

In connection with our discussion regarding the anonymous Christians it can well be asked: In what way then are the Christians better off by confessing Christ explicitly? What is the 'plus' of the explicit faith? In other words: What is the necessity of missionary preaching? The basic justification of missionary preaching, according to Rahner, is not that only the Christians can achieve salvation and the rest of mankind is destined to eternal doom![137a] Rahner also affirms that it is foolish to think that the talk about anonymous Christianity may lessen the importance of mission, preaching, baptizing etc.[138]. He warns against misunderstanding the concept of the anonymous Christians merely as 'a last desperate attempt in a world where Christian faith is fast disappearing to 'rescue' in its ultimate significance all that is good and human for the Church - against every freedom of the spirit' [139]. The 'anonymous Christians', instead of hindering the missionary work, makes it more meaningful and credible. Every anonymous state of man strives towards an explicit expression, towards its full name. There can be different new and higher stages of explicitness in being Christians, the ultimate perfection of it being a consciously accepted profession of Church membership. [140] The proclamation of the gospel, Rahner asserts, 'does not simply turn someone absolutely abandoned by God and Christ into a Christian, but turns an anonymous Christian into someone who now also knows about his Christian belief in the depths of his grace-endowed being by objective reflection and in the profession of faith which is given a social form in the Church' [141] . This explicitation is a part of the development [142] of the anonymous Christianity itself and therefore it is intended by God. The reflex realization of a previously anonymous Christianity, Rahner continues, is demanded by the incarnational and social structure of grace and 'because the individual who grasps Christianity in a clearer, purer and more reflective way, has, other things being equal, a still greater chance of salvation than someone who is merely an anonymous Christian' [143]. The unity of the transcendental and historical revelation, to which we have already referred, also demands that the 'transcendentality' reaches 'categoriality' in human history. [144] Many have, it is true, already found Christ in the smallest of his brothers, without however calling him by name. [145] The world must be brought to an explicit consciousness of the grace which it may have already accepted unreflectively. The Church is the expression and symbol of that what Christ realizes beyond its boundaries [146] and therefore, it is the greatest blessedness of life for a human being to become a Christian in an explicit way! [147] Here attention could be once again drawn to the aspect of the 'plus', the 'newness' or the 'more' of the explicit Christianity to which we had referred also in Chapter VI.B.4.b. That 'more', in short, is Jesus of Nazareth himself, because he is the Christ, the full, unique, definitive irrevocable and sacramental realization of God's salvific presence to man!

The above discussion makes clear once again the basic difference between the positions of Karl Rahner and Raimundo Panikkar, between the 'anonymous Christ' and the 'unknown Christ of Hinduism'. [148] For Panikkar, the 'Christ' without whom is no salvation is, as we have already seen, [149] the universal 'Logos-Isvara-Christ Principle' and not Jesus of Nazareth, the Christ! Panikkar is, as we have already remarked, trinitarian and universal in his Christological approach, but not sufficiently incarnational and historical. [150] In conclusion, it could also be mentioned that the idea of the 'anonymous Christians' in reference to Hinduism does not mean that Jesus Christ is just a 'fulfilment' of the Hindu spiritual aspirations. He is in content 'more' as the definitive and salvific self-giving of God to his creation. Certain aspirations - what is meant here are the possible perversions - in Hinduism will not be fulfilled by Christ, but destroyed! Hinduism has to 'die', has to be transformed, in order to be born again in Christ! This view is also supported by Prof. Ganoczy who maintains that even the legitimacy of having different Christologies does not mean by itself that Christ could be an answer to the existential question of all times and cultures. The inculturization of the Christ-Mystery is meaningful, he argues, only if the cultures are brought into harmony with the Truth of God which is supposed to be mediated by every Christology[151] So, in stressing the salvific value of Hinduism our intention is not to take over uncritically all that we may find in the Hindu faith and culture!

C. 'Khristanubhava' and 'Brahmasaksatkara': Christ (-ology) in Experience

Our evaluation so far of the Indian approaches to Jesus Christ in his universality and uniqueness as the mystery of man and of the human history finally leads us to the consideration and evaluation of the aspect of experience (Anubhava) that is indispensable in man's relation to Christ and in any meaningful talk about him. Indian authors now-a-days are very particular in stressing this experiential aspect in Christology and even talk of, as we have seen,[152] of 'Anubhava' (experience) as the 'Pramana' (source, norm, criterion) of an Indian Christology! It is quite understandable where, as we have observed in the first part, [153]'Anubhava' is validly considered as the essence of religion! The knowledge of Christ, even in the biblical sense ('jada'), is not only a matter of the intellect, but also of the heart and experience. [154] The abstract concepts about God and even the proofs for his existence are meaningful and intelligible only if they are ultimately based on man's God-experience. [155] What we intend to say is not that in Christianity the aspect of God-experience is not stressed, but only that it is not usually given adequate importance in the Christian theologizing as in the Hindu thinking. It would be an appropriate gesture, as Prof. A. Ganoczy observes, to respond to the Hindu openness to the Christian thinking - a fact which can be noted especially in the neo-Hinduism - by a corresponding gesture of openness to the principle of 'experience' that is emphasized by Hinduism because the relationship of the creation to God becomes evident in a secularized society only to the one who can perceive the world with spiritual eyes. [156]

Here naturally the question arises: What is meant by experience? It can, of course, cover a wide range of ideas: life-experience, daily experience , practical experience, political experience, religious experience, faith experience, mystical experience, experience of reason etc. Our concern here being theological, now we are concerned only with religious experience which is one of the principles (Pramana) of theological knowledge. What we have said already in the first and second parts of our work[157] is naturally, to be kept in mind in this section of evaluation which we intend to undertake, as done so far, in the light of the corresponding views of Karl Rahner and Wolfhart Pannenberg. The question here is of course about faith-experience or even mysticism. But, as Rahner himself does, we exclude from the notion of mysticism all those extraordinary phenomna which do not really constitute the true essence of mysticism which, according to him, consists in the 'infused vision' (eingegossene Beanschauung) of God. [158] It is also to be mentioned that for the purpose of our work it is irrelevant to make an elaboration of the 'infused' and 'acquired' aspects of God-experience and we would prefer to concentrate in our evaluation more on God-experience in general, rather than on infused mysticism which, in the opinion of Rahner, does not belong in a strict sense to the essence of Christian life, nor necessary for it, as it cannot be considered as a 'higher stage' of the life in grave! [159]

1. Self-Experience and God-Experience

The highest in man's knowledge of God, Rahner maintains, is a natural, mystical, non-conceptual experience. [160] This is quite in harmony with the Indian vision. We have discussed earlier Rahner's concept regarding the transcendental dimension of human knowledge. [161] What we have said in chapter seven is of great importance also here. Without repeating those points we would rather concentrate here on the religious aspect of man's transcendental experience, and see how the views of Rahner could complement and perhaps even correct the Vedantic position regarding self-experience and God-experience with its application on the question of Christ-experience.

Rahner distinguishes between the 'knowledge of God' and the 'experience of God'. The latter is 'that kind of knowledge that is present in every man as belonging essentially to the very roots of cognition in him, and as constituting the starting-point and prior condition for all reflexive knowledge, and for derived human knowledge in its function of combining and classifying' [162]. This is a non-thematic, non-reflexive and non-scientific knowledge resulting from the transcendental orientation of man to the incomprehensible and ineffable Mystery [163] which constitutes the enabling condition for knowledge and freedom. In other words, the experience of God is the condition of the possibility of the knowledge of God. Therefore, we can say that God-experience is not the privilege of the individual 'mystic', 'but is present in every man even though the process of reflecting upon it varies greatly from one individual to another in terms of force and clarity'[164] . God is the hidden goal 'of the experience of a limitless dynamic force inherent in the spirit endowed with knowledge and freedom' [165] . The God-experience is 'present' irremovably, however unacknowledged and unreflected upon it may be, in every exercise of the spiritual faculties, even at the most rational level in virtue of the fact that every such exercise draws its life from the prior apprehension of the all-transcending whole which is the mystery, one and nameless'[166]. The experience of a transcendental orientation in man is already in its reality the experience of God, whether it is recognized as such or not. [167] Since the experience of God is essentially transcendental in character, it should not be categorized and objectified as though it were one particular experience among others. Except in the case of some extraordinary mystical experiences, Rahner opines, the experience of God is non-objective as constituting the ultimate depth and radical essence of every spiritual and personal experience of love, hope, faithfulness etc. [168].

If the experience of God is so much one with man's experience of his own transcendental horizon, can we speak of an objectively existing reality, God, that is different in essence from man? This is a question that is very important in the Vedantic context. We had discussed this point earlier. [169] The Christian concept of God-experience cannot tolerate any notion of man's identity with Brahman as is suggested in the Vedantic thinking. As Wolfhart Pannenberg asserts, the understanding of God as a personal reality that transcends man and everything finite, is essential for a Christian understanding of the god-man relationship.[170] God-experience or religious experience, Pannenberg argues, cannot be derived automatically from man's structure as a transcendental question 'but from his being met by the reality that is experienced as the answer to the open question of his existence, and thus claims his ultimate confidence as the ground of his existence' [171]. A non-identification of man and God in man's God-experience is insisted very much also by Karl Rahner who affirms that 'even the most radical truth of self-experience recognizes that this subject which we are is finite, even though, precisely as such, and in its sheer transcendentality, it contains an absolute orientation towards the infinite and the inconceivable through which it is this without being identified with it'[172] . There is a unity between the self-experience and God-experience which consists 'in the fact that the original and ultimate experience of God constitutes the enabling condition of, and an intrinsic element in, the experience of self in such a way that without this experience of God no experience of self is possible' and in this sense 'the personal history of the experience of God signifies, over and above itself, the personal history of the experience of the self' and vice versa, i.e., 'the personal history of the experience of the self is the personal history of the experience of God'[173]. At the same time, the transcendence of God and the finiteness of man demands that inspite of this unity in experience, the 'experience of God and experience of self are not simply identical'[174] in a pantheistic sense!

This above view, as is evident, stands in glaring contrast to the Vedantic notion of 'Atmanubhava' and 'Brahmasaksatkara' and the understanding of the mystic state as 'the overcoming' of all the barriers between the individual and the Absolute' and as an achievement (!) through the practice of 'Yoga' and the consequent progressive interiorization of the self transcrossing the five-sheath (Kosa) system enveloping the 'Atman' and thus the 'Atman' coming to the knowledge (Jnana) of being one with the Brahman, who is consciousness itself! [175]

The Vedantic concept regarding God-experience is also problematic from the Christian point of view as far as the immediacy of this experience is concerned. Since 'Atman' is 'Brahman', according to the Vedantic view - in one or another way, it is logical that an immediacy is postulated there which rules out all material and historical mediations in man's God-experience which is irreconcilable with the Christian anthropology which understands the human being as a body-soul integrity immersed in history. Unlike in the case of 'visio beatifica' after death, the 'conversio ad phantasma'[176] is an indispensable aspect of the Christian view of God-experience. Human knowledge is essentially receptive - whether it is infused or acquired is a different question - and it is never innate. That means the human transcendentality is realizable even in the case of mysticism only through an indispensable 'conversio ad phantasma'. The mysticism is never independent of man's materiality and his historicity.[177] Man does not, therefore, encounter or experience the transcendence 'qua transcendence' as if it were an 'object' of actual knowledge; man experiences transcendence only as 'transcendence in a concrete fact'[178].

The mediated character of God-experience stressed by Christian theology has also its implications in the understanding of the role of revelation in man's God-experience. The immediacy of the God-experience is a mediated immediacy and so as Pannenberg insists, the 'immediate religious experience cannot by itself alone establish the certainty of the truth of its content'[179]. Only the historical revelation can be the ultimate criterion of truth. Hence 'Anubhava' alone cannot be the 'Pramana' of theology or Christology.[180] The role of 'Anubhava' in Christology, therefore, has to be understood with the required differentiation. Mysticism can neither exclude the historical Word of revelation, nor can it be in any way superior to the historical revelation.[181] True religious experience cannot be reduced to the personal whims of subjective experiences and the projection of individual feelings.[182] The certainty and reliability of today's Christ-experience is, therefore, necessarily based on what happened in the past, in the history of Jesus of Nazareth as the Christ. Otherwise Christ-experience degenerates into illusion. The importance of experience in theologizing points also to the importance of determining the objectivity and historicity of what happened in the past.[183] Therefore, we could maintain that the Vedantic 'Historiophobia'[184] strikes at the roots of the reliability and credibility of the Vedantic vision of God-experience. Contrary to the position of S. Radhakrishnan we have, therefore, to maintain that apart from the 'certifying' criterion of historical objectivity, god-experience (Anbuhava) is neither self-established (svatassiddha), nor self-evidencing (svasamvedya) and self-luminous (svayamprakasa).[185] The faith-experience does not begin on 'tabula rasa', at point 'o', but from the historical mediation of revelation: Fides ex auditu (Rom 10:17; Jude 3)!"

Our above insistence on the historical revelation to give objectivity to religious experience does not mean that we intend to water down the important role of personal and subjective experience in man's encounter with the divine Mystery. Faith-experience implies not only an objective assimilation of the past data of the definitive revelation at its culmination in the history of Jesus Christ, but also it is necessary to appropriate personally the faith from hearing and to deepen it in confrontation with man's experience at present, which implies also an openness of the faith to the possible experiences of the times to come. The Word of God is not stale and unproductive; it gives origin and inspiration to ever new personal and dynamic experiences.[186] Both objective faith and personal experience will have to go hand in hand, depending on each other and never in opposition to each other. It cannot be accepted, as Karl Rahner asserts, that mystical experience could make the field of revelation and faith superfluous; God-experience has to remain always an experience in faith; otherwise it would be only an illusory gnosis or theo-sophie! [187] On the other hand, faith (ex auditu) has to grow in the reality of one's being and flower into a living God-experience that results ultimately in man's God-realization (Brahmasaksatkara).

Rahner's transcendental method in theology is not meant to lead one to the isolated interiority of one's subjectivity. The transcendental experience that Rahner considers as the starting point of his anthropo-theological considerations is well balanced by his stress on the historical character of human existence. Rahner's transcendental Christology follows the same line of thought and comes to the recognition of the historical reality of Jesus, the Christ, as the ultimate solution to the mystery of man and of the human history. [188] It is this Christological accent in God-experience that constitutes the specificity of the Christian religious or transcendental experience. By the necessary historical and incarnational character of the Christ-reality and Christ-experience (Kristanubhava), God-experience itself becomes necessarily historical and incarnational. That is what V. Chakkarai means when he affirms that Christian God-experience is essentially Christ-experience. [189] Jesus Christ as the one who was yesterday, is today and forever (Heb 13:8) in each man's heart as the indweller (Antaryamin) in union with the Father and the Holy Spirit - we have to evaluate this trinitarian dimension in the following section and is in reality the ultimate criterion for the discernment of 'what is a human misunderstanding of the transcendental experience of God, and what is the legitimate interpretation of this experience' [190]. In this sense, also from the point of view of mysticism, Jesus Christ is the definitive, normative and infallible 'Way', 'Marga' or 'Hodos' (Acts 18:25 etc.) [191] to God-realization!

In this context it is also to be mentioned that what we have already said in reference to the 'anonymous Christians' is also applicable to the reality of Christ-experience. If Jesus Christ is the only norm of God-experience for every human being, then it has to be logically affirmed that there must also be an 'anonymous Christ-Experience'! [191a] Where ever there is authentic

God-experience outside the explicit boundaries of the Church - in our case we are interested first and foremost in the undeniable phenomenon of authentic and deep God-experience in Hinduism [192] - this experience has to be, even in its implicit and unrecognized form, the Christ-experience in one or another way. This is a challenge for Christians to take the reality of God-experience in other religions, especially in Hinduism, in a more earnest and serious way as genuine and inspiring [193] inspite of the fact that 'it is precisely Christianity which makes real this experience of God in its most radical and purest form, and in Jesus Christ achieves a convincing manifestation of it in history'[194]. Every correct interpretation of man's supernatural transcendentality, in whatever religion it may be, has a fundamental meaning for all men,[195] Christians included. Since the non-Christian experience of God is at least implicitly Christian in character, it logically follows that the non-Christians can also teach the Christians something of the mystery of Christ and, as James Dupuis contends, we have to recognize fully also the possibility that certain aspects of the mystery of Christ are more deeply experienced by the non-Christians than they are by many Christians. [196] Hence the need for sharing of God-experience in the Indian context especially between Hinduism and Christianity!

2. The Trinitarian Dimension of Christ-Experience

'The grace of the Lord Jesus Christ, the love of God and the fellowship of the Holy Spirit' (2 Cor 13:13) - this is the goal of the Christian life, as Paul sees it. This is so because the trinitarian dimension is an essential constituent of the Christ-experience itself. We had affirmed this point earlier in chapter six in connection with the Indian Christology. [197] This trinitarian aspect is quite meaningful, of course with necessary modification, especially in the Indian 'Saccidananda' [198] and 'Trimurti' [199] context. 'Isvaranubhava' and 'Brahmasaksatkara' are for the Indian seers, as we have seen in chapter three, integrated in the triadal reality and manifestation of the Parambrahman. A necessary clarification for the Christian thinking in reference to this is, as we have also shown, important for a better understanding of the transcendental and personal aspects of the triune God. [200] In short, what we want to say is that the Vedanta philosophical background in India is a fertile ground for the reception of a Christian spirituality that is indispensably trinitarian in character.

In his notion of mysticism and God-experience, Karl Rahner also stresses the aspect of the self-giving of the triune God, [201] which leads to the personal presence of God to the very reality of man ('Antaryamin', 'interior intimo meo') in a fully gratuitous way. [202] Although the trinitarian formulas are only doxological in character, according to Wolfhart Pannenberg, they are very important in understanding the reality of the Kingdom of God to which all are called because 'the trinitarian doctrine describes the coming God as the God of love whose future has already arrived and who integrates the past and the present world, accepting it to share in his own life for ever. The trinitarian doctrine is, therefore, no mere Christian addition to the philosophical idea of God. Rather the trinitarian doctrine is the ultimate expression for the one reality of the coming God whose Kingdom Jesus proclaimed'[203]. The trinitarian idea of God, Pannenberg thinks, is congruous with the historical process, while the notion of a supreme entity speaks only of a 'divine thing' outside man's history.[204] It is in his personal and trinitarian reality that God establishes his communion and loving relationship with mankind through, with and in Christ!

Since the Christian God-experience is essentially an experience of man's union with God the Father through the Son in the Holy Spirit, it could be reasonably said that God the Father, as the Source of Divinity (pege tes theotetos), [205] to use the expression of Origen or the Source-God (pegaia theotes)[206] is also the Source of our Christ-experience. The theology of God the Father as the only Principle of Divinity (tes theotetos arche)[207] who is without beginning (anarchos)[208] and without origin (agennetos)[209], a fact stressed especially by the Fathers of the East, brings to light the eminent position of God the Father in Christ-experience. St. Augustine also, as a representative of the West, understands God the Father as the source and origin of the whole divinity: 'Fons ergo ipse (Pater) et origo totius divinitatis'. [210] This 'Monarchic' (one source) notion of God is also defended by Bonaventure who considers God the Father as the absolute source of the Divinity [211] although Thomas Aquinas, who considers the 'innascibilitas' as a 'proprietas' of the Father, does not hold it for a positive 'notio personalis' of the Father. [212] In the theology of today Yves Congar declares his preference for the notion of Bonaventure and indicates that in the New Testament the word 'God' refers by and large to God the Father. He points out that

God the Father is the subject of the verb 'agapan', as the bearer of 'Agape' (love). He is Love (1Jn 4:8, 16). [213]the son is the Beloved of the Father (agapetos - Col 1:13). [214] It is the Father who sends (missio) his Word, his Image and the Holy Spirit who is the Gift of all gifts. God the Father, Congar explains, is invisible (Jn 1:18; 6:46; Col 1:15; 1Tim 1:17; 6:16; Rom 1:20) and as the beginningless origin of divinity he makes himself visible to us by sending his Son and has taken abode in us by sending us His Spirit. It is the Father who in his economy of salvation brings us to the sharing of his immanent reality. [215] The economical mission by the Father that corresponds to his immanent mission is the basis and the ultimate principle of man's God-realization (Brahmasaksatkara) and consequently of the Christ-experience (Khristanubhava) that leads to it.

Jesus Christ as the only and necessary mediator between God and man mediates to us the immediacy [216] of God-experience. As Karl Rahner thinks, God as the personal Absolute can be confronted only in him, because it is in him, in the earthly vessel of his humanity that the fullness of the Godhead dwells. In Jesus of Nazareth, the Christ, mysticism and God-experience assumes an historico-incarnational character. Jesus Christ is the highest and unsurpassably the most perfect instance of man's 'Brahmasaksatkara' and he is 'Brahmasaksatkara' itself in tangible form not merely as an event of the past which was of salvific importance for us, but by virtue of the resurrection of historical Jesus, he is now and for all eternity, as Rahner contends, the permanent openness of our finite being to the living God and therefore even in his now glorified humanity he is the same yesterday, today and forever (Hebr. 13:8) he is 'the created reality for us which stands in the act of our religion in such a way that, without this act towards his humanity and through it (implicitly or explicitly), the basic religious act towards God could never reach its goal. One always sees the Father only through Jesus' [217]. So even to-day, the humanity of Jesus Christ is of paramount importance for man's God-experience and God-realization. In other words, Rahner continues, 'if the religious act really wants to reach God, it always and in every case has and must have this 'incarnational' structure' [218]. The importance of the humanity of Christ in God-experience has been always stressed in the tradition of genuine Christian mysticism and especially by St. Teresa of Avila. [219] The Christian mysticism, God-experience, is a down-to-earth mysticism that cannot be reconciled with the Vedantic contempt of this world and the human body in man's search for the ultimate God-realization. In the light of the mystical teachings of seers like Teresa of Avila, we can very well affirm, as Ulrich Dobhan does,[220] that the genuine mysticism has nothing to do with a neo-platonic, dualistic, world vision that promotes contempt and aversion towards the human body and the material aspect of human existence. This is, however, not meant to depreciate the importance of personal asceticism on the way of mysticism. Yogic asceticism[221] is adaptable also in Christian mysticism as a means and help towards God-experience and the idea of self-control[222] is definitely not strange to the Christian view of spiritual life.

While stressing the incarnation and historical dimensions of God-experience realized in and through Jesus Christ, it must also be mentioned that, as far as the humanity of Christ is concerned, our destiny is not different from his. We had discussed this point in reference to the implications of the Hypostatic Union for the whole of mankind.[223] The divinization of the humanity of Christ in the mystery of the incarnation is an irrevocable guarantee for the divinization of the whole of humanity through, with and in Christ. In the Christ-event it is humanity through, with and in Christ. In the Christ-event it is humanity as such that is raised to the divine filiation. Therefore, it is quite reasonable to say that every one who is in union with Christ in an explicit or implicit way is a child of God. We are not only just 'called' or 'considered' as children of God, but in Christ we are really so! The aupanis - hadic 'Mahavakya', 'Aham Brahmasmi' - I am Brahman -, has in this sense a very valuable and undeniable Christian content. The real participation of the trinitarian life being the essence of God-experience, it is fitting and proper to call every one who is in such a real communion with God as the child of God.

The question of the divine sonship in reference to the Christians especially from the standpoint of the Johannine writings has been, as we have already mentioned in Chapter VIII, quite scholarly elaborated by Dr. Matthew Vellanical.[224] We would maintain that the study which he limits to the 'Christians'[225] has definitely wider applications in reference to the whole of humanity and this is especially relevant in the Indian context. While affirming the real divine sonship of Christians according to the Johannine writings,[226] he does not fail to differentiate it in reference to the divine sonship of Jesus, a clarification which is of extreme importance in the Vedantic context. Vella-nickal considers the Johannine expressions 'tekna theou' (Jn 1:12; 11:52 etc.) [227] and 'genēthēnai ek tou theou' (Jn 1:13; 3:3-8 etc.)[228] as decisive in showing the reality of the divine filiation of Christians. Inspite of the hellenistic influences on John regarding the destiny of all human beings to participate in the divine 'Logos', it cannot be ignored that John presents something original regarding the divine filiation by the expression 'genēthēnai ek tou Theou'[229]. Still John is very particular in distinguishing the 'teknon' (Son) he uses for all human beings from the 'hyios' that he reserves for Jesus, the Son of God and the Son of man.[230] Jesus is Son of God by the very nature of his being, but the divine filiation of other human beings is not automatic; they have to become children by supernatural begetting (Jn 3:3-10 etc.),[231] or by super-natural adoption - to use the expression preferred by Paul (Rom 8:14-16,17,21 etc.).[232] The divine filiation of Jesus is an ontological one, but that of other human beings is a 'dynamic sonship'[233] which is all the same not just a title of honour but real through participation in the Divine Sonship of Christ himself (Jn 11:52).[234] These clarifications, we think substantiate biblically what Rahner proposes by his transcendental Anthropo-Christology especially in reference to God-experience. Our God-experience is fundamentally an experience of our divine filiation in the Son, the incarnate Word of God, Jesus of Nazareth, who as Christ is 'yesterday and today and forever' (Heb 13:8).

It is the indispensable role of Jesus Christ in our trinitarian filiation that bases and demands our intimate personal relation and unconditional love towards Jesus. This point has been very much stressed by Karl Rahner. The human reality of Jesus is a constituent factor (inneres Moment) of our God-realization and so, according to him, a personal relation and intimate love towards him belongs to the substance of Christian - implicit or explicit - existence. It is only in our personal relation to the God-Man, who is the historical concretization of 'Brahmasaksatkara', that we can ever reach the immediacy of the trinitarian God in faith, hope and love.[235] It is, therefore, to be stressed in the Indian or Vedantic mystical context that, as Rahner contends, without Jesus of Nazareth, the Christ, 'every absolute of which we speak or which we imagine we attain by mystical flight is in the last analysis merely the never attained, objective correlative of that empty and hollow, dark and despairingly self-consuming infinity which we are ourselves:

the infinity of dissatisfied finiteness, but not the blessed infinity of truly limitless fullness'[236].

The trinitarian dimension of Christ-experiences leads us finally to the role of the Holy Spirit in the process of man's God-experience and God-realization. We had discussed sufficiently the role of Pneumatology for the understanding of Christ-experience especially in the Indian context earlier in chapter six.[237] We had also referred to the lack of precision and clarity that is prevalent by and large in the Indian Pneumatology. [238] The universally present 'Christ-principle' that is emphasized by Panikkar and Klostermaier is better suited in its application to the Holy Spirit than to Christ himself. In both of them we could observe an uncritical and unsubstantiated mixing up of Christology and Pneumatology. Explicit pneumatological aberrations can also be observed in the views which consider the Holy Spirit as the impersonal power of God (Rammohan Roy), [239] as the Christ-force (K.C. Sen), as the resurrected Christ (V. Chakkarai) or as the New Cosmic Energy in evolution (P. Chenchiah).[240] We do not have to repeat here the evaluation regarding these points which we have done in the sixth chapter. We also do not have to elaborate here a theology of the Holy Spirit, which has already been admirable done by theologians like Yves Congar. [241] In connection with the trinitarian dimension of Christ-experience we want only to mention here that it is the Holy Spirit who ultimately realizes and makes efficacious in us the God-realization that has been actualized by Jesus Christ in the name of the whole human race. So our God-experience is the Christ-experience brought about in us by the Holy Spirit. It is the Holy Spirit who makes us into the children of God sharing the filiation of Jesus Christ and who bears witness with our spirit when we cry "Abba! Father!" (Rom 8:15-16).[242] The Holy Spirit, the mutual Love of the Father and the Son, is the Universal Spirit that is present in the core of human existence leading man to his ultimate salvific realization in God. Such a 'mystical' stress in Pneumatology is of great relevance especially in the Indian context of 'Isvaranubhava' and 'Brahmasaksatkara'.

According to Karl Rahner, as to a number of Church Fathers and theologians,[243] the created grace of man's trinitarian life and god-experience is based on the Uncreated Grace, the Holy Spirit. The indwelling presence of God in man is the result of the gift of the Holy Spirit. [244] This is in line with the idea of Thomas Aquinas who describes the Holy Spirit as the 'causa formalis in-haerens' of our divine filiation.[245] The immediacy of God-experience, however, that is effected by the Holy Spirit, Rahner argues, does not dispense with the incarnational and historical dimensions of this experience. Rahner criticizes the faith in the immediacy of the Spirit, at the expense of the historical incarnation as a naive faith in the Holy Spirit.[246] This criticism is also very relevant against those Indian thinkers who, as we have already mentioned, think it possible to develope an Indian Christian experience dispensing with history and incarnation. On the other hand we think that the Pneumatology in the Indian context could make valid contributions to the idea of the woman-liness of God especially because of the fact that in the Hindu tradition the masculine manifestations of the supreme Brahman are always counterbalanced by the corresponding feminine aspects.[247] The womanliness of God has its biblical roots (Is 49:14f., 66:13), but has been by and large neglected in the theological traditions and is now slowly being re-discovered.[248] Avoiding all anthropomorphic exaggerations we could very well affirm that there are aspects in God that correspond not only to the reality of man but also that of a woman; God has after all created the human being as man and woman, corresponding to his own image (Gen 1:27). It would not also be an exaggeration to observe that the divine 'quality' of tenderness ('rahamim' derived from 'rahem' or mother's bosom (Gen 43:30)[249] is more feminine in character than masculine. The same can also be said in reference to love. It would not be improper to say, of course with the necessary reservations, that the Holy Spirit, who is the personification of the love and tenderness between the Father and the Son, is more feminine in manifestation than masculine.[250] In our formation into the children of God, as Y. Congar observes, the Holy Spirit plays the role of a mother who brings us to an intimacy of love with God, our Father and Jesus, our brother.[251] It is the Holy Spirit who actualizes in us the real trinitarian God-realization and God-experience and who brings us, as Pannenberg thinks, to the realization of our eschatological reality in the Kingdom of God.[252]

The Holy Trinity is the community of love. The trinitarian dimension of God-experience which we have discussed so far is an indication also of the dimension of love that forms the substance of this experience. The 'Brahmasaksatkara' that is realized through 'Khristanubhava' is in reality a 'Premanubhava', an experience of love, a love that is not only directed to the trinitarian God but the one that by its very nature embraces also the whole of mankind as we shall see in the following section.

3. The Mysticism of Altruistic Love

The Christian God-experience has an indispensable horizontal dimension. We had stressed this point in reference to the Indian mysticism especially in the sixth chapter of our work. [253] True mysticism leads not to an egoism of a so-called personal spiritual realization, but necessarily to the altruism of human love. Here what we intend is to evaluate the question of altruism in mysticism - a point that is of great relevance in the Vedantic context of Atmasaksatkara - especially from the point of view of Karl Rahner and Wolfhart Pannenberg as we have done so far.

Rahner sees an inseparable unity between the vertical love of God and the horizontal love of neighbour and the condition of the possibility of this unity, according to Rahner, is 'the unity between the experience of God and the experience of self', a point which we have discussed in one of the previous sections. [254] If one can attain the experience of God only through the experience of oneself, it is also true that the only way in which one achieves self-experience and self-realization is through encounter with one's fellow men. It is only in the relation of the 'I' to a 'Thou', as we have mentioned in chapter seven, [255] that our 'life in its full sense is in the concrete achieved in knowledge and freedom' [256]. As Rahner observes, 'the original objectivity of the experience of self necessarily takes place in the subjectivity of its encounters with other persons in dialogue, in trustful and loving encounter. Man experiences himself by experiencing the other person and not the other thing' [257]. In other words, 'he who fails to discover his neighbour has not truly achieved realization of himself either' because 'the subject's experience of himself and of the Thou who encounters him, is one and the same experience under two different aspects' [258]. On the one hand, it can very well be said, the experience of God and the experience of self are one and on the other hand 'the experience of self and the encounter with our neighbour are one, that all these three experiences ultimately constitute a single reality with three aspects mutually conditioning one another' [259] and so one can say that 'man discovers himself or loses himself in his neighbour; that man has already discovered God, even though he may not have any explicit knowledge of it, if only he has truly reached out to his neighbour in an act of unconditional love, and in that neighbour reached out also to his own self[260]. Similarly, in his brief anthropological creed Karl Rahner affirms that a 'person really discovers his true self in a genuine act of self-realization only if he risks himself radically for another. If he does this, he grasps unthematically or explicitly what we mean by God as the horizon, the guarantor and the radical depths of this love, the God who in his existentiell and historical self-communication made himself the realm within which such love is possible. This love is meant in both an interpersonal and a social sense, and in the radical unity of both these elements it is the ground and the essence of the church'[261]. This would mean that the love of neighbour is an act of the love of God itself and that the love of neighbour is not just a preparation, effect, fruit or touchstone of the love of God.[262] The neighbour, therefore, is not just an 'occasion', a 'materia' or a 'verification' of the love of God;[263] the neighbour is not loved just for 'God's sake' and the love of neighbour is not just a commandment that 'guards and defends the other against our brutal egoism'. Rahner warns against considering the neighbour merely as 'an opportunity for pure love of God; 'caritas' means really 'the love of our neighbour himself, a love empowered by God to attain its ultimate radicality and a love which really terminates and rests in our neighbour'[264]. Rahner argues that we love our neighbour 'by an ontological and not merely 'moral' or psychological necessity, that whoever does not love the brother whom he 'sees', also cannot love God whom he does not see, and that one can love God whom one does not see only by loving one's visible brother lovingly'[265].

The love of God and the love of neighbour, according to Rahner, finds its ultimate realization in Jesus Christ, the God-man, because God becomes really concrete in him and because in this concrete man, Jesus of Nazareth, the immediacy of God himself is reached. The absolute culmination of the transcendental and historico-categorial determination of man is attained in the unique God-man unity in Jesus Christ.[266] Love for all other people, so explains Rahner, finds its justification in Jesus Christ and discovers it's ultimate ground, 'and all such love leads to the one man in whom this union of God and man, intended for everyone, appears in its historical uniqueness and utter finality - Jesus Christ'[267]. We had discussed this point sufficiently in Chapter VII.C.1.

In short we can say that Jesus Christ is the guarentee for the fact that God himself is loved in man and that the love towards a human being can be on account of himself or herself, without however by that fact losing God in any way.[268]

A personal and explicit love of Jesus Christ is possible in our encounter with him in the Sacred Scriptures, the Liturgy, in the community of his believers etc.; but, as we have mentioned earlier, Rahner emphasizes very much the fact of man's encountering Jesus Christ implicitly and unthematically in and through the love of one's neighbour. Rahner points out that the criterion of the love that leads one to Jesus Christ is described in the 25th chapter of the Gospel according to St. Matthew; love of neighbour is given there (Mt 25:34-46) as the only explicit standard by which man will be judged, and the cooling down of this love is represented as the content of 'lawlessness' among the afflictions of the last days. What is done to the least of one's brothren is done to Jesus! So the unity of the love of God and love of neighbour finds its basis and radicalization in Christ himself.[269] The smallest act of love towards one's neighbour, carried out even by an unchristian or an unbeliever, reaches truly the Son of man who may remain anonymous, because this Son of Man is one with all sons and daughters of men as implied in the mystery of the divine Incarnation. It is because of that the deeds of the love of neighbour has a definitive character for the eternal life and its ommission would mean definitive damnation. What is done to the smallest of one's neighbour is - and not just 'as if' - done to Jesus. It is in one's neighbour that one encounters knowingly or unknowingly Jesus Christ,[270] who is the ultimate realization of the mystery of man and of the human history. Therefore, we have to say in reference to the socially disinterested Vedantic spiritual tradition that, as Rahner affirms, 'God cannot be truly reached in gnostic-mystic interiority alone'![271]

Hans Urs von Balthasar has critized Rahner's insistence on the unity of the love of God and love of neighbour as promoting indifference to the explicit confession of Jesus Christ, because it is the love of neighbour that ultimately counts! He asks: With what criterion can man, who is basicly a sinner, judge what love is? The performance of the sinful man, he opines, cannot be the criterion to measure God's love! To reduce the love of God to the love of neighbour, he argues, is to reduce Christianity itself to a certain humanism![272]

The same opinion seems to reflect also in Pannenberg who thinks that inspite of St. John's insistence on the love of neighbour, he does not regard the love of God as identical with human fellowship and he argues that 'Christian love is primarily not a question of a human relationship, but of the presence of the God's love in the world and man's sharing in this' [273]. Hans Urs von Balthasar also thinks that Karl Rahner subdues the primacy of the act of religion to the social works of charity. Balthasar contends that the existence of those like the contemplative Carmelite nuns, who live a life of interior prayer and penance, mortifications and acts of expiation for the sins of the world, without any external social works of charity, is really the place where one can perceive the real identity of the love of neighbour and the love of God! [274]

In reference to the above criticism we would say that the fact of Rahner's insistence on the unity of the love of God and the love of neighbour does not mean an outright identification of the two which would make the one disappear into the other. Rahner's position, in order to be understood correctl y, must be seen in the general context of his philosophy of transcendentality and categoriality, which we have discussed already sufficiently especially in the seventh chapter. The primacy of God's love - a point insisted by Baltha-sar and Pannenberg - is fully acceptable also to Rahner, but that does not mean that what is primary has to be also at the same time thematical or categorial, i.e. explicit or objectified. Rahner also would have no hesitation in recognizing the indisputable dimension of love of neighbour in the interior and expiatory life of contemplatives who may not undertake any explicit social development programmes, but withdraw themselves from the hustles and bustles of this world, dedicating themselves to prayer and expiation for themselves and for the whole world! But Rahner would protest against a theocentrism which would consider man 'as unconcerned about God until he systematically conceives the notion of God as one reality 'besides' others and this in the merely dividing distinction from these other realities' [275] .

Like Karl Rahner, Wolfhart Pannenberg, is also of the view that 'Jesus' idea of love has to be understood in close conjunction with his eschatological proclamation of the Kingdom of God', the Basileia. [276] We can speak of the Christian newness and specificity even of the law of love only in the context of the 'Basileia' proclaimed and established by Jesus. It cannot be denied that the primacy of love was stressed by the Jewish rabbis even before Jesus (Tb 4:15 etc.) and the idea of human fellowship was also not unknown outside the Judaism. [277] So the law of love is not something that is absolutely, but only relatively, new. The real newness of the law of love according to the Gospels consists in including also one's enemies in the sphere of one's love (Mt 5:43-45 etc.), [278] the radicality of love that goes even to the point of taking the risk of losing one's life for the sake of others (Ez 34:11-16 etc.), [279] the supremacy of the law of love because what is done for the neighbour is done for Jesus (Mt 5:17 etc.), [280] and finally in the personification of love as the Spirit of God, the Holy Spirit. [281] When one is united with God and with one's fellow men in love, one is in the 'Basileia', the Kingdom of God; this is the specificity of the Christian notion of love and Jesus, as Pannenberg explains, 'above all emphasized that the Kingdom of God is in the man who accepted his message and it is this emphasis that makes the idea of love and human fellowship so characteristic of his teaching' [282].

Like Karl Rahner, Wolfhart Pannenberg is also quite clear regarding the social and humanitarian implications of his concept of the 'Basileia'. The Kingdom of God Jesus proclaimed, observes Pannenberg, is God's own ultimate reality that brings with it the reconciliation of all men in a society of peace and justice. [283] The Kingdom of God breaks in, as Pannenberg contends, 'where men are liberated to humanness, where they enjoy life in gratitude, and where they set over against their own suffering the 'nevertheless' of hope and [try to] remedy the suffering and privations of others' [284]. The human society as we see in the world of today, he declares, is far away from the ideal of the Basileia because what we see today is a 'world which is over-crowded with horror and hunger and satiated self-satisfaction, a world which again and again deteriorates into the madness of war and seldom truly seeks justice, a world which instead verbalizes the great slogans of humanity in order to disguise it's selfishness and evil - such a world is not the Kingdom of God' [285]. Pannenberg blames the so-called Christians of the West themselves who are called to witness the Kingdom of God before the world for being to a great extend responsible for man's inhumanity to man today. He rightly points out that the Christians 'have their population centres in the richest countries of the world, but they don't manage to change the miserable living conditions of the majority of mankind, but rather to contribute to, continue, perpetuate or even aggravate the disasterous occurences of hunger, war and political or economical alienation'[286]. This opinion of Pannenberg reflects very much the criticism of the Hindu intelligentsia against the Christian west, to which we had referred in the sixth chapter.[287] Pannenberg challenges the followers of Christ to action, that corresponds to their confession of Christ, to struggle for a more human form of society and for the peace of mankind. It depends on the Christians, he declares, whether the reality of the Basileia, the Kingdom of God, is eclipsed or illuminated in the world of today![288]

It would be the inalienable task of the Indian Christianity in presenting Jesus Christ as the mystery of man and of the human history, to bring to light and adequately stress also the 'mysticism of altruistic love', as we have already done in the sixth chapter, while emphasizing the importance of 'Khristanubhava' for 'Brahmasaksatkara'. There can be no genuine 'Atmanub-hava' (self-experience), 'Khristanubhava' (Christ-experience), Brahmanubhava (God-experience) and consequently no 'Brahma-'Atma-Saksatkara' God-Self-Experience) without the 'Premanubhava' (love-experience) in all its proper vertical and horizontal implications!

Conclusion to Chapter Nine

For an honest, meaningful and fruitful dialogue in the context of the Vedantic anthropology, the Indian Christology has to affirm in unequivocal terms that Jesus of Nazareth is the Christ! His historical uniqueness does not prejudice his universal relevance; rather, it is the basis of his universality. All the apparent contradiction and polarities of human existence and history find a salvific, non-dual (advaitic) synthesis in Jesus Christ. In our synthesising approach to the question of Christ's transcendental universality and his historical uniqueness in the above chapter we tried to seek out dialogue possibilities to face the universalistic claims of the Vedanta. We based our argument on an evolutionary world-vision and a transcendental anthropology that see Christ in solidarity with the whole of creation which receives in man the gratuitous self-giving of God. The uniqueness of Christ, we stressed, is not an 'exclusive' uniqueness but an all-inclusive one. In this background we also tried to discuss in a credible way the salvific value of Hinduism vis-a-vis the Christian claim that there is no salvation except through Christ. It has also been our concern to approach the disputed question of the 'Anonymous Christians' with the required differentiation insisting that what is important in this matter is not the problematic expression but its content, viz. even the salvation, for example, of a Hindu is to be ultimately traced to Christ. As he is the only mediator between God and man, he is present wherever God's salvation is present, even if he is not recognized explicitly. This is not an arrogant taking over of Hinduism, nor a relativization of Christianity which would strike at the root of all missionary efforts. The 'more' or the 'plus' of the explicit Christianity, we emphasized, is not just a gnostic unveiling or realization of what a non-Christian already is without knowing about it, but the acceptance of the unique, full, perfect, and incarnational self-giving of God in Jesus of Nazareth as the Christ, who is the sacramental realization of God's presence to man in human history, the God-given infallible answer to the transcendental quest of man that transforms one's   life by facilitating the achievement of the goal of one's existence!

In the context of the Indian spirituality and mystical tradition, we are convinced, it is also important that a systematic or dogmatic interpretation of Christ is necessarily linked with the experience of Christ (Khristanubhava) stressing its unity with self-experience (Atmanubhava) and God-experience

(Brahmanubhava) and ultimately with God-realization (Brahmasaksatkara). A dogma that does not blossom into spirituality is sterile; a spiritual theology that is not made credible and based on biblical and systematic theology is on the other hand self-projective and illusory. So we discussed under the notion of 'Khristanubhava' the transforming results that follow the explicit and whole hearted acceptance of Jesus, the Christ, as the mystery of man and of the human history. While dealing with the question of 'Khristanubhava' in its trinitarian dimension, in the background of the concept of 'Saccidananda', we have warned against all illusory divine assimilation of man in a certain pantheistic sense. We have also recognized dialogue possibilities with those aspects of the mystery of Christ which may be ignored or lost sight of in Christianity and which would be re-discovered or at least seen in a new light as a result of Christianity's mystical encounter with Hinduism. We could, for example, speak of a 'Consciousness Christology' that is based on our personal assimilation and appropriation of Jesus' experience of his advaitic unity with God (Jn 10:30., 14:10). In emphasizing the incarnational aspect of the Christian mysticism we have also sufficiently pointed out the necessity of putting spirituality into action for the welfare, including the material one, of the whole of humanity!

Conclusion to Part III

In this part of our work our intention has been to evaluate the Christological synthesis of the mystery of man and of the human history which we had arrived at in the previous part. The apparently contrasting dimensions of Christ's universality and his uniqueness have been critically illumined and evaluated from the anthropological, historical and Christological positions of Karl Rahner and Wolfhart Pannenberg and we have observed that they do in fact make valuable contributions and corrective suggestions - although not explicitly from their part as far as the Indian problematic is concerned - for a dialogue on the implications of a Christology in the Vedantic context.

Rahner's transcendental approach to anthropology and Christology is, as we have seen, an admirable complement for the Indian vision regarding the transcendental horizon in man. Man is the mystery that is oriented to the Mystery of Fullness and by virtue of this orientation he ventures to hope that the absolute Fullness communicates Himself to the mankind that is conditioned by matter and history. This historical hope calls for a historical search, inspired and guided by faith, to verify whether the transcendental orientation of man comes any where in history to its culminating realization. In the light of the divine revelation one can recognize the ultimate realization of the reality of man in God's self-giving in the history of Jesus of Nazareth. The anthropological stress of Rahner, on the other hand is balanced by the historical accent which Wolfhart Pannenberg gives to the understanding of truth and to the God-man relationship that came to its proleptically eschatological realization in Jesus of Nazareth, the Christ. Pannenberg's historico-critical approach to the Sacred Scriptures, his insistence on making faith credible by the criterions of human rationality and his openness towards extra-theological sciences are certainly healthy challenges for the Indian anthropology and Christology to take the multifarious aspects of man and his history more seriously. The Vedantic stress, on the other side, especially on the importance of God-experience in God-knowing and God-talk could also counterbalance and thus contribute to complement the dry intellectualism of the western theology.

The concepts of Christ's metahistorical universality as the 'Logos' and his historical uniqueness as the Son of Man, we have tried to show, are also from the Rahnerian and Pannenbergan points of view by no means two mutually contradicting and irreconcilable theses, but rather one follows the other - we may say as antithesis to thesis - with an inner necessity resulting in a salvific synthesis of the union of God and man with its relevance not only for the historically particular individual, Jesus of Nazareth, but also for the whole of humanity, at the transcendental climax of which he stands recapitulating the whole of creation in himself. If the historical uniqueness of Jesus Christ, as we have insisted, does not prejudice against his universal relevance for the whole of mankind, then it follows that we were right also in considering the salvific relevance of Jesus Christ in the context of the non-Christian religions and especially that of Hinduism. Therefore it was logical to refer to Rahner's notion of the 'Anonymous Christians'.

We have also considered it necessary not to limit our selves to the theoretical plain of God-Man unity in Jesus-Christ, but proceed further to the practical aspects of man's relation to God which attains its culmination in man's loving encounter with God and the lived altruistic love in our every day life!

GENERAL CONCLUDING PERSPECTIVES

Man - History - Christ: these were the dominant themes of our work. In fact, they are not three mutually independent topics but all three are centred on Jesus Christ, as the mystery of man and of the human history, the point on which our investigation has been pivoting all through. We discussed the mystery of Christ in the context of the Indian anthropology, especially of the Vedanta, with special regard for the Christological contributions of some of the prominent Indian thinkers, both Christian and non-Christian. We have also made a serious attempt to bring the Indian anthropo-Christological problematic into contact especially with two knowledgeable representatives mainly of the German theological milieu: Karl Rahner and Wolfhart Pannenberg. Their theological contributions were found to be of extreme relevance for an Indian Christological dialogue with the West, not just because of their different confessional backgrounds, but mainly due to the complementary nature of their Christological approaches: the former has been found to be interesting for his anthropological turn in theology and the latter for his stress on the historico-eschatological dimensions of anthropology and Christology!

On the Problematic

The central problematic of our anthropo-Christological discussion has been that of the apparent contrast between the meta-historical or universal transcendentality and historico-categorial particularity. This implies the metaphysical problem of reconicling the unity and the stability of the Absolute with the multiplicity and mutability of the phenomenal world; in short, the problem of determining the relation between the Absolute and the relative, between the transcendence of God and his immanence in the contingent. It is a dualistic (Dvaita !) problematic that is, from the Christian point of view, aggravated by the prevalent Vedantic non-dualism (Advaita !), in one or another of its forms, which proclaims the spirital, the universal and the transcendental generally at the cost of the material, the particular and the historical! This Vedantic approach has its natural repercussions in the understanding of the status of man and his ultimate goal, and consequently also in a developing Indian Christian theology as far as anthropology, history and Christology are concerned. In the course of our work we have pointed out in sufficient detail the main problems confronting the Indian Christology, viz. the problems which could be traced back to the above mentioned basic problematic.

The Vedantic Darsana, as we have pointed out, reduces the reality of man to that of a spiritual one, the Atman, which is by nature divine. The reality of God is the reality of man, although the inverse of it is not true. There is a certain identification of the transcendental orientation of man with the transcendence itself. The Atman has to liberate himself from the entanglement of the material and the changing world which is the source of desire, ignorance and enslavement to the never ending cyclic process of retributive re-births (Karma-Samsara) and realize his non-duality with the Absolute, the 'Saccidananda' (Being-Awareness-Bliss), who in his empirical manifestation 'accommodates' himself to the principles of the 'Maya' and the changing world through his triadal aspects of Brahma, Visnu and Siva. The problems connected with the notions of 'Karma-Samsara' and 'Maya', for example, the question of sin, the notion of 'Person' applied to the Absolute and the problem of his 'relations' and 'becoming', have been given our special attention. We have indicated that the general Hindu attitude towards the fellow human beings (caste system!) and to the animal kingdom (panpsychism !) are actually determined by the Vedantic vision of man, of the world and of God with a predominantly quasi-pantheistic bend! The theory of 'Karma-Samsara' has also its far reaching consequences on the notion of history. In the cyclic, repeated and endless world-process, an eschatological fulfilment of the history is not conceivable. Since history is a factor of enslavement, one cannot expect the salvation in history itself but only outside it. What is important is the meta-historical and universal principles which are above all changes. God encounters man in the immediacy of his intuition and personal experience (Anubhava) without being conditioned or mediated by the 'sensibles' of history. This problematic 'apauruseya' character of revelation is also a reason for accepting the theological method that considers 'Anubhava' as the most important 'Pramana' (source, means, criterion) of truth. We have sufficiently dealt with the problem of subjectivitiy and illusion in 'Anubhava' if it is taken independently of man's historical conditioning. Since man, according to the Vedanta, is divine, his salvation or self-realization is to be achieved mainly by his efforts (Karma), wisdom (Jnana) and/or loving devotion (Bhakti) to the Supreme. God-experience (Brahmanubhava) and God-realization (Brahma-saksatkara) which are basicly self-experience (Atmanubhava) and self-realization (Atmasaksatkara) belong to the essentials of the Vedantic soteriology. In this effort of self-liberation there are spiritual techniques (Yoga) and spiritual guides (Guru) or even divine manifestations (Avatar) which could be of help to man; but fundamentally salvation is understood by and large as one's own due and achievement. This, however, should be understood with the necessary differentiations to which we have referred in the course of our work: The role of a 'Saviour' is extremely limited! This is a problem which we took seriously from the point of view of Christian Soteriology.

In this context it is quite understandable that the Vedantins see the reality of Jesus Christ from the stand-point of a permanently valid, universal transcendence which ignores the material and the historical. In the advaitic context Christ is seen as the embodiment and realization of the highest possibilities of human existence, as is true in the case of any 'Avatar'. The problem of uncritically identifying the concepts of 'Avatar' and 'Incarnation' is also, as we have mentioned, rather acute. It is the 'Christ-Principle' or the 'Christ-Idea' that would be of interest, and not the Jesus of history! The various attempts so far from the part of Christian theologians to make the person and work of Christ intelligible - these were oft made through the adoption of scholastic and western philosophical categories - were not by and large satisfactory and without surprise they remain unassimilated in the Indian intellectual arena. Similarly there are also problems in the Indian context to explain the uniqueness of the person of Christ as the Son of God in difference to other human beings, the salvific role of Christ as the only saviour of mankind and the vicarious nature of his existence culminating in his death and resurrection. The universally valid ethical principles taught by Christ are for some modern Indian thinkers more important than his person. A deity with a crown of thorns and a body that resurrects into live everlasting are understandably not easy to conceive for a Vedantic mind. In the context of a depreciation of the material and the bodily, the eschatological resurrection of man is irreconcilable with the Vedantic anthropology.

On the Dialogue Possibilities

There are many points, as we have seen, in Hinduism in general and the Vedanta in particular, which are acceptable to the Christian faith and there is an undeniable sharing of concern both in Hinduism and Christianity as far as the ultimate destiny of man is concerned. However, while analysing the Indian anthropo-Christological problematic we have found it to be of extreme importance to submit the Vedantic categories to a healthy process of 'de-hinduization' in order to make them fit as vehicles to carry the Christian faith. That implies a Christian transformation of the Hindu culture as was the case in the first centuries with regard to the Greco-Roman world-vision and life. Our contribution in this process has been to bring in especially Karl Rahner and Wolfhart Pannenberg as examples of dialogues partners for a re-thinking Indian Christology. In the background of their theological perspectives we have tried to make the Christian claim of Christ's universality and his uniqueness credible even in the Vedantic context.

The anthropology of Karl Rahner shares common ground with the Vedanta regarding the question of man's transcendental horizon, through this transcendence, according to Rahner, does not make man identical or essentially one with the Divine in a quasi-pantheistic way nor is to be conceived in a panpsychic sense. The realization of man's transcendence is also, according to him, not the achievement of man himself, but the result of the free and unmerited self-communication of God that crowns man's transcendental orientation by his definitive acceptance into the life and love of the personal triune God through, with and in Jesus of Nazareth, the Christ, the God-Man! Like the Vedantins Rahner stresses the notion of the 'Idee Christi', but unlike them and some Indian Christian theologians, he insists also on the role of the material and the historical both in his anthropology and Christology. Wolfhart Pannenberg supplies additional eschatological dimensions to Rahner's existential approach to history, both of which serve as valuable correctives for the Vedantic approach to the question of history. Contrary to a prevalent misunderstanding we have stressed that neither Rahner nor Pannenberg does ignore the brokenness of history and the tragedy of sin and consequently of man's radical incapacity to save himself or to reach all by himself the realization of his transcendental destiny. The salvific role of Christ is made credible and intelligible in an anthropological and historical conceptual horizon. We have also brought to light the point that both Rahner and Pannenberg, while trying to re-interpret the traditional Chalcedonian approach to Christology, avoid an anthropological and historical reduction of the mystery of Christ. They aim at reconciling both the transcendental universality and the historical particularity in Jesus, the Christ! The central question for the Indian Christology, namely, how the historically limited and unique Christ-event could bring salvation and ultimate realization to the whole of mankind of all times in different geographical and cultural milieu, can only be answered, as we have seen, through a bridging up (Überbrückung) or synthesis of the historically contingent and the transcendentally absolute nature of truth in Jesus, the Christ, as the mystery of man and of the human history. We have found this approach extremely useful for a non-dual (advaitic) synthesis of the realities of man and history, - spirit and matter, eternity and time-in the mystery of Christ, especially in the Indian anthropological context, that is predominantly co-determined by the Vedanta. We have affirmed that it is possible and necessary to proclaim the universality and salvific relevance of Jesus of Nazareth without discriminating against his historical uniqueness as the Christ!

Instead of remaining in the conceptual world of dogmatics and systematics theology, we have found it also of extreme relevance to stress the paramount importance of dogma blossoming into spirituality while the latter is credibly founded on the former. This is the reason for our stress on the question of God-experience (Brahmanubhava) and Christ-experience (Khristanubhava) which strike familiar and acceptable chords for the Vedanta. A living and loving Christ-experience makes the self-giving of God to mankind, to the whole of creation, in Jesus of Nazareth as a life-giving principle in the Holy Spirit a reality not only for the present but also for all times to come. While stressing the trinitarian and incarnational aspects of the Christian God-experience we have pointed out that the sharing in the life of the trinitarian love manifests itself in man's altruistic concern even for the material welfare of his fellowmen. On this point, we have opined, the general Hindu social mentality has to undergo a necessary correction.

On Avenues of Further Research

The above summarization of our analysis of the main problems confronting the Indian Christology in the anthropological context of the Vedanta and our contribution towards making the mystery of Christ more intelligible and credible does not mean that our work is to be naively considered as exhaustive and as the last word in the Indian Christology! We have tried not only to stress the limits, problems and possibilities of Christological dialogue in the Indian context but also to open up avenues for further possible research. A detailed elaboration of these further possibilities would not be required here; our thematic division of sections and sub-sections and our concluding remarks especially in Chapters VII, VIII and IX could serve to indicate such further avenues of research by anybody or for a 'Habilitationsarbeit' by ourselves. Just for example, we could speak of a matter-spirit integration even in the Christian sense based on the symbol of the 'Nataraja' (the dancing Siva) in the Indian context or of applying correctly and with necessary clarifications the notion of 'relation' to 'person' and thus showing the possibility of the concept of person being accepted even by the Vedanta as the summit of the realization of being and consciousness and not as the attribution of a limitation to the Absolute. There are also research possibilities in deepening and critically evaluating the related concepts, for example, of 'Vac' and 'Logos' or of 'Dharma' and 'Basileia'. A further example could be found in a so-called 'Negative Christology' in line with the 'Neti, Neti' approach of the Vedanta to the ineffable mystery, i.e. a Christology based on the experience (Anubhava) of this mystery. The truth of Christ which we may experience is in fact far beyond all its conceptual, categorial and systematic expressions. Such a 'Consciousness Christology' based on Jesus' experience of his 'advaitic' unity with God would consist in personally assimilating and appropriating this 'Advaita' into one's own existence 'so that God may be all and in all' (1 Cor 15:28) by bringing 'everything together under Christ, as head' (Eph 1:10). It is also to be mentioned that such theological investigations in dialogue with the Indian context have far reaching prospects in Christian ecumenism. A joint effort to face theological issues in a new context logically emphasizes the common Christian concern which could help to minimize or even to overcome confessional differences.

Ultimately there are only two words: 'God' and 'Man' who is at the apex of God's creation. Inspite of their apparent duality (Dvaita) they make one Mystery (Advaita) that is made manifest in the Incarnate Word of God, Jesus Christ - the mystery of man and of the human history.

FOOTNOTES

Introduction   577

Chapter I   582

Chapter II   594

Chapter III   604

Chapter IV   623

Chapter V   645

Chapter VI   668

Chapter VII   691

Chapter VIII   718

Chapter IX   740

NOTES: PART I

INTRODUCTION

1. P. Fallon, 'The Gods of Hinduism', in: R. De Smet/J. Neuner (Edd.), Religious Hinduism - A Presentation and Appraisal, Allahabad, 1968, p. 84.

2. Margaret and James Stutley, A Dictionary of Hinduism, Allied Publishers: Bombay, 1977, p. 330.

3. R.C. Zaehner, Hinduism, London, 1962, p. 1. It is also significant to note that one of the well known works of Dr. S. Radhakrishnan has the title 'The Hindu View of Life' avoiding the word 'Religion' (London 1926, third edition 1967).

4. C.B. Papali, 'Vedism and Classical Hinduism', in:Secretariatus pro non-Christians (Ed.), For a Dialogue with Hinduism, Roma, 1970, p.9.

5. Cfr. D.S. Sarma, What is Hinduism, Madras, 1939, p.10.

6. P. Fallon, Art. Cit., p.84.

7. Cfr. S.K. Chatterji, 'The Religions', in: H. Battacharya (Ed.), Cultural Heritage of India, 4 Vols., Calcutta, 1961ff., Vol. 4, p.19 (Original edition: Ramakrishna Mission, Calcutta, 1953-56).
    Cfr. also: Zaehner, Op. Cit., p.21.
    Cfr. also: Stutley, Op. Cit., p.80.
    The proto-Dravidians appear to be the originators of the Indus Valley Civilization with an advanced social and political system.

8. R. Antoine, 'General Historical Survey', in: R. De Smet/J. Neuner (Edd.), Religious Hinduism, p. 23.
    Cfr. also: Stutley, Op. Cit., p. 20.
    Cfr. also: Walter A. Fairsekvis Jr. The Harappan Civilization, New York, 1961., Idem, The Roots of Ancient India, London, 1971, John Marshall et al., Mohenjo-daro and the Indus Civilization, 3 Vols., London, 1931.

9. C.B. Papali, Art. Cit., p.8.
    Cfr. also S.K. Chatterji, Loc. Cit.

10. C.B. Papali, Loc. Cit.

11. R. De Smet, 'Appendix', in: Idem (Ed.), Religious Hinduism, p.323.

12. C.B. Papali, Art. Cit. p.9.
    Cfr. also M. Dhavamony, Classical HInduism, (Documenta Missionalia 15), Rome, 1982, p.1.

13. C.B. Papali, Loc. Cit.

14. R. Antoine, 'Sacred Books and Religious Literature', in: R. De Smet/ J. Neuner (Edd.), Religious Hinduism, p.36.

15. Geoffrey Parrinder, Avatar and Incarnation, London, 1970, p.15.

16. The Latin equivalent is 'Videre', to see. Here 'Vid' refers more to an intellectual vision and knowledge than to a sensory one.

17. Cfr. Geoffrey Parrinder, The Significance of Bhagavad-Gita for Christian Theology, London, 1968, p.44.

18. The Vedas are sometimes reckoned as three in number, ecxluding 'Atharva'. Cfr. Dhavamony, Op. Cit. p.10.

19. M. Dhavamony, Op. Cit. p.2.

20. Stutley, Op. Cit., p.328.

21. S.J. Smartha, The Hindu Response to the Unbound Christ, Madras, 1974, p.46.

22. Ibid., p.47.

23. S. Radhakrishnan, The Principal Upanisads, London, 1978, p.28.

24. 'Samskrta' means 'the refined language' or perfectly constructed, cultivated, literary speech. Cfr. Stutley, Op. Cit., p.267.
Dr. Radhakrishnan writes: "Whatever may be the truth about the racial affinities of the Indian and European peoples, there is no doubt that Indo-European languages derive from a common source and illustrate a relationship of mind. In its vocabulary and inflections Sanskrit presents a striking similarity to Greek and Latin. Sir William Jones explained it by tracing them all to a common source. 'The Sanskrit language', he said in 1786, in an address to the Asiatic Society of Bengal, 'whatever be its antiquity, is of a wonderful structure; more perfect than the Greek, more copious than the Latin, and more exquisitely refined than either; yet bearing to both of them a stronger affinity, both in the roots of verbs, and in the forms of grammar, than could possibly have been produced by accident; so strong, indeed, that no philologer could examine them all without believing them to have sprung from some common source which perhaps no longer exists." S. Radhakrishnan, Op. Cit. p.28.

25. S. Radhakrishnan, Op. Cit p.29. C.B. Papali, Art. Cit. p.41., M. Dhavamony, Op. Cit. p.7.

26. Max Müller, Six Systems of Indian Philosophy, 1899, p.41.

27. Ragozin, Vedic India, 1895, p.114.

28. M. Winternitz, A History of Indian Literature, (translated by S. Ketkar), Vol. I, 1927, p.26.

29. Nicol Macnicol, Hindu Scriptures, 1938, p.14.

30. S. Radhakrishnan, Op. Cit., p.44.

31. Ibid., p.24.

32. Ibid., p.51.

33. Ibid., p.19.

34. Ibid., p.20.

35. Ibid., p.21.

36. Ibid., p.22.

37. Ibid., p.947.

38. R. Antoine, Art. Cit., p.33.
    R. De Smet, 'Ancient Religious Speculation', in: Idem/J. Neuner (Edd.),
    Religious Hinduism, p.40.

39. Svet. Up. 6, 21.

40. S. Radhakrishnan, Op. Cit., pp.22,23.

41. M. Dhavamony, Op. Cit., p.30.

42. R. De Smet, 'Sruti and Divine Inspiration', in: Idem/J. Neuner (Edd.),
    Religious Hinduism, p. 39.

43. C.B. Papali, Art. Cit., p.41.

44. S. Radhakrishnan, Op. Cit., p.17.

45. Quoted from Ibid.

46. Stutley, Op. Cit., p.282.

47. G. Parrinder, Op. Cit., p.19.

48. C.B. Papali, Art. Cit., p.17.

49. Ibid., p.18.

50. S. Radhakrishnan, The Bagavadgita, London, 1958, p.10.

51. Ibid., p. 14.

52. R.C. Zaehner, The Bhagavad-Gita, Oxford, 1969, pp.1,7.

53. Rudolf Otto, The Original Gita, 1939, pp. 12,14. Cfr. also G. Parrinder,
    Avatar and Incarnation, p.32.

54. S. Radhakrishnan, Op. Cit., p.13.

55. Bhagavadgita 15,15.

56.   J.N. Farquhar, The Crown of Hinduism, Oxford, 1915, p.371. Cfr. also: M. Hiriyanna, Outlines of Indian Philosophy, London, 1968, p.116.

57.   Cfr. Fr. Zacharias, An Outline of Hinduism, Alwaye, 1960, p.388.

58.   Cfr. K. Damodaran, Indian Thought, A Critical Survey, London, 1967, p.89.

59.   G. Parrinder, The Significance of Bhagavad Gita, p.8.

60.   M. Dhavamony, Op. Cit., p.11.

61.   J.N. Farquhar, Op. Cit., p.377.

62.   Ibid.

63.   D. Acharuparambil, Induismo, Vita e Pensiero, Roma, 1976, p.22.

64.   Swami Tapasyananda, 'The Religion of the Bhagavad Gita', in: The Cultural Heritage of India, (Ramakrishna Mission edition), Vol. 3, Calcutta, 1953, p.166.

65.   S. Radhakrishnan, Op. Cit., p.12.

66.   R. Antoine, Art. Cit., p. 35.

67.   Stutley, Op. Cit., p. 329.

68.   J.N. Farquhar, Op. Cit., p. 243.
      Cfr. also Swami Chidbhavananda, The Bhagavad-Gita, Tiruparaithurai, 1975, p.3.

69.   G. Parrinder, Avatar and Incarnation, p.50.

70.   J.N. Farquhar, Op. Cit., p.244.
      Cfr. also: Paul Hacker, Untersuchungen über Texte des frühen Advaitavada, 2 Vols., Mainz/Wiesbaden, 1951, 1953.
      E. Deutsch and J.A.B. van Buitenen, A Source Book of Advaita Vedanta, 1971.
      T.M.P. Mahadevan, Gaudapada: A Study in Early Vedanta, Madras, 1952.

71.   Stutley, Op. Cit., p.246.

72.   S. Radhakrishnan, Op. Cit., p.19.

73.   Stutley, Op. Cit., p.330.
      Cfr. also: Paul Deussen, The System of the Vedanta (Tr.by Charles Johnson), Chicago, 1912.

74.   S. Radhakrishnan, Religion in a Changing World, London, 1967, p.61.

75.   Vatican II, 'Nostra Aetate', n.2.
      Cfr. also: A. Hillebrandt, Vedische Mythologe, 2 Vols., Breslau, 1927-1929.
      D.D. Kosambi, Myth and Reality, Bombay, 1962.

76. Cfr. Arthur Cotterell, <u>A Dictionary of World Mythology</u>, London, 1979, p.11.

77. R. Antoine, Art. Cit., p.37.

78. M. Dhavamony, Op. Cit., p.3.

CHAPTER I

1. Arthur Cotterell, A Dictionary of World Mythology, London, 1979, pp.55,56.
    Cfr. also: P. Fallon, 'Image Worship', in: R. De Smet/J. Neuner (Edd.), Religious Hinduism, p.172.

2. A. Cotterell, Op. Cit., p.56.

3. Ibid., p.57. For further explanations on phallic 'lingam'. Cfr. Ch.I.C.3.c.

4. Ibid., p.56.

5. Ibid., p.55.

6. P. Fallon, Loc. Cit.

7. J.N. Farquhar, Op. Cit., p.303. The main Vedic gods as personifications of the powers of nature are: Indra (the god of lightning and thunder), Varuna (the king of the universe who fashions and upholds heaven and earth), Surya (the sun-god), Prajapati (the creator and protector of the world).
    Cfr. P. Fallon, 'The Gods of Hinduism', in: R. De Smet/J. Neuner (Edd.), Religious Hinduism, p.83.

8. J.B. Chethimattam, Consciousness and Reality, An Indian Approach to Metaphysics, Bangalore, 1967, p.22.

9. M. Dhavamony, Op. Cit., p.42.

10. J.N. Farquhar, Op. Cit., p.303. In the whole Rgveda there are only very few references to the images of gods: 4.249; 8.1.5.

11. J.B. Chethimattam, Op. Cit., p.22.
    Buddhism carried the indigenous image worship to Ceylon, Tibet and into every part of Eastern Asia.
    Cfr. J.N. Farquhar, Op. Cit., p.305.
    Cfr. also P. Fallon, Art. Cit., p.172.

12. J.B. Chethimattam, Loc. Cit.

13. A. Huart, 'Pilgrimages and Holy Men', in: R. De Smet/J. Neuner (Edd.), Religious Hinduism, p.149.

14. P. Fallon, Art. Cit., p.175.

15. Ibid., p.178.

16. 'The Omniscient here appears as if subject to men, the Omnipotent as powerless, the rich as needy, the Protector of all as helpless, the Lord as servant, the invisible as visible, the incomprehensible as comprehensible.' So explains Pillai Lokacharya, a theologian of the 13th cen., God's condescension in assuming the idol form. Quoted from

C.B. Papali, Art. Cit., p.45.
Cfr. also: S. Radhakrishnan, The Vedanta according to Sankara and Ramanuja, London, 1923, p.256.

17.   J.N. Farquhar, Op. Cit., p.341. Cfr. also: S. Radhakrishnan, The Hindu View of Life, London, 1980 (1927), pp.24-25.

18.   Ibid., p.340.

19.   P. Fallon, Art. Cit., p.179.

20.   M. Dhavamony, Op. Cit., p.42.

21.   P. Fallon, 'The Gods of Hinduism', in: R. De Smet/J. Neuner (Edd.), Religious Hinduism, p.83.

22.   Ibid.

23.   C.B. Papali, Art. Cit., p.47.

24.   F. Max Müller, Lectures on the Origin and Growth of Religion as Illustrated by the Religions of India, London, 1878.
Cfr. also: M. Dhavamony, Op. Cit., p.41.

25.   M. Dhvamony, Loc. Cit.

26.   Ibid.

27.   P. Fallon, Art. Cit., p.83.

28.   Rgveda 1.164.46: 'Ekam sad vipra bahuda vadanti'.
Cfr. also: 3.55:'Ekam Santi Bahuda Kalpayanthi': The saints imagine the one to be many!

29.   Ibid., 10.114.5.

30.   P. Fallon, Loc. Vit.

31.   Quoted from: P. Fallon, 'Image Worship', p.173.

32.   M. Dhavamony, Op. Cit., p.51.

33.   S. Radhakrishnan, The Principal Upanisads, p.41.

34.   M. Dhavamony, Op. Cit., p.47.

35.   The Vedic concept of Brahman is explained in:
J. Gonda, Notes on Brahman, Utrecht, 1950.
H. Grassmann, Wörterbuch zum Rig Veda, Wiesbaden, 1964.

36.   'Sacred' is the 'Mysterium tremendum et fascinans' (R. Otto).

37.   R.C. Zaehner, Hinduism, p.61.

38.   Tait. Up. 3.10.4-5.

39.   Chand. Up. 1.7.1.etc.

40. R. De Smet, 'Ancient Religious Speculation', in: Idem/J. Neuner (Edd.), Religious Hinduism, p.42.

41. R.C. Zaehner, Op. Cit., p.7.

42. S. Radhakrishnan, Op. Cit., p.52.

43. Stutley, Op. Cit., p.49.

44. Rgveda 10.81.7., 10.71.

45. Ibid., 10.125. Cfr. also Atharvaveda 4.30.

46. Stutley, Op. Cit., p.50.

47. Ibid., p.48.

48. R.C. Zaehner, Op. Cit., pp.61,64.

49. Stutley, Op. Cit., p.49.

50. Sat. Br. 11.2.3.

51. R.E. Hume, Thirteen Principal Upanisads, Oxford, 1921, p.15. He maintains that even the aupanisadic sages misses this notion, which may not be quite correct!

52. S. Radhakrishnan, Op. Cit., p.52.

52a. P. Fallon, 'God in Hinduism', in: R. De Smet/J. Neuner (Edd.), Religious Hinduism, p.76.

52b. R. De Smet, Art. Cit., p.45.

52c. P. Fallon, Loc. Cit.

53. Brhad-aranyaka Upanisad 2.4.12-14. (Hereafter cited Br.Up.).

54. Kena Upanisad 1.3. (Hereafter cited as Ke.Up.).

55. Ibid., 2.2-3.
      Katha Upanisad 1.27. (Hereafter cited as Kat.Up.)

56. Taittiriya Upanisad 2.4. (Hereafter cited as Tait.Up.).

57. Br.Up., 2.8.8., 2.3.6., 3.9.26., 4.2.4.

58. Isa Upanisad 8 (Hereafter cited as Isa Up.).
      For the Madhyamika Buddhists the Absolute is Sunyata or Void!
      Cfr. also: S. Radhakrishnan, Bhagavadgita, p.21., The Principal Upanisads, p.67.

59. Br. Up., 4.2.4., 4.4.22.

60. Ke. Up. 1.4.-8.

61. Isa Up. 5. Cfr. also Mundaka Upanisad 2.1.6.8. (Here after cited as Munda. Up.) Kat. Up. 2.14., Br. Up., 2.37., Svetasvatara Upanisad 3.17. (Hereafter cited as Svet. Up.).

62. S. Radhakrishnan, The Bhagavad-Gita, p.22.

63. Bhagavadgita 2.25.

64. Ibid., 13.15: 'bahir antas ca bhutanam'. Cfr. also Ibid., 13.12., 13.15-17.

65. P. Fallon, Loc. Cit.

66. S. Radhakrishnan, The Principal Upanisads, p. 68.

67. 'Laksana' comes from the root 'laks' which simply means to point, to indicate.

68. S. Radhakrishnan, Op. Cit., p.69.

68a. Kat. Up. 6.12. Cfr. also Mandukya Up. 7 (Hereafter cited as Mandu. Up.).

69. R. De Smet, 'Sankara's Non-Dualism', in: Idem/J. Neuner (Edd.), Religious Hinduism, p.60.

70. Ibid.

71. Ibid.

72. Tait. Up., 2.1.

73. Br. Up., 2.1.20.

74. Ibid., 3.9.28.

75. Ibid., 4.5.13.

76. M. Dhavamony, Op. Cit., p.67.

77. Br. Up. 2.4.12., Tait. Up., 2.1.

78. S. Radhakrishnan, Op. Cit., p.57.

79. Tait. Up. 2.1.

80. Br. Up. 3.9.28. For Sat-Cit-Ananda cfr. also C.D. Sharma: A Critical Survey of Indian Philosophy, Varanasi, 1973, p.26.

81. Tai. Up. 2.1.

82. Tait. Up. 3.

83. S. Radhakrishnan, Op. Cit., pp.56,57.

83a. Taittiriya Upanisad Sankara Bhasya 2.1.

84. S. Radhakrishnan, Op. Cit., p.69.

85. Br. Up. 2.1., 2.3.166.

86. J.B. Chethimattam, Op. Cit., p.48.

87. A.G. Krishna Warrier, 'A New Angle on the Problem of Unreality in Advaita', in: Prabudha Bharata LXIX (1964), p.112.

88. Br. Up. 3.7.

89. J.B. Chethimattam, Op. Cit., p.10.

90. S. Radhakrishnan, Op. Cit., p.59.

91. Chandogya Upanisad 6.1.4-6., 6.2.1-2. (Here after cited as Chand.Up.)

92. J.B. Chethimattam, Loc. Cit.

93. Ibid. p.204.

94. Stutley, Op. Cit., p.50.

95. Munda. Up. 1.1.6.-7.

96. Stutley, Loc. Cit., 'Tajjalana': The One wherefrom we are born (ja), to whom we shall return (la from laya, dissolution) and by whom we breath (an).

97. Tait. Up. 2.12.

98. Ramanuja: Sri Bhasya 1.1.1.

99. Isa Up. Opening Prayer. Cfr. also: Br. Up. 5.1 and Atharva Veda X, viii, 29.

100. Kena Upanisad Sankara Bhasya 2.1., Brahma Sutra Sankara Bhaysa 3.2.21. Quoted from J.B. Chethimattam, Op. Cit., p.154.

101. Chand. Up. 6.2.1.

102. Stutley, Op. Cit., p.213. The three constituents of OM (A,U,M) represent also the deities of the Hindu Triad 'Trimurthi': Brahma, Visnu, Siva.

103. Mandu. Up. 1.1.

104. Maitri Upanisad 6.5.
Mandu. Up. 1.12.
Cfr. also: Heinrich Zimmer; Philosophies of India, ed. by J. Campbell, New York, 1951, pp. 372-378.
Cfr. also: Mircea Eliade, Yoga, Immortality and Freedom, tr. by R. Trask Williad, London, 1958, pp.122-124, 390.

105. Kath. Ip. 2.16-17., Prasna Upanisad 5.7. (Here after cited as Pra. Up.) Cfr. also: Paul Deussen, Allgemeine Geschichte der Philosophie, Vol. 2, pp. 349ff.

106. J.B. Chethimattam, Op. Cit., p.49.

107. Taittiriya Upanisad, Sankara Bhasya 2.1.

108. J.B. Chethimattam, Op. Cit., p.51.

109. Ibid., p.206.

110. Aitareya Upanisad 3.5.3.(Here after cited as Ait. Up.)

111. Brhad-aranyaka Upanisad Sankara Bhasya 1.4.11. tr.by Swami Madhava-nanda, pp.364-366.

112. J.B. Chethimattam, Op. Cit., p.205.

113. Sankara Bhasya on Mandhukya Karika 1.7.

114. Brh.Up. Sankara Bhasya 2.4.9., p.360.

115. Ait. Up. 3.5.3.

116. Vedanta Sutra Sankara Bhasya, Introduction.

117. Munda, Up. 1.1

118. Chand. Up. 6.1.1.

119. Munda. Up. 3.2.9.-

120. Kath. Up. 5.15., Mund. Up. 2.2.10., Svet. Up. 6.14.

121. Chand. Up. 8.3.4.

122. Rgveda 10.129.

123. C.B. Papali, Art. Cit., p.14. Cfr. also: Prabhu Dutt Shastri, The Doctrine of Maya in the Philosophy of the Vedanta, Luzae, 1911.

125. R. De Smet, 'Ancient Religious Speculation', in: Idem/J.Neuner (Edd.), Religious Hinduism, p.46.

126. Taitt. Up. 3., Br. Up. 3.8.

127. Chand. Up. 3.14.3-4., Br. Up. 2.5.14-15., 3.8.6-8. Cfr. also: Mund. Up. 1.1.7.

128. S. Radhakrishnan, Op. Cit., p.82.

129. Svet. Up. 4.9.10.

588

130. S. Radhakrishnan, Loc. Cit.

131. Idem, The Bhagavadgita, p.38.

132. S. Radhakrishnan, The Principal Upanisads, p.80. 'Maya' is said to be the mystery or veil around Brahman. Cfr. also Prabhu Dutt Shastri, The Doctrine of Maya, London, 1911, pp. 7-13.
'Maya' is not so much a doctrine about the ontological status of the world; it is rather a description of the world's relation to God.
Cfr. S.J. Samartha, The Hindu response to the Unbound Christ, Madras, 1974, p.181.
Cfr. also for the classical meaning and the modern interpretations of 'Maya': Idem, Introduction to Radhakrishnan, New York, 1964, pp.57ff.
Cfr. also: M. Hiriyanna, Outlines of Indian Philosophy, London, 1932, p.351.

133. S. Radhakrishnan, The Bhagavad Gita, p.41.

134. Idem, The Principal Upanisads, p.85.

135. Ibid., p.88.

136. Idem, The Bhagavadgita, p.42.

137. Bhagavadgita 7.25., 14.13.

138. S. Radhakrishnan, The Bhagavadgita, p.42.

139. Idem, The Principal Upanishads, p.90.

140. J.B. Chethimattam, Op. Cit., p.16.

141. Quoted from Ibid., p.49.

142. Ibid.

144. Vedanta-Sutra - Sankara Bhasya 1.1.11.

145. R. De Smet, 'Sankara's Non-Dualism', in: Idem/J. Neuner (Edd.), Religious Hinduism, p.61.
For an excellent evaluation of the theory of 'Maya' according to Sankara and Ramanuja cfr. Antony Manalapuzhavila, Nature and Origin of the World according to Ramanuja, (Pars dissertationis ad lauream), Alwaye, 1966, esp. pp.5-14.

146. R. De Smet, 'Ancient Religious Speculation', in: Idem/J. Neuner (Edd.), Religious Hinduism, p.46.

146a. The word 'Purusa' is roughly translated as 'person', but 'purusa' is actually the mythological 'Cosmic Man' or the cosmic giant from whom the world is made. In Samkhya philosophical system 'Purusa' is the masculine creative principle complementing 'Prakrti', passive matter, nature, which is feminine in character. Therefore 'Purusa' can also signify 'man' as complementary to 'woman'. In the Mund. Up. it stands for the 'Supreme Person'-God (2.1).

147. R. De. Smet, Loc. Cit., The notion of 'Person' is intimately connected with that of 'Relation'. God's Trinitarian Relation (as the Christian Theology holds) and His relation to the world are not accidental but metaphysical and constitutive. Such a notion of 'Relation' and 'Person' are applicable also to Nirguna Brahman, because as the Maya theory teaches the world has origin (i.e. methapyhsical relation) only from Brahman. Cfr. also: Idem, 'Categories of Indian Philosophy and communication of the Gospel', in: Religion and Society, Sept. 1963, p.22.

147a. M. Dhavamony, Op. Cit., p.33.

147b. Ibid., p.37. Cfr. also Jan Gonda, 'The Concept of a Personal God in Ancient Indian Religious Thought', in: Studia Missionalia Vol. 17 (1968), pp.121ff. Cfr. also. Svet Up. 3.11., 6.6.

148. Stutley, Op. Cit., p.120., Atharvaveda 7.102.1.

149. M. Dhavamony, Op. Cit., p.55.

150. Stutley, Loc. Cit.

151. S. Radhakrishnan, Op. Cit., p.79.
A comparison may be drawn from the distinction of immanent trinity (Trinity in Himself) and economical trinity (Trinity in relation to the world) as understood by the Christian Theology, of course, mutatis mutandis, because the concept of 'Trinity' is not applicable to 'Nirguna-Brahman' inspite of its designation ans Sat-Cit-Ananda!

152. Ibid., p.84.

153. Ibid., p.70.

154. M. Dhavamony, 'Modern Hinduism', In: For a Dialogue with Hinduism, ed. by. Secretariatus pro Non-Christianis, Roma, 1970, p.78.

155. S. Radhakrishnan, The Bhagavadgita, p.24.

156. Ibid., pp.64,65. Here Plotinus is imitated with his analysis of Reality as One, Nous, Psyche, World! Brahman (absolute and conceived in itself), Isvara (personal God who creates, protects and brings to fulfilment as Brahma, Visnu and Siva), Hiranyagarbha (Spirit moving everywhere in the universe), Viraj (absolutely manifested as the universe). Ibid. p.66.

157. Br. Up. 2.3.1.

158. Bhagavadgita 7.4-5.

159. Ibid., 13.12-17.

160. Ibid., 14.27.

161. M. Dhavamony, Classical Hinduism, p.60.

162. Bhagavadgita 8.3.

163. Ibid., 14.27.

164. Ibid., 14.3.

165. Ibid., 2.72., 4.24.

166. Ibid., 10.12-13.
Dr. Radhakrishnan sees no contradiction between the philosophical idea of God as Spirit (Godhead, Brahman) and the devotional idea of God as person, especially in the context of Hinduis'm acceptance and synthesis of different religious notions from polytheism to pantheism. Cfr. S. Radhakrishnan, The Hindu View of Life, London, 1980 (1927), p.21.: 'The highest category we can use is that of self-conscious personality, we find that it includes cognition, emotion and will, and God is viewed as the supreme knower, the great lover, and the perfect will. Brahma, Visnu, Siva. These are not three independent centres of consciousness, as popular theology represents, but three sides of one complex personality. The different pictures of God which prevailed in the country were affiliated to one or other of this trinity.'
Cfr. also: Ibid., pp.23-24: "Hinduism affirms that some of the highest manifestations which religion has produced require a personal God. There is a rational compulsion to postulate the personality of the Divine. While Hindu thought does justice to the personal aspect of the Supreme, it does not allow us to forget the suprapersonal character of the central reality (...). When we emphasize the nature of reality in itself we get the absolute Brahman; when we emphasize its relation to us we get the personal Bhagavan.'

167. Ibid., 9.16ff., 7.8ff.

168. Ibid., 7.11.

169. Ibid., 11.44.

170. Ibid., 18.64-66., 9.26ff.

171. S.N. Dasgupta, A History of Indian philosophy, Cambridge 1922-55 (5 Vols), p. 474. (Vol.2).

172. R. De Smet, 'Ramanuja and Madhva', in: Idem/J. Neuner (Edd.), Religious Hinduism, p.66.

173. Shri Bhasya of Ramanuja 2.1.9.

176. R. De Smet, Loc. Cit.

178. Shri Bhasya of Ramanuja 2.1.9. Taken from: J.B. Chethimattam, Op. Cit. p.84.

179. S. Radhakrishnan, Op. Cit., pp.17,18.

180. Gita Bhasya 2.12., 2.18., Sri Bhasya 2.1.15.

181. Sri Bhasya 1.1.13.

182. J.B. Chethimattam, Op. Cit., p.83.

183. Ramanuja: Sri Bhasya 2.1.28., 2.3.30.

184. Ibid., 1.2.3.

185. R. De Smet, Art. Cit., p.68.

186. S. Radhakrishnan, The Principle Upanisads, p.137.

187. Ibid., p.66.

188. Idem, The Bhagavad Gita, p.25.

189. Stutley, Op. Cit., p.304.

190. S. Radhakrishnan, Op. Cit., p.26.

191. M. Dhavamony, Op. Cit., p.64.

192. Ibid., p.63.

193. Maitri Up. Ch. 6ff.

194. M. Dhavamony, Op. Cit., p.64.

195. S. Radhakrishnan, The Bhagavad gita, p.26.

196. Arthur Cotterell, Op. Cit., p.57.

197. Ibid., p.65.

198. Stutley, Op. Cit., p.48.

199. A. Cotterell, Op. Cit., p.66. The consort of Brahma is called Sarasvati, the goddess of speech and learning, known also as Vani and Vac.

200. Visnu Puruna translated by H.H. Wilson, I,7, no.5.

201. See below in Chapter II.C, the Hindu notion of History.

202. Stutley, Op. Cit., p.48.

203. Ibid., p.205.

204. P. Fallon, 'The Gods of Hinduism', in: R. De Smet/J. Neuner (Edd.), Religious Hinduism, p.86.

205. R.L. Turner, A Comparative Dictionary of the Indo-Aryan Languages, (School of Oriental and African Studies), London, 1966, 11991.

206. P. Fallon, Loc. Cit.

207. A. Cotterell, Op. Cit., p.85.

208. Stutley, Op. Cit., p.205.

209. P. Fallon, .Art. Cit., p.84.

210. A. Cotterell, Op. Cit., 79.

211. Rgveda 2.33.1-7.

212. Stutley, Op. Cit., p.279.

213. A. Cotterell, Op. Cit., p.79.

214. M. Dhavamony, 'Modern Hinduism', in: For a Dialogue with Hinduism, p.89.

215. A. Cotterell, Op. Cit., p.79.

216. Ibid., p.81.

217. Stutley, Op. Cit., p.209. Cfr. also 'Samudramarthana', churning of the ocean, Ibid., p.265.

218. A. Cotterell, Op. Cit., p.81.

219. Stutley, Op. Cit., p.351.
'Linga' means literally: 'li=to dissolve, 'gam'=to go out. 'Linga' stands for the ultimate reality into whom the creatures of the world dissolve and out of whom they all evolve again. Cfr. S. Radhakrishnan, History of Philosophy: Eastern and Western, Vol. I, London, 1952/3, p.399. This phallic symbol stands to signify the dissolution and the new creation of the world and is the most popular object of saivaite worship. It is estimated to number 30 million in India. Cfr. Coomaraswamy, 'Indian Architectural Terms', in: Journal of the American Oriental Study, 1928, pp.250ff. 'Linga' is the sign of liberation; it is erected to mark the burial place of ascetics and yogins, who are supposed to have attained liberation in this world itself and thus are not in need of the purification of cremation. 'Linga' is also the symbol of death that brings about transformation. Cfr. Edgar Herzog, Psyche and Death (Tr. by D. Cox and E. Rolfe), London, 1966, p.206. Cfr. also: J.M. Allegro, The Sacred Mushroom and the Cross, London, 1970, p.106. The phallic or linga symbol, as an insurance against infertility, are used as amulets by women, presented by bridegroom during the wedding ceremony. In some Christian circles, especially of the Thomas Christians in Kerala, this custom is continued in the form of wedding 'Tali', attached to a necklace. A Cross is engraved on the pendent to give it the Christian character of death and resurrection into new life. The male devotees of Siva especially in S. India are used to wear a miniature 'linga' attached to a necklace. Cfr. Margaret and James Stutley, Op. Cit., p.162.
In Saiva temples the 'linga' stands on a pedestal representing the 'yoni' (female genitals). Their union is the supreme expression of the creative energy. The holy of holies is called 'Barbha Grha' (womb sanctuary) which is the symbol of cosmic fertility and the union of God and man. It is the cosmic womb and the place most suitable for the manifestation of the Divinity and for the union of the devotee with his God.

In this sense, the human heart, the innermost core of one's existence is also called 'Garbha Grha', the holy of holies of the human temple. It is here that the God-man union takes place and the spiritual re-generative energy is radiated into the whole of one's existence.
Cfr. Alice Boner, Principle of Composition in Hindu Sculpture, London, 1962, p.24.
The above mentioned Hindu religious symbols, inspite of their 'pagan' character, contain valuable aspects of Christian spirituality to which we will be referring in the course of our work.

220. Ibid., p.297.

221. M. Dhavamony, Classical Hinduism, p.67.

222. G. Parrinder, Avatar and Incarnation, p.92.

223. Ibid., p.95.

224. Ibid., p.98.

225. Ibid., p.99.

226. Rabindranath Tagore, Gitanjali, L.

227. Young India, 5-8-1925. Cfr. also: G. Soares, 'Mahatma Gandhi', in: R. De Smet/J. Neuner (Edd.), Religious Hinduism, pp.296-307.

228. Aurobindo Ghose, The Divine Life, 1953, p.190.

229. G. Parrinder, Op. Cit., p.110.

CHAPTER II

1. M. Dhavamony, Classical Hinduism, p.112.

2. Ibid.

3. Rgveda 1.44.11., Cfr. also 2.33.13 and 4.37.1.

4. Sat. Br. 13.4.3.3-5., 1.8.1.1-11.

5. Rgveda 10.90.1-14. Purusha Sukta

6. M. Dhavamony, Op. Cit., p.115.

7. Ibid., p.116.

8. Rgveda 10.16.3-4.

9. Ibid., 10.58.

10. Ibid., 8.89.5., Cfr. also: H. Oldenburg, La Religion du Veda, Paris, p.447ff. Translated from Die Religion des Veda, Berlin, 1923.

11. Rgveda 1.113.16., 1.140.8.

12. Sat. Br. 7.5.2.6.

13. Taittiriya Brahmana 3.10.8. (Hereafter cited as Tait. Br.)

14. Rgveda 10.16.4. Cfr. also: H.G. Narahari, Atman in Pre-Upanisadic Vedic Literature, Adyar, 1944.

15. Stutley, Op. Cit., p.31.

16. Rgveda 1.115.1.

17. Stutley, Op. Cit., p.282.

18. Rgveda 9.2.10., 9.6.8.

19. Ibid., 9.85.3.

20. Stutley, Op. Cit., p.31.

21. Kath. Up. 1.2.18.22.
Br. Up. says: Atman (vital force) is not only operative in man, but also in every form of life. Br. Up. 1.3.22.

22. Cfr. M. Monier-Williams, Sanskrit-English Dictionary.

23. Chand. Up., 3.14.

24. R. Antoine, 'Hindu Ethics', in: R. De Smet/J. Neuner (Edd.), Religious Hinduism, p.110.

25. Quoted from S. Radhakrishnan: The Principal Upanishads, p.75.

26. Ibid., p.78.

27. Mand. Up. 7.

28. Taitt. Up. 2.2-8.
    Maitri Up., 2.5.-4.2.

29. S. Radhakrishnan, Op. Cit., pp.90,91.
    Cfr. also: Tait. Up. 1.11.2-5.

30. Ibid., p.91.

31. Kath. Up. 3.11.

32. S. Radhakrishnan, Op. Cit., p.92.

33. Kath. Up. 3.3-4.

33a. The Samkhya school cannot be traced to the aupanisadic source. It
     is a system built on the Upanisad rather than derived from it. It has
     its source in the non-vedic Indian thought.
     Cfr. A.B. Keith, Samkhya-System, London, 1918. Second ed. Calcutta,
     1924, p.7.

34. S. Radhakrishnan, The Bhagavad Gita, p.55.

35. M. Dhavamony, Classical Hinduism, p.131.

36. Bhagavadgita, 15.7.

37. M. Dhavamony, Op. Cit., p.131.

38. Bhagavadgita 3.5.

39. R.C. Zaehner, The Bhagavad-Gita, Oxford, 1969, p.16.

40. Bhagavadgita 14.5-9.

41. J.B. Chethimattam, Op. Cit., p.17.

42. Bhagavadgita 2.41.

43. Ibid., 2.63.

44. M. Dhavamony, Op. Cit., p.133.

45. Bhagavadgita 14.14-18.

46. J.B. Chethimattam, Op. Cit., p.18.

47. S. Radhakrishnan, The Principal Upanisads, p.77.

48. Br. Up. 3.7.23.

49. Chand. Up. 3.14.1.

50. Br. Up. 1.4.10.

51. J.N. Farquhar, The Crown of Hinduism, p.223.

52. Chand. Up. 3.14.3-4.

53. Cfr. the corresponding topic in Ch.I.

54. Br. Up. 2.5.19 and Mand. Up. 2.

55. J.B. Chethimattam, Op. Cit., pp.206,207.

56. Br. Up. 1.4.10.

57. Chand.Up., 6.8.7., 9.4., 10.3.

58. J.B. Chethimattam, Op. Cit., p.207.

59. Ibid., p.209.

61. Br. Up., 2.1.20.

62. Kath. Up., 2.20.

63. Bhagavadgita 2.20-21., Cfr. also Kath. Up. 2.8.

64. Bhagavadgita 15.7.

65. Bhagavadgita 4.10., 8.5., 13.18., 14.19.

66. Bhagavadgita 15.7.

67. Ibid., 3.40., 4.40.

68. G. Feuerstein, Introduction to the Bhagavad Gita - Its Philosophy and Cultural Setting, London, 1974, p.90.

69. R. De Smet, 'Ramanuja and Madhva', in: Idem/J.Neuner (Edd.), Religious Hinduism, p.68.

70. S. Radhakrishnan, Bhagavadgita, p.18.

71. J.N. Farquhar, Op. Cit., p.226.

72. Stutley, Op. Cit., p.264.
    Cfr. also Br. Up. 4.4-5.

73. S. Radhakrishnan, Religion in a Changing World, London, 1967, p.144.

74. Ibid.

75. Sat. Br. 6.2.2.27.

76. S. Radhakrishnan, The Principal Upanishads, p.114.

77. Br. Up. 4.4.3-5.

78. Mahabharata 12.201.21ff. Quoted from M. Dhavamony, Classical Hinduism, p.292.

79. J.N. Farquhar, Op. Cit., p.222.

80. F. Edgerton, The Bhagavad Gita or the Song of the Blessed One, Chicago, 1928, p.21.

81. J.N. Farquhar, Op. Cit., pp.144,145.

82. Rgveda 1.24.9., 1.24.14., 1.24.15.

83. Ibid., 2.28.7., 7.86.3., 7.89.5.

84. Ibid., 2.28.5., 7.86.4., 7.87.7.

85. Ibid., 7.86.6., It also means 'Adharma'.

86. Ibid., 7.86.5.

87. Ibid., 7.88.

88. M. Dhavamony, Op. Cit., p.475.

89. Sat Br. 4.4.5.22-23.
    Cfr. also 13.3.6.5 for Vicarious expiation of sin!

90. Br. UP., 4.2.22.

91. Kausitaki Upanisad 3.1.(Hereafter cited as Kau. Up.)

92. R. De S met, 'Sin and Its Removal', in: Idem/J. Neuner (Edd.), Religious Hinduism, p.130.

93. Bhagavadgita 5.10.

94. Papa=bad., Duritam=ill – going., Duskrta=ill – done., Kalmasa, Kalusa, Dosa=stain., Aparadha=failure etc.
    Cfr. M. Dhavamony, Op. Cit., p.226.

95. Manu Smrti 24.

96. M. Dhavamony, 'Classical Patterns of Hindu Salvation', in: Studia Missionalia, Gregorian, Rome, 1980, p.232.

97. Bhagavadgita 3.27.

98. Ibid., 5.12.

99. Br. Up., 4.4.7.

100. Kath. Up., 2.4., Munda. Up., 1.2.8.

101. M. Dhavamony, Art. Cit., p.233.

102. Bhagavadgita 4.37-38.

103. S. Radhakrishnan, The Bhagavad Gita, p.39.

104. Ibid.

105. Ibid.

106. M. Dhavamony, Art. Cit., p.230.

106a. Stutley, Op. Cit., p.163.

107. S. Radhakrishnan, The Principal Upanishads, p.114.

107a. Betty Heimann, Indian and Western Philosophy - A Study in Contrasts, London, 1937, pp.60ff.

108. Such beliefs can be traced also to other cultures. The orphic texts inscribed on golden leaves which in the 3rd. cen. B.C. were laid in the graves of the dead in Southern Italy as a passport for the journey to the other world shows a similar attitude to the life after death. Cfr. M.P. Nilsson, A History of Greek Religion, Oxford, 1925, p.221.

109. R. Antoine, Art. Cit. ('Hindu Ethics'), p.113. It may also be called a perpetual flux.

110. Betty Heimann, The Significance of Prefixes in Sanskrit Philosophical Terminology, (Royal Asiatic Society), London, Monographs, Vol XXV, 1951, p.14.

111. S. Radhakrishnan, The Principal Upanishads, p.43.

111a. Human beings are judged according to their good and evil deeds (Satapatha Brahmana 11.2.7.33). The good are rewarded in the heavenly world of gods (Rgveda 10.14.10) and the evil ones are punished in the abyss of darkness (Rgveda 7.104.3). Cfr. also above in our work Chapter III.A.1.a.

112. M. Dhavamony, Art. Cit., p.229.

113. S. Radhakrishnan, Op. Cit., p.115.

114. Br. Up., 3.2.13., 4.3.37-38., 4.4.1-6., 4.9.7.
Further on the question of 'Karma-Samsara' Cfr.: Norbert Klaes, 'Tod und Vollendung im Hinduismus und Christentum', in: Theologie und Glaube, 68 (1978), SS. 236-237.
Cfr. also: P. Deussen, The Philosophy of the Upanisads, New York, 1966 (1906), pp.313-318., S.N. Dasgupta, A History of Indian Philosphy I, Cambridge, 1963³, pp.53-57.
M. Hiriyanna, Outlines of Indian Philosophy, London, 1967, pp.79ff.

115. Ibid., 4.4.3-5.

116. Kath. Up. 1.1.6.

117. Ibid., 1.2.1-6.

118. Isa Up. 3., Kath. Up., 1.1.3., Br. Up. 4.4.11.

119. Br. Up. 5.10.1.

120. For more details on this point see the next section on the Hindu Concept of History.

121. Chand. Up. 5.10.1-6.

122. Ibid., 5.10.7. Here the caste system is theologically justified as an inevitable consequence of Karma-Samsara. More about that in the next pages.

123. Bhagavadgita 2.13.

124. Ibid., 2.22.

125. Ibid., 2.26-28.

126. Quoted from G. Feuerstein, The Essence of Yoga - A Contribution to the Psychohistory of Indian Civilization, London, 1974, p.45.

127. C.B. Papali, Art. Cit., p.52.

128. J.N. Farquhar, Op. Cit., 158.

129. M. Dhavamony, Classical Hinduism, p.137.

130. C.B. Papali, Loc. Cit.

131. J.N. Farquhar, Op. Cit., p.159.

132. Rgveda 10.90.11-14., especially 11.

133. M. Dhavamony, Op. Cit., p.140.

134. Rgveda 10.90.11.

135. J.N. Farquhar, Op. Cit., p.158.

136. This rite of initiation is called 'Upanayana'. Cfr. R. Antoine, Art. Cit. ('Hindu Ethics'), p.119.

137. J.N. Farquhar, Op. Cit., p.163.

138. Ibid., In the West the word 'Pariah' is understood often as a synonym for outcastes. The .Pariahs are actually only one of the large outcaste castes of South India. The Outcastes of India were a special concern for Mahatma Gandhi. He preached the equality of all men and gave the title 'Harijan', people of God, to the outcastes.

139. Ibid.

140. Ibid., p.159.

141. Ibid., p.215.

142. Ibid., p.142.

143. Ibid., p.143.

144. R.C. Zaehner, Hinduism, London, 1962, p.10.

145. J.N. Farquhar, Op. Cit., p.148.

146. Brodrock and A. Houghton (Edd.), Animals in Archeology, London, 1972, p.116.

147. The Greek philosopher Pythagoras held a similar view. Cfr. Stutley, Op. Cit., p.265.

148. R.N. Dandekar, 'The Role of Man in Hinduism', in: The Basic Beliefs of Hinduism, ed. by D.S. Sarma, Calcutta, 1955, p.115.

149. R. Antoine, Art. Cit. ('Hindu Ethics'), p.111.

150. C.B. Papali, Art. Cit., p.48.

151. J.N. Farquhar, Op. Cit., p.144.

152. Ibid., p.233.

153. Rgveda 8.90.15.

154. Ibid., 1.73.6.

155. Sat. Br. 2.2.4.15.

156. Atharvaveda 12.5.

157. Stutley, Op. Cit., p.100.

158. G. Soares, Art. Cit. ('Mahatma Gandhi'), p.306.

159. Quoted from R. Antoine, 'Sacred Books and Religious Literature', in: R. De Smet/J. Neuner (Edd.), Religious Hinduism, p.31.

160. Ghosal quoted from the unpublished thesis: Jacob Mendosa, The Concept of Perfection in the Bhagavad Gita and in the Writings of St. John of the Cross, Rome, 1980, p.116.

161. Papali, C.B., Art. Cit., p.49.

162. G. Feuerstein, An Introduction to the Bhagavadgita, Its Philosophy and Cultural Setting, London, 1973, pp.113-114.

163. S. Radhakrishnan, The Bhagavadgita, p.46.

164. Ibid., pp.47,48.

165. Ibid., pp.48,49.

166. S. Radhakrishnan, Religion in a Changing World, London, 1967, p.145.

167. Ibid., p.146.

168. J.N. Farquhar, Op. Cit., p.140.

169. M. Dhavamony, Art. Cit., in: For a Dialogue with Hinduism, p. 90.

170. A. Cotterell, Op. Cit., p.89.

171. J.N. Farquhar, Op. Cit., p.139.

172. A. Cotterell, Loc. Cit.

173. Ibid.

174. J.N. Farquhar, Op. Cit., p.140.

175. Ibid., p.89.

176. A. Cotterell, Loc. Cit.

177. Ibid.

178. Ibid., pp.57,89.

179. B hagavadgita 8.17-19.

180. A. Huart, 'Hindu Calendar and Festivals', in: Religious Hinduism, p.136.

181. M. Dhavamony, Art. Cit., p.90.

182. Idem, Classical Hinduism, p.64.

183. M. Dhavamony, Art. Cit., Loc. Cit.

184. A. Huart, Loc. Cit.

185. A. Cotterell, Loc. Cit.

186. Ibid., p.57. For the sake of clarity we may put the historical calculation
as follows:
360 Human years   =   1 Divine Year
12000 Divine Years =   1 Yuga
4 Yugas   =   1 Mahayuga
2000 Mahayugas   =   1 Kalpa
36500 Kalpas   =   1 Para

187. Ibid., p.89. Cfr. also: S. Schayer, Contributions to the Problem of
Time in Indian Philosophy, Cracow, 1938.

188. G. Parrinder, Avatar and Incarnation, p.38.

189. Bhagavadgita 9.8.

190. A. Cotterell, Op. Cit., p.57.

191. J.N. Farquhar, Op. Cit., p.140.

192. Monier-Williams, Indian Wisdom, London, 1875, repr. 1963, p.197.

193. A. Cotterell, Op. Cit., p.57.

194. 'Numerus motus secundum prius et posterius' - the scholastic definition of time.

195. J.B. Chethimattam, Op. Cit., p.245.

196. A. Cotterell, Op. Cit., pp.11,12.

197. J.B. Chethimattam, Loc. Cit.

198. Ibid.

199. A. Huart, Loc. Cit.

200. The seventeenth-century Anglican divine James Ussher, Archbishop of Armagh, calculated from evidence in the Old Testament that the date of the creation of the earth was 4004 BC. In 1642 Dr. Lightfoot, Vice-Chancellor of Cambridge University, refined the dating and declared it was 23 October 4004 BC, at nine o'clock in the morning - an academic commencement if there ever was one. Although their calculation has long been disregarded, the underlying assumption informs present day thinking in the West, which views events as unique, unrepeatable phenomena.
Cfr. A. Cotterell, Op. Cit., p.58.

201. J.B. Chethimattam, Loc. Cit.

202. S. Radhakrishnan, Op. Cit., p.135.

203. Ibid., p.136.

204. Ibid.

205. Ibid.

206. Ibid., pp.137,138.

207. Ibid., p.147.

208. Ibid., p.143.

209. M. Dhavamony, Art. Cit., p.67.

210. R.C. Zaehner, Op. Cit., p.6.

211. R. Antoine, Art. Cit., p.115.
     M. Dhavamony, Classical Hinduism, p.360.

212. J.B. Chethimattam, Op. Cit., p.196.

213. C.B. Papali, Art. Cit., pp.54,55.

CHAPTER III

1. Br. Up. 1.3.28.

2. S. Radhakrishnan, Religion in Changing World, p.64.

3. Kath. Up. 1.1.27.

4. S. Radhakrishnan, The Bhagavad Gita, p.51.

5. S. Radhakrishnan, The Bhagavad Gita, p.51.

6. Ibid.

7. M. Dhavamony, 'Classical Patterns in Hindu Salvation', in: Studia Missio-nalia, Rome, 1980, p.209.

8. S. Radhakrishnan, Religion in a Changing World, pp. 95,96.

9. Ibid., p.97.

10. Cfr. The Pali Text Society's Pali-English Dictionary ed. by T.W. Ryhs Davids and William Stede.

11. Sat. Br. 12.4.1.1.

12. Svet. Up. 1.8., 2.15., 5.16., 5.13., 6.13.

13. Bhagavadgita 2.39., 9.28.

14. Ibid. 7.29.

15. Ibid. 13.34.

16. Ibid. 2.72., 5.6.24.

17. Ibid. 5.24., 6.27., 14.26., 18.53.

18. Ibid. 8.16.

19. Ibid., 4.9., 7.23., 8.7,10,16., 9.25,28,34., 10.10., 11.55.

20. Ibid., 8.5., 13.18.

21. Ibid. 11.54., 12.8., 18.55.

22. M. Dhavamony, Art. Cit., 218.

23. Bhagavadgita 5.28.

24. Ibid. 17.25.

25. Ibid. 18.66.

26. Ibid. 4.23., 18.40., 5.28., 12.15., 18.7.

27. Ibid. 3.9., 18.26.

28. Ibid. 8.5.

29. M. Dhavamony, Art. Cit., p.210ff.

30. Bhagavadgita 14.18.

31. M. Dhavamony, Art. Cit., p.225.

31a. Brahmaloka: The eternal Brahma-world consisting of infinite wisdom. All distinctions disappear in it.
Cfr. Chand. Up. 8.4.2., Br. Up. 4.3.33.
'The created Brahma has a specific locality and so can be the goal of a journey but not the Supreme Brahman who is present everywhere and in the inner self of the travelling individual selves. When we reach Brahma-loka, we continue to function there until the end of the process, when along with Brahma we enter the Supreme Brahma.'
S. Radhakrishnan: The Principal Upanishads, p.125.

32. S. Radhakrishnan, The Bhagavad Gita, p.75.
The Bhagavadgita speaks of this state as the 'Brahma-Nirvana', an imitation of the Buddist terminology.

32a. Satapatha Brahmana, 17.2.7.33.

32b. Rgveda 10.14.10.

32c. Rgveda 7.104.3.

32d. Norbert Klaes, 'Reinkarnation und Auferstehung', in: Hans Torwesten, Sind wir nur einmal auf Erden? Die Idee der Reinkarnation angesichts des Auferstehungsglaubens, Freiburg/Basel/Wien, 1983, (Nachwort), S.188.

32e. Br. Up. 3.2.13., 4.4.2-6., Cfr. also back to our work Ch.II.B.2.

33. M. Dhavamony, Art. Cit., p.246.
Cfr. also: S. Rodhe, Deliver us from Evil: Studies on the Vedic Ideas of Salvation, Lund, 1946.

34. Maitri Up. 1.3.-4.

35. Munda. Up. 3.2.8.

36. S. Radhakrishnan, The Principal Upanishads, p.121.

37. Nirvana can be compared to the extinction of a flame. It is liberation into the Void!
Cfr. also: L. La Vallee Poussin, de Nirvana, Paris, 1925.

38. 'Sunya' stands for the Indian Mathematical sign for zero.
Cfr. Monier-Williams, Indian Wisdom, p.193.
Sunya is considered also as a symbol for Brahman and Nirvana.

39.   Some consider Sunya also as a 'Plenum' in a philological sense, if not in a philosophical sense. Sunya is neither capable of being made fuller nor. capable of decrease! Cfr. Agehananda Bharati, The Tantric Tradition, London, 1965, p.35, n.5.

40.   M. Dhavamony, Classical Hinduism, p.290.

41.   Ibid.

42.   Ibid.

43.   Ibid., p.291.

44.   S. Radhakrishnan, Indian Philosophy, 2 Vols., London, 1923-1926, 2nd ed. 1929., Vol.2, p.511.

45.   Idem, Religion in a Changing World, p.98.

46.   Idem, Indian Philosophy, Vol.2, p.510.

47.   Idem, The Principal Upanishads, p.95.

48.   Ibid., p.96.

49.   Ibid.

50.   Ibid.

51.   Ibid., p.97.

52.   Ibid.

53.   Ibid.

54.   Ibid., p.99.

55.   Kath. Up. 2.12.

56.   Ibid., 2.20,23.

57.   S. Radhakrishnan, Op. Cit., p.103.

58.   Idem, Indian Philosophy, Vol.2, p.510.

59.   Sankara Bhasya 1.2.8. Quoted from S. Radhakrishnan, Op. Cit., p.511.

60.   Ibid. 1.3.13.

61.   S. Radhakrishnan, Op. Cit., p.513.

62.   Ibid., p.514.

63.   Idem, Religion in a Changing World, p.108.

64.   Ibid., pp.104,105,106.

607

65. Sankara Bhasya 2.1.6.

66. M. Dhavamony, Op. Cit., p.291.

67. Ibid.

68. We will be dealing more with the concept of 'Yoga' in the next title.

69. M. Dhavamony, Op. Cit., p.330.

70. Idem, Art. Cit. from: A Dialogue with Hinduism, p.72.

71. Sri Aurobindo, Essays on the Gita, Pondicherry 1980, p.129.

72. Quoted from M. Dhavamony, Art. Cit., p.75.

73. S. Radhakrishnan, The Principal Upanishads, p.58.

74. M. Dhavamony, Classical Hinduism, p.318.

75. Ibid., p.319.

76. Ibid., p.318.

77. Ibid., p.321.

78. Bhagavadgita 6.30.

79. Stutley, Op.Cit., p.349.

80. Mulik Raj Anand, Hindu View of Art, London, 1957, p.17. Cfr. also: Mircea Eliade, Yoga: Immortality and Freedom, tr. by Williard R. Trask, London, 1958, p.341. Cfr. also: Jacob Wilhelm Hauer, Die Anfänge der Yogapraxis, Stuttgart, 1922.

81. James H. Woods, (Tr.), The Yoga System of Patanjali, Harvard (Oriental Studies). Cfr. also Rajendralala Mitra, (tr.), The Yoga Aphorisms of Patanjali, Calcutta, 1883. Cfr. also: S.n. Dasgupta, A Study of Patanjali, Calcutta, 1920. Cfr. also: Idem, Yoga as Philosophy and Religion, London, 1924.

82. Taitt. Up. 2.4.

83. Kath. Up. 2.12.

84. Mait. Up. 6.25.

85. Franklin Edgerton (tr.), The Beginning of Indian Philosophy, London, 1965, p.37.,n.1.
Cfr. also: Ralph Turner, A Comparative Dictionary of the Indo-Aryan Language, (School of Oriental and Africal Studies), London, 1969, 10526, 10528, 10529. Cfr. also: Jacques Masui, (ed.), Yoga, science de l'homme integral, Paris, 1953.

86. Yoga Sutra, 1.2. (Patanjali).

87. Ibid., 1.3.

88. J. Neuner, 'Yoga', in: Idem/R. De Smet (Edd.), Religious Hinduism, p.185.

89. Yoga Sutra, 2.29-32,49,54; 3.2-3; 1.46,51.
The first step in the 'Astanga-yoga' is 'Yama' (restraint). This is an inner attitude obtained through 'Ahimsa' (non-killing), 'Satya' (truthfulness), 'Asteya' (non-stealing), 'Brahmacarya' (continence) and 'Aparigraha' (abstaining from covetousness). These are the basic virtues expected from everybody and are binding for the 'Yogin' (the one who follows Yoga) like vows. The second step is 'Niyama' (observance) which consists of 'Sauca' (cleanliness), 'Santosa' (contentment), 'Tapas' (austerity), 'Svadhyaya' (self-study) and 'Isvara Pranidhana' (self-surrender to God). By restraint and observances one lays the foundation for the practice of Yoga. 'Asana' is the third step that refers to bodily exercises and postures meant to restore and refresh the body to promote mental concentration. It is followed by the yogic exercises of breath control (Pranayama) through which it is supposed that every part of the body is filled with 'Prana' (vital force). The control of breath is followed by the control of the senses (Pratyahara) by which the senses are withdrawn from their proper objects to ensure the function of the mind. The 'Yogin' who has undergone the above mentioned external preparations enters into the three stages of mediation namely 'Dharana' (concentration), 'Dhyana' (meditation proper) and finally the eighth step in the 'Astanga-Yoga' namely 'Samadhi' (trance) which is the highest level of meditation and the supreme goal of Yoga. 'Samadhi' itself is of two kinds: 'Savikalpa-Samadhi' which is object bound, still containing the seed (sabija) of the changing world and the highest possible state of consciousness called 'Nirvikalpa or Nirbija Samadhi', the seedless trance in which the 'Purusa' is perfectly liberated from the disturbing influences of the 'Prakrti'.
Cfr. also: Sigurd Lindquist, Die Methoden des Yoga, Lund, 1932.

99.   J. Neuner, Art. Cit., p.189.

100. Yoga Sutra (Patanjali), 1,24.

101. Bhagavadgita 2.50., 4.38., 5.6,7., 6.23.

102. Ibid., 2.48., 3.26., 6.23.

103. Ibid., 6.8., 6.10., 6.46.

104. Ibid., 6.15.

105. Ibid., 5.27,28., 6.11-17., 8.10.

106. Ibid., 6.46,47.

107. Ibid., 10.10.

108. Ibid., 12.2.

109. Ibid., 18.78.

110. J. Neuner, Art. Cit., p.191.

110a. There are also other types of Yoga, a detailed presentation of which is irrelevant for our topic. There is, for example, the 'Japa Yoga' or 'Mantra Yoga' in which the spiritual integration is attained through the chanting of sacred formulas. The tapping of the latent energies in man by the mergence or absorption of the mental faculties into the object contemplated or into the inner sound (Anahata Nada) is known by the name 'Laya-Yoga'.

111. Alain Danielou, Hindu Polytheism, London, 1963, pp.254,287.

111a. In the Sahasrara Cakra the final union of Siva (masculine force) and Sakti (feminine force) is believed to take place. In an attempt to hasten the process of Kundalini's rise through the seven Cakras to the brain, some Tantric schools combined particular asanas (positions) with erotic practices. Cfr. Mircea Eliade, 'Cosmical Homology and Yoga', in: Journal of the Indian Society of Oriental Art, V, (1937), p.248. Cfr. also: V.G. Rele, The Mysterious Kundalini, Bombay, 1927.

112. Stutley, Op. Cit., p.350.

113. Chand. Up. 4.9.3., Kath. Up. 1.2.8-9.

114. S. Radhakrishnan, Religion in a Changing World, p.100.

115. Advaya Taraka Upanisad 14-18.
Cfr. also: Alain Danielou, Yoga-The Method of Reintegration, London, 1949, p.118.

116. Betty Heimann, Facets of Indian Thought, London, 1964, p.118.

117. S. Radhakrishnan, The Principal Upanishads, p.102.

118. Stutley, Op. Cit., p.107.

119. Daniel Acharuparambil, 'The 'Guru' in Hindu Tradition', in: Ephemerides Carmeliticae, Teresianum: Rome, XXXI (1980) - I, pp.3,4.

120. Ibid., pp.7,8.

121. Kath. Ip. 2.8-9.

122. Chand. Up., 4.9.2-3.

123. S. Radhakrishnan, The Principal Upanishads, p.102.

123a. Munda. Up. 1.2.12.

124. D. Acharuparambil, Art. Cit., pp.8,9.

125. Ibid., p.10.

126. Ibid., p.11.

127. Quoted from D. Acharuparambil, Art. Cit., pp.26,27. Originally found in: A. Osborne (Ed.), The Collected Works of Ramana Maharsi, London, 1972, p.131.

128. Quoted from D. Acharuparambil, Art. Cit., p.11. Originally found in: Sayings of Sri Ramakrishna, Mylapore, 1960, p.74.

129. Manu 2.44.

130. 'Gayatri' is derived from 'gai', to praise, or from 'gam' with 'tri' to mean three-coursed. It is the name of the metre consisting of a triplet of eight syllables most commonly used in the Rgvedic hymns. Cfr. R.T.H. Griffith (tr.), The Hymns of the Rgveda, 2 Vols., Varanasi, 1963., Vol.1, p.652. Manu 2,148: By means of the Gayatri a Guru obtains for his pupil a second birth, which is real and exempt from old age and death. Gayatri is also personified as the wife of Brahma and the mother of the four Vedas and of the first three castes in their capacity of being twice born!

131. Rgveda 3.62.10.

132. Stutley, Op. Cit., p.97.

133. Ibid., p.79.

134. Ibid., pp.78,79.

135. Sankara, Brahma-Sutra Bhasya, Introduction.

136. Quoted from R. De Smet., Art. Cit. ('Sankara's Non-Dualism'), in: Religious Hinduism, p.54.

137. Stutley, Op. Cit., p.107.

138. Manu 2,44., 2.195-197., 2.226.
Gautama Dharmasutra, 2.21., 2.14-15.
Apastamba Dharmasutra, 1.2.6.1., 1.2.6.13., 1.2.8.25-26.

139. Apastamba Dharmasutra 1.2.6.13.

140. M.P. Pandit, Kularnava Tantra, p.80. Quoted from D. Acharuparambil, Art. Cit., p.24.

141. Apastamba Dharmasutra, 1.2.8.25-26.

142. M. Dhavamony, Classical Hinduism, p.466.

143. Maitri Up., 6.10.
Parama Upanisad 1.
Mukti Upanisad 1,24.

144. Chand. Up., 3.16.17.

145. R. Antoine, Art. Cit. ('Hindu Ethics').

146. M. Dhavamony, Op. Cit., p.334.

147. Rgveda 1.161.1., 4.53.3., 5.63.7., 6.70.1., 7.89.5.

148. Ibid., 1.187.1., 10.21.3., 10.92.2., 10.97.23.

149. R.C. Zaehner, Hinduism, London, 1962, p.3.

150. Rgveda 10.129.6.

151. Taittiriya Aranyaka, 10.63.1.

152. Baudhayana Dharma Sutra 1.1.1 and 3,4.

153. The Manusmrti 2.6.

154. Ibid., 1.108.

155. Chand. Up. 2.23.1.

156. R. Antoine, Loc. Cit.

157. M. Dhavamony, Op. Cit., 356.

158. Ibid., p.357.

159. Ibid.

160. Bhagavadgita, 16.1-3.

161. M. Dhavamony, Op. Cit., p.468.

162. Ibid., pp.159ff.

163. Idem, 'Modern Hinduism', in For a Dialogue with Hinduism, p.84, R. Antoine, 'Rituals and Worship', in: R. De Smet/J. Neuner (Edd.), Religious Hinduism, p.156.

164. M. Dhavamony, Op. Cit., pp.206ff.

165. C.B. Papali, Art. Cit., p.55.

166. R. Antoine, 'The Hindu Samskaras', in: R. De Smet/J. Neuner (Edd.), Religious Hinduism, p.163.

167. Ibid.

168. M. Dhavamony, Op. Cit., p.175.

169. See above.

170. Cfr. A. Huart, Art. Cit., pp.136ff.

171. S. Radhakrishnan, The Bhagavadgita, p.54.
Cfr. also: Friedrich Heiler, Die Mystik in den Upanishaden, München, 1925.

172. Stutley, Op. Cit., p.129.

173. J.B. Chethimattam, Op. Cit., p.14.

174. S. Radhakrishnan, Loc. Cit.

175. M. Dhavamony, Op. Cit., p.478.

176. S. Radhakrishnan, Loc. Cit.

177. Ibid., p.52.

178. M. Dhavamony, Op. Cit., p.477.

179. Munda, Up., 3.1.7.

180. Tait. Up. 2.1.
     Br. Up., 1.4.17., 5.4.
     Chand. Up., 1.2.8.
     Kau. Up. 1.7., 2.13.

181. Kath. Up., 2.20.

182. Mund. Up., 1.2.1.7-11.
     Br. Up. 3.9.6.21.
     Chand. Up. 1.10-12., 4.1-3.

183. Cfr. S. Radhakrishnan, Op. Cit., p.17.

184. Ibid.

185. Bhagavadgita 13.7-10.

186. Cfr. S. Radhakrishnan, Doc. Cit.

187. Bhagavadgita 4.19.

188. S. Radhakrishnan, The Principal Upanishads, p.134.
     The essential means of arriving at valid knowledge (Pramana or criterion
     of knowledge) as accepted in the Hindu philosophy in general are three:
     Perception (pratyaksa), Inference (anumana) and Verbal testimony (sabda).
     Revelation is divine sabda or sruti, what is heard.

189. M. Dhavamony, Op. Cit., p.480.

190. S. Radhakrishnan, Op. Cit., p.134.

191. Ibid.

192. Ibid., p.136.

193. Kath. Up., 2.23. Cfr. also: Sveta. Up. 1.6., 3.20.
     Munda. Up., 3.2.3.
     Katha Upanisad is theistic, while Mandukya Upanisad is non-dualistic
     or monistic.

194. Bhagavadgita 9.32.

195. Stutley, Op. Cit., p.41.

196. Ibid. God (personal) is the supreme object of Bhakti. But respect and devotion towards fatherland, parents, elders, teachers etc. can also be called (analogically) Bhakti.

197. Rgveda 5.85.7-8., 7.87.7.

198. Svet. Up., 6.23. Some consider it a later addition to the Upanisad. Cfr. M. Dhavamony, Op. Cit., p.486.

199. Bhagavadgita 9.27.

200. Ibid., 11.55.

201. P. Fallon, 'Doctrinal Background of the Bhakti Spirituality', in: R. De Smet/J. Neuner (Edd.), Religious Hinduism, p.246.

202. Sandilya Sutra 1.1.2.

203. Narada Bhakti Sutra 2.

204. P. Fallon, Loc. Cit.

205. C.B. Papali, Art. Cit., p.35.

206. M. Dhavamony, Op. Cit., p.484.

207. Ibid., Cfr. also: Idem, Love of God according to the Saiva Siddhanta, London, 1971.

208. Idem, Classical Hinduism, p.184. Bhakti as goal is called 'Sadhya Bhakti' and as means 'Sadhana Bhakti'.

209. P. Fallon, Art. Cit., p.247.

210. Ibid., pp.248,249.
Bhakti is mainly divided into two categories: one is perfect and the other is imperfect. The perfect and pure type of Bhakti is called mukhya (Primary), ahaituki (motiveless,pure), nirguna (absolute), ragatmika (consisting of pure affection) para, parama, siddha (transcendent, perfect). The imperfect Bhakti has also various names: gauni (secondary), haituki (interested, motivated), saugna (related, worldly), vaidhi (law-abiding, formalisitic), apara (imperfect).

211. Further details on Krsna will be discussed below while tackling the topic of 'Avatara'.

212. Bhagavadgita 4.11.

213. Ibid., 6.30.

214. Ibid., 18.64,65.

215. Ibid., 9.30-32.

614

216. Ibid., 9.26,27.

217. Ibid., 9.34., 18.66
Ibid., 18.66.

219. Ibid., 3.5. Cfr. also: w.D. O'Flaherty, Asceticism and Eroticism in the Mythology of Siva, London, 1973; W.A. Well, Sex and Sex Worship, London, 1919.

220. Ibid., 18.62.

221. Ibid., 18.2.

222. Ibid., 3.4.

223. Ibid., 6.1., 18.2.5-6.

224. Ibid., 18.6., 3.6f., 4.18-23.

225. Ibid., 6.10-15.

226. Ibid., 10.10-11.

227. Ibid., 2.72., 5.24., 5.25.

227a. Ibid., 2.72.

228. Bhagavadgita 2.55.

229. R.C. Zaehner, The Bhagavad-Gita, Oxford, 1969, p.36.

230. Ramanuja: Sri Bhasya 1.1.1., Cfr. also Olivier Lacombe, La Doctrine Morale et Metaphysique de Ramanuja, Paris, 1938, p.162.

231. Bhagavadgita 10.10.

232. P. Fallon, Art. Cit., p.248.

233. Kath. Up. 2.23.

234. Bhagavadgita 18.56.

235. P. Fallon, Art. Cit., p.251.
236. Ibid.

237. S. Radhakrishnan, The Bhagavadgita, p.62.
M. Dhavamony, Classical Hinduism, pp.491,492.

238. Ramanuja, Op. Cit., 4.4.22.

239. Advaita and Jnana Marga do not accept and difference in the degree of union once the liberation is definitively reached. Identity with Brahman cannot be described as more or less!
240. Bhagavata Purana 3.29.13.

615

241. Swami Prabhavananda, The Sermon on the Mount according to Vedanta, California 1972, p.44.
242. P. Fallon, Art. Cit., p.248. Cfr. also, the cult of Sakti in Tantrism, 'The worship of Sakti or female energy in conjunction with male energy'. Stutley, Op. Cit., p.298.

243. S. Radhakrishnan, Op. Cit., p.53.

244. Since the mercy of God is the reason for his incorporation, Sandilya considers the Avatars as the objects particularly adapted to Bhakti. Sandilya Sutra 2.46,55., 2.49.

245. Cfr. J.N. Banerje, Puranic and Tantric Religion, Calcutta, 1966, p.31. J. Gonda, Visnuism and Saivism - A Comparison, London, 1970, pp.22-24.
E.J. Rapson (Ed.), The Cambridge History of India, Vols. 6 (1922 - Repr. 1957-1964), Vol.1, p.273.

246. D. Acharuparambil, Art. Cit., p.13.
M. Dhavamony, Classical Hinduism, p.61.

247. S.N. Dasgupta, A History of Indian Philosophy, 5 Vols., Cambridge, 1922,Repr. 1955., Vol. 2, p.525.
This view of Dasgupta . is disputed by E.G. Parrinder: The Significance of Bhagavad-Gita for Christian Theology, London, 1968, p.13.
If Gita is an integral part of Mahabharata or a later work, this affirmation of Das Gupta cannot be correct.

248. Svet. Up. 3.12ff. Such hints are present also in Kath. Up. and Munda. Up. Cfr. also Bhagavadgita 13.13.

249. G. Parrinder, Avatar and Incarnation, p.18.

250. Ibid., p.19.

251. Panini 3.3.120.

252. J. Gonda, Die Religionen Indiens I, Stuttgart, 1960, p.269 says that an Avatar is not a clear incarnation but an 'appearance' (Erscheinung) of God as man or an animal. E. Abegg calls it an 'embodiment (Verkörperung). Cfr. his Der Messiasglaube in Indien und Iran, Berlin,1928, p.39.
253. A. Cotterell, Op. Cit., p.85.

254. G. Parrinder, Op. Cit., p.19. In the Rgveda there are instances of gods assuming various forms at will. Cfr. Rgveda 3.53.8., 6.47.18.

255. S.N. Dasgupta, Op. Cit., Vol.5, pp.7,155.

256. M. Dhavamony, 'Hindu Incarnation', in: Studia Missionalia, Rome, 21 (1972), pp.128,129.

257. Ibid., p.130.

258. G. Parrinder, Op. Cit., pp.72,74.

616

259. Ibid., p.75. Bhagavata Purana contains three lists of Avatars. In 1.3.6-22 twenty two names are given. In 2.7.1ff. twenty three are given and in 11.4.3ff sixteen.

260. Stutley, Op. Cit., p.33.

261. Mahabharatha 12.389.104. (Santi Parva).

262. Stutley, Loc. Cit. It is to be noted that the successive Buddhas and Jaina Tirthankaras are not regarded as divine beings as are Hindu Avatars.

263. Cfr. G. Parringer, Op. Cit., pp.21ff.
M. Dhavamony, Art. Cit., pp.131ff.
A. Cotterell, Op. Cit., pp.85ff.

264. Sat. Br. 1.8.1.1.

265. Mahabharata, Vana-Parva, chs. 1 and 2.

266. Agneya Purana Ch.1., Bhagavata Purana 8.24., 12.8.
Matsya Purana Chs. 1 and 2.
Cfr. also Padma Purana Ch. 36., Visnu Purana 5.10., 6.3.

267. Satapatha Brahmana 7.5.1.5.

268. Prajapati is the chief god of the pantheon of the Brahmanic age.
Cfr. A. Barth, The Religions of India, London, 1882, p.41.

269. Bhagavata Purana 1.3.16., Cfr. also Kurma Purana.

270. Bhagavata Purana 1.3.7.

271. Visnu Purana 1.4.1ff.
Ramayana 2.119.3-4.
Rgveda 1.61., 8.77.
Taittiriya Brahmana 1.1.3.5ff.
Taittiriya Samhita 6.2.4.2-3., 7.1.5.
Satapatha Brahmana 14.1.2.
Mahabharata 3.270., 12.240.
Cfr. also H. Zimmer: Myths and Symbols in Indian Art and Civilization, New York, 1946, pp.77ff.

272. Mahabharata 3.270.
Visnudharmottara Purana 3.119., 3.123., 1.19., 1.196.
Cfr. also Srimad Bhagavata, condensed by A.M. Srinivasacharyar and translated by V. Raghavan, Madras 1937, pp. 133ff.
Cfr. also: Rudolf Otto, The Original Gita, London, 1939 (21), pp.240,241.

273. Ramayana 1.32ff.
Cfr. also Satapatha Brahmana 1.2.5.
Aitareya Brahmana 6.15.
Cfr. also Max Müller, 'Vedic Hymns', in: Sacred Books of the East, Vol.XXXII, p.133.
Kaegi, Rigveda, note 213.
Oldenberg, Religion des Veda, p.228.

Bergaigne, Religion Vedique, Vol. II, p.414.
Wallis, Cosmology of the Rigveda, p.114.
The above given citations are taken from M. Dhavamony, Art. Cit., p.136.

274. Mahabharata 3.115., 5.96.
Srimad Bhagavata, p.231.

275. M. Dhavamony, Art. Cit., p.139.

276. Ibid., p.140.

276a. 'Bala Rama', Rama the strong is sometimes considered as an Avatar of Visnu or of the serpent 'Ananta' on which Visnus sleeps. Cfr. G. Parrinder, Op. Cit., p.73.

277. M. Dhavamony, Art. Cit., p.142.

278. G. Parrinder, Op. Cit., p.26.
Mahabharata 3.139.
Cfr. also E. Abegg: Der Messiasglaube in Indien und Iran, pp.40ff., pp.138ff.
There is also a Kalkin Purana, which, however, is not counted among the 18 great Puranas.

279. A. Cotterell, Op. Cit., p.88.

280. G. Parrinder, The Significance of Bhagavad-Gita for Christian Theology, p.15.
Idem, Avatar and Incarnation, p.27.
Krsna might habe been a non-Aryan 'pastoral' (herdman) god. Cfr. A. Cotterell, Op. Cit., p.88.

280a. Krsna as the monotheistic deity of the Bhagavadgita may be union of at least three strands: the popular (god)-hero of a local tribe, ancient Vedic deity of the ritual religion an the philosophical Absolute of the Upanishads. Cfr. F. Edgerton, 'Prehistory of the God of Bhagavadgita', in his, The Bhagavad Gita, New York, 1944, pp.132ff.
Cfr. also: R. Garbe, Indien und Christentum, Tübingen, 1914, pp.209ff.
A. Barth in his The Religions of India, tr. London, 1882, p.168 holds that Krsna was a tribal god later made man.
Cfr. also: Bhagavan Das, Krshna. A Study in the Theory of Avatars. Madras, 1929.

281. Rgveda 8.74. Especially verses 3 and 4. Cfr. also: M. Dhavamony, Art.Cit. p.148.

282. Chand. Up. 3.17.6.

283. Cfr. Bhagavadgita 8.11-13.
Cfr. also J.Muir, Original Sanskrit Texts, Vol 4, London, 1873, pp.183ff.

284. Mahabharata, Adi Parva, Poona edn., 58., 51f.

285. G. Parrinder, Avatar and Incarnation, p.28. The childhood events of Krsna are elaborately narrated in the much later Bhagavata Purana, Visnu Purana, Harivamsa Purana etc.

286. Mahabharata 2.37f.

287. Ibid., 2.188 and 270.

288. Ibid., 3.270., 7.6., 12.340.

289. Ibid., 16.4.

290. Panini 4.3.98.

291. S. Radhakrishnan, The Bhagavad Gita, p.29.

292. Ibid., p.30.

293. G. Parrinder, Op. Cit., p.32.

294. Cfr. above to the reference to the Gita in the Introduction to the Ist Part.

295. 'Kuru' is the name of a people. 'Kuruksetra' is their land which had Hastinapura as the capital. The historical events relating to Kuruksetra battle, namely the Aryan conquest of India, is dated back to ca. 1400 B.C. Cfr. R.C. Majumdar, et al. (ed.) The History and Culture of the Indian People, Vol 1, p.311. The earliest possible dating is 2000 B.C.

296. G. Parrinder, Op. Cit., p.32.
     M. Dhavamony, Classical Hinduism, pp.85,86,87.

296a. Bhagavadgita 4.5.

297. Ibid., 5.6,8.

298. Ibid., 5.7.

299. Mahabharata 12.326.61.

300. Bhagavadgita 9.11., 15.14.

301. Ibid., 4.6.

302. Ibid., 10.21., 11.9., 18.77.

303. Rudolf Otto, The Original Gita, pp.154ff.

304. W.D.P. Hill, The Bhagavadgita, Oxford 1928, repr. 1953, 1967, p.25.

305. J. Gonda, Die Religionen Indiens, 1960, p.269.

306. Quoted from G. Parrinder, Op. Xit., p.33.

307. Ibid., pp.33,34.

308. Bhagavadgita 4.6.

309. Ibid., 7.4-5.

310. Ibid., 9.11.

311. Ibid., 9.18.

312. Ibid., 7.7.

313. Ibid., 7.26.

314. Ibid., 10.2.

315. Ibid., 10.8.

316. Ibid., 10.39.

317. Ibid., 11.8.

318. Ibid., 11.12.

319. Ibid., 11.15.

320. Ibid., 11.20.

320a. Ibid., 11.44.

321. Ibid., 11.54.

322. Ibid., 11.40. Cfr. also: Ibid., 11.41,42.

324. Ibid., 11.45.

325. Ibid., 7.24.

326. S.N. Dasgupta, A History of Indian Philosphy, Vol.2, p.533.

327. G. Parrinder, The Significance of Bhagavadgita for Christian Theology, pp.16,17.

328. Bhagavadgita 4.6.

329. Ibid., 9.11.

330. Ibid., 4.5.

331. Ibid., 4.14.

332. G. Parrinder, Avatar and Incarnation, p.226.

333. 'Yada yada hi dharmasya glanir bhavati Bharata abhyutthanam adharmasya tada' tmanam srjamy aham. Paritranaya sadhunam vinasaya ca duskrtam dharma-samsthapan' arthaya sambhavami yuge yuge.' English quoted from G. Parrinder, Op. Cit., p.36,37. Bhagavadgita 4.7-8. Cfr. also Ibid., 7.24., 9.11.

334. M. Dhavamony, 'Classical Patterns of Hinduism', p.267.

335. 'janma karma ca me divyam evam yo vetti tattvatah tyaktva deham punar-janma n'aiti, mam eti so, 'rjuna.' English quoted from M. Dhavamony, Art. Cit., p.266. Bhagavadgita 4.9.

336. M. Dhavamony, 'Hindu Incarnations', p.148.

337. G. Parrinder, The Significance of Bhagavad Gita, pp.18,19.

338. Idem, Avatar and Incarnation, p.78.

339. Ibid.. pp.120-126.

340. Ibid., p.61.

341. Ibid., p.48.

342. A.M. Sastri, The Bhagavad-Gita with the Commentary of Sri Sankaracharya, 5th ed., 1961, p.121.

343. G. Parrinder, Op. Cit., p.61.

344. M. Dhavamony, Art. Cit., p.154.

345. G. Parrinder, Op. Cit., p.52.
Cfr. also: K.S. Murty, Revelation and Reason in Advaita Vedanta, 1959, pp.232ff.

346. Cfr. R.C. Zaehner: The Bhagavad-Gita, Oxford, 1969, pp.3ff.

347. Ramanuja: Gita-Bhasya, 1. Quoted from Papali, C.B., Art. Cit., pp.44,45.

348. G. Thibaut, (tr.), The Vedanta-Sutras with the Commentary by Ramanuja, 1904, 2.2.42.

349. See Introduction of Sri Bhagavad Gita with Sri Ramanujacharya's Visishtadvaita Commentary, translated by A. Govindacharya, 1898.

350. Cfr. M. Dhavamony, Art. Cit., pp.156ff.

351. S. Rao Subbha, Bhagavad Gita translated according to Sri Madhwacharya's Bhashyas, 1906, pp.102.
Cfr. also Dasgupta, A History of Indian Philosophy, Vol.4, p.147.
Cfr. also A. Grierson, 'Madhva', in: Encyclopedia of Religion and Ethics, Vol. 8.

352. G. Parrinder, Op. Cit., p.59.

353. Ibid., p.85.

354. M.T. Kennedy, The Chaitanya Movement, 1925, pp.17ff.

355. S.N. Dasgupta, History of Indian Philosophy, Vol. 4, pp.389ff.

356. G. Parrinder, Op. Cit., p.94.
Cfr. also: F.E. Keay, Kabir and His Followers, 1931, pp.69ff.

357. W.H. McLeod, Guru Nanak and the Sikh Religion, 1968, pp.172ff.

358. G. Parrinder, Op. Cit., p.96.

359. J.N. Farquhar, Modern Religious Movements in India, pp.71,80,120ff.
Cfr. also D.S. Sarma, Hinduism through the Ages, 1956.

360. G. Parrinder, Op. Cit., p.233.

361. The Gospel of Ramakrishna, 1947, p.300.
Cfr. also: Teachings of Ramakrishna, Calcutta, 1958, pp.52-89.

362. Sayings of Ramakrishna, 1925, pp.135ff.

363. The Gospel of Ramakrishna, Loc. Cit.
Cfr. also: M. Müller, Ramakrishna, His Life and Sayings. 1951, p.109.

364. M. Dhavamony, Art. Cit., pp.160,161.

365. G. Parrinder, Op. Cit., p.109.

366. Complete Works of Swami Vivekananda, 1931, Vol.4, p.118.

367. M. Dhavamony, Art. Cit., p.162.

368. Ibid.

369. Sri Aurobindo, Essays on the Gita, Pondicheryy, 19591, p.140.
Cfr. also Idem, The Life Divine, 1955, pp.56ff., 189ff., 324ff.etc.
Cfr. also: G. Parrinder, 'Sri Aurobindo on Incarnation and the Love
of God', in: Numen, June 1964.

370. Quoted from G. Parrinder, Avatar and Incarnation, p.104. Originally
found in Young India, 1921.
Cfr. also: Mahadev Desai, The Gospel of Selfless Action or the Gita
according to Gandhi, Ahmedabad, 1948.

371. Quoted from M. Dhavamony, Art. Cit., p.164.

372. Harijan 22 - 6 - 1947.

373. Quoted from G. Parrinder, Avatar and Incarnation, p.104.

374. Ibid., p.103.

375. Vinoba Bhave, Talks on the Gita, 1960, pp.168ff.

376. S. Radhakrishnan, The Bhagavadgita, p.31.

377. Idem, Indian Philosophy, Vol.1, p.545.

378. Idem, The Bhagavadgita, p.35. The eternal Avatara manifests the
immanence of God and the temporal Avatara his transcendence!

379. Ibid., p.32.

380. Ibid., p.34.

381. Ibid.

382. Ibid., p.32.

383. Ibid., p.31.

384. Ibid., p.36.

385. Ibid., pp.32-34.

386. Ibid., p.157.

387. Ibid., p.34.

388. Ibid., pp.156f.

389. Ibid., p.37.

NOTES: PART II

CHAPTER IV

1. Cfr. above Part I passim, esp. the Introduction.

2. Ibid.

3. 'Sanatana Dharma' means 'the Eternal Religion': Here it is important to keep in mind the introduction to Part I in which we had briefly presented some basic informations regarding Hinduism.

4. Cfr. Part I. Chapter III. C. 3.

5. The 'hinduisation' here would mean an uncritical re-interpretation of the mystery of Christ in order to fit it by all means to the Hindu frame of thinking by ignoring the important points of difference.

6. To the number of different Hindu sects we could add here religions like Buddhism, Jainism and Sikhism.

7. The Christianity in India claims its origin as early as the Apostolic times. Cfr. Alfons Väth, Der heilige Thomas, der Apostel Indiens, Aachen, 1925, p. 54.
   For the opinion of the early Church Fathers cfr. PL 14, PL 1134, PL 61, Pl 672, PG 36, PG 228. For further informations cfr. A.C. Perumalil and E.R. Hambye (Ed.), Christianity in India. A History in Ecumenical Perspective, Alleppey, 1972. Special attention could be drawn to the article by A.M. Mundadan, "Origin of Christianity in India", Ibid. pp. 15-29.
   R.R. Hambye, J. Madey, 1900 Jahre Thomas-Christen in Indien, Freiburg (Schweiz), 1972.
   Cardinal Tisserant, Eastern Christianity in India, 1957.
   E. Philipos, The Syrian Christians of Malabar, 1869.
   L.W. Brown, The Indian Christians of St. Thomas, 1956.

8. The Islam began to take roots in India as early as 711 A.D. An expedition under the leadership of the governor of Al-Basrah (Iraq) brought the religion of Mohammed to the region of the Indus. 1200-1757 was the golden period of Islam in India.

9. The Hindu approach to Christianity is predominantly eclectic and synchretic.

10. Ramakrishna Paramahamsa (1936-1886). His original name was Gadadhar. He was not much educated and worked as a priest at the Kali temple of Dakshineswar. His spiritual experiences had been a great inspiration for his disciples, the most prominent of whom was Swami Vivekananda.

11. Swami Prabhavananda, The Sermon on the Mount according to Vedanta, California, 1972, p. xiii.

12. Ibid.

Cfr. also: Cultural Heritage of India (Belur Math, Calcutta, 1953-56). Vol. II, p. 518. The Work has been re-edited by H. Battachary, Calcutta, 1961f. Belur Math is one of the important centres of the Ramakrishna Mission in India.

14. Cfr. back to the notion of 'Anubhava' and 'Saksatkara' in Part I. Ch. III.A.2.

16. Swami Nikhilananda (Tr.), The Gospel of Ramakrishna, New York, 1942, p. 35. This is a typical example of how superficial and naive are most of the Hindu leaders in evaluating the difference between religions!

17. Swami Vivekananda (1863-1902). His early name was Narendranath. As a highly educated disciple of Sri Ramakrishna he brought great prestige to the Ramakrishna movement organized by him with its headquarters in Belur, Calcutta. He is the most prominent advocate of Hinduism as the 'Sanatana Dharma'.

18. Rgveda 1.164.6: Ekam sat vipra bahuda vadanti! One is the reality, but the names are different. Only the wise man can distinguish it and see the fundamental unity in phenomenal multiplicity. It does not, however, explain why there should be an apparently never ending conflict of individuals and ideologies in this world.

19. Bhagavadgita 9.23. This could be interpreted as a doctrine of 'Anonymous devotees of Krishna! Cfr. also Swami Vivekananda, The Complete Works of Swami Vivekananda, 5th ed., Almora, 1931, Vol. IV, pp. 102ff.

20. The Complete Works of Swami Vivekananda, 5th Ed., Almora, 1931 (Hereafter cited as 'Complete Works'). Vol. IV, p. 331. Vivekananda's religious tolerance and generosity is evident here. The various modes belief and worship are only so many attempts of man to grasp the Infinite! In this though-pattern there is no religion that is favoured by a special revelation of God in preference to others. This position is understandable only in the general context of the Vedantic presumption that all men are by nature divine!

21. Ibid. Vol. IV, pp. 51f.

22. Cfr. Yerwada Mandir, Mahatma Gandhi, Ahmedbad, Ch. X.

23. Harijan, February 16, 1934.

24. Harijan, April 6, 1934. According to Gandhi different religions contribute differently in the spiritual progress of mankind.

25. M.K. Gandhi, Christian Missions, Ahmedbad, 1940, pp. 33f.

25a, Harijan, August 8, 1942, passim.

25b. Harijan, March 6, 1937. In Gandhi's opinion Truth is superior to every religion which is only a partial expression of Truth. No particular religion, according to him, has the monopoly of Truth. Gandhiji does not accept that the full Truth is manifest in the Incarnate Word of God, Jesus Christ.

25c. S. Radhakrishnan and J.A. Muirhead (Ed.), Contemporary Indian Philo-sophy, London, 1936, p. 21.

26. M.K. Gandhi, The Message of Jesus Christ, Bombay, 1940, p. 9.

27. Harijan, February 16, 1934.

28. M.K. Gandhi, Christian Missions, p. 13.

28a. Young India, October 14, 1926.

30. S. Radhakrishnan, Eastern Religions and Western Though, London, 1939. Cfr. especially the Chapter on "The Meeting of Religions".

31. Ibid. pp. 313-316.

32. Ibid. But it is not clear how the sum total of conflicting opinions could bring about the full Truth!

33. This Hindu insistence on the experiential aspect of religion does not take seriously how gravely a personal experience could be subjectively disorted.

34. P.C. Mozoomdar's opinion written in the Theistic Quarterly Review is so quoted in: The Life of Ramakrishna, Advaita Ashram, Calcutta, 7th Ed. 1955, p. 276.

35. The Gospel of Ramakrishna, p. 34. Cfr. also Nalini Devda, Sri Ramakrishna, Bangalore, 1965, p. 26.

36. 'Ishtam' is the Sanskrit equivalent of personal liking or preference.

37. Swadeshi: Devotion to one's own immediate milieu and country of birth.

38. Swami Vivekananda, Complete Works, Vol. III, p. 131.

39. Cfr. Ibid. p. 182-184.

40. Ibid., Vol. IV, p. 54.

41. Ibid., Vol. I, p. 22. But the problem is that the spirits of all religions need not necessarily be so mutually complimentary as Vivekananda may suppose!

42. Ibid., Vol. Iv, pp. 52f.

43. Harijan, May 27, 1939.

44. M.M. Thomas, The Acknowledge Christ of the Indian Renaissance, London, 1969, p. 209.

45. M.K. Gandhi, The Message of Jesus Christ, pp. 28f. The statement of Gandhi could be further extended and it could be asked: Could the mission of the Church among cannibals, for example, be aimed at

making them more radical cannibals? This, of course, is not the spirit of his statement. The salvation that Christianity preaches is not principally aimed at making every one 'better' in what one is; there must be a qualitative leap in the realization of human existence. Gandhiji's opposition to missionary conversions was caused by the dubious methods which were often employed in conversion. He also thought that the Indians converted to Christianity could be manipulated as tools of Western colonialism which could destroy peace and stability in the Indian social structure. Gandhi also could not notice any betterment of character in the behaviour of those converted! Cfr. M.M. Thomas, The Acknowledged Christ, p. 230.

46. M.K. Gandhi, Christian Missions, p. 36.

47. Cfr. Idem, The Message of Jesus Christ, p. 29.

48. Ibid., p. 34, Idem, Christian Missions, p. 147.

49. Ibid., p. 174.

50. Idem, The Message of Jesus Christ; p. 6.
    Cfr. also pp. 13, 16.

51. S. Mrthy, Revelation and Reason in Advaita Vedanta, Bombay, 1959.
    Cfr. pp. 219ff.

52. D.S.Sharma, The Renaissance of Hinduism, Benares, 1944. Cfr. pp. 304 etc.

53. Bhagavadgita 7.21f., 9.23,24,27.

54. Here we apply a terminology widely used by the supporters of the view of Karl Rahner and in a different sense by Raimundo Panikkar. We will be discussing later this notion of anonymita. Cfr. Ch. VI.B.4.

55. The Ramakrishna Mission is a movement with centers in different parts of the world. It consists of 'Swami's or monks who lead a life of interiority and social service. Its methods could be compared to those of the Christian missions. The Ramakrishna Mission could be considered as a Hindu response to the Christian challenge.

56. Cfr. above note no. 3.

57. Cfr. The Gospel of Ramakrishna, p. 39.

58. Swami Vivekananda, Complete Works, Vol. I, p. xiii.

59. Cfr. Nalini Devadas, Sri Ramakrishna, Bangalore, 1965, pp. 56-64. Cfr. also pp. 104-133.

60. Swami Vivekananda, Complete Works, Vol. III, pp. 182f.

61. Paul A.Schilpp (Ed.), The Philosophy of Sarvepalli Radhakrishna, New York, 1952, p. 371.

62. In stressing the universal validity of the Vedanta Radhakrishnan follows the lead of Swami Vivekananda. Ibid., p. 25.

63. The Neo-Hinduism is the modernized version of Hinduism that has resulted from India's encounter with the West. It begins from the time of Rammohan Roy's reforms and as it is understood today it tries to co-ordinate the different trends of Hinduism into an organic unity.

64. Cfr.
S.J. Samartha, The Hindu Response to the Unbound Christ, Madras, 1974, p. 98.
Cfr. also P.D. Devanandan, Christian Concern in Hinduism, Bangalore, 1961, p. 98.

65. S.J. Samartha, Op. Cit. pp. 100, 101.
Cfr. also S. Radhakrishnan, An Idealist View of Life, London, 1980, pp. 66ff.

67. M.M. Thomas, Op. Cit., p. 166.

68. Ibid., pp. 167, 171. The question of individualism in the Hindu world-vision as highly responsible for a certain intensitivity towards the miseries of the fellowmen will be dealt with later especially in Ch. VI.C.3.

69. Swami Vivekananda, Complete Works, Vol. III, p. 182.

70. Cfr. S.J. Samartha, Op. Cit., p. 98.

71. This is the title of a book by Swami Akhilananda.

72. The title of our present Chapter.

73. The title of the book by S.J. Samartha. Op. Cit.

74. Ibid., p. 62.

75. Keshub Chunder Sen (1838-1884) was a leader of the Hindu reformation movement. Like Rammohan Roy he worked to purify Hinduism of its idolatry and superstitions especially on the level of the masses.

76. The Brahma Samaj was a continuation of the Spiritual Society (Atmiya Sabha) founded by Raja Rammohan Roy in 1815. The Samaj was called to its proper existence in 1830. It was meant to help religious discussion and communitarian prayer among its members. Dbendranath Tagore, Keshub Chunder Sen and P.C. Mozoomdar were the most prominent leaders who continued the work begun by Roy. They insisted on theism and moral reforms in Hinduism. The Brahma Samaj was a very positive response to the influence of Christian ideals in India.

77. K.C. Sen, Keshub Chunder Sen's Lectures in India, 2 Volumes, London, Vol. I (1901), Vol. II (1904). Hereafter cited as Sen's Lecture.
Cfr. Vol. II, pp. 33-35.

78. Raimundo Panikkar, The Unknown Christ of Hinduism, New Edition,

London, 1981 (Revised and enlarged edition). Regarding the question of salvation in Hinduism cfr. also our work Part II. Ch. VI.B.4.

79. Karl Rahner, "Jesus Christus in den nichtchristlichen Religionen", in: Schriften zur Theologie, XII (1975), pp.370ff.

80. For the ideas of Panikkar cfr. Ch. VI.B.4 and for an evaluation from the standpoint of K. Rahner cfr. Part II, Ch.IX.

81. Sen's Lecture, Vol.II, p. 33. This statement of Sen sounds like the anonymous Christ of K. Rahner. Sen does not, like the Vedantins, reduce Christ to a mere universally present Mystery. The historical uniqueness of Jesus Christ is an important point in Sen's lectures which we will be considering in detail in the next chapter, Ch.V.

82. Sen's Lectures, Vol. I, pp. 391-392.

83. Swami Vivekananda, Complete Works, Vol. VII, p. 14.

84. For a clarification of the concept of 'Jeevanmukta''. Cfr. Part I, Ch. III.

85. Swami Vivekananda, Complete Works, Vol. VII, p. 20. Cfr. also p. 27.

86. M.M. Thomas, Op. Cit., p. 121.

87. The Vedantins think that the application of 'Person' to the Absolute is an anthropomorphism which distorts the reality of Brahman and His (Its) Infinity. But the position of the Vedantic Bhakti schools in similar to that of the Christian concept: God is 'person' par excellence and the human beings are only an image or participation of the Supreme Person in limited forms. A proper theology of the Trinity (the three distinct persons in one Godhead) is inevitable to solve this Advaitic problem in a Christian way.

88. S.J. Samartha, Op. Cit., p. 11.

89. P.C. Mozoomdar (1840-1905) was the follower of K.C. Sen to the Brahma Samaj leadership.

90. P.C. Mozoomdar, The Oriental Christ, Boston, 1883, p. 16.

91. Ibid., p. 17. The orientalisation of Jesus Christ alone can, according to Mozoomdar, make him meaningful in the Indian context. It was a reaction against the westernisation of the image of Christ.

92. Quoted in Manilal C. Parekh, Brahmarshi Keshub Chunder Sen, Calcutta, 1887, p. 95.(Hereafter cited as Brahmarshi Sen.)

93. S.J. Samartha, Op. Cit. p. 63.

94. Cfr. Swami Akhilananda, Hindu View of Christ, Boston, 1971, pp. 36, 55 etc. (First published in 1948).

95. Swami Vivekananda, Complete Works, Vol. IV, p. 140. Cfr. also: S.J. Samartha, Op. Cit., p. 53.

97. Cfr. S.J. Samartha, Op. Cit., p. 52. Vivekananda's claim to understand Christ better than the Christians themselves - whether they be from the West or East - is indeed an arrogant claim that closes oneself to the fullness of truth.

98. P.C. Mozoomdar, The Oriental Christ, p. 46.

99. M.K. Gandhi, The Message of Jesus Christ, p.48.

100. Swami Akhilananda, The Hindu View of Christ, p. 46. But, Akhilananda's View of Christ is itself a superimposition of his Vedantic ideas on the person of Christ.

101. S. Radhakrishnan, Eastern Religions and Western Thought, London, 1939, pp. 304ff.

102. Idem, East and West in Religion, London, 1939, pp. 59f.

103. Cfr. S.J. Samartha, Op. Cit., p. 53.

104. Ibid., p. 59. Jesus' essential oneness with God, according to Vivekananda, is not something that is prerogative of Jesus alone. Every man is by nature divine!

105. Ibid., p. 60.

106. Swami Vivekananda, Complete Works, Vol., IV, pp. 141f. A typical Advaita Vedantic re-interpretation of the Gospel!

107. Ibid., Vol. II, p. 143., Cfr. also Vol. IV, p. 144. Cfr. also: below Chapter VI. Foot note no. 57.

108. "Aham Brahmasmi" - I am Brahman. For explanation cfr. Part I, Ch. II.A.2.a.

109. "Tat tvam asi" - That Thou art! Cfr. Ibid.

110. S.J. Samartha, Op. Cit. p. 55. Here attention should be drawn to the different interpretations of the schools of Sankara and Ramanuja. Cfr. Chapter II.2.a and b.

111. J.R. Chandran, Christian Apologetics in Relation to Vivekananda in the Light of Origen contra Celsum, Unpublished Thesis, p. 179. This is a quotation from Edwyn Hoskyns, The Fourth Gospel, London, 1948, p. 53. Here cited from M.M. Thomas, Op. Cit., p. 133.

112. M.M. Thomas, Op. Cit., p. 133.

113. Manilal C. Parekh, A Hindu's Portrait of Jesus Christ, Rajkot, 1953, p.348.

114. Ibid., p. 349.

115. Ibid. It may be said that Parekh projects upon Jesus Christ the verification to yogic technics!

116. Ibid., p. 374. It is, however, questionable whether the teaching regarding the Fatherhood of God was a concept that is specific to Jesus alone!

117. S. Radhakrishnan, The Bhagvad-Gita, Allen & Unwin, London, 1958, p. 31. Radhakrishnan refers also to Mark 15:34., 13:32., Luke 23:46., John 14:28., 10:30.

118. Cfr. the Conclusion to Chapter I.

119. Paul A. Schilpp, Op. Cit., p. 807.

120. Radhakrishnan, Eastern Religions and Western Thought, p.pp. 169, 171.

121. S.J. Samartha, Op. Cit., p. 63.

122. Ibid., p. 64., Cfr. for required explanations Part I. Ch. III.B.

123. S.J. Samartha, Loc. Cit.

124. Akhilananda, Hindu View of Christ, p. 96. Akhilananda refers to 'four yogas'; to the Karma, Jnana and Bhakti Yogas he adds also Raja Yoga. Such a division is not quite correct since 'Raja Yoga' refers primarily to the physical techniques of 'self-discipline' while the others three are called 'Yoga' only as a synonym to 'Marga', Way of spiritual life. Cfr. III.A.3.a.

125. Akhilananda, Op. Cit., p. 25.

126. 'Samadhi' stands for concentrated thought, profound or abstract meditation, intense contemplation of any particular object, so as to identify the contemplator with the object mediated upon'. By attributing permanent 'Samadhi' state of Jesus Christ, Akhilananda stresses the spiritual perfection and illumination of Jesus Christ. That means, Jesus was always conscious of his identity with the God.

127. Akhilananda, Op. Cit. p. 19.

128. For the 'Law of Karma' Cfr. Part I. Ch. II.B.

129. Further explanations on 'Samsara' Cfr. Ibid.

130. Akhilananda, Op. Cit., p. 18. Cfr. also: J. Baumann, The Character Of Jesus, 1908.
Ch. Binet-Sanglé, The Insanity of Jesus (in 4 Vols.) Paris, 1911-1915.
W.E. Bundy, The Psychic Health of Jesus, New York 1948.
G. De Loosten, Jesus Christ from the Standpoint of Psychiatry, Bamberg, 1905.
H.J. Holtzmann, Was Jesus an Ecstatic?, 1903.
Idem, The Messianic Consciousness of Jesus, 1907.
W. Hirsch, Conclusion of Psychiatrist, New York, 1912.

D.S. Strauß, The Life of Jesus Revised for the German People, 1865.
A. Schweitzer, The Psychiatric Study of Jesus, Boston, 1948.
H. Werner, 'The Historical Jesus of Liberal Theology, A Psychotic',
in: The New Ecclesiatical Journal, 1911 (Vol.22), pp.347-390.

131. For a clarification of the difference between the notions of Avatar
and Incarnation Cfr. Part II.Ch.V.C., Cfr. also: Ch.IV.A.3., Ch. III.C.

132. Sri Aurobindo, Essays on the Gita, 1959, p.15.

133. H. Battachary (Ed.), Cultural Heritage of India, Belur Math, Calcutta,
1961f. Vol.II, p.494.

134. Swami Vivekananda, Complete Works, Vol. III, pp.4f.

135. S.J. Samartha, Op. Cit., p.57.

136. Vivekananda, Complete works, Vol. IV, p.143.

137. Ibid., Vol. III, p.4.

138. For further explanations on the concept of 'Maya' Cfr. Part I. Ch.I.B.4.

139. S.J. Samartha, Op. Cit., p.57.

140. Bhagavadgita 4.7-8.

141. S. Radhakrishnan, The Bhagavad-Gita (Introduction) pp.24,155.

142. Radhakrishnan, Cfr. The Heart of Hindustan. Radhakrishnan proceeds
from the Advaitic principle that every man is by nature divine.

143. Akhilananda, Hindu View of Christ, p. 43.

144. Ibid., pp. 26f.
Cfr also. Sayings of Sri Ramakrishna, XXVII, 58., in the edition of
1971, Nr. 932, pp. 291ff.

145. Akhilananda, Hindu View of Christ, p. 28. Here the 'pre-existence'
is not to be understood in the Christian sense of the term, but according
to the Vedantic anthropology.

146. Ibid., p. 23.

147. Swami Prabhavananda, The Sermon on the Mount according to Vedanta,
California, 1972, p.42.

148. Ibid. p.46. Here Prabhavananda emphasizes the free initiative of God
in the Avatar. It is not the law of nature (Karma) that brings about
an Avatar but the free decision of God!

149. Max Müller, Ramakrishna: His Life and Sayings (Collected Works), London,
1900, Vol 15, p.109, Saying no. 52. 'Ocean' here means the world that
is subject to 'Karma-Samsara'.

150. The Gospel of Ramakrishna, The Vedanta Society, New York, 1947, pp.300-301.

151. Robin Boyd, An Introduction to Indian Christian Theology, C.L.S., Madras, 1979, p.59.

152. S.J. Samartha, Op. Cit., p.45.

153. The Gospel of Sri Ramakrishna, pp.809-810. Quoted from S.J. Samartha, Op. Cit., p.45.

154. For the notions of Anubhava and Saksatkara Cfr. Part I.Ch.III.A,2.

155. Cfr. T.M. Manickam, 'Anubhava as Pramana of an Indian Christology', in: Jeevadhara, A Journal of Christian Interpretation, Vol.I, May-June 1971, No.3.

156. For a clarification of the concept of 'Khristanubhava' Cfr. Part II, Ch.VI. C. and Part III.Ch.IX.C.

157. For the Vedantic concept of History Cfr. Part I,Ch.II,C.

158. Vivekananda, Complete Works, Vol. VII, p.1.

159. Ibid., Vol. IV, pp.147ff.

160. Cfr. Part II,Ch.I.C.

161. Vivekananda, Complete Works, Vol. VII, pp.5f.

162. M.K. Gandhi, The Message of Jesus, pp.54f. Quoted from M.M. Thomas, The Acknowledged Christ, p.204.

163. M.K. Gandhi, Op. Cit. p.36.

164. 'Sambhabvami yuge yuge', Bhagavadgita 4.7-8.

165. M.K. Gandhi, An Autobiography or The Story of My Experiments with Truth, Boston, 1957, p.136.

166. Mahatma Gandhi is not a strict Vedantin. He has his own system of religious syncretism later known as Gandhism. Cfr. Jesuit Scholars, Religious Hinduism, Allahabad, 1968, pp.296-307.

167. For Gandhi the disctinctiveness of Christ lies in the fact that 'he expressed the will and spirit of God as no other could'. Cfr. S.J. Samartha, Op. Cit., p.92.

168. Cfr. Quotation in: Samartha, Op. Cit., p.90.

169. Arthur P. Schilpp (Ed.), The philosophy of Sarvepally Radhakrishnan, p.68.

170. Cfr. Samartha, pp.107, 108.

171. Ibid., p.110.

172. S. Radhakrishnan, Eastern Religion and Western Though, p.184. The universal religious aspiration, as Radhakrishnan means, is one thing and its expression is another thing. Due to the fundamental limitations of man his religious expressions can take also a distorted form!

173. S. Radhakrishnan, Religion in a Changing World, London, 1967, p.132.

174. Arthur P. Schilpp (Ed.), Op. Cit., p.810.

175. Akhilananda, Hindu View of Christ, pp.20, 21, 25. Cfr. also. O. Wolff, Christus unter den Hin dus, Gütersloh, 1965, pp.196-198.

176. Prabhavananda, The Sermon on the Mount, p.45.

177. Ibid., p.xi.

178. Ibid., pp. 42, 43, 44.

179. Ibid., pp.47-48. But, Swami Prabhavananda does not explain how one truth could contradict another truth!

180. Swami Satprakasananda, Hinduism and Christianity, St. Louis, 1975, p.34.

181. Ibid.

182. Ibid., p.35. He also quotes Bhagavadgita 4.7-8. The question of difference between Krishna and Christ from the historical point of view is simply ignored.

183. S.J. Samartha, Op. Cit., p.47.

184. Swami Akhilananda, Mental Health and Hindu Psychology, New York, 1951, pp.126f.

185. Idem, Hindu View of Christ, p.29.

186. Ibid., p.24.

187. Ibid., p.33. This statement is clearly docetic in character. The underlying Vedantic aversion towards matter and body is also evident here!

188. L. Harold De Wolf in: Swami Akhilananda, Spiritual Practices, Boston, 1972 (Posthumous- edited by Alice May Stark and Claude Alan Stark, Cape Cod, 1974 as Memorial Edition with Reminiscences by His Friends, P.172.

189. Akhilananda, Hindu View of Christ, p.36.

190. Geoffrey Parringer Avatar and Incarnation, London, 1970, p.233.

191. Kaj Baago, 'Ram Mohan Roy's Christology - An Early Attempt at Demythologization', in: The Bangalore Theological Forum, 1967, p.31. Our intention here is not to discuss the influence Christ's moral teachings on the Hindu reformers. Here we are concentrating methodologically on the person of Christ. In Ch.VI we will be considering the relevance of Christ's teachings for others.

192. Raimundo Panikkar (*1918) tries to unify the Vedantic and Christian traditions into an organic whole. His work 'The Unknown Christ of Hinduism' has been widely read but its true message is seldom understood as is evident in some of its reviews which wrongly equate Panikkar's idea of 'Unknown Christ' with the 'Anonymous Christ' of Karl Rahner! Cfr. also Note no. 204.

193. Cfr. the concept of 'Isvara' in Part I.Ch.I,C. Isvara is the revealed aspect of the Absolute Deity or the Brahman. He is the personal revelation of the Absolute and the Supreme God of the Bhaktas. The strict Advaitins consider the concept of Isvara as inferior to that of the Nirguna Brahman, the Absolute without attributes. But in the theology of Ramanuja and the Bhakti schools which follow the tradition of the Gita 'Isvara' is even superior to Brahman! For explanation cfr. back to Part I,B,C.

194. Mamen Thomas Madathiparampil (*1916) is a member of the Mar Thoma Syrian Church of Kerala and was the chairman of the Central Committe of WCC. His well known work 'The Acknowledged Christ of the Indian Renaissance', SCM Press: London, 1969, stands in apparent contrariety to the 'Unknown Christ' of Raimundo Panikkar. Thomas' main concern is not to present Christ to a few Advaitic elite of India but to make the Christian message relevant for a modern and secularized India.

195. M.M. Thomas, The Acknowledged Christ, p.x (Preface).

196. Ibid., Chapters IX,X.

197. Ibid., p.306.

198. S.J. Samartha, The Hindu Response to the Unbound Christ, Madras, 1974. German translation, Hindus vor dem universalen Christus, Stuttgart, 1970.

199. J.B. Chethimattam, 'R. Panikkar's Approach to Christology', in: Indian Journal of Theology 23, 1974, pp.219-222.

200. Panikkar, The Unknown Christ, p.48.

201. Ibid. By 'transcendental platform' the reference is to the 'Nirguna Brahman'!

202. Ibid., p.58. Italics his.

203. The title of the book. Underline mine.

204. Panikkar, Unknown Christ, pp.24-25. Italics his. For example cfr. for criticism in S.J. Samartha, The Unbound Christ, pp.140-141.

205. Even an atheist who with a sincere heart searches after truth and follows the dictates of his conscience could be 'religious' in an implicit way!

206. Panikkar, Op. Cit., p.4. Panikkar considers it quite possible to speak also but 'the unknown Christ of Christianity' because the Sruti is according to Panikkar a revelation of 'Christ' for the Hindus, a fact that is not understood normally by Christians. Cfr. Ibid., p.8.

207. Ibid., pp.2-3. The author refers to Jn 1:1., 1:9-10., 8:25.58., 1 Cor 10:4., Ex 17:8., Ps 18:2 etc., Heb 11:24-26.

208. Panikkar, Op. Cit., p.2.

209. Ibid., p.18.

210. Ibid., p.49. Cfr. also pp.57,58. The author cites Prov 8, 34-35., Jn 8,58., Bhagavadgita 9.24.   26.29ff.

211. Ibid., p.20.

212. Ibid., p.29. Panikkar equates this 'Cosmo-theandric principle' with the 'Christ-Principle' that is universally present in different forms of religious convictions and ways of worship. Panikkar ignores however that the mystery of Incarnation is not a matter of universal presence, but of concrete historical manifestation!

213. Ibid., p.30.

214. Ibid., p.49. The author refers to the Vedantic texts regarding the human quest for the ultimate Mystery! *1. Tait. Up. 2.9.1., 2.6.1.
Svet. Up., 2.4., 3.3., 3.9., 3.11., 3.16.
Brhd. Up. 1.4.7., 2.4.5.
Chandogya Up. 3.14.2.

*2. Cfr. Kath. Up. 2.23., Mund. Up. 3.2.3.,
Svet. Up. 1.6., 2.4., 3.4., 3.8., 3.20.,
Chand. Up. 3.15.3., Bhagavadgita 9.23., 10.10-11., 18.56., 58., 62.

*3. Mund. Up. 2.2.2ff., Svet. Up. 3.12.,
Chand.Up. 8.14.1.

*4. Kath. Up. 5.15., Mund. Up. 2.2.9-10 etc.,
Svet. Up. 3.12., 17 etc., Chand. Up. 3.12,8-9., 3.17,7-8.

215. Panikkar, The Unknown Christ, p.20.

216. Panikkar, 'Confrontation between Hinduism and Christ', in: New Blackfriars, Vol. 50., No. 584, Jan. 1969., pp.197.204.

217. Idem, The Unknown Christ, p.26.

218. Rgveda I, 164, 46.
Cfr. also Panikkar, The Unknown Christ, pp.13,23.

219. Ibid., p.169 (Italics his).

220. Idem, Art. Cit. ('Confrontation ...'), p.203 (Italics his).

221. Ibid., p.199. In the context of Panikkar's frame of thinking as seen in 'The Unknown Christ' a comparison between one manifestation of the Christ - principle and another is a contradiction in itself.

224. Panikkar, The Unknown Christ, p.13.

227. Panikkar, The Unknown Christ, p.26.

228. Idem, 'The Meaning of Christ's Name in the Universal Economy of Salvation', in: M. Dhavamony (Ed.), Evangelization, Dialogue and Development, Selected Papers of the International Theological Conference, Nagpur (India) 1971, (Documenta Missionalia 5), Roma, 1972, pp.195-218.

229. Ibid., p.197. It is to be mentioned that Panikkar's understanding of 'name' does not correspond with what is meant by it's use age as we see in the Acts of the Apostles! 'For of all the names in the world given to men, this is the o n l y   o n e by which we can be saved.' (Acts 4:12)!

230. Ibid., pp.197,198.

231. Ibid., p.198.

232. Idem, The Unknown Christ, p.3.

233. Ibid., p.23.

234. Mt. 16, 16.

235. Panikkar, 'The Meaning of Chist's Name', p.200.

236. Ibid. Here the role of Indian Christology is to make clear that everyone is not the Son of the Living God as Jesus Christ is, in an ontological sense. The function of an Indian Christology is not, unlike Panikkar may suppose, to accept every thing one finds in the Vedantic anthropology!

237. Idem, The Unknown Christ, p.3.

238. Ibid., p.27.

239. Ibid., p.23. Here Panikkar means that Jesus Christ is only one of the possible valid expressions of the mystery that is sought after by every man! This would contradict all Christian claims regarding the salvific uniqueness of Jesus Christ.

240. Ibid., p.27, (Italics his).

241. Rgveda 1.164.46. Cfr. also Panikkar, Unknown Christ, pp.13,23.

242. Ibid., p.7.

243. Idem, 'The Meaning of Christ's Name', pp.197,198.

244. Idem, The Unknown Christ, p.27.

245. Ibid., p.26. Panikkar uses 'humankind' instead of 'mankind' and 'Man' (capital) to signify both genders of the human species.

246. Ibid., p.27. Panikkar maintains: Jesus is Christ, but not vice versa, i.e. Christ is Jesus! Christ, the Universal, is according to him more than Jesus! Cfr. also Ibid., p.14.

247. Ibid., p.27.

248. Ibid., p.8.

249. Ibid., p.27. If his work was meant for Hindus he could give it the title 'The Unknown Krishna/Rama of Christianity'! The Christians can in this sense be called 'Anonymous Hindus'!

250. Cfr. Karl Rahner, 'Das Christentum und die nicht-christlichen Religionen', in: Schriften zur Theologie, Band V, Einsiedeln/Zürich/Köln, 1964, SS.136-158.
'Die anonymen Christen', Ibid., Band VI, Einsiedeln/Zürich/Köln, 1965, SS. 545-554.
Cfr. also Panikkar, Unknown Christ, p.13.

251. Rgveda 1.164.46.

252. Panikkar, The Unknown Christ, p.27.

252a. Cfr. Note no. 250.

252b. Cfr. Part II,Ch.VI.B.4.

253. Cfr. Part II.Ch.IV.B.3.

254. Panikkar, The Trinity and World Religions, Madras, 1970, p.42., p.74. Cfr. also Robin Boyd, An Introduction to Indian Christian Theology, p.302.
Trimurth i (Cfr. Part I.Ch.I.C.3) could be compared to the Trinitarian heresy of 'Sabellianism' - God is one having three different aspects or functions without an inherent distinction fo three persons. Authors like Nehemiah Goreh hold that even the concept of 'Trimurthy' could have a preparatory value for the preaching of the Gospel. But mos of the Indian Christian theobgians ignore the Trimurthy concept as a part of the popular and idolatrous Hinduism and concentrate on the 'Saccidananda', the metaphysical Vedantic concept of God which is not marred by myths.
Cfr. also Peter May, The Doctrine of the Trinity, Madras, 1955. The question of the Trinity in Islam is discussed in pp.83ff. This point is irrelevant for our topic.

255. Robin Boyd, Op. Cit., pp.297ff.

Panikkar, Trinity and World Religions, pp.41,58. Cfr. also our discussion on the Margas as given in Chapter VI.C.2.

256. Panikkar, Ibid., p.61.

257. Idem, The Unknown Christ, pp.161,162.
For the concept of Brahman Cfr. Part I.Ch.I.B.

258. Panikkar, Op. Cit., p.161.

259. Saboda Brahman is the self existent eternal 'Sound' (Sphota) that is equal to Brahman and is expressed by the mystical syllable 'OM'. It could be compared with the Greek 'Logos'.

260. Mund. Up. 2.2.4., Mand. Up. 1.if.
Maitri Up. 6.22. 'OM' stands for the ultimate union of Atman in the unqualified Brahman.

261. Cfr. William Ernst Hocking, The Coming World Civilization, New York, 1956, p.98.

262. Panikkar translates 'Logos' as 'Vac' (Word).
Cfr. The Unknown Christ, pp.1,2.

263. William Tempel, Reading in St. John's Gospel, London, 1949, p.10.

264. Panikkar, Op. Cit., Loc. Cit.

265. Ibid., p.169.

266. Ibid., p.1. Would it not be proper to call the Holy Spirit as the Inspirer of all that is good in other religions? Panikkar does not clarify why the Son alone could be called so.

269. Panikkar, The Unknown Christ, p.57.

270. Klaus Klostermaier (*1933). He was born in Munich and was an S.V.D. Missionary who was in India since 1961 making researches in Hindu Philosophy.

271. Klaus Klostermaier, Kristvidhya: A Sketch of an Indian Christology, Bangalore, 1967.

272. Ibid., p.37.

273. Ibid., p.38. 'Christ is unique in the sense Brahman is unique, not in the sense in which one among many sons of God could claim uniqueness.'

274. Klaus Klostermaier, Hindu and Christian in Vrindaban, London, 1969, p.117.

275. Klostermaier, Kristvidhya, p.21.

276. Cfr. Part I.Ch.I.B.3.

277. In the Bhakti tradition 'Isvara' is even greater than Brahman. We have already referred to this point.

278. Panikkar, The Unknown Christ, p.151.

279. Ibid., p.152.

280. In my opinion it would be better to avoid the term 'impersonal' and use 'suprapersonal' instead.

281. Panikkar, Op. Cit., p.153.

282. Ibid., p.154.

283. Ibid., p.155. (Cfr.)

284. Cfr. Ibid., p.153.

285. Taittriya Up. III,1.

286. Panikkar, Po.Cit., p.108, (Italics his).

287. Ibid., p.112. The question could be still further asked: Who is then the cause of Isvara? The Christian theology cannot accept any attempt to deny the causality of this world to the Absolute god.

28 8. Ibid., pp.155,156.

293. Panikkar, Op. Cit., p.156. Cfr. also: Jn. 10:30., 17:11,21,22., 1 Jn 5:7., Jn 1:1., 7.29., 17.5.

294. Panikkar, Op. Cit., pp.156,157,
Cfr. also: Ap 1:8., 2:8., 21:6., col 1:17.,
Phil 2:7., 2 Cor 8:9., Heb 2:14., Jn 1:2.,
2 Cor 4:4., Jn 6:57., Rom 8:29., Col 1:15,18.,
Ap 1:5., Col 1:17., 2:10., 1:16., 1 Cor 8:6., Jn 8:18,21,25,58.

295. Panikkar, Op. Cit., p.158 (Underline mine).

296. Ibid., p.159.

297. Ibid. Panikkar avolids Modalism. But a positive explanation is not given!

298. Ibid., p.160 (Italics his). He refers to Mand. Up. 6. Council of Chalcedon, Denzinger 148.
Cfr. also: 1 Cor 12:12., 15:28., Col 3:8., Gal 3:28., Rom 12:5., Eph 1:23.

299. See above.

300. Panikkar, The Unknown Christ, p.162. The author refers to Eph 1:10., 4.2-13.

301. Ibid., p.161. The difference between Christ and the Holy Spirit is not convincingly clear in Panikkar!

302. Ibid., p.162 (Italics his). He refers also to Jn 12:32.

303. Raimundo Panikkar: 'The Category of Growth in Comparative Religion: A Critical Self-Examination', in: The Harvard Theological Review, 66 (1973), p.128.

304. Cfr. Panikkar, The Unknown Christ, pp.56,57.

305. Ibid.

306. Panikkar, 'The Meaning of Christ's Name', p.217.

307. Idem, The Unknown Christ, p.14.

308. Idem, 'The Meaning of Christ's Name', p.201 (Italics his). The author refers also to Mt 10:40., 11:3., 18:5., Mk 9:37., Lk 9:48., Heb 13:8., Jn 8:58., 1Cor 15:14.
The argument of Panikkar seems to be very naive! It is clear to the Christian consciousness that Christ is not finished with his death on the Cross. In the resurrected suprahistorical state his human body also shares the glory that is proper to the Word. The event of the Incarnation is not ended with the tragedy of Jesus' death. Panikkar seems to ignore the glorification of Jesus' body!

309. Idem, The Unknown Christ, p.27.

310. Ibid., pp.48,49.

311. Cfr. also: Mk 16:15-16., Lk 24:47., Acts 1:8., 2:38., 18:20.

314. The relation between the 'Universal Logos' and Jesus of Nazareth is of cardinal importance here. The faith-expression (Dogma) of Chalcedon is one possible way of expressing this relation; of course, not the only one.
Cfr. Karl Rahner, 'Chalkedon - Ende oder Anfang?' in: Schriften zur Theologie, Band I, Einsiedeln/Zürich/Köln, 1964, SS.169-222.
Cfr. also Grillmeier u. Bacht (Hrsg.). Das Konzil von Chalkedon, Bd.III, Würzburg, 1954, SS.3-40.

315. Panikkar, 'The Meaning of Christ's Name', p.217.

316. Ibid., p.196. Cfr. also Acts 3:16., 3:6., 4:12., 4:10.ff., 5:28., 5:40., 8:12., 9:14ff., 10:43., 10:48., 15:25., 16:18., 19:5., 19:13., 22:16., etc. Mk 9:38., 16:17., Lk 9:49., 10:17.

317. Ibid., pp.214,215. Cfr. also: Jn 8:50., Ap 19:13.

318. Ibid., p.216.

319. Ibid., p.218. 'Christ ... is not the revelation, not the revealed name, but the revelation of the name. The name Christ reveals is a Supername ...' Ibid. This passage is unfortunately very ambigous. 'Christ' here stands for 'Jesus'! Only then could we think of a name above Jesus, a Supername!

320. R. Bultmann, Das Verhältnis der urchristlichen Christusbotschaft zum historischen Jesus und der Christus unseres Glaubens, Wien, 1962, S. 8.

321. H. Schlier, 'Über Sinn und Aufgabe einer Theologie des NT', in: Besinnung auf das NT, Freiburg, Basel, Wien, 1964, SS.7-24.

322. Quoted from Geoffrey Parrinder, Avatar and Incarnation, London, 1970, pp.233,234 (Underline mine).

323. Swami Vivekananda, Complete Works, Vol. III, pp.182f.

324. Ibid., Vol. IV, p.142.

325. Quoted from M.M. Thomas, The Acknowledged Christ, p.129. Cfr. also: C.F. Andrews, 'The Hindu View of Christ', in: International Review of Mission, 28(1939), pp.259-264.

326. Cfr. The Guardian 7.1.1932. Cfr. also Robin Boyd, Op. Cit., p.250.
327. M.K. Gandhi, The Message of Jesus Christ, Bombay, 1940, p.35.

328. Sri Aurobindo, Essays on the Gita, 1959, p.17.

329. S. Radhakrishnan, Eastern Religions and Western Thought, London, 1939, pp.186f.

330. Ibid., p.164.

331. Taken from Paul A. Schilpp (Ed.) The Philosophy of S. Radhakrishnan, New York, 1952, p.807.

332. The influence of the West has also brought in a historical sense gradually into the Vedantic consciousness.

333. Panikkar, The Unknown Christ, pp.164,165.

334. Ibid., p.2.

335. J.B. Chethimattam, Art. Cit. p.220 (in: Indian Journal of Theology, 23 (1974).)

336. Panikkar, Op. Cit., p.83. But, Panikkar does not clarify how the historical aspect of human existence could be taken seriously without finding some historical anchorage even for myths!

337. K. Dockhorn, 'Christ in Hinduism as Seen in Recent Indian Theology', in: Religion and Society, XXI, 1974, p.44.
Original German: 'Christus im Hinduismus in der Sicht der neueren indischen Theologie', in: Evangelische Missionszeitschrift, 30 Stuttgart, 1973, SS.57-75.

338. 'The Great Man' in whom the humanity is restored as a new creation.

339. P. Chenchiah, 'Who is Jesus?', in: The Guardian 1943. Taken from D.A. Thangasamy, The Theology of Chenchiah, Bangalore, 1966, p.217. Cfr. also: Erstgestalten einer einheimischen Theologie, München, 1966. It must also be kept before mind that Chenchiah identifies the resurrected Christ with the Holy Spirit. We will be dealing with this point in greater detail later. Cfr. Ch. VI.B.3.c.

340. Quoted from Robin Boyd, Op. Cit., p.217.

341. Samuel Ryan, 'An Indian Christology - A Discussion of Method', in: Jeevadhara 1 (1971), pp.212-227. Cfr. also: Samuel Ryan, 'Interpreting Christ to India - The Contribution of Roman Catholic Seminaries', in: Indian Journal of Theology, 23 (1974), pp.223-231.

342. S.J. Samartha, Op. Cit., p.143.

343. Panikkar, 'The Meaning of Christ's name', p.204.
Individual: 'In se indistinctum, ab aliis vero distinctum.' It is not necessary that all philosophical systems accept this scholastic definition, because each system has its own categories with their own connotations. What is scientifically important is a coherence of categories in the same system and a coherence of systems among themselves. This rules out the possibility of contradictions inspite of the difference in approaches!

344. Ibid., p.205. This argument of Panikkar regarding the human nature of Christ is not convincing. As there is no humanity apart from individual human beings, so also there is no human nature independently of its individuation. The matter being the principle of individuation, to deny individuality to Jesus Christ as a man is to deny the reality of Christ's incarnate body!

346. Substance: 'Id cui competit esse in se et non in alio tamquam in subjecto inhesionis quod est subjectum inhesionis omnium quae dicuntur de eo.' This scholastic definition has two aspects: the first part speaks about the possibility of existing in itself (-not by itself!) although not its actuality and the second part distinguishes substance from accidents which have an existence only 'in alio'.

347. Suppositum: 'Subsistens distinctum in natura aliqua.' This definition is applicable to all concrete existing things. The scholastic notion of 'Person' is derived from the concept of 'Suppositum'. Thomas Aquinas defines 'Person' as 'Subsistens distinctum in natura intellectuali.' By affirming the intellectual aspect of 'Person' Aquinas makes it applicable not only to rational (human) beings, but also to God and the Spirits who are intellectual but do not require the process of reasoning. This is a correction undertaken by Aquinas on the definition of 'Person' by Boethius: 'Rationalis naturae individua substantia.'! Here the scholastic distinction of 'Supposit' and 'Individual' is also important to note! A 'Supposit' subsists in itself necessarily; it is 'incommunicable.' The 'Individual' on the other hand can subsist, but not necessarily. The 'individual' is called in the scholastic language a 'particularized essence' and since the notion of 'incommunicability' is not attached to it, it has the possibility of being 'assumed'. So we could say that the human

individuality of Jesus could be assumed by the divine person of Christ, without at the same time being destroyed or absorbed by him! The context of Panikkar's arguments the above given clarification is important and in the background of what we have said, Panikkar's position (that Jesus Christ is not a single individual) is untenable even from the scholastic point of view which he himself calls in for support!

348. See above.

349. Panikkar, 'The Meaning of Christ's Name', p.205.

350. This is a misleading sophistication! If Christ is truly man he was one among many human beings. Hence the notion of 'singular' is applicable to Jesus Christ!

351. Panikkar, Art. Cit., p.206.

352. Klaus Klostermaier, Kristvidya: A Sketch of an Indian Christology, Bangalore, 1967, p.38.

353. Panikkar, Art. Cit., Loc. Cit.

354. The concept of 'Communicatio idiomatum' is inseparably related to the notion of 'Hypostatic union'. Communicatio idiomatum could be translated as communication of properties or cross predication and that consists in predicating to the one person of the Incarnate Word, designated after one of his two natures, attributes and predicates which pertain to the other nature. It is the transference of the human characteristics of the Self of the 'Logos' that forms the person. Here we find an 'exchange' of the divine and human qualities in the God-Man. By this we can attribute the properties of human nature to God and the properties of divine nature to this man Jesus Christ, but we shall not attribute human properties to divine nature and divine properties to human nature. Hence we can, for ex. speak of the death of God on the Cross, but not of the death of the Divinity on the Cross!

The main problem in Panikkar's Christology seems to be his identification of the 'Logos' with 'Christ' and the discard for the real distinction of persons in the Holy Trinity. The notion of 'Christ', unlike that of the 'Logos', necessarily includes the humanity of Jesus Christ.

355. Panikkar, Art. Cit., p.213.

356. Ibid., p.212. Cfr. back to the notion of 'communicatio idiomatum'!

357. Ibid. This assertion, however, is questionable especially in the light of the existentialist approach to human existence which is determined by space, time and the totality of human environment.

358. Ibid., pp.212,213.

359. Ibid., p.213.

360. But, without an external discovery there also cannot be an internal or personal discovery. Panikkar ignores this point and that shows his discard for the material and historical aspect of human existence!

644

361. Ibid., p.212.

362. Ibid., p.213.

363. Ibid., p.212.

364. Ibid., p.214. Jesus' resurrection was not a negation of his historicity, but its affirmation!

365. Ibid.

366. Ibid. If we were to follow this opinion of Panikkar, theology itself will have no more right to exist!

367. Panikkar, Salvation in Christ: Concreteness and Universality, the Super-name, Santa Barbara, 1972, pp.32,33.

368. Panikkar, 'The Meaning of Christ's Name', p.208. Does the 'anointing' take place only with the resurrection?

369. Cfr. John 19,34., 20,27.

370. The 'unknown' here should be understood in the sense explained earlier by Panikkar. Cfr. The Unknown Christ, p.26.

371. J.B. Chethimattam, Art. Cit., p.221.

372. Ibid.

373. Ibid.

374. Ibid. Cfr. also: M. Dhavamony's evaluation of Panikkar's 'Unknown Christ' in: Heythrop Journal, 1965, Vol. IV, no.4, p.480.

CHAPTER V

1. The 'personality' of Jesus Christ means not only his 'person' in a philo-
    sophical sense, but the totality of Jesus Christ as an individual in history.

2. Raja Rammohan Roy (1774-1883). He was a prominent Hindu social
    reformer of the 19th century. He is called the father of Indian na-
    tionalism and was the founder of the monotheistic movement 'Atmiya
    Sabha' which developed later into 'Brahmo Samaj'. His approach to
    religion was rationalistic and he insisted that morality is the essence
    of all religions and worked to abolish superstitions, idolatry, caste
    injustice and especially the system of 'Sati' (burning of widows) which
    were prevalent in Hinduism. Although Roy could not accent Jesus Christ
    as God and Saviour, he found the moral teachings of Christ very inspiring.

4. Brahmo Samaj could be literally translated as the society of the wor-
    shippers of Brahman. For explanation cfr. Notes, Ch.IV. no.76.

5. Keshub Chunder Sen. Cfr. Ch.IV. Notes no.75.

6. P.C. Mozommdar, Cfr. Ch.IV. Notes no.89.

7. Our intention is not to deal with all Indian theologians in an exhaustive
    way. By way of 'sample' we concentrate on those who have made some
    significant contribution to the understanding of man and Christ in the
    Indian categories.

8. Jesuit Scholars, Religious Hinduism, Allahabad, 1968, p.287.

9. Ibid., p.276. both of these movements owe their inspiration to the Indian
    encounter with the West especially during the colonial period.

10. The spread of English education helped very much to strengthen the
    influence of Christian values. The Christian values,however, are not
    to be identified with Western values!

11. Here mention could be made of rationalism, positivism etc. which had
    a strong hold on the intelligentia of the 19th century Europe.

12. M.M. Thomas, The Acknowledged Christ of the Indian Renaissance,
    London, 1969, p.111.

13. Jesuit Scholars, Op. Cit., p.278.

14. M.M. Thomas, Op. Cit., p.2.

15. Robin Boy, An Introduction to Indian Christian Theology, Madras, 1979,
    p.25.

16. Rammohan Roy, Second Appeal, Calcutta, 1821. Cfr. in: English Works
    of Raja Rammohan Roy, (Collection) Allahabad, 1906, p.580.

17. Robin Boyd, Op. Cit., p.21.

18. Kaj Baago, 'Ram Mohan Roy's Christology: An Early Attempt at Demythologization', in: Bangalore Theological Forum, 1967, pp.39-40.

19. Rammohan Roy, 'A letter on the Prospects of Christianity', in English Works of Raja Rammohun Roy, Part IV, Calcutta, 1947, p.44.

20. Rammohan Roy, Second Appeal, Calcutta, 1821, p.85.

21. Idem, An Appeal to the Christian Public in Defence of the 'Precepts of Jesus' by a Friend to Truth, Calcutta, 1820, p.22.

23. For the details of the controversy Cfr. M.M. Thomas, Op. Cit., pp.1-28.

24. Rammohan Roy, Second Appeal, Calcutta, 1821, p.88.

25. For details Cfr. M.M. Thomas, Op. Cit., pp.17-19.

26. English Works of Raja Rammohan Roy, Allahabad, 1906, p.172. This passage shows clearly Roy's aversion to polytheism and idolatry. The 'Kenosis' of the Son of God (Phil. 2,6-11) is evidently quite foreign to the rationalistic mind of Roy!

27. Ibid., p.572. Mohan Roy himself gives the summary of these arguments.

28. Ibid., p.811.

29. Cfr. Robin Boyd, An Introduction to Indian Christian Theology, Madras, 1979, p.22.

30. Ibid., p.20.

31. Rammohan Roy, English works of Raja Rammohan Roy, Allahabad, 1906, (Hereafter cited as 'English Works of Rammohan Roy'), pp.573ff.

32. Rammohan Roy, Second Appeal, Calcutta (Baptist Mission Press), 1821, p.110. Roy also denies the title 'Mother of God' to the Virgin Mary.

33. English Works of Rammohan Roy, pp.573-577.

34. Ibid., p.168. The Christian theology of the Holy Trinity is evidently not admitted by Roy. For him to be a son means to be inferior to the father by reason of the causality of origin.

35. Rammohan Roy, Second Appeal, 1821 (Hereafter cited as 'Second Appeal') p.69.

36. English Works of Rammohan Roy, p.582.

37. Ibid., p.577.

38. Ibid., p.579.

39. Ibid., p.577.

40. Second Appeal, p.69.

41. Cfr. English Works of Rammohan Roy, pp.583ff.

42. Ibid., pp.805-808.

44. English Works of Rammohan Roy, p.577.

45. Second Appeal, p.12.

46. Ibid., p.69. We reserve the teachings and ethics of Jesus for Chapter VI.

48. Some followers of Keshub Chunder Sen began to pay him divine honours as the latest of Avatars!
Cfr. G. Parrinder, Op. Cit., p.99.
Cfr. also J.N. Farquhar, Modern Religious Movements in India, 1915, pp.63ff.

49. Jesuit Scholars, Religious Hinduism, p.279.

50. Keshub Chunder Sen, The New Dispensation, 2 Vols. Vol.I (1915), Vol. 2 (1916), Brahmo Tract Society, Calcutta, Here Vol.II, pp.173-175.

51. Eclectism could be explained as a free assimilation of ideas, methods etc. from various sources. It is philosophical in character.

52. Syncretism is a religious tendency to select and compromise illogically at all costs whatever seems to be best in different religions.

53. Whether 'Advaita' can be called pantheisitc or monistic is another problem. As we have seen in the first Part (passim), 'Advaita' is a theory on the non-duality of Being which has received various inter-pretations in different Vedantic schools.

54. Quoted by M.C. Parekh, Brahmarshi Keshub Chunder Sen, Rajkot, 1931, p.110.

55. Keshub Chunder Sen, Keshub Chunder Sen's Lectures in India, Cassel and Co. Ltd., London, Vol. I (1901), Vol. 2 (1904). (Hereafter cited as 'Sen's Lectures').
Sen's Lectures, Vol.I, p.185.

57. Sen's Lectures, Vol. I, pp.257ff.
Cfr. also Ibid., p.216, 387.
Cfr. also Brahmarshi Sen, pp.101f.
This quotation is from the lecture Sen delivered in 1879 under the title 'India asks: Who is Christ?'.

58. Cfr. Part I, Ch.II.A,2.

59. Sen's Lectures I, p.215.

60. Sen's Lectures II, p.20.

61. Sen's Lectures I, p.388.

62. Cfr. above no.57.

63. For informations Cfr. Ch.IV,n.89.

64. P.C. Mozoomdar, The Oriental Christ, Boston, 1883, p.41.

65. Ibid., p.41. In his zeal to refute monism and patheism Mozoomdar rejects also the essential divinity of Jesus Christ!

66. Ibid., p.89.

67. Ibid., p.41.

68. Aiyadurai Jesudasan Appasamy (*1891) is a Hindu convert who later became the bishop of the Church of South India in Palayankottai, Tamil Nadu.He finds Ramanuja's system of thought most appropriate to interpret the Christ-mystery in the Indian context.

69. A.J. Appasamy, What is Moksha? 1931, p.59.

70. Idem, The Gospel of India's Heritage, 1942, p.37.
It is well to keep in mind that Appasamy admits the eternity of the 'Logos' with God, eventhough inferior to him. Arian tendencies are evident in the Christology of Appasamy!

71. Sen's Lectures I, p.388.

72. Cfr. back to A.1.b and c.
Cfr. also: Sen's Lectures II, p.23.
Ibid., p.24. To attribute divinity to Jesus Christ is for Sen equal to calling him a second God! This is unacceptable in the monotheisitc categories of Sen. Only a proper theology of the Trinity can defend the full divinity of Jesus Christ without at the same time postulating a second God!

75. Sen's Lectures II, pp.37,38. Cfr. also pp.20-24.

76. Sen's Lectures II, p.61.

77. Ibid., pp.38-39.

78. Ibid. The Hindu category of 'Avatar' is according to Sen not appropriate to express the mystery of the Incarnation. That would mean that it is God the Father who took a human form, which is absurd!

79. For Rammohan Roy this position of Sen would be tantamount to polytheism in disguise!

80. A.J. Appasamy, What is Moksha?, p.2.

81. Idem, My Theological Quest, Bangalore, 1964, p.27.

82. Idem, The Johannine Doctrine of Life - Study of Christian and Indian Thought, London, 1934, p.59.
This statement of Appasamy would suggest that Jesus Christ was not essentially different from other human beings. His apparent rejection of the full divinity fo Christ cannot be justified in the context of genuine Christian tradition and the Church's condemnation of the early Arian and Semi-Arian doctrines.
Cfr. also: Idem, The Gospel and Indian Heritage, 1942, pp.35,36.

84. Sen's Lectures II, p.24.

85. DS 125.

86. DS 301, 302.

87. DS 166.

88. Karl Rahner, 'Was ist eine dogmatische Aussage', in: Schriften zur Theologie V, 54-81.

89. Pope John's opening speech to the Council, Vat. II on October 11, 1962. Cfr. Walter M. Abbot (Ed.) The Documents of Vatican II, London/Dublin, 1966, p.715.

90. Manilal C. Parekh was a Jain born in Gujarat (1885-1967). He was a disciple of K.C. Sen as a member of his New Dispensation Church. Although he received baptism in 1918, he did not recognize the value of an organized Church and the Sacraments.

91. M.C. parekh, Brahmarshi Keshub Chunder Sen, Rajkot, 1926, pp.165, 173-175.

92. Cfr. Robin Boyd, An Introduction to Indian Christian Theology, p.120.

93. We must guard against making parallels here with the heresies of the first centuries. The philosophical background and the implied nuances are different today!

94. Sen's Lectures I, p.63.

95. Ibid., p.61.

96. Ibid., p.60. When Sen says that Christ's humanity was above ordinary humanity he does not mean in any way Jesus' equality with God in the Christian sense.

97. K.C. Sen, The New Dispensation, Calcutta, 1915, Vol I, p.249.

98. Ibid.

99. Sen's Lectures I, p.373 ('India asks: Who is Christ? 1879). Cfr. also: Mc. Parekh, Brahmarshi Sen, p.98f.

100. Sen's Lectures I, p.369.

101. M.C. Parekh, Brahmarshi Sen, pp.149,150.

102. Sen's Lectures I, p.381.

103. Ibid., p.368. The verse in St. John ('I and the Father are one' - Jn. 10,30) is a subject of contention between the advaitins and the Hindu theistic reformers. The former group sees in this verse the affirmation on the part of Jesus regarding the essential divinity of every human being, while the Hindu theists like Rammohan Roy and Sen see it only as indicating Christ's union of will and submission to God.

104. M.C. Parekh, Brahmarshi Sen, p.104.

105. Sen's Lectures II, pp.25,26.

107. P.C. Mozoomdar, The Oriental Christ, p.89.

108. A.J. Appasamy, The Gospel and India's Heritage, p.207. Appasamy follows Ramanuja's theory of the world as the 'body' of God. Jesus' fleshy organism could be, according to him, considered as a second 'body' of God. Cfr. ibid.

109. Idem, Christianity as Bhakti Marga: A Study of the Johannine Doctrine of Love, Madras, 1928, pp.42,43.

110. Idem, What is Moksha?, p.112.

112. Ibid., p.116.

113. M.C. Parekh, Brahmarshi Sen, pp.90ff.
Cfr. also Sen's Lectures I, p.375,376,379. This position of Sen is very similar to the 'idealism' advocated by Plato in his distinction of the ideal world and the real world of which the former is given a sort of autonomous existence!

114. Sen's Lectures I, p.379.

115. Ibid., pp.375ff.

116. Ibid., pp.374ff.

117. Sen's Lectures II, p.11 (Lecture: 'That Marvellous Mystery, the Trinity', 1882). Cfr. also p.12.

118. Ibid., pp.14,16. This idea of Sen is later shared by Pandipeddi Chenchiah.

119. Cfr. back to Sen's ideas regarding the universal presence of Christ Ch.IV.A.2.a. But it must be well remembered that Sen's idea of universal Christ is very different from that of the Vedantins who insist on the 'Christ-principle' in every man at the cost of Jesus' historical concreteness.

120. Sen's Lectures II, p.34.

121. Ibid., p.32.

123. Ibid.

124. This uniqueness which Sen attributes to Jesus Christ is not admitted by the strict Vedantins.

125. Sen's Lectures II, pp.1,2.

126. Sen's Lectures II, pp.17,18. This identification of the Mystery of the Holy Trinity and the doctrine regarding the 'Saccidananda' on the part of Sen is done very uncritically. The approach of Sen is clearly modalistic. Sen ignores the fact that Christianity believes in a Trinity of persons in God without postulating at the same time any idea of Tritheism!

127. Ibid., p.17.

128. Sen's Lectures II, p.16.

129. Cfr. M.M. Thomas, The Acknowledged Christ of Indian Renaissance, p.65.

130. M.C. Parekh, Brahmarshi Sen, pp.165,171-175.

131. Cfr. Ibid., pp.154-159.

132. Ibid. Quoted from M.M. Thomas, Op. Cit., p.63.

133. Sen's Lectures I, pp.312f.

134. M.C. Parekh, Brahmarshi Sen, pp.154-159. Although Sen does not accept the notion of 'Avatar as applicable to Christ, he sees a valuable truth contained in the Avatara-myths of Hinduism.
It foreshadows the process of evolution that ends up with the Divine Humanity of Jesus Christ: 'The Puranas speak of the different manifestations or incarnations of the Deity in different epochs of the world history. Lo! the Hindu Avatar rises from the lowest scale of life through the fish, the tortoise and the hog up to the perfection of humanity. Indian Avatarism is, indeed, a crude representation of the ascending scale of Divine Creation.' Cfr. 'That Marvellous Mystery, the Trinity', in: Sen's Lectures II, p.13.

135. Ibid., Quoted in M.M. Thomas, Op. Cit., p.63.

136. P.C. Mozoomdar, The Spirit of God, Boston, 1894, p.240.

137. Ibid.

138. Ibid.

139. J.N. Farquhar, Modern religious Movements in India, New York/London, 1915, pp.66f.

140. S.K. Datta, The Desire of India, London, 1908.

140a. Pandipeddi Chenchiah (1886-1959) was the Chief Justice of Pudikottah and the brother-in-law of Vengal Chakkarai. He rejects (unlike Chakkarai) the notion of 'Avatar' as applicable to Christ. Like Sen he adopts an evolutionary frame of thinking in Christology.

141. The Guardian 6.2.1947. Quoted from Robin Boyd, An Introduction to Indian Christian Theology, p.148.

142. P. Chenchiah, Rethinking Christianity in India, 1939, p.158. (Joint author with V. Chakkarai).

143. Ibid., p.54. Quoted from Robin Boyd, Op. Cit., p.149.

144. Ibid., p.166. Quoted from Robin Boyd, Op. Cit., p.148.

145. P. Chenchiah, 'Jesus and non-Christian Faiths', in: Rethinking Christianity in India, p.58.
Quoted from Antony Mookenthottam, Indian Theological Tendencies, Berne, 1978, p.129.

146. Cfr. also: D.A. Thangasamy, The Theology of Chenchiah with Selections from His Writings, Bangalore, 1966, p.17.

147. National Christian Council Review, 1943, p.363.
Adipurusha or Mulapurusha could be translated as 'the original man'.

148. Ibid., p.632.

149. P. Chenchiah, Rethinking Christianity, p.62.

150. Cfr. D.A. Thangasamy, Op. Cit., pp.217,218.
Cfr. also National Christian Council Review, 1943, p.363.

151. P. Chenchiah, Rethinking Christianity, p.168.

152. DS. 302.

153. Cfr. Robin Boy, Op. Cit., pp.149,150.

154. 'Saccidananda' by itself is not properly Trinitarian, but modalistic. What I mean is a Christian re-interpretation of this concept according to the demands of the Christian faith.

155. The approach of Raymond Panikkar to the Christ-Mystery is trinitarian, but supra-historical!

156. Brahmabandab Upadhyaya (1861-1907) was a friend of Ramakrishna Paramahamsa and K.C. Sen and the classmate of Swami Vivekananda. He was born near Calcutta and his original name was Bhavani Charan Banerji. Through Sen he became a member of the Brahmosamaj and later found his way to Christianity becoming a Catholic monk. He remained, however, faithful to his Hindu traditions. He changed his name to the Sanskrit rendering of Theophilus as 'Brahmabandab'. He was a nationalist and also co-operated with Rabindranath Tagore in founding the 'Santiniketan' university. He could rightly be called the Father of Indian Theology.

157. B. Animananda, <u>The Blade: Life and Work of Brahmabandab Upadhyaya</u>, Calcutta, 1947, p.83.

158. B. Upadhyaya, 'An Exposition of the Catholic Belief as Compared with the Vedanta', in: <u>Sophia</u>, Vol. V, no. 1, January 1898, p.11. Cfr. also Kaj Baago, <u>Pioneers of Indigenous Christianity,</u> Madras, 1969, p.40. Cfr. also: Robin Boyd, Op. Cit., pp.71,73,74.

159. B. Upadhyaya, 'Christ's Claim to Attention', in: <u>The Twentieth Century,</u> 1901, May, pp.116, 117.

160. B. Upadhyaya, H induism and Christianity as Compared by Mrs. Basant', in: <u>Sophia</u>, Vol IV, No. 2, Febr. 1897, p.8. Cfr. also: <u>Sophia</u>, Vol.I, No.10. August 25, 1900, p.7.

161. Hymn 'Vande Saccidanandam': Cfr. 'Our New Canticle', in <u>Sophia</u>, Vol. V, Nr. 10, October 1898, pp.146, 147. Brahmabdab's own translation in: Kaj Baago, <u>Pioneers of Indian Christianity,</u> B angalore 1969, p.40. Sanskrit text available also in: Swami Parama Arubi Anandam, <u>Fr. J. Monchanin - A. Memorial,</u> 1959. Other English translations: M.M. Thomas, Op. Cit., p.70. Our translation is taken from Joseph Mattam, SJ, 'Interpreting Christ to India today: The Calcutta School', in: <u>Indian Journal of Theology,</u> 23 (1974), pp.194. This translation is by Fr. Gispert Sauch.

162. Nicea and Chalcedon councils did the same with Greek concepts. They accepted notions such as person, nature etc. from Greek philosophy and re-interpreted them as to fit the Christian faith. There was not only an acceptance of hellenistic ideas, but also a dehellenization!

163. 'Exactly the same'! Cfr. B. Upadhyaya, 'An Exposition of the Catholic Faith as Compared with the Vedanta', in: <u>Sophia</u> Vol. No. 1, Jan. 1898, p.11. Cfr. also K.P. Aleaz, 'The Theological Writings of Brahmabandab Upadhyaya Re-Examined', in: <u>The Indian Journal of Theology,</u> Vol. 28 (1979), 63.

164. Robin Boyd, Op. Cit., p.74.

165. Mahadev Govind Ranade (1842-1901) was a very liberal minded man who served as a judge in the High Court of Bombay. Though he considered the British colonial period a blessing in disguise for India in order to shake her up from her lethargy and the malpractices prevalent in the society, he worked as a patriot for her liberation.

166. G.A. Mankar, <u>Life and Works of the Late Mr. Justice M.G. Ranade,</u> Bombay, 1902, Vol.I, p.195. Cfr. also H.C.E. Zacharias, <u>Renascent India,</u> Lond on, 1933, p.45.

166a. Cfr. also K.C. Sen, 'That Mar vellous Mystery - The Trinity', in: <u>Sen's Lectures, II,</u> pp.1-48.

167. B. Upadhyaya, 'The Incarnate Logos', in: <u>The Twentieth Century,</u> Vol. I, No. 1, Jan. 1901, p.6.

168. Idem, ' Hinduism, Theosophy and Christianity', in: Sophia, Vol. IV, No. 12, Dec. 1897, p.2.

169. Idem, 'Christ's Claim to Attention', in: The Twentieth Century, Vol. I, No. 5, May 1901, p.116. Cfr. also: Idem, 'Incarnate Logos', Art. Cit., p.7.

170. Ibid.

171. K.P. Aleaz, Art. Cit., p.76.

172. In the fourth chapter we have indicated that Raimundo Panikkar does not deny the uniqueness of 'Christ' although Jesus of Nazareth for him is not unique.

173. Fr. Jules Monchanin (1895-1958), from Lyons, France, lived a long time in an Ashram on the banks of Kaveri in South India (Saccidananda Ashram, Kulitalai). He aimed at a dialogue with Hinduism on the level of the Spirit in the tradition of B. Upadhyaya. He changed his name to Parama-arupya-ananda which means joy in the Supreme Formless One.

174. Fr. Henri le Saux (1910-1973) was also a French benedictine who together with Monchanin tried to interpret the Vedantic Saccidananda experience as fulfilled in the experience of the Holy trinity.

175. Quoted from Robin Boy, Op. Cit., p.219.
Cfr. also J.a. Cuttat, The Encounter of Religions, 1960, p.16.

176. Monchanin does not approve of Modalism either in monistic or in mono-theistic forms. Cfr. Swami Parama Arubi Anandam: Fr. J. Monchanin - A Memorial, 1959, p.186. Quoted from Robin Boyd, Op. Cit., p.220.

177. Ibid., p.200, Robin Boyd, p.220.

178. Ibid.

179. Ibid, p.18., Robin Boyd, Op. Cit., p.219.

180. K.P. Aleaz, Art. Cit., p.75. Two of Abhishiktananda's noteworthy works are: Hindu-Christian Meeting-Point within the Cave of the Heart, Bombay/Bangalore, 1969. A Christian Approach to Advaitic Experience, Delhi 1974.

181. The Gospel of St. John is for him 'The Johannine Upanishad' that crowns both the Hindu Upanishads and the Bible. Cfr. Abhishiktananda, Hindu-Christian Meeting-Point, p.51.

182. Ibid., p.97.

183. Prof. Dhanjibhai Fakirbhai (1895-1967) was born as a Hindu in Baroda and was later converted to Christianity as a young man. His thoughts centre on the concept of Love as the essence of Christian religion. He does not accept the advaitic notion of being absorbed into God. He insists on the faith-union of the believers with Christ.

184. 'Adhyatma Darsana' means a vision of spirituality. Cfr. Robin Boyd, Op. Cit., p.331.

185. Robin Boyd, Ibid., p.331,332 (Italics his).
Klaus Klostermaier also refers to the Word as the 'Sabda Brahma', of course, in its universal aspect.
Cfr. Robin Boyd, Ibid., p.27.
Cfr. also Brahma Sutra 3.2.18 for the anylogy of the sun and its rays.
Cfr. also Ait. Up. 3.1.2-4: 'Brahman is Prajnana'.

186. Charles Freer Andrews (1871-1940). He got acquainted with Mahatma Gandhi in South Africa. As an Anglican Missionary he came to India in 1904. He had also cooperated in the erection of the Santiniketanam university with Rabindranath Tagore. Though he remained an admirer of Gandhi all through his life, he could not accept the Gandhian reduction of religion to morality and the puritanism that may presume to achieve one's own salvation without the salvific role of Jesus Christ.

187. Cfr. to our reference in the fourth chapter regarding Gandhi's notion of the universality of Christ!

188. C.F. Andrews, What I owe to Christ, London, 1932, pp.152f.

189. Ibid., p.218.

190. Idem, The Renaissance in India: It's Missionary Aspect, London, 1912, p.174.

191. Ibid., p.163.

192. Sadhu Sundar Singh (1889-1929) was born of Sikh parents in the state of Patiala. Inspite of his original aversion to Christianity he was converted and was baptized as an Anglican in 1905 and became a Christian Sadhu who laid great stress on the personal experience of union with Christ in the form of 'Bhakti'. For him the authority of the organized Church was inferior to that of personal God-experience for which only the Holy Bible is normative. He calls his path of God-realization 'Prema Marga', the path of personal love without identity of being in a monistic sense. He was also a great devotee of St. Francis of Assisi. He understood 'Karma' as the individual and personal sins; the notions of 'Samsara' and transmigration were not acceptable to him.

193. B.H. Streeter and A.J. Appasamy, The Sadhu, 1921, p.54.

194. F. Heiler, The Gospel of Sundhar Singh, 1927, p.162.

195. S.K. Rudra (1861-1925) was an acknowledged Christian leader and Indian nationalist of his time. Susil Kumar Rudra was also the principal of St. Stephen's College, Delhi, and a friend of C.F. Andrews and Mahatma Gandhi.

196. S.K. Rudra, The Christian Idea of Incarnation, Madras/London, 1911.

197. Ibid., pp.6f.

198. His idea of the 'Nirguna Brahman' is highly personal because the definition of person as 'subsistens distinctum in natura intellectuali' is eminently applicable to Brahman. 'Person' does not contain 'per se' the notions of imperfections and limitations we attribute to it!

199. R.V. de Smet, 'Materials for an Indian Christology', in: Religion and Society, 12 (1965), 4., p.7.

200. Cfr. above note no. 198.

201. Vengel Chakkarai (1880-1958) was a lawyer by profession and the brother-in-law of Pandipeddi Chenchiah. As a Hindu convert to Christianity he found it useful to apply Hindu categories to express the Christian faith. Unlike Chenchiah he maintained that Jesus Christ is 'the Avatar' of God. God for him is Nirguna Brahman and Jesus Christ, the Saguna Brahman or the manifested aspect of the one and the same God. He maintained that Christ is the Avatar of God and the Holy Spirit is the Avatar of Jesus Christ in human hearts. It is evident that his understanding of the Holy Trinity is modalistic!

202. Cfr. Robin Boyd, Op. Cit., p.167.

203. V. Chakkarai, Jesus the Avatar, 1927, p.210.

204. Ibid., pp.172, 173.

205. Ibid., p.40.

206. Ibid., pp.40, 41. Chakkarai bases his argument on Jesus' exclusive knowledge of God. In asserting that no one else had ever in history such a knowledge, he seems not to give sufficient attention to the claims of the Vedantic Jnanis!

207. Ibid., p.42.

208. Ibid. Chakkarai follows the Bhakti Marga and ignores the Vedantic claims of the experience of oneness with God.

209. Ibid., pp.48, 49.

210. Ibid., p.45.

211. Ibid., p.53.

212. Ibid., p.54. Jesus should be considered as the Lord of history not only in his eschatological appearence but yesterday, today and forever!

213. Ibid., p.208.

214. Ibid.

215. Ibid.

216. Ibid. This is clearly both a Vedantic and a Hegelian view point!

217. Ibid.

218. Ibid., p.209. In holding the equality of Jesus with God he follows a way of explaining Jesus Christ that is different from the views of Appasamy and P. Chenchiah.

219. Ibid., p.112.

220. Ibid.

221. Ibid., p.207. This view is similar to Chenchiah's evolutionary concept.

222. Ibid., pp.129, 130.

223. Ibid., p.207.

224. Ibid., pp.172, 173.

225. Ibid., pp.40, 41.

226. Robin Boyd, Op. Cit., p.185.

226a. Ibid., pp.180, 174.

227. V. Chakkarai, Jesus the Avatar, p.121. Here Chakkarai unfortunately repeats some of the trinitarian, Christological and pneumatolical errors of the first centuries.

228. Ibid., p.117.

229. Cfr. Ibid., pp.121, 114, 145, 205, 157, 220 etc. Cfr. also: Robin Boyd writes: '... we find a tendency in Indian theology to blur the distinction between the Persons of the Trinity... This tendency is clearest in Chakkarai.' p.242.

230. For an explanation of the concept of 'Maya' Cfr. out Part I, Ch. I, B, 4.

231. In an extreme monistic interpretation 'Maya' means illusion.

232. Robin Boyd, Op. Cit., p.74.

233. Brahmabandab Upadhayaya, 'The True Doctrine of Maya', in: Sophia, Febr March 1899.
Cfr. also Kaj Baago, Pioneers of Indigenous Christianity, Madras, 1969, See Selections, p.148.

234. B. Animananda, The Blade: Life and Works of Brahmabandab Upadhyaya, Roy and Sen, Calcutta 1947 (?), p.84. Sakti refers to the female aspect of God Siva as the personification of his creative power.

235. B. Upadhyaya, 'The True Doctrine of Maya', in: Sophia, Vol. VI, no.2, Febr. March 1899, pp.226f.
Cfr. also: Idem, 'Questions and Answers', in: Sophia, Vol. I, no.6, July 21, 1900, p.8.

Cfr. also: B. Animananda, Op. Cit., p.147.
Robin Boyd, Op. Cit., p.75. Antony Mookenthottam, Op. Cit., p.39.
K.P. Aleaz, Art. Cit., p.70.

236. Pierre Johanns (1882-1955) was born in Luxemburg and came to India
in 1921 and worked as the Professor of Philosophy in St. Xavier's,
Calcutta. Through the periodical 'Light of the East' he tried to make
a Christian synthesis of the philosophies of Sankara and Ramanuja.
Through the Vedanta, he maintained the Hindus could reach Christ,
who is the fulfilment of the Vedantic ideals. He was a Jesuit.

237. P. Johanns, A synopsis of 'To Christ Through the Vedanta', Parts I-
III, Ranchi, 1930-32, Part IV (no date).

238. Idem, Light of the East, V (1927) 5, p.6. Cfr. also: Joseph Mattam,
'Interpreting Christ to India Today: The Calcutta School', in: Indian
Journal of Theology, 23 (1974), p.200.

239. The School of Ramanuja does not accept the identity of the Bhakta
with the Brahman, but every being is essentially divine as part of Brahman, as his 'body'. Cfr. our Part I, Ch. I, B, 4.

240. B. Upadhyaya, 'The True Doctrine of maya', p.228. According to the
Vedantic understanding there cannot be Maya in the liberated state.

241. B. Upadhyaya, 'Questions and Answers', in: Sophia, Vol. I, No. 9, Aug.
11, 1900, p.7.
Cfr. also Sophia Vol. IV, No. 2, Febr., 1897, p.4.

242. Idem, 'Vedantism and Christianity', in: Sophia, Vol. I, nn. 15 & 16,
Sept. 29, 1900, p.6. The scholastic defn. of 'Creation' is: 'Productio
rei ex nihilo sui et subjecti'. It is neither emanation, nor a re-formation
of what already exists in another way.

243. Alfons Väth, Im Kampf mit der Zauberwelt des Hinduismus, Berlin/Bonn,
SS.216 etc.

244. R. Boyd, Op. Cit., p.77.

245. Ibid.

246. R.V. De Smet, 'Materials for an Indian Christology', in: Religion and
Society, 12 (1965) 4, pp.7-13.

247. Ibid., p.10.

248. Ibid.

249. This identification is justifiable, but it needs clarification. Actually
the notions of 'nature', 'substance' and 'essence' view the reality from
different points of view. Nature could be considered in our context
in reference to person, substance in reference to accidents and essence
in reference to existence. While Act and Potency consider Being in
its functional constitutions, Essence and Existence stand, according
to the scholastic frame of thinking, for the real constitution of Being.

250. R.V. De Smet, Art. Cit., p.10.

251. Ibid.

252. Cfr. the Supplement to the Article of De Smet written by Prof.Dr. Paul Hacker. Art. Cit., pp.13-15.

253. Joseph Mattam, 'Interpreting Christ to India Today', p.205. Mattam is of the opinion that a certain freedom of thought patterns or categories is necessary to interpret the Christ-mystery in varying cultural contexts.

254. V. Chakkarai, Jesus the Avatar, p.3!.

255. Ibid., p.30.

256. Ibid., pp.30, 31.

257. Here Chakkarai's approach could be compared and contrasted with the ascending method of Karl Rahner which is philosophico-anthropological.

258. Chakkarai, Op. Cit., p.125.

259. Ibid., p.154.

260. Ibid., p.77.

261. Here 'Purusha' refers to the purusha of the Vedic hymn of creation. Cfr. Part I, Ch. II, A. Cfr. also Rgveda 10.90.1-14.

262. The academic background of V. Chakkarai is not that of a professional philosopher. He was a lawyer and a trade union leader.

263. V. Chakkarai, Op. Cit., p.74.

264. Ibid., p.33.

265. Ibid.

266. Ibid., p.218. Cfr. also: Below Ch. VI. Foot note no. 125. Cfr. also: Robin Boyd, Op. Cit., pp.171, 172.

268. Cfr. DS. 301, 302.

269. 'Hari' literally means pale yellow or red. Hari is the personification of the Sun-god.

270. In the Avatar theory a trinitarian God is not presupposed. Avatar is the manifestation of 'Vishnu' who is just another aspect of God.

271. Robin Boyd, Op. Cit., p.79.

272. The Twentieth Century, 1901, pp.7-8. For C.F. Andrews translation cfr. The Renaissance in India, 1912, Appendix 8. For Kaj Baago's translation. Op. Cit. p.43 (Pioneers).

273. The refrain 'Jai' can mean victory, glory. 'Glory' seems to be better suited here. The change is personal. The usual translation is 'victory'.

274. Both R. Panikkar and V. Chakkarai consider the Vedantic 'Saguna Brahman' as the Johannine 'Word' (Logos). Cfr. Part I, Ch. II, A, 1. Cfr. also Foot notes 28-31.

275. The theory of 'Kosa' is properly found in the Taittiriya Upanisad 2 & 3. But the term 'Kosa' is not used there. We find it in the Mundaka Upanisad. Taittiriya Up. uses the categories of 'Atman' and 'Purusa '; Atman stands for what is meant by Kosa. The last Kosa (Ananda) is variously understood so as to mean the ultimate reality of man or as the ultimate Kosa within which the innermost reality of man is situated. The latter approach is more common and that is also followed by Upadhyaya. Cfr. also: G. Gispert-Sauch, Course on the Indian Religious Texts, Kurseong, 1968-69, p.14. For Sankara's interpretation of the five Kosas cfr. Taittiriya Up. Bhasya, 2, 2,1. Cfr. also: above Ch. II, A, 1.

276. B. Upadhyaya, 'Incarnate Logos', in: The Twentieth Century, Vol. I, no. 1, Jan. 1901, p.7 (also 6-8). Cfr. also 'Notes' in: Sophia, Vol. I, no. 4, July 7, 1900, pp.6-7.
Cfr. also: K.P. Aleaz, Art. Cit., pp.72, 73. Joseph Mattam, Art. p.196. Robin Boyd, Op. Cit., pp.79, 80.
Heinrich Barlage, Christ - Saviour of Mankind: A Christian Appreciation of Swami Akhilananda, St. Augustin bei Bonn, 1977, p.210.
M.M. Thomas, Op. Cit., pp.105, 106.
Kaj Baago, Op. Cit., pp.130, 140.

277. B. Upadhyaya, Art. Cit., Ibid.

278. Ibid.

279. Attention on this question could be drawn to a previous work of mine: Brown's Biblical Approach to Christology, Pontifical Gregorian University, Ro me 1980 (unpublished), Parts I and III.

280. Robin Boyd, Op. Cit., p.80.

281. Regarding the problems involved in a Chalcedonian and non-Chalcedonian Christology, Cfr. Karl Rahner, 'Chalkedon - Ende oder Anfang?', Schriften zur Theologie, Bd. I, Einsiedeln/Zürich/Köln, 1964, SS.169-222. Cfr. also: Grillmeier/Bacht (Hrg.) Das Konzil von Chalkedon, Bd. III, Würzburg, 1954, SS.3-49.

282. Fr. R. Antoine is a Belgian Jesuit born in 1914. Since 1950 he is an Indian citizen. Sanskrit and Indian Classics belong to his main fields of interest.

283. Tait. Up., 2 and 3. According to Upadhyaya the real person is even beyond the fifth Kosa. Cfr. Foot note no. 275.

284. Quoted in Joseph Mattam, 'Interpreting Christ to India Today', p.196.

285. R.V. De Smet, 'Materials for an Indian Christology', in: Religion and Society, 12 (1965), 4, p.13.

286. Ibid., p.11.

287. Ibid. This change is called 'Vivarta', i.e. 'an effectuation through which absolutely nothing new happens to the cause and the whole novelty is on the side of the effect'. Ibid., p.11.

288. Ibid., p.11.

289. Ibid., p.12.

290. Dr. Paul Hacker suggests that 'aikya' or 'ekatva' is better than 'tadatmya'. Cfr. R.V. De Smet, Art. Cit., p.14. This union is not 'Sayujya' (conjunction), nor 'Samanarupata' (mutual conformation as between two persons). 'Satmata' (sharing of a single atman) is good if it implies a personal 'tadatmya'. Cfr. Satapatabrahmana 11,5,6,9.

291. R.V. De Smet, Art. Cit., p.12.

292. The notion of 'Being' is very similar both in Sankara and Thomas Aquinas. What Sankara does by the notion of Maya is done by Thomas by the notion of the Analogy of Being.

293. Cfr. Sastri, A.M., The Bhagavad-Gita with the Commentary of Sri Sankaracharya. 5th Ed., 1961, p.121.

343. E.G. Parrinder, Avatar and Incarnation, London, 1970.

344. Parrinders concern and method are those of comparative religion. So he refers also to the belief in Avatars in other religions than Hinduism.Our concern, however, is restricted to Christ from an anthropological point of view.

345. Fr. Josef Neuner is an Austrian born in 1908. Since 1938 he is in India mainly as the Professor Dogmatic Theology in the Pontificial Athenaeum, Poona. As a 'Peritus' he attended the Second Vatican Council. By his writings he has contributed very much to the Hindu-Christian dialogue on the theological level.

346. J. Neuner, 'Avatara Doctrine and the Christ Mysterium', in: Man and Religion, München, 1964, pp.27,28.
Cfr. also: Joseph Neuner, 'Das Christus-Mysterium und die indische Lehre von den Avataras', in: A. Grillmeier/Bacht (Hrg.), Das Konzil von Chalkedon, Geschichte und Gegenwart, Bd. III, Würzburg, 1954, SS.785-824.

347. J. Neuner, 'Avatara Doctrine and the Christ Mysterium', o.27,28. Cfr. also Bhagavata Purana 10.2.17. Krishna was first present in the 'Spirit' of his parents!

348. J. Neuner, Art. Cit., p.27. Neuner refers also to the 'radical omission of human elements from the Avatar' which is docetic. Further on this question in the following section.

349. Bhagavadgita 4,7. It refers also to the destruction of the evil ones, which constitutes an important difference between Avatar and Christ's Incarnation.

350. Cfr. Part I, Ch.III.C. Cfr. also: Samuel Rayan, 'Interpreting Christ to India: The Contribution of Roman Catholic Seminaries', in: Indian Journal of Theology, 23 (1974), pp.225,226.

351. G. Parrinder, Op. Cit., pp.120f., 224f.

352. That is according to Bhagavadgita. Cfr. also the Hindu notion of history in Part I,Ch.II,C. The four Yugas are taken together as one Yuga in the view of Bhagavadgita. The question regarding the repetition of Avatars is not uniformly considered in different literatures.

353. G. Parrinder, Op. Cit., p.120 etc. Cfr. also: Samuel Rayan, Art. Cit., pp.225,226.

354. But it is to be kept in mind that the different types of Christ's presence is radically different from the repeated manifestations of Avatars!

355. Cfr. G. Parrinder, Loc. Cit., Cfr. also Part I.Ch.III.C.

356. G. Parrinder, Op. Cit., pp.120f.

357. Cfr. the Introduction to Part I.

357a. Rammohan Roy rejects all beliefs in Avatars as mere superstitions. K.C. Sen sees the Hindu belief in Avatars as a 'crude representation' of the cosmic evolution that reaches its climax in Christ. For him also the term 'Avatar' is not applicable to Christ. He calls it 'the lie of Avatarism'. Cfr. Foot note no.75 and no.134. P.C. Mozoomdar considers Christ as the perfect Avatar of God, but not as God!

358. Robin Boyd, Khristadvaita, A Theology for India, Madras, 1977.

359. Ibid., pp.145ff.

360. J. Neuner, Cfr. Foot note above no.346.

361. G. Parrinder, Op. Cit., pp.120ff., Cfr. also: Samuel Rayan, Art. Cit., p.225.

362. Raimundo Panikkar, 'Confrontation between Hinduism and Christ', in: New Blackfriars, Vol 50, no.584, Jan. 1969, p.200.

363. Ibid.

364. Robin Boyd, Indian Christian Theology, p.128. Cfr. also: A.J. Appasamy, The Gospel and India's Heritage, London/Madras, 1942, p.62.

365. H. Zimmer, Philosophies of India, New York, 1961, p.390.

366. J. Neuner, Art. Cit. cited in Samuel Rayan Art. Cit., p.225. Krishna became the victim of the hunter called 'Jara' (old age) and Rama takes leave from this world by crossing a river. In both stories the reality of death is not emphasized as in the case of Jesus Christ!

367. J. Neuner, Art. Cit., in:Man and Religion, p.30.

368. Ibid.

369. Ibid., p.29.

370. L. Harold De Wolf. Opinion taken from H. Barlage, Op. Cit., p.81.

371. For the Vedantic concept of History Cfr. Part I.Ch.II.C.

372. A.J. Appasamy, The Gospel and India's Heritage, p.259.

373. V. Chakkarai, Jesus the Avatar, 1926, 1930.
     Cfr. also: G. Parrinder, Op. Cit., p.227.

374. Robin Boyd, Indian Christian Theology, p.171.
     V. Chakkarai, Jesus the Avatar, 1926, p.133.

375. V. Chakkarai, Jesus the Avatar, 1930, p.136.

376. Bhagavadgita 4.7.

377. The role of the Son is not to condemn but to save! The story of the
     prodigal son is an example of God's pardoning love.

378. G. Parrinder, Op. Cit., p.235.

379. Ibid.

380. J. Neuner, 'Avatara Doctrine and the Christ Mysterium', p.29. The
     term 'Purusha' could be translated as person, but its connotations are
     different from those which are implied in 'person'. Purusha is the counter
     notion of Prakrti (material nature).

381. Ibid., p.27.

382. Ibid.

383. Sen's Lectures, II, p.38. Cfr. also Foot note 357a.

384. Robin Boyd, Indian Christian Theology, p.81 and Joseph Mattam, 'Inter-
     preting Christ to India', p.196.

385. Cfr. D.A. Thangasamy, The Theology of Chenchiah, Bangalore, 1966,
     pp.79, 123, 124, 171.

386. The 'Jnana Marga' is strictly speaking indifferent to the belief in the
     Avatars. Cfr. Klaus Klostermaier, Hindu and Christian in the Vrindaban,
     London, 1969, p.115.

387. Robin Boyd, Op. Cit., pp.127, 128.

388. John Nocol Farquhar (1861-1929) was born in England and went to India
     as a member of the London Missionary Society. He considers the Christ-
     mystery as the 'Crown of Hinduism', but his approach to Hinduism was
     rather polemic!

389. J.N. Farquhar, Permanent Lessons of the Gita, 1912, p.31. Cfr. also: E.J. Sharpe, Not to Destroy but to Fulfil, 1965, p.200. Cfr. also Parrinder, Op. Cit., p.236.

390. Cfr. Part I.Ch.III.C.2.

391. Cfr. Part I.Ch.II.C.

392. S.J. Samartha was born in Karkal, India, in 1920. He worked for a time as the principal of Serampore College, W. Bengal. His theological efforts are directed towards promoting Hindu-Christian dialogue on the basis of the Advaita, however not missing the historical anchorage of the Christ-event. His 'The Hindu Response to the Unbound Christ' is a concrete example of concern for intra-religious dialogue. The German translation: Hindus vor dem universalen Christus - Beiträge zu einer Christologie in Indien, Stuttgart, 1970.

393. Idem, The Hindu Response to the Unbound Christ, Madras, 1974.

394. Ibid., p.154.

395. A. Schweitzer, The Quest for the Historical Jesus, 1910.

396. E. Käsemann, Das Problem des historischen Jesus, 1954. Cfr. also: Essays on New Testament Themes, London, 1964.

397. D.M. Baillie, God was in Christ, New York, 1948, p.28. Cfr. also: E.Fuchs, Studies of the Historical Jesus, London, 1964. G. Bornkamm, Jesus of Nazareth, London, 1960. C.E. Bratten and R.A. Harrisville (Ed.), The Historical Jesus and the Kerygmatic Christ, New Yor, 1964.
Rene Latourelle, Finding Jesus through the Gospels, History and Hermeneutics, tr. by Aloysius Owen, New York, 1978. It gives also a very vast bibliography.

398. Person translation from: Rudolf Bultmann, Jesus Christus und die Mythologie - Das Neue Testament im Licht der Bibelkritik, Gütersloh, 1980, p.17. 'Mythen sind Ausdruck für die Einsicht, daß der Mensch nicht Herr der Welt und seines Lebens ist, daß die Welt, in der er lebt, voller Rätsel und Geheimnisse steckt, und daß auch das Menschenleben eine Fülle von Rätseln udn Geheimnissen birgt. Die Mythologie ist der Ausdruck eines bestimmten Verständnisses der menschlichen Existenz. Sie glaubt, daß die Welt und das Leben ihren Grund und ihre Grenzen in einer Macht haben, die außerhalb all dessen ist, was wir berechnen und kontrollieren können. (...) Man kann sagen, Mythen geben der transzendenten Wirklichkeit eine immanente weltliche Objektivität. Der Mythos objektiviert das Jenseitige zum Diesseitigen.'

399. S.J. Samartha, The Hindu Response to the Unbound Christ, p.156. Cfr. also Idem, The Hindu View of History, Bangalore, 1959.

400. Alfred North Withehead, Process and Reality, 1929. For a vast Bibliography Cfr. John B. Cobb, Jr., David Ray Griffin, Process Theology - an Introductory Exposition, Philadelphia, 1976, pp.162ff.

401. For Bibliography cfr. Cobb and Griffin, Op. Cit., pp.167ff.

402. John B. Bobb, Jr., David Ray Griffin, Process Theology - an Introductory Exposition, Philadelphia, 1976.

404. These 'instances' are the 'micro events' called 'actual entities' in Process Theology.

405. S.J. Samartha, Unbound Christ, p.157.

406. Ibid., p.161. Cfr. also James Robinson and John B. Cobb (Ed.), The Later Heidegger and Theology, New York, 1963, Ch.4: 'Theology as Ontology and History', p.151.

407. S.J. Samartha, Op. Cit., p.162.

408. J.Neuner, 'Avatara Doctrine and the Christ Mysterium', p.31.

409. S.J. Samartha, Op. Cit., p.188.

410. J. Neuner, Art. Cit., p.31.

412. '... Farquhar is surprisingly unsympathetic to Hinduism. He does not, for example, attempt to show how a Hindu conception like Avatara can be of use in an Indian exposition of the Christian faith; rather he points out how inferior the Hindu Avatara is to the Christian understanding of Christ's incarnation.' Robin Boyd, Indian Christian Theology, p.284.

413. Taken from Eric J. Sharpe, Not to Destroy but to Fulfil - The Contribution of J.N. Farquhar to Protestant Missionary Thought in India before 1914, 1965, p.311.

414. J.N. Farquhar, The Crown of Hinduism, Oxford, 1915, p.458.

415. R.C. Das, Convictions of an Indian Disciple, Bangalore, 1966, p.9.

416. Sen's Lectures I, pp.388-9.

417. P.C. Mozoomdar, The Spirit of God, Boston, 1894, pp.246-249 (passim). (Underline mine).

418. William Theodore de Bary (Ed.), Sources of Indian Tradition, London/New York, 1958, p.735.

419. P. Johanns, 'To Christ through the Vedanta', Articles in: Light of the East.

420. Idem, A Synopsis to 'To Christ through the Vedanta', Part I, Sankara, Introduction.

421. Idem, The Light of the East, IV (1925), 1, pp.1-2.

422. Idem, 'To Christ through the Vedanta', in: Light of the East, VIII, (June 1930), 9, p.6.
Cfr. also: Heinrich Barlage, Op. Cit., p. 178.
Joseph Mattam, Land of the Trinity - Modern Christian Approaches to Hinduism, Bangalore, 1975, Ch.I., pp.17-43. Idem 'Interpreting Christ ot India Today', p.199.

423. B.H. Streeter and A.J. Appasamy, The Sadhu, 1921, p.232.

424. Paul Sudhakar: Quoted from Robin Boyd, Op. Cit., p.217.

425. Swami Abhishiktananda, Hindu-Christian Meeting Point within the Cave of the Heart, Bombay, 1969, pp.23-25.

426. Ibid., p.92.

427. Ibid., p.89. In stressing the continuity between the Upanishads and Christ Abhishiktananda seems to ignore that there is also an element of break between the Vedanta and Christ. Christ does not only fulfil but also destroy what cannot be fulfilled because of human distortions!

428. Bede Griffith, Christian Ashram, London, 1966, pp.63-65.

429. Cfr. below Chapter VI.C. on 'Christ-Experience'.

430. Nehemiah Goreh, Proofs of the Divinity of Our Lord, 1887, p.76. Quoted from Robin Boyd, Op. Cit., pp.55,56.

431. R.C. Zaehner, At Sundry Times: an Essay in the Comparison of Religions, London, 1958, p.188.

432. V. Chakkarai, Jesus the Avatar, p.2.

433. P.C. Mozoomdar, The Spirit of God, Boston, 1894, pp.239ff., Cfr. also: The Oriental Christ, Boston, 1883, pp.40-46.

434. N. Goreh, On Objections against the Catholic Doctrine of Eternal Punishmen, Calcutta, 1868, p.81.

435. J. Neuner, 'Avatar Doctrine', p.32.

436. Ibid.

437. Ibid.

438. Quoted from: Samuel Rayan, 'Interpreting Christ to India', p.224.

439. J.N. Farquhar, The Crown of Hinduism, pp.425, 433.

440. Ibid., p.350.

441. The Mystery of the Holy Eucharist could also be given a similar interpretation in the background of the idol worship on the popular level.

442. J. Neuner, Art. Cit. in: Das Konzil von Chalkedon, (Op. Cit.), SS.792-794.

443. Idem, 'Avatara Doctrine', p.33.

444. D.S. Sarma, The Renaissance of Hinduism, Benares, 1944, p.304.

445. P.T. Thomas, The Theology of Chakkarai with Selections from His Writings, Bangalore, 1968, p.123.

446. A.G. Hog maintains that 'whar Christ directly fulfils is not Hinduism but the need of which India has begun to be conscious'. Cfr. Eric J. Sharpe, The Theology of A.G. Hog, Madras, 1971, p.50.

447. James Dupuis, 'The Salvific Value of non-Christian Religions', in: Service and Salvation, ed. by J. Pathrapankal, Bangalore, 1973, pp.209-214. I would maintain that any 'Christian' approach to Christ should be in the line of fulfilment and not merely as 'universal presence' as the Vedantins hold. But the nature of fulfilment could be subject to discussion. It could be asked whether only the Hindu religious aspirations have a salvific role or even Hinduism itself as a religion could contribute in one or another way to the salvation of millions of Hindus. For details on this question cfr. below Chapter VI.B.4.

448. S.J. Samartha, The Hindu Response to the Unbound Christ, p.138.

449. Ibid.

450. Soteriology is in reality not the end of Christology but its beginning. This does not mean that the 'beginning' could not be treated at the end for methodological reasons.

CHAPTER VI

1. Duraisamy Simon Amalorpavadass (*1932) was for a long time the 'main spring' of the National Biblical Catechetical and Liturgical Centre, Bangalore (India). He has made great contributions towards the Indianization of Liturgy and the conscientization of the Indian Clergy, Sisters of religious congregations and the Laity in promoting Indian Spirituality and catechetical and missionary efforts through his regular Seminars in the NBCLC. At present he teaches in the University of Mysore.

2. D.S. Amalorpavadass, The Theology of Indirect Evangelization, Bangalore, 1969, p.18.

3. Cfr. Chapter V above C.2 and 3.

4. S.J. Samartha, The Hindu Response to the Unbound Christ, 1974, p.184.

5. Witness of Jesus' ministry was a criterion for anyone to belong to the group of the Apostles.

6. P.D. Devanandan, Preparation for Dialogue, Bangalore, 1964, pp.137ff.

7. Cfr. DS. 1529.

8. Cfr. back to Part I.Ch.III.B.3. (Bhakti Margha).

9. Cfr. back to the explanation given to the concept of 'Guru' in Part I,Ch.III.A.3.b.

10. Manilal C. Parekh, A Hindu's Portrait of Jesus Christ, Rajkot, 1953, p.246.

11. Ibid., p.247.

12. M.K. Gandhi, The Message of Jesus Christ, Bombay, 1940, p.19.

13. Quoted from M.M. Thomas, The Acknowledged Christ of the Indian Renaissance, London, 1969, p.198.

14. M.K. Gandhi, Christian Missions, Ahmedabad, 19409, p.28. It must be said that the approach of Hindu leaders, including Mahatma Gandhi, to the Christian Sacred Scriptures has been very selective. They take what agrees with their vision of religion and ignore everything else. An objective approach to any religion requires that it is taken in its entirety!

15. Swami Prabhavananda, The Sermon on the Mount according to Vedanta, California, 1971, xi.

16. D.S. Ramachandra Rao, 'The New Testament', in: The Great Scriptures, ed. by T.M. Mahadevan, Madras, 1956, p.127.

17. M.K. Gandhi, The Message of Jesus Christ, p.35. Cfr. also: Young India, December 31, 1931.

19. Sophia Dobson Collet, The Life and Letters of Raja Rammohan Roy, London, 1900, p.41.

20. Rammohan Roy, The Precepts of Jesus:The Guide to Peace and Happiness, Baptist Mission Press, Calcutta, 1820. (The Raja made also a translation of it into Sanskrit and Bengali).

21. English Works of Raja Rammohan Roy (Collection), Allahabad, 1906, pp.484,485.

22. English Works of Raja Rammohan Roy, Part IV, Calcutta, 1947, p.44. Cfr. also: Ray's letter written to Mr. John Digby in 1815. Quoted by J.N. Farquhar, Modern Religious Movements in India, 1918, p.32. Cfr. also: Manilal C. Parekh, Rajarshi Ram Mohan Roy, Rajkot, 1927, p.34.

24. Later dated 18.1.1828. Quoted by Sophia Dobson Collet, The Life and Letters of Raja Rammohan Roy, London, 1900, p.124. Cfr. also: S.J. Samartha, Op. Cit., p.31.

25. M.M. Thomas, Op. Cit., p.10.

26. Rammohan Roy, Second Appeal, in: English Works of Rammohan Roy, 1906, p.615. This position is not accepted either by the Indian Vedantic thinkers nor by Mahatma Gandhi. In accepting the moral uniqueness and pre-eminence of Jesus Christ Rammohan Roy is followed by other Hindu reformers like K.C. Sen, P.C. Mozoomdar and others.

27. Friend of India, No. XX, Febr. 1820. Quoted from S.J. Samartha, Op. Cit., pp.27,28.

28. Cfr. M.M. Thomas, Op. Cit., pp.15ff. Cfr. also: S.C. Collet, Op. Cit., pp.36-61.

29. Rammohan Roy, An Appeal to the Christian Public in Defence of the 'Precepts of Jesus' by a Friend of Truth, 1820. This 'appeal' was followed by a 'Second Appeal' (1821) and a 'Final Appeal' (1824).
In the first appeal Roy wrote: 'Before, however, I attempt to enquire into the ground upon which their attempt to enquire into the ground upon which their objections to the work in question are founded, I humbly beg to appeal to the public against the unchristianlike as well as uncivil manner in which the editor has adduced his objections to the compilation, by introducing personality, and applying the term heathen to the Compiler. I say unchristianlike manner, because, the Editor, by making use of the term heathen, has, I presume, violated truth, charity and liberality which are essential to Christianity in every sense of the term.' cfr. In: English Works of Rammohan Roy, 1906, p.547.

30. Ibid.

31. P.C. Mozoomdar, The Spirit of God, Boston, 1894, p.253.

32. M.K. Gandhi, The Message of Jesus Christ, p.35.

33. Idem, Christian Missions, p.35.

34. Idem, The Law of Love, Ed. by Anand T. Hirigorami, Bombay, 1962, p.27.

35. C.F. Andrews, Mahatma Gandhi's Ideas, London, 1929, p.34.

36. M.K. Gandhi, My Experiments with Truth, London, 1945, p.404.

37. Young India, Nov. 4, 1926.

38. Harijan, October 8, 1938.

39. Harijan, March 14, 1936.

40. Idem, The Message of Jesus Christ, p.79. 'Ahimsa' or non-violence for Gandhi is another aspect of the universal law of Love taught by Christ.

41. Ibid., Preface.

42. Ibid., p.7.

43. Ibid., p.140. The miracles performed by Jesus during his ministry are not of much novelty to the Hindus who believe that by Yogic practices hidden powers could be released in order to do something that is beyond the possibilities of ordinary human beings. The Hindus have no hesitation to accept the miraculous aspect of Christ's life; that does not say anything unique in him. Cfr. also: V. Chakkarai, Jesus the Avatar, Ch.VII, pp.92ff.

44. Mahadeva Desai, Gandhiji in Ceylon, Madras, p.143. Cfr. also: S.J. Samartha, Op. Cit., p.88.

45. M.K. Gandhi, 'What Jesus Means to Me', in: The Modern Review, 1941. Quoted from Op. Cit., p.94.

46. Cfr. back to Gandhiji's remark on the divinity of Jesus Christ in Ch.V.

47. S.J. Samartha, Op. Cit., p.94.

48. S. Radhakrishnan (Ed.), Mahatma Gandhi: Essays and Reflections, London, 1939, p.14.

49. E. Stanley James, Mahatma Gandhi: An Interpretation, London, 1948, pp.80f.

50. S.J. Samartha, Op. Cit., p.95.

51. Vinoba Bhave, Prem Morrthi Eesa (Christ the Love Incarnate) as reported in: The Indian Express, Sunday, Nov. 29, 1064. Quoted from S.J. Samartha, Op. Cit., p.6.
Cfr. also: E. Stanley Jones, Op. Cit., pp.11f:
'Gandhi taught me the spirit of Christ than perhaps any other man in East and West'. Cfr. also Ibid., pp.76, 79, 85.

51a. Quoted from: C.F. Andrews, 'The Hindu View of Christ', in: International Review of Missions, 28 (1939), p.260.

51b. Marshman, The Advantages of Christianity in Promoting the Establishment and Prosperitiy of the British Empire in India, 1813. Cfr. also: S.J. Samartha, Op. Cit., p.24.

51c. M.C. Parekh, A Hindu's Portrait of Jesus Christ, Rajkot, 1953, p.281.

51d. Quoted from: C.F. Andrews, Art. Cit., p.261.

52. Cfr. Ch.IV.A.2.c.

53. Vivekananda, Complete works, 5th Ed. Almora, 1931, Vol. IV, p.143.

54. Ibid., p.145.

55. Here it is important to keep in mind the Vedantic understanding of the question of Sin and Evil in the world. Cfr. Part I.Ch.II.B.1.

56. Vivekananda, Complete Works, VII, p.2.

57. Idem, Complete Works, IV, p.144.

58. S. Radhakrishnan, Eastern Religions and Western Thought, London, 1939, pp.222f.

59. Cfr. Robin Boyd, Op. Cit., p.62.

60. Sri Parananda, The Gospel of Jesus according to St. Mathew, as Interpreted to R.L. Harrison by the Light of the Godly Experience of Sri Parananda, 1898. Quoted from Robin Boyd, Op. Cit., p.62.

61. Swami Prabhavananda, The Sermon on the Mount according to Vedanta, p.18.

62. Ibid., p.85.

63. Swami Akhilananda, Hindu View of Christ, boston, 1971, p.55.

64. Ibid., pp.70, 18 etc.

65. Ibid., pp.23, 24, 196 (Edition of 1948).

66. Idem, Hindu View of Christ, Boston, 1948, p.28.

67. Ibid., p.32.

68. Ibid., p.26. True to his Vedantic traditions Swami Akhilananda stresses here the role of God-experience in human life. But to reduce the role of Jesus Christ merely to that of a promoter of God-experience does not do justice to the Christian faith in Jesus as the Saviour of mankind.

69. Swami Satprakashananda, Hinduism and Christianity, St. Louis, 1975, p.38.

70. Ibid., p.43.

71. Ibid., p.43.

72. Ibid., p.40. In the strict Vedantic each man is his own saviour!

73. J.B. Chethimattam (Ed.) Unique and Universal, Bangalore (India), p.186.

74. Ibid., p.189.

75. Ibid., pp.188, 189. For the Vedantic understanding of 'Guru' cfr. above Part I.Ch.III.A.3.b.

76. A.J. Appasamy, The Gospel and India's Heritage, p.97. In Hinduism the problem of getting liberated from 'Karma' is far more important than the problem of getting rid of sin!

77. Cfr. above Part I.Ch.II.B.

78. The school of Sankaracharya would hold 'Atmasaksatkara' which is the same as 'Brahmasaksatkara' as the final goal of human existence while the followers of Ramanuja see it as the 'Isvarasaksatkara', the realization of the personal God! For details on this topic cfr. above Part I.Ch.III.A.".

79. It must be said that eventhough in theory, according to pure Advaita, there cannot be sin, but only 'Avidhya', 'Kama' and 'Karma', the consciousness of sin on the practical level is very strong in Hinduism especially in the Bhakti tradition. For details cfr. back: Part I.Ch.II.B.1.

80. Nalini Devdas, Swami Vivekananda, Bangalore, 1968, pp.161ff.

81. Quoted from Robin Boyd, Op. Cit., p.61.

82. Nalini Devdas, Sri Ramakrishna, Bangalore, 1965, p.62.

83. Our explanation in the First Part regarding this point is to be kept in mind. 'I am Brahman' does not mean that Brahman can be reduced to me! Cfr. Part I.Ch.II.A.

84. Swami Nikhilananda, The Gospel of Ramakrishna, New York, 1942, p.511.

85. Swami Prabhavananda, The Sermon on the Mount according to Vedanta, pp.94, 95.

86. Ibid., p.97.

87. Cfr. E. Wood, Vedanta Dictionary, New York, 1964, p.175.

88. Ibid., p.238.

89. Vivekananda, Complete Works, 5th Ed., Almora, 1931, Vol. II, pp.130, 168, 1870, 182.

90. Sen's Lectures II, p.366.

91. Ibid., p.362. The gravity of sin in the Christian understanding can be understood only when it is viewed from the radicality of God's love manifested in Jesus Christ. This point seems to be absent in Sen's approach!

92. Ibid., p.368.

93. Ibid., p.367.

94. Ibid., pp.366ff. The question of 'original sin' is, however, not to be confused with that of 'actual sin' for which each individual is personally responsible. Original sin is sin only analogically. Further on this question in chapter VII.

95. M.C. Parekh, A Hindu's Portrait of Jesus Christ, pp.134, 135.

96. Ibid., p.135.

98. P. Chenchiah, Rethinking Christianity, p.165.

99. M.C. Parekh, Brahmarshi Sen, p. 172.
Cfr. also: M.M. Thomas, Op. Cit., p.66.

100. B. Upadhayay, 'Christ's Claim to Attention', p.116.
Cfr. also: 'Questions and Answers', in: Sophia, Vol. I, No.4, July 7, 1900, p.9 and No. 6, July 21, p.8.

102. P.D. Devanandan, Preparation for Dialogue, 1964, p.167.

104. Robin Boyd, Op. Cit., p.309.

105. F. Heiler, The Gospel of Sundar Singh, 1927, p.164.

107. Cfr. back to Part I.Ch.I.A.2 and 3.

111. Iranaeus is against a dualistic separation of the order of creation and salvation in God's redemptive plan. The unity of divinity and humanity in Jesus Christ proves this position. For the theory of 'Recapitulation' (Anakephalaiosis) cfr.: E. Scharl, Recapitulatio mundi. Der Rekapitulationsbegriff des hl. Irenäus, Freiburg i.Br., 1941.

H. Schlier,(kephale), in: Th WNT, III, 673-682;
W. Staerk, 'Anakephalaiosis', in: RAC I, 411-414;
R. Haubst, 'Anakephalaiosis', in: LThK I, 466f.
Cfr. Iranaeus Adv. haer. II, 28, 1 (SC 294, 268-272); IV,9,1; 20,4 (SC 100/2, 476-481; 634-637).
God became man in order that man may be raised to God's sonship:
Cfr. Iranaeus Adv. haer. III,19,2; 20,2 (SC 211,374-379; 388-393); IV,20,4 (SC 100/2, 634-637); V,16,2 (SC 153, 216f).
The same God is the God of creation and salvation:
Cfr. Iranaeus Adv. haer. II,28,1 (SC 294, 268-271); IV,9,1; 20,4 (SC 100/2, 476-481; 634-637).

112. Gregory of Nyssa maintains that God's self-degradation to the level of creation (in order to re-capitulate it in himself) could be done through an overflow of his power, although this was in one sense not according to his nature! Cfr. Gregory of Nyssa, Oratio catechetica magna 24, 1 (PG 45, 64f.).

114. Cfr. back Part II.Ch.V.A.2.

115. Sen's Lectures, II.p.90.

116. Ibid., p.36.

117. Ibid., p.20. (Underline mine).

118. Ibid., p.90.

119. Ibid., (Underline mine).

120. V. Chakkarai, Jesus the Avatar, p.212.

121. Ibid., pp.211, 212.

123. Ibid., p.220.

124. Ibid.

125. Ibid., pp.218, 219. Here Chakkarai stresses that the specifically Christian understanding of God is inseparably connected with the fact of Jesus Christ. It is Jesus Christ who brings us the real 'Jnana' or knowledge of God. It implies that the Vedantic presumption to know God (cfr. Jnana Marga) all by oneself is not acceptable from the Christian standpoint.

126. P. Chenchiah, Rethinking Christianity, p.161.

127. P. Chenchiah, V. Chakkarai and A.N. Sudarisanam (Ed.), Asramas Past and Present, Madras, 1941, p.313.

128. P. Chenchiah, Rethinking Christianity, p.56.

129. Ibid., Appendix pp. 35f. (Underline mine).

130. Ibid., p.59.

131. P.D. Devanandan, I will lift up mine eyes unto the Hills: Sermon and Bible Studies, Edited by S.J. Samartha and Nalini Devanandan, Bangalore, 1963, p.69.

132. P.D. Devanandan, Christian Issues in Southern Asia, New York, 1963, pp.136, 137.

133. D.S. Amalorpavadass, Destinée de l'Eglise dans l'Inde d'aujourd'hui. Conditionnements de l'évangélisation, Fayard-Mame, 1967, pp.258, 259. English translation taken from: Antony Mookenthottam, Op. Cit., p.91.

134. D.A. Thangasamy, The Theology of Chenchiah, p.13.

135. Suffering is meaningless if it is considered from the point of view of 'Karma'. In the Christian vision it is love that makes suffering meaningful: Suffering for the sake of love!

136. In the Vedantic frame of thinking matter is evil, it is a factor that enslaves the true and inner self of man. In such a context the resurrection of the body is meaningless!

137. M.M. Thomas, The Acknowledged Christ of the Indian Renaissance, p.233.

138. Ibid.

139. Idem, The Secular Ideologies of India and the Secular Meaning of Christ, Bangalore, 1976, pp.199, 200.

140. Ibid., pp.198, 199.

141. W. Pannenberg, Jesus - God and Man, London, 1968, p.23.

142. Ibid., p.378.

143. V. Chakkarai, Jesus the Avatar, p.59.

144. Ibid., pp.59, 60. The Vedantic philosophies offer no satisfactory approach to the problem of suffering and how it could be made meaningful even in this life. But suffering is uncritically tolerated as matter of invincible 'karma'. So little is undertaken to alleviate human sufferings!

145. Ibid., p.66.

146. Cfr. back to Chapter V.C.1.

147. G. Parrinder, Avatar and Incarnation, p.213.

148. Ibid., p.238.

149. Ibid., p.239.

150. Ibid., p.214. Cfr. also D.T. Suzuki, Mysticism Christian and Buddhist, 1957, pp.129, 136f.

151. G. Parrinder, Op. Cit., pp.214, 215.

152. Ibid., p.215. Cfr. also: Kamel Hussein, City Wrong, 1959, pp.120, 224.

155. English Works of Rammohan Roy (Allahabad 1906), pp.570-572.

156. Ibid., pp.700f. Suffering of the innocent is an eternal ridle which cannot be understood in terms of justice and injustice. From human experience we can say that suffering is an unavoidable factor in the process of growth and change for the better. Unlike what Roy thinks, the crucifixion of Jesus Christ renders also the suffering of innocents meaningful. This has to be understood especially in the context of humanity considered as a corporate personality.

157. Ibid.

158. Swami Vivekananda, Complete Works, p.326.

159. S. Radhakrishnan, The Philosophy of Rabindranath Tagore, London, 1918, p.15.

164. English Works of Rammohan Roy, pp.700-705. Cfr. also: M.C. Parekh, Rajarshi Ram Mohan Roy, 1927, p.88.

165. Rammohan Roy, Second Appeal, in: English Works of Rammohan Roy, p.571.

166. Ibid., p.608.

167. Swami Satprakasananda, Hinduism and Christianity, p.41. The interpretation of Cross as a process of self-justification on the part of Christ is typically Vedantic, but not Christian!

168. R.C. Zaehner, The Convergent Spirit, London, 1963, p.198. Cfr. also: The Comparison of religion, pp.24, 191.

169. Sen's Lectures II, p.20.

170. For Sen's notion on self-sacrifice cfr. below Foot note no.181.

171. S. Radhakrishnan, Eastern Religions and Western Thought, London, 1939, p.97.

172. Radhakrishnan is quoted here from: S.J. Samartha, The Hindu Response to the Unbound Christ, p.105.

173. An opinion attributed to Sri Ramakrishna Paramahamsa, in: Swami Abhishiktananda, Mental Health and Hindu Psychology, New York, 1951, pp.126ff.

174. Swami Akhilananda, The Hindu View of Christ, p.209. This passage would suggest that the sufferings of Christ was an empirical phenomenon, a matter of appearance! The inner Self of Christ was unperturbed! This Vedantic interpretation does not do justice to the biblical narrations and the Christian faith-traditions regarding the radicality of Christ's sufferings. The Vedantic approach is basicly a docetic one!

175. Quoted from J.R. Chandran by M.M. Thomas in: The Acknowledged Christ of the Indian Renaissance, p.133.

176. M.M. Thomas, Man and the Universe of Faiths, Bangalore, 1975, p.38.

177. M.C. Parekh, Rajarshi Ram Mohan Roy, Rajkot, 1927, p.89. (Underline mine. 'Vice versa' given in italics).

178. Ibid., pp.56f.

179. Idem, A Hindu's Portrait of Jesus Christ, p.575.

180. Sen's Lecture I, p.44.

181. Ibid., p.7.

182. Ibid., p.113.

183. M.C. Parekh, Brahmarshi Sen, p.29. The notion of willingly taking upon oneself the sufferings of others for the sake of mutual love is something that is not very strongly anchored in the Vedantic consciousness. As each one is responsible for one's own 'Karma' one has to retribute it personally and hope for a better lot at least in the next life!

184. Ibid., pp.45-47.

185. Quoted by P.C. Mozoomdar, The Life and Teachings of Keshub Chunder Sen, Calcutta, 1887, p.179.

186. M.K. Gandhi, The Message of Jesus Christ, p.7. Gandhi writes: 'Jesus atoned for the sins of those who accepted his teaching by being an infallible example to them.' Ibid., p.46.

187. Young India, December 31, 1931.

188. E. Stanley Jones, Mahatma Gandhi: An Interpretation, London, 1948, p.127.

189. M.K. Gandhi, The Message of Jesus Christ, pp.36f. Cfr. also: Young India, Dec. 31, 1931.

190. Remark of Mahadeva Desai, the secretary of Gandhiji, in: The Diary of Mahadeva Desai, p.82. Here taken from: S.J. Samartha, Op. Cit., p.92.

191. S. Radhakrishnan, The Heart of Hindustan, p.120. Here taken from S.J. Samartha, Op. Cit., p.111. Cfr. also: Raimundo Panikkar, 'Confrontation between Hinduism and Christ', in: New Blackfriars, Vol. 50, no. 584, Jan. 1969, p.200.

193. M.M. Thomas, The Secular Ideologies of India, p.34. (Underline mine).

194. Chenchiah, Rethinking Christianity, p.164.

195. Cfr. also: Gal 4:4-5., Eph 2:4-10.
God's initiative and gratuity in saving man are central to the Christian concept of salvation!

196. Nalini Devdas, Sri Ramakrishna, Bangalore, 1965, p.98.

198. Cfr. back to the Vedic Sacrifice of Prajapati above in Part I.Ch.II.A. Rgveda 10.90.1-14.

199. K.M. Banerji, The Arian Witness, Calcutta, 1875, p.101.

200. Ibid., p.103.

201. Prajapati is the 'Purusha' (the first Man) begotten before the world and he is also the 'Visvakarma', the author of the universe. Cfr. also: V. Chakkarai, Jesus the Avatar, p.68. Chakkarai also compared Prajapati to Christ.

202. Cfr. Robin Boyd, An Introduction to India Christan Theology, p.283.

203. B. Upadhyaya refers in his 'Hymn of Incarnation' to the 'poison of sin'. Cfr. Chapter V.B.3.

204. Robin Boyd, Op. Cit., p.78.

205. Sen's Lectures II, p.21. Cfr. also: Ibid., p.91-94.
M.C. Parekh, Brahmarshi Sen, pp.194ff.
Cfr. also: Sen's Lectures II, pp.106, 107.

208. 'It washed clear away the slimy sin - Man's heritage! It became also food and drink for him - pure and satisfying!
Thus nou rished the Life of Wisdom ever grew
Yielding the fruit of salvation true!
Such was the blood of our Saviour - Immanuel -
Shed for all - the Living Ganga!'

Cfr. Tamil Christian Poet, (Translation by: R. Rangachary). Here taken from Robin Boyd, Op. Cit., p.47.

212. Hebr. Ch.9., Cfr. also 2, 14-18., 4.14-15 etc.

213. B. Upadhyaya, 'Christ's Claim to Attention', in: The Twentieth Century I, May 5, 1901, pp.115-117.

214. Cfr. the criticism of P. Chenchiah in: Rethinking Christianity, p.164.

214a. The Twentieth Century I, Febr 2, 1901. pp.32f.

215. Cfr. Heiler, Op. Cit., p.150.

216. V. Chakkarai, Jesus the Avatar, p.181.

217. A.J. Appasamy, The Gosepl and India's Heritage, pp.124-125. The reference to the 'payment of costs' could indicate a kind of penal substitution, which can again result in a crude anthropomorphism of God. Any application of human categories to the divine realm cannot fully do justice to the mystery that is beyond human reach. Still man has the right to employ various ways of explaining this mystery without, however, claiming that to be the only valid explanation or category of understanding!

220. M.C. Parekh, Rajarshi Ram Mohan Roy, p.90. God's solidarity with the suffering mankind is the real message of the Cross. That could be understood only in the context of God's love towards mankind. Jesus Christ is the personification of this love.

221. V. Chakkarai, Jesus the Avatar, p.68.

222. A.J. Appasamy, The Gospel and India's Heritage, p.98.

223. Idem, Christianity as Bhakti Marga - A Study of the Johannine Doctrine of Love, Madras, 1928, p.125. Cfr. also: J. Neuner, 'Avatara Doctrine and the Christ Mysterium', p.30.

224. D.S. Amalorpavadass, Approaches in our Apostolate among Non-Christians, Bangalore, 1970, p.28.

225. J. Neuner, Art. Cit., p.31.

226. R.C. Zaehner, Alt Sundry Times: An Essay in the Comparison of Religions, London, 1958, pp.187ff.

227. S. Radhakrishnan, Eastern Religions and Western Thought, p.176.

228. Ibid., p.47. This Advaitic approach to Resurrection does not take earnestly the reality of the body that is involved in this event. The resurrection, in its Christian understanding, is a liberation of the body, not a liberation from the body!

229. Swami Akhilananda, The Hindu View of Christ, 1971, p.217.

230. Sen's Lectures II, p.19.

231. M.C. Parekh, Brahmarshi Sen, pp.113-115. Cfr. also: Sen's Lectures II, pp.420f.

232. Ibid.

233. Sen's Lectures I, pp.384-385.

234. M.C. Parekh, A Hindu's Portrait of Jesus Christ, p.580-

235. Ibid. Parekh's distinction of the gross body and subtle body is only a postulate. This could explain away the 'salvation' of the gross body! But the Christian concern is to explain how the gross body also could share in the salvation of man.

236. P.C. Mozoomdar, The Spirit of God, Boston, 1894, pp.257f.

237. Ibid., p.62.

238. Ibid., pp.250f.

239. V. Chakkarai, Jesus the Avatar, p.221.

240. Ibid.

241. Ibid., p.219. This is a very reasonable explanation of Resurrection. In the event of the Resurrection there is an element of continuity as well as an element of discontinuity. It could be called a qualitative mutation in the direction of the Spirit by the power of God, which Chakkarai calls 'Nava Sakti'.

242. Ibid., p.149 (Italics his).

243. Ibid., p.150 (Italics his.)

244. Ibid., p.149 (Underline mine.)

245. Ibid., p.150. See above the notions of Sen and M.C. Parekh regarding this question.

246. Ibid.

247. P. Chenchiah (with V. Chakkarai and A.N. Sudarisanam), Ashramas Past and Present, Madras, 1941, p.322. (Underline mine except for 'Satyagraha'.)

248. For Chenchiah's of notion of Jesus Christ as 'The New Creation' cfr. Ch.V.A.3.c.

249. P.D. Devanandan,Preparation for Dialogue - A Collection of Essays on Hinduism and Christianity in New India, Bangalore, 1964, p.180.

250. S.J. Samartha, The Hindu Response to the Unbound Christ, p.193.

251. M.M. Thomas, The Secular Ideologies of India and the Secular Meaning of Christ, 1976, p.203.

252. Idem, Salvation and Humanisation - Some Critical Issues of the Theology of Mission in Contemporary India, Bangalore, 1971, pp.30,31.

253. Ibid., Resurrection means not only the salvation of the material aspect of human existence but also the totality of man's history, i.e. man's materiality in its Spatio-Temporal 'relatedness'. This view of Thomas agrees with the position of W. Pannenberg which we will be discussing in Ch. VII.

254. Idem, The Secular Ideologies of India, p.198.

255. S.J. Samartha, The Hindu Response, p.199.

256. A modalistic approach to the doctrine of the Holy Trinity cannot think of a Holy Spirit that is personally different from the Father and the son.

257. Rammohan Roy, Second Appeal, Calcutta, 1821, p.86.

258. Ibid., p.90.

259. Cfr. above Ch.V.A.1.b and c., 3.a etc.

260. Sen's Lectures II, pp.424, 425.

261. Ibid., p.41.

262. Ibid., I,pp.247, 248., II, p.10. Sen identifies 'the Spirit' with God the Father! Cfr. Ibid., p.41.
'The Father manifests Himself first in Creation and then in His beloved Son, Jesus .... When He works within us as the Holy spirit we are con-verted and become new creatures.' Sen's Lectures II, p.41.

263. Sen's Lectures II, pp.32, 33.

264. Sen's Lectures I, pp.420f.

265. Ibid., p.422.

266. Ibid., II., pp.15, 16, 40, 41.

267. Ibid., p. 41.

268. 'Perichoresis' - Compenetration or in-existence of one Person in the other by 'essence', 'relation' and 'origin'.

269. V. Chakkarai, Jesus the Avatar, p.121.

270. Ibid., p.117.

271. For further explanations on this point Cfr. Ch.V. (Passim).

272. V. Chakkarai, Op. Cit., p.114.

273. Ibid., pp.114, 115.

274. Ibid., p. 115.

275. Ibid., p.123. Chakkarai's understanding of the Holy Spirit as the Resurrected Lord is evidently not according to the orthodox Christian belief. The Holy Council of Constantino I (381) promulgated the doctrine of the Holy Spirit, which was not dealt with in the Council of Nicea, against the 'Pneumatomachs'. For details cfr. DS. 150 and also: Oritz de Urbina, Nicee et Constantinople, Paris, 1963I, p.182-205.

276. V. Chakkarai, Op. Cit., p.154 (Italics his.)

277,. Ibid.

277a. Ibid., p.160.

278. Ibid., p.161.

279. Ibid., p.121 (Italics his.) Chakkarai thus stresses a historical incarnation of God and an unbound and universal incarnation in the form of the Holy Spirit!

280. Thangasamy, The Holy of Chenchiah, p.17.

281. Ibid., p.23.

282. P. Chenchiah, Rethinking Christianity, p.57.

283. Idem, Christianity and Hinduism (Pamphlet) 1928, Cfr. D.A. Thangasamy, Op. Cit., Selections p.217.

284. D.A. Thangasamy, Op. Cit., pp.284f.

286. For example: R. Panikkar, The Intra-Religious Dialogue, New York, 1978. P.D. Devanandan, Preparation for Dialogue, Bangalore, 1964. K.M. Banerji, Dialogues on Hindu Philosophy, Calcutta, 1861. Horst Bürkle (Hrg.), Indische Beiträge zur Theologie der Gegenwart, Stuttgart, 1966. J.A. Cuttat, The Encounter of Religions, Desclee Co., 1960. F. Heiler, Der christliche Glaube und indisches Geistesleben, München, 1926. A.G. Hoog, The Christian Message to the Hindu, London, 1947. P. Johanns, Vers le Christ par le Vedanta, Louvain, 1931. Idem, To Christ through the Vedanta, A Synopsis. Part I, Samkara; Part II, Rama-nuja; Part III, Vallabha; Part IV Chaitanya, Ranchi 1944 (3rd ed.), Kulan-dran, Grace: A Comparative Study of the Doctrine in Christianity and Hinduism, London, 1964. Rudolf Ott, Christianity and the Indian Religion of Grace, Madras, 1929. R.N. Smart, Reasons and Faiths: An Investi-gation of Religious Discourse, Christian and Non-Christian, London, 1958, Otto Wolff, Mahatma und Christus, Berlin, 1955. Idem, Christus unter den Hindus, Gütersloh, 1965. R.C. Zaehner, At Sundry Times: An Essay in the Comparison of Religions, London, 1958, etc.

287. S. Radhakrishnan, The Bhagavadgita, London, 1958, p.34.

288. 'Extra ecclesiam nulla salus' (Cyprian)! - This statement means: 'Extra Christum nulla salus'! It is, therefore, to be understood in an all-inclusive sense and not in an exclusivistic way!
The axiom 'extra ecclesiam nulla salus' received a special emphasis in the 3rd cent. from St. Cyprian of Carthage. Cfr.: Cyprian. Carthg., Ep. (73) ad Iubaianum c. 21 (CSEL 3/II, 795-35., PL 3, 1169A). This was taken up by the 4th Lateran Council in the confession of faith against the Albigensians and the Cathars (Cfr. Definitio contra Albi-genses et Catharos DS 802). Cfr. also: DS 3866ff. for the decision of the Church against a too narrow and literal interpretation of this axiom in the controversy involving Leonard Feeney in the U.S.A.

289. Roberto de Nobili, Gnanopadesam Kurippidam (Tamil), Tuticorin, 1955. Taken from Robin Boyd, Op. Cit., p.13.

290. Vatican II, Nostra aetate, no.2.

291. Cfr. above Ch.IV.B.

292. Raimundo Panikkar, The Unknown Christ of Hinduism: Towards an Ecumenical Christophany, (Revised and Enlarged Edition) London, 1981, pp.71ff.

293. Ibid., pp.75ff.

294. Ibid., pp.85f. The main problem with this statement of Panikkar is that he places both Christianity and Hinduism on equal footing as 'agents' of salvation. This is evidently contrary to the self-understanding of the Church as the 'Sacrament of Salvation' - a unique role in God's plan of salvation. The acceptance of the salvific role of Hinduism does not mean that it's role is equal to that of the Church founded by Christ! Panikkar's position is clearly Vedantic, but not Christian!

295. Ibid., p.96.

296. Ibid., p.90. J.B. Chethimattam quotes Panikkar: 'Hinduism, because it is a kind of Christianity in potency, because it has already a Christian seed, because it is the desire of fullness, and that fullness is Christ, is already pointing towards it, already contains, indeed, the symbolism of the Christian reality.' Chethimattam, 'R. Panikkar's Approach to Christology', in: Indian Journal of Theology, 23 (1974), p.220. This quotation is from the 1964 edition of 'The Unknown Christ', pp.59, 60. The New Edition of the same work (1981) rejects the relation between Hinduism and Christianity on the model of potentialactual, seed-fruit, forerunner-real presence, allegory-thing in itself, desire-accomplishment, symbol-reality, death-resurrection as objecitonable on various reasons! Cfr. pp.90ff.

297. Ibid., p.91.

298. Ibid., p.81. Jesus Christ would have only the role of an 'Ishtadeva'!

299. Ibid., p.92.

300. Ibid., pp.92, 93.

301. Ibid., p.94.

302. Ibid., p.93, 94.

303. Ibid., p.95. This position of Panikkar could well be compared with the 'Sarva Dharma Samanatva'-principle of the Vedantins! Here Panikkar is watering down the salvific role of Christianity!

304. Ibid.

305. Ibid., p.19. A religious interpenetration at all levels, without regard for the fundamental differences in doctrines between Hinduism and Christianity cannot certainly serve the cause of truth!

306. Ibid., pp.93, 94.

307. Robin Boyd, Indian Christian Theology, pp.223, 226.

308. Ibid., p.225. Robin Boyd's evaluation is based on the first edition (1964) of Panikkar's work in question. Panikkar himself acknowledges changes in his new edition (1981), p.xi.

309. R. Panikkar, The Unknown Christ, 1981, pp.93, 94.

310. Ibid., p.61.

311. Cfr. back to Chapter IV.A.

312. I Tim. 2w, 4f. etc.

313. R. Panikkar, Op. Cit., pp.26, 27.

314. Vatican II, Lumen Gentium, Ch.I, no.1.

315. K. Rahner, 'Die anonymen Christen', in: Schriften zur Theologie, Bd. VI, Ensiedeln/Zürich/Köln, 1965, SS.545-554. Cfr. also: 'Das Christentum und die nichtchristlichen Religionen', in: Schriften zur Theologie, Bd. V, Einsiedeln/Zürich/Köln, 1964, SS.136-158.

316. Cfr. back to Ch.IV,B. for Panikkar's explanation of the 'unknown'. Dupuis identification of Rahner's position with that of Panikkar is unfortunately not correct! Cfr. James Dupuis, 'The Salvific Value of the Non-Christian Religions', in: Service and Salvation, Ed. by J. Pathrapankal, Bangalore, 1973, p.212.

317. R. Panikkar, Op. Cit., p.13. Cfr. also Rgveda 1.164.46.

318. J. Dupuis, Art. Cit., pp.207-233.

319. Ibid., pp.209f.

320. Ibid., p.212ff.

321. Ibid., p.213.

322. Ibid.

323. Ibid., p.210. The question also depends very much on what one understands by the term 'salvific' when it is applied to religions! The notion of 'religion' also plays a significant role in deciding this issue!

324. Ibid.

325. Ibid., p.211.

326. Ibid., p.229.

327. Vatican II, L.G., no.48.

328. J. Dupuis, Art. Cit., p.229.

329. Ibid. There is also a radical novelty in the Gospel of Christ. Karl Rahner's idea of 'anonymous Christians' cannot be interpreted as to mean that the role of evangelization is only a process of making aware of what is already there in every non-Christian!

330. Ibid., p.230.

331. Cfr. Vatican II, LG, no.17, AG, no.9., NA, no.2.

332. Vatican II, LG, no.16., AG, no.8., UR, no.3.

333. The use of the expression 'subsists' (instead of 'consists') by Vatican II to explain the nature of the Catholic Church in relation to the other Churches could be also used to signify the presence of salvation in Christianity and on-Christian religions. Cfr. Vatican II, LG, no.8.

334. J.B. Chethimattam, Art. Cit., p.219.

335. J. Dupuis, Art. Cit., p.212.

336. Ibid., p.229.

337. T.M. Manickam, 'Anubhava as Pramana of an Indian Christology', in: Jeevadhara 1 (1791), pp.228-244. Cfr. also: Antony Mookenthottam, Indian Theological Tendencies, Berne, 1978, pp.106-110.

337a. V. Chakkarai, Jesus the Avatar, p.11.

338. Ibid., p.12.

339. Ibid. The centrality of Christ in Christian experience of God cannot be replaced by any 'universal principle' as the Vedantins or R. Panikkar may hold!

340. Ibid., p.163.

341. Ibid.

342. Ibid., p.165.

343. Ibid., p.168.

344. Ibid., p.215. The Christian experience is unlike the Vedantic experience highly personal and concrete. It is not a matter of realizing an identity, but entering into communion with God in Jesus Christ!

345. Ibid., p.9.

346. R.C. Das, Conviction of an Indian Disciple, Bangalore, 1966, p.2.

347. S.J. Samartha, The Hindu Response, p.160.

348. Ibid., p.161.

349. Cfr. 'Sayujya' (the final state of union with Good according to the Bhakti tradition) above in Part I. Ch.III.B.3.

350. Sen's Lectures II, p.24.

351. Sen's Lectures I, pp.488-489.

352. Ibid., p.382.

353. Mark Sundar Rao, Ananyatva: Realization of Christian Non-Duality, 1964, p.25.

354. Ibid., p.43.

355. Monchanin (with Abhishiktananda), A Benedictine Ashram, 1951, p.37.

356. Swami Parama Arubi Ananadam: Fr. J. Monchanin, A Memorial, 1959, p.103. Taken from Robin Boyd, Op. Cit., p.221.

357. Abhishiktananda, Saccidananda - A Christian Approach to Advaitic Experience, Delhi, 1974, p.103.

358. Ibid., p.109.

359. Ibid., p.104. It is, however, very important to make a clear distinction between the 'Advaita' of nature in the Holy Trinity and the 'Advaita' that could be spoken of in Christian mystical experience, which is a created and conscious participation in the Trinitarian life!

360. Abhishiktananda, Towards the Renewal of the Indian Church, Ernakulam, pp.1-23., Cfr. also: 'Communication in the Spirit', in:Religion and Society, 17 (1970) 3, pp.33-39.

361. Idem, Hindu-Christian Meeting Point, Bombay, 1969.

362. Ibid., p.131.

363. Sen's Lectures II, pp.85, 86. By this Sen means that any authentic God-experience in any religion cannot stand in contradiciton to the experience of Christ. Whatever contradicts Christ-experience cannot be true! Here we see the importance of the discernment of the spirits!

364. Ibid., pp.58-63. Cfr. also Lectures I, pp.115, 488, 489.

365. Sen's Lectures II, p.84.

366. The Guardian 13.2.1947. Taken from Robin Boyd, Op. Cit., p.162.

367. P. Chenchiah et alii, Ashramas Past and Present, 1941, p.267.

368. Cfr. back in Part I, Ch.III.B.

370. Cfr. also: Mt 11:27., Jn 12:44-45., 14:10., 10:30., Col 1:15., Heb 1:3.

371. Sen's Lectures II, p.39.

372. Ibid., p.40.

373. Ibid., p.15.

374. Lecture on 'Christ and Christianity', in: Keshub Chunder Sen in England (2 Volumes), Brahmo Tract Society, Calcutta 1915, here Vol. I, p.187.

375. Quoted from Joseph Mattam, Catholic Approaches to Hinduism - A Study of the Work of the European Orientalists: P. Johanns, O. Lacombe, J.A. Cuttat, J. Monchanin and R.C. Zaehner, Pontificia Universitas Gregoriana, Roma, 1972 (Only the part dealing with J. Monchanin is published, from which we quote), p.20.

376. Klaus Klostermaier, Kristvidya: A Sketch of an Indian Christology, Bangalore, 1967, p.39.

377. Cfr. L'Abbe Jules Monchanin. (Témoignages, Notes biographiques et textes), Casterman 1960, p.57.
Cfr. also: Monchanin (with Henri Le Saux), A Benedictine . Ashram, Douglas, 1964, p.22.

378. Cfr. back to Part I.Ch.III.B.1.

379. Cfr. Joseph Mattam, 'Modern Catholic Attempts at Presenting Christ to India', in: The Indian Journal of Theology, 1974 (23), p.215.

380. Cfr. the reference to the 'Purusha Sukta' in Part I.Ch.II.A and Rgveda 10.90.1-14.

381. Swami Prabhavananda, The Sermon on the Mount according to Vedanta, pp.81f. Cfr. also Swami Akhilananda, The Hindu View of Christ, pp.92, 93.

383. J.N. Farquhar, The Crown of Hinduism, Oxford, 1915, p.343.

384. Ibid., p.350. Farquhar considers idols as an expression of the human aspiration for a tangible God which is truly fulfilled only in Christ.

385. Samuel Ryan, 'Interpreting Christ to India', p.227. Taken from Joseph Neuner, Art. Cit.

386. J. Neuner, 'Avatara Doctrine and the Christ Mysterium', p.33. Here Neuner speaks in reference to 'Avatars' which for him is also applicable to 'images'.

387. Ibid.

388. P. Chenchiah, Rethinking Christianity, p.190.

389. Cfr. Jnana Marga in Part I.Ch.III.B.2.

390. Samuel Ryan, Art. Cit., p.228.

391. For the notion of 'Truth' in St.John cfr. Ignace de la Potterie, La Vérité dans S. Jean, Roma, 1977. Cfr. especially I: Le Christ et la vérité, pp.181.242. Cfr. also: R. Schnackenburg, 'Cristologia di Giovanni', in: Mysterium Salutis, III/1, Queriniana 1971, pp.425-442., S.A. Panimolle, Il dono della legge e la grazia della verità (Gv 1,17), Roma, 1973.

392. The question of Christ's uniqueness has been already discussed. Cfr. also: Hebr. 1:1ff., John 14:6: 'No one can come to the Father except through me.'!

394. Abhishiktananda, Saccidananda, p.95. By this Abhishiktananda does not, however, reject the distinction between God as 'Prajnana' or 'Cit', ie. pure consciousness, and the limited consciousness of man.

395. Mark Sundar Rao, Ananyatva: Realization of Christian Non-Duality, Bangalore, 1964, p.5.

396. S.J. Samartha, Op. Cit., p.135. It is, however, not possible to bring all dimensions together into one expression. What is intended by Mark Sundar Rao is only the stressing of a particular aspect.

397. Swami Abhishiktananda, Prayer, Delhi, 1967, p.109.

398. Knowledge in the biblical sense is not merely the result of an intellectual process, but the fruit of an inner experience following an inner contact between two persons! Cfr. also: Jn 10:14., 14:17., 17:3,6,25, etc.

399. Cfr. also: 1 John 1,6. Jesus asks the Father to consecrate his disciples in Truth, Cfr. John 17, 17.

400. Cfr. Part I.Ch.III.B.3.

401. Cfr. Foot note above no.403.

402. A.J. Appasamy, Christianity as Bhakti Marga, A Study in the Johannine Writings, London, 1927, p.165.

403. Ibid., p.22.

404. Cfr. back in Part I.Ch.III.B.3.

405. A.J. Appasamy, The Johannine Doctrine of Life - A Study of Christian and Indian Thought, London, 1934, p.117.

406. Dhanjibhai Fakirbhai, The Philosophy of Love, Delhi, 1966, p.2.

407. 'Christ and Christianity', in: Keshub Chunder Sen in England, Vol.I, 1915, p.187.

408. M.C. Parekh, A Hindu's Portrait of Jesus Christ, p.277. A very superficial criticism!

409. Regarding the supreme commandment of man's love towards and fellowmen cfr. Mt 22:36-40., Mk 12:28,33., Lk 10:25-28.

410. Dhanjibhai Fakirbhai, Op. Cit., p.12.

411. Sadhu Sundar Singh, At the Master's Feet, Madras, 1974, p.9.

412. Idem, The Search after Reality, Madras, 1971, pp.39, 40.

413. Idem, The Spiritual Life, Madras, 1970, pp.13, 14. Sadhu Sundar Singh is quite right in making Love the central point in the Christian message.

414. A.J. Appasamy, The Johannine Doctrine of Life, p.117. It is also important to explain the nature of this difference without falling into duality of Being! Mystical union in the Christian sense means unity without implying an identity!

415. Idem, The Gospel and India's Heritage, p.38.

416. F. Heiler, The Gospel of Sundar Singh, 1927, p.170. Sadhu Sundar Singh, like Prof. Dhanjibhai Fakirbhai, sees love as the central factor in Christian existence. A relation of friendship with his fellowmen.

417. Raimundo Panikkar, The Trinity and World Religions, Madras, 1970.

418. God, the Father and the Holy Spirit may not be called 'Persons' in the strict sense, according to Panikkar, because they are not 'manifest' to the extend the Son is! Ibid., p.50. Here we must be careful not to read too much into this statement of Panikkar as to mean a denial of the personal difference that subsists in the Holy Trinity as taught by the early Councils. Panikkar is following the categories of 'Nirguna Brahman' and 'Saguna Brahman', Jesus Christ the concrete manifestation of God standing for the latter! I am personally of the opinion that the concepts of the 'Immanent Trinity' and the 'Economical Trinity' could be expressed in the categories of 'Nirguna Brahman' and 'Saguna Brahman' respectively, but these categories are not adequate to explain the Father, the Son and the Holy Spirit in one God!

419. Raimundo Panikkar, The Trinity and World Religions, p.48.

420. Ibid., p.29.

421. Ibid., pp.29, 32, 38.

422. Cfr. back to Ch.IV, Foot note no.7.

423. Ibid.

424. F. Heiler, Op. Cit., p.266.

425. The Guardian (Madras) June 22, 1967. Quoted from Robin Boyd, Op. Cit., p.197.

426. Samuel Ryan, 'Interpreting Christ to India', pp.229, 230. Cfr. also: Idem, 'An Indian Christology: A Discussion of Method', in: Jeevadhara - A Journal of Christian Interpretation, Vol. I, May-June 1973, no.3, pp.212f.

427. Idem, 'Interpreting Christ', p.230. Cfr. also: Idem, 'An Indian Christology', p.214.

428. Idem, 'Interpreting Christ', p.230 and 'An Indian Christology', p.215.

429. Idem, 'Interpreting Christ', p.230., 'An Indian Christology', p.216.

430. M.M. Thomas, Man and the Universe of Faiths, Bangalore, 1975, p.79.

431. Idem, The Secular Ideologies of India and the Secular Meaning of Christ, Bangalore, 1976, p.194.

432. S.J. Samartha, The Hindu Response to the Unbound Christ, p.171.

433. Samuel Rayan, 'Interpreting Christ', p.231.

434. Ibid., Cfr. also: Idem, 'An Indian Christology', pp.217, 218.

435. Rabindranath Tagore, Towards Spiritual Man, New Dehli, 1961, p.167 (Underline mine).

436. S. Rayan, 'Interpreting Christ', p.231., Cfr. also: Idem, 'Indian Christology', p.217.

437. Lal Bahari Day, 'Narayana Vamana Tilak', in: Indian Christians - Biographical and Critical Sketches, Madras, p.216.

438. S.K. Rudra, The Christian Idea of Incarnation, Madras, London, 1911, pp.10-12.

439. 'Reste á l'Inde un ... Sauveur: le Christ. Nous sovons qu'il n'est pas comme d'autres un 'imposteur' (Mat. 27,62), mais le vrai Rédempteur, le Sauveur unique de l'universe, de toute l'humanité. Son message de salut, l'Evangile, son instrument de salut, l'Eglise, peuvent apporter á l'Inde le remède parfait à ses maux ... La lutte de l' àme indienne pour implanter une spiritualité aux racines profondes dans le structures profanes imposées par la civilisation technico-matérielle est un appel évident à une religion qui est par sa nature méme, une véritable incarnation du spirituel dans le matériel, un appel au Dieu incarné ...' D.S. Amalorpavadass, Destinée de l'E glise dans l'Inde d'aujourd'hui. Conditionnements de l'évangélisation, Fayard-Mame, 1967, pp.86-87. (Underline mine.)

NOTES:PART III

CHAPTER VII

1. Cfr. above Ch.II.B.

2. Cfr. above Ch.I.B.4.

3. Cfr. above Ch.III.A.1. Cfr. also Br. Up. 1.3.28.

4. Karl-Heinz Weger, Karl Rahner - An Introduction to His Theology, London, 1980, p.33-34. (English translation by David Smith).

5. Cfr. Karl Rahner, Geist in Welt. Zur Metaphysik der endlichen Erkenntnis bei Thomas von Aquin, München, 1964, 2.Teil, 3. Kapitel, 4.1., SS.147ff.
    Idem, 'Überlegungen zur Methode der Theologie, in: Idem, Schriften zur Theologie Bd. IX, Einsiedeln, 1970, S.98: 'Eine transzendentale Fragestellung, gleichgültig, in welchem Gegenstandsbereich sie auftritt, ist dann gegeben, wenn und insoweit nach den Bedingungen der Möglichkeit der Erkenntnis eines bestimmten Gegenstandes im erkenndenden Subjekt selbst gefragt wird.'

6. Rahner is, of course, not the inventor of the transcendental method; but it is his credit to introduce it first to theology. Cfr. Karl-Heinz Weger, Op. Cit., Loc. Cit.
    Cfr. also: J.B. Lotz, 'Zur Thomas-Rezeption in der Maréchal-Schule', in: Theologie und Philosophie, 49 (1974), 375-394.

7. Karl-Heinz Weger, Op.Cit., p.50.

8. The 'categorial' in contrast to the 'transcendental' means concrete, limited, objectifiable, particular.

9. Wolfhart Pannenberg, 'Die Frage nach Gott', in: Idem, Grundfragen systematischer Theologie (Gesammelte Aufsätze), Göttingen, 1979 ³, S. 372: 'Die Fraglichkeit des Menschen bedeutet..., daß er das Wesen ist, das über sich hinaus fragt.'

10. Ibid.

11. W. Pannenberg, What is Man? Contemporary Anthropology in Theological Perspective (Translated by Duane A. Priebe), Fortress Press, 1970, p.3

12. Idem, Was ist der Mensch? Die Anthropologie der Gegenwart im Lichte der Theologie Göttingen, 1961 ⁶, S.6.

13. Idem, 'Die Frage nach Gott', in: Grundfragen, S.372.

14. Idem, Was ist der Mensch, SS.10,13.

15. Br. Up. 1.3.28. Cfr. also K. Rahner, 'Nature and Grace', in: Idem, Theological Investigations Vol. IV, Baltimore, 1966, p.183. Heinrich Döring/Franz-Xaver Kaufmann, 'Kontingenzerfahrung und Sinnfrage',

in: Franz Böckle et alii, Christlicher Glaube in moderner Gesellschaft, Bd. 9, Freiburg i.Br., 1983, SS.6ff.
W. Pannenberg, 'Kontingenz und Naturgesetz', in: A.M. Müller/W. Pannenberg, Erwägungen zu einer Theologie der Natur, Gütersloh, 1970.

16. Cfr. above Ch.III.A.2; III.B.2; IV.A.3.b.

17. Cfr. above Ch.III.A.2.

18. Cfr. above Ch.I.B.3.b.

19. Cfr. above Ch.I.B.3.a.

20. 'Aham Brahmasmi'! Cfr. above Ch.II.A.2.a.

21. Cfr. below Ch.VII.A.3.a.

22. Cfr. above Ch.II.A.1.

23. For a critical summary and evaluation of Rahner's 'Geist in Welt' cfr. Andrew Tallon, 'Spirit, Matter Becoming: Karl Rahner's Spirit in the World (Geist in Welt)', in: The Modern Schoolman, 48 (1971), 159-165. In this contect cfr. also: Thomas Pearl, 'Dialectical Panentheism:On the Hegelian Character of Karl Rahner's Key Christological Writings', in: The Irish Theological Quarterly, Vol. XLII (April 1975), No.2, 119-137. John Farrelly, 'Man's Transcendence and Thomistic Resources', in: The Thomist, 38 (1974), 451ff.

24. Thomas Aquinas, Summa Theologica, I, p.84, a.7.
Cfr. also: Ibid., p.84-86.

25. Karl Rahner, Hörer des Wortes.Zur Grundlegung einer Religionsphilosophie, München, 1940.

26. In addition to the above literature cfr. also: Andrew Tallon, 'Spirit, Freedom, History: Karl Rahner's Hörer des Wortes (Hearers of the Word)', in: The Thomist 38 (1974), 908-936.
Brennan Hill, 'Karl Rahner's Metaphysical Anthropology', in: Carmelus, Vol. 18 (1971), Fasciculus 2, 181-194. Hans Urs von Balthasar, 'Rezension von 'Geist in Welt',' in: ZkTh, 63 (1939), 371-379.
U. Browarzik, Glauben und Denken. Dogmatische Forschung zwischen der Transzendentaltheologie Karl Rahners und der Offenbarungstheologie Karl Barths, Berlin, 1970.
Friedemann Greiner, Die Menschlichkeit der Offenbarung. Die transzendentale Grundlegung der Theologie bei Karl Rahner, München, 1978.
R. Masson, 'Rahner and Heidegger: Being, Hearing and God', in: The Thomist XXXVII (1973), 455-488.
W.J. Stohrer, The Role of Heidegger's Doctrine of Dasein in Karl Rahner's Metaphysics of Man, Washington, 1967. Etc.

27. This point has been elaborated by Friedemann Greiner, Op. Cit., 22-82.

28. Karl Rahner, Spirit in the World, London, 1979, liii. (Italics his.)
Cfr. also: Barrie Wilson, 'The Possibility of Theology after Kant. An

Examination of Karl Rahner's 'Geist in Welt',' in: Canadian Journal of Theology, Oct.12,1966, p.251.

29. Karl Rahner, Op. Cit., Loc. Cit.

30. Ibid.

31. Ibid., pp.68-71. Cfr. also Thomas Pearl, Art.Cit., p.123.

32. K. Rahner, Spirit in the World, Ch.III, esp. p.156.
     Idem, Hearers of the Word, London, 1969, p.53.

33. Idem, Spirit in the World, pp.142-145, 153-154, 169.

34. Ibid., pp.142ff.

35. Karl Rahner, Foundations of Christian Faith - An Introduction to the Idea of Christianity, New York, 1978, pp.33, 34. 'Vorgriff' is different from 'Begriff' (concept) that is concrete and acquired. (This work will be hereafter cited as Foundations).

36. Ibid., pp.34, 35.

37. Karl-Heinz Weger, Op. Cit., p.47.

38. K. Rahner, Hearers of the Word, p.53.

39. Frank E. Tupper, The Theology of Wolfhart Pannenberg, Philadelphia, 1973, p.237.

40. Ibid., Cfr. also: 'The Working of the Spirit in the Creation of the People of God', in: Pannenberg et alii, Spirit, Faith and Church, The West Minster Press, 1970, pp.18-19.
     Cfr. also: W. Pannenberg, Was ist der Mensch?, pp.20, 23.

41. K. Rahner, Foundations, pp.35, 36.

42. K. Rahner, Spirit in the World, p.295.

43. Ibid., p.296.

44. Ibid., p.291.

45. K. Rahner, Ich glaube an Jesus Christus. Theologische Meditationen 21, Hrg. Hans Küng, Einsiedeln 1968, S. 17: 'Das Sichanvertrauen ist ein Ereignis (der) Selbstüberbietung...'

46. Ibid., S. 16.

47. Ibid., S.17.

48. W. Pannenberg, Anthropologie in theologischer Perspektive, Göttingen, 1983, S. 116.

49. Idem, Was ist der Mensch?, S. 23.

50. K. Rahner, Ich glaube an Jesus Christus, SS.42, 43.

51. Cfr. above on 'Bhakti Marga', Part I, Ch.III.B.3.

52. Gerald McCool, 'The Philosophy of the Human Person in Karl Rahner's Theology', in: Theological Studies, 22 (1961), p.544.

53. Rgveda, 1.164.46: 'Ekam sat vipra bahudha vadanti'.
    Cfr. above Part I, Ch.I.A.
    Cfr. also: Bernhard Welte, 'Christentum und Religionen der Welt', in: Böckle et alii (Hrg.), Christlicher Glaube in moderner Gesellschaft, Bd. 26, Freiburg im Br., 1981, S.88.

54. Karl-Heinz Weger, Op. Cit., S.65.
    Cfr. also W. Pannenberg, 'The Question of God', in: Idem, Basic Questions in Theology: Collected Essays (Translated by: George H. Kehn), Fortress Press, Vol. II, p.221. (Hereafter cited as: Basic Questions II.)

55. Walter Kasper, Jesus der Christus, Mainz, 1974, S.60: '... der Mensch (ist) in seinem Fragen, Denken und Wollen einerseits größer als ... die Wirklichkeit, weil er fragend, denkend, wollend alles übersteigt; umgekehrt erweist sich aber auch die Wirklichkeit größer als er Mensch; der Mensch kann die Wirklichkeit letztlich nicht einholen.So steht der Mensch vor einem unaufhebbaren Geheimnis; ja, er selbst ist sich ein solches undurchdringliches Geheimnis. Die Wesenslinien seines Daseins lassen sich nicht ausziehen.'

56. Cfr. above foot note no.54.

57. K. Rahner, Foundations, p.80.

58. s. Radhakrishnan, An Idealist View of Life, London, 1980 (1932), p.79.

59. Cfr. above Ch.I.B.2.

60. Br. Up., III.8.8.
    Cfr. also: S. Radhakrishnan, Op. Cit., p.80.

61. K. Rahner, Spirit in the World, p.283.

62. Idem, 'Über den Begriff des Geheimnisses in der katholischen Theologie', in: Idem, Schriften zur Theologie, Bd. IV, Einsiedeln, 1960, S.51.

63. Ibid., SS.60, 61.

64. Ibid., SS.70, 71.

65. Ibid., S.72.

66. Ibid., SS.72, 73. Rahner names the 'Whither' of human transcendence as the 'Holy'. Cfr. S.73.

67. Ibid., Cfr. also: K.-H. Weger, Karl Rahner - Eine Einführung in sein theologisches Denken, Freiburg i.Br., 1978, S.64.

68.   K. Rahner, Do You believe in God?, New York, 1969, p.7.

69.   W. Pannenberg, 'The Question of God', in: Idem, Basic Questions, II, p.225.
Cfr. also: Idem, The Idea of God and Human Freedom, (Translated by: R.A. Wilson), The Westminster Press, 1973, p.107.

70.   Idem, 'Speaking about God', in: The Idea of God and Human Freedom, p.106.

71.   Idem, Was ist der Mensch?, S. 40: "(Der) unendliche Zug ins Offene zielt über alles, was ihm (dem Menschen) in der Welt begegnet, hinaus auf Gott. Darum bedeutet Weltoffenheit im Kern Gottoffenheit. Der Mensch als Mensch ist diese Bewegung durch die Welt hindurch zu Gott hin. In dieser Bewegung ist er unterwegs zu seiner Bestimmung, zur Gemeinschaft mit Gott.'

72.   Ibid., SS. 12, 13: 'Die Weltoffenheit des Menschen setzt eine Gottbezogen-heit voraus ... (Die) Eigenart des menschlichen Daseins, seine unend-liche Angewiesenheit, ist nur als Frage nach Gott verständlich. Die unbegrenzte Offenheit für die Welt ergibt sich erst aus der Bestimmung des Menschen über die Welt hinaus.'

73.   K. Rahner, 'Über den Begriff des Geheimnisses in der katholischen Theologie', in: Op. Cit., SS.68ff.

74.   W. Pannenberg, Op. Cit., S.11: 'Für das Gegenüber, auf das der Mensch in seinem unendlichen Streben angewiesen ist, hat die Sprache den Aus-druck Gott. Das Wort Gott kann nur sinnvoll verwendet werden, wenn es das Gegenüber der grenzenlosen Angewiesenheit des Menschen meint. Sonst wird es zu einer leeren Vokabel.'

75.   K. Rahner, Art. cit., S.76.

76.   Ibid., SS. 77-78.

77.   Ibid., S.80; Cfr. also: Thomas Aquinas, De Pot., p.7,a.5.

78.   Thomas Aquinas, De Pot., q.7, a.5.

79.   Cfr. below Ch.VII.B.2.

80.   K. Rahner, Art. Cit., S.79.

81.   S. Radhakrishnan, Op. Cit., p.80. The other indispensable aspect of 'Neti' is 'Asti'. Cfr. Ch.I.B.1.

82.   Cfr. above Ch.I.B.

83.   Br. Up. 5.1., Cfr. also above: Ch.B.3.a on 'Purnam'.

84.   Atharva Veda 10.8., 10.12. Cfr. especially also 10.8.29.

85.   Cfr. I.A.

86. Cfr. Ibid.

87. God as 'Macht über alles Wirkliche', Cfr. W. Pannenberg, 'Die Frage nach Gott', in: Grundfragen, S. 378.

88. W. Pannenberg, 'Response to the Discussion' in: James M. Robinson/ John B. Cobb Jr. (Ed.), Theology as History, Vol. III of: New Frontiers in Theology, Harper & Row, Publishers, Inc., 1967, p.232. (Hereafter cited only as 'Response to the Discussion').

89. Idem, 'Theology and the Kingdom of God', in: Richard John Neuhaus (Ed.), Theology and the Kingdom of God, Westminster Press, 1969, p.55. (Hereafter cited by article-title).

90. Idem, 'Response to the Discussion', p.232.

91. Idem, 'Dogmatische Erwägungen zur Auferstehung Jesu', in: Kerygma und Dogma, Bd. XIV (1968), S.115. (Hereafter cited only by the title of the article).

92. Idem, 'Theology and the Kingdom of God', p.56.

93. Ibid., p.63.

94. Idem, 'The God of Hope', in: Basic Questions in Theology II, p.244.

95. Idem, 'Theology and the Kingdom of God', p.62.

96. Idem, 'Response to the Discussion', p.232.

96a. Idem, Theologie und Reich Gotters, Gütersloh, 1971, S.22:
'... die schöpferische Macht der Zukunft (wird) nur verständlich ...im Blick auf ihre Konkretion als Liebe. (...) Für ihn (Jesus) offenbarte sich die Liebe Gottes in der Weise, wie seine Herrschaft Gegenwart wird, bevor sie mit unwiderstehlicher Macht anbricht. Jesus sah die Offenbarung der Liebe Gottes in seiner eigenen Sendung zur Ankündigung der anbrechenden Gottesherrschaft und in der Weise, wie sich durch diese Ankündigung der anbrechenden Gottesherrschaft und in der Weise, wie sich durch diese Ankündigung und durch den Glauben, den sie fand, die angekündigte Herrschaft Gottes als gegenwartsbestimmend erwies.'

97. For the concept of the 'Nirguna Brahman' cfr. Ch.I.B.

98. J.g. Fichte, 'Über den Grund unseres Glaubens an eine göttliche Weltregierung', in: Philosophisches Journal, 8(1798), SS.16f. (H. Lindau, Die Schriften Fichtes zum Atheismusstreit, 1912, S.34; also: SS.225ff.)
Cfr. also: F. Wagner, Der Gedanke der Persönlichkeit Gottes bei Fichte und Hegel, 1971, SS.20-96.

99. G.W.F. Hegel, Vorlesungen über die Philosophie der Religion, Hrg. Lasson, Bd.4 (Die absolute Religion), S.57.
Cfr. also: J. Splett, Die Trinitätslehre G.W.F. Hegels, 1965.

100. G.W.F. Hegel, Phänomenologie des Geistes, Hrg. Hoffmeister, SS.528f.

101. Cfr. Ignatius Viyagappa. C.W.F. Hegel's Concept of Indian Philosophy, Documents Missionalia 14, U.G.E., Roma, 1980.

102. Prof. Alexandre Ganoczy explains Hegel's concept of the self-realization of God: '... die letzte und alles umfassende Wirklichkeit in den Augen Hegels (ist) weder Gott noch der Mensch, sondern einfach der Geist.... Der Geist ist Alpha und Omega, sowie auch das, was dazwischen liegt: die nach höchstmöglicher Selbstwerdung strebende Totalwirklichkeit. Als solcher entfaltet sich der Geist sowohl in göttlicher wie auch in menschlicher Gestalt, das Endziel ist aber weder das Aufgehen des Menschlichen im Göttlichen noch das des Göttlichen im Menschlichen. Endziel ist nur die Selbstwerdung des Geistes in allen seinen geschichtlichen Erscheinungen, Gestalten, Momenten.' Cfr. Alexandre Ganoczy, Der schöpferische Mensch und die Schöpfung Gottes, Mainz, 1976, S.46.

103. For St. Augustines 'Psychological approach' to the understanding of the Holy Trinity. Cfr. St. Augustine, De Trinitate. Cfr. also the articles on this topic by Edmund Hill in: Life of the Spirit, Vols.15, 16, 17.

104. Karl Barth, Kirchliche Dogmatik, I/1, 312ff., 375ff. Idem, Die protestantische Theologie, 1947, p.377.

105. K. Rahner, Spirit in the World, p.69.

106. K. Barth, Op. Cit., Loc. Cit., especially S.378.

107. Cfr. K. Rahner, Foundations of Christian Faith, p.134. Cfr. also: Idem, 'Trinität', in: Herders theologisches Taschenlexikon, Bd. 7, SS.349ff. Further on the question of the Holy Trinity cfr. among others: K. Rahner, 'Der dreifaltige Gott', in: J. Feiner/M. Löhrer (Hrg.), Mysterium Salutis. Grundriß einer heilsgeschichtlichen Dogmatik, Einsiedeln, 1965ff., Bd.II, SS.317-319. (Hereafter cited as: Mysterium Salutis).

108. K. Rahner, 'Theology of Symbol', in: Idem, Theological Investigations, Vol. IV (Translated by Kevin Smyth), Baltimore, 1966, p.244. Cfr. also: pp.229-231.

109. Cfr. especially the above mentioned article (no. 107) of K. Rahner in Mysterium Salutis, in Herders theologisches Taschenlexikon, etc.

110. Cfr. above Ch.I.C.

111. Cfr. above Ch.I.B.3.b

112. S. Radhakrishnan, The Hindu View of Life, London, 1980 (1927), pp.23-24.

113. Idem, An Idealist View of Life, London, 1980 (1932), pp.84-85.

114. Idem, The Hindu View of Life, pp.21-24. Cfr. also above: Ch.I.C.

115. Idem, The Hindu View of Life, p.21.

698

116. Cfr. above: Ch.IV.B.1.c., CH.I.B.3.

117. W. Pannenberg, 'Person und Subjekt', in: idem, Grundfragen systematischer Theologie (Gesammelte Aufsätze), Band 2, 1980, S.93. This collection of essays will be hereafter cited as :Grundfragen II).

118. Ibid., S.95: 'Wenn der eine Gott in der Einheit seines Wesens schon Person wäre, dann würde die trinitarische Differenzierung als eine personale in der Tat nicht nur überflüssig sondern auch inkonsistent.'

119. Ibid.: 'Die Pointe der Trinitätslehre liegt gerade darin, daß der eine Gott für sich, abgesehen von den drei Personen, nicht Person ist, sondern jeweils nur in der Person des Vaters und des Sohnes - und auch Person in Gestalt des Geistes.'

120. Ibid., S.93: '... die Differenz zwischen Essenz und Person ermöglicht, daß für jede Person der Trinität das eine göttliche Wesen in den anderen beiden Personen erscheint, und gerade so läßt sich die Einheit des göttlichen Wesens als den drei Personen nicht entgegengesetzt, sondern durch sie vermittelt denken: Jede der drei Personen hat ihre Gottheit nur in den anderen beiden. So ist für den Sohn das göttliche Wesen nur im Vater, und der Geist ist ihm die Bürgschaft der eigenen Gemeinschaft mit dem Vater.'

121. Idem, 'Wie kann heute glaubwürdig von Gott geredet werden?', in: Gottesfrage heute. (Vorträge und Bibelarbeit in der Arbeitsgruppe 'Gottesfrage' des 14. deutschen evangelischen Kirchentages), Stuttgart, 1969, S. 59.

122. Ibid., S. 223; Cfr. also: Idem, 'The Question of God', in: Idem, Basic Questions in Theology II, 230-231.

123. Ibid., p.223., Cfr. also: 'Speaking about God', in: Idem, The Idea of god and Human Freedom, (Translated by R.A. Wilson), The Westminster Press, 1973, p.112.

124. Cfr. above Ch.II.A.

125. Cfr. above Ch.I.B.4; I.C.2; V.B.2.a.

126. Cfr. above Ch.II.A.2.

127. Cfr. above Ch.VII.B.1.

128. Cfr. above Ch.VII.B.3.

129. 'Gratia non destruit naturam, sed supponit et perficit naturam'. For the concepts of 'Nature' and 'Grace' in Thomas Aquinas cfr.: Friedemann Greiner, Die Menschlichkeit der Offenbarung. Die transzendentale Grundlegung der Theologie bei Karl Rahner, München, 1978, SS.160ff. Cfr. also: E. Przywara, Der Grundsatz gratia non destruit sed supponit et perficit naturam', in: Scholastik, 17 (1942), S.182; J. Alfaro, 'Desiderium naturale', in: LThK, III, 1959 , 248ff., B. Stoeckle, Gratia supponit naturam. Geschichte und Analyse eines theologischen Axioms, Rom, 1962., J. Ratzinger, 'Gratia supponit naturam', in: Idem, Dogma und Verkündigung, München/Freiburg, 1973, SS.161-181, etc.

130. Cfr. F. Greiner, Op. Cit., SS.185ff.
Cfr. also: Article by K. Rahner, 'Potentia oboedientialis', in: Idem (Hrg.),
Sacramentum Mundi. Theologisches Lexikon für die Praxis, Bd. III,
SS.1245-1249.

131. J.P. Jenny, 'Reflections on Human Nature and the Supernatural', in:
Theological Studies, XIV, 1953, pp.286-287.

132. K. Rahner et alii (Ed.), Sacramentum Mundi. An Encyclopedia of Theology,
New York, 1968, Vol.5, p.65.

133. Ibid., p.66.

134. Ibid.

135. Ibid.

136. Cfr. also: K. Rahner, 'Über das Verhältnis von Natur und Gnade', in:
Idem, Schriften zur Theologie, Bd. I, Einsiedeln, 1958 , SS.323-345.
Idem, 'Natur und Gnade', in: Idem, Schriften zur Theologie, Bd. IV,
SS.209-236. Especially S. 217.

137. Cfr. above Ch.II.A.2.
'Aham Brahmasmi' (Br. Up. 1.4.10)
'Tat tvam asi' (Chand. Up. 6.8.7., 9.4., 10.3.)

138. S. Radhakrishnan, An Idealist View of Life, p.81.

139. Ibid., p.83.

140. K. Rahner, 'Zur Theologie der Menschwerdung', in: Idem, Schriften
zur Theologie IV, Einsiedeln, 1960, S.140.

141. Ibid., p.141.
Ibid., p.140. Cfr. also: p.141: 'Die Annahme oder Ablehnung des Geheimnisses, das wir als die arme Verwiesenheit auf das Geheimnis der Fülle
sind, macht unsere Existenz aus; das vorgegebene Worauf unserer anneh-
menden oder ablehnenden Entscheidung als der Tat der Existenz ist
das Geheimnis, das wir sind, und dieses ist unsere Natur, weil die Transzendenz, die wir sind und die wir tun, unser und Gottes Dasein beibringt,
und beide als Geheimnis...'

142. K. Rahner, Foundations of Christian Faith, p.216.

143. Rahner owes the expression 'existential' to the philosophy of Martin
Heidegger. Cfr. K.-H. Weger, Karl Rahner - An Introduction, p.87.
'Existential' stands for that which constitutes human existence prior
to one's free choice. 'Existentiell' would refer to the free, subjective
and personal appropriation of some thing to one's own existence. The
former belongs to the 'a priori' structure of man, the latter, on the
other hand, is the result of man's free decisions. Cfr. K. Rahner,
Foundations of Christian Faith, p.16 (foot note).

144. K. Rahner, 'On the Theology of Incarnation', in: Idem, Theological
Investigations IV, London/Baltimore, 1966, pp.105-120.

700

145. Idem, 'Nature and Grace', in: Op. Cit., Vol.I, Baltimore, 1961, pp.302-303.

146. Kenneth D. Eberhard, 'Karl Rahner and the Supernatural Existential', in: Thought XLVI, No. 183 (1971), p.65.

147. K. Rahner, Ich glaube an Jesus Christus, SS.50, 51. Cfr. also: Idem, Foundations of Christian Faith, p.127. K.-H. Weger, Karl Rahner - An Introduction, p.87.

148. K. Rahner, Foundations of Christian Faith, p.128. Cfr. also: Brennan Hill, 'Karl Rahner's Metaphysical Anthropology', in: Carmelus, Vol.18 (1971), Fasciculus 2, p.181. Barrie Wilson, 'The Possibility of Theology after Kant: An Examination of Karl Rahner's 'Geist in Welt',' in: Canadian Journal of Theology, 12, October 1966, p.256.

149. Vorgrimler/Müller, Karl Rahner, Paris, 1965, p.71.

150. Cfr. below: Ch.IX.B.1.

151. K. Rahner, 'Nature and Grace', in: Idem, Theological Investigation, Vol. I (1961), pp.310-311.

152. Ibid., p.313. Cfr. also: Thomas J. Motherway, 'Supernatural Existential', in: Chicago Studies 4 (1965), p.86.

153. K.-H. Weger, Karl Rahner - An Introduction, p.106.

154. The transcendence of man does not make, as Vedanta does, an instrument or means out of God for man's egoistic self-realization. Cfr. K. Rahner, Zur Lage der Theologie. Probleme nach dem Konzil, (Interview), Düsseldorf, 1969, S. 27. 'Wenn man 'transzendental' in dem Sinn auffaßt, daß der Mensch ein Wesen ist, in dem Gott nur als eine Funktion der Selbstvermittlung fungiert, dann ist natürlich die Wirklichkeit Gottes und seiner Offenbarung durch den Menschen und dessen Selbstverständnis vereinnahmt.'

155. W. Pannenberg, Anthropologie in theologischer Perspektive, Göttingen, 1983, SS. 40-71.

156. Ibid., p.73.

157. Ibid., pp.73-74. Cfr. also the literature given there. Lynn White, 'The Historical Roots of an Ecological Crisis', in: The Environmental Handbook, New York, 1970., C. Amery, Das Ende der Vorsehung, die gnadenlosen Folgen des Christentums, 1972.
G. Altner, Schöpfung am Abgrund, 1974, SS.58ff., 81ff.

158. K. Rahner, Foundations of Christian Faith, p.44.

159. Ibid., pp.62, 63.

160. Brennan Hill, Art. Cit., p.181.
Cfr. also: Barrie Wilson, Art. Cit., p.256.

161. K. Rahner, 'Überlegungen zur Methode der Theologie, in: Idem, Schriften zur Theologie, Bd. IX, Einsiedeln, 1970, S.96.

162. Ibid.: 'Wenn man von der Voraussetzung ausgeht, daß jede Philosophie, d.h. jede wirkliche Metaphysik, die diesen Namen verdient, transzendentalphilosophisch arbeiten müsse oder überhaupt nicht sei, dann kann man natürlich sagen, daß jede Theologie, die wirklich reflektiert, denkt und mehr sein will als bloßer heilsgeschichtlicher Bericht, also philosophisch ist, damit auch schon transzendentalphilosophische Theologie, Transzendentaltheologie sei.'

163. Cfr. Ibid., Cfr. also: Idem, 'Theologie und Anthropologie, in: Idem, Schriften zur Theologie, Bd. VIII, Einsiedeln, 1967, SS.43-65., Idem, 'Über künftige Wege der Theologie, in: Idem, Schriften zur Theologie, Bd, X, Einsiedeln, 1972, SS.41-69.
Idem, 'Anthropozentrik', in: LThK I SS.632-634.

164. K. Rahner/E. Simons, Zur Lage der Theologie. Probleme nach dem Konzil, Düsseldorf, 1969, S.25: 'Die transzendentale Methode versucht ... den Glauben dadurch zu erschließen, daß sie nach den Bedingungen der Möglichkeit von Offenbarung im Selbstverständnis des Menschen und seiner Geschichte fragt. Sie bedeutet für die Theologie insgesamt eine anthropologische Wende.'

165. Cfr. K. Rahner, 'Transcendental Theology', in: Idem, Sacramentum Mundi. An Encyclopedia of Theology, New York/London, 1968, Vol.6, p.288.

166. Ibid.

167. Hans Urs von Balthasar, Cordula oder der Ernstfall, Einsiedeln, 1966, SS. 102-103: 'Wer 'Theologie als Anthropologie' zu treiben behauptet, der sagt zumindest, daß jeder Satz, der in dieser Wissenschaft über Gott gesagt wird, auch irgendwie über den Menschen gesagt wird; er läßt aber stillschweigend die Voraussetzung aller Theologie im Schatten, daß sie nämlich Logos des sprechenden Gottes ist, der zunächst den hörenden und nicht auch schon redenden Menschen trifft; das '-logie' in seiner scheinbaren Univozität ist eine Vernebelung.' Cfr. also S.125. For other criticism on Rahner's method, Cfr.: H. Tiefenbacher/A.Schilson, 'Die Frage nach Jesus Christus. a) Karl Rahner - Transzendentrale Theologie', in: Herderkorrespondenz, 26 (1972), S.565.
B. Lakebrink, Klassische Metaphysik - Eine Auseinandersetzung mit der existentialen Anthropozentrik, Freiburg 1967, S. 209.
Hans Urs von Balthasar, Herrlichkeit, eine theologische Ästhetik, Bd. I, 1961, S.142.
H. Fries, Die katholische Religionsphilosophie der Gegenwart, 1949, S. 258.

168. K. Rahner, 'Über künftige Wege der Theologie' (Art. Cit.), S.55: 'Transzendentale Theologie ist nicht bloß Übernahme einer Transzendentalphilosophie in die Theologie. Die Transzendentaltheologie mag geschichtlich ihren Ausgangspunkt von einer solchen Philosophie nehmen, was ja gewiß keine Schande ist. Aber der eigentliche Ansatz einer Transzendentaltheologie ist genuin theologisch.'

169. Henri Niel, 'Honouring Karl Rahner' in: The Heythrop Journal, 6 (1965), p.260.

169a. W. Pannenberg, 'Die Krise des Schriftprinzips', in: Idem, Grundfragen systematischer Theologie, Göttingen, 1979, SS.11,12: 'Eine Theologie, die sich der intellektuellen Verpflichtungen bewußt bleibt, die der Gebrauch des Wortes 'Gott' mit sich bringt, wird sich tunlichst darum bemühen, alle Wahrheit und daher nicht zuletzt die Erkenntnisse der außertheologischen Wissenchaften auf den Gott der Bibel zu beziehen und von ihm her neu zu verstehen (...). Doch recht verstanden ist die Offenbarung Gottes als Offenbarung Gottes eben erst dann bedacht, wenn alle sonstige Wahrheit und Erkenntnis auf sie hingeordnet und in sie aufgenommen wird. Nur so kann die biblische Offenbarung als Offenbarung des Gottes, der Schöpfer und Vollendung aller Dinge ist, verstanden werden.'
Cfr. also: Idem, 'Kontingenz und Naturgesetz', in: A.M. Müller/W. Pannenberg, Erwägungen zu einer Theologie der Natur, Gütersloh, 1970, SS.30-80.

170. Cfr. above Part I.Ch.II.C.

171. K. Rahner, 'Gnade als Mitte menschlicher Existenz', in: Herderkorrespondenz, 28 (1974), 83: 'Ich bin davon überzeugt, daß Transzendentalität nicht ein Metier des Menschen neben der Geschichte ist, sondern in der konkreten Geschichte gelebt und realisiert und in Freiheit bestimmt ist.'

172. F. Greiner, Op. Cit., p.293.

172a. W. Pannenberg, Was ist der Mensch?, SS.35ff.

173. K. Rahner, Hearers of the Word, pp.125, 128, 129.
Cfr. also: W. Kaspar, Jesus der Christus, Mainz, 1974, S.237., F.P. Fiorenza/J.B. Metz, 'Der Mensch als Einheit von Leib und Seele', in: J.Feiner/M. Lohr (Hrg.), Mysterium Salutis, Bd. II, SS.584-636.
Cfr. also: Raphael Schulte, 'Leib und Seele', in: Franz Böckle et alii, (Hrg.) Christlicher Glaube in moderner Gesellschaft, Freiburg/Basel/Wien, 1981, Band 5, SS.6ff.
Alxeandre Ganoczy, Schöpfungslehre, Düsseldorf, 1983, SS.42-46, 112-114.

174. K. Rahnerm, Hearers of the Word, p.128.

175, Ibid., p.125.

176. Ibid., pp.130-132. For Rahner's concept of history. Cfr. especially, Ibid., pp.111-167., Cfr. also: P. Eicher, Die anthropologische Wende, 1970, SS.388ff., L.B. Puntel, 'Zum Denken Karl Rahners', in: ZkTh, 86 (1964), SS.314f.·
E. Simons, Philosophie und Offenbarung, 1966, SS.134ff.
E. Mitterstieler, Christlicher Glaube als Bestätigung des Menschen, 1975, S.47.

177. K. Rahner, Hearers of the Word, pp.132-133.

178. Ibid., p.128. See foot note.

179. K. Rahner, 'Christology in the Setting of Modern Man's Understanding of Himself and the World', in: Idem, Theological Investigations, Vol. XI, London/New York, 1974, p.218., Cfr. also: Idem, 'The Unity of Spirit and Matter in the Christian Understanding of Faith', in: Idem, Theological Investigations, Vol. VI, London/Baltimore, 1969, pp.153-177.

180. K. Rahner, 'The Eternal Significance of the Humanity of Jesus for our Relationship with God', in: Idem Theological Investigations, Vol. III, London/Baltimore, 1967, p.40.

181. Idem, 'Christology in the Setting of Modern Man's Understanding of Himself and His World', in: Idem, Theological Investigations, Vol. XI, p.218.
Cfr. also: Idem, 'The Secret of Life', in: Idem, Theological Investigations, Vol.VI, London/Baltimore, 1969, pp.141-152. K. Rahner/P. Overhage, Das Problem der Hominisation (Quaestiones Disputatae 12/13), Freiburg, 1961.

182. Cfr. Teilhard de Chardin, Man's Place in Nature, London, 1966.

183. K. Rahner, Foundations of Christian Faith, pp.184, 185.

184,. Ibid., pp.187-190.

185. The expression 'Point Omega' is taken from Teilhard de Chardin. Cfr. K. Rahner, Ich glaube an Jesus Christus, S. 34., Cfr. also: Idem, 'Christology in the Setting of Modern Man's Understanding of Himself and His World', in: Idem, Theological Investigations, XI, pp.221,222.

186. For a reconciliation of Creation and Evolution. Cfr. Stefan Niklaus Bosshard, 'Evolution und Schöpfung', in: Franz Böckle et alii (Hrg.), Christlicher Glaube in moderner Gesellschaft, Bd. 3, SS.87ff. Rahner understands the question of 'Miracles' in the context of the self-transcendence of the created reality and not as a direct intervention on God's part into the laws of the world. Cfr. K.-H. Weger, Karl Rahner - An Introduction, pp.83-84.

187. K. Rahner, 'Christology within an Evolutionary View of the World', in: Idem, Theological Investigations, Vol.V, London/Baltimore, 1966, p.160.
Idem, Foundations of Christian Faith, p.181.
Idem, 'Jesus Christ', in: Idem, Sacramentum Mundi - An Encyclopedia of Theology, London, 1968, Vol.3, p.203.

188. K. Rahner, 'Christology within an Evolutionary View of the World', (Art. Cit.), p.172.

189. Thomas Pearl, 'Dialectical Panentheism: On the Hegelian Character of Karl Rahner's Key Theological Writings', in: The Irish Theological Quarterly, Vol XLII (April 1975), No.2, p.130.
Cfr. also: K. Rahner, The Theology of Symbol', in: Idem, Theological Investigations, Vol. IV, Baltimore, 1966, pp.246, 247.

190. K. Rahner, Hominization (Tr. by: W.J. O'Hara), New York, 1965, p.55.

191. Idem, 'Christology within an Evolutionary View of the World', (Art. Cit.), p.164.

192. Idem, Hominization, p.55.

193. Ibid., pp.59-61. Cfr. also: Thomas Pearl, Art. Cit., p.131.

194. K. Rahner, 'On the Theology of Incarnation', in: Idem, Theological Investigation IV, London /Baltimore, 1966, p.113.

195. A. Ganoczy, Der schöpferische Mensch, SS.32ff.

196. Ibid., SS.66-67.

197. Cfr. above Ch.I.B.4.

198. For the view of Brahmabandab Upadhyaya, Cfr. above Chapter V.

199. Frank E. Tupper, Op. Cit., p.25.
     Cfr. also: W. Pannenberg, 'What is Truth?' in: Basic Questions in Theology II, pp.21-26.
     Idem, 'The Significance of Christianity in the Philosophy of Hegel', in: Idem, The Idea of God and Human Freedom, pp.114-177.

200. For the 'Apauruseya' character of the Eternal Truth. Cfr. our Introduction to Part I.

201. Cfr. above Ch.II.A.1. and III.B.".

202. K. Rahner, Foundations of Christian Faith, pp.140-141.

203. Cfr. Thomas Aquinas, Summa Theologica, I,84,7: 'Respondeo dicendum quod impossibile est intellectum nostrum, secundum praesentis vitae statum, quo passibili corpori conjungitur, aliquid intelligere in actu, nisi convertendo se ad phantasmata.' Cfr. also: K. Rahner, Spirit in the World, pp.4-11.

204. Andrew Tallon, 'Spirit, Matter, Becoming: Karl Rahner's 'Spirit in the World' (Geist in Welt)', in: The Modern Schoolman, 48 (1971), pp.151-165, esp. p.160.

205. K. Rahner, Hearers of the Word, p.117.

206. Ibid., pp.140-141.

207. Ibid., p.143.

208. Idem, Spirit in the World, p. xliii.

209. Ibid., p.xliv.

210. Idem, 'The Unity of Spirit and Matter in the Christian Understanding of faith', in: Idem, Theological Investigations, Vol.VI, London/Baltimore, 1969, Cfr. also: p.211.

211. For further on this question, Cfr. A. Ganoczy, Schöpfungslehre, SS.43, 104.

212. Cfr. above Ch. II.B.3.b.

213. K. Rahner, Hearers of the Word, Chapter V, pp.53ff. Cfr. also: William Shepherd, Man's Condition, New York, 1969, p.109ff.

214. K. Rahner, Spirit in the World, pp.67-77., esp. p.71. Cfr. also: Brennan Hill, Art. Cit., pp.187, 188.

215. W. Pannenberg, Was ist der Mensch?, S.6.

216. Ibid., S.7.

217. ibid.,SS.7-10.

218. Ibid., S.13: 'Der Umweltgebundenheit der Tiere entspricht also beim Menschen weder sein Verhältnis zur Naturwelt, noch die Vertrautheit mit seiner Kulturwelt, sondern seine unendliche Angewiesenheit auf Gott. Was für das Tier die Umwelt, das ist für den Menschen Gott: das Ziel, an dem allein Streben Ruhe finden kann und wo seine Bestimmung erfüllt wäre.'

219. Ibid.,SS.34ff.

220. Cfr. below: Ch.VIII.C.3.

221. For the concept of 'Samsara' Cfr. above: Ch.II.B.2. Cfr. also: Ch. VIII.C.3.

222. Cfr. above Ch.VII.B.1.b.

223. Cfr. especially above: Ch.IV.

224. W. Pannenberg, 'What is Truth?', in: Basic questions in Theology, II, pp.20-21.

225. Ibid.

226. Cfr. Gerhold Becker, Theologie in der Gegenwart, Regensburg, 1978, SS.166ff. Cfr. also: Arno Schilson/Walter Kasper, Christologie im Präsens. Kritische Sichtung neuer Entwürfe, Freiburg/Basel/Wien, 1980, SS.90ff.

227. W. Pannenberg, 'Was ist Wahrheit?, in: Grundfragen systematischer Theologie, I, SS.218f., Cfr. also: Idem, 'Über historische und theologische Hermeneutik', in: Op. Cit., S.138: '... die Totalität der Wirklichkeit ist kein Vorhandenes, sondern muß als Prozeß einer Geschichte auf eine noch offene Zukunft hin gedacht werden.'

228. Idem, 'Heilsgeschehen und Geschichte', in: Op. Cit. S.27. Cfr. also: Idem, 'Redemptive Event as History', in: Basic Questions in Theology I, pp.15-80.

229. Idem, 'Heilsgeschehen und Geschichte', (Art. Cit.), S.26., Idem, 'Redemptive Event as History', (Art. Cit.), p.20. Cfr. also: D. Rössler, Gesetz und Geschichte-Untersuchung zur Theologie der jüdischen Apokalyptik und der pharisäischen Orthodoxie, 1960.

230. W. Pannenberg, 'What ist Truth?', (Art. Cit.), p.22. Idem, 'Was ist Wahrheit?', (Art. Cit.), SS.218-219.

230a. Pannenberg quotes Hans von Soden , Was ist Wahrheit? Vom geschichtlichen Begriff der Wahrheit, Marburg, 1927, S.15.

230b. Cfr. above Ch.II.C.

231. W. Pannenberg, 'Glaube und Vernunft', in: Grundfragen systematischer Theologie, I, S.249: 'Jede behauptete Bedeutung beruht auf einem Vorgriff, auf einer Antizipation jener letzten Zukunft, in deren Licht die wahre Bedeutung jedes einzelnen Ereignisses erst und gültig aussagbar wäre.'

232. Frank E. Tupper, Op. Cit., p.58.

232a. Edmund J. Dobbin, Reflections on W. Pannenberg's Revelation Theology, Leuven, 1972, p.20. The 'Telos' or goal at the end of a process is somehow already present in the particular events leading to this end!

233. W. Pannenberg, 'Glaube und Vernunft' (Art. Cit.), SS.249-250. In the light of this Pannenberg's theology could also be called 'Theology of Hope', 'Theology of History', 'Theology of Future' or 'Theology of the Kingdom of God'. Cfr. also: Frank E. Tupper, Op. Cit., p.20.

234. Car. E. Braaten, 'The New Theology of the Future' in: Carl Braaten/ R.W. Jenson, 'The Futurist Option, Paulist/Newman Press, 1970, p.11. Klaus Koch, 'The Discovery of Apocalyptic', in: Studies in Biblical Theology, 2nd Series, No.22, Inc., 1972, esp. p.101.

235. Frank E. Tupper, Op. Cit., p.49.

236. Cfr. below Ch.VIII.C.1.

237. W. Pannenberg, 'Theology and the Kingdom of God', in: Op. Cit., p.55.

238. Edmund J. Dobbin, Op. Cit., p.15.

239. W. Pannenberg, 'Analogy and Doxology', in: Idem, Basic Questions in Theology, I, p.234.

240. Edmund J. Dobbin, Op. Cit., p.15.

241. W. Pannenberg, 'Die Krise des Schriftprinzips' (Art. Cit.), S.12.

242. Idem, 'Dogmatische Thesen zur Lehre von der Offenbarung', in: Idem et alii, Offenbarung als Geschichte, Göttingen, 1961, SS.91-114.

243. K. Rahner/J. Ratzinger, Offenbarung und Überlieferung, 1965, SS.11ff.

244. Cfr. U. Kühn, Natur und Gnade, 1961, S.10.

245. K. Rahner, Hearers of the Word, p.119.

246. On the question of the gratuitous character of Revelation, that is considered by some as problematic in Rahner's writing, see: P. Eicher, Die anthropologische Wende (Karl Rahners philosophischer Weg vom Wesen des Menschen zur personalen Existenz), Freiburg, 1970, SS.373ff. B. Lakebrink, Klassische Metaphysik. Eine Auseinandersetzung mit der existentialen Anthropozentrik, Freiburg, 1967, SS.237ff. K. Lehmann/K.Rahner, in: Bilanz der Theologie im 20.Jahrhundert, Bd. IV, Freiburg/Basel/Wien, 1970, SS.158ff. J.B. Metz, Zur Theologie der Welt, München, 1968, SS.89ff. K.P. Fischer, Der Mensch als Geheimnis. Die Anthropologie Karl Rahners, Freiburg, 1974, SS.206-265. A. Gerken, Offenbarung und Transzendentalerfahrung, Düsseldorf, 1969, S.72.

247. Andrew Thallon,'S pirit, Freedom, History - Karl Rahner's Hörer des Wortes (Hearers of the Word)', in: The Thomist 38 (1974), pp.908-936.

248. K. Rahner, Hearers of the Word, p.120.

249. Ibid., p.172.

250. F. Greiner, Op. Cit., S.255, 254, 265. K. Rahner, 'Christology within an Evolutionary View of the World', (Art. Cit.), p.174., Idem, 'Christology in the Setting of Modern Man's View of Himself and His World', (Art. Cit.), pp.225, 226.

251. K. Rahner, Hearers of the Word, p.172.

252. Ibid., pp.10, 11.

253. Robert Masson, 'Rahner and Heidegger: Being, Hearing and God', in: The Thomist, 37 (1973), p.486., Cfr. also: K. Rahner, 'The Concept of Existential Philosophy in Heidegger' (Tr. by Andrew Tallon), in: Philosophy Today, 13 (1969), pp.131ff.

254. K. Rahner, 'Foreword', to: Louis Roberts, The Achievements of Karl Rahner, New York, 1967, p.viii.

255. M. Heidegger, Being and Time, (Tr. by John Macquarrie and Edmund Robinson), New York, 1966, p.1.

256. Robert Masson, Art. Cit., pp.472, 474, 479-482. K. Rahner, Hearers of the Word, pp.32, 38, 39, 59, 62-64, 67, 158, 161.

257. K. Rahner, Op. Cit., p.159.

258. Ibid., pp.158-159.

259. Cfr. Ch.VII.C.2.

260. Cfr. Ch.IX.A.

261. Cfr. above: Ch.I.C.1., I.C.3., IV.B., V.B.3.a., VII.A.2.

262. K. Rahner, 'Zur Theologie des Symbols', in: Idem, Schriften zur Theologie Bd. IV, Einsiedeln, 1960, S.301. Cfr. also: Idem, 'The Theology of Symbol', in: Idem, 'Theological Investigations', Vol. IV, Baltimore, 1966, pp.224, 229.

263. Cfr. Ch.VII.A. 3.

264. George F. Thomas, Religious Philosophies of the West, New York, 1965, p.288. Cfr. also: Alexandre Ganoczy, Der schöpferische Mensch, SS.43-46.

265. K. Rahner, 'On the Theology of the Incarnation', in: Theological Investigations, IV, p.115.
Cfr. also: Idem, 'Theology of Symbol', (Art. Cit.), pp.236-237.

266. K. Rahner, 'Der dreifaltige Gott als transzendentaler Urgrund der Heilsgeschichte', in: J. Feiner/M. Löhrer (Hrg.), Mysterium Salutis. Grundriß heilsgeschichtlicher Dogmatik, Bd. II, Einsiedeln/Zürich/Köln, 1967, SS.327ff. Cfr. also: H. de Lavalette, 'Dreifaltigkeit', in: LThK III, 543-548.

267. W. Pannenberg, Jesus - God and Man, (Tr. by Lewis L. Wilkins and Duane A. Priebe), (The Westminster Press, 1968), London, 1980, p.180.

268. S. Radhakrishnan, The Hindu View of Life, p.23.

269. P. Schoonenberg, 'Trinity - the Consummated Covenant - Theses on the Doctrine of the Trinitarian God', in: Studies in Religion-Sciences, 1975-6, p.114.
Cfr. also: Idem, 'Spirit Christology and Logos Christology', in: Bijdragen 29 (1977), pp.35-357.

270. Cfr. above: Ch.I.B. and C.

271. Cfr. above: Ch.I.C.3.

272. On the question of myths and idols, Cfr. above our introduction to Part I, C.I.A., II.C., II.A.1., II.B.3.a., III.C., V.C.

273. R. De Smet (Ed.), Religious Hinduism, Allahabad, 1968, p.82.

274. Cfr. also: M. Dhavamony, Phenomenology of Religion (Documenta Missionalia 7), Roma, 1973, pp.137-157. Cfr. also: W. Kasper, Jesus der Christus, S. 49.
Cfr. also: John Navone, The Jesus Story: Our Life as Story in Christ, Minnesota, 1979, passim.

275. W. Kasper, Op. Cit., pp.48ff.
Cfr. also: Hans-Georg Gadamer/Heinrich Fries, 'Mythos und Wissenschaft', in: Franz Böckle et alii, Op. Cit., Bd. 2, SS.30ff.

276. A. Grillmeier, Der Logos am Kreuz, München 1956, Cfr. also: Idem, LThK II², SS.458-467.

277. K. Rahner, Ich glaube an Jesus Christus, SS.39, 40: 'Beim Wesen einer göttlichen Wirklichkeit und Wahrheit kann es außerdem nicht anders sein, als daß eine Formel aus menschlichen Begriffen nicht nur den Zugang zur gemeinten Wirklichkeit eröffnet, sondern auch erschwert, weil jede Formel unweigerlich auch die Gefahr von Mißverständnissen bei sich hat.'

278. Idem, 'Current Problems in Christology', in: Idem, Theological Investigations, Vol. 1 (1961), pp.149-200.

279. Ibid.

280. Ibid., p.150.

281. W. Pannenberg, 'Analogie und Doxologie', in: Idem, Grundfragen systematischer Theologie, I, SS.200, 201.

282. Ibid., SS.186, 187, 196-198, 201. Cfr. also: Idem, Basic Questions in Theology, I, p.218.

283. Idem, 'Analogie und Doxologie' (Art. Cit.), S.84.

284. Hans Urs von Balthasar, Karl Barth, Einsiedeln, 1976, SS.116ff., 175ff.

285. Cfr. above Ch.II.A.2., Ch.V.

286. K. Rahner, 'Grace', in: Idem (Hrg.), Sacramentum Mundi, Vol. II, p.415.

287. Idem, 'The Hiddenness of Being', in: Hearers of the Word, pp.71-82, 91.

288. Ibid., p.91.

289. Ibid., p.92.

290. W. Pannenberg, Was ist der Mensch?, SS. 11f. Cfr. also: 'Die Frage nach Gott', in: Idem, Grundfragen systematischer Theologie, I, SS.361-386.

291. For a detailed exposition of this topic Cfr. G. Fourure, Les châtiments divins, Tournai, 1959.

292. Cfr. above Ch.II.B.1.

293. A. Ganoczy, Die Schöpfungslehre, SS.97ff.

294. On the question of negativity and evil, Cfr. Ludger Oeing-Hankoff/Walter Kasper, 'Negativität und Böses', in: Franz Böckle et alii (Hrg.), Op. Cit., Bd. 9, SS.149ff.

295. A. Ganoczy, Der schöpferische Mensch, SS.23, 33, 37.

296. For S. Radhakrishnan's idea that Growth includes suffering and pain, Cfr. above Ch.III.A.1.a. For an elaborate discussion of the question of suffering,cfr.L. Jerphagnon, Le mal et l'existence, Paris, 1966.

297. Cfr. A.D. Sertillanges, Le problème du mal, I, L'histoire II, La solution, Paris, 1948-1951. Here: II, p.13.

298. Ch. Journet, Le mal. Essai théologique, Paris, 1961, pp.267, 268.

299. Jean Galot, Gesù Liberatore, (Nuova collana di teologia cattolica 12), Firenze, 1978, p.302.

300. K. Kitamouri, Theology of the Pain of God, Richmond, 1965 (Translated from Japanese: Kami no itami no shingaku, Tokyo, 1958.)
J. Moltmann, Der gekreuzigte Gott, München, 1972.
Jean Galot, Il Mistero della Soffrenza di Dio, Assisi, 1975.

301. Cfr. Ch.VIII.B.2.

302. W. Pannenberg, 'Postscript', in: Frank E. Tupper, Op. Cit., p.303.

303. Ibid., p.304.

304. Cfr. above Ch.II.B.1.

305. Idem, Was ist der Mensch?, S. 46: 'Die Ichhaftigkeit, die sich in sich selbst verschließt, das ist die Sünde.'

306. Ibid., p.47. Cfr. also: Idem, 'Christological Foundation of Christian Anthropology', in: Concilium (English), June 1973, pp.93-95.

307. K. Rahner, 'Christology in an Evolutionary View of the World', (Art. Cit., p.85.

308. Idem, Foundations of Christian Faith, pp.192-193.

309. Ibid., p.115.

310. Ibid., pp.103-104.

311. Cfr. above Ch.II.B.

312. Cfr. DS. 1512, 1513, 1515.
Cfr. also: J. Groß, Geschichte des Erbsündendogmas I, 1960, SS. 322ff., 327ff.
M. Flick/Z. Alszeghy, Fundamenti di una antropologia teologica, (Nuova collana di teologia cattolica 10), Firenze, 1973, pp.147-218.
M. Flick, Peccato originale originato-ricerca di una definizione, (Studia patavina 15), 1968, pp.81-93.

313. K. Rahner, Foundations of Christian Faith, pp.107-110. P. Schoonenberg also stresses the 'Situiert-Sein' des Menschen in seinem sozialen Lebenszusammenhang'. This preceds any personal decision of man. This is not merely extrinsic to man, but determined the very existence of man. Cfr. P. Schoonenberg, 'Der Mensch der Sünde', in: J. Feiner/M. Löhrer, Mysterium Salutis, Bd. II, 1967, SS.845-941. Especially 924, 928, 931. Cfr. also: Idem, Theologie der Sünde, Einsiedeln, 1966.

711

314. K. Rahner, Op. Cit., p.114. Cfr. also below Ch.VIII, IX.

315. W. Pannenberg, 'The Christological Foundations of Christian Anthropology', (Art. Cit.), pp.93-96.

316. Ibid., pp.88-90.

317. W.Pannenberg, Cfr. Was ist der Mensch?, SS.40ff., passim.

318. W. Pannenberg, Anthropologie in theologischer Perspektive, Göttingen, 1983, SS.116ff., especially: S. 120: 'Als mythisches Urbild zeigt seine (Adams) Geschichte, was sich in der Geschichte jedes Menschen wiederholt. Als mythisches Urbild hat Adam freilich keine echte Individualität, wie sie erforderlich ist, damit von Verantwortlichkeit für die Sünde im Sinne des Verursachungsprinzips gesprochen werden kann.'

319. Ibid., p.121. For a critical presentation of St. Augustine's concept of 'Original sin', Cfr. A. Ganoczy, Schöpfungslehre, SS.97-101.

320. Cfr. R. Seeberg, Lehrbuch der Dogmengeschichte, II,3, 1923, S.491.

320a. For the ideas of K.C. Sen, Cfr. above: CH.VI.B.1.b.

321. A. Ganoczy, Schöpfungslehre, SS.100-101.

322. Cfr. above Ch.IV.A.2.a.

323. Cfr. above Ch.IV.A.2.c., IV.C.1.

324. Cfr. above Ch.IV.B.

325. Cfr. above Ch.IV.B.1.a.

326. Cfr. above Ch.VII.A. and B.

327. K.-H. Weger, Karl Rahner - An Introduction, p.152.

328. K. Rahner, Grundkurs des Glaubens: Einführung in den Begriff des Christentums, Freiburg i.Br., 1976, S. 227 (Hereafter cited only by the first part of the book's title!)

329. K.-H. Weger, Karl Rahner - Eine Einführung in sein theologisches Denken, Freiburg i.Br., 1978, S.132. (Hereafter cited only by short title).

330. F. Greiner, Op. Cit., S.268.

331. K.-H. Weger, Karl Rahner - Eine Einführung, SS. 132ff.

332. K. Rahner, Grundkurs des Glaubens, SS.208, 210 etc.

333. Idem, Ich glaube an Jesus Christus, S. 29.
Idem, 'Grundlinien einer systematischen Christologie', in: Quaestiones Disputatae 55, SS. 20f., esp. Lehrsatz 10.

334. K. Rahner/W. Thüsing, A New Christology, (Tr. by David Smith and Verdant Green), London, 1980, p.58.

335. K. Fischer, Op. Cit., p.272.

336. K. Rahner, Foundations of Christian Faith, pp.298, 299.

337. D. Wiederkehr, 'Konfrontationen und Integrationen der Christologie', in: Theologische Berichte, 2 (1973), S. 52.

338. K. Rahner, Grundkurs des Glaubens, S.211.

339. Idem, 'Probleme der Christologie von heute', in: Idem, Schriften zur Theologie. Bd. I, Einsiedeln, 1958, S.176.

340. H. Geißer, 'Die Interpretation der kirchlichen Lehre von Gott-Mensch bei Karl Rahner SJ.', in: Kerygma und Dogma, 14 (1968), S.316.

341. K. Rahner, 'Zur Theologie der Menschwerdung', in: Idem, Schriften zur Theologie, Bd. IV, Einsiedeln, 1960, S.151.

342. Ph. Kaiser, Die Gott-menschliche Einigung in Christus als Problem der spekulativen Theologie seit der Scholastik, 1968, S. 286.

343. K. Rahner, Ich glaube an Jesus Christus, S.16.

344. Ibid., p.22. Cfr. also: A. Schilson/W. Kasper, Christologie im Präsens, S. 84.

345. K. Rahner, Grundkurs des Glaubens, S. 289.

346. Idem, 'Auf der Suche nach Zugängen zum Verständnis des gottmenschlichen Geheimnisses Jesus', in: Idem, Schriften zur Theologie, Bd. X, Einsiedeln, 1972, S. 212.

347. Mt 25:31-46., Cfr. also: K. Rahner, Ich glaube an Jesus Christus, S.31.

348. Bert Van der Heijden, Karl Rahner. Darstellung und Kritik seiner Grundpositionen, Einsiedeln, 1973, S.143.

349. K. Rahner, Op. Cit., pp.22, 23, 39.

350. Ibid., pp.24, 25. Cfr. also: Idem, 'I believe in Jesus Christ', in: Idem, Theological Investigations, Vol. 9, London/New York, 1972, p.165: 'The person to whom one ... commits himself can be addressed in the most varied ways depending on the dimensions of one's own self and the nature of one's absolute committal: simply 'Lord', 'Son of God', 'Pardoner', 'Saviour' and a thousand other names which have become his since the New Testament. He can be addressed in an apparently private aspect as the forgiver of one's guilt or in a cosmic perspective as the Omega of the development of the universe, the meaningful conclusion of history.'

351. Idem, Ich glaube an Jesus Christus, S.47: 'Wo sich die Menschen liebend und bedingungslos dem Nächsten anvertrauen, bejahen sie in Gottes Gnade glaubend den Gottmenschen, der in der Liebe zwischen den Menschen seine Endgültigkeit mitteilt.'

352. Idem, Foundations of Christian Faith, pp.295-297.

353. Idem, Ich glaube an Jesus Christus, S. 29.

354. Idem. Foundations of Christian Faith, pp.211, 212.

355. Cfr. above Ch.III.C., Ch.V.C.1., Ch.V.C.3.b.

356. Hans Urs von ·Balthasar, Glaubhaft ist nur Liebe, Einsiedeln, 1963, passim.
Cfr. also: B.v.d. Heijden, Op. Cit., passim.

357. A. Gerken, Offenbarung und Transzendenzerfahrung, Düsseldorf, 1969,
SS.73, 74.

358. W. Pannenberg, 'The Christological Foundation of Christian Anthropology', (Art. Cit.), pp.86 ff.

359. Cfr. to their respective works.

360. K.-H. Weger, Karl Rahner - Eine Einführung, S.134.

361. K. Rahner, 'On the Theology of the Incarnation', in: Theological Investigations, Vol. IV, London/Baltimore, 1966, p.110.

362. Idem, Grundkurs des Glaubens, S. 227.

363. Idem, 'Christology in an Evolutionary View of the World', (Art. Cit.),
pp.157-158.

364. Idem, 'Current Problems in Christology', in: Theological Investigations,
Vol. I, London/Baltimore, 1961, p.186.

365. Ibid., p.187.

366. W. Kasper, 'Kritik und Neuansatz gegenwärtiger Christologie', in: L.
Scheffczyk (Hrg.), Grundfragen der Christologie heute, Freiburg/Basel/
Wien, 1975, S.156.

367. Cfr. above: Ch.VII.B.1.b. and B.2.b.
Cfr. also: K. Rahner, Hörer des Wortes, München, 1941, S.167.

368. K. Rahner, 'Gnade als Mitte der menschlichen Existenz', in: Herderkorrespondenz, 28 (1974), (Ein Interview) S.87. Idem, Hearers of the
Word, pp.161-163, 169. Cfr. also: F. Greiner, Op. Cit., p.252.

369. K. Rahner, Grundkurs des Glaubens, S. 209.

370. K. Rahner/W. Thüsing, A New Christology, p.67.

371. K. Rahner, 'Jesus Christ', in: Idem (Ed.), Sacramentum Mundi (English),
Vol.3, p.204.

372. Ibid.

373. Idem, 'Was heißt heute an Jesus Christus glauben?', in: Idem, Schriften
zur Theologie, Band XIII, Einsiedeln, 1978, SS.175-176.

374. Idem, Current problems in Christology', (Art. Cit.), p.189.

375. We will have to pay more attention to the claims of Jesus in Ch.VIII.

376. K. Rahner, 'Probleme der Christologie von heute', in: Idem, Schriften zur Theologie, Bd. I, Einsiedeln, 1958[3], S.191.

377. K. Rahner, Ich glaube an Jesus Christus, SS.33-34: 'Denn wo ist sonst ein Mensch der hellen, greifbaren Geschichte, der überhaupt auf dieses Ereignis als in ihm geschehen Anspruch gemacht hätte? Wo ist einer, dessen menschliches Leben, dessen Tod und (fügen wir hinzu) Auferstehung, dessen Geliebtsein durch unzählige Menschen den Mut und die geistige Legitimierung dazu geben könnte, sich bedingungslos auf ihn einzulassen, sich auf ihn zu verlassen (im wörtlichen Sinn) - außer eben gerade der biblische Jesus?'

378. Cfr. back to the notion of 'Hearing' as 'paying attention to' (Heidegger): Above: Ch.VII.B.2.b.

378a. K. Rahner, 'Current Problems in Christology', (Art. Cit.), p.186.

379. Cfr. Foot note no. 371, esp. p.289.

380. K.-H. Weger, Karl Rahner. Eine Einführung, S.134.

381. Idem, Grundkurs des Glaubens, S.211.

382. F. Greiner, Op. Cit., p.278.

383. K. Rahner, Op.Cit., pp.227, also: 203, 205, 288.

384. W. Kasper, Jesus der Christus, S.61.

385. Cfr. above: Ch.IV.C.1., IV.B.3.

386. Cfr. above Ch.IV., also: Foot note no. 322-331.

386a. For a discussion of this topic and for a vast bibliography, Cfr. Renè Latourelle, Finding Jesus through the Gospels, (Tr. by Aloysius Owen), New York, 1979.
Cfr. also: José Caba, Dai vangeli al Gesù storico, Roma, 1979.

387. Martin Kähler, Der sogenannte historische Jesus und der geschichtliche biblische Christus, Leipzig, 1892, S.147.

388. Ibid., p.22: 'Der wirkliche Christus (ist) der gepredigte Christus.' Cfr. also the English translation of the same work by Carl Braaten, 'The So-called Historical Jesus and the Historic, Biblical Christ, Fortress Press, 1964, p.66.
Cfr. also: W. Pannenberg, 'Kerygma und Geschichte', in: Idem, Grundfragen systematischer Theologie, Bd. I, SS.79ff.

389. Paul Althaus, Die christliche Wahrheit, 1962[6], SS.423ff. Idem, 'Offenbarung als Geschichte und Glaube: Bemerkungen zur Wolfhart Pannenbergs Begriff der Offenbarung', in: ThLZ, LXXXVII (1962), SS.312ff. esp.325.

390. D.F. Strauß, Das Leben für das deutsche Volk, Bonn, 1891 [6], 2.Teil,
S.387.
Cfr. also: Idem, Das Leben Jesu, kritisch bearbeitet, Bd.1, Tübingen,
1835, S.469.
Idem, Der alte und der neue Glaube, Bonn, 1873[6], S.94.

391. A. Schweitzer, Geschichte der Leben-Jesu-Forschung, Tübingen, 1913[2],
S.4: 'So fand jede der folgenden Epochen der Theologie ihre Gedanken
in Jesus wieder, und anders konnte sie ihn nicht beleben. Und nicht
nur die Epochen fanden sich in ihm wieder, jeder einzelne schuf ihn
nach seiner eigenen Persönlichkeit.'

392. Rudolf Bultmann, Das Verhältnis der urchristlichen Christusbotschaft
zum historischen Jesus, 1962[3], S.13. Cfr. also: Gogarten who is also
in line with the 'Existence Theology' of Bultmann which reduces history
in the history of existence. Cfr. further: W. Pannenberg, 'Heilsgeschehen und Geschichte' (Art. Cit.), SS.22, 23.

393. Oscar Cullmann, Die Christologie des Neuen Testamentes, 1958   ,
Cfr. also: F. Hahn, Christologische Hochheitstitel. Ihre Geschichte im
frühen Christentum, 1963, SS.133-225., 280-333.

393a. Walter Künneth, Glauben an Jesus? Die Begegnung der Christologie
mit der modernen Existenz, Hamburg, 1962.

393b. W. Pannenberg, Grundzüge der Christologie, Gütersloh, 1976   , SS.41-
42. Cfr. Idem, Jesus - God and Man, (Translated by Lewis L. Wilkins
and Duane A. Priebe), London, 1968, p.48.

393c. For further on such a 'Projection Christology' Cfr: J: Jeremias, 'Der
gegenwärtige Stand der Debatte um das Problem des historischen Jesus',
in: H. Ristow/K. Matthiae (Hrg.), Der historische Jesus und der kerygmatische Christus. Beiträge zum Christusverständnis in Forschung und
Verkündigung, Berlin, 1960, S.14.

394. Hermann Diem, Dogmatik. Ihr Weg zwischen Historismus und Existentialismus, 1955, SS.106, 107, 120, 127: Here he questions the need, to go
beyond the Kerygma to the historical Jesus because the history of
Jesus is ever anew in the proclamation. But in his: Der irdische Jesus
und der Christus des Glaubens, Tübingen, 1957, S.12, he admits the
opposite, namely the need to seek Jesus himself behind the evangelists
testimony, as the first phase of the proclamation.

395. E. Käsemann, 'Probleme neutestamentlicher Arbeit in Deutschland',
in: Die Freiheit des Evangeliums und die Ordnung der Gesellschaft,
München, 1952, SS.133-152. Idem, 'Das Problem des historischen Jesus',
in: ZThK, 51 (1954), SS.125-153.

395a. Gerhard Ebeling, Theologie und Verständigung, 1962, S.63.

395b. Wilhelm Hermann, 'Der geschichtliche Christus. Der Grund unseres Glau -
bens', in: ZThK II (1892), SS.232-273.

395c. E. Fuchs, Zur Frage nach dem historischen Jesus, Tübingen, 1965, (2.Auf-
lage), VII.

396. W. Pannenberg, Grundzüge der Christologie, S.17.

397. Ibid. This possibility and necessity have been given concrete expression in a recently published book written by Walter Simonis, Jesus von Nazareth. Seine Botschaft vom Reich Gottes und der Glaube der Urgemeinde. Historisch-kritische Erhellung der Ursprünge des Christentums, Düsseldorf, 1985.

398. Idem, 'Kerygma and History' in: Idem, Basic Questions in Theology, I, p.88. Pannenberg refers also to Gerhard von Rad, Old Testament Theology, Vol. I, p.106.

399. W. Pannenberg, 'Heilsgeschehen und Geschichte', (Art. Cit.) SS.22-23., Cfr. also: Idem, 'Redemptive Event as History', in: Idem, Basic Questions in Theology, I, p.16

400. Finding Jesus historically through the Gospels is essentially a question of Christian credibility. Cfr. René Latourelle, Op. Cit., p.xvii.

401. W. Pannenberg, 'Redemptive Event as History', (Art. Cit.), p.56., Idem, 'Heilsgeschehen und Geschichte' (Art. Cit.), S.59.

402. Ibid. Pannenberg refers also to: E. Troeltsch, Die Bedeutung der Geschichtlichkeit Jesu für den Glauben, 1911, S.40.

403. W. Pannenberg, 'Heilsgeschehen und Geschichte', (Art. Cit.), S.22.

404. Idem, 'Response to the Discussion', in: James M. Robinson/John B. Cobb Jr., (Ed.), Theology as History, (Vol. III of New Frontiers in Theology) Inc., 1967, p.239.

405. Cfr. back to Ch. VII. B.2.

406. W. Pannenberg, 'Einsicht und Glaube' and 'Glaube und Vernunft', in: Idem, Grundfragen systematischer Theologie I, SS.223-251.

407. W. Pannenberg, 'Response to the Discussion', (Art. Cit.), p.271., Cfr. also: Idem, 'Die Krise des Schriftprinzips', (Art. Cit.), S.11.

408. Edmund J. Dobbin, Op. Cit., p.29.

409. W. Pannenberg, Jesus - God and Man, pp.23-25.

410. Idem, The Revelation of God in Jesus', in: James M. Robinson/John B. Cobb Jr., Op. Cit., pp.128-131.

411. Allan D. Galloway, Wolfhart Pannenberg. (Comtemporary Religious Thinkers Series ed. by H.D. Lewis), London, 1973, p.11.

412. W. Pannenberg, 'Einsicht und Glaube', (Art. Cit.), S.225.

413. Edmund J. Dobbin, Op. Cit., p.28.

414. W. Pannenberg, 'Dogmatische Thesen', in: Idem et alii, Offenbarung als Geschichte, 1963, SS.102, n. 15.

415. W. Pannenberg, 'Revelation of God in Jesus', in: James M. Robinson/ John B. Cobb Jr., Op. Cit., pp.130ff.

416. K. Rahner, Foundations of Christian Faith, pp.237, 238, 245, 246, 247, 248., Cfr. also: K.-H. Weger, Karl Rahner - An Introduction, p.152.

417. K. Rahner, 'Christology in the Setting of Modern Man's Understanding of Himself and His World (Art. Cit.), p.222.
Idem, 'Remarks on the Importance of the History of Jesus for Catholic Dogmatics', in: Idem, Theological Investigations, Vol. XIII, London/ New York, 1975.

718

CHAPTER VIII

1. Cfr. back: Ch. VII.C.1 and 2.

2. Cfr. above: Ch. IV.A.2.c., III.A.3.a.

3. Cfr. above: Ch. IV.A.3.a.

4. Cfr. above: Ch. IV.A.2.c.

5. Cfr. above: Ch. IV.A.3.a.

6. Cfr. above: Ch. V.A.3.

7. Cfr. above: Ch. V.B.2.c.

8. K. Rahner, 'Christology within an Evolutionary View of the World', (Art. Cit.), pp.157-192.

9. Cfr. above especially: Ch. VII.B.1.a. and VII.C.1.

10. K. Rahner, 'Allgemeine Grundlegung der Protologie und theologischen Anthropologie', in: J. Feiner/M. Löhrer, Mysterium Salutis, Bd. II, S.416: 'Im Gottmenschen Jesus Christus ist also der Grund und die Norm dessen, was der Mensch ist, in der Geschichte selbst gegeben und zur Erscheinung gekommen.'

11. Ibid., p.417.

12. Idem, 'Incarnation', in: Idem (Ed.), Sacramentum Mundi, (Eng.) Vol. 3, p.110.

13. K. Rahner, Ich glaube an Jesus Christus, S.35: 'Wer Ideen erst dann für ernsthaft und existentiell wahr hält, wenn sie Fleisch und Blut haben, der kann an die 'Idee' des Gottmenschtums doch leichter glauben, wenn er an Jesus von Nazareth glaubt, im Fleisch findet, was der seligste Entwurf der höchsten Möglichkeit des Menschen ist, von dem aus man erst überhaupt weiß, was eigentlich zutiefst Mensch bedeutet.'

14. K. Rahner, 'Probleme der Christologie von heute' (Art. Cit.), S.185.

15. Idem, 'Die anonymen Christen', in: Idem, Schriften zur Theologie, Bd. VI, Einsiedeln/Zürich/Köln, 1965, S.548.

16. Idem, 'Ich glaube an Jesus Christus', in: Idem, Schriften zur Theologie, Bd. VIII, Einsiedeln/Zürich/Köln, 1967, S.216: '... das radikale einmalige Ereignis der Verwirklichung der letzten Wesensmöglichkeit des Menschen.'

17. W. Pannenberg, 'Christologie und Theologie', in: KuD, 21 (1975), S.166. Wenn der Mensch 'in seinem unentrinnbaren Bezogensein auf seinen göttlichen Ursprung und auf seine göttliche Bestimmung ... thematisiert wird, dann wird auch die Gottesgemeinschaft Jesu nicht mehr als etwas dem Menschlichen im allgemeinen Fremdes und Ausgefallenes erscheinen.'

Vielmehr wird dann die spezifische Weise der Gottes-Gemeinschaft Jesu ... als ein In-die-Wahrheit-Bringen des Menschseins überhaupt zugänglich hinsichtlich ... der Gottesbeziehung des Menschen.'

18. Idem, Jesus - God an Man, pp.191, 192.

19. Ibid., pp.195-208.

20. Idem, 'The Christological Foundations of Christian Anthropology', (Art.Cit.), pp.88-89. Pannenberg refers also to: 'Irenaeus, Adv. haer. V,16 I f and H. Langerbeck, Aufsätze zur Gnosis, (Hrg. H. Dörries), Göttingen, 1967, S.56.

21. Cfr. also: J.G. Herder, Ideen zur Philosophie der Geschichte der Menschheit, 1784, IX, S.5 and H. Sunnus, Die Wurzeln des modernen Menschenbildes bei J.G. Herder, Nürnberg, 1971, SS.32ff.

22. Cfr. back to Ch.V.A.1. and V.A.3.

23. A. Hulsbosch, 'Jesus Christus, gekend als mens, beleden als Zoon Gods', in: Tijdschrift voor Theologie, 6 (1966), pp.250-273. For an exposition of similar views further cfr. Jean Galot, Cristo contestato (Nuova collana di teologia cattolica 13), Firenze, 1979, passim.

24. This point is stressed especially in the 'Creeds'.

25. Thomas Pearl, Op. Cit., p.135.

26. K. Rahner, 'Christology within an Evolutionary View of the World', (Art. Cit.), p.178.

27. Idem, 'Incarnation', (Art. Cit.), p.111. (Sacramentum Mundi 3).

27a. Idem, Ich glaube an Jesus Christus, S.34.

27b. Idem, 'On the Theology of the Incarnation', in: Idem, Theological Investigation, Vol. V, London/Baltimore, 1966, pp.111, 117, 118.

28. Idem, 'Christology in the Setting of Modern Man's Understanding of Himself and His World', (Art. Cit.), p.226.

29. Idem, 'Zur Theologie der Menschwerdung', in: Idem, Schriften zur Theologie, Bd. IV, Einsiedeln/Zürich/Köln, 1960, S.142: 'Die Menschwerdung Gottes ist daher der einmalig höchste Fall des Wesensvollzugs der menschlichen Wirklichkeit.' Cfr. also: Idem, 'Chalkedon - Ende oder Anfang?', in: Grillmeier/Bacht (Hrg.), Das Konzil von Chalkedon, Bd. III, Würzburg, 1954,SS. 6, 9, 15, 17.
Idem, 'Probleme der Christologie von heute', (Art. Cit.), passim.

30. Idem, Foundations of Christian Faith, pp.215-218, esp. 217.

31. Idem, 'Probleme der Christologie von heute', (Art. Cit.), S.184, Anm.1.

32. Ibid., S.205., Cfr. also: Idem, 'Current problems in Christology' (Art. Cit.), p.185., Idem, 'On the Theology of the Incarnation', in: Theological Investigations, Vol. IV, London/Baltimore, 1966, p.117.

33. Cfr. above: Ch.VII.A.1.

34. K. Rahner, 'On the Theology of the Incarnatdion' (Art. Cit.), p.120.

35. Ibid.

36. Idem, 'Über den Begriff des Geheimnisses in der katholischen Theologie', in: Idem, Schriften zur Theologie, Bd. IV, Einsiedeln/Zürich/Köln, 1960, SS.51-102. passim.

37. J.B. Metz (Hrg.), Gott in der Welt! Festgabe für Karl Rahner, Freiburg i. Br., 1964, S.9.

38. Cfr. above Ch.VII.A.3. and B.1.

39. K. Rahner, 'Current Problems in Christology', (Art. Cit.), p.162.

40. Idem, 'On the Theology of the Incarnation', (Art. Cit.), p.117.

41. Idem, 'Current Problems in Christology' (Art. Cit.), pp.162-163.

42. Ibid., p.163.

43. On the notion of 'Avatar' Cfr. above: Ch.III.C.

44. Cfr. above Ch.V.B.2.a.

45. Cfr. below Ch.IX.A.

46. DS.301, 302.

47. Cfr. DS. Foot note to no. 302 in p.108. Cfr. also: Ign. Ortiz Urbina, 'Das Symbol von Chalkedon', in: A. Grillmeier/H. Bacht (Hrg.), Das Konzil von Chalkedon, Bd. 1, Würzburg, 1959, S.391, note 4.
R.V. Sellers, The Council of Chalkedon, London, 1953, pp.120ff.

48. DS. 302.

49. Cfr. back to Ch.V.C.1.b. and V.B.1.a.

50. Cfr. back: 'Tadatmya in the Brahmanya Purusha' Ch.V.B.3.c.

51. Cfr. above Ch.V.A.2.a.

52. Cfr. above Ch.V.B.1.

53. Cfr. above Ch.V.A.3.c.

54. Cfr. above Ch.V.A.

55. Cfr. above Ch. V.B.3.b.

56. Ibid.

57. For a detailed presentation of the so-called anti-Chalcedonian authors, Cfr. Jean Galot, Cristo contestato, Firenze, 1979, passim.

58. K. Rahner, 'On the Theology of the Incarnation', (Art. Cit.), p.118., Cfr. also: Idem, Foundations of Christian Faith, pp.289-293.

59. Idem, 'Christologie heute?', in: Idem, Schriften zur Theologie, Bd. XII, Zürich/Einsiedeln/Köln, 1975, SS.354-355.

60. Jean Galot, Le problème christologique actuel, CLD, 1979, p.18: 'Les conciles de Nicée et de Chalcédoine, en définissant l'etre du Christ, ont posé un fundament inaliénable de toute recherche christologique.' In an article on Christology in: La civiltà cattolica, 123 (1972), p.44 Galot affirms: '... dopo Calcedonia, non si tratta più di negare l'unica persona divina e le due nature, ma di percipere meglio ciò che bisogna intendere per persona, per natura e per l'unità affermata.'

61. K. Rahner, Art. Cit., pp.358-360.

62. Idem, 'Jesus Christus'. in: Idem (Hrg.), Sacramentum Mundi II, 1968, S.927: 'Die vordringerdste Aufgabe einer Christologie von heute besteht darin, das Dogma der Kirche - 'Gott ist Mensch (geworden), und dieser menschgewordene Gott ist der konkrete Jesus Christus' - so zu formulieren, daß das in diesen Sätzen Gemeinte verständlich wird und jeder Schein einer heute nicht mehr nachvollziehbaren Mythologie ausgeschlossen wird.'
Cfr. also: Idem, Grundkurs des Glaubens, S.217.
Arno Schilson/Walter Kaseper, Christologie im Präsens - Kritische Sichtung neuer Entwürfe, 1974, S.80.

63. K. Rahner, 'Current Problems in Christology', (Art. Cit.), p.156.

64. Ibid., p.180., Cfr. also: D.L. Gelpi, Life and Light, 1966, p.6.

65. K. Rahner, Art. Cit., p.150.

66. Idem, 'Zur Theologie der Menschwerdung', in: Idem, Schriften zur Theologie, Bd. IV, Einsiedeln/ZÜrich/Köln, 1960, S.138.

67. Idem, Ich glaube an Jesus Christus, S.41.

68. Idem, 'Theologie und Anthropologie', in: Idem, Schriften zur Theologie, Bd. VIII, Einsiedeln/Zürich/Köln, 1967, SS.43-44: 'Christliche Anthropologie erreicht ihren Sinn nur, wenn sie den Menschen begreift als potentia oboedientialis für die 'unio hypostatica'. Und Christologie läßt sich nur betreiben von einer solchen transzendentalen Anthropologie her; denn eben, wenn man heute sagen will, was 'unio hypostatica' ist, ohne in den Verdacht zu geraten, Mythologien vorzutragen, die nicht mehr vollziehbar sind, bedarf es des Aufweises eines transzendentalen Horizontes im begnadigten Menschen und seiner Geschichte für die Idee des Gottmenschen.'
Cfr. also: Ibid., p.54.

69.   Idem, 'I believe in Jesus Christ', (Art. Cit.), p.167.

69a.   Cfr. below: Ch.IX.A.1.

70.   K. Rahner, 'On the Theology of the Incarnation', (Art. Cit.), p.116.

71.   Idem, 'Christology within an Evolutionary View of the World', (Art. Cit.), P.182.
Cfr. also: 'Die Christologie innerhalb einer evolutiven Weltanschauung', in: Idem, Schriften zur Theologie, Bd. V, Einsiedeln/Zürich/Köln, 1962, SS.183-221. passim.

72.   Idem, 'Christology within an Evolutionary View of the World', (Art. Cit.), p.160.

73.   Ibid., pp.180-181.

74.   Ibid., p.179.

75.   Ibid., p.181.

76.   Ibid.

77.   Idem, 'On the Theology of the Incarnation', (Art. Cit.), p.12.

78.   Idem, 'Christology within an Evolutionary View of the World', (Art. Cit.), p.181.

79.   Ibid., p.183.

80.   Ibid., p.182.

81.   Donald J. Beechler, The Centrality of Jesus' Resurrection in Wolfhart Pannenberg's Christology 'from Below', Roma, 1973, p.50.

82.   W. Pannenberg, Jesus-God and Man, pp.116-133. passim.

83.   Cfr. below Ch.VIII.C.

83a.   W. Pannenberg et alii, Offenbarung als Geschichte, Göttingen, 1961, S.9 (Einführung).

84.   Cfr. above: Ch.VII.A.2.c., Cfr. also: W. Pannenberg, 'Person', in: Religion in Geschichte und Gegenwart V, (1961),SS. 230-235., Idem, 'Person und Subjekt', in: Idem, Grundfragen systematischer Theologie, II, Göttingen, 1980, S.91. Idem, Anthropologie in theologischer Perspektive, Göttingen, 1983, S.513. The concept of 'Person' as 'être relationelle', 'l'essere relazionale' - a notion used by St. Augustine in reference to the persons in the Holy Trinity - is applied by Jean Galot to explain also the person of Christ. The concept of person as 'être relationelle', according to him is applicable to both the divine and the human persons. Cfr. Jean Galot, Chi sei tu, o Christo? (Nuova Collana di Teologia Cattolica 11), Firenze, 1977, pp.277, 281-284.

85. Friedrich Gogarten, Der Mensch zwischen Gott und Welt, Stuttgart, 1952, SS.234ff.

86. W. Pannenberg, 'The Christological Foundation of Christian Anthropology', in: Concilium (English), June, 1973 (Translated by David Smyth), pp.99-100.

87. W. Pannenberg, 'Person und Subjekt', (Art. Cit.), S.94.

88. Idem, Jesus-God and Man, p.342, Cfr.also:pp.287, 323.

89. Ibid., p.324.

90. Matthew Vellanickal, The divine Sonship of Christians in the Johannine Writings, (Analecta Biblica 72), Rome, 1977. Cfr. also below: Ch. IX, Foot note no. 224ff.

91. Cfr. above Ch.I.B.

92. Cfr. above Cf.III.C.3. Only the 'body' is assumed and the 'soul' is substituted by Vishnu!

93. Cfr. above Ch.V.A.3.

94. Cfr. above Ch.V.A.2.c.

95. Cfr. above Ch.V.A.2.b.

96. Cfr. above Ch.V.B.1.a. and b.

97. K. Rahner, Foundations of Christian Faith, p.291.

98. Ibid., pp.219-220.

99. Ibid., pp.220-221.

100. Idem, 'On the Theology of the Incarnation', (Art. Cit.), p.113.

101. Ibid., pp.113-114.

102. Idem, 'Bemerkungen zum dogmatischen Traktat 'De Trinitate',' in: Idem, Schriften zur Theologie, Bd. IV, Einsiedeln/Zürich/Köln, 1960, SS.103-136. Idem, 'Der dreifaltige transzendente Gott als Urgrund der Heilsgeschichte', in: J. Feiner/M. Löhrer (Hrg.), Mysterium Salutis. Grundriß heilsgeschichtlicher Dogmatik, Einsiedeln/Zürich/Köln, 1967, SS.317-397.

103. Bernhard Philberth; Der Dreieinige, Stein am Rhein/Schweiz, 1980 [5].

104. Cfr. P. Adnès, 'Matrimonio e mistero trinitario', in: AA.VV. Amore e stabilità nel matrimonio, Roma, 1976, pp.7-25.

105. K. Rahner, Foundations of Christian Faith, pp.223-224, Cfr. also: pp.134-137.

106. Idem, 'Trinitarian Theology', in: Idem (Ed.), Sacramentum Mundi, Vol. 6, p.289.
Cfr. also: E. Simons, Philosophie der Offenbarung: Auseinandersetzung mit Karl Rahner, Stuttgart, 1966.

107. K. Rahner, 'On the Theology of the Incarnation', (Art. Cit.), p.115.

108. Cfr. above Ch.I.C.3.c., Ch.III.C.

109. K. Rahner, Foundations of Christian Faith, p.304.

110. Ibid.

111. K. Rahner/W. Thüsing, A New Christology, p.176.

111a. W. Pannenberg, Jesus - God and Man, pp.150-154.

112. It is the sharing of the 'Logos' that makes man, according to the early Greeks, a 'Zoon logikon' - animal rationale!

113. W. Pannenberg, 'The Christological Foundations of Christian Anthropology', (Art. Cit.), p.97.

114. W. Pannenberg, Grundzüge der Christologie, Gütersloh, 1976, pp.116-167, 345-361.

115. Cfr. above Ch.III.C.1. and 2.

116. R.E. Brown, The Virginal Conception and Bodily Resurrection of Jesus, London, 1974, pp.48ff.

117. Cfr. above Ch.V.C.1.a.

118. Cfr. above Ch.V.C.1.b.

119. Cfr. above Ch.V.A.3.c.

120. Cfr. above V.B.3.b.

121. Cfr. our Work: Mathew Vekathanam, R.E. Brown's Biblical Approach to Christology: A Critical Evaluation, Dissertatio ad Licentiam, Pontificia Universitas Gregoriana, Roma, 1980 (Unpublished), pp.13-34.

122. W. Pannenberg, Jesus-God and Man, p.142.
Cfr. also. Judges 13:5., Jeremiah 1:5., Isaiah 49:5.

123. R.E. Brown, Op. Cit., pp.53, 54.

124. Jean Galot, Etre né de Dieu: Jean 1:13 (Analecta Biblica 37), Roma, 1969. passim.

125. Hans von Campenhausen, The Virgin Birth in the Theology of the Ancient Church, (Translated by Frank Clarke) Studies in Historical Theology 2, Inc., 1964.
Martin Dibelius, Jungfrauensohn und Krippenkind, (Sitzungsberichte der

Heidelberger Akademie der Wissenschaften, Philosophisch-historische Klasse), Heidelberg, 1932, esp. S.30.

126. K. Rahner, 'Virginitas in partu', in: Idem, Schriften zur Theologie, Band IV, Einsiedeln/Zürich/Köln, 1960, SS.192, 193.
R.E. Brown, Op. Cit., pp.34ff.
H. von Campenhausen, Op. Cit., passim.

127. K.S. Frank/K. Kilian, Zum Thema Jungfrauengeburt, Stuttgart,1978,.

128. Karl Barth, Church Dogmatics, I/2.15.3.

129. W. Pannenberg, Jesus - God and Man, p.148.

130. Ibid., p.141.

131. Ibid., p.143.

132. W. Pannenberg, Op. Cit., pp.141-150.
Idem, The Apostles' Creed: In the Light of Today's Questions, (Translated by Margaret Kohl), The Westminster Press, 1972, pp.71-77.

133. Paul Althaus, Die christliche Wahrheit, SS.442, 443.

134. Ambrosius, Ep. 42, 12., (PL 16, 1128).

135. Cfr. O. Piper, 'The Virgin Birth: The Meaning of the Gospel Accounts', in: Interpretation 18 (1964), p.132.

136. Paul Althaus, Op. Cit., S.443.

137. K. Rahner, 'Virginitas in partu', (Art. Cit.), Ss.173-205. Cfr. also: Idem, Zum Thema Jungfrauengeburt, Stuttgart, 1970. passim.

138. K. Rahner, 'Virginitas in partu', (Art. Cit.), S.199: 'Die Geburt der Heiligen Jungfrau entspricht dem einmaligen, gnadenhaften, heilsgeschichtlich wunderbaren Wesen der Heiligen Jungfrau als ganzer.' Cfr. also: pp.196ff., 208ff.

139. Ibid., S.204: 'Weil das Fleisch der Sünde in dieser Geburt gelöst ist, weil hier ein Neuanfang gemacht ist, könnten die Väter mit Recht sich nicht denken, daß hier alles wie sonst sein könnte.'

140. Ibid., p.198.

141. Ibid., S.208: 'wir sagen ... nicht ...: diese Konkretheiten hat es sicher nicht gegeben. Wir sagen nur: die Lehre der Kirche sagt mit dem eigentlichen Kern der Tradition: Die (aktive) Geburt Marias ist, so wie ihr Empfangen, von der Gesamtwirklichkeit her (als ganzmenschlicher Akt dieser 'Jungfrau') auch in sich ... dieser Mutter entsprechend und darum einmalig, wunderbar, 'jungfräulich', ohne daß wir aus diesem Satz ... die Möglichkeit haben, sicher und für alle verpflichtend, Aussagen über konkrete Einzelheiten dieses Vorgangs abzuleiten.'

142. Cfr. above Ch.III.A.3.a.

143. Pope Pius XII, Mystici Corporis (Encyclical letter), AAS XXXV, 1943, p.230.
Idem, Sempiternus Rex, (Encyclical Letter), AAS XLIII, 1961, p.638.
K. Rahner, 'Dogmatic Reflections on the Knowledge and Self-Consciousness of Christ', in: Idem, Theological Investigations, Vol. V, London/Baltimore, 1966, pp.193-215. Especially for the P. Parente and P. Galtier controversy cfr. Ibid., p.210. Cfr. also: P. Parente, 'Unità ontologica e psicologica dell'Uomo-Dio',in: Euntes docete V (1952),pp.337-401. Idem, 'Echi della controversia sull'unita ontologica e psicologica di Christo', in: Euntes docete VI, (1953), 312-322.
P. Galtier, 'La conscience humaine du Christ à propos de quelques publications récentes', in: Gregorianum, XXXII (1951), pp.525-568.,
Idem, 'La conscience humaine du Christ. Epilogue', in: Gregorianum XXXV (1954), pp.225-246.
R. Garrigou-Lagrange, 'L'unique personnalité du Christ', in: Angelicum, XXIX (1952), pp.60-75.
B. Lonergan, De constitutione Christi ontologica et psychologica, Roma, 1956.
Philippe de la Trinité, 'A propos de la conscience du Christ; Un faux problème théologique', in: Ephemerides Carmeliticae XI (1960), pp.1-52.
E. Gutwenger, Bewußtsein und Wissen Christi, Innsbruck, 1960.
J. Ratzinger, Bewußtsein und Wissen Christi', in: Münchner Theol. Zeitschrift, XII (1961), SS.78-81.

144. K. Rahner, 'Current Problems in Christology', (Art. Cit.), p.158.

145. Jean Galot, Chi sei tu, o Cristo, pp.324, 327.

146. K. Rahner, 'Dogmatic Reflections on the Knowledge and Self-Consciousness of Christ', (Art. Cit.), p.203.

147. Ibid., p.216.

148. Ibid., p.203.

149. Ibid., p.206.

150. Ibid., pp.199ff.

151. Ibid., p.208.

152. Ibid., p.211.

153. DS. 3646.
Cfr. also: K. Rahner, 'Jesus Christ', in: Idem (Ed.), Sacramentum Mundi, Vol. 3, pp.207f.
Jesus had the 'immanent expectation', but in its expression this expectation was imprecise. This lack of precision cannot be called 'erroneous' knowledge in Jesus 'because in it a truth appears which is essential even for Jesus' human consciousness, namely, that in Jesus Christ, the Son of Man, the Kingdom of God is irrevocably taking possession of the world'. Cfr. also: Idem, Foundations of Christian Faith, pp.251-254, 287.

154. K. Rahner, 'Dogmatic Reflections on the Knowledge and Self-Consciousness of Christ', (Art. Cit.), pp.210, 216.

155. Idem, 'Theologische Prinzipien der Hermeneutik eschatologischer Aussagen', in: Idem, Schriften zur Theologie, Bd. IV, Einsiedeln/Zürich/Köln, 1960, Ss.401-428, esp. 405-406.
Cfr. also: Idem, 'Chalkedon - Ende oder Anfang?', (Art. Cit.), S.22.

156. J. Mouroux, Le Christ et le temps, Paris, 1962, p.115.
L. Malevez, Le Christ et le foi, in: N.R.Th, 87 (1966), p.1028.

157. K. Rahner, 'Theologische Prinzipien der Hermeneutik eschatologischer Aussagen' (Art. Cit.), passim.

158. Cfr. above Ch.VII.B.1.

159. K. Rahner, 'Visionen und Prophezeiungen', in: Questiones Disputatae, Bd. 4, Freiburg i.Br., 1958, SS.92-97.

160. Ignazio Sanna, La cristologia anthropologica di P. Karl Rahner, Roma, 1970, p.256: '... l'incontro con la realtà empirica non dà un principo sufficiente di spiegazione per la formazione delle conoscenze oggettive che riguardono il futuro.' Cfr. also: Ibid., p.336.

161. W. Pannenberg, Jesus - God and Man, p.334.

162. Ibid., p332.

163. Ibid., p.326.

164. Ibid., p.334.

165. Idem, Grundzüge der Christologie, SS.336-345.

166. Cfr. our Ch.VIII.C.

167. K. Rahner, Transcendental Theology', in: Idem (Ed.), Sacramentum Mundi, Vol. 6, p.289.

168. Cfr. above Ch.V.A.

169. Th. Kaiser, Die Gott-menschliche Einigung in Christus als Problem der spekulativen Theologie seit der Scholastik, (Das spekulative Verständnis der hypo-statischen Union in der neuesten Zeit: Karl Rahner), München, 1968, S.269: 'Menschwerdung ist für uns eben nicht eine ontologische Gegebenheit, die es mit formal-ontologischen Begriffen zu erfassen gilt, sondern sie ist für uns zuerst und vor allem heilsbedeutsam und heilswirksam.'

170. W. Pannenberg, Jesus - God and Man, p.38.

171. Ibid., p.49.

172. Ibid., p.48.

173. For the concept of 'Guru', Cfr. above Ch.III.A.3.b.

174. Cfr. above Ch.VI.A.

175. Cfr. above Ch.III.B.1., III.C.2.

176. Plato, Republic VI, 508 b - 509.

177. Origen, De princ. II,6,3 (GCS 22, pp.141ff.

178. Gregory of Nyssa, Adv. Apoll. 32 (PG 45, 1192 D - 1196 A)., Cfr. also: A.A. Grillmeier/H. Bacht (Hrg.), Op. Cit. Bd. I, SS.147ff., 157ff.

179. Immanuel Kant, Die Religion innerhalb der Grenzen der bloßen Vernunft, 1793, SS.73ff., 127ff.

180. A. Ritschl, Die christliche Lehre von der Rechtfertigung und Versöhnung, 1888 , III, SS.422ff.

181. W. Pannenberg, 'Theology and the Kingdom of God', (Art. Cit.), p.52.

182. Idem, 'the God of Hope', in: Idem, Basic Questions in Theology, II, p.237.

183. Idem, 'Appearance as the Arrival of the Future', in: Idem, Theology and the Kingdom of God, p.133.

184. Idem, 'The Kingdom of God and the Foundations of Ethics', in: Idem, Theology and the Kingdom of God, p.102.

185. Idem, 'Theology and the Kingdom of God', (Art. Cit.), p.52.

186. Idem, Jesus - God an Man, pp.365-378, esp.368.

187. Ibid., p.226. Cfr. also: James M. Robinson and John B. Cobb Jr., (Eds.), Theology as History, p.113.

188. W. Pannenberg, Op. Cit., pp.212, 217.

189. Ibid., pp.13, 217. Nescience is not moral error! Ch.VIII.A.3.c.

190. Ibid., pp.327-328.

191. Ibid., pp.58-63., Cfr. also: H.E. Tödt, The Son of Man in the Synoptic Tradition, The Westminster Press, 1965. passim.

192. W. Pannenberg,Op. Cit., p.53.

193. Ibid., p.65.

194. James Robinson and John B. Cobb Jr., Op. Cit., pp.56-58, 103.

195. W. Pannenberg, Op. Cit., p.66.

196. K. Rahner, Foundations of Christian Faith, p.327.

197. Cfr. above Ch.VI.B.3.a.i.

198. Ibid.

199. Cfr. above Ch.III.A.1.a.

200. Cfr. above Ch.III.A.3., III.B.

201. Cfr. above Ch.VI.B.3.a.i.

202. Cfr. above Ch.VI.B.3.a.

203. W. Pannenberg, Jesus - God and Man, pp.264, 265.
     Idem, The Apostles' Creed, p.80.

204. Cfr. Mk 15:34., Mt 27:46.
     Cfr. also: W. Pannenberg, Jesus - God and Man, p.271.

205. Ibid.

206. Ibid., p.258.

207. Ibid., p.252., Cfr. also: J. Blinzler, 'Gotteslästerung', in: LThK IV, Sp.
     1117-1119.
     Idem, Der Prozeß Jesu, 1960 ^{3}, SS.129ff.

208. W. Pannenberg, Op. Cit., p.252.
     Idem, Apostles' Creed, p.80.
     Cfr. also: P. Winter, On the Trial of Jesus, (Studia Judaica I) Berlin,
     1961, p.41.

209. W. Pannenberg, Jesus - God and Man, p.258.

210. Ibid., pp.254, 255. Compare it with Idem; The Apostles' Creed, p.viii.

211. Cfr. above Ch.III.B.

212. Francis Edward Virgulak, The Death of Christ according Wolfhart Pannen-
     berg: An Exposition and Criticism of Pannenberg's Theology of the Cross,
     rome, 1977, p.23.

213. Ibid., p.25.

213a. Cfr. 1 Co 1:23., Cfr. also: Ulrich Wilkens, Weisheit und Torheit. Eine
     exegetisch-religions-geschichtliche Untersuchung zu 1 Kor 1&2. (Beiträge
     zur historischen Theologie 26), Tübingen, 1959, SS.214ff., 268ff.

214. K. Rahner/W. Thüsing, A New Christology, pp.61, 91.

215. Ibid., p.38.

216. K. Rahner, 'Jesus Christ', (Art. Cit.), p.207.

217. Ibid., p.208.

218. Cfr. above Ch.VI.B.3.a.iv.

219. K. Kitamori, Theology of the Pain of God, Richmond, 1965. (Translated from Japanese: Kami no itami no shingaku, Tokyo, 1958).
H. Mühlen, Die Veränderlichkeit Gottes als Horizont einer zukünftigen Christologie. Auf dem Weg einer Kreuzestheologie in Auseinandersetzung mit der altkirchlichen Christologie, Münster, 1969.
J. Moltmann, Der gekreuzigte Gott, München 1972.
H. Küng, Incarnation de Dieu, Bruges, 1973, pp.640-648.
J. Galot, Il mistero della soffrenza di Dio, Assisi, 1975.

220. Cfr. Ch.VIII.A.3.a.

221. Jean Galot, Gesù Liberatore, (Nuova collana di teologia cattolica 12), Firenze,1978, pp.301ff.

222. Cfr. J. Maritain, 'Quelques réflexions sur le savoir théologique', in: Révue Thomiste, 69 (1969), pp.5-27.

222a. J. Galot, Il mistero della soffrenza di Dio, pp.11-57.

223. Hans Urs von Balthasar, Theodramatik, Band III. Die Handlung, Einsiedeln 1980, esp. SS.297ff.

224. J. Moltmann, Der gekreuzigte Gott, SS.231ff.

225. DS. 1529 (Underline mine.)

226. Cfr. above Ch.II.B.1., II.B.3.c., VI.B.1.c.

227. Cfr. above Ch.III.B.3.

228. Cfr. above Ch.III.C., V.C.1.b.

229. Cfr. above Ch.VI.B.3.a.iii.

230. Cfr. above Ch.VI.B.3.a.iv.

231. Cfr. also: Gal 3:13., 4:5.,., 1 Cor 6:20., 7:23., Col 1:14., Eph 1:7., 1Tm 2:6., Ti 2:14., 1 Pt 1:18f., 2 Pt 2:1f., Heb 9:12,15., Ap 1:5., 5:9., 14:3f.

232. The ransom theory is elaborated by Cfr: Irenaeus, Adv. Haer. V,1,1. Tertullian, De fuga (Pl 2,114) Origen, Contra Celsum 7,17 (GCS.p.169). Idem, in Matthaeum 20, 28 (GCS. 40, p.498) Augustine, De Trinitate XIII, 13 (PL 42, 1026ff.) and XIII, 14, 18 (PL 42, 1028), Idem, Sermo 263,1 (PL 38, 1210
Ignatius of Antioch, Cfr. P.Th. Camelot, Ignace d'Antioche, Polykarpe de Smyrne (Sources chrétiennes 10., 2nd ed., Paris 1951, p.88.
Gregory of Nyssa, Orat. cat. 23f. (PG 45, 62f.),
Gregory the Great, Homil. in Evang. II, 25, 8 (PL 76, 1194f.).

233. Anselm of Canterbury, Cur Deus Homo?, I, 7 & 8 (PL 158, 367-370), I, 21 (PL 158, 393f.), Cfr. also: I,11., I,13., I,20., I,21., II,6., II,11., II.14.

234. Besides the Letter to the Hebrews esp. Ch.9:11-14, cfr. also: Mk 14:24., Mt 16:28., Jn 1:29., Rom 3:25., 1 Cor 5:7., 11:25., 2 Cor 5:21., 1 Pt 1:18f., 2:21., 3:18. Cfr. also: Eduard Lohse, Märtyrer und Gottesknecht:

Untersuchungen zur urchristlichen Verkündigung vom Sühnetod Jesu Christ, Göttingen, 1955, SS.138, 169 etc.

235. Cfr. also: W. Pannenberg, Jesus - God and Man, p.278.

236. Cfr. back Ch.VI.B.3.iv.

237. K. Rahner, 'Current Problems in Christology', (Art. Cit.), pp.192, 193.

238. K.-H. Weger, Karl Rahner - An Introduction, p.174.

239. K. Rahner, Art. Cit., pp.194, 195.

240. K. Rahner/W. Thüsing, A New Christology, pp.38-41.

241. Ibid., pp.64, 65., Cfr. also: K. Rahner, Foundations of Christian Faith, pp.283, 284.

242. K. Rahner, Op. Cit., pp.254, 255.

243. K. Rahner/W. Thüsing, Op. Cit., pp.108, 109. Cfr. also: K. Rahner, 'Der eine Mittler und die Vielfalt der Vermittlungen', in: Idem, Schriften zur Theologie, Bd. VIII, Einsiedeln/Zürich/Köln, 1967, SS.218-238. passim.

244. K. Rahner, 'Christology within an Evolutionary View of the World' (Art. Cit.), p.186.

245. Ibid., p.187. (Underline mine.) For a criticism of Rahner's soteriology cfr. Hans Urs von Balthasar, Theodramatik. Band III. Die Handlung, Einsiedeln, 1980, SS.253ff.

246. W. Pannenberg, Jesus -God and Man, p.275.

247. F. Schleiermacher, Der christliche Glaube, 1830, 104, 4.

248. W. Pannenberg, Op. Cit., p.278., Cfr. also: Nitzsch-Stephan, 'Neuere Lehren von Christi Werk', in: Lehrbuch der Dogmatik, 1912 , 44,3.

249. W. Pannenberg, Op. Cit., pp.247, 250.

250. Besides the given scriptural references cfr. also: 10.25., 14:24., Lk 22:20, 27b., Jn 1:29., 1 Cor 15:3-5., 2 Cor 5:14f., Rom 11:11f., Gal 3:13f., Acts 13:46f., Ap 5:12-13.

251. W. Pannenberg, Op. Cit., pp.258ff., Cfr. also: W. Kasper, Jesus der Christus, SS.140ff.

252. W. Pannenberg, Op. Cit., pp.264ff., Cfr. also: Klaus Koch, 'Gibt es ein Vergeltungsdogma im Alten Testament', in: ZThK LII (1955) 1-42. G.V. Rad, Theologie des Alten Testamentes I, 1957, SS.261ff., 382.

253. Dt 21:1-9. (Substitution of cow): Lv 16:21 f (Substitution of goat). Jer 31:29., Ez 18:2.: Ezechiel preached against the arbitrary application of one's guilt on others, heredity etc. (Ez 18:25-29) and warns against

732

forgetting individual responsibility. But he also affirms the corporate nature of wickedness (Ez 20:18). Cfr. also: Arnold J. Tkacik, 'Ezekiel', in: R.E. Brown et alii, (Ed.), The Jerome Biblical Commentary, Prentice-Hall, Inc., 1968, p.355.

254. F.E. Virgulak, Op. Cit., p.27.

255. W. Pannenberg, Op. Cit., p.268.

256. Ibid., p.263.

257. Ibid., p.269.

258. Ibid., pp.263-264., Idem, The Apostle's Creed, p.89.

259. Idem, Jesus - God and Man, p.245., Cfr. also: Idem, 'Das christologische Fundament christlicher Anthropologie', in: Concilium 9 (1973), S.425.

260. F.E. Virgulak, Op. Cit., p.28.

261. K. Rahner, 'The Two Basic Types of Christology', in: Idem, Theological Investigations, Vol. XIII, 1975, London/New York, pp.215-216. Cfr. also: Jean Galot, Gesù Liberatore, pp.157-184.

Otto Hermann Pesch, Frei sein aus Gnade, Theologische Anthropologie, Freiburg i.Br., 1983, SS.214ff.

262. Cfr. above Ch.VI.B.3.iv.

263. For the 'Purusha Sukta' cfr. Rgveda 10.90.1-14. Cfr. above Ch.II.A.

264. Cfr. above VI.B.3.a.iv.

265. Cfr. Ch.VI.B.3.b.ii., Cfr. also: II.A.1.

266. Cfr. above Ch.VI.B.3.b.iii.

267. W. Pannenberg, Jesus - God and Man, pp.88-106.

268. R.E. Brown, The Virginal Conception and the Bodily Resurrection of Jesus, p.71. Cfr. also: our work: Matthew Vekathanam, Op. Cit., p.71.

269. Cfr. also: Rom 8:11., 10:)., 1 thes 1:10., 1 Cor 6:14., Gal 1:1.

270. Cfr. also: R.E. Brown, Op. Cit., p.81ff.

271. Compare for eg.: Mk 16:7., Mt 28:9-10, 16-20., Lk 24:13-32, 36-53., Jn 20:14-23, 26-29.

272. For a Bibliography of Bibliographies on the question of Resurrection Cfr. Edovard Dhanis (Ed.), Resurrexit, Libreria editrice Vaticana, 1974. Cfr. also: P. Benoit, The Passion and Resurrection of Jesus Christ, New York, 1969.

C.F. Evans, Resurrection and the New Testament, London, 1970., R.H. Füller, The Formation of the Resurrection Narratives, New York, 1971. Lèon Dufour, Résurrection de Jésus et message pascal, Paris, 1971.

W. Marxsen, The Resurrection of Jesus of Nazareth, Philadelphia, 1970.

273. Cfr. also: Gerald O'Collins, The Easter Jesus, London, 1976, pp.29ff.

274. Cfr. also: Ibid., pp.57ff.

275. W. Pannenberg, 'Redemptive Event as History', in: Idem, Basic Questions in Theology, pp.38-80.
Idem, 'Hermeneutik and Universal History', in: Op. Cit., pp.96-136., Idem, 'Postface' to I. Berten, Histoire, révélation et foi, Brussels, 1969, p.113.

276. W. Pannenberg, Jesus - God and Man, p.105.

277. Ibid., pp.89-91., 77, 96.

278. K. Rahner, Foundations of Christian Faith, pp.276, 277.

279. A. Descamps, 'Le structure ... Résurrection', in: Biblica 40 (1959), pp. 726-741.

280. For the different Easter hypothese cfr. W. Kasper, Jesus der Christus, S.154.

281. W. Pannenberg, Op. Cit., pp.101-106.

182. Christian Duquoc, Essai dogmatique. II Le Messie, Paris, 1972, pp.163f.

283. Cfr. L. Evely, The Gospels without Myth, New York, 1971, p.160.

284. G. Lampe, The Resurrection, London, 1967, pp.57, 97, 99.

285. K. Rahner, Op. Cit., p.277.

286. R.E. Brown, Op. Cit., pp.1, 125, 126.

287. G. O'Collins, What are They Saying about the Resurrection, New York, 1978, pp.13-16.
Cfr. also: Idem, The Easter Jesus, London, 1973, esp. pp.29ff., 90ff.

288. W. Pannenberg, Op. Cit., pp.187, 53, 76. Cfr. also: H.Blumenberg, Para-digmen zu einer Metaphorologie, 1961, SS.84ff.

289. W. Pannenberg, Grundzüge der Christologie, S.417. Nachwort zur 5. Auflage.

290. Idem, The Apostels' Creed, pp.109-114.

291. Idem, Grundzüge der Christologie, SS.62-63. Cfr. also: 'Redemptive Event as History' (Art. Cit.), pp.60, 61., Idem, 'On Hisorical and Theological Hermeneutic', Ibid., p.159., Idem, 'Kerygma and Dogma', Ibid., p.94.

292. W. Pannenberg, Jesus - God and Man, p.105.

293. Ibid., p.108., Idem, The Apostles' Creed, pp.114-115.

293a. It is quite understandable that in Rahner's 'Christology from below' the reality of Christ as the God-Man will be more stressed than the question of his resurrection as is done by Pannenberg in his 'Christology from the end'. Still, according to Rahner, the Resurrection is not merely a proof for Christ's divinity as was the case in the scholastic approach for a long time, but it is the central theme of faith as the realization of God's salvific work in human history giving it an eschatological definitiveness! Cfr.: K. Rahner, 'Auferstehung Jesu', in: Idem/A. Darlap (Hrg.), Sacramentum Mundi I, Freiburg/Basel/Wien, 1967, S.420. Cfr. also: Idem, 'Über die Spiritualität des Osterglaubens', in: Idem, Schriften zur Theologie, Bd. XII, Einsiedeln, 1975, SS.335ff. Idem, 'Dogmatische Fragen zur Osterfrömmigkeit', in: Idem, Schriften zur Theologie, IV, Einsiedeln, 1960, SS.157-172. Cfr. further: Hans Kessler, Sucht den Lebenden nicht bei den Toten. Die Auferstehung Jesu Christi in biblischer, fundamentaltheologischer und systematischer Sicht, Düsseldorf, 1985, SS.21ff., L. Ott, Grundriß der Dogmatik, Freiburg, 1959, SS.232f.,

294. K. Rahner, Foundations of Christian Faith, pp.257-264.

295. Cfr. above: Ch.VI.B.3.b.i., IV.A.2.c.

296. Cfr. above VI.B.3.b.iii.

297. W. Pannenberg, 'Dogmatische Thesen', in: Idem (Hrg.), Offenbarung als Geschichte, Göttingen, 1963, SS.107ff.

298. For the apocalyptic tradition in which the resurrection of the dead was cultivated during the time of Jesus, Cfr.: R. Martin-Achard, De la mort à la résurrection d'apres l'Ancien Testament, 1956. Otto Plöger, Theokratie und Eschatologie, Neukirchen, 1959, Paul Volz, Die Eschatologie der jüdischen Gemeinde im neutestamentlichen Zeitalter, Tübingen, 1934, SS.229ff.
Aimo T. Nikolainen, Der Auferstehungsglaube in der Bibel und in ihrer Umwelt, 2 Bdd. Helsinki, 1944/1946.

299. W. Pannenberg, The Apostels' Creed, p.52.

300. Idem, 'Theology and the Kingdom of God', (Art. Cit.), p.53.

301. Idem, 'The Revelation of God in Jesus', in: James M. Robinson and John B. Cobb, Jr., Op. Cit., p.115.

302. Pannenberg, Grundzüge der Christologie, S.53.

303. Cfr. back: Ch.VII.B.2.

304. W. Pannenberg, Jesus - God and Man, pp.82, 83.

305. Idem, 'Dogmatische Thesen' (Art. Cit.), S.105.

306. W. Pannenberg, 'Insight and Faith', in: Idem, Basic Questions in Theology, II, p.45.

308. Idem, 'Wie wird Gott uns offenbart?', in: Radius, No. 4 (1960), S.6.

309. Idem, Jesus - God and Man, pp.106-108.

310. Idem, 'Dogmatische Thesen' (Art. Cit.), S.98.
     Idem et alii, Revelation as History, p.134. Cfr. also: Renè Latourelle, Finding Jesus through the Gospels, p.66.

311. W. Pannenberg, 'Über historische und theologische Hermeneutik', (Art. Cit.), S.156.

312. Ibid., p.157.

313. Idem, 'Was ist Wahrheit?', (Art. Cit.), S.221.

314. Frank E. Tupper, Op. Cit., p.50.

315. W. Pannenberg, 'Heilsgeschehen und Geschichte', (Art. Cit.), S.43. He reacts against R. Bultmann and E. Fuchs who maintain that since Christ is the end of history further interest in history is irrelevant. Cfr. also: R. Bultmann, 'Heilsgeschichte und Geschichte', in: ThLZ (1948), 665. E. Fuchs, 'Christus das Ende der Geschichte', in: EvTh 8 (1948/49), SS. 447-461, esp. 454ff.

316. W. Pannenberg, 'What is Truth?', in: Idem, Basic Questions in Theology II, p.1.
     Cfr. also: 'A Theological Conversation with Wolfhart Pannenberg', in: Dialogue, Vol. XI (1972), p.287.

317. Rosino Gibellini, Teologia e ragione: Itinerario e opera di Wolfhart Pannenberg, Brescia, 1980, p.146: '... Gesù come rivelazione di Dio in forza della risurrezione è visto pure come rivelazione dell'essere uomo dell'uomo, come rivelazione della destinazione dell'uomo alla risurrezione e alla communione con Dio, e come compimento di ogni speranza umana. In breve: Gesù rivelazione di Dio e rivelazione dell'uomo; Gesù rivelazione dell'uomo in quanto rivelazione di Dio.'

318. W. Pannenberg, Jesus - God and Man, pp.396, 397. Cfr. also: pp.365, 367, 381, 388.

319. Idem, 'Dogmatische Thesen', in: Idem (Hrg.), Offenbarung als Geschichte, Göttingen, 1961, S.111.

320. Ibid.

321. Idem, Jesus - God and Man, p.323.

322. Idem, Grundfragen systematischer Theologie, I, S.6 (Vorwort).

323. Idem, Jesus - God and Man, p.224.

324. Ibid., p.137.

325. Ibid., p.321.

326. Ibid., p.137. Cfr. also: Idem, Grundzüge der Christologie, S.136: 'Das Ostergeschehen weist auf den vorösterlichen Jesus zurück, insofern es seinen vorösterlichen Vollmachtsanspruch bestätigt hat. Die Einheit Jesu mit Gott, die im Ostergeschehen begründet ist, fängt daher mit diesem Ereignis nicht erst an, sondern sie tritt von ihm her rückwirkend für den Vollmachtsanspruch im Verhalten des irdischen Jesus in Kraft. Umgekehrt ist der Vollmachtsanspruch des vorösterlichen Jesus als Vorgriff auf seine durch das Ostergeschehen erwiesene Einheit mit Gott zu verstehen.'

327. Ibid., p.141., Cfr. also: Paul Althaus, Die christliche Wahrheit, S.440.

328. W. Pannenberg, 'Dogmatische Erwägungen zur Auferstehung Jesu', in: Kerygma und Dogma, XIV (1968), S.105. Idem, Jesus - God and Man, pp.67-72.

329. K. Rahner, Foundations of Christian Faith, pp.273-276.

330. Ibid., pp.268, 269.

331. Ibid., pp. 277-278, 283-284.

332. Idem, Grundkurs des Glaubens, S.291.
Idem, 'Kirchliche Christologie zwischen Exegese und Dogmatik', in: Idem, Schriften zur Theologie, Bd. IX, Einsiedeln/Zürich/Köln, 1970, S.199.
Idem, 'Auf der Suche nach Zugängen zum Verständnis des gottmenschlichen Geheimnisses Jesu', in: Idem, Schriften zur Theologie, Bd. X, Zürich/Einsiedeln/Köln, 1972, S.213.
Idem, 'Was heißt heute an Jesus Christus glauben', Idem: Schriften zur Theologie, Bd. XIII, Zürich/Einsiedeln/Köln, 1978, S.177.

333. Idem, 'Incarnation', (Art. Cit.), p.11.
Cfr. also: Idem, Foundations of Christian Faith, p.279.

334. Cfr. above Ch.VI.B.3.b.iii.

335. W. Kasper, Jesus der Christus, S.161.
Cfr. also: J. Ratzinger, Einführung in das Christentum. Vorlesungen über das apostologische Glaubensbekenntnis, München 1968², SS.249-257.
G. Marcel, Geheimnis des Seins, Wien, 1952, S.472.

336. Cfr. above Ch.II.B.''., II.A.1.

336a. DS 902.

337. K. Rahner, 'Über den 'Zwischenzustand',' in: Idem, Schriften zur Theologie, Bd. XII, Zürich/Einsiedeln/Köln, 1975, S.459-462.

338. Ibid.

339. Idem, Foundations of Christian Faith, pp.269ff.

340. W. Pannenberg, Was ist der Mensch?, SS.36-38.

341. Idem, Jesus - God and man, pp.86ff.

342. Ibid., p.87.

343. Idem, Was ist der Mensch?, S.37.

344. Ibid. passim.

345. Idem, Jesus - God and Man, p.84.

346. Frank E. Tupper, Op. Cit., p.75.

347. K. Rahner, Foundations of Christian Faith, pp.270-271.

348. Idem, 'Über den 'Zwischenzustand'.' (Art. Cit.), SS.459-462: 'Vielmehr wird es dabei das Ziel sein müssen,zu zeigen, daß sich der Mensch als Wesen der Transzendenz und Freiheit von absoluter Verantwortung in Hoffnung nicht anders denken darf denn als ein Wesen, das durch die eigene Freiheitsgeschichte eine Endgültigkeit vor Gott gewinnt.'

349. Ibid., pp.462, 464., Cfr. also: Idem, 'Der Leib in der Heilsordnung', in: Idem, Schriften zur Theologie, Bd. XII, Zürich/Einsiedeln/Köln, 1975, SS.407-427.

350. W. Brugger, 'Seelenwanderung', in: LThK 9 (1964), Spp.576-578.

351. Cfr. above Ch.II.B.2., III.A.1.a.

352. Cfr. above Ch.II.C.

353. Cfr. above Ch.III.A.1.b.

354. Hans Torwesten, Sind wir nur einmal auf Erden? Die Idee der Reinkarnation angesichts des Auferstehungsglaubens, Freiburg/Basel/Wien, 1983, SS.21-22: 'Ist im Menschen etwas potentiell Göttliches angelegt, so muß er sich auf der relativen Ebene, in Zeit und Raum, so lange entwickeln, bis er seine wahre Natur verwirklicht hat, bis das in ihm Schlummernde voll manifestiert ist. Da ein einziges Menschenleben in den meisten Fällen zur kurz ist (was nicht so sehr aus logischen Überlegungen sondern eben aus unseren Erfahrungen abzuleiten ist) und da der Tod dem Menschen nicht automatisch die Erleuchtung bringt, bedarf es dazu einer Reihe von Leben....' Cfr. also: Ibid., S.205. Further on the question of 'Seelenwanderung' or Re-incarnation, Cfr. H. Küng, Ewiges Leben, München, 1982, SS.83-94., L. Scheffczyk, 'Die Reinkarnationslehre und die Geschichtlichkeit des Heils', in: MThZ 31 (1980), SS.122-129.
H. V. Glasenapp, 'Seelenwanderung', in: RGG, 5 (1961) Spp. 1937-1939., Paul Althaus, 'Seelenwanderung', in: RGG, 5 (1961), Spp. 1939-1940.

355. H. Torwesten, Op. Cit.,pp.26f.

738

356. Ibid., pp.111ff.

357. Norbert Klaes, 'Reinkarnation und Auferstehung' Nachwort in: H. Torwesten, Op. Cit., S.190: 'Das Christentum hat es sehr schwer, die verschiedenen biblischen Bilderworte zu eschatologischen Aussagen so zu inter-
pretieren, daß nicht der Eindruck erweckt wird, es handle sich um vorüber-
gehende raum-zeitlich begrenzte Geschehnisse. Wie sind Wiederkunft
Christi, letztes Gericht, zeitlich begrenztes Fegfeuer und Nicht-Gleichzeitigkeit von Vollendung des Einzelnen und Ende der Welt zu verstehen,
ohne daß sie letztlich in den Wechsel der Zeiten und in Karma als Grund-
gesetz des Werdens und der Veränderung eingeordnet werden? - Für
den Hindu sind alle diese Wirklichkeiten verständlich als Momente der
einen relativen, sich ewig umwandelnden Welt. Sie gehören noch in den
Bereich von Maya.'

358. Ibid., p.191.

359. Ibid., p.196., Cfr. also: Idem, 'Tod und Vollendung in Hinduismus und
Christentum', in: Theologie und Glaube, 68 (1978), SS.233-266, esp. 255ff.

360. W. Brugger, Loc. Cit.
'Die Seelenwanderung nicht im Sinn eines Hindurchgehens der Seele
durch verschiedene Zustände und Umwelten nach dem Tod oder als Wieder-
annahme ihres Leibes in der Auferstehung, sondern als echte Einkörpe-
rung in einen anderen Leib widerspricht der Wesenseinheit des Menschen.'

361. W. Pannenberg, What is Man? Contemporary Anthropology in Theological
Perspective (Translated by Duane A. Priebe), Fortress Press, 1970, p.79.

362. K. Rahner, Foundations of Christian Faith, p.437.

363. Ibid., p.441.

364. Ibid., pp.431-434.

365. Ibid., p.441.

366. Ibid., p.435, 443, 444.

367. Ibid., p.442.

368. Ibid., pp.271, 272.

369. W. Pannenberg, Was ist der Mensch?, S.57: 'Durch die Brücke der Ewig-
keitstiefe unserer Lebenszeit sind wir also schon jetzt identisch mit
dem Leben, zu dem wir künftig auferweckt werden.'

370. Ibid, pp.57-58.

371. Idem, What is Man?, p.80, Idem, The Apostles' Creed, pp.172ff.

371a. Pannenberg identifies the destiny of the whole cosmic reality with the
transformation of man. Cfr. Idem, 'Über historische und theologische
Hermeneutik (Art. Cit.), S.149. Cfr. also: Idem, 'Kontingenz und Naturgesetz', in: A.M. Müller/W. Pannenberg (Hrg.), Theologie der Natur,
Gütersloh, 1970, SS.34ff.

372. W. Pannenberg, 'Futurity and Unity', in: Ewert, H. Cousins (ed.), Hope and the Future of Man, Fortress Press, 1972, pp.70-71.

373. W. Pannenberg, Was ist der Mensch?, S.38.

374. K. Rahner, 'Über den 'Zwischenzustand',' (Art. Cit.), SS.459-462.

375. Ibid., pp.455-456. Cfr. also: DS. 1000-1002.

376. K. Rahner, Art. Cit., pp.462-464.

377. Idem, Foundations of Christian Faith, p.278.

378. Norbert Klaes, 'Reinkarnation und Auferstehung', S.195: '... die eschato-logischen Aussagen (geben) keine Informationen über das Leben nach dem Tod ... sondern (erhellen) auf bildhafte Weise das jetzige Leben...' Cfr. also: Ibid., SS.192-193: 'Grundsätzlich geht es bei eschatologischen Aussagen um die Gegenwart des konkreten Menschen, insofern er ein Wesen ist, das von Gott gewollt und so auf die absolute Zukunft Gottes geöffnet ist. Im Zentrum stehen also immer die gegenwärigen Erfahrungen des Menschen mit sich und mit Gott in Christus, deren Zukunftsdimensionen dem Menschen gerade sagen, was er im Tiefsten jetzt ist und soll. - 'Zukunft' ist nicht so zu verstehen, als gäbe es sie schon als feste Größe, über die man wie in einer Reportage alles mögliche berichten könnte und auf die wir Menschen uns nur hinzubewegen brauchten. Es wird also nicht von einer festgelegten Zukunft etwas in die Gegenwart projiziert. Vielmehr werden die gegenwärtigen heilsgeschichtlichen Erfahrungen und verschiedenen Dimensionen des Menschen in ihrer Tendenz auf die Zukunft hin ausgelegt und konkret in vielfältigen Zukunftsbildern vorgestellt, um das Jetzt zu erhellen.' Cfr. also: Ibid., S. 193: '... die Vorstellung von der leiblichen Auferstehung (ist) die Aussageform für den Offenbarungsglauben, daß der jetzige Mensch als ganzheitliches, leib-seelisches Wesen nicht dem Nichts verfällt, sondern in Gott seine Zukunft hat. Die Vorstellung von der Vollendung der Welt am Jüngsten Tag könnte eine Aussageweise des Inhaltes sein, daß der heutige Mensch als Glied einer Gemeinschaft und einer universalen Geschichte seine Beseligung in Gott findet.' Cfr. also further for the question of death and resurrection: Gisbert Greshake, 'Tod und Auferstehung', in: Franz Böckle et alii (Hrg.), Op. Cit., Bd. 5, SS.64ff.

CHAPTER IX

1. J.B. Chethimattam (Ed.), Unique and Universal - Fundamental Problems of Indian Theology, Bangalore, 1972.

2. Cfr. above Ch.IV.A.3.b.

3. Cfr. above Ch.II.C., V.C.1.b.

4. Cfr. above Ch.IV.A.3.b., III.C.

5. Cfr. above Ch.V.C.1.a.

6. Cfr. above Ch.IV.A.3.a.

7. Cfr. above CH.IV.A.1.a.

8. Cfr. above Ch.IV.A.1.b.

9. Cfr. above Ch.IV.A.1.c.

10. Cfr. above Ch.IV.B., IV.B.3., IV.C.2.a.

11. K. Rahner, Ich glaube an Jesus Christus, S.31: 'Wie kann ich sagen, daß dieser Mensch, der am 'Akt' des absoluten Sichselbstanvertrauens an den Anderen, in diesen Anderen bejaht wird, gerade Jesus von Nazareth ist und niemand sonst.

12. Ibid., S.32: 'Warum gerade Er und nur Er unter unzähligen Menschen diese Wahrheit des Menschen darstellt? Warum nicht ebensogut ein anderer?'

13. Ibid., p.13.

14. Idem, 'Current Problems in Christology' (Art. Cit.), pp.197, 198.

15. K.-H. Weger, Karl Rahner - An Introduction, pp.10, 11. Cfr. also: Ignazio Sanna, Op. Cit., p.298. He formulates Rahner's historical problem setting as follows: 'Una domanda che può benissimo essere posta e di fatto fu posta è: perché io, uomo del XX secolo devo prestare attenzione a ciò che è stato detto e fatto da un oscuro predicatore che visse più 1900 anni fa, in un remoto angolo del Medio Oriente? Non sembra sia tanto facile rispondere questa domanda, in un modo tale che l'uomo di oggi la trovi rilevante, se non si può mostrare che l'uomo ha il dovere di ascoltare nella storia una possibile rivelazione di Dio Assoluto.' (Underline mine.)
    Cfr. also the references given by the same author: J. Doncell, The Philosophy of Karl Rahner, Albany, 1969, p.19., E. Ridau, 'Y a-t-il un monde profane?', in. NRTh, 87 (1966), pp.1062-1082.
    J. Sudbrack, 'Der Gott-Mensch als Sinn des menschlichen Daseins', in: Geist und Leben, 39 (1966), SS.165-182.

16. K. Rahner, 'Über die Spiritualität des Osterglaubens', in: Idem, Schriften zur Theologe, Bd. XII, Zürich/Einsiedeln/Köln, 1975, S.339:

741

'Wie kann eine Geschichte aus Endlichkeiten eine Bedeutung absoluter und endgültiger Art haben vor einem unendlichen Gott? Warum vergeht für das geistige und gnadenhaft erhobene Subjekt nicht alle Geschichte als wesenlose Vorläufigkeit, wenn es unmittelbar wird zu dem Gott über aller Geschichte?'

17. Idem, Foundations of Christian Faith, pp.234, 235. F. Greiner, Op. Cit., p.263.

18. K.-H. Weger, Karl Rahner - An Introduction, p.10, 11. A. Schilson/W. Kasper, Op. Cit., p.84.

19. W. Pannenberg, 'The Revelation of God in Jesus', in: James M. Robinson and John B. Cobb Jr., (Edd.), Op. Cit., p.133.

19a. James Dupuis, 'The Salvific Value of Non-Christian Religions', in: J. Pathrapankal (Ed.), Service and Salvation, Bangalore, 1973, pp.207ff.

20. K.-Weger, Op. Cit., pp.10, 11.

21. K. Rahner, 'Current Problems in Christology', (Art. Cit.), p.198.

22. DS. 302.

23. K. Rahner, Foundation of Christian Faith, p.454 (460), Cfr. also: Idem, 'Two Basic Types of Christology' (Art. Cit.), p.215.

24. Idem, Art. Cit., p.216.

25. W. Pannenberg, Jesus - God and Man, pp.191-282.

26. Idem, Grundzüge der Christologie, Gütersloh, 1976 , S.43: 'Alle soteriologischen Motive haben nun einen Zug gemeinsam, der für die Gestaltung der Christologie wichtig ist. Sie bringen zum Ausdruck, daß in Jesus die Bestimmung des Menschen schlechthin ihre Erfüllung findet, sei diese nun als Vergottung in dieser oder jener Weise, als Gerechtigkeit vor Gott im Sinne der Rechtfertigung oder des Gerechtgesprochenwerdens verstanden, als Bestimmtheit des Weltverhältnisses durch das fromme Selbstbewußtsein, als Befreiung für die sittliche Aufgabe oder zum reinen Personensein. Immer geht es darum, daß das Menschsein des Menschen überhaupt durch Jesus erfüllt ist.'

27. Cfr. F. Greiner, Op. Cit., p.281 and W. Pannenberg, Op. Cit., S.193. and Idem, 'Das christologische Fundament christlicher Anthropologie', in: Concilium 9 (1973), S.426.
Die 'Bestimmung des Menschen (ist) nicht schon durch das Dasein der Menschheit gewährleistet', sondern 'die Bestimmung der Menschheit (hängt) an der besonderen Geschichte dieses einen Individuums...' weil die Bestimmung der Menschheit von außen her auf sie als ihre Zukunft zukommt, 'darum kann es die Besonderheit Jesu ausmachen, daß mit ihm dasjenige, was die Bestimmung des Menschen überhaupt ist, einmalig an einem Individuum erschienen ist und so den übrigen nur durch diesen einzelnen zugänglich wird.'

28. K. Rahner, 'Christologie within an Evolutionary View of the World', (Art. Cit.), pp.187, 188.

29. Idem, Foundation of Christian Faith, p.233.

30. K.-H. Weger, Karl Rahner - An Introduction, pp.20, 21.

31. K. Rahner, Art. Cit., pp.174, 175.

32. Ibid., pp.175, 176.

33. Idem, 'Current Problems in Christology', (Art. Cit.), pp.198, 199.

34. W. Pannenberg, 'Dogmatische Thesen', (Art. Cit.), S.98.

35. Idem, 'Heilsgeschehen und Geschichte' (Art. Cit.), S.29. or: 'Redemptive Event as History' (Art. Cit.), p.24.

36. Idem, 'Response to the Discussion' (Art. Cit.), pp.240, 241.

37. Idem, 'What is a Dogmatic Statement', in: Idem, Basic Questions in Theology I, p.199.

38. Idem, 'Über historische und theologische Hermeneutik', (Art. Cit.), S.155.

39. Cfr. back: Ch.V.C.2.b.

40. K. Rahner, Ich glaube an Jesus Christus, S.32.

41. Idem, 'Jesus Christ', (Art. Cit.), p.205.

42. Idem, Foundations of Christian Faith, pp.174-175.
Idem, Ich glaube an Jesus Christus, Ss.35-36: Jesus ist 'die Zusage Gottes zur Welt und die Annahme der Welt in Gott hinein in Person und als Person ..., gewiß das unüberholbare, endgültige und eschatologische Ereignis. Nach ihm kann - sonst wäre er nicht der Gottmensch - keine religiöse Erfahrung und kein Prophet mehr kommen, der ihn überholen könnte, etwas, wodurch ein Neues und Besseres, das Alte ablösend, an die Stelle des Bisherigen treten könnte. Wie sollte es auch möglich sein? Es gibt doch zwei unüberholbare Worte bzw. Wirklichkeiten und damit deren Konvergenz: der Mensch als die unendliche Frage und das unendliche Geheimnis als die unendliche absolute Antwort, indem es Geheimnis bleibt: Mensch und Gott. Darum ist der Gottmensch unüberholbar; ein neuer Prophet kann es nicht zu mehr bringen, kann hinter der Antwort, die der Gottmensch ist, höchstens zurückbleiben oder diese Antwort kopieren.'

43. K.-H. Weger, Op. Cit., pp.160ff.

44. K. Rahner, 'I believe in Jesus Christ', (Art. Cit.), p.168.

45. W. Pannenberg, Jesus - God and Man, p.217.
Cfr. also above: Ch.VIII.B.1.

46. Idem, Grundzüge der Christologie, S.23: 'Die Aufgabe der Christologie ist es ... aus der Geschichte Jesu die wahre Erkenntnis seiner Bedeutung zu begründen, die sich zusammenfassend durch den Ausdruck umschreiben läßt, daß in diesem Menschen Gott offenbar ist.'

47. Idem, 'Response to the Discussion', (Art. Cit.), pp.232, 239, 240. Cfr. also: Idem, 'Einführung', in: Idem et alii, Offenbarung als Geschichte, S.12.

48. O. Cullmann, Christ and Time, London, 1952, passim.

49. W. Kasper, Jesus der Christus, S.13: 'Sinn und Grund der Kirche ist aber nicht irgendeine Idee, kein Prinzip und kein Programm, sind auch nicht einzelne Dogmen und moralische Gebote, schon gar nicht bestimmte kirchliche oder gesellschaftliche Strukturen. Das alles hat an seinem Ort sein Recht und seine Bedeutung. Grund und Sinn der Kirche ist jedoch eine Person, die einen konkreten Namen hat: Jesus Christus.'

50. K. Rahner, Foundation of Christian Faith, pp.235, 236.

51. A. Ganoczy, 'Die Bedeutung des christlichen Schöpfungsglaubens für die Einheit der Menschheit', in: W. Strolz/H. Waldenfels, Christliche Grundlagen des Dialogs mit den Weltreligionen, (Quaestiones Disputatae 98), Freiburg i.Br., 1983, SS.128-129: 'Wesentliche Inhalte des Christusbekenntnisses wie die Auferstehung des Gekreuzigten, seine Messianität und Gottessohnschaft, machen Christus gewiß zum Stein des Anstoßes bei den meisten Nichtchristen, während die Christen ihn gerade aufgrund solcher einmalig-endgültigen Einheit mit dem Schöpfer als den Versammler aller Menschen und Geschöpfe verstehen'.

52. Cfr. above Ch.IV.A.3.b.

53. W. Kasper, Op. Cit., 14: 'Das Bekenntnis 'Jesus ist der Christus' ist die Kurzformel des christlichen Glaubens, und Christologie ist nichts anderes als die gewissenhafte Auslegung dieses Bekenntnisses.' (Italics his). We had seen that Christ's uniqueness is stressed by Indian theologians like P. Johanns, Abhishiktananda and Bede Griffiths. The theory of 'universal presence' and the 'Fulfillment theory' are actually, according to our opinion, not in contrast to each other as some may think, but they are actually complementary. Cfr. also: James Dupuis, Art. Cit., pp.209ff.

54. K. Rahner, 'Grundlinien einer systematischen Christologie', in: Quaestiones Disputatae 55 (1972), Lehrsatz 10, 20f.

55. Idem, 'Christology in Evolutionary World View', (Art. Cit.), p.186.

56. Idem, Foundations of Christian Faith, pp.271,272.

57. Idem, 'Die Christologie innerhalb einer evolutiven Weltanschauung', in: Idem, Schriften zur Theologie, Bd. V, Einsiedeln/Zürich/Köln, 1964, SS.203f.

58. Cfr. above Ch.VI.B.3.b.ii.

59. Frank E. Trupper, Op.Cit., p.50.

60. W. Pannenberg, What is Truth?, (Art. Cit.), p.9.

61. Idem, 'Über historische und theologische Hermeneutik', (Art. Cit.), S.158.

62. Idem, Was ist der Mensch?, S.54.

63. Idem, 'Analogie und Doxologie', in: Idem, Grundfragen systematischer Theologie, I, S.197.

64. K. Rahner, 'Current Problems in Christology', (Art. Cit.), p.165.

65. W. Kasper, Das Absolute in der Geschichte, Mainz, passim.

66. On the question of the 'Anonymous Christians' cfr. esp. the following contributions of Rahner: 'Anonymer und epxliziter Glaube', in: Stimmen der Zeit, 192 (1974), SS.147-152., 'Über das Verhältnis des Naturgesetzes zur übernatürlichen Gnadenordnung', in: Orientierung, 20 (1956), 8-11., 'Der Christ und seine ungläubigen Verwandten', in: Idem, Schriften zur Theologie, Bd. III, Einsiedeln/Zürich/Köln, 1956, SS.419-439. 'Das Christentum und die nichtchristlichen Religionen', in: Op. Cit., Band V, 1964, SS.136ff., 'Die anonymen Christen', in: Op. Cit., Bd. VI, 1965, SS.545-554., 'Jesus Christus in den nichtchristlichen Religionen', in: Op. Cit., Bd. XII, 1975, SS. 370-383, 'Mission und 'implizite Christenheit',' in: Idem (Hrg.), Sacramentum Mundi, III, Freiburg i.Br., 1969, SS.547-551, etc. A rich bibliography is available also in the following contributions towards the topic:
Elmar Klinger (Hrg.), Christentum innerhalb und außerhalb der Kirche, (Quaestiones Disputatae 73), Freiburg/Basel/Wien, 1976, H. Kruse, 'Die 'anonymen Christen' exegetisch gesehen', in: MThZ, 18 (1967), SS.2-29. K. Riesenhuber, 'Der anonyme Christ nach K. Rahner', in: ZKT, LXXXVI (1964), SS.286-303., Anita Röper, Die anonymen Christen, Mainz, 1963. H. Waldenfels, 'Die neuere Diskussion um die 'anonymen Christen' als Beitrag zur Religionstheorie', in: ZMRW 60 (1976), SS.161-180, etc.

67. Cfr. above Ch.VI.B.4.

68. Cfr. above Ch.I.A., IV.A.1.a., IV.A.3.b.
69. Cfr. Ch.VII.A.3.b.

70. K.-H. Weger, Karl Rahner - Eine Einführung, SS.99ff.
Idem, Karl Rahner. An Introduction, pp.112ff.

71. K. Rahner, 'Anonymous Christians', in: Idem, Theological Investigations, Vol.VI, London/Baltimore, 1969, p.393. Col 1:15-20., 1 Cor 15:23-28.

72. K. Rahner, Art. Cit., p.394.

73. Ibid.

74. Ibid., Cfr. also: Idem, Foundations of Christian Faith, pp.227, 228.

75. K.-H. Weger, Karl Rahner - An Introduction, pp.127ff.

76. K. Rahner/J. Ratzinger, Offenbarung und Überlieferung, (Quaestiones Disputatae 25), Freiburg i.Br., 1965, S.13.

77. K. Rahner, 'Glaube zwischen Rationalität und Emotionalität' in: Idem, (Hrg.), Ist Gott noch gefragt, 1973, S.135.

78. Idem, 'Bemerkungen zum Problem des 'anonymen Christen',' Idem, Schriften zur Theologoie, Bd. X, Zürich/Einsiedeln/Köln, 1972, S.537.

79. Idem, 'Atheismus und implizites Christentum', in: Idem, Schriften zur Theologie. Bd. VIII, Einsiedeln/Zürich/Köln, 1967, S.188.

80. K.-H. Weger, Karl Rahner - An Introduction, pp.112ff.

81. K. Rahner, 'Gnade als Mitte der menschlichen Existenz', in: Herderkorrespondenz, 28 (1974), S.87.
Cfr. also: Idem, 'Grundlinien einer systematischen Christologie', (Art. Cit.), S.22.

82. K.-H. Weger, Op. Cit., pp.127ff.

83. Ibid., p.136ff.

84. K. Rahner, 'Über den Begriff des Geheimnisses in der katholischen Theologie', (Art. Cit.), S.55.
Cfr. also: Idem, 'Wort Gottes', in: LThK X, 1965, S.1238.

85. K. Rahner/J. Ratzinger, Op. Cit., p.15.

86. K. Rahner/E. Simons, Zur Lage der Theologie, Düsseldorf, 1969, S.15.

87. Cfr. above Chs. VII, VIII, IX.

88. K. Rahner, Foundations of Christian Faith, pp.153-154.

89. Ibid., pp.142-143.

90. Cfr. above Ch.VII.B.2.

91. W. Pannenberg, 'Redemptive Event as History', in: Basic Questions in Theology, I, pp.41-42.

92. Idem, 'Dogmatische Thesen' (Art. Cit.), Thesis 3, S.98.

93. Idem et alii, Offenbarung als Geschichte, SS.113-114.
Idem et alili, Revelation as History, pp.155.

94. Idem et alii, Offenbarung als Geschichte, S.99.
Idem et allii, Revelation as History, p.136.
Cfr. also: 2 Cor 4:4.

95. Cfr. above Ch.VIII., Ch.IX.A.

96. LG 16., GS 22., AG 7., NA 1ff.

96a. Elmar Klinger, 'Perspektiven des Christlichen im Begriff der anonymen Christlichkeit', in: Idem (Hrg.), Christentum innerhalb und außerhalb der Kirche, (Quaestiones Disputatae 73) Freiburg i.Br./Basel/Wien, 1976, S.12: '... auf dem Boden transzendentaler Theologie des Christentums ist der Audruck anonym eine Bezeichnung, womit Christentum als etwas f ür menschliches Verhalten selber Konstitutives bezeichnet wird.'
Cfr. also: Idem, 'Anonymes Christentum', in: Mayers Enzyklopädisches Lexikon II, Mannheim, 1971, S.261.

746

97. K.-H. Weger, Karl Rahner - An Introduction, p.134.

98. K. Rahner, Foundations of Christian Faith, pp.151-152. Cfr. also: Idem, 'Reflections on the Unity of the Love of Neighbour and the Love of God', in: Idem, Theological Investigations, Vol. VI, London/Baltimore, 1969, p.29.

99. Idem, 'On the Theology the Incarnation', in: Idem, Theological Investigations, Vol. IV, London/Baltimore, 1966, p.119. Cfr. also: Idem, 'Jesus Christ' (Art. Cit.), pp.208ff.

100. Idem, 'Über die Möglichkeit des Glaubens heute', in: Idem, Schriften zur Theologie, Bd. V, Einsiedeln/Zürich/Köln, 1962, S.17: '... ich (sehe) überall ein anonymes Christentum..., weil ich in meinem ausdrücklichen Christentum nicht eine Meinung neben anderen, ihm widersprechenden, erkenne, sondern in meinem Christentum nichts erblicke als das Zusichselbergekommensein dessen, was als Wahrheit und Liebe auch überall sonst lebt und leben kan n.

101. Idem, 'Atheismus und implizites Christentum', (Art. Cit.), S.187: 'Implizites Christentum - man könnte es auch 'anonymes Christentum' nennen - heißt der Zustand jenes Menschen, der einerseits im Zustand der Rechtfertigung und Gnade lebt und andererseits mit der ausdrücklichen Predigt des Evangeliums noch nicht in Berührung gekommen ist, also auch nicht in der Lage ist, sich selber 'Christ' zu nennen.'

102. Cfr. Acts 11:26., 26:29., 1 Pet 4:16. On the extra-Christian origin of the name 'Christian' Cfr. Elmar Klinger (Hrg.), Op. Cit., Ss.9-10., also: 13. Cfr. also: H. Karpp, 'Christennamen', in: Reallexikon für Antike und Christentum, Bd. II, Stuttgart, 1951-1954, 1114-1138.

103. K. Rahner, Foundations of Christian Faith, pp.227, 228.

104. Idem, 'On the Theology of the Incarnation', (Art. Cit.), p.119., Cfr. also: Idem, 'Über die Möglichkeit des Glaubens heute', (Art. Cit.), SS.11-32, esp. 15-17.

105. Idem, 'Anonymous Christians', (Art. Cit.), p.391. Idem, 'Das Christentum und die nichtchristlichen Religionen', (Art. Cit.), p.147. Idem, 'Das neue Bild der Kirche', in: Idem, Schriften zur Theologie, Bd. VIII, Einsiedeln/Zürich/Köln, 1967, SS.329-324., Idem, 'Kirche, Kirchen und Religionen', in: Op. Cit., SS.355-373., Idem, 'Anonymes Christentum und Missionsauftrag der Kirche', in: Idem, Schriften zur Theologie, Bd. IX, Einsiedeln/Zürich/Köln, 1970, Ss.498-518.

106. Hans Urs von Balthasar, Cordula oder der Ernstfall, Einsiedeln, 1966, SS.103-103: 'Wer von 'anonymen Christen' redet, der kann nicht (und will wohl auch nicht) eine letzte Univozität zwischen Christen mit dem Namen und Christen ohne den Namen abwehren, infolgedessen kann es - trotz aller nachträglichen Proteste - doch nicht erheblich sein, ob man den Namen bekennt oder nicht. (...) Aber während wir unsere Partner sehr ehrlich als anonyme Christen ansprechen können, falls sie immer Treue und Redlichkeit üben, und der liebe Gott ihre Tugenden immer

schon übernatürlich als Glaube, Hoffnung und Liebe aufwertet und inter-
pretiert, werden sie uns gewiß Gegenrecht halten, indem sie uns als
anonyme Atheisten begrüßen, da unsere ganze angebliche Dogmatik
nur noch ein ideologischer Überbau sei über einem Feld-, Wald- und
Wiesen-Humanismus und seiner Anthropologie. Haben sie Unrecht?

107. James Dupuis, Art. Cit., p.229.

108. Ibid.

109. Ibid.

110. Ibid.

111. Ibid., pp.208, 298.

111a. Cfr. M.K. Gandhi's opinion on this point above in our work Ch.IV.A.1.b.

112. Walter Kasper, 'Are Non-Christian Religions Salvific?'. in: J. Pathrapankal
(Ed.), Op. Cit., pp.197-198.

113. K.-H. Weger, Karl Rahner - An Introduction, pp.112f. Cfr. also: H. Küng,
Christ sein, München, 1974, SS.89-90.

114. Ibid.

115. James Dupuis, Art. Cit., pp.229-230.
Cfr. also: G. Thils, Propos et problèmes de la théologie des religions
non-chrétiennes,Tournai, 1966, p.194.

116. K. Rahner, 'Anonymous Christians', (Art. Cit.), p.398.
Cfr. also: Bayerischer Rundfunk II, Nachmittagsstudio, 'Fragen unserer
Zeit'. Gespräch zwischen Leonhard Rheinisch und Karl Rahner. 6.04.84.
Following Rahner's demise on 31.3.1984. (Personal recording): '... das,
was ich mit diesem problematischen Schlagwort des anonymen Christen
sagen wollte, das ist an und für sich mindestens heute, der Sache nach,
wenn vielleicht auch nicht hinsichtlich dieser Terminologie, eine im kathol.
Christentum selbstverständlich angenommene Sache. Diese ganze Problematik ist doch von Leben herausgegeben. Ich bin Christ, ich möchte katholischer, römisch-katholischer Christ sein, unbedingt und selbstverständlich und gleichzeitig sehe ich, daß so und so viele Menschen, die ich
schätze, die ich liebe, eine andere Meinung, eine andere Lebensanschauung
haben, und da muß ich mich doch als katholischer Christ fragen: wie
ist es mit diesen anderen Menschen, die doch im Grunde genommen
von der Liebe des einen und selben Gottes, dem ich zu dienen versuche...,
und dann komme ich eben auf diese Dinge, die an und für sich ganz
allgemein katholisch mindestens heute sind, daß jeder, der seinem Gewissen
folgt und ihm getreu ist, mag er auch meinen, Atheist zu sein, einer
anderen christlichen Konfession anzugehören oder einer anderen großen
Kulturreligion anzuhangen - alle diese sind und bleiben selbstverständlich,
wie gesagt, wenn sie nicht sich in einer tödlichen Weise gegen ihr eigenes
Gewissen versündigen, umfangen von der einen rettenden Liebe des
einen ewigen Gottes, dessen absolute Zusage für mich in Jesus Christus,
dem gekreuzigten und auferstandenen Herrn, erschienen ist.'

748

117. Cfr. Wolfgang Feneberg, 'die Kirche hat gelernt tolerant zu sein', in: Georg Sporschill (Hrg.), Karl Rahner - Bekenntnisse - Rückblicke auf 80 Jahre, Wien/München, 1984, SS.92-93.

118. K.-H. Weger, Op. Cit., pp.112ff.

119. Elmar Klinger, 'Perspektiven des Christlichen im Begriff der anonymen Christenheit', in:Idem (Hrg.), Op. Cit., SS.12, 15.

120. Ibid., p.23, 21, 17.
121. Ibid., pp.15, 16, 20.

122. Ibid., p.22.

123. K. Rahner, 'Zur Theologie des ökumenischen Gesprächs', in: Idem, Schriften zur Theologie, Bd. IX, Einsiedeln/Zürich/Köln, 1970, S.78., Cfr. also above: Ch.IV.A.1.c.

124. Otto Hermann Pesch, Frei sein aus Gnade, Theologische Anthropologie, Freiburg/Basel/Wien, 1983, SS.243ff., 184ff. In reference to this question Cfr. also: Gerald A. McCool (Ed.), A Rahner Reader, London, 1975, pp.211-223.
Yves Congar, Außer der Kirche kein Heil. Wahrheit und Dimension des Heils, Essen, 1961.
H. Küng,Die Kirche, Freiburg/Basel/Wien, 1967, SS.371-378, Idem, Christ sein, SS.81-108.
Walter Kern, Außerhalb der Kirche kein Heil?, Freiburg i.Br., 1979.
Karl Forster (Hg.), Religiös ohne Kirche? Eine Herausforderung für Glaube und Kirche, Mainz, 1977.
W. Kasper, (Hrg.), Absolutheit des Christentums, Freiburg i.Br., 1977.
Horst Bürkle, 'Der christliche Anspruch angesichts der Weltreligionen heute', in: W. Kasper (Hrg.), Op. Cit., SS.83-104.
Karl Lehmann, 'Theologische Reflexionen zum Phänomen 'außerchristlicher Religiösität',' in: Ludwig Bertsch/Felix Schlösser (Hrg.), Kirchliche und nichtkirchliche Religiosität. Pastoraltheologische Perspektiven zum Phänomen der Distanzierung von der Kirche, Freiburg i.Br., 1977,SS.47-90.

125. Eberhard Jüngel, 'Extra Christum nulla salus - als Grundsatz natürlicher Theologie? Evangelische Erwägungen zur 'Anonymität' des Christentums', in: ZThK, 72 (1975), SS.337ff., also in: Elmar Klinger (Hrg.), Op. Cit., pp.122-138.

126. A. Ganoczy, 'Außer Gott kein Heil?', in: Lebendiges Zeugnis, 32 (1977), SS.55-56.

127. Cfr. above Ch.IX.A.

128. Leszek Kalakowski, 'Toleranz und Absolutheitsansprüche', in: Franz Böckle et alii (rg.), Op. Cit., Band 26, SS.6ff. (A vast bibliography is available there).

129. Georg Sporschill (Hrg.), Op. Cit., p.93.

130. K. Rahner, 'Christianity and Non-Christian Religions', in: Idem, Theological Investigations, Vol.V, London/Baltimore, 1966, p.118. Cfr. also H. Bürkle, Art. Cit., pp.83-103.

131. W. Kasper, 'Are Non-Christian Religions Salvific?', Art. Cit., pp.193-194. Cfr. also: Y. Congar, 'Non-Christian Religions and Christianity', in: J. Pathrapankal (Ed.), Op. cit., pp.168-169.

132. James Dupuis, Art. Cit., pp.230ff.

133. W. Pannenberg, Jesus - God and Man, pp.269ff. Cfr. also: W. Bieder, Die Vorstellung von der Höllenfahrt Jesu Christi, Zürich, 1949, SS.110ff.

134. James Dupuis, Art. Cit., pp.224ff.

135. H. Küng, 'The World Religions in God's Plan of Salvation', in: J. Neuner (Ed.), Christian Revelation and World Religions, London, 1967, pp.25-66.

136. James Dupuis, Art. Cit., p.227.

137. K. Rahner, 'Anonymous Christians', (Art. Cit.), p.398. Idem, 'Christianity and the Non-Christian Religions', (Art. Cit.), p.134.

137a. Idem, 'Der Christ und seine ungläubigen Verwandten', in: Idem, Schriften zur Theologie, Bd. III, Einsiedeln/Zürich/Köln, 1959, SS.426-427. Cfr. also: A. Ganoczy, 'Absolutheitsanspruch. Begründung oder Hindernis der Evangelisation', in: Concilium, 134 (1978), SS.221-226.

138. K. Rahner, 'Anonymous Christians', (Art. Cit.), p.397.

139. Ibid., p.396.

140. Ibid., p.395. Cfr. also: Idem, Ich glaube an Jesus Christus, SS.50, 51. 'Man ist immer Christ um es zu werden.' Rahner maintains that the grades of church membership cannot be fixed with academic clarity. Even in a Christian it is a progressive transition. Its basis is man's 'übernatürliches Existential, d.h. die seiner Freiheit angebotene Selbstmitteilung Gottes'.

141. Idem, 'Christianity and the Non-Christian Religions', (Art. Cit.), p.132.

142. Idem and E. Simons, Op. Cit., p.15.

143. Idem, Art. Cit., Loc. Cit.

144. Idem, 'Bemerkungen zum Problem des 'anonymen Christen',' in: Idem, Schriften zur Theologie, Bd. X, Zürich/Einsiedeln/Köln, 1972, S.545.

145. Idem, Ich glaube an Jesus Christus, S.64.

146. Idem, 'Das Christentum und die nichtchristlichen Religionen', (Art. Cit.), S.156.

147. Idem, Ich glaube an Jesus Christus, S.65.

148. For the details on R. Panikkar's position cfr. back to our work Ch.IV.B. and C., Ch.VI.B.4.a. and b.

149. Cfr. above Ch.VI.B.4.

150. Ibid.

151. A. Ganoczy, 'Jesus der Christus für alle Zeiten?', in: TThZ, 84 (1975), SS.338-350., bes. S.347.: 'Ist das historisch konstatierbare Faktum, daß es bereits im Neuen Testament verschieden konzipierte, strukturierte und gewendete Christologien gab, ein hinreichender Grund dafür, daß derselbe Jesus als der Christus für verschiedene Zeiten und Kulturen die Antwort auf die Existenzfrage geben kann? Dazu sei gesagt: allein die Faktizität der genannten Vielfalt kann ihre Begründung und Legitimation nicht in sich tragen. Sie zeigt sich in ihrer Sinnhaftigkeit erst dann, wenn sie mit der Wirklichkeit Gottes selbst, welche durch jede Christologie letzten Endes vermittelt wird, im Einklang steht.' (Italics his). Cfr. also above to our conclusion to the Ch.V.

152. Cfr. above Ch.IV.A.3.b., Cfr. also: III.A.2., VI.C.

153. Cfr. above Ch.III.A.2. and 3., IV.A.1.a. Cfr. also: S. Radhakrishnan, The Hindu View of Life, London, 1980, (1927), p.13.

154. W. Kasper, Der Gott Jesu Christi, Mainz, 1982, S.108. Cfr. also: A.M. Hass, 'Die Problematik von Sprache und Erfahrung in der deutschen Mystik', in: W. Bierwaltes/H.U.von Balthasar/A.M. Haas, Grundfragen der Mystik, Einsiedeln, 1974, S.75, Anm.1.

155. W. Kasper, Op. Cit., pp.106-107: 'Wie alle Erkenntnis bedarf ... auch die Gotteserkenntnis einer erfahrungsmäßigen Grundlage.' Cfr. also: H. Ogiermann, 'Die Problematik der religiösen Erfahrung', in: Scholastik 37 (1962), SS.481-513 and 38(1963), SS.481-518.
A. Gerken, Offenbarung von Transzendenzerfahrung, Düsseldorf, 1969.
R. Egenter, Erfahrung ist Leben, München, 1974.
C. Heitmann/H. Müller (Hrg.), Erfahrung und Theologie des Heiligen Geistes, München, 1974.
J. Sudbrack (Hrg.), Das Mysterium und die Mystik. Beiträge zur Theologie der christlichen Gotteserfahrung, Würzburg, 1974.
K. Rahner, 'Erfahrung des Geistes und existentielle Entscheidung', in: Idem, Schriften zur Theologie. Bd.XII, Zürich/Einsiedeln/Köln, 1975, SS.41-53. Idem, 'Die enthusiastische und die gnadenhafte Erfahrung', in: Ibid., SS.54-76.
R. Bragne, 'Was heißt christliche Erfahrung?', in: Intern. kath. Z. 6 (1976), SS.481-496.
H.U.von Balthasar, 'Gotteserfahrung biblisch und praktisch', in: Ibid., SS.497-509.
L. Scheffczyk, 'Die Frage nach der 'Erfahrung' als theologisches Verifikationsprinzip', in: W. Ernst/K. Feiereis/F. Hoffmann (Hrg.), Dienst der Vermittlung, Leipzig, 1972, SS.353-373.
E. Schillebeeck, Christus und die Christen, Freiburg i.Br., 1977.
N. Schiffers, 'Gnadenerfahrung. Überlegungen zur Auferstehung und Geisterfahrung im Anschluß an Röm. 8,11Å, in: Mysterium der Gnade (Festschrift für J. Auer), Regensburg, 1975, SS.105-118.
W. Beinert, 'Die Erfahrbarkeit der Glaubenswirklichkeit', in: Ibid., SS. 132-145.

L. Scheffczyk, 'Die Erfahrbarkeit der göttlichen Gnade', Ibid., SS.146-159.

156.　A. Ganoczy, 'Die Bedeutung des christlichen Schöpfungsglaubens für die Einheit der Menschheit', (Art.Cit.), SS.149-150: 'Der relativen Rezeptionsbereitschaft eines sonst selbstbewußten Neuhinduismus gegenüber jüdisch-christlichen Gedanken sollte m.e. die christliche Bereitschaft entsprechen, das Prinzip 'Erfahrung' vom Partner mehr und mehr zu übernehmen. Denn der Gottbezug der Schöpfung erschließt sich in der säkularisierten Gesellschaft nur noch jenem, der Welt und Umwelt mit spirituellen Augen wahrnehmen kann.' (Italics his).

157.　Cfr. above Ch.III.A.2.3., B., VI.C.1.2.3.etc.

158.　K. Rahner, 'Ein Brief von P. Karl Rahner', in: Klaus Fischer, Der Mensch als Geheimnis. Die Anthropologie Karl Rahners, Freiburg/Basel/Wien, 1974, SS.405f.: 'Was eigentlich 'Mystik' ist, das ist eine Frage, die wohl auch in der katholischen Theologie noch keine einhellige Antwort erhalten hat. Man kann natürlich sagen, daß die 'eingegossene Beschauung' das eigentliche Wesen der Mystik ausmachte und Phänomene zusätzlicher und sekundärer Art (Ekstasen, Elevationen und ähnliche Dinge, die entweder parapsychologischen Phänomenen oder solchen Phänomenen ähnlich sind, die sich in anderen Religionen oder außergewöhnlichen seelischen Zuständen finden) nicht mit diesem eigentlichen Wesen der Mystik verwechselt werden dürfen. (...) Ich meine ..., daß die erste und ursprüngliche Erfahrung des Geistes ... auch der innerste Kern dessen ist, was man Mystik nennen kann, und daß von daher, weil diese ... Geisteserfahrung im eigentlichen und ursprünglichen Sinn die Glaubenserfahrung ist, Mystik (im üblichen Sinn des Wortes) nicht eine höhere 'Stufe' über dem normalen Glauben ist, sondern eine bestimmte Weise, eben dieser Glaubenserfahrung, eine Weise, die 'an sich', in ihr selbst, der natürlichen Psychologie und den natürlichen Möglichkeiten des Menschen für 'Versenkung', Konzentration, Leerwerden des Geistes usw. angehört.'

159.　K. Rahner, 'Mystische Erfahrung und mystische Theologie, in: Idem, Schriften zur Theologie, Bd. XII, Zürich/Einsiedeln/Köln, 1975, SS.428-438, Here 437. Cfr. also: Foot note no. 158 above.

160.　K. Rahner, Hearer of the Word, pp.77-78.

161.　Cfr. above CH.VII.

162.　K. Rahner, 'Experience of Self and Experience of God', in: Idem, Theological Investigations, Vol.XIII, London, 1975, p.123.

163.　Idem, 'The Experience of God Today', in: Idem, Theological Investigations, Vol.XI, London, 1974, pp.155ff. Cfr. also: Rudolf Otto, Das Heilige. Über das Irrationale in der Idee des Göttlichen und sein Verhältnis zum Rationalen, München, 1979, (1917). He describes the Holy Mystery as the 'mysterium tremendum et fascinosum', which implies a contrast-harmony between the repelling distance and attracting nearness of the Holy! (Cfr. K. Rahner: Loc. Cit.).

164.　K. Rahner, Art. Cit., p.153.

752

166. Ibid., p.159.

167. Ibid., pp.156, 159.

168. Ibid., pp.154, 156.

169. Cfr. above Ch.VII.A.2.

170. W. Pannenberg, 'Speaking about God', in: Idem, The Idea of God and Human Freedom, The Westminster Press, 1973, pp.102ff., Cfr. also: Idem, The Apostles' Creed, pp.115-17.

171. Idem, 'Response to the Discussion', (Art. Cit.), p.225, no.2.

172. K. Rahner, 'Experience of Self and Experience of God', (Art. Cit.), p.125.

173. Ibid., p.125.

174. Ibid., Cfr. also: Idem (Hrg.), Herders Theologisches Taschenlexikon 5, Freiburg/Basel/Wien, 1973, S.145. ('Mystik').

175. S. Radhakrishnan, an Idealist View of Life, London, 1980 (1932), p.83., Cfr. also above: Ch.I.B.3.b., II.A.1., III.A.2., III.A.3.a., VI.C.1., VI.C.2., VII.A.3.

176. Thomas Aquinas, Summa Theologica, I, 84,7.
Cfr. also: K. Rahner, Hearers of the Word, p.77.
Idem, Spirit in the World, pp.2-54.

177. Idem, Hearers of the Word, p.150.

178. Idem, Spirit in the World, pp.52, 53, 211, 217, 226.
Thomas Aquinas, De veritate, q.14, a.8, ad.4.
Cfr. also: K. Rahner, 'Gotteserfahrung heute', in: Idem, Schriften zur Theologie, Bd. IX, Einsiedeln/Zürich/Köln, 1970, SS.172ff.
Idem, Grundkurs des Glaubens, SS.75f.
J.B. Lotz, Transzendentale Erfahrung, Freiburg/Basel/Wein, 1978. passim.

179. W. Pannenberg, 'Responsae to the Discussion' (Art. Cit.), p.239.

180. Cfr. above Ch.IV.A.3.b., VI.C., III.A.2.
Here attention could be drawn once again to T.M. Manickam's article: 'Anubhava as Pramana of an Indian Christology', in: Jeevadhara, 1 (1971), pp.228-244, esp. p.241. There he fortunately qualifies his notion of 'Anubhava' attributing to it the three dimensions of Revelation, Ecclesial Faith and Reason which are presupposed in the traditional 'Fundamental Theology' and to which he gives the Indian expressions:
1. Sruti-yojyata: agreement with the Revelation,
2. Sabha-Yojyata: conformity with the believing community,
3. Yukti-yojyata: compliance with the requirements of human reason.

181. K. Rahner, Hearer of the Word, p.78.

182. W.Kasper, Der Gott Jesu Christi, pp.110-111. On false mysticism or erroneous pseudo-mysticism, Cfr. DS. 866., 2181-2192., Cfr. also DS. 891-899, 2201, 2223, 2226, 2263, 2268, 2365, 2366, 2367, 2371.

183. W. Pannenberg, Jesus - God and Man, p.28.

184. Cfr. back to our Ch.VII.C.3. It is however to be mentioned that as a result of the inevitable contact with the Christian West, some neo- Vedantins like S. Radhakrishnan are discovering the value of history and the mediated character of God-experience. Cfr. S. Radhakrishnan, An Idealist View of Life, p.78.

185. Ibid., p.73.

186. W. Kasper, Op. Cit., p.108.

187. K. Rahner, 'Mystik', in: Idem, Herders Theologisches Taschenlexikon, Bd. 5, S.146.

188. F. Greiner, Op. Cit., SS .259-260: '... die transzendentaltheologische Methode muß nicht in die transcendentale, d.h. in die isolierte Innerlichkeit religiöser Subjektivität führen. Demgegenüber ... kann die Unmittelbarkeit der religiösen Erfahrung allererst das Resultat eines anthropologisch notwendigen Ausganges in die Geschichte sein. Dies in ausdrücklicher Weise darzutun, unternimmt Rahner in der Entfaltung der transzendentalen Christologie.'

189. Cfr. above Ch.VI.C.1., Cfr. also: James Dupuis, 'Knowing Christ through the Christian Experience', in: Indian Journal of Theology, 1969, pp.54-64.

190. K. Rahner, Foundations of Christian Faith, pp.157, 158.

191. Cfr. or discussion on the 'Marga' above: Ch.VI.C.2 and Ch.III.B. Cfr. also: Mt 21:32., 26:16., Act 16:17., 22:4., 24:14., 2 Pt 2:2.

191a. K. Rahner, Ich glaube an Jesus Christus, S.50.

192. Cfr. above Ch.III.A.2.

193. K. Rahner, 'Experience of God Today', (Art. Cit.), p.163.

194. Ibid., p.164.

195. Idem, Foundations of Christian Faith, p.161.

196. James Dupuis, 'The Salvific Value of Non-Christian Religions', (Art. Cit.), p.232.

197. Cfr. above Ch.VI.C.1.

198. Cfr. above Ch.I.B.3.

199. Cfr. above Ch.I.C.3.

200. Cfrf. above Ch.VII.A.2., IX.C.1.

201. K. Rahner, 'Mystik', (Art. Cit.), S,137: Mystik ist das 'Bewußtwerden der Erfahrung der ungeschaffenen Gnade als Offenbarung und Selbstmitteilung des dreieinigen Gottes.'

202. Ibid.

203. W. Pannenberg, 'Theology and the Kingdom of God', (Art. Cit.), p.71.

204. Ibid.

205. Origen, In Ioan, II,II.20.

206. Pseudo Dynonysiu, De div. nomi. II,7 (PG 3,645 B)

207. Gregory of Naziance, Or. 2, 38 (PG 34, 445).

208. Idem, Or. 25, In laudem Heronis Philos., 15. (PG 35, 1220., Cfr. also: PG 36, 348).

209. Gregory of Nyssa, C. Eunom. (PG 45, 929).

210. Quoted by the Council of Toledo (Mansi XI, 132., XII, 640), DS. 525, 568., Cfr. also: St. Augustine, De Trin. IV, 20, 29 (PL 10, 90., 108., 120).

211. Cfr. O. Gonzalez, Misterio trinitario y existencia humana. Est. hist. teol. entorno a S. Bonaventura. Madrid, 1966. passim.
Cfr. also: A. de Villalmonte, 'El Padre plenitud fontal de la deidad', in: S. Bonaventura 1274-1974, Bd. IV, 2, Roma, 1974, pp.221-242.

212. Thomas Aquinas, I Sent. 26 q2 a.3., Summa theologica I.q.32 a.3., q.33 a.4., q.30 a.3 ad.3.

213. Cfr. also: 1 Cor 13:11., 2 Cor 13:13., Eph 2:4., Jn 3:14., 1 Jn 2:15.

214. Cfr. also: Mk 1:11 and parallels, Mt 12:18., 17:5., 2 Pt 1:17.

215. Yves Congar, Der Heilige Geist, Freiburg i.Br., 1982, SS.414-417, esp. 417.

216. K. Rahner, Ich glaube an Jesus Christus, S. 57.

217. Ibid., pp.55-56., Cfr. also: Idem, 'The Eternal Significance of the Humanity of Jesus for Our Relationship with God', in: Idem, Theological Investigations, Vol. III, London/Baltimore, 1967, p.44.

218. Idem, Art. Cit., p.45.

219. Cfr. the 'Vida' of St. Teres of Avila, Ch.22, especially 22:6-7.12.14.

220. Ulrich Dobhan, Gott-Mensch-Welt: in der Sicht Teresas von Avila, Frankfurt am Main/Bern/Las Veagas, 1978, SS. 365ff. (Die Bedeutung der Verehrung der Menschheit Christi für das gesamte geistliche Leben).

Cfr. also: SS.383-396, esp.S.394.

221. Cfr. above Ch.III.A.3.A.

222. Cfr. above Ch.II.A.1.

223. Cfr. above Ch.VIII.A.1., Cfr. also: W. Pannenberg, Jesus - God and Man, p. 40, Cfr. also: Iranaeus, Adv. haer. V Praefatio (PG 7/2, 1120) Athanasius, De Incarnatione, I:3., 13., 14. Origen, Dialogue with Heraclides, Sources Chret, 67, (1960), p.70. Gregory of Naziance, Ep. 101 (PG 37, 181C).

224. Matthew Vellanickal, The Divine Sonship of Christians in the Johannine Writings (Analecta Biblica 72), Rome, 1977. Cfr. also above: Ch.VIII, Foot note no. 90.

225. Ibid., p.4.

226. Ibid., p.353: 'The use of (tekna Theou) as antithetically parallel to (tekna tou diabolou) and in parallelism with (einai ek tou Theou) shows in the children of God a moral connection of derivation from and dependence on God. But the use of (gegenetai ek tou Theou) in the perfect exclusively for the divine sonship of man shows that, unlike the diabolic sonship, it is based on an initial communication of life from the part of God, which remains active throughout and which determines the nature of the children of God. It is by virtue of this communicated life that one grows into a (teknon Theou). Thus the two phrases (gegenetai ek tou Theou) and (tekna Theou einai) seem to be identical in sense. Hence for Jn the divine sonship of Christians is more than a mere moral relationship, is essentially dynamic, destined to growth and development to full maturity.'

227. 'tekna theou': Cfr. also: 1 Jn 3:1,2,10., 5:2.

228. 'genethenai ek tou theou': Cfr. also: 1 Jn 2:29., 3:9., 4:7., 5:1,4,18.

229. For 'genethenai ek tou Theou': Cfr. M. Vellanickal, Op. Cit., pp.353, 364, 369, 11.

230. Ibid., p.3., ('teknon' and 'hyios').

231. Ibid., pp.163-226. Cfr. also: 1 Jn 4:12-13., 3:23-24.

232. Cfr. also: Rom 9:7f., 1 Cor 4:15., Gal 4:4-6., Phil 2:15.

233. M. Vellanickal, Op. Cit., pp. 353-358. Cfr. also: Mt 5:9, 43-48., Lk 6:27-28., 32-36., 20:36.

234. Ibid., pp.74-76. Cfr. also: Ibid., pp.66ff., pp.214-223 and also: Mt 11:25-27., 12:48-50., 17:25-27., 1 Cor 4:15., Gal 3:26-28.

235. K. Rahner, Ich glaube an Jesus Christus, SS.40, 58. Cfr. also: M. Vellanickal, Op. Cit., pp.295-316, 317-330, 331-352.

236. K. Rahner, 'The Eternal Significance of the Humanity of Jesus for our Relationship with God' (Art. Cit.), pp.43-44.

237. Cfr. above Ch.VI.B.3.c.

238. Cfr. also: Ch.IV.B.1.b.

239. Cfr. also: A. Ganoczy, 'Der Heilige Geist als Kraft und Person', in: G. Becker/H. Bürkle (Hrg.), Communicatio fidei, Regensburg, 1983, SS.111-119.

240. Cfr. above Ch.VI.B.3.c.

241. Yves Congar, Der Heilige Geist, Freiburg i.Br., 1982.

242. Cfr. also: Jn 3:3,5,6., Rom 8: esp. 14-17., Gal 4:4-7.

243. J.C. Martinez-Gomez, 'Relación éntre la inhabitación del Espíritu santo y los dones criados de la justificación', in: Est. Ecles. 14 (1935), pp.20-50.

244. K. Rahner, Zur scholastischen Begrifflichkeit der ungeschaffenen Gnade', in: Idem, Schriften zur Theologie, Bd. I, Einsiedeln/Zürich/Köln, 1954, SS.347-376.

245. Thomas Aquinas, III Sent. d.10 q.2 a.1 sol.3.
The Holy Spirit is the 'Causa formalis inhaerens' of our divine filiation.

246. K. Rahner, 'Interview zum 70. Geburtstag', in: Herderkorrespondenz 28 (1974), S.91.

247. Cfr. above Ch.I.C.3.

248. Cfr. also. Anita Röper, Ist Gott ein Mann?, Düsseldorf, 1979. Cfr. also for the same question: Christa Mulack, Die Weiblichkeit Gottes. Matriarchale Voraussetzungen des Gottesbildes, Stuttgart, 1983. Inge Wenck, Gott ist im Mann zu kurz gekommen, Gütersloh, 1982.

249. Cfr. also: 1 Kgs 3.26., Prv 12:10

250. Y. Congar, Op. Cit., pp.424-432.

251. Ibid., p.432.

252. W. Pannenberg, Grundzüge der Christologie, S.170.

253. Cfr. above CH.VI.C.3.

254. Cfr. Ch.IX.C.1. Cfr. also: K. Rahner, 'The 'commandment' of Love in Relation to Other Commandments', in: Idem, Theological Investigations, Vol. V, London/Baltimore, 1966, pp.439-459.

255. Cfr. above: Ch.VIII.A.1.c., also: K. Rahner, 'Reflections on the Unity of the Love of Neighbour and the Love of God', in: Idem, Theological Investigations, Vol.VI, London/Baltimore, 1969, pp.242-243.

256. Idem, 'Experience of Self and Experience of God', (Art. Cit.), p.127.

257. Ibid., Cfr. also: Idem, 'Reflections on the Unity of the Love of Neighbour and the Love of God', (Art. Cit.), p.241.

258. Idem, 'Experience of Self and Experience of God', (Art. Cit.), p.128.

259. Ibid.

260. Ibid., pp.128-129., Cfr. also: Idem, 'Reflections on the Unity of the Love of Neighbour and the Love of God', (Art. Cit.), p.238, Cfr. also: Idem. Ich glaube an Jesus Christus, SS.18-19: 'Wenn diese Liebe den Menschen wirklich radikal und ohne Vorbehalten an den Anderen wagt ..., dann ist darin inwendig und, vielleicht namenlos, aber wirklich, das erfahren, was mit 'Gott' eigentlich gemeint ist. (...) Der Akt radikaler Liebe des Nächsten (ist) schon ein Akt der Liebe zu Gott ... und in diesem Akt (mindestens unthematisch) angeht, was mit 'Gott' eigentlich gemeint ist.'

261. Idem, Foundations of Christian Faith, pp.456, 460.

262. Idem, 'Reflections on the Unity of the Love of Neighbour and the Love of God'. (Art. Cit.), p.236.

263. Idem, Ich glaube an Jesus Christus, Ss.20-21.

264. Idem, Art. Cit., p.244.

265. Ibid., pp.246f.

266. Idem, Op. Cit., pp.60-61.

267. Idem, 'I believe in Jesus Christ', (Art. Cit.), p.168.

269. Idem, 'Reflections on the Unity of the Love of Neighbour and the Love of God', (Art. Cit.), p.234.

270. Idem, Op. Cit., pp.26-28.

271. Idem, Art. Cit., p.235.

272. Hans Urs von Balthasar, Cordula oder der Ernstfall, Einsiedeln, 1966, SS.103-104: '... wer die Identität der Gottes- und Nächstenliebe proklamiert, und die Nächstenliebe als den primären Akt der Gottesliebe hinstellt, darf nicht erstaunt sein (und ist es wohl auch nicht), wenn es gleichgültig wird, ob der Mensch einen Gott bekennt oder keinen. Die Hauptsache ist, daß einer die Liebe hat. Zugegeben, wenn er weiß, was die Liebe ist. Aber nach welchem Maßstab mißt ein Mensch, der wesentlich ein Sünder ist, die Liebe? Doch wohl nach dem, was er, mit einer gewissen Anstrengung, etwa noch zu leisten imstande ist. Genügt dieser Maßstab und kann er (mit Gottesgnade) als caritas ausgelegt werden? (...) Gelänge es, das ganze Christentum auf einen Humanismus zu reduzieren ... man habe im Minimalpunkt durch Kompression das Maximale untergebracht (nämlich die Gottesliebe in der Nächstenliebe)...' Cfr. also: Rom 5:8., 1 Jn 3:16., 4:10. Cfr. also: Idem, Glaubhaft ist nur Liebe, Einsiedeln, 1963. A. Ganoczy, 'Wahrheitsfindung durch Liebe', in: E. Biser et alii, Das Prinzip der Liebe, Freiburg/Basel/Wien, 1975, SS.36-58.

273. W. Pannenberg, 'The Christological Foundation of Christian Anthropology', (Art. Cit.), p.92.

274. Hans Urs von Balthasar, Op. Cit., SS.95-96: 'Was ist eine karmelitanische Existenz? Angebot des gesamten eigenen Seins an den Gott Jesu Christi, damit er dieses Sein nach seinem liebenden Wohlgefallen für das Erlösungswerk verwende und verzehre. Man erkennt an ihr die wahre Identität der Nächstenliebe mit der Gottesliebe, aber nicht so, wie K. Rahner sie schildert: der 'religiöse Akt als solcher' ist gerade primär.' Balthasar continues: 'Die Überspringung des Kreuzes und seines ganzen Zusammenhangs verharmlost zudem die Sünde; eine Existenz für die Sühne der Weltschuld erscheint, was die Nächstenliebe angeht, recht wenig 'operativ'.'

275. K. Rahner, 'Reflections on the Unity of the Love of Neighbour and the Love of God', (Art. Cit.), p.244.

276. Ibid., p.234., and Cfr. also: W. Pannenberg, Art. Cit., p.91.

277. W. Pannenberg, Art. Cit., ibid. Cfr. also: Lv 19:18.34., Pss 15(14), 24(23). Is 1:16-17., 26:2-3., 33:15., Mi 6:6-8., Zech 8.16-17., Ez 18:7-9., Dt 6:45.,

278. Cfr. also: Lk 10:25-37., Pss 139:21-22., 125:5., 137:7., 15:4.

279. Cfr. also: ss:38-40., 25:31-46., Jn 13:34-35., 15:12., Rom 12:3ff., 12:8-10., 1 Cor 8:1., Gal 5:13., Phil 2:3., Eph 4:28., 1 Thes 2:9., 2 Thes 3:8., 1 Tm 1:5., 1 Jn 4:11., Jas 2:8., Acts 20:34-35.

281. For the above Cfr.: S. Lyonnet, 'The Newness of the Gospel', in: J. Pathrapamkal (Ed.), Op. Cit., pp.96-110.

292. W. Pannenberg, Art. Cit., p.91., Cfr. also: Idem, 'Theology and the Kingdom of God' (Art. Cit.), p.65.

283. Idem, 'Future and Unity', in: Ewert, H. Cousins (Ed.), Hope and the Future of Man, Fortress Press, 1972, p.65.

284. Idem, 'Wie kann heute glaubwürdig von Gott geredet werden?', in: Friedebert Lorenz (Hrg.), Gottesfrage heute, Stuttgart, 1969, S.64 (Translation taken from: Frank E. Tupper, Op. Cit., pp.301f.).

285. Ibid., S.63.

286. Idem, 'The Working of the Spirit in the Creation of the People of God', in: Pannenberg et alii, Spirit, Faith and Church, The Westminster Press, 1970, p.24.

287. Cfr. above Ch.VI.A.3.

288. W. Pannenberg, 'Wie kann heute glaubwürdig von Gott geredet werden?', (Art. Cit.), p.64.

A SELECT BIBLIOGRAPHY

1.	General Bibliographical Aids	761
2.	General Lexical Aids	761
3.	Principal Hindu Sources and Translations	762
4.	Related Works on Hinduism	764
5.	Principal Works in Indian Christological Thinking	771
6.	Related Readings in Indian Christian Theology	774
7.	Works by Karl Rahner	779
8.	Works on Karl Rahner	783
9.	Works by Wolfhart Pannenberg	785
10.	Works on Wolfhart Pannenberg	788
11.	General Literature for the Evaluative Part	790

1. General Bibliographical Aids

AIYER Ramaswami, A Bibliography of Indian Philosophy, 2 Parts, Madras, 1963/1968.

BAAGO Kaj, Library of Indian Christian Theology. A Bibliography, Madras,1969.

BLEISTEIN Roman/KLINGER Elmar (Hrg.), Bibliographie Karl Rahner 1924-1969, Freiburg/Basel/Wien, 1969.

BLEISTEIN Roman (Hrg.), Bibliographie Karl Rahner 1969-1974, Freiburg/Basel/Wien, 1974.

DANDEKAR, R.N., A Vedic Bibliography, 3 Vols. Bombay 1946, Poona 1961 & 1973.

2. General Lexical Aids

BAUER Johannes B., Bibeltheologisches Wörterbuch, 2 Bdd. Graz/Wien/Köln, 1967 (3.Aufl.).

BLOOMFIELD M., A Vedic Concordance, The Harvard Oriental Series, Vol.X, Cambridge/Massaschusetts, 1906.

COTTERELL Arthur, A Dictionary of World Mythology, London, 1979.

DOWSON J., A Classical Dictionary of Hindu Mythology and Religion, London, 1950.

GALLING Kurt et al. (Hrg.), Die Religion in Geschichte und Gegenwart. Handwörterbuch für Theologie und Religionswissenschaft, Bdd. 6, Tübingen, 1957-1962.

GRASSMANN H., Wörterbuch zum Rgveda, Wiesbaden, 1964, Leipzig, 1973.

HEIMANN Betty, The Significance of Prefixes in Sanskrit Philosophical Terminology, Royal Asiatic Society-Monographs, Vol. XXV, London, 1951.

HÖFER J./RAHNER K. (Hrg.), Lexikon für Theologie und Kirche, Bdd. 10, Freiburg i.Br., 1957-1965.

JACOB G.A., A Concordance of the Principal Upanishads and the Bhagavadgita, 1891.

KÖNIG Fr. (Hrg.), Religionswissenschaftliches Wörterbuch, Freiburg i.Br., 1956.

MAYRHOFER M., A Concise Etymological Sanskrit Dictionary, 2 vols., Heidelberg, 1953/1963.

MONIER-WILLIAMS Monier, A Sanskrit-English Dictionary, Oxford, 1964 (1890).

RAHNER Karl et al. (Hrg.), Sacramentum Mundi - Theologisches Lexikon für die Praxis, Bdd. 4, Freiburg/Basel/Wien, 1967-1969. (English translation in 6 Vols., London/New York, 1968-1970).

RAHNER Karl (Hrg.), Herders theologisches Taschenlexikon, 8 Bdd., Freiburg/Basel/Wien, 1972-1973.

STUTLEY Margaret and James, A Dictionary of Hinduism Its Mythology, Folklore and Development 1500 BC - 1500 AD, London/Bombay/Bangalore, 1977.

TURNER; R.L., A Comparative Dictionary of the Indo-Aryan Languages, London, 1966.

WOOD, E., Vedanta Dictionary, New York, 1964.

3. Principal Hindu Sources and Translations

AYYANGAR Narasimha, Vedanta Sara of Bhagavat Ramanuja with Original Text and Translation, Madras, 1953.

BOXBERGER, R. (Tr.)/GLASENAPP H. (Hrg.), Bhagavadgita - das Lied der Gottheit, Stuttgart, 1965.

BUITENEM J.A.B.van, Ramanuja's Vedartha Samgraha - Critical Edition with Original Sanskrit Text and English Translation, Poona, 1956.

DEUSSEN P., Sechzig Upanishads des Veda, Leipzig, 1897.

IDEM, Sixty Upanishads of the Veda, 2 Vols.(Tr.), Delhi, 1980.

DEUTSCH E./BUITENEN J.A.B.van, A Source Book of Advaita Vedanta, 1971.

EDGERTON F. (Tr.), The Bhagavad-gita, Harvard, 1944.

EGGELING Julius (Tr.), The Satapatha Brahmana, 5 vols. S.B.E. Vols: 12, 26, 41, 43, 44, Delhi, 1963 (Repr.).

GANGULI K.M. (Tr.), The Mahabharatha, 12 vols., Delhi, 1972, ff.

GELDNER K.F. (Tr.), Der Rig-Véda, 4 Bdd., Harvard, 1951.

GOVINDACHARYA A. (Tr.), Sri Bhagavad Gita with Sri Ramanujacharya's Visishtadvaita Commentary, 1898.

GRIFFITH R.T.H. (Tr.), Atharvaveda, Benares, 1897.

IDEM (Tr.), The Hymns of the Rgveda, 2 Vols., Varanasi,1963 (Repr.).

IDEM (Tr.), The Hymns of the Samaveda, Varanais, 1963 (Repr.).

GRIFFITH W., Hymns of Yayur Veda, Benares, 1961 (Repr.).

HILL W.D.P., The Bhagavadgita (Translation and Commentary), Oxford, 192 8, (Repr. 1953, 1967).

HUME Robert Ernest (Tr.), The Thirteen Principal Upanishads, Oxford, 1921 (Repr. 1949).

MAX MÜLLER F. (Ed.), Sacred Books of the East, 50 Vols., Oxford/Delhi, 1879 ff.

MITRA Rajendralala (Tr.), The Yoga Aphorisms of Patanjali, Calcutta, 1883.

MUIR John, Original Sanskrit Texts on the Origin and History of the People of India. Their Religion and Institutions, 5 Vols., 1858-1872 (Repr. 1967).

RADHAKRISHNAN, Sarvepalli (Tr.), The Principal Upanishads, London, 1953, (Repr. 1978).

IDEM The Bhagavadgita - With an Introductory Essay, Sanskrit Text, English Translation and Notes, London, 1958.

IDEM (Tr.), The Brahma Sutra, London, 1960.

RAGHAVACHAR S.S., Vedartha Samgraha of Sri Ramnuja. With Original Text and Translation, Mysore, 1956.

SAMPATKUMARAN M.R. (Tr.), The Gitabhasya of Ramanuja, Madras, 1969.

SARMA D.S. (Tr.), The Bhagavad-gita, Mylapore, 1936.

SASTRY A. Mahadev (Tr.), Sankara's Gitabhasya, Madras, 1961.

IDEM (Tr.), Bhagavad-gita with the Commentary of Sri Sankarachary, Madras, 1929, (Repr. 1961).

SHATRI, H.P. (Tr.), The Ramayana, 3 Vols., London, 1952-1959.

SUBBHARAO S. (Tr.), Vedanta Sutras with the Commentary of Sri Madhvacharya, 1936, (2nd ed.).

THIBAUT George (Tr.), Vedanta Sutras with the Commentary of Sankaracharya, S.B.E. Vols. 34 & 38, Oxford, 1890 & 1896.

IDEM (Tr.), Sri-bhasya. The Vedantra Sutras with the Commentary of Ramanuja, S.B.E. Vol. 48, Oxoford, 1904.

VARII AUCTORI (Tr.), Sacred Books of the Hindus, Vols. 1-31 and extra vols., Allahabad, 1909-1926 (Repr. in 46 Vols., 1974).

VARII AUCTORI (Tr.), Srimad Valmiki-Ramayana, 2 Vols. Grorakphur, 1974.

VEIRESWARANDA Swami (Tr.), Brahma-Sutras with the Commentary of Sankara, Almora, 1936.

VIDYALANKARA Isvaradatta (Tr.), Ramanuja's Commentary on the Bhagavadgita, Jaspur, 1930.

WARRIER A.G. Krishna (Tr.), The Sakta Upanishads, Adyar, 1967.

WILSON H.H. (Tr.), The Vishnu Purana, Calcutta, 1961 (Repr.).

ZAEHNER R.C. (Tr.), The Bhagavad-Gita. With a Commentary based on the Original Sources, Oxford, 1969 (Repr. 1973).

4. Related Works on Hinduism

ABEGG E., Der Messiasglaube in Indien und Iran, Berlin, 1928.

ACHARUPARAMBIL Daniel, Induismo, Vita e Pensiero, Roma, 1976.

IDEM, 'The 'Guru' in Hindu Tradition', in: Ephimerides Carmeliticae, (Teresianum), Roma, XXXI (1980), I, pp.3-28.

ANTES P., 'Das Neue im modernen Hinduismus', in: ZMR, 57 (1973), SS.99-116.

ARTHUR Paul (Ed.), The Philosophy of Sarvepalli Radhakrishnan, New York, 1952.

AUROBINDO Sri, Essays on the Gita, Pondicherry, 1980 (1959).

BANERJEE N.V., The Spirit of Indian Philosophy, New Delhi, 1973.

BASHAM A.L. (Ed.), A Cultural History of India, Oxford, 1975.

BATTACHARYA H. (Ed.), The Cultural Heritage of India, 4 Vols. Calcutta, 1961 ff. (Original edition by Ramakrishna Mission Calcutta, 1953-1956).

BLOOMFIELD M., Religion of the Veda, New York, 1908.

BROWN N., 'The Sources and Nature of Purusa in the Purusa-Sukta, RV 10.90', in: JAOS 51 (1931), pp.144ff.

CHARPENTIER J., Brahman - Eine sprachwissenschaftlich-exegetisch-religionsgeschichtliche Untersuchung, Uppsala, 1932.

CHATTERJEE, S.C./DATTA D.M., Introduction to Indian Philosophy, Calcutta, 1950.

CHATTOPADHYAYA/DATTA D.M., Indian Philosophy, Calcutta, 1962.

CHETHIMATTAM J.B., 'Psychology and Personality in the Indian Tradition', in: IES 7 (1967), pp.101-117.

IDEM Consciousness and Reality - An Indian Approach to Metaphysics, Bangalore, 1967.

IDEM, Patterns of Indian Thought - A Student's Introduction, London, 1971.

DAMODARAN K., Indian Thought - A Critical Survey, London, 1967.

DANDEKAR R.N., 'The Role of Man in Hinduism', in: Sarma D.S. (Ed.), Basic Reliefs of Hinduism, Calcutta, 1955, pp.115ff.

DANIÈLOU Alain, Yoga - The Method of Re-integration, London, 1949.

DAS Bhagavan, Krshna - A Study in the theory of Avataras, Madras, 1929.

DASGUPTA S.N., A Study of Patanjali, Calcutta, 1920.

IDEM, Yoga as Philosophy and Religion, London, 1924.

IDEM, Hindu Mysticism, Chicago, 1927.

IDEM, History of Indian Philosphy, 5 Vols., Cambridge, 1961 ff (1922 ff.).

DEUSSEN P., The System of the Vedanta, Cicago, 1912 (Tr. by Charles Johnson).

IDEM, Indische Philsophie, 3 Bdd., Leipzig, 1922.

IDEM, The Philosophy of the Upanishads, New York, 1966 (1906), (Tr. by Geden A.S.).

DEVANANDAN P.D., The Concept of Maya - An Essay in Historical Survey of the Hindu Theology of the World with reference to the Vedanta, Calcutta, 1954 (London, 1950).

DEVDAS Nalini, Sri Ramakrishna, Bangalore, 1965.

IDEM, Swami Vivekananda, Bangalore, 1968.

DHAVAMONY Mariasuasi, 'The Quest for Salvation in Hinduism', in: Secretariatus pro non-Christianis (Ed.), Religions-Fundamental Themes for a Dialogic Understanding, Rome, 1970, pp.175-203.

IDEM, 'Hindu Incarnations', in: Studia Missionalia 21 (1972), pp.127-169.

IDEM, Classical Hinduism, (Documenta Missionalia 15), Rome, 1982.

EDGERTON F., Beginning of Indian Philosophy, London, 1965.

ELIADE Mircea, Yoga, Immortality and Freedom, London, 1958.

IDEM, Myth and Reality, London, 1964.

IDEM, Patanjali and Yoga, New York, 1969.

FAIRSERVIS Walter A.Jr., The Harappan Civilization, New York, 1961.

FARQUHAR J.N., Modern Religious Movements in India, New Delhi,1977(1914).

FEUERSTEIN G., The Essence of Yoga - A Contribution to the Psychohistory to Indian Civilization, London, 1974.

IDEM, Introduction to the Bhagavad Gita - Its Philosophy and Cultural Setting, London, 1974.

FRANWALLNER E., Geschichte der indischen Philosophie, 2. Bdd. Salzburg, 1953-1956.

GISPERT-SAUCH G., Course on the Indian Religious Texts, Kurseong, 1968-1969.

GLASENAPP H. von, Der Hinduismus, München, 1922.

IDEM, Entwicklungsstufen des Indischen Denkens, Halle, 1940.

IDEM, Das Indienbild deutscher Denker, Stuttgart, 1960.

GONDA Jan, Noten on Brahman, Utrecht, 1950.

IDEM, Die Religionen Indiens, 2 Bdd., Stuttgart, 1960f.

IDEM, 'The Hindu Trinity', in: Anthropos 63 (1968), pp.212-226.

IDEM, 'The Concept of Personal God in Ancient Indian Religious Thought', in: Studia Missionalia 17 (1968), pp.121ff.

IDEM, Visnuism and Sivaism - A Comparison, London, 1970.

GUENON René, Man and His Becoming According to the Vedanta, London, 1928.

HACKER Paul, Untersuchungen über Texte des frühen Advaitavedanta, Mainz, 1950.

IDEM, 'Eigentümlichkeiten der Lehre und Terminologie Sankaras', in: ZDMG, 100 (1950), SS.246-286.

IDEM, Vivarta, Wiesbaden, 1953.

IDEM, 'Der Dharmabegriff des Neuhinduismus', in: ZMRW, 42 (1958), SS. 1-15.

IDEM, 'Zur Entwicklung der Avataralehre', in: WZKSO IV (1960), SS. 47-70.

IDEM,'Dharma in Hinduismus', in: ZMRW 49 (1965), SS. 93-106.
HALBFASS W., Indien und Europa, Basel, 1981.

HAUER Jacob Wilhelm, Die Anfänge der Yogapraxis, Stuttgart, 1922.

IDEM, Die Yoga - Ein indischer Weg zum Selbst, Stuttgart, 1958.

HEILER Friedrich, Die Mystik in den Upanishaden, München, 1925.

HEIMANN Betty, Studien zur Eigenart indischen Denkens, Tübingen, 1930.

HILLEBRANDT A., Vedische Mythologie, 2 Bdd., Breslau, 1927-1929.

HIRIYANNA M. (Ed. and Tr.), Vedanta-sara, Poona, 1929.

IDEM, Outlines of Indian Philosophy, London, 1951 (1932).

IDEM, Essentials of Indian Philosphy, London, 1951.

IDEM, The Quest after Perfection, Mysore, 1952.

ISHERWOOD Christopher, Vedanta for the Western World, London, 1949.

IYENGAR P.T.S., Outlines of Indian Philosphy, Benares, 1909.

JACOBI H., Entwicklung der Gottesidee bei den Indern und deren Beweise für das Dasein Gottes, Bonn/Leipzig, 1928.

JESUIT SCHOLARS, Religious Hinduism - A Presentation and Appraisal, (Ed. by Smet de R./Neuner J.), Allahabad, 1968.

JOAD C.E.M., Counter Attack from the East - The Philosophy of Radhakrishnan, London, 1933 (1927).

KEITH Arthur Berriedale, Samkhya System, London, 1918.

IDEM, The Religion and the Philosophy of the Vedas and the Upanishads, 2 Vols. (Harvard Oriental Series Vols. 31 & 32), Cambridge, 1925.

KLAES Norbert, 'Hindu Reformer und Reformbewegungen der Neuzeit', in: Studia Missionalia, 34 (1985), SS.141-179.

KLOSTERMAIER Klaus, Dr. S. Radhakrishnan und die Fundamentalreligion des Geistes, Rom, 1961.

KRIES F., 'Hegels Interpretation der indischen Geisteswelt', in: ZDK 7 (1941), SS.133-145.

KUPPUSWAMY B., 'A Modern Review of Hindu Dharma', in: Jdh Vol. I, July 1976.

LACOMBE Olivier, La doctrine morale et métaphysique de Ramanuja, Paris, 1938.

LAL B.K., Contemporary Indian Philosophy, Delhi,1978 (2nd ed.).

LUKE K. 'Some Aspects of the Rgvedic Conception of 'Vak,' in: Jeevadhara 1 (1971), pp.176-189.

MACDONNEL A.A., A History of Sanskrit Literature, 1970 (1889).

MAHADEVAN T.M.P., Gaudapada - A study in Early Vedanta, Madras, 1952.

IDEM, Outlines of Hinduism, Bombay, 1960.

MANALAPUZHAVILA Antony, Nature and Origin of the World According to Ramanuja (Pars dissertationis ad lauream), Alwaye, 1966.

MANICKAM T.M., 'Manu's Vision of the Hindu Dharma', in: JDh 1 (1975), pp.101-117.

MARSHALL John et al., Mohenjo-daro and the Indus Civilization, 3 Vols., London, 1931.

MASUI Jacques (Ed.), Yoga, science de l'homme intégral, Paris, 1953.

MATHOTHU Kurian, The Development of the Concept of Trimurthy in Hinduism, Rome, 1973.

MAX MÜLLER F., Lectures on the Origin and Growth of Religion as Illustrated by the Religions of India, London, 1878.

IDEM, The Six Systems of Indian Philosophy, Oxford/London, 1891 (Repr. 1961).

IDEM, Ramakrishna - His Life and Sayings, (Collection), London, 1900.

IDEM, Vedanta Philosophy (Three Lectures), Calcutta, 1950 (Repr.).

IDEM, Heritage of India, Calcutta, 1951 (Repr.).

MONIER-WILLIAMS Monier, Hinduism, Calcutta, 1877.

MURTHY, K.S., Revelation and Reason in the Advaita Vedanta, 1959.

NARAHARI H.G., Atman in Pre-Upanisadic Vedic Literature, Adyar, 1944.

NARAVANE V.S., Modern Indian Thought, Bombay, 1967 (2nd ed.).

NIKAM N.A., Some Concepts of Indian Culture - An Analytical Interpretation, Simla, 1973.

NIKHILANANDA Swami (Ed.), The Gospel of Ramakrishna, New York, 1942.

OBERHAMMER, G. (Hrg.), Offenbarung, Geistige Realität des Menschen - Arbeitsdokumentation eines Symposiums zum Offenbarungsbegriff in Indien, Wien, 1974.

O'FLAHERTY W.D., Asceticism and Erotism in the Mythology of Siva, London, 1973.

OLDENBERG H., Die Religion des Veda, Berlin, 1923.

OTTO Rudolf, The Original Gita (Tr.), London, 1939.

IDEM, Mysticism, East and West, New York, 1939.

PANDEY R.B., Hindu Samskaras - A Sociological Study of the Hindu Sacraments, Benares, 1949.

PANIKKAR Raimundo, 'The Myth of Incest as Symbol for Redemption in Vedic India', in: Zwi Werblowsky R.J:/Bleeker C.J. (Edd.), Types of Redemption, Leiden, 1970, pp.130-143.

IDEM, 'Some Aspects of Suffering and Sorrow in the Vedas', in: Jeevadhara, 2 (1972), pp.387-398.

IDEM, The vedic Experience, London, 1977.

PAPALI Cyril Bernhard, Hinduismus, 2 Vols., Roma, 1953, 1960.

IDEM, The Advaita Vedanta of Cnkaracarya, Roma, 1964.

PARRINDER G., 'Revelation in Other Scriptures', in: Studia Missionalia 20, Rome, 1971.

RADHAKRISHNAN Sarvepalli, The Vedanta According to Sankara and Ramanuja, London, 1923.

IDEM, Indian Philosophy, 2 Vols., London, 1923, 1927 (Repr. 1958).

IDEM, The Hindu View of Life, London, 1927 (Repr. 1980).

IDEM, Die Lebensanschauung des Hindu, (Tr. by Schomerus H.W.), Leipzig, 1928.

IDEM, The Idealist View of Life, London, 1932 (Repr. 1980).

IDEM/MUIRHEAD J.A. (Edd.), Contemporary Indian Philosophy, London, 1936.

IDEM, Eastern Religions and Western Thought, London, 1939.

IDEM (Ed.), History of Philosophy: Eastern and Western, 2 Vols., London, 1952, 1953.

IDEM/MOORE Charles A. (Edd.), A Source Book of Indian Philosophy, Princeton, 1957.

IDEM/RAJU P.T., The Concept of Man - A Study in Comparative Philosphy, London, 1966.

IDEM, Religion in a Changing World, London, 1967.

RAGOZIN, Vedic India, 1895.

RAJU P.T., Thought and Reality - Hegelianism and Advaita, London, 1937.

RELE V.G., The Mysterious Kundalini, Bombay, 1927.

RENOU L., 'On the Word 'Atman',' in: Vak 2 (1952), pp.151-157.

IDEM, Religions of Ancient India, New York, 1968.

IDEM, Der Hinduismus, Gütersloh, 1981.

ROY Raja Rammohan, English Works of Raja Rammohan Roy, (Collection), Allahabad, 1906.

RUBEN W., Geschichte der Indischen Philosophie, Berlin, 1954.

SAKSENA S.K., Nature of Consciousness in Hindu Philosophy, Benares, 1944.

SAMARTHA S.J., The Hindu View of History, Bangalore, 1959.

IDEM, Introduction to Radhakrishnan - The Man and His Thought, New Delhi, 1964.

SARMA D.S., What is Hinduism?, Madras, 1939.

IDEM, Studies in the Renaissance of Hinduism, Benares, 1944.

IDEM, The Basic Beliefs of Hinduism, Calcutta, 1955.

SATCHIDANANDA MURTHY K., Revelation and Reason in Advaita Vedanta, Waltair, 1959.

SCHAYER S., Contribution to the Problem of Time in Indian Philosophy, Cracow, 1938.

SCHILPP Paul Arthur (Ed.), The Philosophy of Sarvepalli Radhakrishnan, New York, 1952.

SCHREINER P., Begegnung mit dem Hinduismus, Freiburg, 1984.

SECRETARIATUS pro non Christianis (Ed.), For a Dialogue with Hinduism, Rome (1970).

SHASTRI Bhattacharya, Studies in Post-Sankara Dialectics, Calcutta, 1936.

SHASTRI Prabhu Datt, The Doctrine of Maya in the Philosophy of the Vedanta, Luzac, 1911.

IDEM, The Conception of Freedom in Hegel, Bergson and Indian Philosophy, Calcutta, 1914.

SINHA J., History of Indian Philosophy, 2 Vols., Calcutta, 1956.

SIRCAR M., Hindu Mysticism, New Delhi, 1974 (Repr.).

SMET R. de/NEUNER J. (Edd.), Religious Hinduism - A Presentation and Appraisal (by Jesuit Scholars), Allahabad, 1968.

SOMMERFELD S., Indienschau und Indiendeutung romantischer Philosophen, Zürich, 1943.

SRIVASTAVA R.S., Contemporary Indian Philosophy, Delhi, 1965.

STRAUSS O., Indische Philosophie, München, 1925.

TAGORE Rabidranath, The Religion of Man, London, 1953 (4th ed.).

IDEM, Towards Spiritual Man, New Delhi, 1961 (Repr.).

VEMPENY I., Inspiration in the Non-Biblical Scriptures, Bangalore, 1973.

VIVEKANANDA Swami, The Complete Works of Swami Vivekananda, 7 Vols., Almora, 1931ff., (7th ed. 1946-1947).

VIYAGAPPA Ignatius, G.W.F. Hegel's Concept of Indian Philosophy, Documenta Missionalia 14), Rome, 1980.

WARRIER A.G. Krishna, The Concept of Mukti in Advaita Vedanta, Madras, 1961.

IDEM, 'A New Angle on the Problem of Unreality in Advaita', in: Prabudha Bharata, LXIX, 1964.

WEBER Albrecht,'Vac und Logos', in: Indische Studien IX, Leipzig, 1865, SS.473-480.

WOLFF O., Indiens Beitrag zum neuen Menschenbild, Hamburg, 1957.

WOODS J.H., Yoga System of Patanjali, Harvard, 1914.

YOUNG R.F., Resistant Hinduism. Sanskrit Sources on Anti-Christian Apologetics in the Early Nineteenth Century India, Vienna, 1981.

ZACHARIAS Father, An Outline of Hinduism, Alwaye, 1956.

ZAEHNER R.C., Hinduism, London, 1962.

ZIMMER Heinrich, Maya - der indische Mythos, Stuttgart, 1936.

IDEM, Myths and Symbols in Indian Art and Civilization, (Ed. by J. Campbell), New York, 1946 (Repr. 1972).

IDEM, Philosophies of India,(Ed. by J. Campbell), New York, 1951.

5. Principal Works in Indian Christological Thinking

ABHEDANANDA Swami, Why a Hindu Accepts Christ and Rejects Christianity, Calcutta, 1965 (11th ed.).

AKHILANANDA Swami, Hindu View of Christ, Boston, 1971.

ANDREWS, C.F., 'The Hindu View of Christ', in: IRM, 28 (1939), pp.259-264.

APPASAMY A.J., Christianity as Bhakta Marga - A Study of the Johannine Doctrine of Love, Madras, 1928.

IDEM, The Johannine Doctrine of Life - A Study of Christian and Indian Thought, London, 1934.

BAAGO Kaj, 'Ram Mohan Roy's Christology - An Early Attempt at Demtyhologization', in: The Bangalore Theological Forum, 1967, pp.31ff.

BARLAGE Heinrich, Christ Saviour of Mankind - A Christian Appreciation, of Swami Akhilananda, St. Augustin bei Bonn, 1977.

BERGEN, L.F.M., 'Eine indische Christologie', in: H. Bedtscheider (Hrg.), Das asiatische Gesicht Christi, St. Augustin bei Bonn, 1976, pp.35-47.

CAMPS A., 'Person and Function of Christ in Hinduism and in Hindu-Christian Theology', in: Bulletin Secretariatus pro non-Christianis, 1971, pp.189-221.

CHAKKARAI Vengal, Jesus the Avatar, Madras, 1929.

IDEM, The Cross and the Indian Thought, Madras, 1932.

CHENCHIAH Pandipeddi, 'The Vedanta Philosophy and the Message of Christ', in: IJT, October 1955, p.18 etc.

CHETHIMATTAM J.B., 'Theology as Human Interiority: Search for one Teacher', in: Idem (Ed.), Unique and Universal - Fundamental Problems of an Indian Theology, Bangalore, 1972, pp.183-177.

IDEM, 'Indian Approaches to Christology - Contribution of the Syro-Malabar Church', in: IJT 23 (1974), pp.176-180.

IDEM, 'Raymond Panikkar's Approach to Christology', in: IJT 23 (1974), pp. 219-222.

DOCKHORN K., 'Christ in Hinduism as Seen in Recent Indian Theology', in: Religion and Society, XXI (1974), pp.39-57.

DUPUIS James, 'Knowing Christ through Christian Experience', in: IJT, 1969, pp.54-64.

FAKIRBHAI Dhanjibhai, Shri Khrist Gita, Delhi, 1969.

IDEM, Khristopanishad, Bangalore, 1965.

FARQUHAR J.N., The Crown of Hinduism, Oxford, 1915.

GANDHI M.K., The Message of Jesus Christ, Bombay, 1940.

IDEM, What Jesus means to Me, Ahmadbad, 1959.

GOREH Nehemiah, Proofs of the Divinity of Our Lord, Bombay, 1887.

GRIFFITHS B. (Ed.), Christ in India (Essays), New York, 1966.

JESUDASAN S., Unique Christ and Indigenous Christianity, Bangalore, 1966.

JOHANNS Pierre, Vers le Christ par la Vedanta (Cankara et Ramanuja), Louvain, 1932.

IDEM, To Christ through the Vedanta. A Synopsis, Part I (Samkara), Part II (Ramanuja), Part III (Vallabha) Part IV (Chaitanya), Ranchi, 1944.

KELLER Carl, 'The Vedanta Philosophy and the Message of Christ', in: IJ, March, 1955.

KLOSTERMAIER Klaus, Kristvidya - A Sketch of an Indian Christology, Bangalore, 1967.

KRÄMER, A., Christus und Christentum im Denken des modernen Hinduismus, Bonn, 1958.

KUMARAPPA J.C., The Practice and Precepts of Jesus, Ahmedabad, 1945.

LEDERLE Matthew J., 'Interpreting Christ through Indian Art', in: IJT 23 (1974), pp.232-241.

MANICKAM T.M., 'Anubhava as Pramana of an Indian Christology', in: Jeevadhara. I (1971), pp.228-244.

MATTAM J., 'Interpreting Christ to India Today: The Calcutta School', in: IJT 23 (1974), pp.191-205.

IDEM, 'Modern Catholic Attempts at Presenting Christ to India', in: IJT 23 (1974), pp.206-218.

MELZER Friso, Christus und die indischen Erlösungswege, Tübingen, 1949.

MOFFIT J., Journey to Gorakpur - An Encounter with Christ beyond Christianity, New York, 1972.

MOZOOMDAR Pratap Chunder, The Oriental Christ, Boston, 1881.

NEUNER Joseph, 'Das Christus-Mysterium und die indische Lehre von den Avataras', in: A. Grillmeier/H. Bacht (Hrg.), Das Konzil von Chalkedon - Geschichte und Gegenwart, Bd. III, Würzburg, 1954, SS.785-824.

IDEM, 'Avatara Doctrine and the Christ-Mysterium', in: Man and Religion, 1965, pp.27-33.

PANIKKAR Raimundo, 'Confrontation between Hinduism and Christ', in: New Blackfriars 50 (January 1969), pp.197-204.

IDEM, 'The Meaning of Christ's Name in the Universal Economy of Salvation', In: M. Dhavamony (Ed.), Evangelization, Dialogue and Development, (Selected Papers of the International Theological Conference, Nagpur, India, 1971 - Documenta Missionalia 5), Rome, 1972, pp.195-218.

IDEM, Salvation in Christ: Concreteness and Universality, the Supername, Santa Barbara, 1972.

IDEM, The Unknown Christ of Hinduism - Towards an Ecumenical Christophany (New Edition, Revised and Enlarged!), London, 1981 (Original Edition: London, 1964).

PAREKH Manik Lal, A Hindu's Portrait of Jesus Christ, Rajkot, 1953.

PARRINDER, E.G., Avatar and Incarnation, London, 1970.

PRABHAVANANDA Swami, The Sermon on the Mount according to Vedanta, California, 1972.

PRAJNANANDA Swami, Christ, the Saviour, Calcutta, 1961.

RANGANATHANANDA Swami, The Christ We Adore, Calcutta, 1955.

RAYAN Samuel, 'An Indian Christology - A Discussion of Method', in: Jeevadhara 1 (1971), pp.212-227.

IDEM, 'Interpreting Christ to India: The Contribution of Roman Catholic Seminaries', in: IJT 23 (1974), pp.223-231.

ROY Rammohan, The Precepts of Jesus: The Guide of Peace and Happiness, Calcutta, 1820.

IDEM, An Appeal to the Christian Public in Defence of the 'Precepts of Jesus' by a Friend of Truth, Calcutta, 1820.

IDEM, Second Appeal, Calcutta, 1821.

IDEM, Final Appeal, Calcutta, 1824.

RUDRA S.K., The Christian Idea of Incarnation, London/Madras, 1911.

SAMARTHA S.J., The Hindu Response to the Unbound Christ, Madras, 1974.

SATPRAKASANANDA Swami, Hinduism and Christianity - Jesus Christ and His Teachings in the Light of the Vedanta, St. Louis, 1975.

SEN Keshub Chunder, Keshub Chunder Sen's Lectures in India, (Collection), 2 Vols., London, 1901, 1904.

IDEM, The New Dispensation, 2 Vols., Calcutta, 1915, 1916.

SINGH Surjit, Preface to Personality - Christology in Relation to Radhakrishnan's Philosophy, Madras, 1952.

SIVANANDA Swami, Life and Teachings of Jesus Christ, Rishikesh, 1959

SMET R. de, 'Materials for an Indian Christology',in: Religion and Society 12 (1965) 4, pp.7-13.

THOMAS M.M., The Acknowledged Christ of the Indian Renaissance, London, 1969.

IDEM, The Secular Ideologies of India and the Secular Meaning of Christ, Bangalore, 1976.

UPADHYAYA Brahmabandab, 'The Incarnate Logos', in: The Twentieth Century, Vol. I, No. 1 (January 1901), pp.6 etc.

IDEM, 'Christ's Claim to Attention', in: The Twentieth Century, Vol. I, No. 1 (January 1901), pp.116ff.

WARREN M.A.C., 'The Universal Christ - The Missionary Problem with Interpretation', in: Religion and Society 17 (1970), pp.75etc.

WOLFF Otto, Christus unter den Hindus, Gütersloh, 1965.

6. Related Readings in Indian Christian Theology

ABHISHIKTANANDA (Dom le Saux), Sagesse hindoue - mystique chrétienne. Du vedanta à la trinité, Paris, 1965.

IDEM, 'Christians Mediate on the Upanisads', in: Logos 6 (1965), pp.1-16.

IDEM, Hindu Christian Meeting Point within the Cave of the Heart, Bombay, 1969.

IDEM, 'The Upanisads and the Advaitic Experience', in: Clergy Monthly, 38 (1974), pp.474-487.

IDEM, Saccidananda: A Christian Approach to Advaitic Experience, Delhi, 1974.

ALEAZ K.P., 'The Theological Writings of Brahmabandav Upadhyaya Re-Examined, in: IJT 28 (1978), pp.55-77.

AMALORPAVADASS D.S., Destinée de l'Eglise dans l'Inde d'aujourd'hui. Conditionnements de l'evangélisation, Fayarel-Mame, 1967.

IDEM, Theology of Evangelization in the Indian Context, (Inaugural Address at the Nagpur Theological Conference), Bangalore, 1973.

IDEM, The Theology of Indirect Evangelization, Bangalore, 1967.

IDEM (Ed.), Research Seminar on Non-Biblical Scriptures, Bangalore, 1974.

ANDREWS C.F., The Renaissance of India: Its Missionary Aspect, London, 1912.

ANIMANANDA B., The Blade: Life and Work of Brahmabandab Upadhyaya Calcutta, no date (1947 ?).

APPASAMI Aiyadurai Jesudasan, What is Moksa: A Study in the Johannine Doctrine of Life, Madrdas, 1931.

IDEM, The Gospel and India's Heritage, London/Madras, 1942.

IDEM, The Cross is Heaven: The Life and Writings of Sadhu Sundar Sing, London, 1956.

IDEM, My Theological Quest, Bangalore, 1964.

BAAGO Baj, Pioneers of Indigenous Christianity, Madras, 1969.

BACHMANN P.R., Roberto Nobili 1577-1656. Ein missionsgeschichtlicher Beitrag zum christlichen Dialog mit dem Hinduismus, Rom, 1972.

BOYD Robin, An Introduction to Indian Christian Theology, Madras, 1969.

IDEM, Khristavaita - A Theology for India, Madras, 1977.

BÜRKLE Horst, Dialog mit dem Osten. Radhakrishnans neuhindustische Botschaft im Licht christlicher Weltanschauung, Stuttgart, 1965.

IDEM/ROTH W.M.W. (Hrg.), Indische Beiträge zur Theologie der Gegenwart, Stuttgart, 1966.

CHENCHIAH Pandipeddi/CHAKKARAI Vengal, Rethinking Christianity in India, 1939.

CHERUKARAKKUNNEL A., 'Indianization among the St. Thomas Christians in Kerala', in: Jeevadhara 1 (1971), pp.361-373.

CHETHIMATTAM J.B., 'The Spirit and Orientation of an Indian Theology', in: Jeevadhara 1 (1971), pp.452-462.

IDEM (Ed.), Unique and Universal - Fundamental Problems of an Indian Theology, Bangalore, 1972.

CUTTAT J.A., Expérience chrétienne et spiritualité orientale, Paris, 1967.

DAHMEN P., Robert de Nobili. Ein Beitrag zur Geschichte der Missionsmethode und der Indologie, Münster(Wfl.) 1924.

DÊCHANET J.M., Christian Yoga, London, 1960 (1971).

DEVANANDAN P.D., Christian Concern in Hinduism, Bangalore, 1961.

IDEM, Preparation for Dialogue (Ed. by Nalini Devanandan and M.M. Thomas), Bangalore, 1964.

DHAVAMONY M., 'Christian Approaches to Hinduism - Points of Contact and Difficulties', in: Gregorianum 53 (1972), pp.89-114.

FAKIRBHAI Dhanjibhai, The Philosophy of Love, Delhi, 1966.

FARQUHAR J.N., Gita and Gospel, 1904.

GANDHI M.K., Christian Mission, Ahmedbad, 1940.

GARBE Richard, Indien und Christentum, Tübingen, 1914.

GEORGE S.K., Gandhi's Challenge to Christianity, Ahmedbad, 1960.

GOREH Nehemiah, A Letter to the Brahmos from a Converted Brahman of Benares, Allahabad, 1868.

IDEM, Christianity not of Man but of God, Calcutta, 1888.

GRIFFITHS B., Christian Ashram - Essays towards a Hindu-Christian Dialogue, London, 1966.

IDEM, 'Indian Christian Contemplation', in: Clergy Montly 35 (1971), pp.277-281.

HEILER, F., Der christliche Glaube und indisches Geistesleben, München, 1926.

HOGG A.G., The Christian Message to the Hindu, London, 1947.

KLOSTERMAIER Klaus, Hindu and Christian in Vrindaban, London, 1969.

MANICKAM T.M., Dharma according to Manu and Moses, Bangalore, 1977.

MATTAM J., Catholic Approach to Hinduism - A Study of the Works of the European Orientalists: J. Johanns, O. Lacombe, J.A. Cuttat, J. Monchanin, R.C. Zaehner, Rome, 1972.

IDEM, Land of the Trinity - A Study of the Modern Christian Approaches to Hinduism, Bangalore, 1975.

MELZER F., Indische Weisheit und christliche Erkenntnis, Tübingen, 1948.

MOFFIT J., 'Christianity Confronts Hinduism', in: Theological Studies, 39 (1969), pp.207-224.

MOOKENTHOTTAM Antony, Indian Theological Tendencies, Berne, 1978.

IDEM, Towards a Theology in the Indian Context, Bangalore, 1980.

MOOZOMDAR P.C., The Life and Teachings of Keshub Chunder Sen, Calcutta, 1887.

NAMBIAPARAMPIL A., 'Dialogue in India - An Analysis of the Situation, reflection experience', in: JDh 1 (1976), pp.267-283.

NOBILI Roberto de, Gnanopadesam Kurippidam (Tamil), Tuticorin, 1955.

OHM Th., Das Christentum im neuen Indien, St. Ottilien, 1948.

OHM Th., Asiens Nein und Ja zum westlichen Christentum, München, 1956.

OTTO Rudolf, Christianity and the Indian Religion of Grace, Madras, 1929.

PANIKKAR Raimundo, Die Vielen Götter und der eine Herr-Beiträge zum ökumenischen Gespräch der Weltreligionen, Weilheim Obb., 1963.

IDEM, Kultmysterium in Hinduismus und Christentum - Ein Beitrag zur vergleichenden Religionstheologie, München, 1964.

IDEM, Kerygma und Indien - Zur heilsgeschichtlichen Problematik der christlichen Begegnung mit Indien, Hamburg, 1967.

IDEM, The Trinity and World Religions, Madras, 1970.

IDEM, The Intra-Religious Dialogue, New York, 1978.

IDEM, 'Rtatattva: A Preface to a Hindu-Christian Theology', in: Jeevadhara 49 (1979), pp.6-63.

PARANANDA Sri, An Eastern Exposition of St. John, London, 1902.

PAREKH Manilal C., Brahmarshi Keshub Chunder Sen, Calcutta, 1887.

IDEM, Rajarshi Ram Mohan Roy, Rajkot, 1927.

PARRINDER E.G., Upanishads, Gita and Bible, 1962.

IDEM, The Significance of Bhagavad-Gita for Christian Theology, London, 1968.

PATHRAPANKAL Joseph (Ed.), Service and Salvation (Nagapur Theological Conference on Evangelization), Bangalore, 1973.

PERIGALLOOR J., Salvation through Gita and Gospel, Bombay, 1972.

778

RAO Mark Sundar, Ananyatva: Realization of Christian Non-Duality, Bangalore, 1964.

SCHOMERUS H.W., Die indische theologische Spekulation und die Trinitäts-lehre, Berlin, 1919.

IDEM, Indische Erlösungslehren - Ihre Bedeutung für das Verständnis des Christentums für die Missionspredigt, Leipzig, 1919.

IDEM, Indien und das Christentum, 3 Bdd. Halle/Saale 1931-1933.

IDEM, Indische und christliche Enderwartung und Erlösungshoffnung, Gütersloh, 1941.

SHARPE E.J., Not to Destroy but to Fulfil - The Contribution J.N. Farquhar to Protestant Missionary Thought in India before 1914, Calcutta, 1965.

SINGH Sadhu Sundar, Visions of the Spiritual World, London, 1926.

IDEM, The Spiritual Life, Madras, 1970.

IDEM, The Search after Reality, Madras, 1971.

SMET R. de, 'Categories of Indian Philosophy and Communication of the Gospel', in: Religion and Society, Sept. 1963.

IDEM, 'Die Theologie in Indien', in: H. Vorgrimler et al. (Hrg.), Bilanz der Theologie im 20. Jahrhundert, Freiburg, 1967, SS.419-442.

IDEM, 'Recent Developments in the Christian Approach to the Hindu', in: Lumen Vitae, 12 (1974), pp.515-520.

SUDBRACK J., 'Faszination aus dem Osten', in: Geist und Leben, 44 (1971), SS. 424-439.

THANGASAMY D.A., The Theology of Chenchiah with Selections from His Writings, Bangalore, 1966.

THOMAS, M.M., The Christian Response to the Asian Revolution, London, 1966.

IDEM, Salvation and Humanization. Some Critical Issues of the Theology of Mission in Contemporary India, Bangalore, 1971.

IDEM, The Realization of the Cross, Madras, 1972.

THOMAS P.T., The Theology of Chakkarai with Selections from His Writings, Bangalore, 1968.

UPADHYAYA B., 'Hinduism and Christianity as Compared by Mrs. Basant', in: Sophia Vol. IV, No. 2 (Febr. 1897), pp.8 etc.

IDEM, 'An Exposition of the Catholic Belief as Compared with the Vedanta', in: Sophia, Vol. V, No. 1 (Jan. 1898), pp.11 etc.

IDEM, 'Our New Canticle', in: Sophia Vol. V, No. 10 (Oct. 1898), pp.146 etc.

IDEM, 'The True Doctrine of Maya', in: Sophia Vol. VI, No. 2 (Febr.-March 1899), pp.226ff.

VÄTH Alfons, Im Kampf mit der Zauberwelt des Hinduismus, Berlin/Bonn, 1928.

WAGNER H., Erstgestalten einer einheimischen Theologie in Südindien, München, 1963.

ZAEHNER R.C., At Sundry Times - An Essay in the Comparison of Religions.

7. Works By Karl Rahner

a. Schriften zur Theologie, 16 Bdd. u. Register-Band, Zürich/Einsiedeln/Köln, 1954-1984. (English translation: Theological Investigations, 13 Vols. London, 1961-1975, New York, 1972-1975.
(The following articles are worthy of special mention. The reference here is to the German edition).

'Probleme der Christologie von heute', I (1954), SS. 162-222.

'Über das Verhältnis von Nature und Gnade', Ibid., SS.323-345.

'Auferstehung des Fleiches', II (1955), SS.211-225.

'Würde und Freiheit des Menschen', Ibid., SS.339-373.

'Die ewige Bedeutung der Menschheit Jesu für unser Gottesverhältniś', III (1956), SS.47-60.

'Der Christ und seine ungläubigen Verwandten',Ibid., SS.419-439.

'Über den Begriff des Geheimnisses in der katholischen Theologie', Ibid., SS. 51-102.

'Bemerkungen zum dogmatischen Traktat 'De Trinitate',' Ibid., SS.103-136.

'Zur Theologie der Menschwerdung', Ibid., SS.137-155.

'Virginitas in Partu', Ibid., SS.173-205.

'Natur und Gnade', Ibid., SS.209-236.

'Zur Theologie des Symbols', Ibid., SS.275-311.

'Theologische Prinzipien der Hermeneutik eschatologischer Aussagen', Ibid., SS.401-428.

'Weltgeschichte und Heilsgeschichte', Ibid., SS.115-135.

'Das Christentum und die nichtchristlichen Religionen', Ibid., SS.136-158.

'Die Christologie innerhalb einer evolutiven Weltanschauung', Ibid., Ss.183-.221.

'Dogmatische Erwägungen über das Wissen und Selbstbewußtsein Christi' Ibid., SS.222-245.

'Einheit von Geist und Materie im christlichen Glaubensverständnis', Ibid., SS.185-214.

'Über die Einheit von Nächsten- und Gottesliebe', Ibid., SS.277-298.

'Die anonymen Christen', Ibid., SS.545-554.

'Abgestiegen ins Totenreich', VII (1966), SS.145-149.

'Begegnungen mit dem Auferstandenen', Ibid., SS.166-173.

'Theologie und Anthropologie', VIII (1967), SS.43-65.

'Atheismus und implizites Christentum', Ibid., SS.187-212.

'Ich glaube an Jesus Christus', Ibid., SS.213-217.

'Der eine Mittler und die Vielfalt der Vermittlungen', Ibid., SS.218-238.

'Gotteserfahrung heute', Ibid., SS.161-176.

'Kirchliche Christologie zwischen Exegese und Dogmatik', Ibid., SS.197-226.

'Christologie im Rahmen des modernen Welt- und Menschenverständnis', Ibid., SS.227-241.

'Die Sünde Adams', Ibid., SS.259-275.

'Anonymes Christentum und Missionsauftrag der Kirche', Ibid., SS.498-515.

'Selbsterfahrung und Gotteserfahrung', Ibid., SS.133-144.

'Menschliche Aspekte der Geburt des Herrn', Ibid., SS.203-208.

'Auf der Suche nach Zugängen zum Verständnis des gottmenschlichen Geheimnisses Jesu ', Ibid., SS.209-215.

'Die zwei Grundtypen der Christologie', Ibid., SS.227-241.

'Bemerkungen zum Problem des 'anonymen Christen', Ibid., SS.531-546.

'Erfahrung des Geistes und existentielle Entscheidung', XII (1975), SS.41-53.

'Die enthusiastische und die gnadenhafte Erfahrung', Ibid., SS.54-76.

'Anonymer und expliziter Glaube', Ibid., SS.76-84.

'Glaube zwischen Rationalität und Emotionalität', Ibid., SS.85-107.

'Der eine Jesus Christus und die Universalität des Heils', Ibid., SS.251-282.

'Über die Verborgenheit Gottes', Ibid., SS.285-305.

'Fragen zur Unbegreiflichkeit Gottes nach Thomas von Aquin', Ibid., SS.306-319.

'Um das Geheimnis der Dreifaltigkeit', Ibid., SS.320-325.

'Jesu Auferstehung', Ibid., SS.344-352.

'Christologie heute?', Ibid., SS.353-369.

'Jesus Christus in den nichtchristlichen Religionen', Ibid., SS.370-383.

'Die theologische Dimension der Frage nach dem Menschen', Ibid., SS.387-406.

'Der Leib in der Heilsordnung', Ibid., SS.407-427.

'Mystische Erfahrung und mystische Theologie', Ibid., SS.428-438.

'Über den Zwischenzustand', Ibid., SS.455-466.

'Die menschliche Sinnfrage vor dem absoluten Geheimnis Gottes', XIII (1978), SS.111-128.

'Tod Jesu und die Abgeschlossenheit der Offenbarung', Ibid., SS.159-171.

'Was heißt heute an Jesus Christus glauben?', Ibid., SS.172-188.

'Transzendenzerfahrung aus katholisch-dogmatischer Sicht', Ibid., SS.207-225.

'Erfahrung des Heiligen Geistes', Ibid., SS.226-251.

'Über die Heilsbedeutung der nichtchristlichen Religionen', Ibid., SS.341-350.

'Zum Verhältnis von Naturwissenschaft und Theologie', XIV (1980), SS.63-72.

'Kleine theologische Bemerkung zu dem 'Status Naturae Lapsae',' Ibid., SS. 91-109.

'Ewigkeit aus Zeit', Ibid., SS.422-432.

782

b. **Other Works by Karl Rahner** (For his articles in lexica Cfr. the above mentioned lexical aids especially 'Lexikon für Theologie und Kirche', 'Sacramentum Mundi', 'Herders theologisches Taschenlexikon'.)

Geist in Welt. Zur Metaphysik der endlichen Erkenntnis bei Thomas von Aquin, Innsbruck, 1939. Überarbeitet und ergänzt von Johannes Baptist Metz. 2. Auflage, München 1957. (English Translation: Spirit in the World, London, 1979 (1968)).

Hörer des Wortes. Zur Grundlegung einer Religionsphilosophie, München, 1940 (Überarbeitet und ergänzt von Johannes Baptist Metz, 2. Auflage, München, 1963). (English translation: Hearers of the Word, London/Sydney, 1969.

'Über das Verhältnis des Naturgesetzes zur übernatürlichen Gnadenordung', in: Orientierung, 20 (1956), SS.8-11.

'Natur und Gnade nach der Lehre der katholischen Kirche', in: Una Sancta 14 (1959), SS.74-81.

'Erlösungswirklichkeit in der Schöpfungswirklichkeit', in: Catholica 13 (1959), SS.100-127.

On the Theology of Death, New York, 1961.

'Die Forderung nach einer 'Kurzformel' des christlichen Glaubens', in: Concilium, 3 (1967), SS.202-207.

'Der dreifaltige Gott als transzendenter Urgrund der Heilsgeschichte', in: J. Feiner/M. Löhrer (Hrg.), Mysterium Salutis. Grundriß heilsgeschichtlicher Dogmatik, Bd. II, Einsiedeln/Zürich/Köln, 1967, SS.317-401.

'Allgemeine Grundlegung der Protologie und theologischen Anthropologie', in: Ibid., SS.405-420.

Ich glaube an Jesus Christus, (Theologische Meditationen 21, Hrg. Hans Küng), Einsiedeln, 1968.

Grace in Freedom, New York, 1969.

'The Concept of Existential Philosophy in Heidegger', in: Philosophy Today, 13 (1969), pp.126-137. (Translated by Andrew Tallon).

'Grundlinien einer systematischen Christologie', in: Quaestiones Disputatae, 55 (1972), Lehrsatz 10, 20f.

Christologie - systemtatisch und exegetisch, Freiburg i.BR., 1972 (Mit Wilhelm Thüsing - English Translation: A New Christology, London, 1980.)

'Gnade als Mitte der menschlichen Existenz', in: Herderkorrpspondenz, 28 (1974), SS.77-92. (Interview zum 70. Geburtstag).

Grundkurs des Glaubens - Einführung in den Begriff des Christentums, Freiburg i.Br., 1976. (English Translation: Foundations of Christian Faith - An Introduction to the Idea of Christianity, New York, 1978).

8. Works on Karl Rahner

BALTHASAR Hans Urs von, 'Zur Soteriologie Karl Rahners', in: Idem, Theodra-matik III. Die Handlung, Einsiedeln, 1980, SS.253-262.

IDEM, 'Rezension von 'Geist in Welt',' in: ZkTh, 63 (1939), SS.371-379.

BECHTLE Regina, 'Karl Rahner's Supernatural Existential', in: Thought 4 (1973), pp.61-77.

BRANICK Vincent P., An Ontology of Understanding: Karl Rahners' Meta-physics of Knowledge in the Context of Modern German Hermeneutics, St. Louis, 1974.

BROWARZIK U., Glauben und Denken: Dogmatische Forschung zwischen der Transzendentaltheologie Karl Rahners und der Offenbarungstheologie Karl Barths, Berlin, 1970.

DONCEL Joseph, The Philosophy of Karl Rahner, Albany, 1969.

EBERHARD Kenneth D., 'Karl Rahner and the Supernatural Existential', in: Thought 46 (1971), pp.537-561.

EICHER P., Die anthropologische Wende. Karl Rahners philosophischer Weg vom Wesen des Menschen zur personalen Existenz, Freiburg i.Br., 1970.

FABRO C., La svolta antropologica di Karl Rahner, Torino, 1974.

FARELLY John, 'Man's Transcendence and the Thomistic Resources', in:Thomist, 38 (1974), pp.453 etc.

FISCHER K.P., Der Mensch als Geheimnis. Die Anthropologie Karl Rahners, Freiburg i.Br., 1974.

GEISSER H., 'Die Interpretation der kirchlichen Lehre vom Gottmenschen bei K. Rahner', in: KuD 14 (1968),SS.307-330.

GELPI D.L., Life and Light - A Guide to the Theology of Karl Rahner, New York, 1966.

GREINER Friedemann, Die Menschlichkeit der Offenbarung. Die transzendentale Grundlegung der Theologie bei Karl Rahner, München, 1978.

GRÜN A., Erlösung durch das Kreuz. K. Rahners Beitrag zu einem heutigen Erlösungsverständnis, Münsterschwarzach, 1975.

HEIJDEN Bert van der, Karl Rahner - Darstellung und Kritik seiner Grundposi-tionen, Einsiedeln, 1973.

KASPER Walter, 'Die anthropologisch gewendete Christologie', in: Idem, Jesus der Christus, Mainz, 1977, SS.50-60.

IDEM, 'Karl Rahner - Theologie in einer Zeit des Umbruchs', in: Th Q 159 (1979), SS.263-271.

KLINGER El mar/WITTSTADT Klaus (Hrg.), Glaube im Prozeß. Christsein nach dem II. Vatikanum, Freiburg/Basel/Wien, 1984.

KRUSE H., 'Die 'anonymen Christen' exegetisch gesehen', in: MThK 18 (1967) SS.2-29.

LAKEBRINK B., Klassische Metaphysik. Eine Auseinadersetzung mit der existentialen Anthropozentrik, Freiburg i.Br., 1967.

LEHMANN K., 'Karl Rahner', in: Bilanz der Theologie im 20. Jahrhundert, IV, Freiburg/Basel/Wien, 1970, SS.143-181.

IDEM/RAFFELT A. (Hrg.), Rechenschaft des Glaubens - Karl Rahner Lesebuch, Freiburg i.Br./Einsiedeln, 1979.

MASSON, 'Rahner and Heidegger: Being, Hearing and God', in: The Thomist XXXVII (1973), pp.455-488.

McCOOL Gerald A., (Ed.), A Rahner Reader, London, 1975.

METZ J.B. et al. (Hrg.), Gott in Welt - Festgabe für K. Rahner, Freiburg/Basel/ Wien, 1964.

IDEM, 'Karl Rahner ein theologisches Leben. Theologie als mystische Biographie eines Christenmenschen heute', in: Stimmen der Zeit, 192 (1974), SS.305-316.

MITTERSTIELER E., Christlicher Glaube als Bestätigung des Menschen. Zur 'fides quaerens intellectum' in der Theologie Karl Rahners, Frankfurt, 1975.

MOTHERWAY Thomas J., 'Supernatural Existential', in: Chicago Studies, 4 (1965), pp.79-103.

PEARL Thomas, 'Dialectical Pantheism - On the Hegelian Character of Rahner's Key Christological Writings', in: IThQ XLII (1975), pp.119-137.

PUNTEL L.B., 'Zum Denken Karl Rahners', in: ZkTh 86 (1964), SS.304-320.

RATZINGER J., 'Rahners Grundkurs des Glaubens', in: Theologische Revue, 74 (1978), SS.186 etc.

RIESENHUBER K., 'Der anonyme Christ nach K. Rahner', in: ZKT LXXXVI (1964), SS.286-303.

RÖPER Anita, Die anonymen Christen, Main, 1963.

SANNA Ignazio, La cristologia antropologica di P. Karl Rahner, Roma, 1970.

SIMONS E., Philosophie der Offenbarung - Auseinandersetzung mit Karl Rahner, Stuttgart, 1966.

SPECK J., Karl Rahners theologische Anthropologie, München, 1967.

SPORSCHILL George (Hrg.), Karl Rahner - Bekenntnisse. Rückblick auf 80 Jahre, Wien/München, 1984.

STOHRER W.J., The role of Heidegger's Doctrine of Dasein in Karl Rahner's Metaphysics of Man, Washington, 1967.

TALLON Andrew, Spirit, Matter, Becoming - An Analytical Study of K. Rahner's Spirit in the World',' in: Modern Schoolman, 48 (1971), pp.151-165.

IDEM, 'Spirit, Freedom, History - An Analytical Study of Karl Rahner's 'Hearers of the Word',' in: Thomist 38 (1974), pp.908-936.

VORGRIMLER H., Karl Rahner: Leben - Denken - Werke, München, 1963.

WALDENFELS H., 'Die neue Diskussion um die 'anonymen Christen' als Beitrag zur Religionstheologie', in: ZMRW 60 (1976), SS.161-180.

WEGER Karl-Heinz, Karl Rahner. Eine Einführung in sein theologisches Denken, Freiburg/Basel/Wien, 1978 (Translated by David Smith: Karl Rahner - An Introduction to His Theology, London, 1980).

WILSON Barrie, 'The Possibility of Theology after Kant. An Examination of Karl Rahner's 'Geist in Welt',' in: Canadian Journal of Theology, Oct.12 (1966), pp.251 etc.

9. Works by Wolfhart Pannenberg

'Mythus und Wort - Theologische Überlegungen zur Karl Jaspers Mythusbegriff', in: ZThK LI (1954), SS.167-185.

'Neue Wege katholischer Christologie', in: ThLZ, LXXXII (1957), Ss.95-100.

'Dialektische Theologie', in: RGG II, Tübingen, 1958, SS.168-174.

'Wie wird Gott uns offenbar', in: Radius IV (1960), SS. 3-10.

'Jesu Geschichte und unsere Geschichte', in: Radius I (1960), SS.18-27.

(Hrg.), Offenbarung als Geschichte, Göttingen, 1961. English translation by David Granskon/Edward Quinn, Revelation as History, London/Sydney, 1969.

'Wirkungen biblischer Gotteserkenntnis auf das abendländische Menschenbild', in: Studia Generale XV (1962), SS.586-593.

Was ist der Mensch? Die Anthropologie der Gegenwart imLichte der Theologie, Göttingen, 1962 (6. Auflage 1981). English translation by Duane A. Priebe, What is Man? Contemporary Anthropology in Theological Perspective, Philadelphia, 1970.

'Einsicht und Glaube - Antwort an Paul Althaus', in: ThLZ 88 (1963), SS.81-92.

Grundzüge der Christologie, Gütersloh, 1964, English translation by Lewis L. Wilkens/Duane A. Priebe, Jesus - God and Man, London, 1980 (1968).

'Erscheinung als Ankunft des Zukünftigen', in: Studia Philosophica, XXVI (1966), SS.192-207.

'The Revelation of God in Jesus of Nazareth', in: Theology as History (Ed. by James M. Robinson and John B. Cobb Jr.), New Frontiers in Theology, Vol. III, Harpter & Row Inc., 1967, pp.101-133.

'Response to the Discussion', in: James M. Robinson/John B. cobb Jr. (Edd.), New Frontiers of Theology, Vol.III, pp.221-276.

Grundfragen systematischer Theologie (Gesammelte Aufsätze), 2 Bdd., Göttingen, Bd. 1: 1969/1971/1979., Bd. 2: 1980. English translation of the Ist. Volume by G.H. Kehm, Basic Questions in Theology, 2 Vols., London, 1970 & 1971.

'Dogmatische Erwägungen zur Auferstehung Jesu', in: KuD 14 (1968), SS.105-118.

Was ist das - der Mensch? Beitrag zu einer modernen Anthropologie, München, 1968.

'Wie kann heute glaubwürdig von Gott geredet werden', in: Lorenz Friedeberg (Hrg), Gottesfrage heute, Stuttgart, 1969.

'Unser Leben, unsere Geschichte - in Gottes Hand?', in: Gerhard Rein (Hrg.), Dialog mit dem Zweifel, Stuttgart, 1969, SS.78-83.

Theology and the Kingdom of God, Philadelphia, 1969. German edition: Theologie und Reich Gottes, Gütersloh, 1971.

'Kontingenz und Naturgesetz', in: A.M. Müller/w. Pannenberg (Hrsg.), Erwägungen zu einer Theologie der Natur, Gütersloh, 1970, SS.33-80.

'The Church and the Eschatological Kingdom', in:Idem et al., Spirit, Faith and Church, The Westminster Press, 1970, SS.108-123.

'Weltgeschichte und Heilsgeschichte', in: Hans Walter Wolff (Hrg.), Probleme biblischer Theologie - Festschrift für Gerhard von Rad, München, 1971, SS.349-366.

'Wie wahr ist das Reden von Gott?', in: Evangelische Kommentare, IV (1971), SS.629-633.

'Erfahrung der Wirklichkeit. Fragen an Karl Friedrich von Weizsäcker', in: Evangelische Kommentare IV (1971), Ss.468-470.

Die Bedeutung des Christentums in der Philosophie Hegels, Kyoto, 1971.

The Apostles' Creed - In the Light of Today's Question, (Tr. by Margaret Kohl), London, 1972.

Christentum und Mythos. Späthorizonte des Mythos in biblischer und christlicher Überlieferung, Gütersloh, 1972.

Gottesgedanke und menschliche Freiheit, Göttingen, 1972.

'Die Geschichtlichkeit der Wahrheit und die ökumenische Diskussion', in: Begegnung. Festschrift für Heinrich Fries, Graz/Wien/Köln, 1972, SS.31-43.

'Warum nennen wir Jesus Gottes Sohn', in: Zur Debatte. Themen der katholischen Akademie in Bayern, 2.Jg., 11/12, München, 1972.

'The Doctrine of the Spirit and the Task of a Theology of Nature', in: Theology 75 (1972), pp.8-11.

Das christologische Fundament christlicher Anthropologe', in: Concilium 9 (1973), 427 etc. For the English translation see the English edition of Concillium June (1973), pp.86-100.

'History and Meaning in Lonergan's Approach to Theological Method', in: ITgQ 40 (1973), pp.103-114.

'Eschatologie und Sinnerfahrung', in: KuD, 19 (1973), Ss.39-52.

'Tod und Auferstehung in der Sicht christlicher Dogmatik', in: KuD 20 (1974), SS.167-180.

'Christologie und Theologie', in: KuD 21 (1975), SS.159-175.

'Gottesebenbildlichkeit und Bildung des Menschen', in: Theologia Practica. 12 (1977), SS.259-273.

'Die Auferstehung Jesu und die Zukunft des Menschen', in: KuD, 24 (1978), SS.104-117.

Die Bestimmung des Menschen. Menschsein, Erwählung und Geschichte, Göttingen, 1978.

'Zur 'Aporie der Zweinaturenlehre' (Brief an Christoph von Schönborn)', in: FZPT 25 (1978), SS.100-103.

'Die Bedeutung der Kategorien 'Teil' und 'Ganzes' für die Wissenschaftstheorie der Theologie', in: Theologie und Philosophie, 53 (1978), SS.481-497.

'Vom Nature der Eschatologie für die christliche Theologie', in: KuD, 25 (1979), SS.88-105.

Anthropologie in theologischer Perspektive, Göttingen, 1983.

10. **Works on Wolfhart Pannenberg**

ALTHAUS Paul, 'Offenbarung als Geschichte und Glaube - Bemerkungen zu Wolfhart Pannenbergs Begriff der Offenbarung', in: ThLZ LXXXVII (1962), SS.321-330.

BEECHLER Donald J., The Centrality of Jesus' Resurrection in Wolfhart Pannenberg's Christology from below, Rome, 1973.

BERTEN Ignace, Geschichte - Offenbarung - Glaube: Eine Einführung in die Theologie Wolfhart Pannenbergs, München, 1970.

BETZ Hans Dieter, 'Das Verständnis der Apokalyptik der Theologie der Pannenberg Gruppe', in: ZThK 65 (1968), SS.257-270.

BLASQUEZ Pèrez, La resurreción en la cristologia de Wolfhart Pannenberg, Vittoria, 1976.

BRENA Gian Luigi, 'La teologia di Wolfhart Pannenberg', in: La Civiltà Cattolica 1975, III, pp.368-386.

IDEM, 'La cristologia di Wolfhart Pannenberg', in: Ibid., 1975, IV, pp.350-357.

IDEM, 'Epistomologia e teologia nel pensiero di W. Pannenberg', in: Ibid., 1976, I, pp.241-251.

DOBBIN Edmund J., Reflections on W. Pannenberg's Revelation Theology, Leuven, 1972.

DUFORT Jean-Marc, 'Wolfhart Pannenberg et la théologie d l'espérance', in: Science et Esprit, 22 (1970), pp.361-377.

FLÜCKIGER Felix, Theologie der Geschichte. Die biblische Rede von Gott und die neuere Geschichtstheologie, Wuppertal, 1970, SS.93-103.

GALLOWAY Allan D., Wolfhart Pannenberg (Contemporary Religious Thinkers Series edited by H.D. Lewis), London, 1973.

GEYER Hans-Georg, 'Geschichte als theologisches Problem. Bemerkungen zu W. Pannenbergs Geschichtstheologie', in: Evangelische Theologie, 2 (1962), SS.92-104.

GIAVINI Giovanni, 'La linea theologica di W. Pannenberg riesposizione e note', in: La Scuola Cattolica, 2 (1970), pp.147-152.

GIBELLINI Rosino, Teologia e Ragione. Itinerario e opera di Wolfhart Pannenberg, Brescia, 1980.

GOEBEL Hans Theodor, Wort Gottes als Auftrag. Zur Theologie von Rudolf Bultmann Gerhard Ebeling und Wolfhart Pannenberg, Neukirchen, 1972.

GÖPFERT M., Heilsgeschichte in der neueren Theologie: Offenbarung als Geschichte bei W. Pannenberg, St. Augustin bei Bonn, 1972.

789

HAMILTON William, 'Die Eigenart der Theologie Pannenbergs', in: James M. Robinson/John B. Cobb Jr., (Hrg.), Theologie als Geschichte (Neuland in der Theologie Bd. 3), Zürich/Stuttgart, 1967, SS.225-251.

KIENZLER Klaus, Logik der Auferstehung. Eine Untersuchung zu Rudolf Bultmann, Gerhard Ebeling und Wolfhart Pannenberg, Freiburg/Basel/Wien, 1976.

KLEIN Günter, Theologie des Wortes Gottes und die Hypothese der Universalgeschichte. Zur Auseinandersetzung mit Wolfhart Pannenberg, München, 1964.

McDERMOTT B.O., The Personal Unity of Jesus and God according to Wolfhart Pannenberg, St. Ottilien, 1973.

NEIE Herbert, The Doctrine of Atonement in the Theology of Wolfhart Pannenberg, Berlin/New York, 1979.

O'COLLINS G.G., 'The Christology of Wolfhart Pannenberg', in: Religious Studies, 1967, pp.369ff.

PAGANO Maurizio, Storia ed escatologia nel pensiero di W. Pannenberg, Milano, 1973.

PASQUARIELLO R., Reality as History - An Introduction of W. Pannenberg's Understanding of Reality, New York, 1972.

SECKLER Max, 'Zur Diskussion um das Offenbarungsverständnis W. Pannenbergs', in: MThZ, 2 (1968), SS.132-134.

SEGUERI Pier Angelo, 'La storia di Gesù come rivelazione di Dio. Ontologia della transcendenza e dalla immanenza di Dio nella cristologia di W. Pannenberg', in: La Scuola Cattolica, 103 (1975), pp.202-245.

STEIGER Lothar, 'Offenbarungsgeschichte und theologische Vernunft: Zur Theologie W. Pannenberg's, in: ZThK, 59 (1962), SS.88-113.

SUHL Alfred, 'Zur Bedeutung der Überlieferung von der Auferstehung Jesu in Wolfhart Pannenbergs 'Grundzüge der Christologie',' in: NZSTR, 12 (1970), SS.294-308.

TUPPER Frank E., The Theology of Wolfhart Pannenberg, Philadelphia, 1973.

VIRGULAK Francis Edward The Death of Christ according to Wolfhart Pannenberg. An Exposition and Criticism of Pannenberg's Theology of the Cross. (Excerpta ex Dissertatione), Rome, 1977.

790

11. General Literature for the Evaluative Part

ALFARO J., Christologia e anthropologia, Assisi, 1972.

ALTHAUS Paul, Die christliche Wahrheit, 1962 (6.Aufl.).

BALTHASAR Hans Urs von, Herrlichkeit. Eine theologische Ästhetik, Band I, Einsiedeln, 1961.

IDEM, Glaubhaft ist nur Liebe, Einsiedeln, 1963.

IDEM, Cordula oder der Ernstfall, Einsiedeln, 1966.

IDEM, Karl Barth. Darstellung und Deutung seiner Theologie, Einsiedeln, 1976 (1951).

IDEM, 'Gotteserfahrung biblisch und praktisch', in: IkZ, 6 (1976), SS.497-509.

IDEM, Theodramatik. Die Handlung (Band III), Einsiedeln, 1980.

BECKER Gerhold, Theologie in der Gegenwart, Regensburg, 1978.

BEINERT W., 'Die Erfahrbarkeit der Glaubenswirklichkeit', in: Mysterium der Gnade, (Festschrift für J. Auer), Regensburg, 1975, Ss.132-145.

BERTEN I., Histoire, révélation et foi, Brussels, 1969.

BIERWALTERS W. et al., Grundfragen der Mysthik, Einsiedeln, 1974.

BLINZLER J., Der Prozeß Jesu, 1960 (3. Aufl.).

BLOCK E., Das Prinzip Hoffnung, Frankfurt am Main, 1959.

BÖCKLE Franz et al. (Hrg.), Christlicher Glaube in moderner Gesellschaft, Bdd. 30, Freiburg/Basel/Wien, 1981-1982.

BRAGNE R., 'Was heißt christliche Erfahrung', in: IkZ 6 (1976), SS.481-496.

BRATTEN C.E./HARRISVILLE R.A. (Edd.), The Historical Jesus and the Kerygmatic Christ, New York, 1964.

BROWN Raymond E., Jesus: God and Man - Modern Biblical Reflection, London, 1968.

IDEM, The Virginal Conception and the Bodily Resurrection of Jesus, London, 1974.

BULTMANN Rudolf, Jesus, Tübingen, 1926.

IDEM, Jesus Christus und die Mythologie - Das Neue Testament im Licht der Bibelkritik, 1958 (Gütersloh, 1980).

IDEM, Das Verhältnis der urchristlichen Christusbotschaft zum historischen Jesus und der Christus unseres Glaubens, Wien, 1962.

BÜRKLE Horst, 'Der christliche Anspruch angesichts der Weltreligionen heute', in: W. Kasper (Hrg.), Absolutheit des Christentums (Questiones Disputatae 79), Freiburg i.Br., 1977, SS.83-103.

CAMPENHAUSEN Hans von, The Virgin Birth in the Theology of the Ancient Church (Studies in Historical Theology 2. ed. by Frank Clarke), Alec R. Allenson, Inc., 1964.

CHARDIN Theilhard de, Le milieu divin, London, 1960.

IDEM, Man's Place in Nature, London, 1966.

COBB John B. Jr./GRIFFIN David Ray, Process Theology - An Introductory Exposition, Philadelphia, 1976.

CONGAR Yves, Außer der Kirche kein Heil. Wahrheit und Dimension des Heils, Essen, 1961.

IDEM, Der Heilige Geist, Freiburg i.Br., 1982.

CORETH E., Heidegger und Kant', in: Kant und die Scholastik heute, 1955, SS. 206-255.

CULLMANN Oscar, Die Christologie des Neuen Testamentes, 1958 (2. Aufl.).

DIEM Hermann, Dogmatik. Ihr Weg zwischen Historismus und Existentialismus, 1955.

IDEM, Der irdische Jesus un der Christus des Glaubens, Tübingen, 1957.

DUFOUR Leon, Résurrection de Jésus et message pascal, Paris, 1971.

DUPUIS J., 'The Salvific Value of non-Christian Religions', in: M. Dhavamony (Ed.), Documenta Missionalia 5 (1972), pp.169-193.

EGAN Harvey D., Christian Mysticism. The Future of a Tradition, New York, 1984.

ENDRES J., 'Menschliche Natur und übernatürliche Ordnung', in: FZPT, 4 (1957), SS.3-18.

EVELY L., The Gospels without Myth, New York, 1971.

FIORENZA F.P./METZ J.B., 'Der Mensch als Einheit von Leib und Seele', in: J. Feiner/M. Löhrer (Hrg.), Mysterium Salutis. Grundriß heilsgeschichtlicher Dogmatik, II, Einsiedeln/Zürich/Köln, 1967, SS.584-636.

FLICK M., Peccato originale originato - Ricerca di una definizione (Studia pataiana 15), 1968.

IDEM/ALSZEGHY Z., Fundamenti di una anthropologia teologica, Firenze, 1973.

FÜLLER R.H., The Formation of New Testament Christology, London, 1965.

IDEM, The Foundation of the Resurrection Narratives, New York, 1971.

GALOT Jean, Etre né de Dieu: Jean 1,13 (Analecta Biblica 37), Rome, 1969.

IDEM, Il mistero della soffrenza di Dio, Assisi, 1975.

IDEM, Chi sei tu, o Cristo?, Firenze, 1977.

IDEM, Gesú liberatore, Firenze, 1978.

IDEM, Cristo contestato, Firenze, 1979.

IDEM, Le problème christologique actuel, CLD, 1979.

GALTIER P., 'La conscience humaine du Christ. Epilogue', in: Gregorianum XXXV (1954), pp.225-246.

GANOCZY Alexandre, 'Jesus Christus für alle Zeiten?', in: TThZ, 84 (1975), SS.338-350.

IDEM, 'Wahrheitsfindung durch Liebe', in: E. Biser et al., Das Prinzip Liebe, Freiburg/Basel/Wien, 1975, SS.36-58.

IDEM, Der schöpferische Mensch und die Schöpfung Gottes, Mainz, 1976.

IDEM, 'Außer Gott kein Heil?', in: Lebendiges Zeugnis, 32 (1977), SS.55-66.

IDEM, 'Absolutheitsanspruch. Begründung oder Hindernis der Evangelisation?', in: Concilium, 134 (1978), SS.221-226.

IDEM, Biblische Grundlegung dogmatischer Rede', in: Concilium, 158 (1980), SS.587-591.

IDEM, Schöpfungslehre, Düsseldorf, 1983.

IDEM, 'Die Bedeutung der christlichen Schöpfungslehre für die Einheit der Menschheit', in: W. Strolz/H. Waldenfels, (Hrg.), Christliche Grundlagen des Dialogs mit den Welt-Religionen (Quaestiones Disputatae 98), Freiburg i.Br., 1983, SS.127-150.

IDEM, 'Der Heilige Geist als Kraft und Person', in: G. Becker/H. Bürkle (Hrg.), Communicatio Fidei, Regensburg, 1983, SS.111-119.

GARRIGOU-LAGRANGE, R., L'unique personalité du Christ', in: Angelicum XXIX (1952), Pp.60-75.

GERKEN A., Offenbarung und Transzendenzerfahrung, Düsseldorf, 1969.

GOGARTEN Friedrich, Der Mensch zwischen Gott und Welt, Stuttgart, 1952.

GRILLMEIER A./BACHT H. (Hrg.), Das Konzil von Chalkedon. Geschichte und Gegenwart, 3 Bdd. Würzburg, 1951, 1953, 1954.

GUTWENGER E., Bewußtsein und Wissen Christi, Innsbruck, 1960.

HACKER Paul,'The Religions of the Nations in the Light of the Holy Scripture', in: ZMRW, 54 (1970), SS.161-185.

IDEM, 'Religion of Gentiles views by Fathers of the Church', in: ZMRW 54 (1970), SS.253-278.

IDEM, 'Christian Attitude towards non Christians', in: ZMRW 55 (1971), SS.81-97.

HEISLBETZ J., Theologische Gründe der nichtchristlichen Religionen, Freiburg, 1967.

HEIDEGGER M., Vom Wesen des Grundes, Frankfurt, 1965 (5. Aufl.).

IDEM, Sein und Zeit, Tübingen, 1967 (11.Aufl.).

HEITMANN C./MÜLLER, H. (Hrg.), Erfahrung und Theologie des Heiligen Geistes, München, 1974.

HILLMAN E., The Wider Ecumenism: Anonymous Christianity and the Church, London, 1968.

HINKE N., Kants Weg zur Transzendentalphilosophie. Der dreißigjährige Kant, Stuttgart/Berlin/Köln,1970.

HOOFT Vissert W.A., No other Name. The Choice between Syncretism and Christian Universalims, Philadelphia, 1963.

JERPHAGNON L., Le mal et l'existence, Paris, 1966.

JOURNET Ch., Le mal. Essai théologique, Paris, 1961.

JÜNGEL Eberhard, 'Extra Christum nulla salus - als Grundsatz natürlicher Theologie? Evangelische Erwägungen zur 'Anonymität' des Christentums', in: ZThK, 72 (1975), SS.337ff.

KÄHLER Martin, Der sogenannte historische Jesus und der geschichtliche, biblische Christus, Leipzig, 1892.

KÄSEMANN E., 'Das Problem des historischen Jesus', in: ZThK 51 (1954), SS.125-153.

KASPER Walter, Jesus der Christus, Mainz, 1974.

IDEM, Absolutheit des Christentums (Quaestiones Disputatae 79), Freiburg i.Br., 1977.

IDEM, Der Gott Jesu Christi, Mainz, 1982.

KITAMOURI K., Theology of the Pain of God (Translated from Japanese: Kami no itami no shingaku, Tokyo, 1958), Richmond, 1965.

KLAES Norbert, 'Tod und Vollendung im Hinduismus und Christentum', in: Theologie und Glaube, 68 (1978), SS.233-266.

IDEM, 'Reinkarnation und Auferstehung' (Nachwort), in: Hans Torwesten, Sind wir nur einmal auf Erden? Die Idee der Reinkarnation angesichts des Auferstehungsglaubens, Freiburg i.Br., 1983, SS.183-202.

KLINGER Elmar (Hrg.), Christentum innerhalb und außerhalb der Kirche (Quaestiones Disputatae 83), Freiburg i.Br., 1976.

KRUSE H., 'Die 'anonymen Christen' exegetisch gesehen', in: MThZ, 18 (1967), SS.2-29.

KÜNG Hans, Menschwerdung Gottes. Eine Einführung in Hegels theologisches Denken als Prolegomena zu einer künftigen Christologie (Ökumenische Forschung II), Freiburg i.Br., 1970.

IDEM, Christ sein, München, 1974.

KÜNNETH Walter, Glauben an Jesus? Die Begegnung der Christologie mit der modernen Existenz, Hamburg, 1962.

KUNNUMPURAM Kurien, Ways of Salvation - The Salvific Meaning of non-Christian Religions according to the Teachings of Vatican II, Poona, 1971.

LATOURELLE René, Finding Jesus through the Gospels. History and Hermeneutics, (Tr. by Aloysius Owen), New York, 1978.

LIEBART J., 'Christologie: Von der apostolischen Zeit bis zum Konzil von Chalkedon (451)', in: M. Schmaus/H.Rahner/A. Grillmeier, Handbuch der Dogmengeschichte, Bd. III,1a, Freiburg i.Br., 1965, SS.19-127.

LOHSE Eduard, Märtyrer und Gottesknecht - Untersuchungen zur urchristlichen Verkündigung vom Sühnetod Jesu Christi, Göttingen, 1955.

LONERGAN B., De constitutione Christi ontologica et psychologica, Roma, 1956.

LOTZ J.B., Transzendentale Erfahrung, Freiburg/Basel/Wien, 1978.

IDEM, 'Zur Thomas-Rezeption in der Maréchal-Schule', in: Theologie und Philosophie, 49 (1974), SS.375-394.

MARÉCHAL J., Le point de départ de la métaphysique. Lecons sur le developpment historique et theorique du problème de la connaisance, Cahier I-V, Louvain, 1922-1926.

MARTINI Carlo M., Il problema storico della risurrezione negli studi recenti, Roma, 1980 (1959).

MARXSEN W., Die Auferstehung Jesu von Nazareth, Gütersloh, 1968.

MATTHIAE K. (Hrg.), Der historische Jesus und der kerygmatische Christus. Beiträge zum Christusverständnis in Forschung und Verkündigung, Berlin, 1960.

METZ J.B., Zur Theologie der Welt, München, 1968.

MOLTMANN Jürgen, Theologie der Hoffnung - Untersuchungen zur Begründung und zu den Konsequenzen einer christlichen Eschatologie, München, 1969 (1964).

IDEM, Der gekreuzigte Gott. Kreuz Christi als Grund und Kritik christlicher Theologie, München, 1972.

MÜHLEN H., Die Veränderlichkeit Gottes als Horizont einer zukünftigen Christologie, Münster, 1969.

MÜLLER M., Erfahrung und Geschichte - Grundzüge einer Philosophie der Freiheit als transzendentale Erfahrung, München, 1971.

NEUNER J. (Ed.), Christian Revelation and World Religions, London, 1967.

OBERHAMMER G. (Hrg.), Transzendenzerfahrung - Vollzugshorizont des Heils, Wien, 1978.

O'COLLINS G., The Easter Jesus, London, 1973.

OTTO Rudolf, Das Heilige. Über das Irrationale in der Idee des Göttlichen und sein Verhältnis zum Rationalen, München, 1979 (1917).

PANIMOLLE S.A., Il done della legge e la grazia della verità (Gv. 1,17), Roma, 1973.

PARENTE P., 'Unità ontologica e psicologica dell'Uomo-Dio', in: Euntes Docete, V (1952), pp.337-401.

IDEM, 'Echi della controversia sull'unità ontologica e psicologica di Cristo', in: Euntes Docete Vi (1953), pp.312-322.

PESCH Otto Hermann, Frei sein aus Gnade. Theologische Anthropologie, Freiburg i.Br., 1983.

PHILBERTH Bernhard, Der Dreieinige, Stein a.R. (Schweiz), 1980 (5. Aufl.).

POTTERIE Ignace de la, La vérité dans S. Jean, Roma, 1977.

PRZYWARA E., 'Der Grundsatz, gratia non destruit, sed supponit perficit naturam', in: Scholastik, 17 (1942), SS.178-186.

RATZINGER J., 'Bewußtsein und Wissen Christi', in: MThZ XII (1961), SS.78-81.

SCHARL E., Recapitulatio mundi. Der Rekapitulationsbegriff des hl. Iranaeus, Freiburg i.Br., 1941.

SCHEFFCZYK I. (Hrg.), Grundfragen der Christologie heute, Freiburg/Basel/Wien, 1975.

IDEM, 'Die Erfahrbarkeit der göttlichen Gnade', in: Mysterium der Gnade, (Festschrift für J. Auer), Regensburg, 1975, SS.146-159.

IDEM, 'Die Frage nach der 'Erfahrung' als theologisches Verifikationsprinzip', in: W. Ernst/K. Feiereis/F. Hoffman (Hrg.), Dienst der Vermittlung, Leipzig, 1972, SS.353-373.

SCHILLEBEECKX E., Jesus. Die Geschichte von einem Lebenden, Freiburg i.Br., 1975.

SCHILSON A./KASPER W.,Christologie im Präsens - Kritische Sichtung neuer Entwürfe, Freiburg/Basel/Wien, 1974.

SCHNACKENBURG Rudolf, Gottes Herrschaft und Reich. Eine biblisch-theologische Studie, Freiburg i.Br., 1965 (1959).

IDEM, Das Johannesevangelim, 3 Teile (Herders theologischer Kommentar zum Neuen Testament), Freiburg/Basel/Wien, 1967, 1971, 1975.

IDEM, 'Christologie des Neuen Testamentes', in: J. Feiner/M. Löhrer (Hrg.), Mysterium Salutis. Grundriß heilsgeschichtlicher Dogmatik, Bd. III, Einsiedeln, 1970,SS.227-388.

SCHOONENBERG P., 'Spirit Christology and Logos Christology', in: Bijdragen 29 (1977), pp.335-357.

SCHWEITZER A., Geschichte der Leben-Jesu-Forschung, Tübingen, 1913 (2. Aufl.).

SELLERS R.V., The Council of Chalkedon, London, 1953.

SERTILLANGES A.D., Le problème du mal I, L'histoire II, La solution, Paris, 1948-1951.

SIMONIS Walter, Jesus von Nazareth. Seine Botschaft vom Reich Gottes und der Glaube der Urgemeinde. Historisch-kritische Erhellung der Ursprünge des Christentums, Düsseldorf, 1985.

SPLETT J., Die Trinitätslehre G.W.F. Hegels, 1965.

STEGGINK O., et al., Mystik 2 Bdd., Düsseldorf, 1983, 1984.

STOECKLE B., Gratia supponit naturam. Geschichte und Analyse eines theologischen Axioms, Rom, 1962.

SUDBRACK J. (Hrg.), Das Mysterium und die Mystik. Beiträge zur Theologie der christlichen Gotteserfahrung, Würzburg, 1974.

VELLANICKAL Matthew, The Divine Sonship of Christians in the Johannine Writings, (Analecta Biblica 72), Rome, 1977.

WAGNER F., Der Gedanke der Persönlichkeit Gottes bei Fichte und Hegel, Gütersloh, 1971.